THE YEAR BOOK OF EDUCATION
1956

CONTENTS

v

CONTENTS

SECTION II: THE ACQUISITION AND DISTRIBUTION OF RESOURCES

Acquiring Resources
(Some Historical and Case Studies)

PAGE

Chapter One

PROVISION FOR EDUCATION IN THE FREE CITIES OF ITALY 118
R. R. Bolgar, M.A., Ph.D., Fellow of King's College, Cambridge; formerly Research Fellow, Durham University Institute of Education

Chapter Two

THE FOUNDING OF CHRIST'S HOSPITAL 130
H. L. O. Flecker, C.B.E., M.A., Principal of Lawrence College, Murree, Pakistan; formerly Head Master of Christ's Hospital, 1930–55

Chapter Three

THE DISSOLUTION OF THE SOCIETY OF JESUS IN THE EIGHTEENTH CENTURY AND ITS FINANCIAL CONSEQUENCES 137
N. Hans, Ph.D., D.Litt., formerly Reader in Comparative Education, University of London, King's College

Chapter Four

CHURCH AND STATE IN THE UNITED KINGDOM 147
Canon R. Bailey, M.A., Ph.D., Secretary of the Schools Council of the Church of England Council for Education and General Secretary of the National Society

Chapter Five

THE LAND-GRANT COLLEGES AND UNIVERSITIES OF THE UNITED STATES 155
Russell I. Thackrey, B.S., M.S., LL.D.(Hon.), Executive Secretary, Association of Land-Grant Colleges and Universities of the U.S.A.; formerly Dean of Administration and Director of the Summer School, Kansas State College, Manhattan, Kansas

Chapter Six

EDUCATIONAL PROVISION THROUGH PHILANTHROPY AND FOUNDATIONS 160
John K. Weiss, Assistant Vice-President of the Fund for the Advancement of Education, New York

Chapter Seven

RESOURCES FOR EDUCATION IN NEW YORK STATE 171
Howard A. Shiebler, Master of Laws, Coordinator of Public Relations, New York State Education Department, Albany, N.Y.

Chapter Eight

SUBSIDIES TO UNIVERSITY STUDENTS IN NORWAY 177
Helge Sivertsen, Cand.Philol., University of Oslo; Under Secretary, Norwegian Ministry of Church and Education

The Tax System
Chapter Nine

THE INCIDENCE OF TAXATION AND OF STATE PROVISION FOR EDUCATION: UNITED KINGDOM 180
W. H. Burston, M.A., Lecturer in Education, University of London Institute of Education

Educational Provision through Private Agencies and Supplementary Services

Paying Teachers

INTRODUCTION

THIS volume of THE YEAR BOOK, the fourth prepared under the joint editorial responsibility of Teachers College, Columbia University and the University of London Institute of Education, is on a theme which compared with those of its predecessors is mundane. Education is a costly business for any country that takes it seriously—costly in money and in the intellectual resources of the country. In one form or another every government has to face the questions of the extent of the provision for education it would like to make and the extent it can afford to make. There is always a gap between the answers to the two, and then the further question arises of the ways and means whereby the limited resources available can be used to the best effect. It usually emerges that the scale of the provision for education is such as to make it a major item in the organization of national resources, and it has to stand in competition with economic development, social service and defence.

The reader will discover, however, that the volume is necessarily concerned with much more than the mechanics of finance. It is of the nature of education that any discussion in this narrow field invariably raises broader questions about the purposes of education. The problem would be much simpler if it were possible to regard education as a national luxury and proceed to determine the extent of indulgence we can afford without regard to other forms of national activity. It does not work out in this way, for it soon becomes apparent that the maintenance and development of the national effort in every direction ultimately depends upon education, whether in school or out of it. From this point of view education is the means by which a country organizes its human ability for the purposes of every form of national effort. You cannot have a due supply of engineers, doctors and administrators, or meet the personnel needs of industry and commerce unless you have good schools and institutions for higher education.

The problem, however, runs to a deeper level. The people of every country have their own private hopes for their national future. If these hopes are realized the tone of the national life twenty-five or fifty years ahead will not be a mere reproduction of the present. Education in all its manifold forms is the instrument by which a nation transforms itself from what it is into what it hopes to be. Thus, the nature and intensity of the national effort for education provide a peculiarly reliable index of the national will for the future. A virile people with great hopes for the future will give active care to education; the first sign of national pessimism is a neglect of education.

In accord with our invariable practice, our Editors have invited contributors to write on different aspects of this theme from their own experience in different countries. They have attempted no censorship and accordingly the responsibility for each article remains solely with the author over whose name it appears.

HOLLIS L. CASWELL,
President: Teachers College, Columbia.

G. B. JEFFERY,
Director: Institute of Education, London.

WILLIAM F. RUSSELL

IN the YEAR BOOK OF EDUCATION the best tribute I can pay to my old friend President Russell is to tell the story of how the YEAR BOOK became a joint venture of the sister institutions, Teachers College, Columbia, and the Institute of Education, London. On one of his visits to London in 1951, we spent an evening together, in accordance with our custom, discussing this and that, and somehow the conversation turned to the building of an educational transatlantic bridge buttressed on our buildings in London and New York. Russell's mind was big enough for big ideas, but he liked to shape them into practical form. He wanted to know what we were going to do about it. He told me that he and his colleagues had been discussing the possibility of reviving Kandel's *Educational Year Book*, and he wanted to know whether I had any advice to offer in the light of our experience of the YEAR BOOK. One of us, I forget which, suggested that we might join forces. It would be a rather complicated operation to secure agreement across the Atlantic in the planning of successive volumes, inviting contributions and making all the arrangements necessary for publication in our two countries. I said that I thought it could be done somehow, but " somehow " was not good enough for Russell. We discussed the problem backwards and forwards, and very late that night we made two fair copies of a detailed scheme which we could put before our Governing Bodies for approval and use as a basis for negotiation with Evans Brothers as publishers. That scheme with hardly any change was later embodied in the tripartite agreement between Teachers College, the Institute of Education and Evans Brothers, under which the YEAR BOOK is published today. At the time of our talk a good many decisions had already been taken about the 1953 volume, but here again Russell's passion for striking while the iron was hot came into evidence. I told him how far we had got with the preparation of the volume and he said, " That sounds good to me, why can't 1953 be the date of our first joint volume?", and it was so.

That is how I shall always remember Russell—as a man who saw his job in a big way and got on with the doing of it. In America he will be remembered as one of the great educational figures of his time. We in England will hold him in grateful remembrance as one who fundamentally believed in the spiritual unity of the English-speaking peoples and of their great and common destiny.— G. B. JEFFERY.

Education and Economics

IN the south-east corner of Iran, close to the frontiers of Pakistan and Afghanistan, there is a nomadic tribe which ranges over an area about the size of France. This tribe, the Baluchi, are best known to the few tourists who visit them for the beautiful rugs they weave and the enormously impressive moustaches which their men affect. They are an ancient people, proud and highly effective in their nomadism, although almost completely illiterate. They are, indeed, almost the prototype of a technologically under-developed society, and their economic level is amongst the lowest in the world. It has been shown that the Baluchis are incapable of providing even a minimum of formal education for their children, in spite of any possible utilization of their present economy. Even if they did not spend a single penny on food, clothing, or shelter, and if they saved nothing for future security or defence, they would still not create enough wealth to cover the exceedingly modest cost of the elementary education made compulsory by Iranian law.

A situation like this raises a basic question : How much education can a society afford? To which Americans would probably reply that the real question was rather whether any society could ' afford ' to do without education. This is correct for rich and complex societies, where a literate and highly trained population is needed, but misleading when applied to impoverished or relatively primitive ones. In the U.S.A., education is recognized and rewarded materially and spiritually. There is a widespread belief that man has it in his power to modify his situation and to improve his lot through his own efforts. This faith is rooted in the deep-seated optimism of a young, dynamic, and growing society in which there is little fear of defeat or failure. It is sustained by a national economy capable of providing almost any level of material well-being, provided the apparatus at hand is used intelligently, forcefully, and skilfully. Education, then, appears as a social instrument through which man can guide his destiny and shape his future.

Human societies do not all enjoy the wealth and natural resources of the U.S.A., nor share the energy and optimism of Americans. Often, there is fear of the future and love of the past; the will to seek modest security rather than dangerous greatness. The essential point for the philosopher is to note that everywhere ideas on the upbringing of the young stem from and reflect historical experiences, geographical conditions, and patterns of culture.

It is a truism that all societies have an adequate educational system, for if they did not they would vanish. All cultures teach a language which, however primitive in form or restricted in vocabulary, is adequate for immediate needs. All transmit the essential secrets of sex and reproduction, as well as the knowledge needed to survive. The Baluchi, for example, teach their young an array of difficult and complex skills by which they secure the minimum necessary requirements in one of the most cruelly arid regions of the globe. It is difficult to know just what advice could be given to them by even the most skilled Western consultants, unless new sources of wealth were discovered.

It seems that our question might well be re-stated as: "What is the level of education which is desirable for a given group?" The answer would be that this level is determined in part by the economic capacity of the group, in part by the skills required for survival, in part by the values accepted. The ability to find water and to maintain direction in a desert waste have high priority with a nomadic tribe. They have no importance in New York city. The American youngster is given intensive instruction in safety rules and traffic problems, while attention is paid to the vocational choices which he will have to make in a highly industrialized environment. The Baluchi do not need to read or write, but do need to understand the psychology of camels. The young American can hardly recognize a camel when he sees one in the Bronx Zoo, but may well have the movements of his eyeballs analysed to improve his speed of reading. And he will study the psychology of group processes while learning the complicated human relations which occur in industrialized societies based upon scientific technology.

These are extremes. But similar, though smaller, differences are noted between cultures which are superficially alike. Only a narrow channel separates Britain from France, only a political frontier lies between Germany and Belgium. Yet there are marked differences between the educational practices these nations pursue. Take another example: both the U.S.A. and the U.S.S.R. are dedicated to the education of the masses. In some ways, the outer structures of their school systems resemble each other. Yet how different are the results! It is the social and political philosophy adopted which shapes the aims: as is society, so is education.

In order to clarify the point, let us consider another simple case or model. The *guru* of Ancient India served his community as an educator. Through him the lore of the *Vedas* was passed on. He was the

agent through whom learning was disseminated; social norms per-
petuated; religious, political, and medical knowledge imparted; the
arts of war preserved. His task required lengthy training and the
utmost devotion. In time, it became the privilege and responsibility of
the Brahmins. Each teacher had a small number of pupils, who lived
with him. Those who could not pay for the education they received
were expected to gather fuel, collect food by begging, and do household chores for the *guru*. Students often lived for as many as twelve
years with their teacher and, understandably, the number living in the
household at any time was restricted to fewer than two dozen. Education was thus provided in the powerful institution of the household
and family.

For his support the *guru* fulfilled certain important social tasks. He
officiated at ceremonies and was responsible for religious ministrations. His class, the sacerdotal, was the first to acquire the rigidity of
caste and to become impregnated with various taboos which helped to
maintain its sanctity.

In the light of events, it can be seen that the education thus provided made for a stable society, slow to change and regulated by the
esoteric knowledge of a minority, for the literature which was its
special concern included instructions and information on every aspect
of social life. The auxiliary sciences were both theoretical and practical. The system strengthened existing institutions, particularly the
family, and was supported by them. The material needs of the teacher
were met through the family, he was freed from other duties in order
to devote himself to study and teaching, and he either remained within
the precincts of a particular house or travelled from one household to
another. Begging and patronage were regarded as justifiable methods
of acquiring support. The Brahmin lived simply, without ostentation,
but enjoyed the highest prestige as a result of the duties he performed.
Evidently what was, and continued to be, a service to the community
became a vested interest and remained so in India until very recently.
Under these circumstances education was turned into the privilege
of a few and enabled these to maintain their position, sometimes to
the disadvantage of the rest of society. For the traditional forms of
education may be in conflict with the aspirations of large groups of the
people, especially in periods of change. This, however, is another
point to which we shall return.

The Economic Aspects of Education

For the present, let us content ourselves by noting that the amount
as well as the kind of education demanded is related to the totality of
social forms, to the cultural pattern as a whole. One aspect of that

pattern is, of course, the economic : the way in which the material goods are produced, distributed, and exchanged. It is the purpose of the present YEAR BOOK to examine the relations which exist between the educational and the economic aspects of the total pattern. What we have said should make clear that we do not think this exhausts the discussion. It is obvious that every human activity has its economic aspect, but we reject the view that the latter is essential or fundamental or primary. Undoubtedly, all education has economic aims and its form and content are affected by the economic capacity of the community being served. But that is not the whole story, nor even, perhaps, its most significant or interesting chapter.

In order to study the relations between education and economics, it is helpful to think for a while of the former as if it were a commodity like any other, such as, for example, music or—shall we say?—soap, and then to ask what sorts of question would arise if such goods were being considered. First, of course, would come the problem of demand. What makes a population desire music or soap? What influences bring about an increase or a diminution in demand? Can it be stimulated or diminished? Then, secondly, to produce goods like music or soap resources have to be provided : manpower, materials likely to be scarce, buildings, and so on. How are these resources acquired and allocated? Is the matter left only to the initiative of private persons? Is there any interference by the authorities—as might happen negatively with harmful drugs or positively with religious buildings? Thirdly, what problems of management arise? How are the workers trained? What fixes their remuneration? Fourthly, what determines the price of the product? Are there varying qualities of it, for which varying prices will be paid? Are there subsidies? Fifthly, what economic consequences flow as a result of producing just these goods? A distinction is often drawn here between producer-goods, the supply of which increases the capital resources of a community (that is, its capacity to produce what it desires), and consumer-goods, which disappear when used. Is education to be classed among producer-goods or among consumer-goods? Or are there various kinds of ' education ', some of which belong to one class while the rest belong to the other?

These are some of the questions which came to our minds when we decided to study the intricate problem we had set ourselves—that of the relation of education to economics. The approach was evidently fruitful and stimulating. But, unfortunately, we soon discovered a quite appalling shortage of factual inquiries. It appeared that far too little work had been done to make it possible for us to realize our plan with complete success. The studies and papers presented in this YEAR BOOK are, in many cases, little more than tentative explorations of almost virgin land. There is here an almost unlimited field for educational research of high significance at this period of rapid technological change; research which would provide a solid base for the planning of the educational statesman.

The Demand for Education

Let us begin, then, by considering the forces and influences which create a demand for education. Among the Baluchis, evidently, it is as weak as the demand for soap! But in ancient India, the religious and philosophical outlook of the population led them to attach value to what the *guru* taught. The Indians met problems in their daily life and perplexities within their minds which, as they saw, could be solved or simplified if the counsel or instruction of the teacher were accepted. In general, indeed, the religious sentiment has everywhere and always led to the stimulation of demand for instruction of a particular kind: in the right rituals and ceremonials, in the skills needed to read the sacred texts, in the philosophical interpretation of the sayings and epigrams of the holy men. It is here, too, that belong the activities of missionaries, whether Christian, Muslim, or Buddhist. They, too, by spreading religious faith, helped to stimulate demand for a particular kind of education.

At first, religious teachers are always maintained willingly by gifts of food or hospitality or alms. But already this support involves a diversion of material resources: only seldom, as in the medieval monasteries of Christendom, do wise and holy men actually till the soil or engage in the manipulation of materials. Usually they produce goods that are desired, as are music and art. By so doing they help to maintain individual and social harmony, cohesion and morale. Indirectly, no doubt, this helps the production of fundamental necessities —food, shelter, defence—but only indirectly. At a later stage, these same religious men may also teach crafts and usable skills : as did the monks who introduced the plough and a knowledge of the working of metals to the barbarians of the North. Here they intervened directly, and contributed to economic well-being. Perhaps, however, this should be considered rather as an instance of intercultural contact than as an example of the effect of the religious sentiment. And quite certainly, one of the permanently powerful agencies stimulating the demand for education is precisely the external stimulus due to such contacts. A vigorous and expanding people—the Romans in the Ancient World or the British in the eighteenth or nineteenth centuries—extends its dominion and its trading area. The indigenous population with which it has relations—the Gauls or the Indians—desires to possess the knowledge which brings power. The conquerors, on the other hand, need the services of clerks, administrators, and soldiers. They allot resources for education and training. The demand exists, the supply is created.

And sometimes the whole society, while retaining political independence and even autonomy, changes within itself in the effort to acquire what is possessed by those who are richer or more advanced. The rulers of the less-developed society may set themselves both to create demand and to organize supply—as happened in Russia a generation ago and is happening in China now. Here a new factor nearly always comes in. The rulers desire not education in general, but education of a particular kind : aimed at industrial advance and at political docility. They look for a selective valve. There can be little doubt that the complex *Kanamajiri* system of writing in Japan was deliberately used as such a valve through which only the knowledge which the ruling groups desired the people to have was transmitted. The entire structure of the Japanese state, developed under the theory of the *Kokutai*, depended upon the proper functioning of this valve. There is just as little doubt that the enormous and expensive educational system of Soviet Russia has for thirty-five years been used not only to transmit vocational skills but also to control political and social beliefs. Even in countries which pride themselves in offering great freedom of dissent to individuals, in the U.S.A., Great Britain, Sweden, Switzerland, or Chile, for instance, one finds that the population is surprisingly susceptible to the manipulation of thoughts, beliefs, attitudes, and emotions by the very educational apparatus which is believed to be the instrument and guarantee of freedom.

As social change proceeds, the nature of the demand for education changes too. What satisfied at an earlier time no longer does. In medieval Europe, schools and colleges were built by the direct labour of monks or by the money provided by wealthy bishoprics. The Church dominated the educational process and provided the ideological leadership needed to direct military and social power into acceptable channels. No doubt the prime purpose was the maintenance and expansion of the institution itself, but incidental benefits accrued. When conditions changed through the voyages of discovery, the development of mechanical invention, and the incipient industrial revolution of the seventeenth century, the nature of the demand changed too. Milton asked for an education " which fits a man to perform justly, skilfully, and magnanimously all the offices both private and public of peace and war ", thus expressing his dissatisfaction with the wordy, literary education suited to earlier times. His curriculum extended far beyond grammar—though he starts with that—to the study of applied agriculture and engineering, to household economics, politics, law, and the highest matters of theology. The study of politics was, he thought, desirable for these students collected together in groups of about one hundred and fifty in spacious houses set aside for the purpose in "every city throughout the land". Through it "they may not in a dangerous fit of the Commonwealth be such poor, shaken uncertain reeds, of such tottering conscience, as many of our great counsellors have lately shown themselves, but steadfast pillars of the State".

The needs of the time were for men trained in the applied sciences—trigonometry, architecture, engineering, and navigation. Commercial enterprise was creating a demand for trained personnel which could not be provided by the traditional schools and universities. Milton recognized the need. He also wrote as one committed to a defence of parliamentary democracy against a king who based his authority to rule on 'Divine Right'.

Thus in Milton is found an educational pioneer who recognized the needs of commerce and the needs of political democracy. Whilst vested interests have continued to resist the demands of groups interested in these aspects of education, the latter have gradually come to the forefront. To their claims has been added the social demand for technically trained personnel. This is a late-nineteenth- and twentieth-century demand.

Historic examples can be quoted of institutions which owe their birth, or extension, to one or several of these three demands. The rapid growth in nineteenth-century England of the 'Public' school was connected with an increasing demand for educated people who would run England's expanding commercial enterprises. These had involved the annexation, subjection, or simple occupation of many foreign countries for the purposes of trade. An Empire needed administrators, and it is due to more than chance that the nineteenth-century English 'Public' schools were able to supply it.

German education stands in the same period as an example of a system responding to various social demands, one of the most significant of which was industrialization, which required technical-vocational training. The efficiency of the German *Fachschule*, *Berufschule*, and *Technische Hochschule* system bears witness to the clarity with which the leaders of German unification and nationalism saw the role of education in the international race for industrial supremacy.

The original intentions of the early European settlers in America to provide education in order to defeat the old deluder Satan were transformed after the Revolution into a clear-cut desire to maintain through an educational system the democratic institutions which the founding fathers cherished and which they thought the best defence against the Satan of personal power and the corruption which it brings.

Allied to all such demands has been yet another, due to the creation

of sovereign states. Nationalism itself has been a powerful incentive
and stimulus to the provision of education on a wide scale. It has
taken many forms, depending upon where national leaders have
thought security to lie, but it has aways involved a demand for an
education that would help to produce good, loyal, patriotic citizens.

Then there are the changes in the class-structure of society which
come from changes in trade, political organization, and industrial life.
Though the Marxian predictions and prophecies of doom are unacceptable to Western people, yet Marx's analysis of the economic
conditions promoting social change has much to commend it. The
development of a very large middle-educated class capable of industrial
management and control has made it possible for some societies to
avoid the ultimate and final clash between *bourgeoisie* and proletariat.
This development is the result of a combined demand by the leaders
for an education that would safeguard democracy and by the masses
for educational opportunities that would lead to higher social and
economic status and, perhaps incidentally, would help them to participate in the government of their country.

If the Marxian thesis is wrong, it must be possible for those who
control the means of production, on the one hand, and for the wage-
earners on the other, to recognize their interdependence and so to
modify their attitudes and institutions as to lead to mutual satisfaction
and confidence. An educational system explicitly accepting the aim
of fostering institutions through which these processes take place is
marked off from all past systems. It implies that the acquisition of
education need not out of sheer necessity lead to the acquisition of
the political power and to the domination of one class by another.

The democratic ideal also creates its own demand for education. It
is expressed, as are all demands for education, through institutions and
through groups of people. Commercialism, industrialization, nationalism, and democracy have contributed in various degrees to make the
demand for education in most present-day societies a popular one.
Clearly, in countries which have recently become independent, like
India, there is ambivalence. Her leaders hope that education can make
the country democratic and economically prosperous at one and the
same time. What do the masses want? As likely as not, their chief
concern is with the economic fundamentals of life. Such popular
desires are stirred in the twentieth century by the speed of communication and the presence of mass media like the press and the radio.

Acquiring Resources for Education

When there is a strong demand for education or instruction, it is of
course provided. This means that resources have to be allocated to

it: manpower is withdrawn from other activities, special buildings may be erected, books and materials provided. Only very seldom, however, is either the total amount or the kind of education left to the ordinary mechanism of supply and demand, that is, to the desires of individual persons prepared to pay the full cost. It is true that there have long existed private academies or schools which charge their customers fees so high as to cover the real cost and which provide exactly the kind of teaching that is desired by the consumers. But even in the Free Cities of the Middle Ages, the burghers saw that some members of their class or estate needed help, at least at a certain period of their life, and they were prepared to club together to maintain schools which were either free or at least charged amounts much below the real economic cost. As for the Church, its spiritual and moral power was such that it was able, and still is, to persuade some people to give their services freely as schoolmasters: the aim being to promote the public good through the support of an institution which guards it. Many a father, sceptical and anti-clerical, has sent his sons to a Church school, giving them an education of which he approved only in part, because it was provided at much less than cost.

It might indeed be argued that education differs from other economic goods because its price has never anywhere been left simply to the play of market demand. The authorities and the *élites* have always interfered. Both have always wanted to have more education than was available and usually education different in kind from that called for by consumers.

They have expressed their will by placing material resources at the disposal of education—on stated conditions. Thus, in the Middle Ages, kings, bishops, and nobles gave land—the source of material wealth—to endow colleges or schools. Rich men left scholarships for deserving boys in their wills, or endowed Chairs of Philosophy at universities. And even to-day, in countries as progressive and liberal as the United States, so full of faith in the wisdom of private enterprise, we find that federal aid is provided to correct the market in order to enlarge the supply of technological, commercial, or agricultural instruction. And, everywhere, the central government provides instruction for the armed forces, thus helping to keep down the cost of the specialized services it needs and uses.

In a complete treatise on the relation of education to economic life, this would be the place to consider and to survey carefully the character of the material resources which the provision of educational facilities requires. We should consider what was and what is demanded in the way of manpower, equipment, buildings. We should take into account how these can be enlisted: it would be necessary to

weigh up against one another the efficacy of the ideological or
humanitarian appeal to which missionaries respond, and the strength
of promising security, holidays, and pensions in recruiting personnel for the schools. We should discuss what sort of resources can
be directed towards education: whether land or specialized personnel
are properly to be thus made available (e.g.: it has recently been suggested that scientists and technologists ought to be ordered to teach.
What would be the effect of this? We should take into account the
by-products of such action on the general economy). We should think
about the sales of services or of goods produced by students, not over-
looking Mahatma Gandhi's schemes. We should also pay attention to
the sale of services rendered by faculty-members—to royalties, patents,
consultations, fees—for these are quickly becoming a major source of
income, especially to the senior staff of universities who are thus compensated for teaching instead of entering the world of commerce and
industry. This would lead us to the contribution made by private
industry, by either the provision of courses within their concerns, the
payment of special taxes, or the release of employees.

Then would come a study of the effects of the philanthropic impulse
manifested to-day in the activities of the Foundations. It would be
fascinating to trace the history of institutions such as the Rockefeller,
Carnegie, Ford, or Nuffield Foundations: the economic effects of the
transfer of funds from industry to education and research, the implicit
conditions associated with the gifts, the final effect of this allocation of
resources.

It goes without saying, however, that the most important questions
to-day arise in connexion with the multifarious operation of the tax
machines controlled by public authorities. Education was one of the
first social services to be subsidized from taxation. Much of the money
made available to it came from the obvious source of wealth of that
time, i.e., land and property. As this form of wealth has become less
and less important there has been a shift in the base of taxation. In
England, the cost of education is shared between taxes raised locally
through rates, and those raised nationally on incomes and consumer
goods. Local taxes are assessed on the supposed value of real estate.
The proportion of money from central funds has continued to rise not
only in England and France but in most industrialized countries. This
may have come about as a result of the inability of local taxation
systems quickly to follow changes in the source of 'wealth'. It may
also account for the generally low investment in education in periods
of inflation. For whilst the selling price of property may rise sharply,
its value for the purposes of taxation may lag very considerably. Yet
the property tax is one which can be administered locally more easily

than it can on a national level. The willingness of communities to pay high 'rates' or property taxes reflects their preparedness to support education.

The implications of this are important. The operation of tax systems needs to be analysed if a better understanding of educational problems is to be obtained. Some of the relevant questions relate to the willingness of taxpayers to support education as a social service compared with their willingness to support it as an item of personal consumption. From this point of view Dr. Peacock and Dr. Wiseman's analysis of the acquisition of resources for education in England and the distribution of benefits is very significant.

Where the majority of money is provided from central funds, and therefore to-day from non-property taxes, it seems likely that a larger proportion of the national revenue will be spent on education than under conditions where the money is raised locally. A typical example of this—indicated in Dr. Thabault's article—is France, where the percentage is as high as eight. This reflects the appreciation of the political leaders of the social importance of education. Rejection of an educational programme by refusing to pay taxes would have to be on a national level. The extent to which French municipalities are shifting the burden of education to the central government illustrates the difficulties experienced in raising money locally. This in turn reflects, perhaps, the lowered value of education in France as a consumer-item.

It cannot be assumed that the amount of money raised will be proportionately less where money is raised for education largely on a local tax base. If the type of education provided is of a kind which the public appreciate, i.e., if it is a consumer-item, then it is likely that local taxation will bring in more money than central funds. The situation in the United States should be studied in these terms. How far has its flexibility, its ability to modify curricular offerings, its comparative freedom from hard and fast traditional educational norms, made it possible to raise locally such a large proportion of the money needed to finance education? And how far has the system of decentralized control made education more modifiable in terms of consumer-demand?

If education is to be regarded as a consumer-item it has to be responsive to consumer-demand. Decentralized control makes this possible. It is pointless, for example, to deplore the reluctance of municipalities in France to shoulder the burden of education if curriculum, organization, appointment, and dismissal of teachers and so on are centrally controlled. Of course, if education is seen as a social service, central administration has many advantages provided the institutions operating alongside the schools make it difficult for the latter to be manipulated to political ends by unscrupulous people. The central government may then be expected to provide most of the funds. It can explain its policy in terms of social usefulness, and respond to suggestions for improving this usefulness. It is worth repeating that many administrations fail to distinguish between a social service and a consumer-item. They justify their policy in terms of consumer-demand when in fact it is a kind of social service. This justification allows them to administer the service as though it were a consumer-item, but with 'experts' deciding what the consumer wants.

The Allocation of Resources

In any modern society, many other public services compete with education for trained personnel, buildings, and equipment. In England the atomic research establishment at Harwell, for example, attracts to its service large numbers of the most highly qualified scientists and technicians who might otherwise teach in schools. The armed forces themselves call for many technically trained men and women. Governmental priorities in the United Kingdom and elsewhere often place at the disposal of these armed forces resources far in excess of what the national economy can easily support. Few deny the need for armaments, but it is doubtful whether the large absorption of personnel is cheerfully accepted by the majority of people.

Other political and vote-catching policies tend to attract resources towards areas where popular demand is strong, for example to housing schemes and other social services. Frequently such resources are distributed as a result of powerful labour pressure. The employment of a very high number of supernumerary workers on the railways and in public transportation is a case in point.

The health service is an example of a policy which enjoys the support of a very wide public. Medical knowledge has advanced very rapidly in recent years. With the aid of new drugs, antibiotics, and improved anaesthetics, the power of the medical profession to prevent and cure illness has raced ahead. Health is thought to be within the grasp of all who can avail themselves of the latest medical knowledge and experience. Since most people would rather be alive than educated, this is a field in which popular demand is extremely strong. In most countries resources are being found, both in cash and in kind, to maintain an efficient medical service. This appears to be so whether under a socialized or national health scheme, as in the United Kingdom, or under a free enterprise system, as in the United States.

Education, indeed, is at a disadvantage *vis-à-vis* all these public services, and this fact is reflected in the generally low salaries of teachers throughout the world—a situation described in the 1953 YEAR BOOK

OF EDUCATION on the *Social Position of Teachers*. More often than not, school buildings are more out of date than others. The criteria of efficient education which can be measured in terms of economic resources, like teacher–pupil ratios, space per pupil, the quantity and quality of specialized equipment, playgrounds, audio-visual aids, and textbooks, are usually laid down by educators. The provision of these necessary ingredients nearly always falls far below the level regarded as adequate.

This level, incidentally, is rising all the time. A hundred years ago all that was needed for an elementary school was a blackboard, rough furniture, and a few cheap booklets. Cheap microscopes, knives, and porcelain dishes sufficed to equip a medical faculty. To-day television sets, movie projectors, gymnasiums, and playing-fields are often provided even for young children, while professors of medicine ask for lavish supplies of expensive chemicals, electron microscopes, and laboratory technicians. And universities find it necessary to invest millions on electronic computing gear and the staff needed to operate it. Just as a modern factory needs expensive modern machinery, so does a modern teaching plant—but the latter is always far behind what would be thought proper for the former. The equipment of schools is usually a generation or two behind the times.

When the total amount of support to be devoted to education has been decided, usually with very little insight into the nature of the pressures that have determined the answer, there remains the vast problem of how to distribute the support within education itself. In a money economy, this problem appears as one of somehow reconciling conflicting financial claims within a limited budget. For example, vocational and technical education compete with general education or with mass-literacy campaigns; higher education with secondary or primary schooling; teachers' salaries with the provision of buildings, textbooks, and apparatus. The policy which determines the wise apportioning of resources is influenced by all kinds of factors and conditions vary from country to country. For example, in France, the rapid development of secondary and technical education might be secured by giving money to the Catholic Church—but this would offend a politically influential section of the people. In the southern regions of the U.S.A. much capital has been invested during the last twenty years in the attempt to improve the educational facilities available to Negroes: this was a response to the claims of liberal social thought as well as to the pressure exerted by the coloured population.

Furthermore, there are always decisions to be made connected with the most effective use of existing resources. Thus—should industry, commercial organizations, government departments, or the armed forces rather than schools and colleges undertake certain kinds of vocational training? Would efficiency be increased if they did? If the state bears the cost of technical colleges, industry is provided with recruits which it would otherwise have to train—is this a disguised subsidy to some industries? Who should benefit from this investment? Evidently, the answers given to such questions in highly industrialized countries may differ very much from those appropriate to agricultural ones undergoing mechanization.

Education and Production

It would be easier to arrive at a wise and acceptable policy for allocating available resources if one really knew how to assess the return on educational investment. Unfortunately, only vague and general estimates can be made. For our present purpose, it must suffice to say that the investment should lead to economic improvement. Now, classical economists list four basic elements which, operating jointly, determine the level of production within a community. These are: capital and capital goods, including tools, plant, cash, and credit; a supply of raw materials which is either controlled by or at least accessible to the producing units; transportation from the source of supply and to the markets; and labour. This last factor, which concerns us particularly, consists of skilled labour in the form of a trained working force and managerial talent with skills in leadership and in industrial judgment.

The factors which limit the development of skilled labour can themselves conveniently be grouped under four categories. The first is the availability of inborn, inherited talent. It might be argued that, under special conditions, a society could concentrate selected characteristics through selective breeding. This could, of course, take place without conscious direction simply as the result of social or natural factors in the environment. Whether it has occurred in the past or not is a matter for speculation, but it is certain that no modern society, whatever its political or social structure, attempts to modify the quality of its working force by planned breeding of human beings.

The second factor which determines the size of the work-force is the availability of institutionalized instruction and of appropriate cultural tools: schools, teachers, libraries, research, language. The Inca Empire was stopped in its growth and ultimately disappeared because it failed to make the indispensable cultural invention of a writing system capable of accumulating and transmitting knowledge. The Baluchis have no schools and cannot support 'non-productive members of society' such as teachers. Their language is an inadequate vehicle for advanced and systematic thought.

The third factor, which we have already discussed, is the availability of support. In many parts of the world, this material base, on which an educational system could be founded, simply does not exist. It still has to be created: and this creation may involve a change in the very nature of the cultural pattern itself. For instance, nomadic tribes wandering over a desert followed by a few camels and fat-tailed sheep will have to settle down in fixed abodes. Many, though not all, pastoral economies will have to change to the more productive small-grain agriculture. For some societies, with high population densities, even intensive land utilization like wet-paddy rice culture may prove inadequate, and manufacturing industry may have to be developed.

A fourth element might be called the ' social climate ': unless there exists within a society a pattern of attitudes which accords a higher status to an educated than to an uneducated man, people will not seek education. The ' social climate ' should include traditions of personal drive in the effort to secure training and skill, as things which are both necessary and desirable. It should also make it possible to grant to those who succeed in acquiring great learning a prestige as high as that given to those who have gained wealth or power by controlling factories or armies.

The real measure of a society's attitude towards education is the recognition it gives to those who are engaged in it and by its willingness to support non-productive members of a society during the process. It will be measured, too, by the use made of skilled talent once it is trained, and by a generalized willingness to accept changes in the cultural mores when these are dictated by the research and experience of educated *élites*. It may well be argued, indeed, that in the development of an economy, the education of the general public is as important as that of a skilled work-force because it determines the general attitude to what is desirable as well as the disciplines and restrictions which will be accepted in the effort to attain it.

This point is so important to-day in England and, indeed, in most European countries, that it deserves elaboration. It is certain that more resources are being devoted than can be afforded to the study of subjects and activities having little or no industrial importance and contributing not at all to national prosperity. Furthermore, powerful and age-hallowed institutions, such as the older universities and the ' Public ' schools, contain within themselves elements which are gravely prejudicial to the public welfare. As a result of their operation, talent is led away from science and technology towards studies having only traditional reputability, while resources are expended for the upkeep of useless posts and buildings at the cost of those upon which survival depends. The problems arising from the complex relations set up within modern industry are ignored. The reasons for the fall of ancient empires are studied, those that might lead to the decay of modern societies are avoided. Traditional disciplines are revered, technology is considered unworthy of real university status. Degrees are granted to those who specialize for a few years in modern or ancient languages, and refused to others of equal ability who devote themselves to less reputable but more useful aspects of human activity, calling for just as high a degree of ability. Blind tradition, operating through outworn institutions, blocks the path to progress and creates troubles which cannot be understood or dealt with. In spite of all that has been said recently about the imperative need for trained scientists and technologists, the idea still prevails in England that at least as many university students should be trained in the 'liberal arts' as in the sciences—as if there was an endless reservoir of high talent and as if there was something sacred and absolute in these 'fair shares'.

Under-developed countries illustrate the same principles just as clearly. Many nations claim to want the material benefits of technology but are unwilling to pay the social price which would make its adoption possible. A Muslim nation may want the material benefits of the factory system, but be unwilling to utilize its women as factory labour. Yet it can be demonstrated that such a society cannot compete with a Western society which utilizes all its population. A South American nation may dream of the material advantages of industrialization, but be unwilling to abandon the security and the comfort of a semi-feudal system. Such attitudes may in the long run be more significant for national economy than the direct training of labour. It is fairly easy to teach a man from the most primitive of societies basic skills which, when brought together in the carefully organized pattern of large-scale industry, lead to the fabrication of steel, the weaving of textiles, the refining of oil, and the operation of railways and airlines. The development of the managerial skills needed to organize these simpler skills and to guide the enormously complex enterprise of modern industry can also be developed, though with much greater difficulty, by formal education and extended experience. But all this will count for naught if the society itself in which the new industries operate is not adequately prepared for them. Lack of social and political cohesion among the population of France may well bring disaster, in spite of the intelligence of its leaders and the technical skill and inventiveness of its people. The rapid recovery of Germany is the reward for the willing acceptance of the disciplines of industrial life, although the reverse of the medal—political docility—was the condition for the disasters that overwhelmed her. The amazing wealth and expanding economy of the U.S.A. come not merely from the vast natural resources: indeed, the modern frontier and the untapped wealth are in the laboratories and in the minds of its people. Yet not all the training of its industrial army nor the education and experience of its managers could explain its success. The deepest roots of this expansion lie in a national attitude of daring and in a continuing optimism in the possibilities of the future—though doubt and strain may worsen the ulcers and thromboses produced by wrong feeding.

Once again we are led to the view that it is society's attitude to education, the institutionalized expressions of its social philosophy, which determine the way in which its schools contribute to economic well-being.

Five Types of Attitude towards the Support of Education

(1) Education as a Human Right

When considering typical national attitudes towards the purposes of education, one comes across five basic patterns. The first is also the most novel and most popular. It has been consecrated in the Bill on Human Rights prepared by the United Nations and assumes that every human being on earth, by the mere fact of birth, has a right to be educated just as he has an absolute and inalienable right to life, liberty, the pursuit of happiness, and—some would add—the enjoyment of private property. What Jeremy Bentham would have said about this new ' natural and inalienable right ' can well be imagined—in any case, the ideal it expresses is probably unattainable and perhaps unreasonable. Our purpose here is not to argue this point but rather to suggest that, even if education *per se* is a good thing, too much even of a good thing may do ill. This is true for education, although most Americans would hate to admit it. It seems almost certain that modern techniques of education can develop the potential qualities of many individuals in a society to a degree so high that few, if any, societies can adequately absorb the talent produced. It is all very well to argue that widespread non-functional education merely serves to give the society a high cultural level, though Dr. Bolgar's article on humanist education in the Free Cities of Italy should be read in this connexion. In fact, however, with the increased educational level, there comes an increase in ' felt needs ' and social demands, which the society cannot supply. Inevitably there comes ' unemployment ', social unrest, and individual frustration. The country of Lebanon has for fifty years developed more talent through education than its economy can absorb, and the only solution has been to export population—not the poor and uneducated immigrants with which the Western world is familiar, but the highest cultural products of that society. This is obviously a fantastic economic and social loss. The new country of Israel is also an example of too high a concentration of education in an economy unable to support it. Using scientists and scholars with doctoral degrees as simple labourers in the development of the Negev may provide dramatic propaganda, but it is hardly an economic utilization of manpower. No society operating such a system can be stable.

(2) *Education as an Indispensable Service*

In the U.S.A. and, to a varying degree, in other advanced countries it is widely held that a society cannot afford less education than the maximum it is able to finance. Superficially convincing proofs, some of a negative kind, are adduced. It is clear, for instance, that both in England and in the U.S.A., there are dismaying shortages of technically competent manpower. Official reports have been published in both countries which stress the gap between need and supply. The really disturbing shortage of teachers of science and mathematics is deplored: the long-range implications on the future training of engineers is evident. It seems, too, that only about half the personnel required is being produced, and that many large plants have hundreds of posts which they cannot fill. Furthermore, about half of all college or university graduates are needed to staff the schools. Yet, in the U.S.A., only 20 per cent have actually been entering teaching. Americans estimate that the need for new university teachers during the next ten or fifteen years will far surpass the total number of doctoral degrees awarded in that period. The quality of instruction must therefore inevitably fall: by 1970 only 20 per cent of college teachers will have a Ph.D. degree, instead of the 40 per cent who now hold it. Similarly, it is extremely doubtful whether the new English higher technological colleges, on the building of which vast sums are to be spent, will be able to recruit adequate numbers of competent teachers. It seems that both countries have in the past invested too little in higher education and that they are now to pay the price of neglect. What is known about the training of scientific and technological personnel in the Soviet Union high-lights the situation and gives it dramatic urgency.

Another superficially convincing proof put forward is that the U.S.A. is the richest nation on earth and that it has the highest general level of education; the two facts being causally related. Some observers, of course, have doubts about the quality of American education. This is a matter of judgment and of values. But no one can challenge the statistical facts that the United States has overwhelmingly the highest concentration of secondary school graduates, with twelve years or more of formal education, of college graduates, with sixteen or more years of formal education, and of persons holding standard doctoral degrees (representing nineteen or more years of formal education). The United States has 1,806 recognized institutions of higher learning, comparable to universities or independent university colleges in Europe. For the past five years American college enrolment has been running at approximately 2½ million. It is estimated that between 1966 and 1971 this enrolment is likely to be doubled. Even the so-called depressed minorities among the American population have educational benefits far surpassing that of any other nation on earth. Thus, the Negroes have a substantially higher percentage of university graduates than that of any European nation.

It would be easy, therefore, to draw the conclusion that America's income is largely or solely the result of this very high concentration of educational investment. There is certainly a correlation between a nation's income and its educational investment, but it is not a simple one. The United States could not possibly have achieved, nor could it maintain, its economy without very large investments in education, but it does not at all follow that this is the sole or even the dominant reason. During a period when the national income has expanded by about five, the expenditure on education has expanded by less than 50 per cent, and this with no adjustment for the inflation which has approximately doubled the cost of living. The explanation, of course, is in part the lag between the educational investment and the resultant change in national economy. America, like England, is living on the educational investment of twenty years ago, and the predicted manpower—and hence industrial—difficulties in the next ten years can be directly traced to a failure in educational policy during and immediately after World War II.

(3) Education creates Élites

Traditionally, the French, and to a less degree the English, think of education, especially at the higher level, as something intended for a small and select group. Qualities of mind are thought to be the essential requirement for leadership: the wise should lead and wisdom comes from the right education. This view is supported in part by simple traditional reverence and in part by an appeal to the outworn psychological theory of ' formal discipline '. The French, for instance, argue that intensive study produces a toughening of the mind analogous to the strengthening of muscles through exercise. They hold that the study of languages and mathematics is ' good ', whether or not these subjects will be used. The English argument is slightly different: it is the view that the qualities of character and personality needed to lead men are developed through contact with the liberal and humane disciplines, through literature, language, philosophy, history, and that it is essential to develop a proper misunderstanding of the role and function of science by continually pointing out its ' limitations '. Here one perceives the importance of the Platonic illusion that men can know absolute truth—an illusion which denies to man the supreme satisfaction of struggling to escape other illusions.

All these beliefs are linked to another myth, namely that somehow there should be restrictions on numbers receiving higher education if the quality of the latter is to be maintained as well as the social position of those who have enjoyed its benefits. In order to achieve this double aim, a complicated system of barriers, in the form of examinations, has been established. Candidates pass or are rejected on the basis of an almost savage elimination of those who fail to meet arbitrary standards. In principle, these standards should be deliberately adjusted so that society would receive precisely the number of doctors, lawyers, engineers, professors, chemists, and so on that the economy needs. This would involve being able to forecast future needs accurately, and agreeing upon the type of society desired. In point of fact, what happens is that society receives an alarming number of defeated frustrates, while the way in which both France and England stagger from one economic and financial crisis to another, hampered dreadfully by shortage of trained manpower, dramatizes the inaccuracy of forecasting and the failure of foresight.

The application of the *élite* theory to other areas of social organization has produced interesting phenomena. One of these is the ' downward filtration ' theory in colonialism. If the leader should be that one who is distinguished by intellectual or educational or social attainments, it naturally follows that the best method of raising the cultural standards of colonial areas is to educate leaders and allow them to raise the standards of the masses of their people. The technical success and the political chaos which this system has produced are only too painfully apparent in many areas of the world.

The economic result of this educational policy is extensive and evident. It has produced an economic class-society with built-in limits on the development of purchasing power of the masses, with a clear-cut hierarchy of economic power, and with a dangerous inherent antagonism between management and labour. It fails to develop an adequate reserve of talent which could be made available for rapid economic growth and for adjustment to rapidly changing conditions. It tends to reward intellectualism and hence, unfortunately, verbalism, while it tends to disregard practical skills and individual initiative. It lays stress on stability and individual security, and develops a large class of civil service bureaucrats and inflexible workers in an undynamic economy resistant to change.

(4) *Education as Thought-control*

The concept of education as a centrally controlled instrument for manipulating the minds of a people goes back to the ancient world but has been illustrated by the practices of the Italian Fascists, the Nazis, the militarists of Japan, and the Communists. The system of schools and universities serves as a selective valve through which flows only the kinds of knowledge and skill which the ruling groups consider good. In its less objectionable form this is not very different from the control of education by religious organizations, so that the religious but uninstructed believers will not be confused or led astray by intellectually superior non-believers. In its most vicious and amoral forms it leads to brain-washing and regimentation. Somewhere in between, education has consciously or unconsciously been used by all societies as an instrument of economic and social control.

We pride ourselves, for example, on ' consumer courses ' in which we attempt to teach values and judgment in the appraisal and purchase of material or cultural goods. We develop a subtle attitude towards taste, economic values, and even towards the products offered in our markets. Thus, the smell of flowers or musk has social status, while the odour of onions or garlic requires masking by chlorophyll. We teach that ownership of a house implies one set of social standards, while ownership of a television or a refrigerator or a motor-car has another. There can be no denying that education of this sort conveys real benefits by achieving the kind of society which a people desire, but the line between education and propaganda, between learning and advertising, between political consciousness and regimentation, is a very difficult one to draw. There can be little doubt that in the freest of societies man is easily susceptible to the development of an uncritical submissiveness to mass opinion. We follow the fads and fashions of our times in political ideas as well as in clothing.

(5) *Education for National Development*

The last of the five typical patterns of social attitudes towards education is that which considers it the tool *par excellence* for achieving national unity as well as for technological development. For instance, the leaders of under-developed societies argue that " the great nations of the world are great because they have available trained leadership and skilled personnel. If we have the same, we can develop our own country, utilize our resources, and achieve our rightful position in the world's community of nations."

The concept of education as the essential element for national development is based in part on a recognition of the status and prestige of those who do have education and who live within the under-developed area. Even a relatively modest degree of education sets the individual apart. In addition there exists a belief that education is directly correlated with political, economic, and social power. Finally, this belief is based on the idea that only lack of education stands in the way of technological and economic development. The individual who has already achieved status through education, but aspires to greatness both for himself and for his people, tends to forget that the powerful and rich nations of the world have an accumulation of experience and of capital, together with powerful alliances and economic links with societies and markets which only a long history can provide.

The example of Iran makes this quite clear. That country has enjoyed a relatively high level of educational opportunity for the past thirty years. There exists in its population a large body of personnel with advanced university degrees from distinguished institutions in Europe and the United States. Iran has one of the best systems of technical schools and, proportionately, one of the largest systems of secondary schools, in the Middle East. It has a national university and several faculties of a second university. Yet Iran has been unable to absorb its existing trained personnel. In 1949 a census showed that there were approximately fourteen thousand university graduates who were not practising their professions and who could not be located in the general population. One of the major problems which has faced the oil industry, both before and after nationalization, has been the crippling necessity of maintaining on the pay-roll very large numbers of technical personnel for whom there is no real need and no economic justification. As long as such a situation exists, far from being beneficial, education tends to depress the economy and to create a potentially explosive social situation. It will be extremely difficult, if not impossible, for Iran's major industry, oil, to compete in free world markets if it must carry the heavy burden of continued employment of trained but unnecessary personnel. Yet it is equally difficult, from a political and social point of view, to leave unemployed this surplus of technical personnel. It may well be questioned whether other existing or potential industries in Iran can in the foreseeable future absorb the excess. In such circumstances a drive to increase educational opportunity can certainly be seriously questioned.

Not all under-developed areas have basic restrictions such as those of Iran, however. Brazil, for example, has such unlimited possibilities for population growth, and such enormous natural resources, that there is likely to be almost an unlimited market for trained personnel at any time in the foreseeable future. Where intensive education in an under-developed area might very well produce an over-supply of trained personnel in certain industries or regions, the very size and potential richness of Brazil, together with its diversified pattern of industries, make possible an almost infinite number of readjustments so that it is unlikely that a situation like that in Iran could arise.

The United States can hardly be called an under-developed area. Yet the very rate of change and the speed of its growth have indicated that national development is entirely a relative matter. The U.S.A. represents an outstanding example of what Brazil may become through investment in education and industry. One of the major reasons for the constant need for education and training, in a nation which already has such a high level of educational attainment, is precisely the fact that a dynamic economic system rapidly makes skills obsolescent and produces serious dislocation in the employment of the work-force. It is estimated that the average industrial worker in the United States must be retrained every six or seven years, because of technological changes. This is possible only if the work-force originally possesses a relatively high level of general education. The difficulty is overcome only through an enormous annual expenditure, much of it hidden and contributed by the industries themselves in constant retraining of personnel.

Policy and Management of Resources

Against the background of societal attitudes—such as we have described above—those who control education frame their policy. That is to say, they decide how to acquire resources, how to allocate them, and how to administer them efficiently. To-day, all these problems are couched in terms of finance. It should be noted, however, that peculiar problems arise in societies changing quickly from the old barter economies towards those based on money. The transitional period is a difficult one. Once tribal or family living begins to break down, services in kind and the functional social organization of work tend to be replaced by wage structures, and consumer-goods are bought for money. More important, social organization tends to be determined economically with *entrepreneurs* distorting the general pattern of the efficient use of resources. Non-essential goods are often produced, if there is a sale for them from which profit is derived, which profit is not necessarily reinvested into society. Personnel no longer work in occupations in which, in a vague sense, they are most ' useful ' socially; very often they are encouraged to move into better-paid occupations which benefit the few rather than the many. The criteria of guidance, selection, and maintaining personnel in various jobs change. Time, accommodation, high social prestige, and status can no longer be set aside for people fulfilling useful functions as they were in small self-supporting societies. If there is a demand for certain kinds of skill, other incentives have to be found to attract them and other resources placed at their disposal.

The transition from one kind of economy to another involves changing from one source of 'wealth' to another in acquiring resources for any service—and for education. In primitive and pre-industrial societies the sources of wealth were land and property. Many educational systems have been created and maintained on these. It is necessary to look only at the Church schools and the land-grant colleges · in the United States to recognize this.

As the economy changes so do the criteria of evaluating the services provided. In a money economy an education which leads to a better-paid job is likely to be valued highly. Social evaluations on the desirability of this or that kind of education are extremely difficult to make. Even correlations between national productivity or national income and education are not easy to draw. Let us turn once more to advanced societies. It has been said already that the policy-maker is concerned, in the first place, with the search for resources. Here, three questions immediately arise. The first is whether the sources to be tapped are reputable. Some money is socially unacceptable in most societies, as for example, the returns on gambling, taxes on liquor, licence fees on prostitutes. Certain money is socially acceptable in many societies but unacceptable in some, as for example, money from religious sources, federal funds for equalization of opportunity, and foreign aid. And some funds are acceptable everywhere, as for example, individual tuition fees and local taxation.

Closely linked with all this is the problem of side-effects resulting from drawing on such income. In the United States, for example, most people would welcome federal funds to assist education, yet for a wide variety of reasons probably a majority are unwilling to accept them—because of fear of racial miscegenation, the possibility of religious influence, the fear of federal control, the possibility of excessively high taxes, local fear of a flight of capital, the possibility of slums and blighted areas, and so on.

Whatever the current or local attitudes, almost all societies finance education from six basic sources. These are: credit in the form of municipal or district bonds or loans; taxes or rates, including tax benefits such as exemptions for non-profit and philanthropic agencies; tuition or individual payment for educational services; profits arising from the sale of goods and services produced directly or indirectly by the educational institutions; income from endowment or other productive investments; and non-recurring income from gifts, charity, or bequests.

The second major problem in financing is that of the management of expenditures. Here, there is inevitably a conflict between 'efficiency' and 'effectiveness'. In earlier and less sophisticated times, business managers tended to measure efficiency in terms of *per capita* and unit costs. This is obviously misleading, if not meaningless, since education is efficient only if it is effective, and the measurement of effectiveness is not a financial but primarily a social matter. The educational system of pre-war Japan, for example, was one of the most efficient in the world from the point of view of *per capita* expenditure. It might even be considered efficient from the point of view of immediate and superficial attainment—such as the degree of literacy or the percentage of the population who attained secondary and higher levels. But seen historically, Japan's educational system was a catastrophic failure, for it produced a regimented, docile population which was duped by its leaders and led to defeat and disaster.

In the management of expenditure, methods of accounting inevitably influence cost. Skill in drawing up budgets and forecasts (either dividing up the available money or doing the job regardless of ultimate expense) basically affect the efficiency. Audit, appraisal, and control of the actual finances of a school or system are certainly important in maintaining accuracy and accountability. In all this, educational finance is no different from any other type—whether government, industrial, or personal—except in the evaluation of results.

Perhaps the major obstacle to developing a good appraisal system for education is the time-lag which inevitably exists. The effects of an educational procedure are seldom immediately apparent. Johnny may not learn to read and this, in a gross sense, is a condemnation of the quality of the education he has received. But in most educational systems Johnny *does* learn to read, and the real test of whether his education was 'good' or not is determined only much later in life when one can see what Johnny does with his reading. Failure to learn some skills is dramatically more apparent in some cases than in others. Thus, a poorly trained navigator or pilot crashes his plane, and a poorly trained surgeon or physician kills his patient. But the difference in the life pattern of Johnny, whether he is well or poorly trained in reading or in social attitudes, may take a generation to become apparent, and the result may even then not be closely identified with the cause.

There is also the difficulty of comparing intangibles. What is an attitude worth in comparison to a skill? There were few societies in the world with more highly developed skills than Nazi Germany, yet the failure to develop proper attitudes led to the greatest catastrophe the world has yet seen. There is the problem of relative values. In every society and economy, long-range changes take place which are difficult to evaluate and which may not become apparent for so long a time that modification of the educational system is difficult or impossible. Thus, for example, through education a man may gain life and lose his soul—he may improve his material well-being but abandon worthy ethical standards. Even some of the characteristics presumably most desirable over a short range of time may prove to be disastrous in the end. Thus, in the free world there are few who would deny that individualism and the willingness to stand against the crowd are desirable characteristics, yet this very characteristic has proved disruptive to French society. On the other hand, we may laud teamplay and the subordination of one's personal interest to the good of the group, yet this led to regimentation and to the enslavement of the individual in Nazi Germany.

Another important question is the effect of education on the total economy. This has received far less attention and is probably less susceptible to accurate research than simple matters of educational finance. By its very nature, it must be studied in terms of indirect results.

It was earlier noted that the productive pattern of any economy depends upon capital, raw materials, transportation, managerial skill, and trained labour. The relative importance in any single organization of the trained work force and of the consumer is an indirect measure of educational attainment. Three examples will suffice to illustrate this. The first is that of mechanization, and especially of automation. Whether the change takes place as a result or as a cause of an educational endeavour, it is nevertheless certain that education will be a major limiting factor upon the extent and the success of such an organization of work. Without high levels of education, some forms of organization are not possible.

A second example is that of technological development. One of the tragic mistakes which most under-developed nations make is in their belief that because they can learn successfully to operate an existing industry, they have in fact achieved the ability to compete in that industry. Nothing could be further from the truth—because the success and survival of industry in the modern world depend upon the dynamic qualities of continued and intensive industrial research, and most industries become obsolescent and non-competitive almost immediately unless supported by such researches. Obviously scientific research cannot be carried on without an adequate educational system.

A third example is the development of consumer attitudes, again a highly specialized but nevertheless an extremely important element in the economic effects of education. In 1954 one of the three most powerful automobile corporations in America faced serious economic reverses because it was unable accurately either to gauge or to modify public taste. In the following year it almost completely reversed its disadvantageous economic position by successfully meeting these two needs. On three occasions major British aeronautical companies suffered the dismaying economic consequences of inadequate engineering. In each case the deficiency in engineering was ultimately corrected, but the loss to the economy could not be recouped so readily. In one case the prototype of an aircraft had to be removed from service; in another, failure of a wing structure delayed the utilization of the model until the design was approaching obsolescence; and in the third case, England lost her unchallenged position in the jet-propulsion field. It would be inaccurate to state that education was responsible for the immediate errors or omissions of the engineers who were concerned. But it can be argued that lack of an adequate body of trained engineers and technicians limited the amount of research and testing, and hence delayed the successful building of acceptable models. Germany in World War II suffered from this same lack of trained personnel as a result of its educational system. That country could not adequately man five major programmes simultaneously—radar, submarines, guided missiles, jet propulsion, and atomic fission.

The indirect and intangible results of education have enormous effects upon any economy. It is a popular pastime for Europeans and Asians to laugh at the American preoccupation with bathrooms, television sets, cars, and electric refrigerators. Yet no one can deny that the economy of the United States might collapse and bring economic ruin to all the world if a chain reaction were set up in which its public lost interest in canned and frozen foods, Sunday afternoon drives, the sacred daily bath, and the favourite T.V. comedian. These tastes and attitudes are inextricably linked with the economic organization of society. Complex economies run on intangibles—attractive packaging, recognition trim on new models, a preference for certain trade names and brands, and the presumed necessity of using special types of soaps and powders, toothpaste, and cigarettes if one's health and allure and professional competence are to be preserved. Even the stern and politically generated attitudes towards economic life common among European nations are based not alone on simple patriotic slogans and propaganda, but also have their roots deep in the lives of the people and the bringing-up of their children. The Germans were induced to accept guns instead of butter as much by the schools as by the political orator. England's austerity with " fair shares for all " came as much from school-inspired ethics of good sportsmanship as it did from party programmes and political editorials. It would be a mistake to think that America's economy rests solely on the skills of the radio huckster and of the advertising man. It stems fundamentally from a national conviction in the possibility of an expanding economy, which is one of the fundamental characteristics of American life.

The third measurable effect of investment in education is that provided by the growth of national income. Such a measure has many limitations. It is an attempt to correlate a complex end-result, of many interlocking factors, with a single one of those factors. It has the limitation of measuring only one of the effects—the material one —out of a large number of observable results from the educational endeavour. It has the disadvantage that a time-lag exists between the investment and the national profit. And, above all, it suffers because the relationship between educational investment and resultant national income is so complex that it seems almost impossible to establish precise statistical results. With all these limitations, the fact remains that a correlation between educational investment and national income does exist, and in rough terms probably can be determined. Such a measure of the effectiveness of an educational system has a very real attractiveness to many people. In their individual lives they are willing to accept this measure regardless of its imperfections. Parents make sacrifices and youth invests its best years in an educational investment which they know offers the greatest single chance for economic as well as social benefit.

ROBERT KING HALL.

J. A. LAUWERYS.

THE DEMAND FOR EDUCATION

(Setting the Goals)

THIS section is devoted to an analysis of the ways in which a demand for education is created. Two basic demands can be distinguished : one stems from parents, the other from society generally. Neither excludes the other and at times the interests of parents are closely identified with those of society. The former, consumer demand, can be recognized by the willingness of parents to pay high fees, or under some circumstances high taxes, for the education of their children. The overriding needs of a complex society are much less easily discerned and assessed.

Here, however, the demand for education as a social service receives special attention. Every society provides a minimum amount of education for its members. In simple cultures taboos, imitation, ridicule, praise and initiation ceremonies play an important part in the process of passing on information thought necessary for social harmony and economic viability. In more complex societies we have to look at the activities of numerous social groups and institutions concerned with the provision of education. Consensus rarely exists between them. Nevertheless, a study of their objectives and the efforts they make to provide education makes it possible to judge community feeling and the status accorded to education.

Many factors influence the climate of opinion. Religious and political convictions, the strength and wish for social advancement, the needs of industry and of national defence play their part. All create a demand for education and influence the form of response. A particularly important factor in industrialized societies is the belief that education promotes economic well-being by spreading necessary skills and enabling fresh sources of talent to be tapped. Another strong stimulus to-day is a social philosophy which finds expression in slogans such as "equality of educational opportunity" and "secondary education for all". Not always, however, can the economy support what is desired.

Our analysis, then, suggests that at least FOUR broadly conceived factors should be considered. They are neither comprehensive nor, in practice, can they be isolated one from the other. Evidently the pattern of an educational demand in a modern society is very complex. Nevertheless we recognized that *The Religious Traditions in Education* had been important. Operating through the churches, they created a demand for an educated *élite* or aimed at the recruitment of believers. Professor Phenix discusses some aspects of this in the first article.

In the second, Professor Grue-Sorensen analyses *The Social Factor in Education*; it is seen as operating through the agency of the family, small informal groups, and governments. The problem for any social philosophy is how far we are justified in manipulating education to further social stability—that is to transmit culture—and to what extent is the individual to be allowed freedom of development. *The Effects of External Stimuli* is the third important question discussed. To-day mass media of communication have made a very large public conscious of the apparent benefits of Western education. In varying degrees it is in demand everywhere. But as articles by Mr. Griffiths and by Mr. Lawrence point out, doubts exist about the suitability in this century of nineteenth-century Western education. In some cases these doubts amount to apathy.

The fourth, and perhaps most significant, factor is seen as the process of industrialization. Technically trained personnel is required at all levels. Industry to-day must have adequate research staffs and well-qualified executives. With an increase in the number of specialists, however, the need arises for a general education which will enable economically fragmented societies to cohere socially and politically. New processes of selection have had to be devised in order to make full and efficient use of available manpower.

The kind of education demanded by an industrializing society in order to improve material conditions often conflicts with that thought most desirable in a previous age. Acute problems arise when the primary task of education is no longer to transmit a somewhat static culture but to meet the economic needs of a rapidly changing society. The solutions have to be sought in a clearer understanding of the educative processes and in a reorganization of educational systems. Thus the dual task for educators is to discover, as far as possible, and retain those aspects of the tradition which are generally held to be essential to the stability of society and to become aware of social needs and parental wishes in order to modify the educational structure and curricular offerings in these terms.

In a technological age these are tremendously complicated and involve more than a simple assessment of the economic return on educational investment as both Dr. Bowden and Dr. McCloskey point out. The problem goes to the very heart of educational evaluation and policy. The final article by Professor Shavin indicates how the recognized need in the U.S.S.R. for technically trained personnel is being met.

THE EDITORS.

CHAPTER ONE

The Religious Tradition in Education

THERE are three essential components to education: content or sub-ject-matter, motivation, and a principle for evaluation and selection of the content. These three essentials all enter into the formulation of what Ortega called " the principle of economy in education ". Accord-ing to Ortega, education comes into being because in the civilized community the number and complexity of things to be learned (con-tent) and demanded for assured, free, and efficient living (motivation) far outstrip the capacity to learn and hence necessitate a standard of choice between alternatives. " Scarcity of the capacity to learn is the cardinal principle of education. It is necessary to provide for teaching precisely in proportion as the learner is unable to learn." [1] Thus in its essence education is an economic phenomenon. It has to do with the problem of distributing scarce goods, the capacity to learn. Education is an economic concern in a still broader sense, since human beings have other interests and engage in activities other than learning. All of these interests compete for the limited supply of available human and material resources.

The Religious Factor in General

Religion is one of the major factors which has entered into the creation and resolution of this economic-educational problem. It has provided content, motivation, and criteria for choice. The extent of this provision depends upon whether religion is conceived in a basic functional sense or in a conventional and traditional manner. In a basic sense religion may be defined, following Tillich, as that which concerns us ultimately, i.e. as one's centrally controlling loyalties or life-commitments. By such a definition, religion clearly provides the central motivation for conduct and criteria for decisions. In particular, it furnishes both power and direction for the educational enterprise. It supplies the basis on which the relative importance of various learn-ings is assessed and by which judgment is rendered on education in comparison with other human concerns. Religion, fundamentally conceived, thus supplies the answer to the economic problem.

Conventionally conceived, religion is merely one interest among others, a specialized and limited set of concerns and activities. It is

---

[1] *Mission of the University* (Routledge & Kegan Paul, London, 1946), p. 53.

then no longer *the* determinant of the economic problem but merely one factor among many. The religious interest is only one source of motivation for education, providing only a part of the content of education, and competing with other special interests, including education, for available resources.

This distinction between religion as ultimate concern and as special interest is crucial for the economic problem. The degree of ultimacy is a measure of the extent to which the economic problem is subsumed under the religious question. In an intentional religious community religious conviction governs the whole of social and personal existence, and the question of content, motive, and distribution of education is decided on religious grounds. In a predominantly secular society religion takes its place alongside political loyalties, business and professional interests, and the concerns of the manifold voluntary associations in competition for resources. It might be added that there are also societies (e.g. communistic) which are nominally secular but which actually function as communities with an ultimate religious concern, in that they have an ideology which provides criteria for the organization of all phases of life.

Life-affirmation and Life-denial

We propose now to deal in succession with some of the major aspects of religion which relate to the demand for education. The first of these is the principle of life-affirmation or of life-denial.

Religions may be distinguished with respect to their positive or negative attitude towards existence. Life-affirming religions tend to create a demand for education; life-denying religions tend to discourage education. If the world is regarded as essentially good, there is a motive for elaborating that good in cultural creations and in transmitting these from generation to generation; if the world is regarded as evil, the multiplication of misery through culture and education will be avoided.

The religion of Israel is an example of life-affirmation. According to the Genesis story, God looked upon the world He had created and saw that it was good. He commanded men to multiply and to enjoy the fruits of the earth. Israel's God was no metaphysical principle, nor remote spectator of the cosmic drama. He was an active participant in the historical existence of His people, showing concern for individual and nation, guiding, strengthening, punishing, fighting battles, and giving laws. Knowledge of Him and devotion to Him presupposes serious concern with the processes of temporal existence. Hence education has been of major importance in the Jewish community. Learning is a religious duty and privilege. It is through education that one can participate in the life which God has created and sustained.

Christian faith shares in this Hebrew affirmation of life and supports it further with the belief in the divine Incarnation. For the Christian not only is God manifest in history, but He is fully revealed in the person of Jesus Christ. That God should take upon himself the garment of flesh and blood is to Christians the supreme instance of God's interest and participation in temporal existence. Hence in Christian civilization the life and culture of men and the education which promotes them are important.

Confucianism is a life-affirmative religion of a non-theological kind. In it the emphasis is on education in right social relationships, and more particularly in the requirements of skilful political management.

Hinduism is an illustration of a life-denying religion. Time and history are regarded as illusion, and material existence is a bondage from which one seeks deliverance. Under these circumstances culture and its transmission through education are at best unavoidable concomitants of earthly travail.

In general, religious mysticism shares this world-denying outlook. Philosophically, mysticism rests upon a preference for the one as against the many, a desire that multiplicity be swallowed up in unity. But education requires a due respect for the plural, a recognition of and interest in the manifold richness of the world. Hence mystical tendencies serve to diminish the demand for education.

The case is more complex with regard to the *ascetic* element in religion. Asceticism is world-denying with respect to material goods, but it may be basically life-affirming. The denial of physical pleasure may be in the interests of a heightened intellectual or spiritual life. Perhaps all education rests upon a certain asceticism—a renunciation of simple biological satisfactions for the sake of more complicated cultural attainments. Puritanism is an example of a qualified asceticism united with a vigorous concern for education.

The Nature of Man

At the heart of every religion and of every educational programme is a view of the nature of man. All religions without exception take human life seriously. By its very nature religion involves a deep concern for the meaning of man's existence. Every religion presupposes that the human drama is not an insignificant by-product of the cosmic process, but that man's life is in some degree a reflection of, or a clue to, the meaning of the whole.

Religious teaching about human nature has generally centred about the idea of the *soul*. Man's soul is his innermost essence, his true being or nature. It is that reality which makes him uniquely human. The conduct of education is dependent upon a guiding doctrine of the soul, or of essential manhood. The attempt to reduce man to physio-chemical mechanism or to explain human behaviour solely in bio-logical terms not only contradicts the religious testimony regarding the soul but in the religious view undermines the very foundations of education by according to man's highest and distinctively human attainments a subordinate and derivative status.

In Western religion, especially in Christianity, there have been two contrasting aspects of the doctrine of man which have influenced the demand for education. One is the belief that man bears the image of the divine nature. This may mean that man, like God, has capacity to create, that he possesses freedom, that in his rational powers he shares in the divine *logos*, that he is a temple of the Holy Spirit, or that he contains a ' divine spark' or ' inner-light '. For the most part this high view of man has been a stimulus to education. It has encouraged the development of the highest human powers by affirming that they are akin to the divine ground of all things. It has provided cosmic sanc-tion for creativity and invention, the search for truth, the production of beauty, and the attainment of virtue. It is the theological support for the belief in the " infinite worth of human personality " which plays such a central role in the modern demand for universal education. There is no sufficient empirical justification for this belief. It is only in the light of an ultimate commitment to ideals of equality and justice that such an educational programme can be defended, and this commit-ment in turn rests either explicitly or implicitly upon the religious faith of which the *imago dei* doctrine is the classic expression.

The other aspect of the Christian view of man which has been educa-tionally important is the doctrine of sin. Man is not only created in the divine image but that image has been defaced. From his state of original innocence he has fallen into a state of estrangement from his fellows and from God. According to this view, man cannot be trusted to use his powers rightly; he will seek to employ them for his own selfish purposes rather than in the service of love, truth, and justice. Education will only aggravate the disease by increasing the power which man can pervert.

A strong doctrine of sin would appear to diminish the demand for, and the relative prestige of, education by fostering distrust of human powers and of autonomous culture, yet the evidence does not support this. The Calvinists, for example, believed in total depravity yet also in education. The explanation lies in the relation of education to redemption. The redeemed sinner can profit from education, and even for the unregenerate, education may serve to warn and condemn, pre-paring the way for redemption. A doctrine of sin, by itself, would discourage education, but attended by a belief in the possibility of salvation it serves as a stimulus to learning.

In orthodox Christian teaching the basic sin is pride, the clearest form of which is the demand for self-sufficient autonomy. Redeemed man acknowledges his creature-hood and dependence upon God. Modern naturalistic humanism is based upon the principle of autonomy and assumes that education will play a major role in achieving it. Yet there is much weight in the religious view that dependent man will maintain a more consistent and fruitful demand for education than autonomous man, since the latter is estranged from the true sources of his being while the former maintains connexion with the fountain of life from which all culture ultimately proceeds and in which all education has its primal reason for being. On the other hand, a religious faith which pushes human dependence to the extreme, making of man a pawn of arbitrary divine omnipotence and the highest righteousness an unquestioning obedience, does undermine the value of education. Probably the relative weakness of education in Islamic civilization is due in part to this factor. The maximum religious motive for education would seem to be in a view of man as free and responsible, capable of sin, yet heir also of saving grace.

The Destiny of Man

Another factor in the demand for education is religious belief concerning life after death. Belief in rewards and punishments in a life to come stimulates a sense of urgency and importance of the use of time which heightens the significance of education. As compared with the view that there is no life beyond this one it also tends to promote an interest in education continuing throughout life. There is little incentive to learn for older people who see no consequence of their effort in a life after death.

The belief in reincarnation (as in Hinduism), as contrasted with immortality or resurrection (as in Christianity), tends to diminish the importance of education in any one life-span. On the other hand, it does provide motivation for progressing to higher stages of existence and eventually for release from the cycle of rebirth. The ultimate necessity for education, if not its urgency, is certified by the law of *karma*, according to which every deed has its inexorable consequences in the next stage of incarnate existence.

Faith, Reason, and Works

One of the major tensions within the religious tradition has been the contrast between belief in salvation by faith as contrasted with works or reason. The moral and logical rigour of primitive Buddhism is opposed to the short-cut formula for salvation in the cult of Amitabha Buddha. Hinduism has its " Way of works " (cf. the *Code of Manu*) and its " Way of Knowledge " (cf. the *Upanishads*), but also its " Way of Devotion " (cf. the *Bhagavad-Gītā*). In Christianity there is the Pauline-Augustinian-Lutheran emphasis on justification by faith alone as opposed to all legalistic or moralistic formulae. There is also the contemporary challenge of a strong doctrine of revelation (e.g. in Karl Barth) to rationalistic and natural theologies.

Education, as a deliberate enterprise in guiding human development, inescapably involves reason and moral effort. To the extent, then, that any religion emphasizes faith at the expense of intellect and will, the demand for education is diminished. Confidence in fulfilment by simple trust and devotion may serve to console those who do not have the opportunity or the ability to profit from education. Popular faith-cults may thus quiet the demand for widespread education.

It is possible, of course, for faith to be in fruitful union with reason and moral effort and thus to encourage education. Luther, for example, had no use for scholarship for its own sake but valued it highly for the defence and exposition of the faith; Calvin taught that the keeping of the moral law was proof of the faithful man's election and vital union with Christ, and to-day's dialectical theologians make great use of the critical intellect and vigorously pursue ethical concerns.

Sacred Books and Rites

The religious tradition is embodied for the most part in certain sacred writings and in cultic ritual. The effect on the demand for education is two-fold. First, the sacred books and rites constitute a definite and tangible corpus which is to be transmitted from generation to generation. They provide the substance of a curriculum for religious education. This curriculum may be comprehensive in scope. It may encompass not only belief and the conduct of worship, but such matters as dress, personal morality, and business practices. In Judaism the *Torah* and the *Talmud* together contain regulations for every aspect of the life of the Jewish community. The *Qu'ran* and the traditions serve similarly for the orthodox Muslim. The orthodox Hindu also has a definite tradition of wide scope for the regulation of his conduct.

The second effect of sacred books and rites is to restrict or circumscribe education. It is characteristic of religious movements to crystallize their traditions in authoritative writings and in standardized rituals. The fixed tradition then tends to become the norm for all future generations and to resist alteration or accretion. From this spring exclusivist and monopolistic attitudes, wherein the faithful consider themselves in possession of the truth and do not welcome instruction in any other ideas and practices. When a Protestant Christian confesses that the Bible is the sufficient rule for faith and practice, he *may* imply that psychiatry or modern history or anthropology add nothing essential to the guidance or interpretation of life. The Muslim is convinced that Allah has not left him without sufficient light—in the *Qu'ran*—and the Jew searches the Law for guidance in every age.

These two effects of the religious tradition—the one in stimulating religious education of a very definite sort and the other in discouraging other kinds of education—re-enforce one another in relation to the economic problem. Both effects increase the demand for available educational resources by religious interests in comparison with other agencies. The extent to which a monopoly condition results depends upon the degree to which the religion involved is an ultimate concern as contrasted with the conventional-nominal type.

The Religious Institution

The mode of organization of the religious community has much to do with the demand for education. In general, a highly organized, authoritarian, hierarchical church limits the demand for education, while a democratic type of church extends it. The most striking historical example of this was the movement for popular education under the stimulus of the Protestant Reformation. If each Christian was to read and interpret the Bible for himself, under the direct guidance of the Holy Spirit, and if each believer was to serve as priest to his neighbour, then all must be educated. In the hierarchical church the need for education is limited to the higher clergy, whose function it is to interpret God's truth and then mediate it to an unquestioning and obedient laity.

Judaism has also stood for the education of all the people, because of a deeply rooted democratic and lay tradition and a profound sense of the responsibility of each person for the well-being of the community. In the case of Islam there are in theory no clergy and a strong tradition of equality amongst believers, yet its powerful authoritarianism, more political than religious in character, exacting full obedience and submission, has hindered the advance of popular education. The caste organization of Hinduism reserves education for the Brahmins, who as an *élite* mediate divine wisdom to the lower orders of humanity. Similarly, Confucian education in the classics was reserved for the small group of scholar-officials, who were then expected to use their wisdom for the wise governance of all the people. Buddhism, on the other hand, especially the Hinayana, being generally egalitarian in character, has encouraged wide diffusion of learning.

A church with a clerical *élite* creates a demand for higher education.

In ages of popular ignorance and violence the monasteries of Europe were virtually the only centres of learning. Theological studies were for centuries a major part of the curriculum of the universities of Europe. The earliest American colleges were established principally to supply an educated clergy.

With advancing secularization theological training has receded into the background and taken its place as one of the specialized disciplines. As such, it competes with law, medicine, business, and other callings for able personnel and financial support. At the present time in the United States there is keen competition for the most able students, and the theological seminaries are making a strong and increasingly successful bid for them, backed by substantial financial resources. This phenomenon, which reflects the contemporary wave of popular interest in religion (with its resultant demand for clergy) and the remarkable revival of theological scholarship, is a final striking example of the influence of the religious tradition upon the economic problem in education.

PHILIP H. PHENIX.

CHAPTER TWO

The Social Factor in Education

EDUCATION always takes place in a society and is, more or less, woven into the texture of the life of the society. The few instances that are known of education being carried on in isolation are of interest only as curiosities and play no part in a general consideration of this subject. They are so few that it is not possible to generalize from them and the information we have about them is so questionable and inadequate that it is not possible either, through a study of these isolated cases, to gain a reliable picture of what the social factor means in education.

We must not let the fact that education takes place in a society mislead us into assuming that education is an out-and-out social phenomenon without other components. A given education can have its social and non-social features. People of an extremely sociological way of thinking, for example, Émile Durkheim, would probably be inclined to regard education exclusively as a function of the society in which it takes place. In which case education becomes simply one of the forms in which the life of the community expresses itself, and no component part of education would be without its social contingency. It could be advanced in support of this view that education varies according to social conditions and manifests itself differently in different groups, classes, and other forms of human society. But this proves really nothing more than that education has its clearly marked social contingency, and not that it cannot at the same time have other aspects which are not a function of society.

In order to determine if this be the case, we need a clearer definition of what comes within the concept of education and, in addition, we require a distinctive characteristic by which we can decide whether a given influence is to be labelled social or non-social.

Education from Nature, Things, and Men

If we think for a moment about Rousseau's old distinctions between the education received from nature, from things, and from men, it soon becomes apparent that neither the education received from nature nor the education received from things is social. It is true that what Rousseau calls the education received from nature could perhaps be social in one sense, namely, in regard to its capacity for developing an instinct or urge towards social life, but that is quite another matter.

The concept ' social factor in education ' does not allude to any purpose at which natural development may aim, but refers to whether a given factor is social in its origin; and with this interpretation we must maintain that in Rousseau's meaning the education received from nature and from things does not contain any social component. Nor does the human development which occurs as a result of these factors often fall within the concept of education, except in a very extended and transferred meaning of the word.

Only in the third kind of education, education received from men, can we expect to find the social factor, and the question at once arises as to whether this factor is always present. It serves no purpose to refer to the fact that this education takes place in the form of a social relationship, namely that of teacher and pupil : for if this were the meaning of the presence of a social factor in education, the subject would be too trivial. The crucial point is whether the person who carries out the education represents something social and not only his own individual wishes and intentions; whether he transmits something which by its very nature must be called social—something which in a broad sense is demanded by society.

To get a general view of the importance of the social factor or factors in education, it is expedient to regard education as a *function*; and the very ambiguity of this word can be used to gain the general view we desire. Function can mean something that takes place, simply a process, or it can mean the dependence of one thing on another, and it is from this latter meaning we can say that education is a function—but of what?

The education of a particular individual depends on many things: the intelligence and temperament of the parents, their taste and manners, their valuations and morals, and their economic and social circumstances. In addition, it is a function of the same factors in the other teachers with whom the individual comes into contact. Further, it depends upon public opinion and prevailing traditions, on the country's political structure and the educational system. In other words, the demand for education is a function of an endless number of factors in the sense that it varies with them—and, in addition, with differing effects according to the individual's own character. It is, among others, this last condition which makes it so difficult to develop an exact, empirical, scientific doctrine of education; for " the same fire that melts butter, hardens the egg " (G. W. Allport).

The task now is to select from all these demands for education the ones that are social. It is probable that they form a hierarchy in which some are more superior and generally active, others more subordinate and particular in operation.

The Influence of Social Groups

In certain respects education undoubtedly reflects the objectives of the political community and its particular organization, for example, whether it is a liberal democracy or an illiberal dictatorship. We have had clear evidence of this in our own times and need not go to history to be convinced that this function is important. We have had opportunity, too, of seeing how education is made to accord with the national political form when for some reason it has come into disharmony with it. This happened in the Soviet Union, where educational ideas during the 1920's were fairly radical and actually implied an extreme individualism. They had been adopted because they were revolutionary and represented a form of revolt in the *bourgeois* Western Europe and America where they were practised. However, this form of education was out of harmony with the interests of a collectivist, authoritarian government, with the result that a change was made in the 1930's, when a new pedagogy was adopted in which the emphasis was laid on discipline, order, obedience, and the like.

This serves to show education as a function of the political community and its particular system, even in the case where there was not full agreement between them at the beginning. Where it is a case of a stabilized society, the relation is quite obvious. Greek children in olden times were brought up to be Greeks, and if they were Spartan children they were educated to be Spartans and if Athenian to be Athenians; Roman children were educated to be Romans, and in our times English children are brought up to be English and German children to be Germans. In each case, having regard not only to the general culture pattern, but also to the system of government. The relation is particularly marked where education of the young is regarded actually as the main duty of the state, a view expressed by Plato, Aristotle, and others. In doing so they merely expressed what was common practice in the Greek city-state.

But education depends not only on the structure of the large society, the state, it is also dependent on its various sub-groups, e.g., the social class with its particular outlook, way of life, and ideology. Even the family can be regarded as a small society with its own kind of solidarity, traditions, and concepts of the need for education, and though these may vary considerably from one family to another, many of the influences that emanate may be described as social in character. The family, too, is one of the intermediate links through which many of the other social influences make themselves felt, e.g., class influence or the influence of the religious communities. Actually it is often difficult to separate these two kinds of influence, that of the parents on the children firstly as a family influence and secondly as an influence from a larger group to which the family happens to belong, such as the Catholic Church or the Quaker Society, the working class or the middle class. Though we must not forget that class influence and the influence of the religious community usually flows, too, through channels outside the family.

The Social Process and Methods of Transmission

At the same time we must distinguish between the psychological process that takes place and through which the individual is moulded in harmony with the social standards and norms which are current in the various social groups, and the result itself in the form of a social character of a more or less distinct kind. But if we stick to our description of education as responding to the demands of society, it is sufficient, as a matter of principle, to consider the result in the form of a particular social character or type, without bothering about the psychological processes by which the result came about. It is analogous to knowing, in a purely descriptive way, a physical dependence between two factors, e.g., the tide and the position of the moon, without knowing the physical theory which explains it.

Sociologists have often taken the view that they could study social phenomena and their inter-relations independently of any possible psychological explanation of the origin and transmission of these phenomena, and it is a point of view that can very easily be upheld. These social phenomena are usually uniformities in ways of thinking, feeling, or acting, which are transmitted to the next generation through education. And we need only ascertain their presence in the younger generation to know that education has exerted an influence. From a sociological point of view we need not know the psychological processes by which it has happened, e.g., what part imitation, identification, suggestion, direct teaching, coercion, threats, and warnings with attendant fear have played in the transmission.

This view, which can be described as the principle of the psychological irrelevance of sociology, or *vice versa*, has been met in the French school of sociology, and it has not been without significance for the elucidation and study of social phenomena and their inter-relations. It keeps to the purely descriptive and abstains from the explicative technique, and for a positive science which would stay on safe empirical ground it is not a bad principle to follow.

However, such a methodological one-sidedness is hardly fruitful in the long run. For if we intend to influence progress, it is surely advantageous to know the processes through which transmission takes place. Here, however, closer examination is a matter only of a description which goes more into detail and includes in the picture the psychological nature of the individuals. Where we use a psychological description to elucidate something which we already know from a sociological description, we have at the same time some kind of explanation.

If Durkheim and the many others who agree with him are followed in regarding education as a socialization of the child, i.e., as an implanting of all the characteristic traits of a group in the individual, the sociologist will often be satisfied with the bare proof that such an implanting takes place, whilst the social-psychologist will, in addition, understand and explain the whole process from what is known of the individual's psychic constitution, needs, and reaction mechanisms. Sometimes the psychology is carried so far that it deduces the child's social adaptation from its biological nature, e.g., a tendency to reduce tensions by falling into line with certain ways of life, a particular social pattern. If this interpretation is carried to extremes one can look upon social adaptation as a training in which the child experiences pleasure in being in harmony with the social norms and dislike in being in disagreement with them, a learning process which takes place according to Thorndike's ' law of effect '.

In this case, however, one is on the way to denying the real social factor. If there is such a factor, it is tantamount to a confirmation that the process of socialization cannot consist of a learning process after the pattern of training through pleasure and displeasure, and which is conditional on an individual's biological constitution. In an earlier age, too, philosophers assumed that, because people saw it was advantageous to unite together, society was based on some kind of agreement or pact. Here again the social factor was underestimated as a separate form of reality—social behaviour being deduced from biological need.

This is not to say that there is nothing in the individual which predisposes him to social ways. On the contrary, it can be said that the social factor, such as is found outside the individual, must correspond with something in the individual's own nature, in order for him to become socialized. What this is, however, can often be defined only in terms which are limited to recording the fact itself, e.g., if I am able to regard others as my true fellows and treat them as my true fellows, I must have a fellow feeling. Here it is possible to record only the fact that one has a characteristic psychical disposition which cannot be derived from others. And instead of deducing the social element from the psychological, one rather deduces the psychological from the social. The closest we have come to an explanation of the socialization of man from purely individual psychological ideas has probably occurred through the use in psycho-analysis of concepts such as identification and especially introjection, the latter being understood as the process by which prohibitions and precepts of other people, their moral attitudes and valuations, are incorporated in the child's own personality. By this means a super-ego is formed which becomes in part a representative of society in the individual. These concepts, however, are matters of hypothetical formation, and their advantage over other concepts in giving positive information about the nature of the process of socialization is still in dispute.

The Danish philosopher, Hoeffding, has described conscience as the social echo, and has thereby contended that there is within the single person a sounding-board for the social element, a quality by which man feels himself allied with and bound by the society in which he grows up, first of all with the concrete society with all its special traits, and also possibly with an idealized, unrealizable form of society.

The social factor is sometimes regarded as a separate reality of supra-individual nature. Its manner of existence can be difficult to grasp, but such a supra-individual reality is considered by some sociologists and even more social-philosophers to be a necessary assumption to the understanding of the social phenomena. The very question of existence is a metaphysical one which we can safely leave aside; what matters here is to find a legitimate use of the word 'supra-individual' as a characteristic of the social factor. When the psycho-analysts call the representative of society in the individual a super-ego, it is mainly because this factor in the individuality has assumed a certain control over the ego and is superior to it in authority. But it can also be taken to mean that the super-ego is representative of the super-individual. In this way we get some understanding of the assertion which is advanced by certain philosophers, for instance, Paul Natorp in his *Sozialpäda-gogik* (1899), that society is just as much in the individual as the individual is in society.

Education as Social Assimilation

The interpretation outlined here can be dangerous in that it is often connected with an interpretation according to which the social demand is valued more highly than that of the individual, though there is not necessarily any connexion between the two. A statement of facts, or should we say presumed facts, is one thing, and their valuation quite another. The society which can sometimes take possession of the individuals, and involve their implicit loyalty for the community, may be of a perverted kind. The interpretation does not really make any order of preference between the individual factor and the social, nor does it express any opinion on the question of individualism *versus* collectivism. The substance of mankind is divided into individuals; these in turn live in groups, societies, communities, and the like, and their individualities take colour from them. From this point of view, even if the social factor does have a very strong hold on the individuals, it could be argued that it is just as much the duty of society to enrich the lives of the individuals as it is the duty of the individuals to allow their individualities to be submerged in the fellowship of community, as demanded by the collectivists.

If we want a realistic interpretation of the social factor in education, we should best be served by keeping as far as possible to the descriptive. And if we look for the most obvious and most direct educative effect of living together in some form of community we must surely admit that it consists in the fact that people become more like each other. Society has a kind of equalizing or uniforming influence on the individuals. The same effect can be observed where individuals are brought together who have not had anything to do with each other previously, e.g., where a number of new pupils are brought together to form a new class or school. And if a community already exists, the new pupils become imbued with already established dominant traditions and collective habits.

This is society's mildly unifying influence, which in its simplest form can be expressed by saying that all reciprocally educate each other. It is not therefore a unification which obliterates all individual peculiarities, but simply a mild equalizing through example and imitation. Though it can at times be reinforced, particularly if there exists within the society an ideal for unification which has sufficient power behind it. Examples of this have been seen in the authoritarian states, where not least the German Nazis tried to force a *Gleichshaltung* on all spheres of life. But such a forced uniformity is very different from the assimilation through which the individuals adjust themselves to each other or according to the prevailing norms in the society. The role of the school in either of these processes is, of course, important.

Assimilation takes place through education; one can even say that education to a very great extent consists of precisely this. And the main task for a descriptive science of education consists in getting as close as possible to a detailed knowledge of this assimilation-process, which demands psychological and sociological, and especially social-psychological, insight.

The question naturally arises as to how the process is influenced by the individual teachers who take part, whose distinctive personal characters also become an element in the formation of pupils. They usually receive their authority from a society of one kind or another, either clearly expressed or implied and taken for granted; they can represent the state or a church community, or they can represent a particular rank or class. But they can also feel themselves to be first and foremost representatives of their own ideals and ways of life and give to education a leaven of their own nature. But since they themselves have received their characteristics from a society, their activities can be regarded as variations of a theme which is fundamentally social and only the variations are individual. In judging an education we can make the mistake of presuming that the most striking and most conspicuous elements mean more than they really do. Many of the educating influences lie beneath the theshold of the conscious both in their transmission and reception, and even when considered by an outside observer. Comprehended as the sum of all the human influences that go to characterize the individuals, their knowledge and opinions, their behaviour and ways of life, education can perhaps be compared with an iceberg, one-tenth of which is visible above the water-level and nine-tenths hidden. It is difficult to decide if this gives the exact relative strength between the individual and the social factors, both because it can vary from case to case and because a quantitative comparison is almost impossible to carry out.

The Demand for Social Individuals

The social demand which has been dealt with here as that which is responsible for the equalizing effect that asserts itself in society, can now be considered both more abstractly and more concretely than has been the case. In a more abstract sense it can be regarded, on the whole, as that which makes individuals social without reference to any particular society. In which case the predominant feature becomes the education towards a certain solidarity with those who are one's group fellows. The main emphasis is laid on solidarity and not conformity, as expressed by Pericles in his famous speech for the fallen in the Peloponnesian war : " Far from exercising a jealous surveillance over each other, we do not feel called upon to be angry with our neighbour for doing what he likes, or even to indulge in those injurious looks which cannot fail to be offensive, although they inflict no positive penalty. But all this ease in our private relations does not make us lawless as citizens. Against this fear is our chief safeguard, teaching us to obey the magistrates and the laws."

Pronounced egoism, asociality, and lack of solidarity become general defects, but the demand for conformity is weakened. The social factor does not therefore assert itself according to the formula " to be different is to be indecent ", but is restricted to a general requirement for reasonable consideration for others, mutual respect for the interests of each other, and equality in duties and rights.

Such are the conditions in a marked liberal and individualistic

society, where the citizens are guaranteed a wide liberty and independence, and are free agents with regard to religion, mode of life,
occupation, taste, and so on. Even the demand for solidarity can be
reduced to a minimum and replaced by a demand for abstract justice.
In such a society the social factor is also reduced and asserts itself
essentially as an abstract moral instruction. That would in any case
be its natural form of expression in these conditions. From a realistic
psychological and sociological point of view it is a state of affairs
which appears somewhat utopian; it is to a greater extent motivated
ethically with the effect that the social demand cannot attain too great
an influence.

The Influence of Classes within a Society

What we understand by the social factor can at the same time be
taken for something much more concrete than we have yet done.
Every society has its own special structure and most often it is characterized by an order of preference. The social status of the individuals
is different and the social stratification will be among the factors which
assert themselves in education. The social classes can be regarded as
a kind of sub-society, each of which has its own way of life, and from
this view everything that has been said generally about the relation
between society and education should apply to the relation between
class and education. Much of it does, but not all. This is due to the
fact that the class-society is open and allows traffic between the
different strata. The boundaries are not too sharply drawn, and by
belonging to the same large society the individuals are already in many
respects endowed with a certain likeness. Another factor of importance
for this social mobility, and in the eyes of most people the decisive one,
is the different prestige the various classes possess. One hears of
higher, more distinguished, and of lower, less reputable strata.

What influence has this social factor, stratification, on education?
At the outset it must be acknowledged that there are relations in the
class divisions which are inconsistent both with our democratic ideals
and with our Christian conscience. Children are never deliberately
taught the existence of class divisions; rather are they taught their
non-existence, e.g., through such expressions as " one man is as good
as another ", " fundamentally we are all equal ", " many people in
poor circumstances are as good and as valuable as many in better circumstances ", " a man's position in society is no indication of his
human worth "; and therefore these false distinctions are of no great
importance. Nevertheless class division plays an important part in
the individual's outlook and way of life, and most people know it well
enough in spite of the lack of direct teaching or the teaching to the

contrary. It filters in through all the observations they make, and this serves to show how effectively society itself acts as educator and teacher in spite of the well-meant but misleading teaching of others.

This factor has other consequences for education; for people not only observe the social stratification, they react to it. Teachers react and the children themselves do. These reactions may be different and are very often unconscious. W. Lloyd Warner, the American sociologist and anthropologist, describes how some people become climbers and strainers on the social ladder, others remain static, while others cling to their status at the risk of losing it. Whatever attitude is taken is usually dependent upon the parents' outlook, which is induced in the children, positively or negatively, but most often without either knowing it. The structure of the educational system may encourage or discourage this mobility. Throughout the world there is an increasing demand for education which gives equal opportunities to all children.

Here the term 'social factor' gets a more concrete interpretation. It is the stratification itself with its various strata which, by manifesting itself in numerous ways for all to see, exercises its influence. This is a factor which not only characterizes education in the home and its nearest geographical and social surroundings, but also involves the school, because, for one thing, school education is one of the means by which we move socially. The school itself, in regard to both its content and its organization, will be influenced by the structure of the society; it has its social function even in many of the efforts which seem only to serve the individual development. A more detailed account of all the ways in which the social reality is reflected, refracted, and transformed in school would, however, be a chapter to itself.

The term 'social factor' is in certain aspects an ambiguous one, and can be traced back to the ambiguity which is found in the words 'society' and 'social'. Some of the most important meanings should by now have been brought to light, and the leitmotiv which can be seen to run through them all is the influence which society radiates to mould the personality of the individual. This influence manifests itself in numerous ways, some of which we know quite well, others only slightly. Indisputably, we know too little about the subject. We know too little, and often we do not know, either, how to begin to gain knowledge which is not only true but essential. There are still many problems for a sociology of education.

K. GRUE-SORENSEN.

CHAPTER THREE

Industrial Societies : Education for What?

THE twentieth-century cornucopia of industrial production has poured out goods and services on a scale undreamed of a hundred years ago. A drastic speed-up in social change has resulted. New values, new yard-sticks for social organization and behaviour have emerged.

Concurrently there has been a tremendous growth and development of educational processes: from kindergarten to the doctorate level. In the U.S., the eighteenth-century dream of the founding fathers to provide an education for each young citizen has, for all practical purposes, come true. The schools to-day set out to expose each member of society during his formative years to certain areas of human knowledge and culture. Ideally, they propose to ' educate ' each one within the limits of his capacities so that he can carry his rightful share as a free man in a free, modern, industrial society. The fast pace of social change has thrown new burdens on the educational process. Continually, the question arises, " Education for what, to what end, by what means?" The intelligent choice of these educational ends and means raises unique difficulties and perhaps unique urgency.

The concurrence of large-scale industrialization and equally large-scale formal education is a characteristic particularly of American society. To most Americans the everyday reality of industrialization is so pervasive that they take it for granted; no less a part of their experience is the presence of all kinds of formal education from the primary grades up through the most advanced research and graduate studies. While the complex inter-relationships of these two basic activities in American society are only vaguely sensed by most of us, they have become in recent decades the subject of increasing analysis and study.

It is hard to find any aspect of living in America that is not coloured by the presence of industrial activity. It appears not only in the highly complex division of labour of the American community, providing a fabulous range of goods and services, but in the magnitude of our systematically organized facilities for mass production. The variety and quantity of consumer market activities result in a material standard of living without historical parallel (1).

This division of labour extends into education and results in specialized training of wonderful intensity and variety. We educate ourselves and our children in schools offering a wide range of specialized subjects being taught by professionally trained teachers who have fifteen years or more formal education. Through graduate and adult evening course programmes formal education can continue almost indefinitely.

Historical Background

All societies, whether primitive or civilized, carry on some form of education. In form and substance it tends to be appropriate to the society's needs and values by reason of history and circumstance. Hence, while the educational processes of primitive societies may appear to us rather clumsy, crude, or unimaginative, their adequacy for the primitive situation is probably not less than ours are for modern industrial society.

However, at a given moment, there tends to be a lag between the adequacy of educational effort and the needs of a society. The degree of lag probably depends primarily on the wisdom of the society's real leaders and the size of the organizational problem. Nor can the fortuitous circumstances of history be overlooked. The range, scope, and variety of modern education may be almost bewildering in their complexity, but the underlying purposes are probably not greatly different from those of primitive societies. Not the least of these is the training of a sufficient number of persons in a sufficient range of skills to take care of the material wants of the society. How important material wants are, as compared with various non-economic needs, depends on the value-system of the society. In India and China non-material wants are prominent; in modern industrial society material wants tend to dominate. In primitive societies, for example, education deals in a rudimentary way with the relatively simple skills of hunting, fishing, agriculture, and military protection. In modern industrial society the division of labour has proliferated in a tremendous number of directions and created the need for many varieties of technical education.

What do we have in mind when we use the term 'industrialization'? Many students have studied its origins (2). They call attention to such influences as natural resources, population growth, climate, religious and cultural values, and the operation of chance.

If we confine attention to the U.S.A., the availability of a wide range of natural resources is an historical fact. But this was available to the American Indians for at least a thousand years before European exploration started. The same can be said about favourable climate. Neither of these factors stimulated large-scale population growth or industrial activity. Favourable natural resources also prevailed in western Europe long before the rise of industrialization. So attempts to explain industrialization must look at the values and cultural ideas of a people.

Modern industrial activity is commonly thought to have its origin in the Industrial Revolution of seventeenth-century England and western Europe. In America its growth closely paralleled and then its tempo eventually surpassed that of Europe. Some students have suggested that the Industrial Revolution probably received a large part of its impetus from a religious sanction which fostered the pursuit of knowledge for its own sake and for ' the glory of God '. From the seventeenth century the theological protection of ignorance and superstition about the natural world gradually lost its hold, and scientific knowledge of nature, as we know it to-day, began to develop more rapidly (3). This made possible the technological developments necessary to factory production, which in turn made possible the mass market.

Students of the history of science have suggested that religion also gave another push to industrial development through its view that the production and accumulation of worldly goods through hard work and perseverance was one way to achieve personal salvation. The individual accumulation and moral use of material wealth acquired the cloak of respectability (4).

More or less simultaneously various *entrepreneurial*-minded groups developed in reaction against the extremely restrictive control of produced goods and services by the handicraft guilds. In such a climate these *entrepreneurs*, forerunners of the modern business man, turned to invention and innovation, which had become possible through science and economically profitable through growing commercial opportunities.

As production, wealth and the demand for goods increased, the material wants of people expanded; better machines and manufacturing techniques came to be seen as having competitive value. As competition grew keener the earlier religious justifications sank more and more into the subconscious thinking of the people, and innovation, production, and improvement became a basic preoccupation not only in machine technology but in techniques of factory organization, production, distribution, and management. The resulting increases of productive capacity were in turn a stimulus to factory population growth and to urbanization. All these social and economic processes gathered momentum more easily in America than in Europe and Great Britain.

Broadly speaking, the differing rates of industrialization in the various countries of western Europe and America in the last three hundred years are probably best understood in terms of the relative importance of ' tradition ' *versus* ' experiment ' and ' innovation ' in the minds of people generally. Nowhere, historically, have experiment and innovation been encouraged more widely than in America; nowhere has industrialization become so complex and on such a large scale. The use of science and education to raise the material and cultural standards of living for all people has become an integral part of the American *ethos* (5). This has gone hand in hand with the ideas of freedom of thought and religion which were rallying-points in the establishment of the nation.

By contrast, the weight of tradition and an influential Church have perhaps supported the " old ways " (technological and educational) more persistently in Western Europe and England. It may be that the receptivity to change in the latter country has been influenced considerably by the continuing emphasis on the importance of tradition in political, economic, and social life. These are perhaps significant factors in the relative slowness to discard hand methods and to accept machine technology in English industry.

Demand for Technically Trained People

With only 6 per cent of the world's population and 7 per cent of the land area, America to-day produces approximately 40 per cent of the world's industrial goods (6), consumes half the world's steel and oil, uses three-fourths of the world's cars and appliances (7). The population in America has grown from about 23 million in 1860 to 151 million in 1950. Accompanying this there has been a shift in the rural-urban distribution. In 1850 almost 85 per cent lived on farms or in rural territory. With temporary variations in the rate of shift to urban living, the percentage in rural areas in 1950 had declined to about 41. The population living in cities of 100,000 or more in 1850 was less than 5 per cent; in 1950 it was over 40 per cent (8).

The growth of educational need has to some extent paralleled the growth of industrialization and urbanization. Until about 1880, when compulsory public education laws became prevalent, public education was relatively slow to spread. ' Free education ' above the primary level is relatively recent. But, historically, there was a belief in the importance of education being available to all regardless of social, economic, or religious differences. It was an early belief among businessmen that public schools would develop responsible citizens in support of the *status quo*. By 1910 almost 60 per cent of the population of 5 to 19 years of age was enrolled in primary or secondary schools; by 1950 the percentage had risen to 80 (9). This, of course, does not mean that the percentage graduating has been equally high.

Actually and typically it has been much lower. In higher education similar growth is noted. In 1900 there were 969 public and private schools above the secondary level; by 1950 this number had grown to 1,851.

" Expenditures per pupil (in primary and secondary schools), when adjusted for price changes, were four times as great is 1950 as in 1900 —$259, compared with $62 in 1949–50 dollars " (10).

The occupational profile has changed. A recent overall study of payroll changes by the Bureau of Labour Statistics indicates that the number of jobs concerned with services has risen from about 14 million in 1919 to 30 million in 1955. During the same period, jobs in the production of goods have risen from 26 to 28·3 million (11). While the full implications of this are not clear, it reflects the growth of mechanization and automation. Our productive capacity is so great that we can afford to have more people on services. Added to this, an increased number of people are on retirement incomes and the age at which young people enter the labour market has risen—these increase the demand for services and especially for education.

As technology and automation have taken over more and more of the simple, repetitive jobs in mass-producing industry, there has been an increase in the demand for the semi-skilled and specialized employees. The unskilled population with no formal education is gradually becoming smaller in favour of the grade school and high school graduate who can be trained, with his formal-education background, to do semi-skilled and skilled jobs. Tables I and II give some indication of the extent to which education and technical training has spread into the working population.

TABLE I

RISE, PERCENTAGE OF THE LABOUR FORCE, 1870 TO 1940

	Per cent
Clerical occupations	0·7– 8·2
Professional services	2·6– 6·7
Public service (not elsewhere classified) . .	0·7– 1·8
Transportation and communication . .	4·2– 7·9
Trade	6·8–12·5

TABLE II

RISE AND DECLINE, PERCENTAGE OF THE LABOUR FORCE, 1910 TO 1940

Important Rises	Per cent of Total
Professional workers	4·4– 6·5
Clerks and kindred workers . . .	10·2–17·2
Semi-skilled workers	14·7–21·0
Important Declines	
Proprietors, managers, and officials . .	23·0–17·8
Unskilled workers	36·0–25·9

Source: Seymour Harris, *The Market for College Graduates* (Harvard, 1949), p. 191.

This shift in occupations has given impetus to an extension of the period of formal education, to the rise of professional education, and to shifts in choice of profession. While, at first, professional training was predominantly in law, medicine, and the ministry, Chart I shows how the professions of engineering, education, and business have grown : Chart 2 shows the rapidity of this growth from 1900 to 1953 compared with the humanities. The number of graduates in all fields has increased, but the outstanding increases in popularity have been in the fields of business, education, and engineering.

CHART I

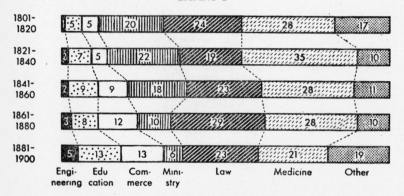

Percentage of graduates of 37 colleges entering major professions, 1800–1900

Source : D. Wolfle, *America's Resources of Specialized Talent* (N.Y., 1954), p. 36.

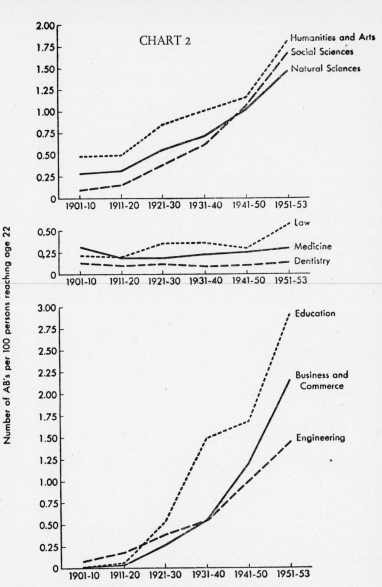

Growth trends of bachelor's and first professional degrees in selected fields of specialization

Source : D. Wolfle, *op. cit.*, p. 32.

The emphasis on industrially important fields of specialization is also apparent in the trend of doctors' degrees away from the humanities towards the natural sciences. Chart 3 shows this trend from 1900 to 1953. The reasons for it are obviously complex, but the overall market for higher training in particular fields is an important influence

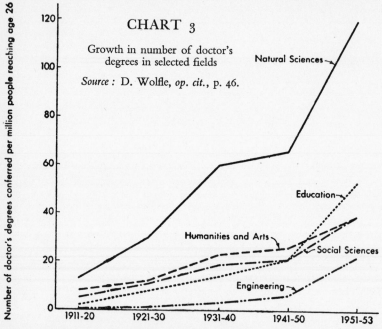

CHART 3

Growth in number of doctor's degrees in selected fields

Source : D. Wolfle, *op. cit.*, p. 46.

on the decision of an individual to take up a career in one of them. Chart 3 lends support to the idea that industrialization is exerting an effect. Dr. Wolfle, in his extensive study of these trends, observes that :—

> Traditionally the Ph.D. degree has been awarded for scholarly research and has been granted to students who planned on careers in research and teaching. But other markets for men and women with doctors' degrees have been expanding, in industry, in government service, and in private practice or consulting work (12).

The contemporary supply-and-demand picture in various fields of specialization is shown in Table III. The inadequacy of supply in the natural sciences and in all levels of teaching reflects the economic basis for supply. As industry has grown, its demand has also grown for natural scientists who can develop economically important innovations in product and manufacturing processes. And this general

TABLE III

SUPPLY AND DEMAND IN THE SPECIALIZED FIELDS

Size, Current Demand, and Supply-demand Prospects in the Principal Specialized Areas

Field	Estimated Number Employed at Professional Level in 1953	State of 1953 Demand	Adequacy of Prospective Graduates in 1953–1957 to meet Anticipated Demand
Natural sciences .	237,000	High	Insufficient at both A.B. and Ph.D. levels
Psychology .	22,000	Increasing	Insufficient at Ph.D. level; adequate at lower levels
Social science .	47,000	Increasing	Moderate shortage at Ph.D. level; adequate at lower levels
Humanities .	114,000	Increasing	Insufficient at Ph.D. level; adequate at lower levels
Engineering .	633,000	30,000 a year	Insufficient
Applied biology .	246,000	Variable	Sufficient in agriculture and forestry; insufficient in home economics
Health fields:			
Dentistry .	84,000	More needed	Insufficient
Medicine .	185,000	More needed	Insufficient
Nursing .	340,000	More needed	Insufficient
Pharmacy .	91,000	Moderate	Sufficient
Business and commerce	1,372,000	Flexible	Will absorb many graduates from other fields
School teaching .	1,141,000	160,000 a year	Insufficient by 60,000 a year
College teaching	200,000	Increasing	Insufficient
Other professions:			
Law .	202,000	Moderate	Sufficient
Ministry . .	168,000	Moderate	Sufficient
Social work .	77,000	Variable	Variable
Other professions . .	118,000	Variable	Variable

Source: D.Wolfle, op. cit., Table V.1, p. 77.

demand leads to further specialization. But at the same time the economic attractiveness of *teaching* natural science has declined along with a general loss of prestige for teaching as a profession—industry and government have been able to pay more for such training than have educational institutions. The financial rewards for teaching other subjects have by comparison lost even more ground, and the results to-day are a serious shortage of teachers at all levels (13).

This competition between industry, government, and education for specially trained people would seem to be short-sighted, and is so regarded by some students of the situation, but it is probably more the result of industry's preoccupation with its needs and society's pre-occupation with earning a living than the result of any intention to compete with education. Another view, perhaps unconsciously operating, is the traditional one of the business man that the process of supply and demand should be left alone rather than controlled. Whether the supply of technically trained people is adequate has in fact been left largely to chance and to what the educators could do to anticipate need in a fickle market.

The ability of educators to cope with this problem has been handi-capped by the indifference of industrial management to long-range estimations of its own needs. Such indifference has been encouraged by the logic of the industrial process, requiring, as it does, productive flexibility and quick changes in product and style which are basic to free-market economy. If free-market conditions of supply and demand change rapidly on a short-term basis, naturally industry's own demands for technically trained people fluctuate in similar fashion.

The educational problem is further complicated by industry's dual training demands—in production engineering (ability to adapt what we already know to recurring problems) and in research engineering (to discover new basic knowledge). Educationally these demands are difficult because of the programme variations required to develop specialists in the industrially important fields.

As a result of these circumstances there have been periods of over- and under-supply in the engineering and research fields. In periods of over-supply the graduate engineer finds his training depreciated in the employment market and he ends up with work that uses his training only partially and inefficiently, or in work in which his training is actually irrelevant; in periods of under-supply the graduate engineer finds his value inflated by industry competing for his services. This in turn stimulates college students to enter engineering and, with in-dustry's demand, to build up the overall demand to a level beyond the capacities of the engineering schools. The main detriment to the schools is the strain of conflicting pressures for quality and quantity. This kind of consequence runs the gamut of education—whether in-dustry steps up its demand for workers at the unskilled, semi-skilled, or highly skilled levels, the pressure on education is to sacrifice quality for quantity. In recent years much has been done by large industries to plan and forecast their needs and to work with the universities to meet them. The fluctuation and lack of correlation between supply and demand are probably inevitable in a free economy, but the economic waste of such a lag is more than offset by the resulting adaptive, productive power of free enterprise. This is one of the costs of a growing economy and an improving standard of living.

The Guidance Problem

Despite the progress that is being made in helping education to serve society and in helping the individual to select his programme wisely, it is estimated that not more than 30 per cent of our best minds go on to college and professional training. It is also claimed that a substantial number of those who do go to college should not be there: their personal gain from the experience is negligible, and their presence contributes to the over-taxing of existing staff and facilities. Educational leaders like Dr. Conant, formerly President of Harvard University and presently U.S. Ambassador to Germany, have concerned themselves with how to improve education so that more than 30 per cent of the best minds will want to go to college (14).

Scholarship funds have been set up to overcome the obstacle of financial inability which faces many of the potentially qualified. Vocational guidance specialists in the secondary schools have taken up this problem in recent years, and industry has supported studies to improve the processes of identifying talented young people. College-entrance screening procedures are also helpful within their limits of predictive accuracy, but these are not the crux of the problem.

The difficulties with these efforts, again, stem from the fact that, in the past, education—neither as a personal attribute nor as a career— has had any close connexion with the prevailing rewards of industrial society. The opportunities for personal achievement and material reward in the socially fluid, economically oriented culture of America have been available largely without educational qualifications.

The indifference to higher education is understandable when high school students observe that they can do as well or better financially without going on to college than most teachers or other educated people. Perhaps the long-run earning value as well as the prestige of a college education *per se* in industry have been rising in recent years. But only recently have any figures been obtained that offer any approximate value of a college education in earning ability (15). Charts 4, 5, 6, and 7 suggest how education may affect earnings. Because most college graduates go into business this, again, weighs against the teaching profession.

If the information contained in the following charts could be communicated to high school students it might perhaps stimulate them to better scholastic performance and to go on to college. At the same time it would not be valid to infer that education necessarily gives a

Men who graduated from college and men who didn't— the jobs they hold

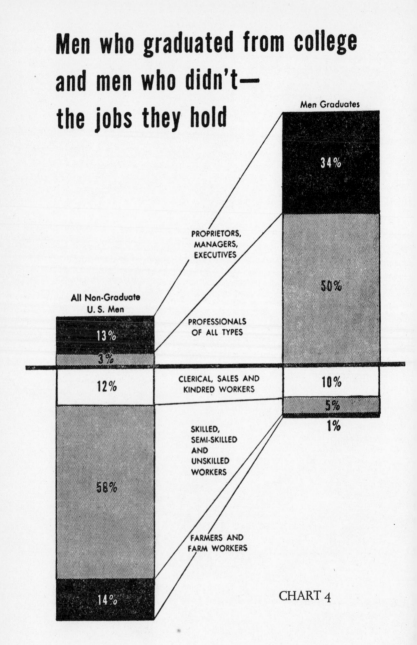

Men Graduates

34%

50%

All Non-Graduate
U. S. Men

13%

3%

PROPRIETORS,
MANAGERS,
EXECUTIVES

PROFESSIONALS
OF ALL TYPES

CLERICAL, SALES AND
KINDRED WORKERS

12%   10%

5%
1%

SKILLED,
SEMI-SKILLED
AND
UNSKILLED
WORKERS

58%

FARMERS AND
FARM WORKERS

14%

CHART 4

CHART 5

The cash value of the degree.
It increases with age

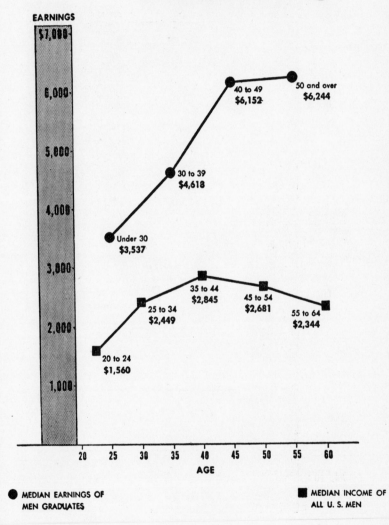

EARNINGS

$7,000
6,000
5,000
4,000
3,000
2,000
1,000

40 to 49
$6,152

50 and over
$6,244

30 to 39
$4,618

Under 30
$3,537

35 to 44
$2,845

25 to 34
$2,449

45 to 54
$2,681

55 to 64
$2,344

20 to 24
$1,560

20   25   30   35   40   45   50   55   60

AGE

● MEDIAN EARNINGS OF
MEN GRADUATES

■ MEDIAN INCOME OF
ALL U. S. MEN

CHART 6

Financial rewards differ by occupation

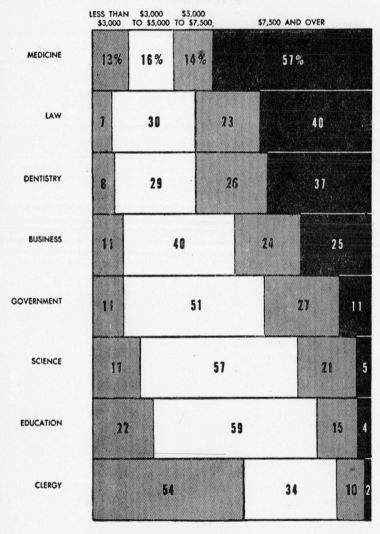

Percent of Graduates who earn

	LESS THAN $3,000	$3,000 TO $5,000	$5,000 TO $7,500	$7,500 AND OVER
MEDICINE	13%	16%	14%	57%
LAW	7	30	23	40
DENTISTRY	8	29	26	37
BUSINESS	11	40	24	25
GOVERNMENT	11	51	27	11
SCIENCE	17	57	21	5
EDUCATION	22	59	15	4
CLERGY	54	34	10	2

CHART 7

How business pays graduates

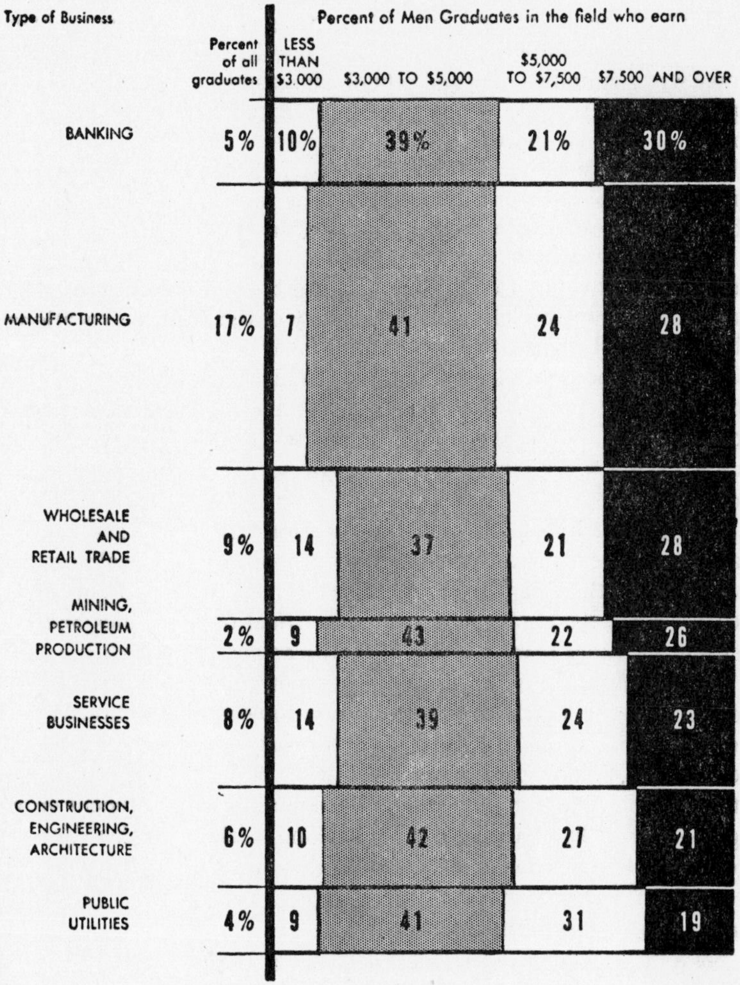

Type of Business	Percent of all graduates	LESS THAN $3,000	$3,000 TO $5,000	$5,000 TO $7,500	$7,500 AND OVER
BANKING	5%	10%	39%	21%	30%
MANUFACTURING	17%	7	41	24	28
WHOLESALE AND RETAIL TRADE	9%	14	37	21	28
MINING, PETROLEUM PRODUCTION	2%	9	43	22	26
SERVICE BUSINESSES	8%	14	39	24	23
CONSTRUCTION, ENGINEERING, ARCHITECTURE	6%	10	42	27	21
PUBLIC UTILITIES	4%	9	41	31	19

Percent of Men Graduates in the field who earn

man a higher price in the employment market; as certain studies have suggested, the influence of education on earning power is more apparent than real (16). It may be that those who have the drive to go through college, also have the drive to advance to positions of greater responsibility where greater income tends to be found : success may be due to ' motivation ' rather than to ' education '.

Another facet of the guidance problem is the negative effect on the student of poor teaching. Mediocre and poor teaching are responsible for much of the distaste for education. This is a long-range problem requiring general improvement of salary levels, so that more capable people will go into teaching and school administration. A solution will depend on the extent to which the public attitude towards teaching as a profession can be improved.

Effective guidance is also complicated by the problem of curricula construction in an industrial society. The increasing complexity of job specialization in industry has confused the educator : shall he train in highly specialized skills and semi-skilled vocational work and fail to prepare the individual for development and broader responsibilities, or shall he train more broadly and make many of the available vocational jobs distasteful to graduates? The educator tries to resolve this dilemma without conspicuous success. Whichever way he goes, he is faced with the present inability to select the high-potential student from the low, and the inability to advise effectively in vocational choice. Much work is in progress, but we seem far from really useful tools.

For the majority of intellectually superior high school graduates it may be more realistic to emphasize their ability to pursue almost any occupation with a higher education behind them, and to encourage them to make the choice in terms of personal opportunities and circumstances rather than in terms of temperament and skills.

The accelerating social change that comes with industrialization complicates the curricula-construction problem and indirectly the problem of vocational guidance. In the last fifty years it has been increasingly difficult to develop a synthesis of past knowledge in the arts and sciences which intrigues and makes sense to the student growing up in a rapidly changing and questioning world. Obsolescence has become no less a problem in textbooks than in technology.

The Demand for Executives

The growth of industrialization in America has also created a special need for managerial skills. As business enterprises have grown in size, the problems of management have required increasing explicit attention. They can no longer be left to the random appearance of intuitive skills among rank-and-file workers or among the sons of owners. We do not yet have sufficient systematic knowledge of human organization and communication problems to understand fully what effects the size or organizations may have on them, but there is probably a point—whether it is two hundred and fifty employees or two thousand five hundred—at which the managerial problems of an industrial organization begin to change in both form and content as well as in magnitude. At this point informal, family-centred, personal types of organization and procedure must give way to fairly explicit policy, practice, and procedure. The replacement of a single supervisor or manager, which occurs only occasionally in the small organization and can then be handled without previous planning, becomes in the large organization a question of replacing many people within a relatively short period of time, and cannot be done without planning.

This requires training in the ways in which managerial jobs are changing in content and scope. For a period of time in the industrialization of America there was a general inclination on the part of business leaders to ignore the need to think ahead, and to meet the problem by hiring, as needed, executive replacements from the outside market. This ' pirating ' still continues, but in terms of the size of the problem and the negative reactions of existing personnel to bringing outsiders into the managerial group it is no solution. When the importation of men at high management levels is tried as a policy (whether stated or implicit) it undermines the incentive of ' promotion from within ' which is probably important to the morale of the existing team. The incoming executive is not only handicapped by his lack of acquaintance with the technical aspects of the business (which are taking more and more time to learn), but he does not know the people, the human organization, the subtle ways of thinking which are important to the equilibrium of the total organization. Although this acquaintance and comprehension can be accelerated by programmes which encourage self-development, to a large extent they must be learned first-hand through the development of good working relationships with subordinates, colleagues, and superiors. All this takes time.

In addition to the factors already mentioned, there is an increasing need for executives in modern industry to think effectively about the co-ordination of specialists. As an industrial organization grows and its division of labour becomes more complex, the relations between specialist groups need specific executive attention. Finding this ability by chance in the labour market is impracticable. Educational specialization has gone so far that the lack of administratively minded graduates has aggravated rather than ameliorated the situation. Only a few schools recognize this problem in its full implications. The tendency is to devise new 'specialized' training for 'generalists', which in approach represents a premature distillation of the problem. We are perhaps too sure that analytical and administrative ability can be narrowed down and trained for in a simplified drill manner, like other abilities needed in industry. This is particularly evident in the modern diversification of personnel and human-relations training (we are trying to solve the problems of specialization with more specialists). This is indeed compounding an educational felony.

Finally, one particular concomitant of this shift to the more rationalized type of organization which should be mentioned is the formalization of retirement policies calling for mandatory retirement at the age of 65. This, plus the normal attrition of management through death, has intensified the need for a constant pool of men capable of taking on, as vacancies occur, heavier duties at all management levels.

Only recently has industry concerned itself seriously with the need to educate people explicitly for managerial positions. Although the Wharton School of Finance and Commerce was founded in 1881 by a business man, it stood almost alone until 1898. From 1898 to 1950 the growth of business training was quite rapid. Over 617 schools were offering courses and granting degrees in business and commerce in 1950, and 80 schools were granting degrees in administrative or industrial engineering (17). This growth was, to a large extent, the result of the educators' efforts rather than through encouragement or assistance from business. Business men historically have been indifferent to their own interests in education, and some modern corporations still are. This indifference stems not only from the factors already mentioned but from an early and long-standing belief that higher education is largely irrelevant to a man's success in business: the Horatio Alger myth (18) had enough substance behind it to influence thinking. One of its implications was the idea that every man's growth and development are his own responsibility, and that they could not be got out of books. This implies an inherently wasteful approach to talent, which perhaps 'worked' in the past in small concerns where the demand was small, and could therefore be left to chance. But it cannot be left to chance where the general desirability of self-development is obscured by the constriction of interest through training which tends to be typical of the specialist. To-day, a fair comprehension of several fields of knowledge is not as possible as it may have been in the past, and the individual takes a broad education at the risk of being labelled a dilettante.

The question is: How can more men in industry and public life be encouraged to develop themselves to meet the greater responsibilities of their present management jobs and to take on those of higher levels when needed? It is this kind of question that business schools and business managers are trying to answer in a variety of ways. Here again, the demand for men with a general outlook and specific abilities vital to modern management exceeds the supply educational institutions can provide on a short-term basis. This has led industry to develop its own internal programmes to speed up, if possible, the broadening of outlook and stimulation of personal interest in self-development. More and more industries are studying their long-range needs in management manpower and what kinds of preparation are necessary. The internal efforts range from supervisory-technique training for those who are just starting to assume management responsibilities to broad development programmes for higher levels of management where stress is placed on reflective and analytical thinking with regard to underlying problems of social, economic, and political change.

Industry's Aid to Education

While internal programmes are receiving increasing attention, the concern of the business man for the economic health of education is also making considerable headway. It is apparent that industry needs the help of education and that education needs the help of industry: internal programmes alone cannot meet the need. In an extensive study of the financial problems of higher education, Millett (19) refers to a Russell Sage Foundation estimate that private benefactions from industry to colleges and universities in 1950 were approximately 40 million dollars. This amounted to approximately 38·5 per cent of the 104 million which Millett reports colleges received from all outside sources in 1950. The break-down between groups was as follows:—

	Per cent
Corporations and business	38·5
Foundations	24·0
Churches	24·0
Alumni funds	13·5

The percentage contributed by foundations since 1950 has probably increased significantly as a result of the activity of the Ford Foundation, which has been especially concerned with the financial problems of educational institutions. Similar increases have probably occurred in the contributions of industry through scholarship funds and direct grants to universities by the larger corporations.

Although this is encouraging, the amount of money spent on education is still relatively small. In 1950 the total expenditure of institutions of higher education was slightly more than $2·2 billion when the gross national product was $283 billion : meaning less than 1 per cent for higher education. At the same time the American people spent $4 billion on tobacco, $11 billion on recreation, and $19 billion on automobiles. Even if expenditures for primary and secondary education (which were slightly more than double that for higher education) are included, the percentage is small in relation to other expenditures. Public and general education has been taken for granted as a right of every citizen, but there has been no corresponding public acceptance of the responsibility for the costs or the maintenance of quality. America's value-system gives prior emphasis to raising the material standard of living. An interesting evidence of this has been the public's generally more favourable response to appeals for building funds than to appeals for higher teachers' salaries.

The rising cost of living which has come with industrialization has directly affected the economics of education. Of the present outlay by institutions of higher education only about 75 per cent is for the educational programme—the other 25 per cent is for such auxiliary expenses as dormitories, dining-halls, and other facilities. The cost of these items has been largely outside the control of educational administrators and has typically risen faster than income.

Increases in income must come either from student fees, local taxation, federal subsidy, or private gifts. From 1940 to 1950, student fees increased by 50 to 60 per cent. This is a hardship on the student and may exclude talented aspirants from poor economic backgrounds. To some extent this is being alleviated by the increase in industrial contributions to scholarship funds, but support is still far from adequate. Local or federal taxation is a remedy not available to the privately endowed university, although it has kept the state university in reasonably good economic health. Private gifts to endowment funds are especially important to the privately endowed institutions, but they have not kept pace with rising costs. It is even less adequate than the total amount of gifts might indicate, because a considerable portion of them are restricted for particular uses. This restriction curtails the ability of the educational administrator to meet the fluctuations in operating costs.

In an industrial economy like America's, education has been financially handicapped because it has no tangible service to sell. The raising of funds for the expansion of productive facilities to sell goods or tangible services in industry has been a relatively solvable problem: pricing and improved performance have been effective roads to solution. But how can a price be put on the quality and quantity of education? What is the consumer of education ' buying '?

Federal Aid to Education

Federal financial support of education has become a major development since 1940, particularly in two ways; through the War Veterans' educational benefits programme and through contract research. The Veterans' programme as such was established as a temporary and indefinite action following World War II. Its direct assistance has practically ended, but the implications have given rise to a controversy on academic freedom and government control. The large-scale government expenditures in contract research with universities have evoked the same controversy. The universities, in need of income, have reluctantly accepted this restricted source of income. The business community has shared the apprehensions of the educators regarding the political aspect of the acceptance. Government funds for research carry a potential threat to untrammelled, pure research and to effective administrative control. Whether government subsidy gains headway in the future depends largely on the amount of financial support which is forthcoming from the business community and other private sources. The business community faces a dilemma. Will unrestricted funds be wisely used? Will restricted funds save the universities? (20).

This same controversy over control of education carries into the secondary and primary schools. In economically poor regions, to what extent should federal funds aid education? And where educational programmes deemed vital to the national interest at these levels are not being established by local or state government, should the federal government step in? These are by no means issues near resolution in America. The sentiment for local autonomy in public schools is still quite strong. Only in time of war does federal intervention seem acceptable.

The Need for General Education

Industrialization has intensified the need for general education in several ways. This need arises primarily from the development of specialized, technical, and professional education. As new knowledge increases and these programmes delineate themselves, the graduates find it harder to communicate with others in terms of their specialized vocabulary and viewpoint. They are trained to ignore all aspects of a situation except those of their speciality. The achievement of "knowing more and more about less and less" carries with it the handicap of "knowing less and less about more and more". Understanding the inter-relatedness of special fields of knowledge becomes more important.

But it is not only a problem of knowledge—it is a matter of viewpoint. For example, the engineer by virtue of this training ignores certain aspects of a problem so that he can give expert attention to those in which he is trained; so do the accountant and the lawyer. These specialists and others need a broader knowledge not only if they are to be considered for managerial positions but even to do a satisfactory job as a specialist. To some extent, but not enough, the graduate professional schools are expanding their curricula to meet this problem. The medical doctor is being asked to view the patient as a person living in a complex social situation as well as a physiological organism; the lawyer is asked to look at the social and extra-legal aspects of legal action; the engineer is being urged to consider the socio-economic and political consequences of his engineering.

Over and above this, those already in managerial positions need general education. Without this, present-day managers fall behind in the long-range thinking that is necessary to develop and maintain the flexible work force vital to the continued growth of the industrialization process.

Finally, the gradual lowering of the retirement age in industry, the decline in average work-hours, and the rise in average life-span, all emphasize the question of what to do with free time. An education which prepares the individual to obtain full satisfaction from free time is clearly essential. The ways and means are not at all clear, but they point to an education that widens the scope of interests and develops a taste for self-education when leisure arrives.

Looking Ahead

The development of science, technology, and automation has given a momentum and direction to the industrialization process that will probably continue for very many years. In a study predicting American economic growth, the editors of *Fortune* magazine recently estimated the future as shown in Chart 8. Whereas productivity has

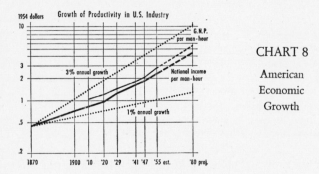

CHART 8

American
Economic
Growth

increased at the rate of 2 per cent during the last eighty-five years, it is expected to accelerate to 3 per cent for the next twenty-five years.

This impetus, as we have tried to indicate, comes not only from the massive accretions of knowledge (historical and pragmatic) in the last one hundred years, but from a philosophy of change, innovation, and improvement. While the evidence is more obvious in the material side of living, the social side is also affected. The drive for change in moral values, work habits, and other living habits has been more strongly resisted than change in industrial processes, and at times it may have appeared that technological progress has been at too great a cost, but social changes have eventually been accepted. So this atmosphere of change raises a crucial question for educational leaders : Education for what?

Throughout history there have been iconoclasts, but never have they been so prevalent—never have traditional values had less weight *sui generis*. Where the industrial processes of a society seem committed to change, can (or should) the educational process be likewise committed?

In 1919 A. N. Whitehead perceived a problem which has subsequently become sharper :

> The War has afforded the most astounding proof of what can be effected by an intense concentration upon invention, provided that you utilize the trained ability. Now the same effect can be produced in most departments of industry, not merely for a short period, but continuously—granted that your science advances, and you train the men to apply it. Now you cannot think that these lessons have been overlooked by other nations. Of course they haven't. The Americans, the French, the Italians, the Germans, the Japanese, will concentrate inventive faculty upon every detailed process of their manufactures. In the State of the future to use obsolete industrial methods will be little short of a criminal offence. However, it will be unnecessary for the police to prosecute, for bankruptcy will automatically overtake the offenders.
>
> Thus the old conception of industry in a static state, forever employing the old methods and producing the old goods, will not fit the facts. Managers, designers, and artisans must be equipped to adapt themselves to circumstances which are ever changing. Now, to produce this adaptability there is only one method, and that is education. This education must not be conceived on narrow lines. It is of no use to train the young in one very special process which will probably be superseded before they are middle-aged (21).

Elton Mayo, in his studies of modern industrial society (22), suggested that with the Industrial Revolution we departed from an 'established' type of society where the traditional ways of living stayed essentially the same from one generation to the next, and headed for an 'adaptive' society where change, improvement, and free inquiry have become of central importance. We find ourselves in a difficult transition phase where the balancing forces of the 'established' society have lost most of their power, but we have not yet developed adequate equivalents. Education has a vital role in the development of them and has struggled under many handicaps (internal and external) to fulfil its responsibility. To develop them in a climate where change in the material side of living induces change in the social side is almost an educational contradiction—how can people be educated to preserve social order where change is dominant?

Education, like established religion, has been concerned with the transmittal of a more or less sacred body of knowledge, beliefs, and practices. As the spirit of free inquiry has taken hold new knowledge has revised the old, and the body of stabilizing sacred data has steadily lost its appeal: sacred ideas and ritual, contrary to their role in traditional societies, have slight appeal *per se* in a changing society. Knowledge of the past needs to be translated into modern terms, but much is lost in the translation.

The efforts of education to adapt have hardly touched the problem, concentrating as they have on techniques and superficial modification to the neglect of points of view and content. This has occurred partly through the disposition of educators to misinterpret the merit of detachment from the 'madding crowd'. The advantage of the 'halls of ivy' is not real unless the residents have ample acquaintance with the profane activities of the market-place on which to base their reflections. They must also maintain periodic contact with profane activities to revitalize and revise the impressions on which they reflect and objectify for the benefits of students. Otherwise they validate Whitehead's suggestion that "the secondhandedness of the learned world is the secret of its mediocrity". 'Misplaced concreteness' is the special hazard of curricula construction in a world of social and economic change. This has stimulated a search for the basic wisdom that must underly all human relations regardless of social organization or process, and has given rise to an emphasis on "general education" (23).

In the future, even more than in the present, if education is to gain the respect and support it needs, it must lead students to a far more active interest in self-development than it has heretofore, and delegate to the libraries the job of *conveying knowledge*.

One of the basic, unsolved problems of an industrial society committed to accelerating change is how to educate people to live effectively in it. Some of the crucial questions are: What frames of reference shall we hang on to? What knowledge, what skills, and what point of view shall we teach our children if there is so much that may have to be revised or discarded as irrelevant in face of future changes? Should there be any limits to our encouragement of change?

Classical examples of skills rendered obsolete by technological changes are those of the coal miners and steel rollers. New coal-mining machines have displaced manual skills, and the increasing competition of other fuels has put additional pressure on coal miners to transfer to other occupations. This occurred even more strikingly twenty years ago in the steel industry, when automatic continuous strip mills replaced the hand-rolling operations completely. Such a skill or occupation carries with it human associations that easily become essential to personal equilibrium and integrity, and can involve the whole person. Learning a new skill or occupation is not a simple matter of learning new techniques. It is a matter of acquiring new habits, new knowledge, and making new human associations.

One approach to this situation is to attempt a control of technological inventions and changes so that they do not occur at a socially detrimental pace. The government's role has at times been conceived as slowing the pace; at others as taking care of the victims. Some students reject this as a remedy not really available, on the grounds that we cannot go backward in social or economic process, and attempts to restrict creative effort tend to weaken the growth and adaptive powers of the society. They would say that education's role must include the general development of adaptive and critical capacities, so that social trends towards anomie and rigidity can be kept in balance, while the benefits of change occur.

An alternative direction of effort has been to break down industrial work into more and more simple operations, so that workers can learn any operation easily and quickly, and thus move without personal, social, or economic disturbance from obsolete operations to new ones. The adverse consequences of this approach have been the loss of challenge in the job, the decline of the 'instinct for workmanship', and resulting low morale. These consequences had a part in stimulating the development of mechanization and automation as a way to get repetitive operations done in quantity and with quality. The adverse consequences also gave impetus to the recent trend towards job enlargement in industry.

In the ' adaptive ' society of to-day and the future, some observers maintain that group life is likely to be more superficial and ephemeral in its involvements and may have a more negative, internalized orientation while it lasts. In the face of change, new groups tend to form in reaction—however subtle—to the destructive effects of change on group life. The solution is probably not in the direction of legal controls or policing efforts but in education that will help people to live with the ephemeral type of group life, get acquainted easily in changing situations, and reject the negative orientation.

The basic human needs which are satisfied in the 'established' society—personal and social security and easy communication—are still with us, but they cannot be satisfied now in the same ways. The social climate is quite different. By contrast the opportunities for recognition and new experience are probably greater in the adaptive society, but with them goes the onus on the individual to develop more inner security so that he may approach his changing world with a sense of equanimity, a mature attitude toward anxiety and ritual, an attitude of experiment and adventure. In the past this has generally come to the individual only with age and long trial-and-error experience. At the rate our world is changing, now and in the future, this may not be soon enough.

The educators' problem has been the one faced in a more extreme form by the leaders of established religions : the seeming irrelevancy of the past and of ritualistic learning to the problems of the person in the present. In an industrial society, where the profane activities of making a living so heavily overshadow the sacred, education and religion alike grope uncertainly in their search for a recognized function. The educator's function to-day tends to be clear and secure only in those fields which have a direct or tangible bearing on the profane activities of business and industry.

It might seem from the foregoing discussion that education is less important in modern industrial society because there is less relevant educational content to communicate. Actually the opposite is true. The amount of scientific knowledge will continue to increase, yet the rationale for learning will not be for knowledge *per se*, but rather for the purpose of understanding the past, for orientation to the future, and for improving our response to change. We must learn better how to be selective and to get the essence where detail is a hindrance, to grasp the detail where it is critical to the essence.

It might also appear from the foregoing that the educational process in a changing industrial society is more difficult than in an established society. This, too, is open to doubt. While it may be easier in a stable environment to determine the important knowledge and skills to be learned, the motivation for learning and acceptance of self-discipline may be harder to communicate to the younger generation. The rationale for effort and attention is lacking. Where the problems of adjustment have been simplified and made easy, there is less awareness of inadequacy at the point of action here and now. The motivating challenge of this inadequacy is probably at the core of most learning and personal achievement.

Finally, it might seem that if we accept accelerating change as an unmixed blessing, the educational task is almost hopeless. Whether change is an unmixed blessing (or when it may not be) are questions to which education can give uniquely important answers. For example, should change be curbed when it causes break-downs in communication or is this a question of communicating skills? Can people with greater communicating skills live and work in an atmosphere of more rapid change?

Education has been depended upon for the long view, the perspective that helps men to assign the right values to human effort and experiences in the present. In relying on education for this we place upon educators the heavy responsibility of keeping in touch with the pulse of the community and with history in such a way that they do not teach either a worship of the past, the *status quo*, or of change for its own sake. Education must communicate a point of view that evaluates change and resistance to change with the same discriminating judgment.

So 'education for what?' remains the crucial unanswered question of industrial society. We have committed ourselves to a faith in the spirit of free inquiry and the application of scientific knowledge to the solution of technical industrial problems. We must use this faith and knowledge to solve our educational problems.

GORDON T. BOWDEN.

REFERENCES NOTED

(1) See *The Changing American Market*, Ed. by *Fortune* (New York, 1955).

(2) E.g., see G. Unwin, *Industrial Organization in the 16th and 17th Centuries* (Oxford, 1904); B. F. Shields, *The Evolution of Industrial Organization* (London, 1928); J. A. Hobson, *The Evolution of Modern Capitalism* (Scribners & Sons, New York, 1917); Witt Bowden, *The Industrial Revolution* (New York, 1928); G. T. Jones, *Increasing Return* (Cambridge, 1933).

(3) R. K. Merton, *Science, Technology and Society in 17th Century England* (Bruges, 1938).

(4) Max Weber, *The Protestant Ethic and the Spirit of Capitalism* (trans. by Talcott Parsons) (London, 1930).

(5) B. Barber, *Science and the Social Order* (Allen & Unwin, London, 1953); H. R. Tawney, *Religion and the Rise of Capitalism* (London, 1928).

(6) Dewhurst and Associates, *America's Needs and Resources* (New York, 1955), p. 892.

(7) *The Changing American Market*, p. 13.

(8) Dewhurst *et al*, *op. cit.*, pp. 71-2.

(9) *Ibid.*, p. 381.

(10) *Ibid.*, p. 384.

(11) See also H. Barger, *Distribution's Place in the American Economy Since 1869* (Princeton, 1955), p. 3 ff.

(12) D. Wolfle, *America's Resources of Specialized Talent* (New York, 1954), p. 47.

(13) See *Teaching Salaries Then and Now*, by Ruml and Tickton (Fund for Advance of Education, New York, 1955).

(14) J. B. Conant, *Education in a Divided World* (Harvard, 1949), D. Wolfle, *op. cit.*, p. 8.

(15) Haveman and West, *They Went to College* (New York, 1952).

(16) Standard Oil Company of New Jersey, *Employee Relations Research*, pp. 113–14 and A21 (New York, 1955); H. P. Longstaff, " Analysis of Some Factors Conditioning Learning in General Psychology," in *Journal of Applied Psychology*, Vol. 16, 1932, pp. 9–48 and 131–66.

(17) L. Urwick, *Management Education in American Business* (A.M.A., 1954), p. 14.

(18) See Warner and Abegglen, *Big Business Leaders in America* (New York, 1955).

(19) J. D. Millett, *Financing Higher Education in the U.S.* (Columbia, New York, 1952).

(20) See W. M. Daniels, *Education Opportunities for Youth* (New York, 1955); G. C. Lee, *The Struggle for Federal Aid* (Columbia, 1949); Paul R. Mort, *Public School Finance* (New York, 1951); *Problems and Issues in Public School Finance*, edited by Johns and Morphet (Columbia, 1952); *The Economic Outlook for Public Education* (National Educational Association Committee on tax education and school finance, 1952); U.S. Dept. of Health, Education and Welfare, *Expenditures for Education at the Midcentury*, Hutchins and Munse (Washington Govt., 1953); Council for Financial Aid to Education, *The Role of the Corporation in Aiding Higher Education* (New York, 1953).

(21) A. N. Whitehead, "Education and Self-Education", in *Essays in Science and Philosophy* (New York, 1947), p. 168.

(22) Elton Mayo, *The Social Problems of an Industrial Civilization* (Harvard, 1945).

(23) *General Education in a Free Society* (Harvard Committee Report, 1945); Edwards and Richey, *The School in the American Social Order* (Boston, 1947); G. K. Chalmers, *The Republic and the Person* (Chicago, 1952); National Education Association, *Public Education and the Future of America* (Washington, 1955); N. M. Pusey, "The Exploding World of Education", *Fortune*, September, 1955; J. R. Oppenheimer, *The Open Mind* (New York, 1955), Chapters VII and VIII.

Charts 4, 5, 6, and 7 based on charts from *They Went to College* by Ernest Havemann and Patricia Salter West. Used by permission of Harcourt Brace & Company, New York, 1952.

CHAPTER FOUR

The Effects of External Stimuli

THE world has been brought so close together that nowadays in every country education is stimulated by competition (commercial and political) with other countries, by the desire for world status, and by the influence of other people's educational ideas. But the countries most affected by external stimuli are the dependent territories and, to a lesser degree, those countries newly independent but still with large under-developed areas. This article will be concerned mainly with the British dependent territories.

In these territories the type of education in the schools is Western—that is, an imported one. Such indigenous forms of training as existed have been unable to compete and are now of diminishing importance. In all but the most remote and unsophisticated areas the demand from the people for the Western kind of schooling is now so great that it sometimes seems to have an element of hysteria in it. This was not always so. In the early stages of contact with Western ways many peoples, of advanced culture as well as the unsophisticated, showed an aversion to it almost as great as their present-day passion for it.

Western education in dependent territories, therefore, did not begin in response to a demand from the people of those territories, but in response to a demand from interested elements amongst the ruling people—missionaries, employers (government and foreign firms), humanitarians, and politicians.

Missionary Interest

The Christian Missions, inspired by the spiritual revival of the latter half of the eighteenth century and the early nineteenth century, were almost without exception the first in the field with Western schools. Their primary aim was evangelization, but as Hailey remarks, " The missionary in Africa came at an early stage under the influence of the fact that he was often the sole agent of civilization ".[1] For various reasons the form missionary endeavour took was to civilize on European lines rather than to attempt a synthesis of cultures.[2]

---

[1] Lord Hailey, An African Survey, Royal Institute of International Affairs Series, Oxford University Press, p. 1,235. See also African Education (O.U.P.), p. 44.
[2] H. S. Scott, Year Book of Education, 1938 (Evan Bros.), pp. 704 ff.

The governments in British territories were content to leave the field to the missionary, just as, until the latter part of the nineteenth century, the home government left education to the churches and other voluntary bodies. The only exception was in areas where there existed vigorous and widely organized non-Christian religions. There Christian mission schools were limited by government in their activities, as in India, or the development of schools had to await the initiative of other interests, as in Northern Nigeria and the Northern Sudan.

The pressure of missionary interest in education has not been confined to the field. The influence of the parent organizations on the metropolitan governments has been very great. An outstanding example of this influence is seen in the formation of an advisory committee by the United Kingdom government in 1923—a committee which eventually became the Advisory Committee on Education in the Colonies.[3]

The missions and the local churches, which have now taken over much of their work, still play a great part in the inspiration of education and the management of schools. It is estimated, for instance, that in East Africa they still control about three-quarters of the schools. But they are no longer an important factor in the huge demand for education, having been surpassed by the rising tide of nationalism and economic claims. Their influence is, however, important not so much for professional efficiency, in which they are sometimes weak, but for a spiritual basis to education, a basis specially needed with the breakdown of tribal sanctions. The tendency for missionary bodies now is to concentrate their limited resources on strategic points, creating a few good schools as examples and focusing on teacher training.

Business Interests

From the earliest days there was another and more practical kind of demand for the education of indigenous peoples. This was the demand from government and foreign firms for clerks and other subordinate officers who could be employed at less expense than imported Europeans. The missions themselves were anxious to educate local men to be pastors and teachers. The result of this demand was the growth of secondary schools of the grammar type.

In this development the authorities were soon encouraged by the response from the people. To most families dependent on the traditional economy the prospect of a son able to supplement that economy by regular money contributions was attractive. To none more so

---

[3] The outcome of another missionary enterprise, the first thorough educational survey of Africa, *Education in Africa*, 1920–21 (Edinburgh House; Phelps-Stokes).

than to the freed slaves, for whom the first schools in British territories (apart from India) were established.

Although from time to time the supply of academically trained youth has been inadequate to meet the demands from government and trade,[4] on the whole the demand from the people for grammar schools has exceeded that of business and government for its products.

Managerial and senior posts of responsibility have been a different matter. The demand for local people to fill such posts has been a later development. First, dependent peoples had to come to feel that they were capable of filling these posts and to have confidence in each other; while European people in authority had to reach a conviction that the qualities of character were there as well as the knowledge and intelligence. As questions of power were also involved at this level it is not surprising that where the climate was friendly to European settlement (e.g., in Kenya and the British West Indies) the demand from employers for non-European senior employees, and even junior employees, has been much slower to develop than in, for instance, West Africa, where the climate 'kept the ring' for Africans and Crowther, a Nigerian, became a bishop in the nineteenth century.

Education in dependent territories has shown a largely academic bias, but there have been periodical attempts to establish vocational training of other types, in spite of the greater cost of these types of education and difficulties of securing staff. These attempts have proved successful where there was a ready field of employment for their products, as for instance in the development of railways and of road transport or of mining operations. Often such schools have been run by the department of government or the firm concerned.[5] There has been very little success in developing training for artisans and agriculturalists who would make a living within the ordinary economy of the area, mainly because, until the wants of the people are materially increased in both quantity and quality, there is little demand for their trained services.[6]

Humanitarian Interests

Just as the missionary and the employer thought the prospect of

---

[4] For example, on the West Coast of Africa after the First World War (see Lord Lugard's *Memorandum* of 1918 quoted by S. Phillipson in *Grants in Aid of Education in Nigeria*, 1948), and in most territories during the present post-war expansion.

[5] See articles in *Year Book of Education*, *1954* (Evans Bros.).

[6] See H. S. Scott, *Year Book of Education*, *1938* (Evans Bros.), p. 731; J. S. Furnivall, *Colonial Policy and Practice* (Cambridge University Press), pp. 379–83.

The *East African Royal Commission 1953–5 Report* points out (p. 176) that while all clerical work requires a modicum of education, many other avocations can at present be pursued, however inefficiently, without it.

salvation or a job, respectively, were sufficiently strong attractions to lure unwilling pupils to Western-type schools, so the humanitarians thought, with less justification, that people would want what was good for them. It is difficult to separate the humanitarian interest from that of the missionary on the one hand and the political on the other, but in the nineteenth century and up to roughly the First World War it comprised all those who believed that the West, and in Britain especially the British, had a civilizing mission in the world.[7] This concept of a mission, strong in the early part of the nineteenth century with the freeing of the slaves, suffered a long spell of apathy during the latter half. One of the last examples of its influence was the founding of the non-Christian Gordon College in Khartoum by Lord Kitchener in 1902.[8]

The humanitarian interest took a different form after the First World War. Then, with the self-confidence of Western Civilization shaken, the often unhappy social effects of Western-type education prominent, the findings of anthropologists of increasing relevance, and trusteeship the new political doctrine, humanitarian interests pressed not so much for more education as for a different kind of education; one which should be distinguished by, to quote a heading in the 1925 White Paper, its " adaptation to native life." [9]

In most areas this change of emphasis was not acceptable to the people. They continued to demand an education recognized as European and suspected that this adapted education might, in fact, be an inferior education, as indeed, with a lack of source-books and properly-worked-out material for children, it very often was.[10]

A third and post-Second-World-War stage can be distinguished, where the pressure from humanitarian interests is less for any particular kind of education than for pushing on with the provision of all kinds of schools and of widespread informal education of adults. It is a pressure, too, which is now on governments rather than on voluntary effort, and expresses itself most strikingly through the various bodies of the United Nations Organization.[11] These formalize and make vocal a

[7] In the early nineteenth century often compared with that of Rome. See A. Mayhew, *The Education of India, 1926* (Faber & Faber), pp. 32 ff.

[8] K. D. D. Henderson, *Survey of the Anglo-Egyptian Sudan, 1898–1944* (Longmans, Green), p. 26.

[9] *Educational Policy in British Tropical Africa* (HMSO, 1925), Cmd. 2374, p. 4.

[10] L. J. Lewis, *Educational Policy and Practice in British Tropical Areas* (Nelson, 1954), pp. 56 ff. H. S. Scott, *Year Book of Education, 1938*, pp. 697–8.

[11] The UNESCO General Conference, the UNO Committee of Information, the UN Fourth Committee, and the Sub-Commission of the Human Rights Commission which is inquiring into discrimination in education.

world conscience and enable practical expression to be given to this
new demand.

Political Interests

The later British colonial empire inherited the nineteenth-century
liberal tradition that the political goal of dependent territories was
self-government, but while this has been the accepted ultimate aim, its
achievement was thought to lie in a distant future and the details of ·
the political structure of each territory were left for time and experience to dictate.

The responsible authorities have sought help from education in three
directions: first, in the education of sons of chiefs; secondly, in the
training of a local bureaucracy; and thirdly, in the spread of literacy
and a greater understanding of affairs amongst the mass of the people.

The special schools opened for sons of chiefs (e.g., in Sierra Leone,
Tanganyika, Aden) flourished for a time, but diminished with the
general spread of education.[12]

The education of prospective government officials has been a main
task of post-primary education, but, as Hailey points out, it is at the
higher level (post-secondary) that the considerations deciding the type
of education given are largely political, depending on the view taken
of the place in society which the educated are expected to fill.[13] And,
as he adds, there are few instances in British colonial history
when the future of the educated native of the area has been consciously determined. In contrast to French governments, British
governments up to just before the last war have, on the whole, been
content to wait until the products of local secondary education or
university education gained overseas have asserted their claim to positions in the political and administrative life of the country.[14] But
from the time of the 1937 Commission on Higher Education in East
Africa[15] there has been a remarkable development of university
colleges in Africa, the West Indies, and South-East Asia, at very considerable expense to the governments of the territories concerned.[16]

The third demand has been for education of the masses through the
spread of primary education and latterly through work with adults.
There has, perhaps, been too great a tendency to believe that literacy
by itself can be an important factor in ensuring the success of self-

---

[12] Lord Hailey, *op. cit. supra*, p. 1,257.
[13] Lord Hailey, *ibid.*, p. 1,288.
[14] Lord Hailey, *ibid.*, p. 1,289.
[15] *Higher Education in East Africa, 1937* (HMSO, London).
[16] See Inter-University Council for Higher Education Overseas, 1946–54
(HMSO).

government.[17]   But the rapid rise of nationalist sentiment during the last two decades has encouraged those responsible for educational policy to more thorough attempts to enlighten the masses through programmes of community development undertaken both by government and by voluntary bodies.[18]   In this they have been helped by the Fundamental Education programme of UNESCO.

Education, however, has not developed in an atmosphere of universal approval. In its early days, some chiefs and people were suspicious of its tendency to undermine tribal cohesion and traditional customs; some administrators have been doubtful of the wisdom, balance, and loyalty of its products; and where there has existed a plural society the more advanced communities have often opposed the education of the less advanced.

On the other hand, the people themselves have come increasingly to look upon education, and particularly post-primary education, as a chief means to political advancement; and nationalist leaders have urged more higher education to produce the necessary leaders and the development of technical education to enable the economic basis of political independence to be secure. A weaker response has been that to community development, where at least initially there has often been widespread apathy.[19]

Of present-day external political influences affecting educational programmes, the chief are the interest in the metropolitan countries of those political parties which are prepared to press ahead and take a risk, for instance the Fabian interest in the British Labour Party, the voices in UNO of countries which have recently become independent, and the special assistance offered by countries opposed to communism, in particular the United States of America.

The Development of Internal Demand

The demand from outside has met with an increasing response from the peoples of the territories, but not an unselective response. Dr. Margaret Read has suggested that there may be a common pattern in the transition from an initial aversion to European schools, through an increasing acceptance of new ways and rejection of old, to an eventual new selection by the people themselves of those elements in traditional culture and in the European culture which they wish to incorporate

---

[17] Furnivall, *op. cit. supra*, pp. 392–5.

[18] See *Mass Education in African Society* (HMSO, 1944, London); *Education for Citizenship in Africa* (HMSO, 1948, London).

[19] Margaret Read, *Education and Social Change in Tropical Areas* (Nelson), p. 90.

in their education. But this last stage appears to come only after a feeling of parity with the rest of the world has been achieved.[20]

So far, education in practice has been almost exclusively something external to the local cultural pattern, a means of obtaining a salaried job. Hence the response to opportunities for girls to be educated has lagged behind that of boys.

Another and perhaps inevitable difference between the external demand and the demands of the people has been over the quantity of education. Conscious of the standards of education elsewhere, of the costs of schools and problems of absorbing their products, the external interests have been restrained in their demands for quantity. Not so the people. Once they began to want education, they pressed for the opening of schools oblivious of any standards but those of examinations, of costs, and of the capacity of the country to absorb the products. With the *laissez-faire* tradition in education, the governments have let missions and private bodies go ahead, provided that they, the governments, have not had to foot the bill. When, as in recent years, they have had increasingly to bear the cost of education, there have been sharp differences of opinion on what constitutes a reasonable proportion of the budget to devote to education.

If one can take what the newly independent countries express through UNO and UNESCO as indicative of what the more advanced parts of the population want in most dependent territories, the chief demands at the present day are : for European ' know-how ' as quickly as possible, universal primary education, and, in the larger language areas, the development of their own tongue for general local use rather than any of the world languages.

Education and the Economy
How Far Has Education Contributed to the Economic Progress?

On the whole, education does not seem to have been able to produce the adventurous type prepared and able to work his way up against all odds from small beginnings to big business. It has excelled at training up the civil servant and has undoubtedly made a big contribution in supplying governments and commercial firms with considerably cheaper staffs than could be obtained from abroad. This valuable contribution, however, has been partly offset by the practice, probably inevitable, of relating local salary scales to the rates for European staff rather than to the internal market rate.[21]

---

[20] Margaret Read, *op. cit. supra*, pp. 105–11.

[21] It is usually reckoned that an imported European costs about 30 per cent more in salary and allowances than a locally recruited non-European. The figure varies according to the territory.

Primary education has been accused of encouraging a drift from country to town, and so long as schooling is not universal and the amenities of the country are so far behind those of the town, it is natural that those with even a little education should be attracted to the city. But there is a general consensus of opinion that, for any initial adverse economic effects of schooling—and not all the effects are by any means adverse—widespread education is a prerequisite of any big economic advancement in the under-developed territories, just as it has been in the more advanced territories. The problem is to make it an effective education.

Financing Education—Size and Nature of the Problem

It is generally agreed that lack of money and not lack of demand is now the number one problem in educational development.[22] In all except the wealthiest territories the money available is nothing like enough to meet the new demands for education. And these demands are not just for any kind of education, they insist on education to Western standards—including expensive university and vocational education. The economic resources of each territory are very limited, and mostly of an agricultural nature. Direct revenue, for instance, ranges from about £1 to £15 per head per annum, as compared with £80 per head in the United Kingdom.[23] At the same time many of the territories are experiencing a leap forward in population due mainly to the recent revolutionary improvements in the control of disease.[24] Thirdly, with some governments the status of education has been that of one of several competing social services whose demands can be satisfied only after the needs of ' essential ' services and expenditure on economic development have been met.[25]

One of the most difficult administrative problems in the distribution of funds is to find a principle by which grants can be given to voluntary

---

[22] See *Education in the United Kingdom Dependencies*, 1954, p. 11. Hailey, *op. cit. supra*, p. 131.

[23] *Education in the U.K. Dependencies, op. cit. supra*, pp. 61 and 63.

[24] The British West Indies population is increasing at the rate of 25 per thousand (*Development and Welfare in the West Indies, 1954* (HMSO), London, p. 62); Malaya now has 20 per cent of its population in the 6–12 age group, compared with 9·5 per cent in the U.K. and U.S.A. (*Education in U.K. Dependencies*, p. 63).

[25] Examples of percentage of central revenue spent on education in recent years : Barbados 17·6, Hong Kong 9·4, Fiji 12·5. Where self-government is coming in there is usually a marked rise in the percentage devoted to education, e.g., Western Nigeria, 1955–6, approved estimates 27·8 per cent. That there are limits to this urge to spend on education may be seen in the recent decision of the Gold Coast government to postpone some of the more ambitious items in its educational programme.

bodies for schools reaching a defined standard without at the same time committing government, if not legally, at least in the public eye, to an unlimited policy of expansion.[26]

The Prospect of Increasing Resources

Taxation: central government taxes in each territory have risen generally. It is difficult to say whether they could be further increased. In the British West Indies the opinion seems to be no [27]; on the other hand, the Barnes Committee on Malay Education seemed to think the community (a comparatively wealthy one) could afford to spend more.[28] It would seem that in many areas where demand is rising, people are quite prepared to pay an additional local rate for education, sometimes " with joy in every heart ".[29] This is a promising development, but it has its dangers in the possible neglect of the less popular services.

Apart from local rates, voluntary assistance from the community is another source of help for education. For instance, religious and lay bodies have done a great service in providing the buildings for so many schools. Voluntary assistance is usually more successful when the object is a limited one than when continuous support is required, such as for the payment of salaries. The stimulus of the community-development movement may perhaps augment this source of help.

From outside the territories financial aid for certain purposes is available. While the missionary societies are no longer able to contribute as they did in the past, the metropolitan governments are now more generous. The United Kingdom, through its Colonial Welfare and Development Acts (the first of which was in 1929), has provided some £220 million, of which about £28 million has been allocated to education up to March 1955. The United States [30] government has spent large sums, particularly on furthering vocational training, and the big charitable trusts, such as Carnegie, Rockefeller, Ford, and Nuffield, have also made substantial contributions. It is usual for this outside help to be restricted to (i) capital expenditure, (ii) running costs of a

---

[26] African Education in Kenya (Beecher Report), 1949; and S. Phillipson, Grants in Aid of Education in Nigeria (Nigerian Government Printer, 1948).

[27] Record of Proceedings of the British Caribbean Education Conference in Barbados, 1951.

[28] Report of the Committee on Malay Education (Government of Malay Printer), p. 74.

[29] " Report of the West African Study Group " in African Education (Oxford University Press), 1953, p. 55.

[30] Walter R. Sharp, International Technical Assistance (Public Administration Service, Chicago), 1952.

new project during the first few years of experiment, and (iii) scholar-ships for training local staff. Another form of help has come from UNESCO in the form of loans of expert staff and training scholarships.

These various sources, both internal and external, do not nearly meet the demands of the countries concerned, and though they may be increased, they are unlikely in the near future to approach the sums required. The problem, then, is how to cut out the less essential parts of the educational system and to use existing resources most effec-tively. Among measures taken or proposed in various territories are the use in the primary schools of one building and one set of teachers to teach two sets of children, one in the morning the other in the afternoon (e.g., in Puerto Rico and Tanganyika), the reduction in the length of primary schooling (e.g., proposed in the British Caribbean, but not so far carried out), dilution of staff with untrained teachers and pupil teachers (widespread), and economy in the provision of books and apparatus. While the double-shift system and a shortening of school life may be preferable to gross overcrowding in school, the use of untrained teachers and economy in books and equipment are much more serious in their effects, except where offset by special schemes for assisting the inadequately trained teacher (e.g., as in the Gold Coast and the Sudan).

The main difficulty in devising a suitable policy in these circum-stances is the ignorance of a newly powerful public opinion on educa-tional and financial matters and their demand for universal primary education and a Western level of further education. Where a terri-tory is still dependent on an outside power, there is suspicion of the motives of the government as well as ignorance of educational prin-ciples and finance.[31] Perhaps the new universities and university colleges could perform a useful function here, as they possess a certain initial status of independence and prestige.

V. L. GRIFFITHS.

---

[31] It is perhaps significant that in a discussion by educationists on educa-tional expansion in Africa (Cambridge Conference, 1952), only one out of thirty-four speakers referred to finance (*African Education*, p. 158). It is also interest-ing that the International Team reviewing *Teachers and Curricula in the Secondary Schools in India* (1954) (Ford Foundation, New Delhi) devoted one of the four parts of its report to " The Development of Public Understanding of Education ".

CHAPTER FIVE

Apathy : An Example from the British Cameroons

HER MAJESTY'S Government in the *Cameroons Report for 1952* says, " Development of primary education in the Southern Cameroons is limited not by the supply of schools or teachers, but by the demand for education. In some areas there is little demand, and existing schools are by no means full ",[1] and in a subsequent report for 1954, " The governing factor in the development of primary education in the Southern Cameroons is still the lack of genuine demand. . . ." [2] These statements point out a general apathy towards education within the Cameroons, but in this study, one small, typical area has been chosen in order that the conditions might be considered more directly.

Principles of Selection

The area to be studied has been chosen in consideration of the five following principles :

(1) It would not be well to study an extremely rural district even if it were typical of the Cameroons, because there would be the tendency just to assume that the apathetic view of education arose from lack of contact with Western culture. This would overlook the apathy that exists even when a people is well aware of education and Western culture.

(2) On the other hand, it would not be well to choose a district that has had considerable contact with the West. Such areas usually have experienced rapid growth in the past few years, and are definitely marked off from the normal situation in the Cameroons. In addition, there seems to be very little apathy towards education in the more Westernized areas, and in many cases quite the contrary seems to exist.

(3) As a result of the two foregoing conditions, we must choose a district that is rural, but not too far removed from contact with Western culture, as exemplified in principal seaports or large Westernized towns.

(4) Economically speaking, the area, in order to be typical, must have as its principal industry that which is the largest within the Cameroons (i.e., one employing a large percentage of the population and producing

---

[1] *Cameroons Report, 1952, Colonial No. 299* (H.M.S.O., London, 1954), p. 146.
[2] *Cameroons Report, 1954, Colonial No. 318* (H.M.S.O., London, 1955), p. 106.

the largest proportion of wealth). F. J. Pedler, in his book *Economic Geography of West Africa*, points out that, " The production of local foodstuffs in West Africa greatly exceeds, in value, the production of crops for export ".[3] In his case-study of Nigeria, of which Cameroons is a part, he shows that, " Production for local use yielded five-sixths of their real incomes; though not of their cash income, since much of what was grown was consumed by the producers and was never turned into cash ".[4]

(5) The people of the Cameroons, in general, are driven by the economic motive, not only to produce goods for subsistence, but to have a surplus with which to trade for European goods such as cloth, salt, soap, and other items rare to the Cameroons. This motivation extends even to the extremely rural sections, perhaps because of the influence of the Hausa and Fulani traders and herdsmen who have lived in the territory for so long.[5] Thus it can be assumed that Western culture will continue to advance, and those primitive areas within the Cameroons will become more and more Westernized. If, then, the district chosen is to be allowed in any way to deviate from what would be considered typical, it would be best that it deviate towards a more Westernized culture, as eventually most of the primitive areas will arrive at that place and have essentially the same problems of apathy. There is virtually no possibility of regression from Westernization, now that the economic motive has been grasped so fully.

The District of Mongo

For the purposes of this study the district of Mongo, approximately ten miles from Tiko, and thirty miles from Victoria, the two principal seaports of the Cameroons, has been chosen. It is located on the left bank of the Mongo River and includes the islands that are situated just where the river breaks into the vast expanse of mangrove swamp forming the delta of the river. There is no road into the Mongo area. Most of it will remain rural because of the nature of its industry, but the building of a road to Mudeka, the principal village of the area, would certainly transform it into a large trade centre. As it is, the people of Mongo must take their produce to Tiko, by canoe or overland on their heads, in order to exchange it for the goods they desire. A few traders purchase goods in the Mongo area from the farmers or fishermen and transport them to Tiko, acting as middlemen.

The population of Mudeka is about 900. It is the residence of the

---

[3] F. J. Pedler, *Economic Geography of West Africa* (Longmans, Green and Co., London, 1955), p. 40.

[4] *Ibid.*, p. 40.

[5] *Op. cit., Cameroons Report*, 1954, pp. 52–3.

chief of the area, Gabriel Eta, who is also the district head, i.e., the elected president of the native council. Both the old and the new systems of government are incorporated under the same man. The chief formerly lived in the village of Mongo itself, but moved away because Mudeka became considerably larger than Mongo. Apart from Mudeka, the district is made up of small villages and hamlets, as would be expected in an agricultural and fishing community. The population of these villages varies from ten to one hundred and fifty.

The principal occupations of the area are given here in the order of importance.

Agriculture and its connected occupations include raising cassava, cocoa yam, yam, plantains, coconuts, groundnuts, bananas, mangoes, and palm oil. Cassava in the form of Ngari, yams, plantains, and groundnuts are exported to Tiko and Victoria by the traders of the district, who bring back European goods for sale. The village of Kongae is particularly noted for making Ngari, a staple food, out of cassava. The latter is grated and left to drain overnight, and fried the following day in palm oil. Practically the whole village is involved in this work.

Fishing and its connected occupations are the catching of fish, drying, salting, and otherwise preparing them for market; the making of canoes, fish nets, sinkers, gaffs, and hooks (blacksmithing).

Trading is carried on by those who occupy themselves taking the goods produced in the area to places such as Victoria and Tiko and exchanging them for European goods to sell in the markets at Mongo.

Palm-thatch-mat making : the making of mats for the roofing of houses is from rafia palm leaves. Some are exported to Tiko and Victoria for native use, but the greatest proportion of them are purchased by the Cameroons Development Corporation for roofing the houses of their employees.

Local building has stimulated the production of carraboards on rather a large scale, and the collection of mangrove sticks and reeds. In some instances the houses are made of sun-dried mud bricks, and a more recent innovation is the use of planks and scantlings produced from the limited supply of large trees in the area. In a very few cases zinc and cement have been used in building, but to a very limited extent because of transportation difficulties.

About one-half of the people of Mongo are *Duala* or *Buckweri*, one quarter are *Effik* from around Calabar, and the remainder come from all over West Africa. The *Duala* people are principally farmers, a few being fishermen, while the *Effiks* are principally fishermen or traders, particularly involved in the production and sale of Ngari. The *Duala* are the principal landowners. Chief Gabriel Eta has set up a fairly representative form of government and has continued to insist that every group have some representation. Consequently he is particularly popular among the strangers of the community. He is very ambitious, and takes great pride in the progress of his district. It is interesting to note that he was chosen from all the district heads to act as temporary chairman of the Victoria Federation of Native Authorities in the absence of the permanent chairman. He is particularly interested in education and is constantly striving to have educational conditions improved within his district.

Aspects of Apathy

There are two schools within the district of Mongo, a native authority school at Mudeka that has four classes (i.e., standard II), and a Roman Catholic school at a small village about three miles from Mudeka with four classes. In addition to this there are several vernacular classes, run indirectly by the Basel and Baptist missions. The vernacular classes are very limited in their scope and usually consist of only one class of infants, taught by the local catechist, within the local church.

Several facts reflect the apathetic attitude towards education within this area. The total enrolment of the two schools is only about 25 per cent of the school-age population. The parents of these children hold positions as clerks, or school teachers, or are traders or in some other occupation that has come about as a result of Westernization. It is difficult to keep the enrolment sufficiently high, at times, to keep the two existing schools open. The force exerted by the chief and his close associates has thus far maintained the minimum level.

Poor attendance also indicates that even those who have supposedly sent their children to school because of their interest in education, apparently are not convinced that it is important. At certain times during the year the teacher finds that he has very few pupils because of some important activity connected with the occupation of the parent.

Apathy towards education is also reflected in the respect paid to the teacher within the community. The teacher most certainly receives respect and far more than the average individual, but the respect given seems to be given with an attitude of doubt. The teacher can read and write, but so can others. The teacher can do arithmetic and solve mathematical problems in their simple economy, but so can others. It is the general opinion that the teacher is the teacher because he could not succeed at any other work that required education. They never carry their reasoning far enough. They do not see that, but for the teacher, there would be no educated persons, and thus the teacher is of great importance. The limited demand for educated people keeps the status of the teacher comparatively low. The contributions of the teacher are intangible, and outside his own profession he is judged by his personal, social, and academic ability, and not by the attributes that make a good teacher (i.e., teaching ability, teaching methods, ways of handling children, and results).

Apathy is also reflected in the poor condition of the schools and equipment. But for the efforts of the chief they would not even reach minimum requirements.

The apparent attitude towards education differs from the real attitude towards education. When asked direct questions, community leaders or individuals seem to be all in favour of education and are quite willing to support any effort put forth to extend the system within their community. One goes away with the feeling that at last progress is going to be made. However, on returning, one usually discovers that nothing has been done, and, on closer investigation, that nothing will be done. Apparently people are quite in favour of education and think it is a good thing. In reality they have put it at the bottom of the list of many things they would like to have. The average Englishman would say that a car is a nice thing to have, and if one were given to him without any obligation or effort he would take it, but if it involved effort, it would be just one of those things he would like to have, but would be quite far down on his list.

The question is asked : " Why this apathetic attitude towards education?" It must be pointed out that, for the purposes of this paper, apathy has a meaning that is extended beyond the dictionary definition of ' indolence of mind ' or ' without feeling '. Apathy is here extended to include passive resistance and opposition, in order to include those districts of the Cameroons in general that appear to be apathetic because they are doubtful whether education can offer them something more than they already have, or have seen the effect of education in changing their way of life and do not wish to be changed.

Apathy is expressed in different terms and shades, depending on the district and the surrounding conditions. In an extremely rural area like Misako Mongo, apathy is really scepticism, and the people seem to offer a passive resistance to education. They associate it with the white man, and do not see that his way of life can help them. The white man is always rushing about and working hard and seems to be no better off than they, from what they have seen. In fact, if it is suggested that they would be better able to build a house and raise crops if they were educated, the reply would most likely be that they are perfectly satisfied with their house and they do not need any more food than they already have. In cases such as this, either they have not come under the influence of the economic motive, or they have no desire to change their way of life. Misako has definitely been under the influence of the economic motive, but to no avail. The people simply do not want to change their way of life, even for economic wealth. They measure their wealth by other standards.

The foregoing situation is by no means typical of the area, and in fact is an isolated instance. The greatest problems of apathy are located in the larger agricultural and fishing villages and within the town of Mudeka. Here the people have gone through a stage of enthusiasm for education, and the few posts that require education have been filled. Now the people have come to the point where they believe that education can help only a very few people. They are spurred on by the economic motive, and they do not see how education will help them catch more fish or raise better crops in order to get the money they desire. It is difficult to overcome this particular outlook because they are not long-range planners. They expect immediate results. They do not want to take time from their present gainful employment in order to receive the education, even if they are convinced that ultimately it would help. The same reasoning is applied to the education of their children. They would rather have the child's labour and assistance at the present time than wait for him to receive his education. They consider education desirable, but at present they cannot take time off to acquire it for themselves or their children, because of the ever-pressing economic motive.

Hostility to Education

In addition to this attitude, they sometimes become very hostile to education. For generations these people have been farmers or fishermen. Instruction has been passed down from father to son. Now the white man comes along and offers education in order to help. But they have learned that for the most part education breaks up their way of life and tears down their tribal system. Little or no respect is paid to the elders by those who have been educated. The children leave the village, and their father's occupation, in search of employment that demands the education they have received. The parents are opposed to this, just as most societies are opposed to rapid change, and consequently they do not send their children to school, they refuse to pay education rates, and are very reluctant to help in any matter that assists educational progress. The apparent apathy that they demonstrate is actually opposition towards an educational system that breaks up their way of life.

What can be done? Certain obvious steps have already been taken, such as establishing what are called ' Village Education Committees ' in order to discuss the problems that education causes the people. As a result, education has been made more accessible. Fees have been reduced to a minimum and in many instances to nothing. Arrangements have been made so that school will not conflict to such a great degree with harvest-time and fishing seasons. But these committees are difficult to operate because most of the people refuse to serve on them, and even so, the committee cannot solve the problem of the children leaving home.

Adult education would help considerably to overcome apathy. Most of the people have a desire to be able to read and if possible to write a little, in order to read the few publications that are available, and as a matter of prestige. Present adult education schemes usually do not take up a great deal of time and do not interfere with the day's work. Thus, the people, if it were not for the fees involved, would gladly come in order to learn to read and write. This creates the opportunity of offering practical courses that will help them in their work and at the same time raise the value of education in their eyes. If the people see some immediate results in their own lives, they will be more willing to make a sacrifice in order to send their children to school.

The Value of Propaganda

Propaganda has fallen into disrepute recently, and there seems to be a constant protest against 'selling' education, but this would undoubtedly assist in overcoming scepticism and apathy. It is generally assumed that education is good for any society and every means seem to be used to foster Western systems of education among primitive peoples, but when proposals are made to convince people, through posters and educational exhibits of their need for education, the line is drawn. Propaganda could be very effective in showing the connexion between education and the society in which the people live. At present they look upon education as something foreign to their own society, and unless they are convinced of its usefulness and their connexion with it they will continue to reject it.

The introduction of more reading material, essentially material that is understandable and useful, as against material that is merely trying to present some particular organization's ideas, would arouse curiosity on the part of the people and aid in adult education as well as education in general. Public libraries, even if small, would certainly be of assistance and a local paper would be of great help. There is not much sense in making a person literate if there is nothing to read.

Perhaps the most difficult suggestion to put into operation, but the most effective in the long run, would be the introduction of a more practical curriculum in the schools. The present curriculum is years ahead of the society in which it is being used. It is time that the curriculum was changed to help the people live within their own society. It is easy to say that the people need to advance and consequently the curriculum must be set high in order to help them advance, but it is also possible to put it so far out of reach that they will not even try. The society is changing and the curriculum must change with it. It must give growth and direction, but never be out of reach.

Much has been said and a little done about starting trade schools. The capacity to which the existing trade schools in the Cameroons are filled speaks well of the people's estimation of them. The practical nature of the curriculum is really the problem of the teacher on the spot, and as such should possibly be dealt with in the teacher training institutions. A vicious circle, however, has to be broken. Those people who have received sufficient education to become teachers generally look down upon manual labour. This is reflected in the schools, and as a result is carried back to the parents, creating trouble over again. The vast majority of the people in a society such as is found at Mongo must use their hands to earn their livelihood, and the curriculum must have a practical application to that society. Perhaps in some cases a trade school with a literacy campaign attached to it would be of more value than the ordinary school. The people would readily accept such a system, and once they became accustomed to the idea of education, the curriculum could be slowly changed, with the advance of the society, to give a more balanced academic education.

The introduction of an outboard motor, by a local trader, in fishing has had an outstanding effect upon the school at Mudeka. Several parents realized that if their sons could learn enough to run and care for a motor of that sort, they would personally gain by it in a short time, and they have sent their children to school. However, the present system will only make them capable of learning about the motor. It will not give them the desired results without some additional help.

It would seem, then, that the principal reason for the apathetic attitude towards education is that, driven by an economic motive, the people are not convinced that education can help them to earn money and raise their standard of living any faster than at present. This becomes more apparent when we consider Victoria and Tiko. Here the economic motive and education have been related. Here the schools are overcrowded. The people must be convinced of the usefulness and their need of education, and the curriculum must above all be useful to them as well as academic.

G. B. LAWRENCE.

CHAPTER SIX

Education for Economic Efficiency

MANKIND is wonderful. So is nature. The earth's people have demonstrated an amazing range of physical, intellectual, and spiritual capacities. As we are now so busily discovering, the physical world offers a fantastic array of natural resources which educated men can use and develop to make life satisfactory.

We are just beginning to comprehend the vastness of the human capacities, the natural resources, and the heritage of knowledge we have to use or waste. Perhaps that is why statesmen, industrialists, farmers, homemakers, social scientists, teachers, and others are asking more avidly than ever old and new questions about ways we can educate, organize, and work to use these capacities and resources in humanly satisfactory ways.

Economic efficiency is widely accepted as a worthy human objective, but experience indicates that acceptable and practical efforts to achieve it depend partly on how people define it. For the purpose of this analysis economic efficiency is defined as arrangements and actions which enable people voluntarily to use their innate capacities, knowledge, and natural resources to fulfil their needs and wants.

Some readers may wish to modify this definition. If so, do it, because the practical tasks of developing educational programmes that contribute to economic efficiency are inevitably influenced by varying concepts of what it is. For that reason let us consider briefly some variations involved in most concepts of economic efficiency.

First, around the world there are wide differences of feeling and opinion about just what arrangements and actions will best enable people to use their capacities and resources. For example, there are differences of opinion about how farm land should be owned and used, how banking systems should be organized and regulated, the extent to which various economic aspects of life shall be financed publicly or privately.

Since individual and national feelings about such matters differ, there are equally divergent feelings about just what specific human capacities and skills are of most economic worth and the extent to which they should be developed by public or private schools. For example, what percentage of a population needs to develop an ability to use higher mathematics? What resource-conservation concepts and skills shall be taught to how many youth? What kinds of vocational skills are of most value to individuals and social orders, and how much effort shall schools place on vocational education? How far shall schools go in helping youth develop discrimination and skills that aid them in choosing from the plethora of commodities and services produced by modern technology? Any one of these questions would lead to a prolonged and inconclusive argument in almost any pub or club.

Likewise, people have widely divergent concepts of needs and wants. The value judgments, traditions, resources, and current living conditions of individuals and nations influence concepts of acceptable living conditions. What types of housing and diet shall be considered minima for health and decency? How much and what types of economic security are of value? Shall public services be expanded or contracted? How much, or how little governmental control over individual judgment and effort complies with ancient concepts of the dignity of man and the stimulation or discouragement of individual creativity and responsibility? Such large questions continue to be subjects for debate in political campaigns, parliaments, churches, trade associations, and cocktail lounges.

The pages that follow will explore relationships between education and economic efficiency in nations where it is intended that people shall have large amounts of freedom to: (1) select and change occupations; (2) identify themselves with producer, seller, and consumer organizations; (3) consume products and services of their choice, and (4) vote, directly or indirectly, for or against various types of public enterprise and governmental economic regulation. This limitation does not reflect any lack of concern for the economic and educational problems of nations in which people lack those freedoms or have them in only slight degree. But most means by which education can actually contribute to economic efficiency appear sufficiently different in these two types of social orders that it appears most practical to consider them separately.

As a matter of fact, considerable popular control over the economic aspects of government and freedom for individuals to work and consume as they wish are inherent in the above definition of economic efficiency. Experience suggests that promoting these freedoms is one basic way of promoting efficient ways of creating products and services that contribute to the well-being and dignity of men. Of course, there is some evidence that forced labour of voteless citizens can be mobilized in ways that yield large quantities of some commodities and services. There is also evidence that even those specifics are produced more efficiently by voluntary workers who are voting citizens. In any case, the long history of slavery and serfdom indicates that compulsory efficiency is generally so much in conflict with human welfare and dignity that it defeats the humanitarian objectives of economic activity.

This analysis is also limited to relationships between education and economic efficiency in countries where people desire to use technology to obtain material goods, services, and leisure. This limitation is not intended as either a blanket endorsement of industrialization, as it has developed, or a criticism of peoples who prefer to avoid it. But since most of the world appears to be tending towards further use of technology, this analysis deals with developing the kinds of knowledge, skills, and human relationships which appear to help people do so in satisfactory ways.

Relationships between Education, Production, and Distribution

Production and distribution of commodities and services are basic aspects of economic life. So it is elementary to consider the relationship between those functions and schooling. For a long time both public and private education has been supported partly on the assumption that schools can help people obtain knowledge and develop skills that will increase their ability to produce useful commodities and services. What is commonly called general education has been expected to do part of that job. Various types of vocational education have been justified as means of doing other parts of it. Educational programmes in the contemporary Western world include varying amounts of both general and vocational training.

So let us start by assessing what we have. Then on that base we can consider some next best steps.

General Education in Elementary and Secondary Schools

For centuries many countries have recognized the economic values of what is commonly termed general education—instruction in reading, writing, mathematics, and the sciences. From the standpoint of developing and operating modern economic facilities, the experience of those countries indicates that such interest has been fruitful. Analysis of modern production and distribution techniques shows clearly that only people who have ability to obtain facts, explore ideas, communicate, calculate, keep accurate records, and use scientific processes can operate modern farms, stores, factories, laboratories, and transportation systems. As industrialization proceeds, individuals who lack that elemental training are becoming less able to perform modern economic tasks. Schools have proved that they can teach large masses of young and elderly people to read, write, communicate, calculate, and understand scientific theory and fact. These are reasons why citizens and educators in industrialized countries continue to expand and improve means of helping people develop these skills. For similar reasons countries in which industrialization is getting under way are quite reasonably making widespread general education one of their first objectives. Contemporary India, Pakistan, Mexico, Burma, and China are cases in point.

A growing number of industrial personnel directors are also pointing out that general ability to reason, exercise initiative, accept responsibility, and work co-operatively with colleagues are essential to the efficient operation of modern economic enterprises. The relative importance of such abilities and the mastery of factual knowledge has been debated at least since the time of Plato. But recent research and experiments indicate that those abstract human qualities influence efficiency of production quite as much as knowledge of facts, or the mastery of more specific skills. Both appear to be valuable economic contributions of general education.

Let us benefit from experience and provide first things first. In any country seeking to make good use of technology, elementary and secondary school programmes which provide high-quality universal general education are basic.

General Education in Colleges and Universities

Liberal arts colleges have long been regarded as means of helping people acquire knowledge, values, ethical concepts, and ability to reason which contribute to the ' good life '. Many thoughtful people question how successful they have been. Conceding many regrettable limitations, two facts remain. First, colleges and universities are a major means by which most nations attempt to perform that general educational function. Second, in contemporary, interdependent industrialized social orders, that function is more important than ever.

The 1955 Atoms for Peace Conference in Geneva was a dramatic reminder that it is now possible for industrialized countries to produce and distribute fantastic quantities of useful or useless and tragically detrimental commodities and services. Nations moving towards industrialization are becoming more able to do likewise. Technology is amazingly fertile—it is also amoral and indiscriminate. Two recent world wars, slums, imperialism, and the large-scale production of nostrums raise questions about the ends for which technology shall be used that are more critical than ever. Such matters can be considered best by citizens informed about ideas and values which in the past have proved beneficial or detrimental. Wise decisions can yield mankind unprecedented benefit. Mistakes or unethical decisions can endanger and impoverish millions. The premium on men capable of comprehending values and disposed to consider them is at an all-time high. This fact is basic to any realistic approach to education for economic efficiency.

Facts about the extreme interdependence of people, groups, and nations in the highly specialized industrial world indicate the practical importance of a training which prepares men to comprehend and work with the many local and international inter-relationships of producers, sellers, and consumers. This practical necessity places large economic value on the intangible qualities of broad vision, tolerance, restraint, and capacity to communicate. Liberal arts college and university training is a major existing means of developing those qualities.

Let us be sure that a legitimate interest in developing technicians does not obscure the basic economic importance of liberal arts education. In the name of economic efficiency we could become so busy with the technical training of farmers, accountants, engineers, managers, and economists that we would neglect to develop the general principles of civil organization and the goodwill needed to prevent the moral or atomic obliteration of every farm, factory, and office in all economic systems.

Just how much of what kinds of general education should be made universally available has long been a subject of professional and public debate. Of course, it would be culturally tragic to consider this matter exclusively on the ground of what quantities and types do or do not contribute to economic efficiency. There are other, perhaps more important, aspects of life. However, since economic efficiency can contribute so much to cultural aspects of life, one question citizens and educators of all nations can reasonably ask is, " Are we providing all youth with enough general education to enable them to work effectively in the contemporary world?" It is doubtful if citizens of any nation can answer, " Yes ". Statistics of school enrolments and literacy in many countries suggest definitely negative answers. It sounds elementary and trite to say so, but there is little doubt that in most countries economic efficiency can be increased by providing more general elementary, secondary, and collegiate education for more youth.

Vocational Education and Economic Efficiency

The question of how much effort should be allocated to general education and how much to specialized vocational training is old. Quite rightly, discussions of it usually involve consideration of both cultural and economic objectives. At present there appears to be general agreement that elementary schools can contribute most by concentrating on general education. But with respect to secondary and collegiate.......

levels, the debate continues. Advocates of either point of view can, and do, assemble impressive arguments.

However, after both viewpoints are examined it remains obvious that to use modern technology many kinds of specialists must be trained. It is equally obvious that somehow schools, colleges, or industry must train them. So the appropriate question becomes how much and what kinds of vocational training can best be provided by various types of schools and by industrial and commercial enterprises. Three questions may help us reach some practical working decisions: (1) What types of special training can schools and colleges provide best? (2) What types can industry provide best? (3) What types can be provided equally well either by educational institutions or by industry?

Of course, answers to these questions will be influenced by tradition and by existing social and economic arrangements: and the violent arguments of extremists seeking to defend either educational or industrial vested interests frequently obscure sincere efforts to find rational answers.

However, even in the heat of controversy, experience provides some evidence suggesting a reasonably effective division of effort and points to some possible next step.

Vocational Training for Non-college Youth

Practically all industrialized countries have relied partly on public and private secondary schools and trade schools to provide some basic training for the millions of craftsmen, mechanics, clerks, and secretarial workers required to do routine work in productive and distributive enterprises. Courses in typing, accounting, radio, television, automobile mechanics, agriculture, retail selling, welding, carpentry, are examples of ways schools perform that function. Industrial and commercial employment procedures indicate that the tremendous amounts of such training these schools have provided, and are providing, is economically useful.

At the same time in most of these same countries industrial and commercial organizations have provided similar types of on-the-job training. These efforts commonly take the forms of apprenticeships, orientation programmes for new employees, and special training which helps employees acquire new skills or further develop old ones. We should aim at maintaining, relating, and modifying the vocational training efforts of secondary schools, trade schools, and industries in accord with the stages of development and desires of various nations or regions.

As evolving technology continues to create new occupational

patterns, educators in each country should make more systematic efforts to provide the largest possible number of youth with vocational training that fits their abilities and the contemporary occupational facts. Three types of specific effort appear essential.

(1) Authentic up-to-date facts about contemporary occupational opportunity and need should continually be made available to school administrators, teachers, and counsellors, who should accept responsibility for keeping well-acquainted with them.

(2) Vocational instruction programmes should be continually adapted to fit changing occupational facts.

(3) Great emphasis should be placed on the vocational guidance of every young person. In the stresses that accompany industrial change it is more important than ever to remember that the state exists for individuals. At a mimimum, vocational guidance programme should include tests which indicate the capacities and interests of each person. Also each youth should be provided with information about the nature, training requirements, and probable economic returns of various occupations.

(4) With the above information freely available, each youth should be helped select and obtain training for occupations that fits his capacities and interests.

As Harold F. Clark [1] pointed out so clearly in 1931, the reasonable full development of youths' ability to produce depends largely on the availability of technical training. Rapidly evolving technology increases the importance of that fact. There is now general agreement among students of occupational trends that in the immediate future a greater percentage of workers will need increased technical training. Those who lack it will be less able to produce or earn. Some of this increasingly essential training can be provided for secondary school-age youth by full-time public or private schools. There appears little doubt that enrolments in the vocational programmes of secondary and trade schools must be greatly expanded in all industrialized nations.

Of equal importance is the fact that as technology develops it makes existing occupations obsolete and creates new ones. It is becoming plain that a growing percentage of workers will have to change their occupations one or more times during their lives. In many cases these

---

[1] Harold F. Clark, *Economic Theory and Correct Occupational Distribution* (Bureau of Publications, Teachers College, Columbia University, New York, 1931), p. 146.

mid-life changes will necessitate new training. This means that industries and educational systems will need to expand and modify adult vocational training programmes.

Regardless of what institutions are assigned the tasks of providing vocational training, it is well-known that the families of many able youth cannot pay the cost. Yet, nations wishing to benefit from youths' contributions and wishing to provide it with economic opportunity in accordance with democratic principles have no choice but to make more elaborate training available on an unprecedented scale. In many countries this plainly calls for a great expansion of support for secondary and vocational schools and more student subsidies or scholarships. Obviously, the financial cost will be greater than is now commonly recognized. The necessary instruction programme re-organization of many local and state and national educational systems will be drastic. Failures to provide adequate funds or to make needed adjustments will result in serious economic lags. What is worse, such failures will deny to a growing percentage of individuals the opportunity to fit themselves for successful living in the modern world. Educators and statesmen have an unprecedented responsibility to inform citizens of these facts.

Vocational Training Tasks for Colleges and Universities

Economic systems which make use of modern technology require the services of increasing numbers of highly trained people. The percentage of workers needing such training goes up steadily as more advanced technology evolves. It is obvious that only highly trained chemists, biologists, physicists, engineers, and managers can operate modern laboratories. Only people with similar training can develop the thousands of new products that appear each year in industrialized countries and design the complicated machinery that produces and transports them in such huge quantities. Equally specialized training is needed by the physicians, teachers, and social scientists upon which a nation depends for modern health, educational, and governmental services. Obviously, a nation will be more productive if colleges, universities, and industries provide adequate advanced professional training in fields such as science, engineering, medicine, and health education, social sciences and government. Since that is so, the matter of how freely such training shall be made available to all capable students becomes a crucial problem. The costs of college training are clearly beyond the means of many able youth. The 1947 *Report of the President's Commission on Higher Education* stated that in the United States " at least as many young people who have the same or greater intellectual ability than those now in college do not enrol because of low family income ".[2] In many other countries this percentage is substantially higher. If we are to talk seriously about relationships of education and economic efficiency in this age, we have no choice but to confront this problem head on. So long as the income structures of nations are such that families of able youth cannot afford to pay the costs of necessary training, it is essential that other agencies consider means of doing so. In the United States the President's Commission of Higher Education recommended that the federal government provide a broad programme of scholarships. To date that has not been done. In the meantime numerous foundations, corporations, and industrial associations are providing an increased number of collegiate scholarships. So far these admirable efforts have assisted only a fraction of the capable youth who cannot afford college training. Other parts of the current need are being partially met by the development of two-year junior colleges and adult education programmes. These make available at lower costs some types of training.

This problem of how reasonable amounts of collegiate vocational training shall be provided is further complicated by a vague combination of academic traditions which give many educators and laymen some rather arbitrary ideas about who is, or is not, " capable of benefiting from college training ". That trite clause is vague and not necessarily appropriate to the needs of nations seeking to operate modern economies efficiently. College faculties and many laymen are reasonably concerned about the problems of maintaining ' high-quality instruction '. Certainly that is a primary responsibility of any college. But for those concerned with economic efficiency there is another equally important consideration. Colleges also have a responsibility to provide whatever kinds and amounts of training contribute most to individual and national welfare. In the present rapidly changing technological age the concept of such training may, or may not, coincide with old concepts of what intellectual qualities best fit a youth to benefit from traditional college training. Now three other questions become relevant and urgent.

(1) What kinds of advanced training are most necessary and desirable to prepare youth of varying abilities to perform the technical tasks that emerge as industrialization proceeds?

(2) Shall nations hold rigidly to higher education systems based on old concepts of college training for only those who are considered most able, or shall they explore the desirability of providing whatever

---

[2] " Equalizing and Expanding Individual Opportunity ", *President's Commission on Higher Education. Higher Education for American Democracy*, Vol. II (U.S. Government Printing Office, Washington D.C., 1947), p. 6.

training appears most useful to those who have abilities not previously considered?

(3) More important, as rising populations increase the numbers applying for college entrance, shall facilities be expanded or shall we 'raise standards' and maintain existing facilities to train a relatively constant number of the most able?

At present, a growing number of colleges in the United States are following the latter procedure. Many private, and some state, colleges have raised entrance requirements and are now refusing admittance to students who would have been admitted a few years ago before the number of applicants strained existing facilities. These decisions are understandable, and temporarily may represent a practical means of making the best use of available facilities. But, since many students who are now refused entrance would a few years ago have been accepted, such decisions contribute little to the provision of the college training urgently needed for growing numbers and to the promotion of national welfare.

The question of expanding college and university training programmes in accord with population increases cannot reasonably be confused with the fact that there are limits to the percentage of youth who can benefit from college training, and to the kinds of college training that will contribute to economic efficiency. Of course there are limits. And there are well-recognized differences between colleges and trade schools or rehabilitation institutions. It would be disastrous to clutter colleges with students of such limited capacities that instructors would be unable to train those who can benefit. But at a time when the college-age population is increasing, and when the efficient operation of social-economic orders based on technology depends on larger percentages of people having advanced training, taking sophomoric refuge in old arbitrary concepts of who is capable of benefiting will not help college staffs expand the urgently needed programmes. Social-economic conditions are changing. It is only reasonable that colleges adapt their work to make themselves as serviceable as they can be under these circumstances.

Special Economic Education and Economic Efficiency

In addition to, or as a part of, general and vocational education, schools and colleges can make some special efforts to help people understand the characteristics of the contemporary economic world and some of the specific new opportunities and problems that are integral parts of it. In spite of the effect of technology on economic life, the basic facts about the immense technical capacity to produce, the relationships between productive capacity and buying power, the facts of interdependence and the importance of intelligent mass consumption are still generally unrecognized or inadequately understood. As a result many people are unaware of how large are contemporary opportunities for satisfactory living. Thinking and acting in terms of concepts or traditions that grew from an outmoded past, they fail to recognize, or they resist, changes that are necessary to make reasonably full use of modern capacities to produce, distribute, and consume.

Four general concepts need to be more widely understood.

(1) *Modern technology makes it possible to produce tremendous quantities of commodities and services. Material poverty and insecurity are becoming less necessary and less defensible.* By using modern knowledge and machines, even under-developed countries can add much to peoples' well-being and security. Recent developments in electronics and atomic energy are adding to the already amazing capacity of highly industrialized countries to produce abundance.

A more widespread comprehension of these facts is important because many people believe that a low level of economic living is the natural and more or less inevitable lot of most people. So long as this is so they lack the vision and incentive to make the quite practical, individual, and social adjustments needed to make fuller use of modern productive capacities. A more accurate picture of how productive they can be will help show them that hopes and efforts to improve their lot are very practical: that living can be improved.

As records of recent progress in numerous under-developed regions show, such knowledge rapidly broadens outlooks, creates new hopes, and encourages people to take individual and political actions that result in much better use of human energies and natural resources. In highly industrialized countries, where some types of production are artificially restricted, poverty and insecurity are quite indefensible. It is important that citizens of these countries be fully informed about the high levels of production and consumption they have capacity to achieve.

(2) *Technically specialized workers are locally, nationally, and internationally interdependent. Each person depends on thousands of others to produce the things he uses and to buy the things he makes.*

To live and work effectively, all people need to consider this fact in their daily working relationship and when voting on association or governmental policies. Thorough consideration will increase their ability to produce and trade. Failure to give adequate consideration results in inefficient production and inadequate markets.

Because economic interdependence is so real, citizens of democratic countries have voted to establish various types of government regulations. Producers, sellers, and buyers have also voluntarily established trade associations, co-operatives, and labour unions as means of making joint economic decisions which in their judgment will best promote their common interests. These familiar means of adjusting to inter-dependence have proved useful and need to be better understood. In the meantime, the constant efforts of pressure groups to obtain legisla-tion giving special privileges to manufacturers, retailers, farmers, or labour, the current difficulties involving in organizing the European Defence Community or of implementing the general agreements on tariffs and trade illustrate the far-reaching importance of creating a more thorough and widespread understanding of how extensive eco-nomic inter-dependence is—and what a price the entire world pays for failure to understand.

(3) *To pave the way for the distribution of the large quantities of goods men and machines can produce, the total incomes of people must be large enough to pay the total prices charged for all of those goods and services.* This means that more people must be helped understand the logic of basing wage, salary, and pension payments on the productivity of men and machines instead of on an ' iron law of wages ' or abstract concepts of ' what workers are worth '.

Of course there are, and will be, variations in the ways informed people in nations or regions can adapt to this fact. In some areas rising wages, unemployment compensation, and pension programmes, voluntary industrial efforts to mass produce and sell goods at low prices, and governmental limitations on prices charged by public utilities, have already gone far to help people act in accord with this fact. At the same time needlessly low wages, price-fixing cartels, artificial restrictions of production by some industries and some labour organizations, tariff barriers and other types of trade restrictions repre-sent widespread efforts to deny or evade it. The general need for creating buying power that equals productive capacity has been well documented by scholars and statesmen. More educational effort to develop wider and more thorough understanding of that need will help people work and vote in ways that result in fuller use of modern productive capacities.

It is important to observe that courses in *descriptive* economics seldom develop the above concepts. Classical descriptions of economic arrangements as they are, or have been, are obviously not enough. Citizens need more training designed to help them *analyse* existing economic arrangements and to evaluate them in terms of how fully and purposefully they enable people to use their capacities, knowledge, and resources. Experience shows that such instruction runs the hazard of being criticized or opposed by some individuals or groups who resist technological development or wish to hide it from citizens.

For that reason, development of analytic instruction should be accompanied by carefully planned methods of showing that economic analysis and adjustment are in accord with tradition, and in the interests of citizens and industries.

(4) *The purpose of economic activity is to provide people with commodities and services they need and want. Economic arrangements are man made. They can be, and are, modified and directed by human beings—not by immutable natural laws. For those reasons it is beneficial for all people to consider just what commodities and services yield the most satisfaction—just what purposes they want their economic system to serve.*

As was indicated on page 95, any reasonable concept of economic efficiency must include a consideration of the human purposes it is to serve. The well-organized production of relatively useless or detrimental goods cannot be regarded as the efficient use of human energies or resources. Modern technology can, and in some highly industrialized regions does, turn out such a plethora of relatively useful and useless products and services that it is difficult for most people to know which ones best meet their needs and wants. It is becoming increasingly important that free people be capable of making purposeful consumer choices.

Of course, around the world there are widespread differences of opinion about what needs and wants are, and about what products and services best fulfil them. Traditions and values rightly influence individual and group choices. But in many cases intelligent choice is obscured by lack of understanding of what the basic physical needs are. For example, in the United States, where food-supplies are plentiful, millions of inadequately fed families choose to spend large sums on unneeded clothing. Other millions lack facts needed to help them select and buy goods of reasonable quality at reasonable prices. The facts are similar in other countries. As a result, many human energies and natural resources are being used to produce and distribute commodities and services that yield little human satisfaction. Some even contribute to frustration, discontent, and poverty. Many social scientists have long pointed out that this represents a tragic and needless waste, and that people will benefit from more thoughtful consideration of what types of consumption best serve their needs and desires.

The writer will not presume to construct any list of specific products or services that will best fulfil the needs and wants of all people. He has too much admiration and respect for the infinity of mankind's desires and appreciations for that. However, an elementary knowledge of physiology and a general observation of what contributes to human welfare and misery indicate some classes of economic goods that are important in the lives of all people. Primary among these are food, housing, health services, clothing, education, and recreation. It appears obvious that in a world where insecurity, illness, and poverty are widespread, school systems which help people arrive at reasonable decisions about how they can best use knowledge and resources to produce and consume such items can, and do, contribute much to economic well-being.

Current educational efforts to enlighten consumers take a variety of forms. Some secondary school and college courses in history, geography, sociology, economics, and political science deal with large human objectives and market procedures that influence the consumption of necessities and luxuries. Considerable portions of elementary school arithmetic instruction give practice in buying and selling calculations. Home-making courses include studies of family budgeting and means of selecting, purchasing, and using commodities and services. Some schools and colleges offer specialized courses in buying and consumption. Perhaps most hopeful are the efforts some schools and colleges are making to integrate materials from various fields of social studies and general science by relating them to contemporary living opportunities and problems. These efforts are enabling a growing number of students to become informed about the historic, economic, sociological, scientific, and governmental aspects of individual and national efforts to obtain adequate food, housing, health service, education, and leisure.

A General Consideration

Contemporary interest in the ways education can contribute most to economic efficiency holds promise of helping the earth's people enrich their lives in many ways. Certainly they will benefit if education helps them make more satisfactory use of their capacities and resources. As educators, we are obligated to evaluate school and college programmes to see what types of instruction contribute most to rational and humane economic outlooks, decisions, and actions. But, as this analysis has indicated at several points, educational efforts to increase economic efficiency are, as a matter of fact, related closely to the general intellectual and ethical aims of education. Current interest in designing school programmes that will contribute to economic living represent a hopeful development. But this important interest should not lead to any careless inference that economic education can, or should be, set apart from other aspects of education. As a matter of fact, the exact opposite appears to be true. Economic efficiency has long been one educational goal. Much of what we have been doing for generations has been designed and accepted partly as a means of moving towards that goal. Now, as expanding technology and improved communications give us new means of achieving better levels of economic living, it will be well for those who are particularly interested in the relationships between this fact and schooling to look both forward and backward. Apparently effective economic education is closely related to modern concepts of general and vocational education. Of course, some aspects of existing school programmes can and should be modified or given new emphasis to take advantage of new economic facts and opportunities. We are obligated to seek ways of doing that. We are also obligated to keep in mind that life is only partly economic. The economic aspects of life are not ends. They are means. So, let us pursue our very worthwhile special interest with constant regard for the relationships between economics and man, and for the other equally important purposes of education.

GORDON MCCLOSKEY.

CHAPTER SEVEN

Technical Education in the U.S.S.R.

SCIENTIFIC research is conducted on a steadily growing scale in the U.S.S.R. where science plays an increasingly important part in advancing the development of industry, transport, construction, and agriculture. Progress of scientific thought and engineering leads to the construction of new, more economical machines, equipment, instruments, and materials; to the development of more efficient technological processes. The national economy of the Soviet Union requires an increasing number of specialists, and paramount importance is therefore attached to the progress of higher and specialized secondary education. Millions of skilled specialists for all branches of economy have been trained in Soviet years. There are at present in the U.S.S.R. more than five million specialists with a college or secondary education, whereas they numbered fewer than 200,000 in Russia, in 1913.

The college attendance in the middle of 1955 was 1,732,000 (173,000 more than in 1953). Attendance in the technical and other specialized secondary schools approximated 1,790,000 in 1954 (144,000 more than in 1953). More than 560,000 young specialists received their diplomas last year at the colleges and specialized secondary schools. About 280,000 college-trained specialists swelled the ranks of the workers employed in national economy, in 1955.

The rapid development of industry, construction, agriculture, and transport creates a very great demand for specialists in industrial and civil construction, electric power production, mechanization of agriculture, technology of machinery production, and other fields, but supply lags behind this demand. The 1954 national economic plan, therefore, provided for a greater enrolment into technical colleges. The actual enrolment at technical colleges was 37·2 per cent of the total college enrolment, and 160 per cent above the 1940 figure.

Technical Schools

Technical schools in the Soviet Union may be broadly classified as follows:

Polytechnical and industrial engineering schools, which educate engineers for the machine-building industry, for construction, railway maintenance, and motor transport, geology, mineral prospecting, oil and gas technology, technology of chemical production, light industry, etc.

Electric power and electrical equipment production, engineering, radio engineering, and physio-technical schools, which train specialists for all fields of electrical and radio engineering, electrification of industrial enterprises and factories, automatic plants, remote control and electric meters, electronic equipment, turbine construction, boiler-making, etc.

Mechanical engineering, shipbuilding, aircraft engineering, and poly-graphical schools, educating engineers for the car and tractor industry, specialists in internal-combustion engines, agricultural and transport machinery construction, hot and cold treatment of metals under pressure, foundry technology, machinery production, metal-cutting lathes and tools, hoisting machines, welding equipment and tech-nology, shipbuilding and ship repairs, printing presses, polygraphic technology, etc.

Higher schools for training specialists in geology, mining, oil, peat, and metallurgical industries. These educate engineers who specialize in the production of raw materials for heavy industry; geologists, mining engineers, technologists in specific branches of production, coal-mining, oil and metallurgical equipment, electrical specialists for the mines, specialists in mine construction and in the treatment of metals under pressure.

Chemical engineering schools, which train specialists for all the branches of chemical production : technological engineers, engineers specializing in machines and equipment for the chemical industry, technologists for pulp and paper production, etc.

Higher schools of the food and fish industry, which educate engineers specializing in the technology of bread-baking and confectionery production, grain storage and processing, in the technology of all types of food production and its machines and equipment, refrigerating and compressing equipment, specialists in the technology of fish-smoking, canning, etc., specialists in commercial fishing.

Higher schools of the light industry, which train specialists familiar with fibrous materials and their processing, skin and fur dressing, garment and leather industries, machines and equipment for light industry, heat and power production.

Construction engineering, geodesy, automobile, and road engineering schools, which educate construction engineers for industrial and civil construction, hydrotechnical construction, city construction, construc-tion in the mining industry, the construction of motor roads, etc.

Transport and communication schools, training rolling-stock and railway maintenance engineers, railway, tunnel, and bridge construction engineers, transport electrification specialists, engineers for marine and river transport, ship repair and port maintenance specialists, radio communication and broadcasting, telegraph and telephone communication specialists.

Mechanical and electrical engineers for agriculture are educated at the agricultural colleges.

Specialists for which the demand in national economy is especially acute are also trained in the other higher schools. For example, engineers for industrial and civil construction are educated not only by the construction engineering schools, but also by a number of polytechnical schools. The point is that the specialized higher schools are not distributed evenly throughout the territory, and chairs and faculties for training engineers in the most widespread fields are therefore maintained also at the non-specialized higher schools.

It should be emphasized that the geographical distribution of the technical schools has changed greatly in the last few years. Changes in economic geography naturally necessitate the training of greater numbers of specialists in the east of the Soviet Union in order to obviate the need for sending specialists to that part of the country from the central and western regions.

The relationship between the education of college-trained and secondary school-trained specialists is so calculated as to have at least two to four specialists with a secondary school training (depending upon the nature of the specific branch of national economy) for every college-trained specialist in industry, construction, and transport. Every stage in the development of national economy, science, and engineering presents new demands with regard to the specialization in the higher school. In all cases, however, it is expedient to educate college-trained specialists suitable for a number of fields. The training of specialists for a limited field narrows down their background and makes it difficult to distribute the specialists after graduation from the technical college. Allocation of a very great number of hours for the subjects necessary for a limited speciality inevitably lowers the general standard of knowledge and often obliterates the dividing line between the standards of the engineer and technician.

General Education of Specialists

The number of limited specialities is being now reduced in the colleges in order to equip the specialist with a better general background. He must be thoroughly familiar with the latest scientific discoveries and their application in his specific field, so as to be able to use them in practice. The general scientific education with the special training must be closely connected in order to equip the specialist

with a good general background. This is the trend of the new programme now being prepared for the technical colleges. Stress on the
education of specialists with a wider background naturally creates the
need for broadening the fields of some of the chairs and faculties in the
higher schools. This reorganization is being conducted at present in
all the technical colleges.

Readjustments in the list of specialities in which training is given
at the colleges makes it possible to improve the educational programmes through their contraction and transfer of some of the subjects
from the general to the special programmes of the faculties.

Much is being done to improve the programme by eliminating undue
repetition in different years and excluding unimportant material. This
readjustment will make it possible to reduce the number of hours in
the classrooms and allocate a greater number of hours to the students
for independent work.

Contact between science and production, i.e., the unity of theory
and practice, is a vital necessity. An important part in the training of
Soviet specialists is therefore played by the organic combination of the
theoretical and practical training in the colleges. Production practice
is undergoing a radical reorganization at present. Every technical
higher school will be able to send its students for practical training to
definite enterprises.

The factories and mills, construction jobs and railways chosen for
practical training must be up to the highest technological standards.
During their practical training the students perform independently
the duties in positions corresponding to their specific knowledge and
training. Production practice is directed by professors, lecturers, and
the most skilled specialists employed in production. Personal responsibility for the organization of production practice is borne by the
chief engineers of the factories and mills, and by the directors of the
Machine and Tractor Stations and state farms.

During their studies the students prepare independently three to
four annual projects and three theses. At the conclusion of his studies,
the student prepares and defends his graduation project before a state
examination commission appointed by the Ministry of Higher Education and composed of eminent specialists in the respective branches of
economy. On the basis of the merits of this project, the commission
issues to the graduating student the diploma of an engineer.

Specialists of the middle categories (technicians) are trained by the
specialized secondary schools.

Technicians are trained in a greater number of specialities than
engineers; in other words, the technician is skilled in a more limited
field than the college-trained engineer.

The technical and other specialized secondary schools function under the respective special Ministries.   There are about four thousand technical and other specialized secondary schools in the U.S.S.R.   One of the advantages arising from their subordination to the respective Ministries is that these Ministries are in a position to select instructors in the special subjects also among the engineers employed in production.   Specific features of concrete branches of production, transport, and construction are taken into account in the programmes and plans of these schools.   The respective Ministries render considerable assistance to the technical schools in providing equipment for the workshops and laboratories.   All that brings the training of the specialists closer to the nature of their future work.

The future specialists may or may not work while studying (they may be taking a college correspondence course, or attend an evening school after work).

Part-time Education

The evening schools and colleges admit people employed in production, in offices or institutions.   Classes are held four times a week (in the evening).   The students come for lectures, seminars, laboratory practice, etc.

Those who have not the time to attend school may continue their education and acquire a profession by taking a correspondence course. Correspondence courses may be taken with schools or colleges in the place of residence or elsewhere.

Correspondence students must submit a definite number of written papers in each subject.   These papers are controlled under the respective chairs and faculties of the institutes or technical schools. The correspondence students must take annual exams and submit graduation projects, just as the students in the regular colleges.   The worker who takes a correspondence course or attends an evening college is entitled to an extra paid holiday from work for taking the examinations and defending the graduation thesis or project.

Admissions to Higher Technical Schools

The higher schools admit persons with a secondary school education, and the specialized secondary schools—graduates of the seven-year school.

Enrolment is based on the results of the examinations.   Youths and girls have equal right to a college education in any field they choose.

College students receive state grants which depend upon the progress they make in their studies, and dormitory accommodation.   The necessary textbooks and other literature are supplied to the students.

The duration of the studies in the higher technical schools varies from five to five and a half years, depending upon the future profession.

The specialized secondary schools have a one- to two-year course for graduates of the ten-year school and a three- to four-year course for graduates of the seven-year school.

The graduate of the higher or secondary technical school receives an appointment in his specific line. Specialists trained at the evening colleges or through correspondence courses are as a rule promoted to positions for which they are fitted at the enterprise where they are employed; the specialist, should he so desire, may also be transferred to a higher position at another enterprise.

Graduates of the day schools or colleges receive at the conclusion of their studies a paid holiday of one month at the expense of the undertaking where they are to commence work.

A. F. SHALIN.

THE ACQUISITION AND DISTRIBUTION OF RESOURCES

ANY educational system makes claims on the economic resources of a society. It needs trained personnel, buildings, and equipment. The type of society and the nature of the demand will, however, determine in part what resources have to be made available for education. Tribal societies might not need a special corps of teachers. Where the demand springs from a particular social group or institution, education might be provided by and restricted to its own members. Industrialized societies have their own problems of providing mass education and have developed techniques for acquiring and allocating resources for this purpose.

Aspects of the evolution of national systems of education are presented in the first part of this section. The gradual transference of responsibility from institutions like the churches and municipalities to national governments has not been uneventful. Some of the important implications of the competition between Church and State for the control of education are made clear in articles by Mr. Bolgar, Dr. Hans, and Canon Bailey. Each describes how resources were acquired for education and what happened as states became more interested. Other case-studies show how a famous English 'Public' school was founded (Mr. Flecker), how land was made available for educational purposes in nineteenth-century U.S.A. (Dr. Thackrey), and how university students in Norway are helped by loans (Mr. Siversten). In the task of acquiring sufficient resources for education, the role of philanthropy and voluntary effort is not forgotten. Dr. Weiss outlines the extent of the American foundations' contribution to the finance of education, and in describing their policies indicates the importance of their 'risk capital'.

Increasingly, however, the major burden of educational provision is met by the state. Education, as one of several social services, is now supported by a well-developed tax system. Different attitudes exist in various countries to particular kinds of taxes—to local state and national taxes and to direct and indirect taxation. These have implications for educational provision. In theoretical articles Mr. Burston and Dr. Erviti analyse some aspects of taxation in the United Kingdom and the U.S.A. respectively.

Fundamentally the problem of distribution of resources in any economy is one of reconciling competing demands. Education is competing with industry and commerce for real resources. It also competes with other social services for a share of that proportion of the national income which is allocated to them. Its chief competitors are public works; health insurance and pension schemes; national defence; agricultural subsidies, and so on. What proportion is allocated to education will ultimately depend on some order of priorities—whether explicit or merely implicit. The second problem is that of reconciling the competing demands within an educational programme. Vocational and technical education compete, for example, with general education or with mass literacy campaigns; teachers' salaries with the provision of buildings, textbooks, and equipment. Decisions have to be made regarding the most effective use of resources. Should industry, commercial organizations, or governmental departments rather than the schools or colleges undertake certain vocational training?

None of these policy decisions will be easy to make, for the return on educational investment is not obvious. A case for increased investment in technical-vocational education can be countered by one in favour of a broad general programme of studies. The task is particularly onerous when general education and social reform is planned.

Dr. Seymour Harris introduces the third part of this section with a general article devoted to aspects of this problem. Other contributors give critical accounts of the economic problems associated with educational reforms in their own country which involve a considerable increase in educational opportunity. Mr. Holmes analyses in these terms the implementation of the English 1944 Education Act. Under circumstances of inflation the problems of financing an adequate educational programme are particulaly acute. Dr. Haralambides outlines the task of social reconstruction in Greece. Other articles deal with the special problems of extending education to disadvantaged groups under difficult economic conditions. Mr. Henderson reviews the reform of education in New Zealand, with special reference to the Maoris. Mr. Saiyidain's article is concerned with the tasks of reform in India, and Mr. Ghioldi describes some of the efforts and consequences of the Peronist five-year plans of reform.

All illustrate the central problem of acquiring sufficient resources to meet what are regarded as desirable educational objectives when other services are pressing for their share of trained personnel, raw materials, and manpower for building and for the special equipment needed in modern education.

THE EDITORS.

ACQUIRING RESOURCES

(Some Historical and Case Studies)

CHAPTER ONE

Provision for Education in the Free Cities of Italy

IF we take freedom to mean political democracy, we shall find that very few of the Italian cities were free for any length of time. We shall give the title to Florence at the beginning of the fifteenth century, but deny it to Milan; and we shall deny it to Florence under the Medici. We shall deny it to Ferrara, where Guarino had his famous school, and almost certainly to Venice. We shall, in short, commit ourselves to a distinction which has its uses for the political historian, but which has little significance in the field we are considering. Whether a city was at any particular moment a democracy, an oligarchy, or a tyranny did not make much difference to the development of its educational institutions.

The Development of Capitalism

The period from the thirteenth to the sixteenth century was characterized in Italy by two educational revolutions: the growth of the great universities, and the emergence of Humanism. The origins of both can be traced to the development of capitalism, which led to the rise of the middle class. Whatever their form of government, all the Italian states in the northern half of the peninsula were organizing their economy along capitalist lines. All the states were free in the sense that their citizens were not unduly fettered by the bonds of inherited status, and a high degree of social mobility based on wealth was permitted. The growing prosperity of agriculture, the revival, extension, and organization of industry and commerce combined to establish the political and economic life of the towns as a field of activity independent of the feudal order and the administrative dominance of the Church. The effects of this revolution were felt with equal force in every part of northern and central Italy.[1]

---

[1] V. Rossi, *Il Quattrocento: Storia Letteraria d'Italia 16* (new ed., Milan, 1945), pp. 2–3.

It was during the twelfth century that the Lombard cities first achieved a measure of independence; but the triumphs associated with the peace of Constance (1183) had been preceded by a long period of preparation; and even at that early stage the educational system of the Lombard communes possessed many features which did not conform to the common medieval pattern. The monastic schools in Italy had never attained the distinction they enjoyed in the north while the cathedral schools were associated in men's minds as much with the city in which they stood as with the ecclesiastical power that controlled them. Already in the tenth century we have a Bishop of Verona using the phrase " educated in our city ", and the same bishop talks also of private teachers.[2] Furthermore, by the eleventh century we find the Italians taking an exceptional interest in law—obviously derived from the growing complexity of their social and economic relationships. At this juncture, law was not yet clearly distinguished from rhetoric; but the old schools of grammar and rhetoric were introducing more and more legal instruction into their courses, and nowhere was this tendency so marked as in Italy. Pavia, which produced Lanfranc, was perhaps the most famous of these early half-legal, half-rhetorical schools. There were others, however, at Reggio, at Ravenna, and Bologna[3]; and as knowledge increased and problems were clarified, the study of Roman Law came into prominence. With Irnerius in the twelfth century we have the appearance of what is properly a law school in Bologna and what is to be the first of the great universities.

Studia Generalia

The history of the early universities bristles with problems, not the least of which concerns the exact significance of the name by which they were described. We find them referred to as *studia generalia*. Later this term was to acquire a precise connotation; but at first its use was informal, and, as Rashdall suggests, probably meant no more than that the school in question had a plurality of masters, offered at least one of the common subjects of higher education, law, theology, or medicine, and attracted students from all parts. But before we consider how these *studia* were organized and financed, there is one incidental feature we must mention, because it serves to distinguish Italy from the north of Europe. The great schools of Italy in the twelfth and early thirteenth centuries were primarily schools of law or medicine. Theology, which dominated the teaching of Paris and Oxford

---

[2] Ratherius of Verona, *Syndica 15* (Migne, *Patrologia Latina*, 134, col. 49).

[3] H. Rashdall, *The Universities of Europe in the Middle Ages* (ed. F. M. Powicke and A. B. Emden, Oxford, 1936).

and held a prominent place in such early foundations as Toulouse
(1229) and Palencia (1208–9), took third place south of the Alps. There
were migrations by the Bologna lawyers to Vicenza (1204), to Arezzo
(1215), and to Padua (1222)—where we hear of a twelfth-century law
school—and Pisa (1338); and in addition, we hear of law teaching at an
early date at Siena, Piacenza, Perugia, Treviso, Florence, Pavia, and
Ferrara.[4] Medicine, which had found its first home at Salerno, was
also represented at many of these centres, but theology was taught
almost exclusively by the friars in their convent schools, whose connexions with the universities were slight, and whose pupils had to go
to Paris to graduate.

It is not intended to suggest that the interest in law and medicine
was confined to Italy. There existed a medical school at Montpellier,
famous law schools at Angers and Orleans; and foreign students came
to Italy in great numbers. But the predominance of these secular disciplines was Italian. The forces working to create the new order of
the Renaissance were everywhere in Europe; but they were pre-
eminent in the Italy of the free cities. Elsewhere, the new developments in learning were to a great extent pressed into the service of the
established feudal and clerical order as it grew and attempted to maintain its hold on a changing environment.

Professional Learning

Professional learning then was the first intellectual product of the
nascent capitalism of the free cities. Their famous schools had grown
up from small beginnings, from classes where young boys were taught
the elements of grammar. There had been a time when any man
could set up as a teacher if he could find pupils to listen to him, when
no qualifications were demanded, with the possible exception of a
bishop's licence. But the individual teacher naturally found it convenient to settle near an existing school which in a way prepared his
pupils for him. Well-known teachers took assistants when they
attracted more hearers than they could adequately supervise; and a
city like Pavia, which had acquired a reputation, naturally produced
more specialists. Bologna, where Irnerius taught in the twelfth century, seems by 1150 to have had a sizeable community of teachers, and
probably they formed themselves into an informal guild for their
mutual protection. Dependent on fees, their position was not enviable.

Nor were their students in a much better case. Such of them as
were strangers to the city, whether from abroad or from other parts of
Italy, were given little protection by the laws; and they too banded

[4] H. Rashdall, ibid., Vol. II, pp. 5–58.

themselves together. Masters and pupils had in their isolation one potent weapon. They could depart; and in the smallish communities of the twelfth and thirteenth centuries, the departure of a school was a serious matter. When the University of Padua moved to Vercelli in 1228, the city authorities agreed to place five hundred of the best houses at their disposal. The presence of such a sizeable student population meant considerable gains for landlords and shopkeepers, quite apart from the distinction bestowed on the city by the possession of famous teachers; and it was the fear of financial loss rather than any special goodwill towards learning on the part of the citizens that enabled the infant university to extort valuable privileges.

Employers and the Employed

In Italy the organizations formed by students were very strong and for a time effectively controlled all but the most distinguished of the masters. They were the employers, the masters the employed. In the twelfth century the latter were wholly dependent on fees they could collect for their lectures, the amount of which was decided by bargaining. Later, however, their position improved. When other towns tried to follow the example of Bologna by establishing schools which would draw foreign students, they began to offer fixed salaries as an inducement to well-known teachers. One of the earliest instances of this comes not from Italy but from Palencia in Spain. The practice soon became common, however: in 1246 we find the authorities at Siena hiring a doctor of civil law; in 1260 the town statutes of Padua provide for the salaries of doctors; and by 1280 Bologna itself was forced to show an equal generosity. In 1289 there was a chair of civil and two of canon law at Bologna with salaries of 100 and 150 *librae* for two canonists and 50 for a civilian. But before another ten years had passed we hear of a famous jurist who was offered 500. These salaries seem to have been additional to whatever the professors could collect from fees, though later we come across instances where the amount of the fee was limited or fees were altogether abolished. By 1381 Bologna had as many as twenty-three salaried doctors of law, whose payments varied from 100 to 620 *librae*. Ferrara in 1474 had twenty-three salaried professors in law and twenty-nine in medicine and philosophy; and with the power of the purse went the power of making appointments. The practice of allowing the students to nominate their professors lapsed. Soon no teacher could afford to forfeit the goodwill of the city fathers whose favour had gained him his post. A circumstance which the more quarrelsome of the fifteenth-century Humanists had reason to regret.

Teachers also benefited from the presents which a candidate was

supposed to give when taking his doctorate. These varied in character. At Bologna the doctors and university officials taking part in
the ceremony received a cap, gloves, and a box of sweetmeats; and
the new doctor was expected in addition to provide a feast for his
colleagues and friends. Wealthy students spent money freely on such
occasions, even to the extent of organizing tilts and tournaments.

Organizational Expenses

The money paid to individual teachers did not represent the whole
cost of education. There were also organizational expenses. In the
student-universities of Italy these were for the most part connected
with the exercise of the rectorship—consequently the individual holding the office had to be a man of means. But the rector could levy fines,
a moiety of which went towards his personal expenses. Students who
misbehaved, booksellers whose wares were not up to standard, landlords who proved too extortionate—all contributed. In addition, the
statutes permitted levies for special purposes. But as the universities
grew in importance, these irregular sources of income proved insufficient, and eventually in this field too the university was forced to rely
on municipal support.

Let us for the moment, however, consider only the universities in
their early days. They had no buildings, their organization was simple,
their professors comparatively unassuming; and the greatest part of
the cost of their maintenance came out of the private pockets. What
is more, in the twelfth and thirteenth centuries before the vast influx
of students from beyond the Alps laymen predominated over ecclesiastics; middle-class students over the cadets of noble houses. The
university rose to fame as a middle-class institution, the direct product
of the new interests in the city states.

With time, however, all this changed. First of all, the number of
beneficed ecclesiastics increased. We find them in particular among
the northerners.[5] They still paid fees. But in the final analysis these
fees must be regarded as coming from the resources of the Church
rather than out of private pockets. A benefice given to a student was
an indirect method of endowing education. Nor was this the only
form of help. Those who had not yet secured benefices were often
privately aided by well-to-do ecclesiastical patrons. So, for example,
the humanist John Free was sent to Italy by Bishop Bekynton and had
from him gifts of money wherewith to buy books.[6] We may also cite

---

[5] H. Rashdall, *ibid.*, Vol. I, p. 150; see also G. Barraclough, *Papal Provisions*
(Oxford, 1935), pp. 27–8, 73–4, 101–3.

[6] R. J. Mitchell, *John Free* (London, 1954), pp. 41, 75–8.

the fourteen hundred poor students whom Pope Urban V is said to have supported.[7] Furthermore, churchmen took a notable part in the foundation of colleges.

In Italy these were primarily hostels for students of moderate means who needed help with their living expenses. At Bologna we have the College of Avignon, founded by a bishop of that city for eight students in 1267; the College of Brescia, founded by a Bolognese Archdeacon in 1326; the College of Spain for thirty students, founded by Cardinal Albornoz in 1367; the Gregorian College, founded by Gregory XI in 1371. Cardinal Capozzi founded the Gregorian College in Perugia for forty students, and Sixtus IV was responsible for one at Turin—to take only a few examples.

The Role of Princes and Municipalities

As we move on in the fourteenth and fifteenth centuries to the universities which were deliberately founded, the part played by princes and municipalities becomes increasingly important. The first migrations from the older universities in the thirteenth century seem to have been caused by discontents at home rather than by solicitations from abroad. But we know from the case of Vercelli in 1228 that careful arrangements were negotiated, and it is plausible to suppose that the cities which received the migrants expected to benefit. Later we have evidence that cities competed for migrant professors and scholars, and, as has been mentioned in connexion with salaries, generous offers were frequently made to attract individual teachers. When the advantages of possessing a university became clear, the cities took the initiative. The municipality of Siena appears to have been the first to attempt to set up a university as a matter of deliberate policy, and its example was followed two years later by Piacenza (1248), by Perugia (1308), by Treviso (1314), by Florence (1321), and in the next century by Ferrara, Turin, and Catania. By this time the nature of a *studium generale* was clearly enough understood to be formulated in legal terms. Charters from the Pope or Emperor conferred on the new foundations the status of Bologna or Padua, though, as Naples and Florence discovered, the guarantee of status was not a guarantee of success. However, by the fourteenth century, the municipalities were the agencies responsible for bringing universities into being and paid and controlled the teachers.

The money was sometimes drawn from the general city funds. At others, a particular tax was earmarked to supply the needs of the university: an ox-tax and wagon-tax at Padua, a tax on ecclesiastical

---

[7] G. Mollat, *Les Papes d'Avignon* (Paris, 1912), pp. 107, 110.

property at Florence, and a bridge-toll at Turin. The Florentine method deserves to be noted. In 1342 the Pisans tried to make their newly founded *studium* a charge on the revenues of the diocese. Benedict XII refused their application, but later Sixtus IV agreed to the raising of 5,000 *ducats* by a tax on the clergy. Here again we find the Church making its contribution. Nor did the despots who seized power in so many of the Italian cities prove less generous. Padua owed her first university building to Francesco Carrara in 1399, and the bridge-toll which supplied the fifteenth-century university of Turin was supplemented by a salt-tax raised in the dominions of the reigning Duke of Savoy.

Humanism

If professional training in law and medicine was the first educational product of the new social and economic order which was emerging from the feudalism of the Middle Ages, the programme of the Humanists in all its subtle manifestations was undoubtedly the second. Life in a free society (using the term ' free ' in its widest sense to cover more than just political freedom) requires not only familiarity with certain techniques, but also the general acceptance of certain values, and of certain patterns of behaviour. The Roman system of law might be described, without undue paradox, as a technique for organizing human relationships within the framework of a free society.[8] While one section of the Italian middle class had been mastering its intricacies in the schools, another section had been busy learning informally in the market place and the counting house the parallel techniques of the rational pursuit and management of wealth. It was not until these techniques had been adequately mastered that the less obvious cultural difficulties presented themselves. The impossibility of investment in a society that labelled the taking of interest as usury—the cloud cast on the worth of civic dignities by the esteem reserved for birth—the conflict between habits of faith and habits of reason—between deliberate asceticism and the habits of luxury—all served to underline the need for a new outlook. Already in the thirteenth century, in the court of Frederick II, a way of life was emerging that broke with the medieval tradition; but it was not until considerably later that the task of formulating new standards was

---

[8] The identification of ecclesiastical benefices with secular types of property is an example of how medieval institutions were transformed by the influence of the categories of Roman law: C. Gross, *Das Recht an der Pfruende* (Graz, 1887), pp. 122–40. The fact that the study of Roman law militated against the survival of the established medieval order was not hidden from the men of the time: Bernard of Clairvaux, *De Consideratione* (ed. Migne, *Patrologia Latina*, Vol. 182, cols. 727–807).

effectively undertaken by Petrarch. Then the ancient world with its civic ideals, its hedonism, and its rationalism was called in to supply a model for the men of the Renaissance.

Humanism in the fourteenth and fifteenth centuries had two faces. On the one hand, it was a movement for the revival of classical learning whose leaders concerned themselves with the recovery of manuscripts, the niceties of Latin grammar, and the popularization of Greek. On the other hand, it was a movement concerned with the elaboration of ideas which had in most cases an echo in the ancient classics, but which proliferated in a multitude of new guises. A long series of incidental writings prepared the ground for Machiavelli's rational politics, Castiglione's *Courtier*, Alberti's vision of civic dignity, Ficino's vision of an ideal love, for the liberalism of Erasmus and the scepticism of Montaigne.

Such a complex movement was not well fitted to influence organized education. Its intellectual appeal was to the adult mind through the commerce of ideas. Its strength lay in its literary propaganda and in the impact it made upon the arts. Its educational programme never amounted to much more than the encouragement of an all-round development, of the body as well as the mind, and a zeal for teaching correct Latin and Greek. Although the early Humanists talked much about education, little of what they said applies usefully to the work of the classroom. They were scholars and propagandists rather than educators. If many of them taught in universities and schools, they did so rather from necessity than from choice, since they had no other way of earning a living. To a great extent Petrarch's refusal to give up his Padua canonry for a university chair in Florence and Filelfo's remark that he would as soon keep a lodging-house as open a school must be taken as typical of the Italian Humanists, in spite of the educational achievements of a Guarino or a Vittorino da Feltre.

The Humanists who tried to make a place for themselves as teachers had in any case to work within a system that made shamefully poor provision for their special interests. Although the universities had their Arts faculties, the study of Arts was only a preparation for law, theology, and medicine, and of all the Arts, rhetoric and grammar were the least esteemed.[9] Arts students were, owing to their youth, excluded from many of the rights and privileges of their elders; and Arts teachers never commanded the salaries offered in other faculties. Grammar masters, moreover—although under the jurisdiction of the university—were not even required to be graduates.

This cult of ancient literature was slow to make its impact on the

---

[9] H. Rashdall, *ibid.*; Vol. I, pp. 238, 242.

universities. We have Valla at the beginning of his career Professor of Eloquence at Pavia for a stipend of 50 *scudi* when eminent jurists could earn 600 to 800; and in 1453 an undistinguished Humanist like Lauro Quirino had to be prepared to hold his chair of rhetoric at Padua for a miserable 40 *ducats*, less than a tenth of what he would have earned as a canonist or civilian. Admittedly a man who had a great reputation as a scholar or publicist could on occasion make better terms. Filelfo on his return from Constantinople (when he was reputed to have mastered Greek learning more thoroughly than any Italian before him) was offered 450 *scudi* to lecture at Bologna and later received equivalent, or even slightly greater, salaries at Florence and Milan. But Filelfo was an exception; and when we compare his income with that of the jurists, we must bear in mind that he could not supplement his earnings by private practice and that he had no security of tenure, but was forced to wander from city to city.

Humanism in Florence

Since Humanism represented in the field of ideas the social and political movement which had given birth to the free cities, it will be convenient to glance at its history in Florence, where the new freedom had the longest sway. In the early days when rhetoric and law were still taught together, Florence had provided Bologna with some of her leading stylists. Latin was a useful accomplishment in a merchant community with international interests, and the schools we hear about towards the end of the thirteenth century were probably of long standing. In 1321 an unsuccessful attempt was made to establish a university after the manner of Bologna. John XXII refused to issue the necessary Bull and the Florentines failed to secure the services of the professors who had just seceded from Bologna. A law school was opened without university status, but did not flourish, although we hear of the well-known jurist, Cino da Pistoia, teaching there in 1334. Fourteen years later the effort was repeated—this time with better results. An annual sum of 2,500 *florins* was set aside to meet the expenses of the new foundation, and in 1349 Clement VI granted the necessary Bull to establish a *studium generale*. Even so, the university enjoyed only moderate success. The very prosperity of Florence was a bar to its academic progress. The city was crowded, lodgings were expensive and hard to find, and it is questionable if the population would have welcomed a great influx of students from outside. Poggio, who was educated in Florence near the beginning of the fifteenth century, complains of the uninspired character of the teaching. Most of his time was apparently spent in learning by heart the common *formulae* of legal correspondence; and after the middle of the fifteenth century the law school seems to have died out altogether. In one way, however, the weakness of the traditional faculties was an advantage. It left the door open for freer experiment. Florence was the first university in Italy to have an effective theological faculty (1349); the first to establish a chair of Italian literature with lectures on Dante whose holder was no less a person than Boccaccio (1373–4) and the first to elect a Professor of Greek, when the visiting Byzantine scholar, Manuel Chrysoloras, was appointed at a salary which was soon raised to 250 *florins*. These experiments reflect the lively interest of a certain section of Florentine society in all new ideas. In consequence, the rhetorical faculty in the otherwise undistinguished University of Florence became during the first half of the fifteenth century a forum for the expression of Humanist ideas. The lectures attracted audiences of brilliant amateurs. The position of the lecturers was analogous to that of those who spoke publicly at the Collège de France and the Collège de Beaux Arts and thus enlivened the intellectual life of nineteenth-century France. We must compare them to Cousin, Taine, and Bergson rather than to the professors of a modern English or American university. Guarino taught at Florence from 1410 to 1414, Filelfo was Professor of Greek and Eloquence from 1429 to 1434, Carlo Marsuppini from 1434 to 1444. Marsuppini became Chancellor in 1444, but continued to lecture irregularly until his death nine years later; then we hear of a curious incident which sheds a light on the intellectual life of the city. After two years with no Humanist lecturer, the signoria was pressed by the partisans of the new learning to make a fresh appointment in 1455. Instead of voting a salary sufficient to attract some eminent Humanist, however, the signoria refused to do more than establish two badly paid chairs. These were to be filled from local talent. In this the anti-Humanist party was supported by the aged Poggio, who declared that lectures were, anyway, a waste of time. Eventually, the two parties agreed to leave a low stipend for one chair for a young Florentine, while the other was endowed with an annual 400 *florins* and was offered to a distinguished Byzantine exile.

The incident shows that, far from being wholeheartedly Humanist, Florentine society was divided on the subject. We recognize here the now familiar division between an intellectual *élite* and the great mass of practical men.[10]

---

[10] The division was formally recognized by Cardinal Bessarion whose plan for training young Greeks in Italy divides the students into two groups, some receiving a literary, others a technical education. A. G. Keller, " A Byzantine Admirer of Western Progress, Cardinal Bessarion ", *Cambridge Historical Journal* (October, 1955), Vol. XI, 3.

The Florentine Élite

In 1455 the Florentine *élite* was just entering upon its period of greatest glory. Marsilio Ficino was back in the city and was soon to embark on that series of translations which earned him the name of a second Plato. Soon he was to collect round him that circle of friends which later ages were to call the Florentine Academy. The death of Cosimo de' Medici, Ficino's patron, merely marked another forward step. His successor, Lorenzo, whose rule marked the end of Florence's political freedom, proved the most magnificent patron that the Humanists had ever known. Writers and scholars found themselves welcome at court, and the life of the intellect was supported by all the resources of political and economic power. The monuments of Florentine Humanisn, the writings of the Neoplatonists, the poetry of Lorenzo himself, of Pulci and of Politian, the Medicean Library and Lorenzo's collections of works of art were all the products of an activity which lay outside the bounds of organized education. In this florescence of Humanism, the university played an undistinguished part. After 1472 it was transferred to the subject city of Pisa, where it flourished but lost much of its earlier unorthodox character, and much also of its intimate connexion with Florence.

But the discussions at Lorenzo's palace and the lectures of the professors of Greek and Eloquence shaped the minds only for a minority. It was another form of education altogether that produced the men to whom Florence owed her wealth. Even a Humanist like Vergerio takes it for granted that a young man will enter his father's business. He recommends a general education, not as an alternative, but as a useful supplement to the training of the counting-house. The men who opposed the appointment of Humanist lecturers in 1458 had no doubt served their apprenticeship in business and were satisfied with the result. There must have been quite a few Florentines who, like Bartolomeo Masi, attended school for only two and a half years, just long enough to learn to read and write, before entering his father's shop.[11]

In general, six years was the most that a middle-class boy, who was not destined for a learned profession, counted to spend in the classroom. A substantial number appear to have learnt Latin, which had some value in commerce; but more went to arithmetical schools. In Florence in 1339 there were four large Latin schools, and no fewer than six where arithmetic and accounting were taught to some twelve hundred pupils in all.[12] These schools were privately run for fees,

---

[11] This was from 1488–90, between his eighth and his tenth year. *Ricordanze*, (ed. Corazzini Florence, 1906), p. 15.

[12] R. Davidsohn, *Geschichte von Florenz*, IV, iii, 114, commenting on the well-known chapter in Villani's Chronicle (xi, 94).

and to judge by their textbooks—the *Abaco* of Pietro Borgi or the *De Aritmetica* of Luca Pacioli—their curriculum was relatively advanced, covering matters like the rules for double entry. Later the curriculum increased in difficulty.[13] After this training, the youth entered a trade or spent some time apprenticed to a craftsman. Apprenticeship was, we must remember, another avenue to learning, and for some crafts—pottery and glaziery, for example—there exist technical manuals of some excellence dating from this period.[14] The men who received this education did not as yet clearly picture themselves as sharing a particular sort of culture that distinguished them from those with a more theoretical training. But the beginnings of a division were already there, and it is one which reflects clearly the specialization inherent in free, capitalist societies. Humanism in its broadest sense could not attract more than a minority, because once the standards of individualism were established, only a minority was needed to act as their guardians. In a literate world, no culture can exist without finding intellectual expression for its traditions, and no culture can afford to leave the formulating of that expression wholly unorganized. But the *élite* that is trained for the task need not be large. Admittedly, if it is too small, there is a danger that its preoccupations will appear a mystery to the community at large, and its consequent isolation will make it blind to those contemporary cultural developments which ought to be its especial concern. So all modern states have had to strike balance between the risks of promoting that isolation and the high costs of what one might call ' pure ' education on a large scale. The Florentines of the fifteenth century struck the balance with un-usual generosity in the favour of their Humanists. But even so, the latter remained a minority.

With the sixteenth century, the Italian cities lost their place in the vanguard of economic development as they had already lost their political freedom. Their education was circumscribed by the severities of the Inquisition, and their schools, which had once reflected the needs of a local culture, passed into the hands of the Society of Jesus. By 1550 the period which had begun so hopefully in the eleventh cen-tury was definitely over. A new order was established in Europe, but the city states which had been its first embodiment in Italy lay gripped in the shackles of an inglorious servitude. Venice alone retained her independence; and her collapse was soon to come.

R. R. BOLGAR.

---

[13] A. Fanfani, "La Préparation intellectuelle et professionnelle à l'activité économique, en Italie, du XIVe au XVIe siècle," *Le Moyen Age*, LVII (1951), pp. 327–46.

[14] *Ibid.*

CHAPTER TWO

The Founding of Christ's Hospital*

*A Royal, Municipal, and National Foundation of the Tudor Age
for the Education and Maintenance of Poor Children*

" AND euen foorthwith by the meanes of the sayd Cromwell all the orders of superstitious and begging Fryers, as White, Gray, Blacke, Augustine, Croched Friers, and likewise all the puling Nonnes, with their Cloysters and Houses were suppressed and put downe." So *Grafton's Chronicle* on the year 1537. Wriothesley, dealing more particularly with the Capital, records that on November 12th, 1538, " all the houses of fryers in London were suppressed and the fryers clene put out, and the goodes taken to the Kinges use."

Of those in authority few seem to have foreseen the consequences of the suppression of the monasteries except one section of the clergy. " Bishop Latimer moved strongly that two or three of these religious houses might be left in every county for pious uses. But Cromwell . . . invaded all." [1] For the religious houses, however just or unjust may have been the accusations levelled against them, had at least always dispensed a measure of charity and assisted the sick, the lunatic, the destitute, the children. " The abbeys were very serviceable places for the education of young people : every convent had one person or more assigned for this business. Thus the children of the neighbourhood were taught grammar and music without charge to their parents. And in the nunneries, those of the other sex learned to work, and read English with some advances into Latin." [2] In their attempt to preserve the charitable and educational work of the monasteries, Cranmer and the bishops of the ' New Learning ' went so far as to incur the displeasure of Henry VIII. " These prelates could not be brought to a thorough complaisance in parliament. They were willing the abbeys of royal foundations should return to the crown : but for the rest, they insisted upon their being turned into hospitals, schools, and such other establishments of public service. It was thought the king's resentment of

---

* [The author and publishers acknowledge the courtesy of Messrs. Hamish Hamilton, Ltd., London, for permission to reproduce extracts from *Christ's Hospital, Four Hundred Years Old* (1953).]
[1] This quotation and the two following are from Collier's *Ecclesiastical History*.
[2] *Ibid.*

this incompliance brought him to the thought of the Six Articles." [3] The neglect of the wise counsel given by the bishops of the ' New Learning' led to a social crisis, which naturally was first evident in the greatest city of the realm. In London the growing number of vagrants and unemployed presented a twofold threat to the well-being of the City. The able-bodied paupers, who had profited in former times from the indiscriminate distribution of alms by the monasteries, resorted increasingly to crime, and, in so doing, corrupted street-children deprived of monastic protection. Relief was not only a Christian duty; it was a political and social necessity. But the King's Council, having instructed local authorities to maintain the impotent poor and to appoint overseers to administer relief, dismissed the matter from its mind. Extravagance at Court, the costs and debts of war, and the debasement of the currency left the Treasury in no position to render financial aid, even had the King's Chancellors so wished.

Transfer of Social Services to Laity

The urge for the laity to take over from the Church the essential social services came from those whose eyes must daily convince them of the need for action. It was the deplorable condition of the London poor that induced the Council of Aldermen repeatedly to approach Henry VIII for assistance. In particular they petitioned for the transfer to the City of some of the monastic properties to become centres of social relief. Sir Richard Gresham's letter to the King, written in 1538, is extant. No immediate result was produced by it or by a series of further appeals from Gresham and his successors in the office of Lord Mayor. The Common Council even offered £700 as a maximum price for the four chief religious houses in London, proposing the levy of ' a fifteen ' on the citizens and inhabitants to provide the money. This offer Henry indignantly rejected as too small and stigmatized the citizens as ' pynche pence.'

There the matter might have rested, but for a circumstance which both increased the need for action and affected the crown more directly. The wounded from the war in France swelled the number of the London destitute and induced the King to reconstitute St. Bartholomew's as a hospital for them on June 23rd, 1544. The restored hospital was controlled by royal nominees. It was not until December 27th, 1546, that the indenture was signed which secured St. Bartholomew's, Bethlem, and Greyfriars to the City of London.

There may have been other reasons besides the emptiness of the Treasury which made Henry reluctant to transfer religious houses to the City. It was one thing for the supreme Head of the Church in

---

[3] *Ibid.*

England to seize such property: it was a different matter to hand over the great houses in the Capital to the laity. But it was presumably economy which provided St. Bartholomew's alone with a royal grant. As to Greyfriars, "the church was shut vp for a time and vsed as a Store house of Goods, taken prises from the French: but in the year 1546 on the third of Januarie, was againe set open. On the which day preached at Pauls crosse the Bishop of Rochester,[4] where he declared the king's gift thereof to the citie, for the releeing of the poore." [5] Yet it remained empty until 1552. The economic depression had hit the London merchants no less than the King, though Latimer's sermons suggest that their lack of generosity was as greatly responsible as their lack of means.

During the last years of the reign of Henry VIII and the first of his successor the condition of the London poor went from bad to worse. " At that tyme y[e] nomber of the poore did so encrease of all sorts that the churches, streates and lanes Were fylled daylye wth a number of Loathsome Lazars botches & sores so that St. Bartholomewes hospitall Was not able to receyve the tenthe parte of those that then were to be provided for." [6]   Other public-spirited men took up the cause championed by Sir Richard Gresham, and found a spokesman in Nicholas Ridley, Bishop of London. It was he who set matters in motion by a sermon preached before Edward VI in February 1552 on the theme of charity. The young king immediately responded to this exhortation. At the conclusion of the service he sent for Ridley and sought his advice.

The ' Mansion House Appeal '

Despite the indifference of the Council, which had failed to implement an Act of Parliament providing for the founding of free schools, Edward determined to send letters to the Lord Mayor of London, Sir Richard Dobbs, encouraging him and his citizens to raise funds to furnish hospitals, which the King would provide, for " every sort and category of the poor ", and especially for the young. The Lord Mayor needed only such a mandate. He and the leading citizens took prompt and vigorous action. They surveyed the field, drew up the necessary plans and appealed to the Londoners for support. The response to this, perhaps the first ' Mansion House Appeal ' in history, was genuine and whole-hearted. Its thoroughness will bear comparison with any modern campaign for charitable funds. The Committee started with a levy on themselves and afterwards solicited the help of their fellow

---

[4] Ridley.

[5] Stow, *Survey of London* (The Clarendon Press, 1908), Book I, Chap. XXVI.

[6] From John Howes' MS. account of the foundation of Christ's Hospital.

citizens. They got money from the Corporation; they canvassed the preachers to plead their cause: they provided the preachers with a sermon; they put collecting-boxes in the inns and in the halls of the great City Companies: they sent to every householder a " byll printed wherein there was a glasse wyndowe lefte open for his name and for his some of money".[7] Those funds were first needed for the repair of the buildings, which had long lain neglected. Wriothesley records: " The 20 of July the house of Grey Fryers beganne to be builded for the fatherless children. Allso the latter end of that moneth the church of St. Thomas hospitall in Southwarke was begunne to be builded for poore and impotent persons, lame and sicke." John Howes gives a more detailed account: " ffyrste they devysed to take oute of the streates all the fatherless children and other poore mens children that were not able to keep them & to bringe them to the late dissolved house of the Greie ffryers w[ch] they devysed to be an hospitall for them where they shoulde have meate drincke & cloths, lodging and learning and officers to attende vppon them." They renamed Greyfriars Christ's Hospital. It is important to note that from its very foundation Christ's Hospital was not exclusively an orphanage; and that it always combined education with maintenance. And so it came about that " The 23 of November the poor children of the City of London were taken into Christes Hospitall, late the house of the Grey Fryers in London."

The King had given the buildings which his father had seized and some financial privileges. The City of London gave the ideas that were to govern the Hospital and also the funds to set its work in operation. It was expected that the continuing expense of educating and maintaining the children would be met partly by the Wards of the City from which the children were introduced, partly by private benefactions. In the event it was the latter which produced most of the revenue.

The expenses must have been considerable and can be gauged from the list of the first officers of the House and the salaries paid them. They consisted of a Wardeine, a Clarke, a Stewarde, a Buttler, an Under-buttler, a Cooke, Porters, a Gramer Schoole Mayster, a Gramer Usher, a Teacher to write, two Schoole-Maisters for the Petties A.B.C., a Schoole-Maister for Musicke, two Chirurgiones, a Barbor, a Taylor, a Coale keeper, a Mazon scourer, a Matron, twenty-five Systers and a Bruer. Most of these officials exist to-day—many of them with title unchanged; but alas, the Bruer is no more!

No fewer than six of these men were teachers—a very handsome provision for those days. And their titles are evidence of a design to

---

[7] Howes, *op. cit.*

give these poor children a complete education up to college standard. The 'Teacher to write', the 'Two Schoole-Maisters for the Petties A.B.C.', and the 'Schoole-Maister for Musicke' were for the youngest children. Out of music or song schools had grown the English system of elementary education. For it was only the choirboys of the cathedrals and large churches who were taught the simple art of reading in the early Middle Ages.

The 'Gramer Schoole Mayster' and the 'Gramer Usher' are also an inheritance from the earliest days of the Church in England. Latin was not only the living language of European scholars; more importantly, it was the language of the church service: to worship intelligently, one must be able to speak Latin. The first Christian missionaries, therefore, who came from Rome to England in 597, brought the Bible in one hand, and, perforce, the Latin Grammar in the other. Grammar was the gateway to Latin: Latin was the gateway to knowledge. The Grammar School included in the foundation of Christ's Hospital gave, for the first time in history to such poor children, the same chances of learning and of advancement in life as William of Wykeham gave to the scholars of Winchester and Henry VI to those of Eton. The governors of the Hospital laid it down that the children committed to their charge should in due course be " put forth to service " with freemen of the City of London, but that such of the children " as be pregnant and very apt to learning be reserved and kept in the Grammar School in hope of preferment to the university ". In 1566 the Hospital sent its first son to Cambridge and, as a matter of course, paid his expenses there.

The need to find money was a constant preoccupation of the Governors. The annual Spital Sermon, for instance, was pressed into service, and it was not unknown for a deputation to wait upon the preacher beforehand and make his duty clear to him. In 1653, when there seems to have been a threat of economy, a preacher said to the City Fathers in his sermon : " The time may come when you will stand in need of scholars and would be glad to have them for your money, and, if ye be not careful to cherish them and maintain them, where will ye have them? If ye set not young plants, where will ye have grown trees? These are not like Jonah's gourd to come up in a night."

Private benefactions continued to be a main source of revenue and, as the reputation of Christ's Hospital grew, it made a national appeal and received the charity of others besides Londoners.

The Seventeenth Century—the Royal Mathematical School

In the seventeenth century a notable addition was made to the foundation. A Governor of Christ's Hospital, Richard Aldworth, left considerable property to the foundation by his will, which is dated December 21st, 1646. But his executors disputed the will, and it was not until 1660 that the courts awarded Christ's Hospital the sum of £7,667.[8] Of this all but £240 was secured upon the arrears of the excise revenue—a very doubtful security. Aldworth's bequest stipulated for the establishment of a distinct group of forty boys within the wider body of Christ's Hospital. It seems to have been Sir Robert Clayton, a great benefactor of the House, who conceived the idea of securing the money by proposing an additional object for its use of such a nature as to arouse the personal interest of Charles II. The Dutch wars revealed an alarming scarcity of competent naval officers and the proposal was that these forty boys should " bee bound out as Apprentices for seaven yeares to some Captaines or Comanders of Shipps ".[9] The idea reached the Secretary to the Admiralty, who recorded that, " a Warr wth Hollnd administering a naturall Argument " the scheme "was [upon a Foundation wholly new and specially calculated for ye Advancement of Navigation] happily consumated 1673 " but only " upon Mr. Pepys being call^d to ye Secretariship of ye Admiralty; and noe sooner." [10]

A vocational school for boys of this age was indeed something new. The Charter laid down that candidates for admission to the Royal Mathematical School must be such boys from the main body of Christ's Hospital as had " attained to a competent skill in the Grammar and Comon Arithmatique to the Rule of Three ". They were now to be " instructed in the Art of Navigacon and the whole Science of Arithmatique."

The first difficulty encountered by the new school concerned the apprenticing of the boys. By the time the first batch was ready, there was no war and consequently no demand for them in the Royal Navy. Merchant captains expected a fee for taking an apprentice, and the problem of finding this money was solved only when Pepys persuaded the King to give to the Royal Mathematical School " an establishment for ever of £370 10s. per annum for the binding forth of these children to merchant masters only ".[11] This is the only considerable benefaction Christ's Hospital has ever received from ' Government ' funds.

This independence has continued to the present day. A few local educational authorities send boys or girls (the two schools have been separated for nearly two hundred years) to Christ's Hospital and pay the cost. But its main financial support is the generosity of private

[8] To-day £1 = approximately $2.8.
[9] From the Charter of the Royal Mathematical School.
[10] Pepys MS. Collection of Matters relating to Christ's Hospital.
[11] Pepys, Letter to Governors of Christ's Hospital, April 2nd, 1694.

individuals through the ages, not least of those who have received their education there and prospered in later life. It is their gratitude to the school, together with the high estimation that it holds in the eyes of the public, that have enabled Christ's Hospital to survive even the inflationary periods which have followed the two great wars of our time. A contributing factor has been the personal interest taken in the Foundation by the Royal Family. Since the middle of the nineteenth century the Hospital that owed so much to the Boy King has been honoured by a Royal President.

H. L. O. FLECKER.

The Dissolution of the Society of Jesus in the Eighteenth Century and its Financial Consequences

THE present article is not concerned with the Jesuit educational system as such, their *Ratio Studiorum* or their role in the struggle between State and Church in the eighteenth century. Our subject is limited to the problems of finance and administration in the establishment of a state maintained and controlled national system of schools. In most countries of the world present legislation provides for universal free education, usually accompanied by compulsory attendance laws. Apart from rich industrialized nations in Europe, America or Japan, these provisions often remain a dead letter. Universal education even at the primary level is still an ideal hardly realizable in the near future in most under-developed countries. There is no doubt of the sincere intention of governments to establish a universal free school system, as there is no doubt of the widespread demand for it among the populations of these countries. However, there are too few buildings available, no adequate financial resources, and no adequate cadre of trained teachers to staff the required number of schools. In the eighteenth century this situation was common to all European countries. The physiocrats, the encyclopædists, and the *philosophes*, the enlightened autocrats and their ministers all agreed that a state maintained and controlled school system should replace the traditional Church system, which was neither universal nor modern enough to meet the economic and social needs of the century. But no state in Europe, not even the northern Protestant countries, was able to build up a national school system without the co-operation of the various Churches and their trained personnel. In the Catholic countries the position was more acute because education was legally a monopoly of the Roman Church and was actually in the hands of religious orders.

Among many orders which maintained their own schools none could rival the international Society of Jesus. In 1749 the Society had its last pre-dissolution census of its institutions. The statistics were collected for Jesuit provinces. These did not coincide with national frontiers or sovereign countries, and therefore the numbers here given are according to the Jesuit classification. In the year 1749 the Society possessed : in France 89 colleges and 32 clerical seminaries for the training of priests; in Italy 133 colleges and 22 seminaries; in Spain 105 colleges and 12 seminaries; in Portugal 20 colleges and 3 seminaries; in Germany and Austria 101 colleges and 41 seminaries; in Bohemia 26 colleges and 25 seminaries; in Belgium 36 colleges and 10 seminaries; in Poland 44 colleges and 32 seminaries. Hungary was not mentioned, but had about 15 colleges. Outside Europe, in Spanish colonies, the Society had 89 colleges and 32 seminaries. The totals as given by the Society (669 colleges and 176 seminaries) are not identical with the summing up by country, evidently through the incorrect classification of some colleges as seminaries. The main fact is that the Society maintained and controlled in Europe about 720 secondary schools for the training of an intellectual *élite*. The universities and other Catholic orders, especially the Piarists and Barnabites in many countries and the Oratorians in France, also possessed many schools, but their combined numbers were less than the schools of the Society of Jesus. The relative strength of the Jesuit schools varied from country to country, yet in some the Society enjoyed almost a monopoly.

As a rule in the Jesuit colleges no fees were charged. Local colleges received cash subsidies or buildings from municipal authorities, but seldom any grants from the central government. Their main source of income was the rent from estates bequeathed by pious landowners. They also possessed a central fund in their Rome headquarters, and local cash funds for separate provinces and individual colleges. In administration the Jesuit colleges were highly centralized under the General in Rome and Provincials in each Jesuit province. Thus the whole system was quite independent of national governments both in administration and in finance. Because of their international organization and considerable wealth the Society pursued a policy often opposed to that of the national government and to the particular interests of individual countries. The Piarists, the Barnabites, or the Oratorians in each country where they had schools worked in agreement with the government and identified themselves with the interests and traditions of each country. French Oratorians, for example, were French in organization and promoted French studies and traditions. In these circumstances, whenever there was a conflict between a king and his royal government and the Roman *Curia*, the Jesuits invariably sided with the Pope, whilst other orders backed the king. When the French encyclopædists and *philosophes* started their campaign to emancipate national education from the control of the Church, inevitably their attacks were concentrated on the Society of Jesus. The spread of English Masonry in all European countries, with their Protestant-deistic creed, further strengthened the anti-Jesuit campaign, and in the middle of the eighteenth century it was evident that the Society of Jesus was moving towards a major crisis. All the encyclopædists and Freemasons advocated the foundation of a secular state school system. The enlightened autocrats of Austria, Spain, Portugal, Naples, Sardinia, Parma, and Toscana, the Masonic king of Poland, and even Louis XV of France, backed their Masonic ministers and started founding secular, modern institutions maintained by their governments or secular foundations. But their resources were not sufficient to maintain a nation-wide state system which could replace the old-fashioned Church system. With envy they observed the magnificent institutions of the Jesuits, and it was natural that the idea occurred to them of confiscating Jesuit funds and buildings to start national school systems. Such a policy would have whole-hearted support not only of secularist *philosophes*, but among Catholic orders and liberal clergy, who hated the Jesuits as successful rivals with special privileges awarded to them by many Popes.

Portugal, Spain, and France

The first step was taken in 1759 by the prime minister of Portugal, Pombal. Initiated into English Masonry by Frederick, Prince of Wales, Pombal conceived the idea of a Church of Portugal, similar to the Church of England, independent of Rome, but established, maintained, and controlled by the secular government of the king of Portugal. Having, in the name of the king, autocratic powers, Pombal ruthlessly proceeded with his plan. He appointed his brother as Chief Inquisitor of Portugal and promptly accused the Society of heresy. The leading Jesuit theologian, Malagrida, was convicted and executed. An attempt on the king's life was ascribed to Jesuit propaganda and Pombal expelled the whole Society from Portugal with unnecessary cruelty and ruthlessness. It did not prevent him from appointing the Jesuit astronomer Da Rocha to a chair and vice-rectorship of the University of Coimbra when the latter agreed to follow his instructions. All the funds and buildings of the Society of Jesus were confiscated and Pombal was in a position to start the first state-maintained school system in Europe. His example was followed by Aranda in Spain and Choisel in France. But in these two countries the confiscated funds and buildings were only partially used for the establishment of secular state schools. In Spain three military colleges were founded and financed by Jesuit funds, the majority of the colleges were given to the secular clergy to secure their continuity, as the Spanish government had no secular teachers and training institutions. When Spanish physiocrats and Masons started their *Sociedades de los Amigos del Pais*, the government allocated subsidies to their modern schools from Jesuit sources. The opportune moment, however, was lost and a large proportion of Jesuit wealth found its way back to the Church.

The same story was repeated in France, where a few colleges were taken over for military schools (*La Fléche*, the college of Descartes, was one of them), but the rest of them were distributed among other Catholic congregations and municipal authorities. It must be remembered that the expulsion of the Jesuits from Portugal, Spain, and France happened before the dissolution of the order by the Pope in 1773, and the three governments were cautious not to alienate the secular clergy by general anti-clerical legislation. The expelled Jesuits left their native countries with no pensions, destitute, and full of hatred towards their national governments. Some of them found asylum in Italian principalities, in Habsburg lands, but many sought protection in Protestant Prussia and Orthodox Russia. They were allowed to teach, and in Russia, Catherine II allowed the Society to exist as an organized order in spite of the dissolution of 1773. D'Alembert wrote to Frederick the Great on June 16th, 1769 : " It would be madness for the Pope to destroy his body guard to please the Catholic princes. . . . It is strange that their most Catholic majesties want to annihilate these staunch defenders of the Holy See and that Your most Heretical Majesty is the only one to defend them." It is pertinent to ask whether Frederick II would have been so magnanimous if the Jesuits had possessed buildings and large funds in Prussia. Probably he would have confiscated their wealth as eagerly as the Catholic monarchs had done. In fact, the Jesuits presented no danger in Prussia and Russia, and they brought with them much needed skills and knowledge.

The Imperial Chancellor Kaunitz, who ruled the Habsburg lands in the name of Maria Theresa, was more prudent than his Masonic friends of the three Latin countries. So was King Stanislas Augustus of Poland. Although both were Masons and anti-clericals, they preferred to wait for the official dissolution of the order by the Pope before starting their policy of the secularization of education. The Pope tried to use this delay to maintain Church control of Jesuit property and to divert it to the Church. Maria Theresa categorically refused to accept this, as the Portuguese, Spanish, and French governments had already confiscated and used all Jesuit funds without the Pope's consent. The Pope was obliged to give in and the Imperial and Polish governments acquired Jesuit property to use as they wished. Being now in the possession of immense funds, the two governments could plan a national system from the centre without dissipating the Jesuit millions on separate measures or individual institutions.

Habsburg Lands

The dominions of Maria Theresa included the four kingdoms of Bohemia, Hungary, Northern Italy, Austrian Netherlands, and the Grand Duchy of Austria. In addition her husband Francis, and after his death her son Joseph II, were Holy Roman Emperors. Thus her prime minister Kaunitz was also the Imperial Chancellor and wielded almost autocratic power over half Western Europe. He and his assistants, Van Swieten, Von Pergen, and Von Sonnenfels, had for years wished to reform the educational system according to a central plan, but all their schemes broke down owing to the lack of economic resources. Nevertheless a blue-print was ready and the central training college (*Normalschule*) in Vienna was in working order. With the dissolution of the Society of Jesus and the confiscation of its property they were able at last to realize their dreams. The leading statesmen, including the Vice-Chancellor Kobenzl and all the governors of separate lands, were Freemasons and fully agreed on the structure and character of the new secular state system. Kaunitz and his friends did not commit the mistakes of their brother Masons in the three Latin countries. They did not expel the Jesuits; on the contrary, they invited ex-Jesuits to continue teaching in reformed state institutions under the supervision of state inspectors and as established civil servants. Dozens of ex-Jesuits joined the Masonic order and about four hundred agreed to become civil servants. Those who had religious objections were awarded state pensions from Jesuit funds. Thus the Austrian statesmen had trained personnel to start the reform immediately, and gradually filled the vacancies with a new cadre of secular teachers. The total number of Latin colleges, counting the non-Jesuit institutions as well, was more than Austria needed, and Kaunitz rightly decided to convert at least half the Jesuit colleges into German modern schools with a four-year course, instead of the six years of the Jesuits. Thus the government saved money, for primary education and a well-thought-out system of modern schools was created.

A central commission was appointed (all Masons) as a kind of ministry of education with its own inspectors and its own training colleges in all the lands of the Habsburg Empire. An Imperial graded scale of teachers' salaries was introduced, with a system of pensions and comparative security of tenure. As tolerance was now the guiding principle, it was possible to appoint non-Catholics to new chairs of science in the universities and to invite Protestant specialists from northern Germany. All these measures required considerable financial resources, but the Jesuit buildings, equipment, and funds covered the needs. I have the detailed accounts only for Bohemia and the Austrian Netherlands. Yet the other countries had similar amounts. Bohemia and Moravia had about fifty well-equipped buildings for secondary schools, and a total capital of 8,405,000 silver *zloty*.[1] It consisted largely of estates which brought in a revenue of about one million *zloty* per annum. This was a large sum in terms of the eighteenth century, and put the whole school system on a sound basis.

A very important feature of the state system was the substitution of the native languages of the pupils for Latin as the medium of instruction in the Jesuit colleges. Thus in Austria proper and in the German areas of Bohemia it was German, and Czech in Czech-speaking areas. In the Serb-speaking Orthodox provinces of the frontier it was Serbian (Illyrian, as it was then called), with an Orthodox catechism for religious instruction. This made the new schools popular despite the objections of the diehard clergy and the opposition of the Roman *Curia*.

The Austrian Netherlands

The position in the Austrian Netherlands was slightly different. Maria Theresa was represented by a viceroy, her brother-in-law, Charles of Lorraine, who had to take into account native traditions and the old system of self-government. Although Kaunitz was still, in fact, the overlord, he was a foreigner in the eyes of the Belgians and had to be cautious. But among the Belgian Masons he found a brilliant administrator of Irish origin De Neny (McNeny), who was appointed a royal treasurer and who, under the benevolent protection of the viceroy (Charles of Lorraine was also a Mason), enthusiastically initiated a policy of secularization. But the Belgian clergy, especially the Flemings, were much more stiff-necked than the easy-going Austrians or heterodox Czechs and Hungarians. In Austria two archbishops, eight bishops, and about two hundred canons and priests were members of Masonic lodges. In Belgium, only in Liège, which was an independent enclave, were the bishop and some clergymen Masons; in the Austrian Netherlands they were opposed to the new policy almost to a man. The Belgian Jesuits were reinforced by many exiled Jesuits from French Flanders, who were embittered and hostile to state intervention. When the colleges were confiscated and converted into Theresian secondary schools, not a single Belgian ex-Jesuit consented to serve as a civil servant. According to the proclaimed principle they were all to receive pensions. During the transition period the Belgian Jesuits employed all possible means to obstruct the transfer; they included perjury and concealment of funds. According to a report of Kaunitz to Maria Theresa, about 100,000 *florins*[2] were either divided among

---

[1] To-day 11·20 *zloty*=£1=$2.8.
[2] To-day 10·64 *florins*=£1=$2.8.

members of the dissolved order or concealed by forged receipts. Nevertheless, when the financial ' operation' was completed the government possessed 387,000 florins annual income from Jesuit estates. The budget of the Fond Jesuit in 1780 was as follows : Various expenses, including payments to churches, 64,000 florins; pensions to ex-Jesuits, 116,000 florins; public education, 78,000 florins; École Militaire at Anvers, 34,000 florins; Military Hostel at Malines, 3,000 florins. A total of 295,000 florins, which left a surplus of 92,000 florins for that year. With the increase of expenditure on new schools the surplus disappeared and in a few years there was a small deficit. From this budget it can be seen that about one-third of the income was spent unproductively on pensions for ex-Jesuits. Owing to the organized opposition of the Church, the Flemish Catholics did not send their sons to the new colleges in sufficient numbers and illegally employed some ex-Jesuits as private tutors. When Maria Theresa died, Joseph II tried to break the opposition of the clergy by confiscating all monastery funds and establishing state seminaries for the training of the clergy under the control and supervision of imported Masonic priests. As is well known it resulted in the Brabançonne revolution in 1789, which was organized and led by the Church.

Reform in Poland

What is usually called Poland in Western Europe was in fact a commonwealth (Rzeczpospolita) of three ' nations ': Poles, Lithuanians, and Russians (or the White Russians and Small Russians as distinguished from the Great Russians of Moscow). The two states which formed the confederation, the kingdom of Poland and the Grand Duchy of Lithuania-Russia, had definite political frontiers, separate legislation (in Russian in the Grand Duchy), and separate school systems. Poland proper was Catholic with a few Protestant communities, Lithuania was mixed—Catholic, Protestant, and Orthodox, whilst the Russian-speaking provinces were Orthodox with a Slavonic liturgy. When the Jesuits arrived in the Commonwealth they established the best secondary schools in the country and succeeded in converting the Lithuanian nobility, Protestant and Orthodox, and the Russian princely families to Catholicism and Polish nationality. The overwhelming majority of Lithuanians and Russians were not influenced by the Jesuits and remained true to their national and religious traditions. This resulted in continuous civil wars, in which the Protestants appealed to their Protestant neighbours (Sweden and Prussia) and the Russians to their co-nationalists under the Moscow Tsars, later Emperors. Thus the Jesuits were unable to consolidate the Commonwealth and their ultramontanism was one of the main causes of the partition of Poland. The Polish ruling families, educated abroad and members of English and French Freemasonry, clearly understood that the only salvation of the Commonwealth lay in the foundation of a state secular school system accompanied by a policy of tolerance and social reform. However, to follow the example of Pombal, by expelling the Jesuits and secularizing their schools against the open opposition of the Roman *Curia* under Polish conditions, meant starting a general civil war, with the inevitable destruction of the whole Commonwealth. King Stanislas Augustus and his Masonic advisers had to wait for the official dissolution of the Society of Jesus before taking possession of the Jesuit wealth and establishing a state system. As subsequent events proved, the reform came too late and only for a time revived the hopes of the patriots. The very success of the reform convinced the three neighbours, Russia, Prussia, and Austria, that they had to proceed immediately with their plans of partition whilst Poland was still in a state of transition and could not offer effective resistance.

This was the background to Polish reform and secularization. The Jesuits had a dominant position in the field of education. The University of Cracow was a church institution under the influence of the Society of Jesus. The University of Vilna was a Jesuit academy maintained and controlled by the Society. Out of some 140 secondary schools (University colleges, Catholic congregational, Piarist, Dominican, etc.; Basilian (Orthodox-Uniates) as well as Orthodox and Protestant), the Jesuits owned 65 colleges and seminaries, with better buildings and equipment than the rest. The Jesuits had from their estates an annual income of 386,000 *zloty* in the kingdom and 494,000 *zloty* in the Grand Duchy. If we divide the income in terms of linguistic areas we get the approximate figures: in Polish-speaking areas (Catholic), 215,000 *zloty*; in Lithuanian-speaking areas (Catholic and Protestant), 284,000 *zloty*; and in Russian-speaking areas (Orthodox and Uniate), 390,000 *zloty*. This distribution of income from estates shows quite clearly that Jesuits concentrated their efforts on the conversion of Protestant and Orthodox gentry and that the largest estates were in the Russian areas. In addition to the land, the Jesuit had cash funds which amounted to 5,300,000 *zloty* for the kingdom and 2,400,000 *zloty* for the Grand Duchy, which meant a 250,000 *zloty* income for the kingdom and 110,000 *zloty* for the Grand Duchy. In 1783, ten years after confiscation, the income of the Commission of Education from ex-Jesuit property was given as follows: from real estate, in the kingdom 383,820 *zloty*, in the Grand Duchy 522,848 *zloty*; from cash funds 362,154 *zloty*, and from various ex-Jesuit property 43,054 *zloty*. The total annual income from ex-Jesuit sources thus amounted to 1,311,876 *zloty*. The Commission's expenses for the same year (1783) were:

		zloty
University of Cracow	. . . .	150,000
University of Vilna	. . . .	150,000
Teachers' salaries (kingdom)	. . . . . .	180,000
Teachers' salaries (Grand Duchy)	. . . . .	185,000
Teachers of modern languages and drawing	. . . .	23,000
Grant to Piarists	. . . .	32,000
Grant to Basilians	. . . .	9,000
Teachers' seminaries and hostels for poor students	. . .	76,200
Two inspectors for the kingdom	. . . . .	8,000
Two inspectors for the Grand Duchy	. . . .	7,000
Extraordinary expenses	. . . .	60,000
Pensions for ex-Jesuits	. . . .	192,000
Officials of the Commission	. . . . . .	90,350
Concordats with the Church	. . . . . .	54,286
Publication of textbooks (for primary schools)	. . . .	10,837
Library	. . . .	8,957

Total Expenditure	. . . . . .	.1,236,630
Surplus	. . . .	75,246
(It should be)	. . . .	73,856

One striking difference compared with the Austrian Netherlands is the proportion of income spent on ex-Jesuit pensions. Whereas in the Netherlands the ex-Jesuit pensions consumed 30 per cent of the income, in the Polish Commonwealth it amounted to only 15 per cent. This was the result of many ex-Jesuits continuing to work under state supervision in the reformed schools. The salaries of teachers were paid according to a state scale, which was uniform for the whole country. As a rule the university professors received 6,000 *zloty* per annum, and as many foreign professors of first rank agreed to accept positions at this salary, one may presume it was tempting enough to attract them. The rectors of colleges (head masters of secondary schools) received 2,180 *zloty*; the prefects and six masters of each college, 1,200 *zloty*; the masters of modern languages and of drawing, 800 *zloty*. In addition, most teachers gave private lessons to wealthy pupils, sometimes getting four times as much as their state salaries. The new state school system was similar to the Theresian system in the Habsburg lands. Each province had a college (a full seven-year secondary school), each district an intermediate four-year secondary school, and many parishes had primary schools, which formed a ladder crowned by two universities: Cracow for the kingdom and Vilna for the Grand Duchy. The curriculum was modernized and new scientific subjects were added. In the universities new chairs were created and well-known professors from abroad (French, German, and Italian) were appointed. The colleges of the Piarists and the Basilians were subordinated to state supervision and received grants. This Polish system survived the partition and continued to exist almost unchanged under the Russian Emperors till 1830, when it was Russified after the Russo-Polish war. It also served as a model, side by side with the French state system of the Convention, for the school reform of Alexander I of Russia.

Conclusion

The school system of the Society of Jesus provides an excellent example of an international organization of education maintained by bequests of lands and cash. It had, however, a fundamental defect: it was devised for the intellectual *élite* only and had no primary schools as regular feeders of Latin colleges. When the national governments decided to build universal state systems they had to consider the elementary education of the masses as well and to create a national ladder of schools from primary to university level. Such an enormous task was beyond the means of any European country and has been realized only in our time after two centuries of gradual reform. The confiscation of the property of the Society of Jesus provided a sufficient economic basis for the first step only. But it gave the governments the opportunity of planning national education; of establishing a trained teaching profession as a part of the civil service, and of modernizing the curriculum. Most important was the principle of secular control and religious tolerance, which was incompatible with the Jesuit system. It was evident in the eighteenth century that whilst the Jesuits dominated and controlled seven hundred and twenty secondary schools in Europe no effective change in education, more adapted to the new economic and social conditions, was possible. The confiscation of their wealth by the state was the *conditio sine qua non* of the reform. There is another conclusion which can be drawn from the story of the dissolution. In those countries where secularization took place under conditions of persecution and even cruelty, the success of the reform was only partial and temporary. It split the nations into two hostile factions, which continue their cold civil war even to-day. In the Austrian lands and Poland the policy of tolerance and even collaboration with the ex-Jesuits resulted in a more permanent reform, which served as a basis for subsequent educational systems.

N. HANS.

BIBLIOGRAPHY

Josef Lukaszewiz, *History a Szkol w Koronie i w Weilkem Ksiçstwe Litewskem* (2 vols., Poznan, 1849); Paul Bonenfant, *La suppression de la Companie de Jesus dans le Pays Bas Autrichiens*, 1924; Baron A. v. Helfert, *Geschichte der Oesterreischen Volksschulen*, 1866; Thomas Bilek, *Statku a jmêni kolleji jesuitskych . . . v. kralovstri Českim ad cisare Josefa II Zrušenych* (Prague, 1893).

CHAPTER FOUR

Church and State in the United Kingdom

THE Church has from the beginning considered education as an essential part of her mission. In the New Testament itself we find both the dominical commission in the first Gospel and the parallel strands of preaching and teaching in the apostolic tradition. In England, schools were set up almost at the same time as the coming of Christianity, and it was the Church who founded English education. Throughout most of our history, men not only regarded the Church as the institution responsible for education, but looked to the Church for its provision.

For the purposes of this article the Church will be normally understood to be the Church of England, but the story of education may be interpreted on a broad basis as that of the relationship between religious and secular life. As long as these were united in an integrated and single outlook, there could hardly be any distinction between Church and state in education. Until long after the Reformation, education was essentially religious because life was religious. Thus in the ancient and religious foundations of colleges and schools, and in the varied provision of Grammar school, Song school, and Charity school of the Middle Ages, the Church and education were at one, while in unsettled times the monastery was the guardian of culture and learning. It is probable that before the Reformation considerable elementary education was provided by the clergy, not only for boys but also for girls, and that some at least of the Grammar schools provided teaching free. At the Reformation, it was the closure of the Chantries which really struck the hardest blow at the existing system.

In spite of the destruction of the means of education caused by the Reformation, the Church continued its close relationship with teaching. Both Edward VI and Elizabeth I ordered the clergy to teach reading and writing to their parishioners. Church of England canon law in 1605 required all teachers in school or private house to be licensed by the bishop, which secured Church control. The growth of the provision of education for the poor sprang from a religious sentiment, and there is no doubt that both bishops and other clergy took a leading part in promoting this development. Bishop Ken is said to have established a school in every parish in his diocese.

The Charity School Movement

The movement to provide Charity schools and, after 1811, National schools by the Church had the clear intention of provision for the poor. What motives prompted this work and how were resources provided? "The able men at the head of the Charity school movement", writes Professor Trevelyan,[1] "introduced the principle of democratic co-operation into the field of educational endowment. They did not depend merely on the support of a few wealthy founders. The policy at headquarters was to excite the local interest in a parish in setting up a school. Small shopkeepers and artisans were induced to subscribe and to collect subscriptions, and were taught to take a personal interest in the success, and a personal part in the control of the school for which they helped yearly to pay." No doubt fear of political and social unrest was one motive. Another was the belief in the connexion between morals and religious belief. Parents could find in schools protection for their children from the real moral dangers of the times, and the strongest remedy was religious faith and duty. There was, nevertheless, a genuine desire to provide education. That great supporter of the Charity school movement, Bishop Butler, preaching on the subject in 1745, declared that "though education were nothing more than informing children of some truths of importance to them, relating to religion and common life, yet there would be great reason for it, notwithstanding the frivolous objections concerning the danger of giving them prejudices. But when we consider that such information itself is really the least part of it; and that it consists in endeavouring to put them into right dispositions of mind, and right habits of living in every relation and in every capacity; this consideration shows such objections to be quite absurd." [2]

Before the nineteenth century, the French and Industrial Revolutions were exercising their influences. One bishop, speaking to the House of Lords, condemned Sunday Schools on the grounds that they encouraged the views of the French Revolution. Moreover, radicalism was spreading under the leadership of Bentham. At times of war and unrest, when the sense of social and economic security is threatened, men turn their attention to education. The monitorial system of Lancaster and Bell provided the means for a new advance. This soon issued in the division between Church and Nonconformist schools, although a not insignificant contribution had already been made by both bodies in the Sunday School movement. But the Industrial Revolution had brought large numbers of children to the towns, and even infants might find employment in a pit or mill.

---

[1] *English Social History* (Longmans Green & Co., 1944), p. 327.
[2] *Sermons by Joseph Butler* (The Clarendon Press, 1826), p. 358.

The method of providing resources for education by the Church remained the same. The local community was encouraged to help itself, assisted by grants from central sources. Often the squire would contribute the site and a donation, and sometimes he would erect the school, but it was the many rather than the few who provided the means, though much was done by the clergy, both by their own contributions, in the raising of funds, and in organization and teaching. Reasons given for the rejection of proposals for universal education do not always take sufficient account of either the facts or the circumstances. There is certainly evidence of fear—fear of education above status; fear of loss of child labour; fear that children might be educated outside Church control—but the practical difficulties were enormous. Nor were social conditions promising. Bishop Henson asserts that " the mass of the population has not emerged from medieval superstition. At the beginning of the nineteenth century the English people generally was illiterate, lawless, and depraved." [3] The condition of the children was, in fact, appalling.

State Support

From 1833 onwards the first parliamentary grants began to appear, and the Church continued to provide schools with growing assistance from the state. The denominational conflict continued to exert its dominating influence. The Bill for factory schools was rejected on this issue. Few were more devoted to the cause of education than Lord Shaftesbury, who supported the Ragged Schools with all his energy. Yet he regarded as disastrous any provision for education which was not made by a voluntary agency.

The Board schools appear to have stimulated the Church to new efforts, for many more school places were provided. But towards the end of the century the renewed enthusiasm waned. After the 1902 Education Act, in spite of a fresh indication of denominational conflict, the contribution of the Church began to decrease, so that by 1921, when the next act appeared, the number of Church schools was significantly less, and this decline continued, although at a slow rate. By then the local authorities were responsible for the salaries of the teachers. The Education Act of 1944 gave increased financial assistance to voluntary schools.

Abroad, principally in India, China, and Africa, the Church has founded or promoted colleges and schools. The close relation which has existed with the state is still evident in Africa and elsewhere. In

---

[3] *The Church of England* (Cambridge University Press, 1939), p. 189.

this sphere, as in others, the Church is faced with the urgent problem of providing teachers with a full sense of vocation, able to work as partners with local teachers, and of providing the necessary funds.

The Resources at Her Disposal

The resources at the disposal of the Church are threefold—traditional learning, faith, and finance. For centuries the Church was regarded as the sole institution for the provision of education. Until recent times classics was the hall-mark if not the foundation of any education, while Latin was the language of the Church. The scholarship of the parsonage is still to be found, and not solely in the arts, although the science master whose clerical collar surmounts his dissecting coat may not be a common sight.

Faith indicates the authority of the Transcendent. The Church could exhibit the sense of vocation, speak in the name of Him who was the Friend of children, and point to the teaching office as a response to dominical command. Thus the financial support of education was in obedience to the divine will. Endowments for education were built up and, partly by bequests, educational trusts were established which at present form a considerable part of the Church's material resources, some of which are in the form of buildings.

Fees were always paid for education, and the penny of the village school is still recalled by old people. Reference has already been made to the principle of self-help and co-operation. The Church has always encouraged local support. Appeals have been another form of provision. In 1955, a new Church secondary school was erected for which the Church's share of the cost was provided by the laymen of the Diocese.

The basis of the Church's wealth and power is thus derived from her supernatural foundation and claims, and from the essential link between the Church and education.

Financing Denominational Schools

From the beginning of the last century various proposals were urged for some form of universal education. Increasing financial assistance was given to voluntary organizations, until the stage was reached when grants were made for the salaries of the teachers, for equipment, and for other subsidiary expenses. This continued until 1944, but inevitably, as the local authorities took an increasing part, their organization and power grew. The numbers of children in Council schools became greater than those in Church schools, although in some areas, particularly in rural counties, the majority of schools remained Church schools. The Education Act of 1944 required the L.E.A.s to provide a complete development plan for future school provision. It also made the local authorities generally responsible for all ' secular ' education. This recognized that the state had in fact become the authority for the provision of statutory education.

The task of maintaining voluntary schools in such circumstances can be seen by recognizing the bases of their support. Funds for the provision of voluntary schools have been obtained from the contributions of Church members, of others interested in schools, legacies, endowments, and grants from charities.

The contributions from Church members and others have been obtained in a variety of ways. In rural areas, the site was often given or rented at a nominal cost, and sometimes the squire would build the school at his own expense. But in the majority of cases, funds were raised by local effort under the leadership of the local clergy. Even when grants were available, they were given only on condition that some part of the cost was raised locally, and in some schools a plaque can still be seen inscribed with the sources which provided the cost of its erection. Two societies took a leading part in the provision of Church of England schools. The Society for Promoting Christian Knowledge was founded in 1698, and had as its first object the creation and support of schools, which were known as Charity schools. In London in 1708 there were sixty Charity schools with 2,248 children: 1,874 of these were also clothed, and 862 were apprenticed. For this purpose annual subscriptions provided £536, collections after sermons £1,434, and gifts £5,861. The National Society was founded in 1811, and in the first seven years of its existence made grants of £37,568 for Church of England schools. The Society's income rose from £2,842 in 1838–9 to £17,339 in 1839. In 1843 a special fund was started, to which £151,985 was contributed. Between 1811 and 1870, £6,270,577 was expended in erecting Church of England schools and £8,500,000 on their maintenance, from voluntary contributions. Between 1870 and 1893 an additional £7,125,402 was contributed. Legacies and endowments date back to at least the Middle Ages, and in course of time many schools possessed some endowment even though it was often small. The most notable charity is Betton's, which has an interesting story. Mr. Betton left half his money to the London Church Schools and half to redeem slaves captured on the Barbary Coast. In due course there were no more slaves to be redeemed and the funds accumulated, until by an action in Chancery it was decided that the money should provide assistance for Church schools in England.

The modern trend has been to centralize the financial organization of Church schools. It has always been the case that the local Church and parish—represented in the case of an existing Church school by

the managers—are ultimately responsible for the provision and maintenance of the school.   There were, however, associations of managers,
and in some cases they provided some scheme of mutual assistance.
Since the last Education Act administration has grown considerably.
This was recognized by the Diocesan Education Committees Measure;
formulated by the Church Assembly and passed into law.   The changes
which have taken place may be illustrated from the case of one diocese
where the managers and parish make annual fixed contributions for
both maintenance and improvement, in return for which the managers'
share of these costs is met by the diocese, who organize a regular
inspection of buildings.   Some organization of this kind is now the
practice in most dioceses.

Additional funds have recently been derived from the mobilization
of disused endowments where the trust has failed.   In this way funds
which can no longer fulfil their original purpose have been made
available for present needs.

Colleges, Public Schools, and Sunday Schools

The ancient universities are Church foundations, symbolized by the
college chapels with their deans and chaplains.   Most of the ' Public '
schools also have a Church foundation, and some of them are controlled by Church educational trusts.   Some Church Grammar schools
are now ' direct grant ' schools, which means that they are now
assisted by grants made directly by the Minister of Education and thus
retain relative independence.   Next in historical order are the Sunday
Schools.   This remarkable movement developed towards the end of the
eighteenth century and provided at least a modicum of education for
children who had no other chance.   It was based on a religious impulse
and had as its ideal the provision of universal popular education.   By
1803, there were 7,125 Sunday Schools reported to be in Great Britain
with 8,860 teachers and 844,728 scholars, yet even in 1839 the day
schools under inspection contained only 700,000 pupils.   The Church
training colleges have made a notable contribution to education, and
since 1944 the Church has made determined and successful efforts to
bring her twenty-five existing colleges up to date.

The Financial Task

In the circumstances of the two previous centuries, the Church took
a leading part in the provision of education.   This was due to the
traditional relation of the Church with education, and to the religious
convictions of her leaders in this field.   How far those convictions
did in the last century hold up the growth and development of education is not easy to determine.   There was certainly denominational

antagonism, and feelings ran high. On the other hand, men had deep convictions about education, which they were willing to support by action, voluntary service, and even sacrifice. It is also possible to ignore the economic circumstances of the times, and the limits of what was possible. Even denominational differences acted as a stimulus.

With the development of state participation in the earlier part of this century, the position was changed. Church schools have grown old, while state schools were new. But at no time has there appeared a conflict between Church and state. This has been at least in part due to the wide interest of the Church in education generally, and to the denominational conflicts. The increasing need to provide universal secondary education, which appeared at the beginning of the century, called for the state to take an increasing part. Church resources were insufficient to meet the need.

There were significant reasons why the Church of England has found the task increasingly difficult. The Free Churches confined their efforts to a limited number of schools. The Roman Catholic Church has continued her determined efforts to retain and provide schools. The Church of England has been first affected by the decline in religious conviction. The philosophical and religious atmosphere has changed. The immense progress of science, the belief in material progress, the disintegrating effects of modern warfare, and the growth of materialism, have produced a different outlook.

Moreover, those concerned for Christian education have been concerned for all children. Church teachers taught in Church and state school alike. The recognition by the Church of her responsibility for Christian education in all schools has imposed a double loyalty, and as the number of children in state schools have grown, some question the value of Church schools. But the practical reason has been the financial demands. " Why ", it was asked, " should those who already pay rates and taxes for education need to pay a second time? Could not some such system as the Scottish solution be adopted, which allowed Church parents such religious facilities as they wished for their children?"

Hope was raised by the offer, in the Education Act of 1944, of grants of half the cost of maintenance and improvement, but this was offset by constantly rising costs which more than doubled, and by the very high standards laid down by the Minister of Education for school buildings. A school which in 1938 cost £20,000 may now cost £100,000. Even the improvement of the sanitation for fifty children can cost over £2,000, while a new building for a hundred and twenty children may well be £20,000. When, at the end of 1954, the Minister of Education issued a circular proposing that the reorganization of rural secondary and primary schools should be speeded up, he challenged the Church to improve its rural ' Aided ' schools within seven years, and agreed that this would impose a financial strain on the Church, which had made financial plans to extend the work over a long period. The Church authorities are now considering what steps they should take in view of the financial problem which faces dioceses and managers of their schools. Meanwhile, there is a steady expenditure of funds on improvements, and in the erection of new buildings, including Special Agreement Church Secondary schools which attract a 75 per cent grant from the state.

Another factor was the invention of Church ' Controlled ' schools, which relieved the Church of all costs and at the same time provided opportunities for Church teaching. A few have regarded this as the only solution, but it is widely thought that unless the contribution of the Church is maintained by an adequate number of ' Aided ' schools— that is, Church schools in the historic sense—the Church will lose her influence in statutory education, and secularism may increase.

One aspect to which some reference should be made is organization. In modern circumstances, some think that greater central administration, perhaps especially on the financial side, would have been of great assistance. Under such an arrangement, parishes would then contribute fixed annual amounts. However, the Church has always attached importance to local control and responsibility, and to the personal factor.

Increasing costs (including salaries) may also affect the position of Church and other independent schools. Archbishop Temple attached social importance to a variety of types of school in education, and to the value of the preservation of a degree of independence. To-day the trend is to throw all the responsibility on the Welfare State, which is expected to have an almost bottomless purse.

It remains to be seen how far there is a real conviction about the value of schools which are directly founded on an historic worshipping community, and whether this is sufficient to enable the Church to maintain her valued partnership with the state in education. There are at present signs that this conviction is growing.

ROLAND BAILEY.

CHAPTER FIVE

The Land-Grant Colleges and Universities of the United States

THE Land-Grant Colleges and Universities of the United States were founded as a national system as a result of congressional action offering to each state grants of federally-owned land. This land was to be sold and the proceeds used as a permanent fund for the " endowment, support, and maintenance " of " at least one college "—with a new educational emphasis—in each state.

The Morrill Act

The Act, sponsored by Senator Justin Morrill of Vermont, was signed by President Abraham Lincoln on July 2nd, 1862. The nation was in the midst of a bitter war which threatened its continued existence; the federal government was heavily in debt; ' printing press ' money (unsecured by bullion deposits) was a fact; inflation was rampant; and the tide of war was against the federal government. It was in these circumstances that a substantial portion of the nation's resources—about 10 million acres of land were eventually involved—was given as an act of faith in what higher education might contribute to the nation.

Conditions of the Act were few and in broad terms: The new colleges were to emphasize " agriculture and the mechanic arts " (the latter now interpreted as engineering), but were not to exclude (and therefore were to include) " other scientific and classical studies ". The grand object was " to promote the liberal and practical education of the industrial classes in the several pursuits and professions of life ". All proceeds from the endowment were to be used for instructional purposes—the states must provide the buildings and equipment—but instruction was to be given " in such manner as the legislatures of the states may respectively prescribe ", thus clearly prohibiting federal control. Later amendments provided for additional funds in the form of annual appropriations, and required equitable provision for the higher education of Negroes in all the states.

In 1887 the Congress passed the first of a series of acts authorizing annual federal grants-in-aid for agricultural research in the Land-Grant institutions. The term is broadly defined in practice, and includes support of basic research in the natural sciences as well as a wide variety of applied research. This early and continuing support of scientific research in each state and territory has been a major factor in the development of the universities as research centres in the United States. The Land-Grant institutions early furnished " a sympathetic nursery for the scientific spirit and method ".

In 1914, extension work of the Land-Grant institutions and the federal Department of Agriculture were combined in one co-operative system, operated by the Land-Grant institutions of each state and financed by federal, state, and local (chiefly county) funds.

Influence of the Act

The " revolution in American higher education " represented by the Morrill Act has profoundly affected all American higher education, and all American life, both economically and culturally. It was fostered by men and women who believed profoundly that higher education should do more than offer preparation for the law, the ministry, medicine, and for a leisured and governing class. There were many in existing colleges who believed this, also, and were among the leaders in the new movement, but they possessed neither the influence nor the financial support to effect the needed changes rapidly enough. Farm leaders, educators, and some spokesmen for a growing industry were leaders in the agitation over a period of many years prior to passage of the Morrill Act, a period which saw many unsuccessful (and a few successful) attempts to establish new " people's colleges " under state and private auspices.

The influence of the Land-Grant movement is sometimes spoken of as having been primarily to make higher education " more practical ". This was not the case. Existing colleges were highly practical in terms of the few fields they recognized. The Land-Grant movement made higher education more inclusive, more democratic in scope and in availability.

The significance of the federal contribution to the Land-Grant institutions, aside from the fields of agricultural research and extension, lies not in its amount (which in 1952–3 constituted only 3·3 per cent of a combined instructional budget of more than $850 million), but in the stimulus it gave to the establishment of colleges with a new outlook and emphasis, and, particularly, to state support of higher education. Instructional programmes of the Land-Grant institutions to-day are in general primarily supported by state appropriations, student fees, and some private gifts and endowments.

They vary widely in character and support, including on the one hand Massachusetts Institute of Technology (almost wholly privately supported aside from research funds) and Cornell University (which has both private and state colleges), and on the other the typical state university dependent primarily on public funds and student fees, but with some other sources of income. In all, there are sixty-nine Land-Grant colleges and universities, located in each state, Alaska, Hawaii, and the Commonwealth of Puerto Rico, eighteen states having designated two Land-Grant institutions for instructional purposes. They vary in size from the University of Alaska, with some three hundred students in 1953-4, to the University of California, with nearly thirty-four thousand full-time students on its several campuses. The majority are designated as State Universities; many of the rest are complex institutions offering professional work in a wide variety of fields, and graduate work through the doctorate. All but one are co-educational. In a complex and rapidly changing South, Negro students are now attending (particularly for graduate and professional work) many institutions which formerly excluded them, and white students are beginning to enrol at some former " Negro " institutions. In other areas no such distinctions have ever been made.

In the fall of 1954 the Land-Grant colleges and universities collectively enrolled 456,000 students on an annual basis, or more than 18 per cent of those in American higher education. Their significance in advanced training is shown by the fact that they confer 38 per cent of all doctoral degrees. In professional fields, they graduate 40 per cent of all U.S. engineers, award about 90 per cent of all degrees in agriculture and veterinary medicine, 40 per cent in home economics, 20 per cent of all medical doctors. With all this professional emphasis, 37 per cent of all students in Land-Grant institutions are in the arts and sciences.

Contributions of the Land-Grant Institutions

American colleges and universities are playing a major role in the U.S. technical co-operation programme for less economically developed areas of the free world, through contracts involving U.S. and host country funds under which the U.S. institution works directly with a counterpart abroad in improving teaching, research, and extension programmes. About two-thirds of all such contracts are with Land-Grant colleges and universities, whose staff members are working in many areas of the Far East, Near East, Africa, and Latin America. Oklahoma Agricultural and Mechanical College (whose late president was first U.S. director of technical co-operation) found it necessary to develop secondary schools in Ethiopia as a basis for the establishment of an imperial university, a development following the early pattern of many U.S. Land-Grant universities. The University of Nebraska is working both with an established university in Turkey and in the development of the completely new Ataturk University along " Land-Grant " lines. Land-Grant institutions working in India and Pakistan are finding that the well-established colleges and universities there have much to contribute to, as well as to benefit from, mutual co-operation, which is true in many other areas. The non-political character of the Land-Grant institutions, and their experience in working with people to improve their living standards and productivity, has fitted their staffs particularly for this type of international co-operation.

In agricultural research and extension work, as well as in college instruction, the stimulus of federal aid combined with state and institutional responsibility for programme, is evident. In a recent year, federal support of $19 million for agricultural research was only one-fifth of expenditures of the Land-Grant institutions for that purpose. Federal grants of $39 million for co-operative agricultural and home economics extension work were less than half total expenditures.

The economic value of the contributions of the Land-Grant institutions may be illustrated by the development of hybrid corn, brought to economic practicability in food production largely, though not exclusively, by research workers in their agricultural experiment stations. In one year (1947), increased production through use of hybrid seed is estimated to have increased the value of the U.S. corn crop by $1 billion, more than thirty times the expenditures of all Land-Grant institutions for agricultural research in that year. Within three years after the discovery of streptomycin by a research worker in the New Jersey Agricultural Experimental Station of Rutgers University, the investment by industry in buildings and equipment alone for its production was nearly twice the entire expenditure on agricultural research at Rutgers in the sixty-five years of the history of its experimental station to that point. The discovery was the result of continuing fundamental investigations started half a century previously and carried on by Dr. Selman A. Waksman, who subsequently received a Nobel Prize for his work. In another area, atomic energy, the University of California, a Land-Grant institution, has been the chief centre for U.S. research, and the Land-Grant institution of North Carolina established in 1953 the first university-owned nuclear reactor, for research and teaching purposes. The second such reactor was at Pennsylvania State University, also a Land-Grant institution.

In 1890 Sir William Crookes, President of the British Association for the Advancement of Science, predicted that " almost certainly the United States within a generation will be driven to import and will scramble for a lion's share of the wheat crop ". This was a sound prediction on the basis of evidence at the time. Between 1910 and 1950, however, the United States achieved a 75 per cent increase in agricultural production, with only a 14 per cent increase in factors going into production (labour, capital, arable land). In the same period, costs of food products to the consumer, in relative terms, were reduced 10 per cent. The Land-Grant institutions have been a major factor in this achievement, fundamental to the maintenance of a rising standard of living with a rapidly increasing population and a relatively fixed amount of arable land.

Reliance for increased food production no longer is on the pioneer and his family opening up new lands, but upon the pioneers of research and education, pushing back the frontiers of the possibilities of agricultural production. The Land-Grant institutions, their staffs and graduates have made great contributions in other areas as well: in science and industry, in atomic energy, in business, in the improvement of family living, in art, literature, and music, and in public life. They owe much to the British and European universities: a debt they gratefully acknowledge. At the same time, they have made their own unique contribution to the long history of higher education in the Western world by broadening the scope of higher education, making it more accessible to the talented from whatever walk of life or field of interest, and by emphasis on service activities which bring the benefits of research into application in meeting the needs and problems of the people. This emphasis has won for them support in their own states and communities far exceeding the dreams of their founders, and has justified the magnificent act of faith in the future enacted in the Nation's darkest hours nearly a century ago.

RUSSELL I. THACKREY.

CHAPTER SIX

Educational Provision through Philanthropy and Foundations

THE first Pharaoh who endowed a college of priests to honour his name by religious observance would hardly recognize the modern, giant foundation as an outgrowth of his whim. But like other enduring cultural ideas, philanthropy has grown and adapted to an increasingly complex civilization which, in turn, reflects its values and progress through its institutions. The Pharaoh had one mind with but a single thought, to perpetuate his name, but the idea of endowment itself stood on its own strength and gathered cultural force with more dedicated purposes.

Ptolemy's endowment of the library at Alexandria, Plato's establishment of the Academy, and the younger Pliny's gift of a school, a library, and public baths to his native town of Como are all early indications of the more serious purposes for which private funds are given to-day. During the Roman period, not only did emphasis shift from honouring gods, family, and cultural rites to promoting education and welfare, but some of the finer legal aspects emerged. The concept of a legal heir as opposed to a natural heir and the idea of a corporate personality allowed private gifts a freedom from family which could point only to a concern for public welfare. Municipal foundations were established throughout the Empire " to aid in the feeding, clothing, and educating needy legitimate children ".[1] Such palliative ministrations were assumed later by the Church under Constantine and led to the ecclesiastical foundations, which continued through the Middle Ages as the dominant agency of philanthropy.

Under Henry VIII, monasteries were dissolved and their vast fortunes, estimated to be one-third to one-half of the total wealth of the kingdom, were transferred to the state. Foundations were now state licensed, and could receive bequests of land for the public good. Philanthropy, however, was promoted not by the new, landed aristocracy but by the emerging middle class, whose pooled contributions became substantial enough to necessitate state protection and allocation. The Statute of Charitable Uses (43), passed in the reign of

---

[1] Quoted in *American Foundations for Social Welfare* (Russell Sage Foundation, New York, 1946), p. 14.

Elizabeth I, comprehended in smaller scope the major areas of health, education, and welfare in which philanthropy and foundations are active to-day.

The Industrial Revolution and the Age of Reason, with its faith in man and his possibility for progress, added new dimensions to philanthropic giving, for the one provided the opportunity to accumulate vast fortunes and the other provided the objectives to which these fortunes could be dedicated. Philanthropic relief societies soon became merely token gestures to handle the mounting ills of a runaway industrialization. Too frequently, moreover, relief nourished the very conditions it tried to eradicate. As early as 1834, a commission set up to investigate the Poor Laws in England had this to report : " The places intended to be favoured by large charities attract an undue proportion of the poorer classes, who, in the hope of trifling benefits to be obtained without labour, often linger on in spots most unfavourable to the exercise of their industry. Poverty is thus not only collected, but created, in the very neighbourhood whence the benevolent founders have manifestly expected to make it disappear." [2]

To achieve any measure of social progress, philanthropic foundations borrowed methods from industry and science. The idea of the modern foundation, then, emerged from a faith in social progress applied to the fortunes of industrial progress.

The Modern Foundation in America

Only a handful of foundations were established in America before the turn of the twentieth century. Benjamin Franklin's fund for " young married artificers of good character ", or the Philadelphia Magdalen Society's perpetual trust set up in 1800 " to ameliorate the distressed condition of those unhappy females who have been seduced from the paths of virtue, and are desirous of returning to a life of rectitude ",[3] cannot be considered foundations in the modern sense. Even the Smithsonian Institution, established in 1846 " for the increase and diffusion of knowledge among men ", cannot be included since it was a direct ward of the government at the bequest of the English scientist, James Smithson. But when George Peabody set up the Peabody Education Fund in 1867 with a sum of $2 million for the advancement of education in the South, he defined the foundation as it is known to-day—a non-governmental, non-profit organization with a principal fund of its own, established to conduct or aid activities which serve the welfare of mankind. " Up to this time philanthropy was palliative; now it seeks to lay hold on the age to come," [4] wrote Elbert Hubbard of the new fund.

---

[2] *Ibid.*, p. 19.　　　[3] *Ibid.*, p. 17.　　　[4] *Ibid.*, p. 21.

Approximately six more foundations followed this new trend until Andrew Carnegie virtually turned trend into tradition with his definitive 'gospel of wealth'. "The millionaire," he said, "will be but a trustee of the poor, entrusted for a season with a great part of the increased wealth of the community, but administering it for the community far better than it could or would have done for itself. . . . The man who dies thus rich dies disgraced." [5] More than ear-marking private fortune for public good, Carnegie appointed the foundation as an instrument of progress and self-advancement rather than relief. "The best means of benefiting the community is to place within its reach the ladders upon which the aspiring can rise."

Early American Giving and the Public Attitude

From this point on, foundations became a distinctly twentieth-century phenomenon. Small and vast fortunes, representing such names as Carnegie, Rockefeller, Mellon, Sloan, Stanford, Harkness, and others, were dedicated to the public good through foundations rather than bequeathed to their respective families. Such was the signal contribution of foundations during the early years that in 1913, the Carnegie Corporation and the General Education Board (Rockefeller) contributed more than 15 per cent of the income for nine hundred colleges and universities in the country. To-day, with twice as many institutions, the combined incomes of the Rockefeller Foundation, the Carnegie Corporation, and the General Education Board represent less than 1 per cent of the budgetary needs of our educational institutions.

During the decade between 1921 and 1930, American philanthropic giving rose sharply, with an average yearly contribution of over two billion dollars. The pattern of giving which emerged has been largely maintained both by foundations and by philanthropy in general. Religion received 49 per cent of the total contributions; education, 8.4 per cent; and health, 9 per cent. Of the half-billion dollars given by a hundred large foundations during this period, 90 per cent went for education, health, and social welfare. Education received the largest single share, $223 million, or 43 per cent. Within the twelve educational divisions, over 60 per cent of that sum was designated for higher education, almost 15 per cent for elementary and secondary education, and 4 per cent for adult education.

For contributing unprecedented sums to the public welfare, the giant philanthropists received criticism as well as praise. They were charged variously with trying to purify 'tainted money', to make peace with an uneasy conscience, to perpetuate their names, or to maintain and promote the conservative element in society. Since a discussion of

---

[5] *Ibid.*, p. 19.

motives must be based on speculation rather than fact, it not un-naturally invited a host of charges founded solely on personal belief. By 1915, criticism was strong enough to warrant official investigation of foundation activities by the United States Industrial Relations Commission. The fact that foundations were not subsequently abolished or brought under public control did not deny the justness of the accusations, but it did prove a significant point : that no matter how variously motivated philanthropists might be, the actual results of their contributions were socially constructive and vital to cultural progress.

The Structure of the Foundation

Although the depression of the 'thirties largely reduced U.S. surplus wealth, the income tax and the deduction allowed for philanthropy encouraged the creation of new foundations. This legal method of reducing taxes indicated the important role which philanthropy had assumed, and helped to organize and clarify its function in national life. The family foundation mushroomed, since it served as a reservoir for receiving, holding, and later distributing contributions, now 20 per cent for individuals instead of 15 per cent, but still 5 per cent for corporations. For families who owned corporations, it has distinct advantages : in the face of high inheritance taxes, it allows the family to retain control of the business after the death of the principal owner, even though the actual ownership is transferred to the foundation. The foundation is given either non-voting stock, as in the case of the Ford Foundation, or voting stock, as in the case of the Pew Memorial Fund.

Setting up a foundation also allows more intelligent giving, since it enables a more careful selection of organizations to be aided and a more even distribution of funds through uneven business periods. By serving as arbiter between fund-raiser and donor, it discourages random, wasteful, often victimizing appeals and promotes well-directed, intelligent campaigns for funds.

Foundation activities usually fall into two categories, depending on the size of their endowment. Those which make grants to other organizations or individuals are called non-operating, and those which conduct their own research are termed operating. In some instances, such as the Ford Foundation, they do both. The large foundations, with permanent endowments of $50,000 or more, and especially the giant foundations with assets in the millions, are generally active in a specific area such as education, medicine, the physical sciences, or welfare. They are concerned with comprehensive programmes or projects and only with specific organizations or locations as they serve to implement a programme.

Typical and largest of these foundations is the Ford Foundation, which in 1955 gave away $65 million.[6] Its resources are concentrated in five major areas, and since 1951 it has apportioned them as follows:—(1) promotion of international understanding and world peace, 25 per cent; (2) strengthening of democratic institutions and processes, 10 per cent; (3) advancement of economic well-being, 5 per cent; (4) improvement of education, 50 per cent; and (5) advancement of behavioural sciences, 5 per cent.

The vast majority of family foundations, however, with assets of under $50,000, usually contribute to the annual operating budgets of local or familiar organizations and institutions in which there is some personal interest. They do not conduct research in broad fields, but concentrate on a few institutions which they essentially support by carrying through their operations. Though their contributions do not compare in size to those of the larger foundations, they are indispensable in implementing the results of research underwritten by the largest foundations.

Marginal Types of Foundations

For a variety of reasons the exact number of foundations existing to-day is not available. Estimates range from four thousand to thirty thousand, while those that satisfy the definition as it is considered in this discussion number approximately five thousand. There are numerous marginal types which carry out typical foundation work but which are not legally set up as such. Many colleges have such foundations which are simply endowment funds, alumni funds, or memorial bequests establishing a chair, a lectureship, a library collection, or a special department. Similarly, certain businesses and industries have set aside funds for restricted purposes, either for the benefit of the employees and their families or for commercial profit through research.

Then, too, many family foundations have published no reports as to their activities or even locations, making it impossible to count them or even determine whether their funds are being expended for the public good or at all.

Concerning the type of foundation created in perpetuity for some highly restricted purpose, Andrew Carnegie had this to say: " No man of vision will seek to tie the endowment which he gives to a fixed cause. He will leave to the judgment of his trustees, as time goes on, the question of modifying or altogether changing the nature of the

---

[6] Its recent $500 million grant to the nation's schools and hospitals is part of the 1956 grants.

trust so as to meet the requirements of the time." [7] Carnegie's foresight is high-lighted to-day by the number of foundations which have
outgrown their original objectives.

Finally, the community trust exemplifies another organization engaged in foundation work but not strictly a foundation. It is a federation of endowments created to serve the changing needs of a particular
community and administered co-operatively by local bank trustees and
the individual foundation trustees.

The Place of Foundations in American Philanthropy

Excluding all these marginal types, the resources of the five thousand
general philanthropic foundations total $4·5 billion. Seven giant foun-
dations possess $1·5 billion, or 33 per cent of the wealth; 78 founda-
tions control $3·1 billion, or almost 70 per cent of the wealth; and 718
foundations control $4·2 billion, or 93 per cent of the resources. The
$150 million contributed annually by all foundations, however, is
actually less than 3 per cent of the philanthropic dollar : the remaining
97 per cent is from other sources. The great base of philanthropy is
the individual taxpayer, whose gifts represented 80 per cent of the
total philanthropic contributions of $4·5 billion in 1950. It is estimated
that gifts to philanthropy in 1955 totalled $5·5 billion.

The major sources of giving, aside from individual taxpayers, are
charitable bequests, property gifts, and corporations. Corporate gifts
represented $500 million, or three times as much as foundations in
1952. In recent years, philanthropy has been distributed annually
according to the following pattern : religion, 50 per cent; welfare, 23
per cent; hospitals and health, 9 per cent; higher education, 8 per cent;
other education, 3 per cent; foreign relief, 3 per cent; and foundations,
3 per cent (approx.).

It appears, then, that foundations play a unique and crucial role in
the progress of public welfare which far outweighs their actual financial contributions to philanthropy. " The foundation was created
primarily as an instrument for wise giving ",[8] and as such its uniqueness lies in the strategic placement of that 3 per cent on the frontiers
of progress. Foundation work represents experimental, pioneering
research and service which focuses attention on important new areas
for substantial contribution from other sources. By stressing the
" development of the unknown rather than the remedial ",[9] it can do
work which could not otherwise be done by public funds. " It [the
philanthropic foundation] has the important additional opportunity of

---

[7] Howard J. Savage, *Fruit of an Impulse* (New York, 1953), p. 29.
[8] *American Foundations, op cit.,* p. 76.
[9] John Price Jones, *The American Giver* (New York, 1954), p. 100.

offering the 'risk capital' of philanthropy. This represents moneys which, because the project may 'fail', might not be forthcoming from public or from other private sources. It is this capital, identifying dead-end streets in the maze of scientific investigation, that has so often lighted the right road to brilliant discoveries, such as penicillin."[10]

Not only do foundations open up new areas for private philanthropy, but, in many cases, services which they once performed have been assumed by federal or local government. The work they do is a dynamic, continuing process of exploring the unknown, filtering out those aspects which promote the common welfare, and incorporating them into the accepted cultural pattern as the jumping-off place for further investigation. The foundation resembles nothing so much as a laboratory where hypotheses are tested, discarded, or utilized with an eye on the future and progress of mankind. "True culture is always futuristic," said Eduard Lindeman in 1936, and "if their [the philanthropists] disbursements of funds are to have true cultural meaning, each decision must be tested in terms of a desired but imagined future."[11] It is this emphasis on ultimate goals which distinguishes foundation philanthropy from random giving. It also carries tremendous cultural implications, for it places on those who disburse the funds the burden of selecting long-range goals desirable for society.

Such a burden, however, must be assumed if progress is to be more than a random affair. Frederick P. Keppel, the late president of the Carnegie Corporation, foresaw the foundation as one of the very few organizations in society which could afford " the risk of being called impractical and visionary, of waiting till the Greek Kalends for results, the risk of making mistakes, even costly ones, in the hope of ultimately contributing something of value to mankind ".[12]

Time has borne out his judgment. As research has proven its value, foundations have increasingly turned to areas, such as the social sciences and humanities, where the results of investigation are less readily achieved and less easily evaluated. The disadvantages of prolonged experiments and delayed outcomes which prohibit the investment of public funds are the very problems with which foundations should and do concern themselves. " Certainly the continuity and independence of foundations would seem to lay upon them a special responsibility for taking the long view, and for dealing with problems whose treatment is neither popular, and thus easily supported, nor

---

[10] *Ibid.*, p. 100.
[11] Eduard C. Lindeman, *Wealth and Culture* (New York, 1936), p. 61.
[12] *American Foundations, op. cit.*, p. 94.

likely to be handled by other agencies, nor capable of quick or easy solution." [13]

Considering these objectives, there are certain areas in education, especially in higher education, for which 'risk' capital would not serve its unique function. Such capital would not be purposefully used towards a college endowment, because it empowers future college trustees with the disbursement of funds and endowment needs are, in fact, too vast for assistance to be effective. Another area in which capital would lose its risk value is that of current operating expenses. Such grants would tend to maintain the *status quo* and perpetuate operational difficulties which can often be eliminated under economic pressure.

Nor is education generally advanced by using 'risk' capital to cover deficits, though colleges sometimes incur such deficits through risking their own capital. Foundation grants for this purpose would be in the nature of relief rather than prevention or cure and would tend to delay change.

Similarly, grants for buildings and construction gain much maintenance but little progress. Mrs. Walter G. Ladd, in a letter of gift to the Macy Foundation in 1930, realized this and hoped that " the Foundation will take more interest in the architecture of ideas than in the architecture of buildings and laboratories." [14]

Areas of Operation

Identifying areas for the investment of risk capital, however, demands imagination rather than elimination, and it is in such unexplored areas that foundations fulfil their purpose. Perhaps the most far-reaching effects of applied imagination have been felt in the field of medical education. In 1910, the Carnegie Foundation for the Advancement of Teaching engaged Abraham Flexner to investigate the shocking situation which existed in the 155 medical schools in the country. As a result of the detailed study he made, at a cost of $60,457, John D. Rockefeller and the General Education Board appropriated over $45 million to make a few medical schools so outstanding that the rest would have to raise their standards or close. Consequently, half of the medical schools were closed during the next twenty-five years. By 1928 the original gift, though expended, had drawn in $600 million to American university medical schools. Risking capital had produced unprecedented high standards of medical education, both in the United States and throughout the world.

Foundations to-day follow the same principle of aiding high-quality programmes, so that low-quality programmes must improve if they

---

[13] *Ibid.*, p. 94.   [14] *Ibid.*, p. 77.

are to continue. The Fund for the Advancement of Education, for example, has given grants to clarify the functions of schools, colleges, and teachers; to re-define educational programmes according to clarified aims; to reorganize budgets by management surveys; to introduce programmes for the preparation of college teachers; and to utilize the professional skills of elementary and secondary school teachers more fully by supplying aides to perform routine duties. These are areas which suggest a total re-thinking of the methods of education in our society. The efficiency of business and industry, once inimical to the academic world, is now essential to it if foundations are to prevent and cure rather than relieve.

Scholarship Programmes

Many foundations concerned with education devote an important part of their programme to scholarships and fellowships. The Guggenheim Foundation contributes significantly to the long neglected areas of the arts and humanities through its graduate fellowships. Instead of sponsoring group projects, it has re-emphasized the value of individual work and personal cultivation in an age of group-mindedness and research teams.

To promote the international exchange of scholars, the Rockefeller Foundation has given approximately $20 million to seven thousand five hundred individuals. This has implications for world peace far beyond the benefit to the individual recipient, for it envisages and could encourage foreign travel by large numbers and intercultural exchange through many media of communication.

In the area of general undergraduate scholarships, the available resources do not begin to approach the vast financial need. Not only is the need great, but the distribution of available funds does not utilize them to the maximum degree. A recent study in the United States estimated that half of the scholarship funds in the country are concentrated in fifty colleges and universities. Regardless of their national reputation, these institutions can reach only a fraction of the able but indigent youth who want and ought to go to college.

Many students are further prevented from going to college by the numerous restrictions which donors place on scholarship gifts. Scholarships may be restricted to a geographical area, a specific college or colleges, a special field of study, religion or national origin, membership in the sponsoring organization, or any other attribute which the donor deems worthy. Frequently there are more scholarships for a specified purpose than there are candidates qualified to meet the specifications, so that funds are wasted. An expert on the American scholarship situation has estimated that half of all college students change their plans of study during college, indicating that many scholarships for special studies show no profit to the donor and that many students become eligible for certain scholarships too late. Thus the student, the institution, and the donor himself are damaged by scholarship restrictions. The expert summed up the situation by saying that " ' a vast segment of the population ' is not covered by any existing scholarship programme ".[15]

Unrestricted programmes and impartial agencies, such as the Ford Foundation's National Merit Scholarship Program and the College Entrance Examination Board's College Scholarship Service, have been and are being set up to distribute money to more students in a more equitable fashion. Such programmes identify able students and acquaint them with the advantages and availability of college education. National programmes also enable small companies to contribute funds where they could not otherwise establish a scholarship programme of their own.

Similar to the scholarship idea is the system of loans whereby a student receives financial aid repayable at a small interest-rate. Harvard University has proved this plan workable for both the student and the college, since the small loss on principal is more than compensated by the interest paid. The Technology Loan Fund, set up by the Massachusetts Institute of Technology in 1931, has loaned 4,045 students a total of $2,074,000 and has been repaid $2,085,000. It has collected $254,000 in interest and has lost only $9,600 on principal. Harvard, M.I.T., Ohio State University, and Yale University have found that the loan plan not only helps to retrieve students otherwise lost to education, but that the serious student is willing to assume a measure of responsibility for his education.

Sources of Giving to Education

Philanthropic funds for scholarships and higher education in general are largely contributed by alumni, business corporations, foundations, bequests, and religious organizations. According to a recent study, these groups contributed $336 million in 1954–5 to 728 higher educational institutions representing 70 per cent of the nation's college students. Of the total gift, 71·5 per cent was given for current operations and 28·5 per cent for endowment. Of the total contribution, more was given unrestrictedly, 28·5 per cent, than for any single purpose. Restrictions were designated in the following proportions: buildings and grounds, 22 per cent; research, 17 per cent; faculty salaries, 10 per cent; and student aid, 7·7 per cent.

[15] Council for Financial Aid to Education, *College Scholarships—Too many? Too Few?* (New York, 1955), p. 13.

The private, non-church-related colleges, comprising 25 per cent of those reporting, received 47·4 per cent of the total contribution. The largest gift from any single source was given by alumni, who contributed over $52 million, or 15·5 per cent of the total. Of the $50 million given by foundations, $24·4 million went to the private, non-church-related colleges. This was the largest amount given by any source to any of the four types of institutions. Corporate gifts of $39·5 million do not include sums given for contract research. Reliable estimates indicate that corporate giving to all the nation's college and universities might well exceed $75 million in 1954–5.

Increasingly substantial gifts from corporations indicate that a new economic factor has entered the philanthropic scene. Private fortune is no longer gained at public expense, but is dependent on the general economic prosperity of the nation. When education was recognized as an effective instrument for achieving economic success, it became an area of vital interest to business. Corporate resources hold such potential for education that colleges will be forced into self-improvement programmes more than ever before in order to attract its funds. The same principle of forced competition which raised the standards of medical education thirty years ago, could be extremely effective in improving the state of school and college education to-day.

The Foundation's Commitment

Just as independent colleges must be responsible to the non-academic world which supports them, so must foundations be responsible to the public which ultimately acts upon their work. Foundations must educate the public concerning their activities in order to bridge the gap between research and action, between the discovery of knowledge and its diffusion. Communicating through publications, lectures, conferences, and consultations is equally important, in order to avoid unfounded accusations, which often range from ultra-conservatism through irresponsibility to subversion. Since 1950 two congressional committees have investigated charges that foundations were engaged in subversive activities or were trying to influence legislation through political propaganda. The record of the foundations was found generally to be good and, although no legislation resulted, the investigations pointed up the need for closer contacts between foundations and the public. Informed public opinion is of the essence if foundations are to retain their independence and freedom of action. Finally, the public attitude towards foundations, which is as dispassionate as it is informed, will affect the establishment of future foundations.

JOHN K. WEISS.

CHAPTER SEVEN

Resources for Education in New York State

THE earliest schools were conducted by the Dutch. They were free. The first schoolmaster in New York State was a salaried official of the West India Company receiving a compensation of 360 florins or approximately $144 per year. There is some reason to believe that this pioneer in the army of school teachers took in washing to increase his income.

In the year 1638 appears the record of the first tax for the maintenance of schools, the following law having been proposed:—

> Each householder and inhabitant shall bear such tax and public charge as shall hereafter be considered proper for the maintenance of clergymen, comforters of the sick, schoolmasters, and such like necessary officers.

In *Annals of Public Education in the State of New York*, Mr. Pratt states that:—

> as early as 1642, it was customary, in marriage contracts, whenever the bride was a widow having children, for the parties to " promise to bring up the children decently, according to their ability, to provide them with necessary clothing and food, to keep them at school, to let them learn reading, writing, and a good trade"; to which was sometimes added " as honest parents ought and are bound to do, and as they can answer before God and man."
>
> About 1648 a small private school was opened which was tolerably well patronized. The best families had generally their own private tutors direct from Europe; but there were enough to support a school besides, and the new teacher found himself fully occupied.

An act was passed by the Legislature (Chapter 75, Laws of 1795) entitled " An Act for the encouragement of schools ". The act provided that twenty thousand pounds should be appropriated annually for five years for the encouragement and maintenance of elementary schools throughout the state. This sum was apportioned to school districts upon their raising an amount equal to their distributive share, which they were required by law to do. Upon the expiration of the five-year period the appropriation was not renewed. This " act for the encouragement of schools " marked the beginning of the cleavage which existed for more than one hundred years between the Regents and the administrators of the common school system. The act did not vest in the Regents the power of supervising the common schools that were to be encouraged, but left that function to town commissioners.

The next formal step by the Legislature was " An Act to raise a fund for the encouragement of Common Schools " (Chapter 66, Laws of 1805). This act was the beginning of the common school fund which is now ' preserved inviolate ' in the Constitution (Art. XI, 3). By this act the ' net proceeds ' of the sale of five hundred thousand acres of vacant and unappropriated lands in the state was established as a " permanent fund for the support of common schools ". The fund was to be loaned by the State Comptroller and after the accumulation of fifty thousand dollars the interest was to be " distributed and applied for the support of common schools" in the manner directed by the Legislature.

Since the special appropriation in 1795 and the establishment of the permanent common school fund in 1805 by-passed the Regents, it is not surprising that the next formal step by the Legislature, though still delayed seven years, was the passage of " An Act for the establishment of Common Schools" (Chapter 242, Laws of 1812), enacted June 19th, 1812. This act provided for the appointment of a Superintendent of Common Schools to be named by the Council of Appointment at an annual salary of $300. The broad duty of the superintendent was " to digest and prepare plans for the improvement and management of the common school fund, and for the better organization of common schools ".

State Support of Education

There are familiar steps in the early history of the public support of education in New York. The Dutch implanted the principle when they established, in 1638 in New Amsterdam, their first school, which was supported in part by public taxation. Under later English rule feeble efforts were made to provide for the support of common schools. In 1732 provision was made for the partial public support of a school in New York City for teaching of " Latin, Greek and mathematiks ".

It was not until 1795 that the state took its first step towards the support of common schools, when a direct grant of 20,000 pounds ($50,000) was made for a period of five years " for the purpose of encouraging and maintaining schools in the several cities and towns ". At the end of the five-year period this appropriation was not renewed. A permanent common school fund was established in 1805. The fund was augmented in 1838 by allocations from the United States Deposit funds and again in 1846 by constitutional provision for the addition each year of $25,000 of the revenues of these funds. The establishment of a state-wide system of common schools in 1812 provided a stable and more permanent basis for state support, and a local tax was mandated in 1814. Thus the public support of common schools as a joint responsibility of the state and the local school districts was determined a hundred and seventy-six years after the Dutch established the principle.

Difference in Ability

During the nineteenth century little change was made in either the amount or the method by which the state participated in the support of schools. By 1900 the total amount provided by the state was slightly more than $3,700,000, or about 11 per cent of the total cost of public education. Just after the turn of the century the amount of state funds to be distributed was based for the first time upon the assessed valuation of the taxable property within the district. This was the first recognition of the difference in the ability of school districts to support education.

For a period of twenty years after the passage of the Unification Act in 1904 numerous methods were adopted for increasing the amount of state support by means of special quotas. In 1908, quotas for special teachers were established. In 1909 the district quotas were increased and revised. In 1916, quotas were provided for physical training teachers. In 1919, additional teachers' quotas were set up and a mandated salary clause inserted. In 1920 the academic quota was increased from $100 for each academic department to $200 for each year of academic instruction. In 1921, teachers' quotas were increased. In 1923, quotas for special classes for mentally retarded children were established and the training-class quota was raised from $700 to $1,200. In 1924, quotas were established for medical inspectors, school nurses, health teachers, and special classes for physically defective children. As a result, during the period from 1904 to 1924 the state aid was increased from $4,105,000 to $41,402,497.

Ensuring Adequate Support

The cumulative effect of these various enactments was a total of twenty-five various bases used for the distribution of state aid. These procedures reflected the concern of the state for the welfare of its school system, but the piecemeal method was clearly not the best for ensuring adequate support. The rising costs as a result of World War I, the desperate financial straits of the cities restricted by constitutional tax limitations, and the increasing tax burden upon the property tax caused a great deal of concern. As a result a legislative commission was appointed in 1919 which bore the title of the Special Joint Committee on Taxation and Retrenchment. In 1920 the U.S. Commissioner of Education called a conference of citizens to study the cost of the expanding school system. As an outgrowth of the conference a committee was named which outlined the scope of an inquiry into the financing of education and proposed that a commission be appointed to undertake the study. With grants from several foundations the American Council on Education conducted the study. The scope of the inquiry was nation-wide, but concentrated on certain states, of which New York was one. One volume of the report dealt directly with the problem of financing schools in the state. This report clarified the principle of equalization of educational opportunity and support.

Committee of Twenty-one

While these two studies were under way the Committee of Twenty-one undertook the Rural School Survey of New York. The report of the study of this committee was published in 1922 in eight volumes. Volume III outlined a plan of financial support. This report called attention to the great differences in the ability of localities to support schools. Thus in the early 'twenties there were three major studies of the problem, one national in scope, one a legislative commission, and a third by a group of interested citizens. All three contributed to the understanding of the problem and its scope. The Joint Legislative Commission accepted the principle of equalization of support as clarified and defined by the Educational Finance Inquiry and in 1925 proposed legislation embodying that principle in a small measure in the now historic Cole-Rice law.

The Commission had available a sum of $10,000,000 to provide for increased state aid. It proposed that $6,000,000 of the amount be made available to increase teacher quotas and quotas to one-room schools, and that $4,000,000 be made available as an equalization fund to be distributed to the localities, so that every locality making a minimum contribution will have the equivalent of $1,200 for an elementary teacher and $1,600 for a high school teacher.

Principle of Equalization

Thus in 1925 the principle of equalization of support was finally adopted as state policy and effectively established in law, twenty-three years after the need for some form of equalization was first felt in the meagre effort of adjusting to the varying ability of the local communities in the law of 1902. The fact that other states have since followed New York's example attests to the wisdom and foresight of the public-spirited groups who aided in the development of the plan.

In addition to the establishment of the equalization principle, the legislation of 1925 also made another very significant contribution in the improvement of the public school system of the state when it pro-

vided for a more generous apportionment of state aid to those communities which saw fit to join their small inefficient school districts
into a central rural school district. Provisions for such districts had
been made as early as 1914, but it was not until the Cole-Rice law of
1925 that this movement began. The next twenty-five years saw
remarkable progress in the improvement of the facilities for education
in rural areas of the state. The history of education will perhaps
mark this legislation as the most significant in the history of the state
up to the present time.

Financing in Cities

As remarkable as the Cole-Rice law was, sufficient funds were not
provided at that time to meet fully all the critical situations which
existed. A special commission was appointed to which was assigned
the problem of financing of education in cities. A number of the
larger cities were seriously handicapped by a 2 per cent tax limit
which proved to be inadequate to meet all the needs of both schools
and city government. Various unsound practices of financing were
virtually forced upon these cities. The Friedsam Commission bearing
the name of its chairman, Michael Friedsam, after studying the plight
of these cities, presented a plan for greatly increasing the amount of
state aid as a means of providing tax relief. In providing this relief
the commission recommended legislation increasing the amount of
state aid from about $54,000,000 in 1925 to an anticipated $89,000,000
by 1930. It adhered to the principle of equalization first incorporated
in the Cole-Rice law, and thereby accomplished the two primary functions of state support: one, the equalization of educational opportunity and support, and the other, the relief of the property tax, by
distributing state funds derived from other than property taxes to the
localities that did not have recourse to such forms of tax.

Depression Years

The planning done in the mid-'twenties of the twentieth century was
so thorough and sound that no major revision or change in either the
amount or the method of distributing state support was called for for
another twenty years except for several 'stand-still' arrangements
made during the depression years of the 'thirties. The provisions of the
Friedsam law served the purpose well and should be credited with
having safeguarded the schools during those trying years. No schools
were closed, no terms were shortened, and no serious curtailments
were made in the character and quality of the educational programme.

With the inflation following World War II, the increased costs and
the lowering value of the dollar necessitated further revisions in the

equalization formula, particularly those relating to the measure of the cost of a minimum or foundation programme. The figure of $1,500 for each elementary and $1,900 for each secondary teacher were no longer realistic. Consequently, beginning in 1945, a series of revisions in the amounts became necessary. In 1945 the basic factors were increased, and while the pupil was substituted as the unit of measure instead of the teacher, there was no change except in the upward revision of the dollar amounts. In 1945, the minimum programme for the foundation level was adjusted upward to $100 for each elementary pupil and to $130 for each secondary pupil. The legislation of 1945, however, made no provision for changing the apportionment to central school districts, so in 1946 and again in 1947 legislation revising the apportionment to such districts was made. In 1948, coincident with the revision of the minimum-salary law, the factors were again increased to $200 and $240 per pupil, and in 1951, with the further revision of the salary law, the factors were increased to $220 and $274 respectively. The state has said to the local districts in effect :—

If you levy a tax of $6.20 on each $1,000 of the true valuation of the taxable property in your district we, the state, will make up the difference between the amount that you receive from this $6.20 tax and the total sum necessary to provide the $220 for each elementary school child and the $274 for each high school child. If the state did not do this, children living in districts where property values are low would have lesser educational opportunity than children living in districts where property values are high.

A Sound System

The fifty years just concluded are outstanding in the development of a sound system of state-supported education. In that period there was clearly established the realization that the support of schools is the joint responsibility of the state and the local communities; that the state is obligated to maintain an adequate level for the support of the schools regardless of the ability of the local communities; and the recognition that the burden of supporting education should fall equitably upon all tax sources. The state has met well the constitutional mandate that " the legislature shall provide for the maintenance and support of a system of free common schools, wherein all the children of this state may be educated ".

HOWARD A. SHIEBLER.

CHAPTER EIGHT

Subsidies to University Students in Norway

IN Norway there are at the moment nine universities and institutes of the same standing with some five thousand eight hundred students altogether. In addition, some two thousand students are studying abroad, which is a higher proportion than in most countries.

Studies at Norwegian universities and institutes are free. The students pay no tuition fees. With one exception (the private institute of theology) all the institutions draw their money from the state. The financial problem, from the students' point of view therefore, has been reduced to raising the money to live. That may be serious enough, especially so as most institutions prefer long courses. The entrance examination (*examen artium*) is normally passed at the age of 19, after that, a student who is going to teach in secondary schools spends six to eight years at the university, the average age at which the final examination is taken being, at the moment, about 30. This is later than for most professions, but normally a student must be able to spend four to six years on his university studies.

Student Organizations

It is no surprise in Norway, where in this century various organizations have become very important factors in democratic life, that the students themselves have built up strong and efficient organizations for the purpose of tackling their economic and social problems. Since 1939 their organizations have been granted special rights by law. They get an entrance fee, that was earlier paid to the state; further, they are entitled to membership fees from all students. The state subsidizes their activities by some 500,000 Norwegian *crowns* [1] a year.

The student organization of Oslo (*Studentsamskipnaden i Oslo*), which is the largest one, had a total turnover of 3,778,290 Norwegian *crowns* in 1954. The organization has seven cafeterias (luncheon, 1·90 Norwegian *crowns*); further, a student's village, Sogn, with six hundred rooms (75 Norwegian *crowns* a month for furnished single room of a high standard), a students' travel bureau, book store and editing house, health service for students, etc. Also the students' bank (*Statens Lånekasse for studerende ungdom*) was founded on the initiative of the students' organization of Oslo. However, this bank is a separate institution with its own law dating from 1947. The founding

---

[1] 7·15 Norwegian *crowns* = 1 U.S. *dollar*.

of the students' bank is a typical example of the co-operation between students' organizations and the government.

The government wants to stimulate the students' desire to help themselves, their social initiative, and their organizational work. There is no doubt that the responsibility placed on students and their organizations has become an important part of the students' education, and that the various undertakings are very well run.

The policy formed with the co-operation of students, parents, and the government is based on some basic principles :—

We are working towards a situation where all youth, regardless of the home environment and the economic status of their parents, may have the education they want and are gifted for.

The responsibility has been placed with the home for the children's education up to *examen artium* or equivalent education or training.

In cases where the home cannot afford the education, the state should grant the necessary allowances. With increasing productivity and a rising standard of living, the country should outgrow this system of subsidies because there will be fewer cases where help is needed.

Further studies beyond the *examen artium* or, more generally speaking, beyond the age of 19–20, should be financed by the student himself, by loans or work. Those who want to go beyond the general level of education, do so for the purpose of getting a job that is better paid or more enjoyable than others, and expenditures in that connexion may be considered as personal investments to an economic end. But some students, in fact, have to work too hard in order to pay for their studies. A paid vacation job is not enough, they have to work during term. This hampers their studies. Therefore an increase is planned in the amount of grants to students (1956–7 some 2·5 million *crowns* for university and teacher training).

Loans to Students

The students' bank has grown rapidly since its start in 1947. By 30th June, 1955, the total number of clients was 16,130 and loans granted totalled some 71·2 million Norwegian *crowns*. The popularity of the institution is, of course, due to the fact that the loans are free of interest during the period of study. After the final degree the candidate still has eighteen months to find a job and establish himself financially before he begins paying back. The whole amount is then due over a period of fifteen years. The students' bank does not ask for any security. The student gets his money on his honest face. Two persons who know him guarantee his honesty, but not the money. There were many pessimists when this system was launched. All the other banks ask for guarantees, and usually very secure ones. This system of rigorous guarantees was presumably built on experience. The optimism of the founders of the students' bank regarding people's honesty seemed therefore unwarranted. Students, who earlier had to beg for guarantees (in some cases they had to convince as many as thirty underwriters, who later followed their progress with Argus-eyes), now feel themselves free individuals. The result is that the system of trust in human nature seems to work in this banking business. The students have, so far, paid back rather more quickly than their contracts oblige them to. An amendment, recently proposed by the government in the taxation laws, entitles payments on such loans to be deducted from income liable to taxation.

The proportion of students taking loans varies from institution to institution and also from faculty (school) to faculty in the universities. At the University of Oslo, 31 per cent of the students take loans from the students' bank. (In pharmacy the percentage is 63, in medicine 54, in language and history 22·5, and in theology 19·5 per cent.) At the University of Bergen the average is only 20 per cent, possibly reflecting the fact that a higher proportion of the students there come from the town and close vicinity and therefore may live at home. At the other academic institutions the percentage of students borrowing from the students' bank is even higher, 57 as an average. The Institute of Odontology tops the list with 75 per cent; while at the technical University of Trondheim 59 per cent have loans from this bank.

Also students abroad are covered by the students' bank, and expensive as their studies often are, this system is of great value.

The whole system of financial aid for education has recently (1954) been reviewed by the Norwegian parliament, the *Storting*. The importance of enabling young people to live at home as long as possible was stressed, but on a whole Parliament accepted the principles on which, up to now, subsidies have been built. The government estimated that a total of 25 million Norwegian *crowns* a year was necessary to carry over the principles efficiently into practical work. At the moment about half of this amount is available. The increase will be obtained through the budgets from 1956 onwards and on the advice of a permanent 'Grants Board' which was appointed in June 1955. The main effort will take place in the field of direct grants to pupils (homes) for secondary school education, vocational schools included. For the economy of the university students it is especially important that grants for the *gymnasium* should be greatly increased. The selection of students for this 'track' or stream in the school system has been good, but there are still intellectual reserves that have not yet been mobilized. We need them more than ever before.

HELGE SIVERTSEN.

CHAPTER NINE

The Incidence of Taxation and of State Provision for Education: United Kingdom

THE real cost of providing education, as of providing anything else, is not the money spent on it, but the real resources, in terms of capital and labour, which are devoted to it. With education, these real resources include such items as the number of people engaged in teaching, in building schools, and equipping them, and in administering them, together with the raw materials and capital involved. It includes, too, the time and work of members of governing bodies or of county education committees, in so far as this time and energy is given at the expense of other productive work. Finally, it may include those who, by devoting all or part of their time to learning as pupils in schools or other institutions, are reducing or postponing their own direct contribution to production; but this last factor may well be outweighed by the increased skill of the educated person who is therefore contributing a greater share to the total supply of labour after his education than he would have done before.

It is clear that the greater part of this real cost is likely to be substantially the same, whether education is provided by the state or by private enterprise. But the distribution of the burden of this real cost among different members of the population, on the one hand, and the allocation of the benefits of education among them on the other, depends upon the method by which education is financed. When education is provided by private enterprise, the consumer who purchases it and who wishes to enjoy its benefits pays a price to cover the cost of providing it. When education is provided by the state, the same system may prevail as it does with state-managed concerns like the Post Office and the nationalized industries. Most commonly, however, with the provision of education, the state proceeds by a radically different method. Although it pays a price for buildings and salaries for teachers and so forth, it raises the money to cover these costs not by prices to the individual consumer but by taxation of the community in general.

Nature of Taxation

Professor Taussig defined a tax as follows : " The essence of a tax, as distinguished from other charges of government, is the absence of a direct *quid pro quo* between the tax-payer and the public authority. It follows that a tax is necessarily a compulsory levy. The Post Office illustrates the payments which are different from taxes. A charge is made by it for each letter; no one is compelled to contribute towards its revenue unless he makes use of the service . . . each individual user pays . . . in proportion to the service he gets. . . . But when the government maintains streets, a fire service, a police-force, it supplies the several services free to everyone. On the other hand, everyone is called upon to contribute. It is immaterial whether the individual citizen happens to be benefited directly or indirectly; a great deal, a little, or not at all. What he pays to the government for a postage stamp is in the nature of a price for a specific service. It is very different from a tax, which is exacted from all alike and without any regard to the individual's use of the service provided." [1]

The point of this, as far as we are concerned, is that a tax is a compulsory payment in return for which nothing specific, or *pro rata*, is promised to the individual payer of the tax. This arises in part from the nature of the services which a Government originally sought to provide from taxation. Police supervision and the fire brigade, the public highway and national defence—with none of these can we assess the benefit to a particular citizen or individual tax-payer. Such a costing operation is impossible. In part, the compulsory tax with its absence of a specific *quid pro quo* is linked with the principles on which taxation has been levied. These have traditionally been two: the first, that since everyone benefits from a communal service, everyone should contribute a proportion of his income, either directly or through his necessary expenditure; and the second that, since the distribution of capital and income among different classes of the community is unequal, taxation should depend on ability to pay, and be not proportional but progressive, so that the higher the income of the tax-payer, the greater the proportion of it would he contribute to the common fund.

In modern times incomes of the most populous groups in the community have risen considerably and the large national expenditure of

---

[1] F. W. Taussig, *Principles of Economics* (Macmillan, 1933), Vol. II, p. 505. There may be an element of taxation in the purchase of a postage stamp if the Post Office makes a profit on its activities and if this profit is handed over to the Government revenue department. Equally, there may be a subsidy, if it makes a loss which the revenue makes good. But these qualifications do not affect the main point of Professor Taussig's argument.

the modern state can no longer be financed from the surplus incomes of the rich. These factors have produced the position that all citizens contribute *something* to the common fund. They do not, of course, all contribute the same proportion of their earnings, but no citizen avoids the burden of taxation in some shape or form.

The raising of money and the spending of money are thus conceived by the state as two separate and distinct operations, governed by different principles, and, as far as taxation is concerned, it is usual to examine not particular taxes but the total system of taxes in any state, in order to estimate the incidence of taxation and discover on whom the burden falls. Particular taxes, such as outlay taxes on necessities, may well be regressive, but when combined with a heavily progressive income tax, the result is a progressive system of taxes, taken as a whole. From this there follows an important consequence for our purpose. It is not possible to balance education or any other specific service of the state against a specific tax or set of taxes which may be said to pay for it. If all free or state-subsidized education were abandoned, no one could say which tax or group of taxes would be reduced as a result, for the reduction would normally be considered from the standpoint of total tax policy, and not from that of the service curtailed or abolished. Nor, if education expenditure were suddenly to be doubled, could anyone say which tax or taxes would be raised to meet the increase.

This all arises fundamentally from the nature of taxation—that it is compulsory and that no specific *quid pro quo* is due to the tax-payer in return. There is one exception to this general rule, which arises with local government. In England, local government expenditure is financed partly by Exchequer grant, and partly by its own local taxation. This local taxation is confined to a single tax—the rate on property—and the result is that an increase or decrease in local government expenditure will produce a rise or fall in one particular tax—the rate. When a public service like education is provided through the agency of local authorities, we can therefore impute part of its cost to a particular tax. Even then, however, we must be careful not to overstate the position. Although local authorities in England habitually attach a statement to their rate demand showing how much of the total rate is allocated to each service, this statement does not constitute a contract with the tax-payer. If the expenditure on education falls short of the estimate, the surplus is not earmarked for education, or for corresponding reduction in rates: it goes to the general fund of the authority to be spent as it thinks fit, most usually on meeting excess expenditure on some other service, such as roads. A local rate is still, in essentials, a tax.

Local Taxation or Rates

It is, however, possible for a rate to be a mixture of a tax and a price. The water rate in England is basically a tax, being levied according to the rateable value of a property. But excess water rate is charged on certain conditions thought to denote excess use of water—the possession of a garden hose, for example. Here, there is an element of paying according to the use one makes of a service—a principle alien to taxation, but the essence of paying a price. If a similar principle operated in regard to education, there would be a basic education rate for all, assessed on rateable value, and an excess rate to the parents of large families. The same idea in reverse lies behind the suggestion that those who educate their children at their own expense at independent schools should be allowed the fees, or part of them, as free of income tax. There are arguments for and against this proposal, but, in whatever form it is put forward, it rests on the assumption that tax liability should be adjusted for the individual in proportion as he makes use of a public service: such an assumption is invalid according to traditional ideas of taxation.

In view of the special connexion of the local rate with the provision of state education, it is worth noticing some of the main considerations which affect its incidence. It is a tax on property, and is traditionally classed as a 'direct' tax. This classification is an administrative rather than an economic one, and from the economist's point of view, the local rate is more properly regarded as an 'outlay' tax—that is, a tax not on income but on expenditure. It is a tax upon expenditure on property. Like other outlay taxes, it can be and frequently is passed on from the landlord to the tenant, from the tenant to the lodger, and from the shopkeeper in highly rated premises to his customers, in the form of enhanced prices. On the other hand, it may not fall on all property in a locality, for in practice modifications of the rate system occur. In certain states of the U.S.A., the home-dwelling is derated; in England, agricultural land is entirely derated, and industrial premises pay only one-quarter of the full rate. The effect of such devices is a subsidy to the derated categories of property, a disturbance of the general incidence of rates, and a higher rate for the remainder of the ratepayers in order to obtain the same total revenue.

Since the rate rarely rests on the immediate person on whom it is levied, but is generally passed on in surreptitious or overt fashion, it is difficult to draw definite conclusions about its incidence upon different classes in the community. But we can observe the incidence of the local rate in distributing the tax burden among different parts of the country. Heavily populated areas, constituting a heavy demand for social services such as education, may not be wealthy. The rate burden will tend to be high, the low rents and capital values will discourage building and the settlement of wealthy people in the area. A wealthy area, with a small demand for social services, may have high property values and low rates. Thus the local rate does not distribute the burden in accordance with need: the areas needing most local expenditure are frequently those least able to afford it.

Percentage and Equalization Grants

In England these differences between areas are reduced by a system of Exchequer grants. These are: first, a percentage grant related to particular services; and second, an equalizing grant relating to all services. As far as education is concerned, the central authority bears, by means of a percentage grant, some 60 per cent of all local authority expenditure on education. The equalizing grant is designed specifically to bring the poorer areas up to the standard of the average in ability to finance local authority services. It is based on the difference between the rateable value *per capita* in the area, and the national average, and on the ' needs ' of the area, as measured by its expenditure. Its only weakness, about to be remedied, is the lack of a standard system of valuation of property throughout the country. With this ensured, the equalizing grant is both simple, and should be effective.

These grants carry with them a measure of control by the central authority. A percentage grant from the Ministry of Education gives the latter power to exact standards of service in education. Although it appears as an aid in education, it may well be an effective lever to force the local authority to spend more than it would otherwise have done. Hence it may not reduce rates, but increase them, not by increasing the cost of social services, nor by throwing their whole burden on the authority, but by increasing their scope and standard. But the effect of this on poorer authorities is offset by the equalizing grant which goes some way to compensate the weaker brethren for the high level of local expenditure forced on them by national control of their activities. In practice, this grant may be substantial: in Somerset, not by any means a poor county, it was recently nearly one-third of the total expenditure. But it is complicated, from the local authority's point of view, by the fact that the grant starts as an estimate, continues as a revised estimate, then as an estimated grant on actual expenditure, and ends as a finally agreed grant. Four years may be taken to agree the grant for one year. The more substantial the grant is, the more irksome is this delay, and the more does it inhibit effective planning by the local authority. But the second of the two terms of reference on which it is based—the ' needs ' of the area as measured by its expenditure—appear to make this procedure unavoidable.

The final result of both percentage and equalization grants to local authorities, coupled with the great expansion of social services administered by them, is to change the relative burden as between local and national taxation. In a recent book,[2] figures are quoted showing that in 1938-9, the burden of educational expenditure was shared in roughly equal proportions by local rates and Exchequer grants. In 1953-4 the Exchequer contribution is roughly two-thirds of the whole. Hence, in trying to compare any individual's tax-burden with the benefit he may receive in education, we cannot rely on the one tax to which this particular benefit can be imputed—the local rate —for it does not bear the main part of the burden. And with national taxation, it is the total burden of all taxes we must consider, and the willingness to bear this for the relatively small part of it spent on education is best considered in relation to the manner in which the state distributes its provision of education.

State Provision in Practice

The state provides education in ways which range from the direct and obvious, such as state schools, to the hidden provision of education contained in apprenticeship and similar schemes which take place during national service in the Armed Forces. An accurate statement of how much is spent on education is not therefore to be obtained merely by examining the annual vote of supplies to the Ministry of Education. Further, this vote itself contains items, such as school meals and milk, which are not strictly ' education '. Finally, the vote includes a contribution to local expenditure on a borderline item— transport to and from school, a sum which in some counties exceeds £100,000 per year. To the economist, transport may properly be regarded as one of the costs of education, for it is the cost of distributing education to the final consumer. The total state expenditure on education would therefore include most of the Ministry of Education expenditure, the expenditure of local authorities, that part of expenditure on the Armed Forces devoted to general or vocational education, and finally, in Great Britain, the grant to universities which is made direct from the Treasury, and not through the Ministry of Education.

For the purposes of this article, we may confine ourselves to the more overt forms of state provision of education. There are first,

---

[2] G. A. N. Lowndes, *The British Educational System* (Hutchinson's, London, 1955), pp. 44-5. Expenditure on education is now by far the largest single item in local authority expenditure.

schools which the public authorities provide, own, and control. These are built and maintained entirely at public expense, and their teachers remunerated from the public purse. These in Great Britain are known as ' Maintained Schools ', and they constitute by far the majority of the schools under the full and direct control of the local authority. In virtually the same category, from the standpoint of economics come the ' voluntary-aided ' schools—schools with an independent foundation, and perhaps a very small independent income, drawing their main finances from the public funds, and therefore under corresponding control by the local authority.[3]

Secondly, the state may seek to extend facilities for education by using, and offering financial aid to, independent schools. In England this aid takes two forms. First, there are ' Direct Grant ' schools: these are schools with an independent foundation and income who receive a direct grant from the Ministry of Education, and not from the local authority. The grant consists of thirty pounds per year for each pupil in the school, and a further forty pounds per year for each pupil in the Sixth Form. In return for this aid, the school fees have to be approved by the Ministry of Education, and may not be raised without its sanction, not readily granted. Further, the school is required to offer a proportion of its places—not less that twenty-five per cent, and possibly more—to the local authority as free places: it thus makes a contribution to the free grammar school education of its area. The remainder of its places are ' residuary ' places to be awarded by the school subject to two conditions. First, no boy may be debarred from admittance by reason of the poverty of his parents. Any parent earning less than £470 a year is entitled to full remission of fees, and a sliding scale operates thereafter, taking size of family into account. This is not free education, but it is the removal of the financial barrier to education : since the poor gain more than the rich from this it is, unlike free education, an equalizing device. Second, no boy may be admitted who is not up to the standard for grammar school admission in the area. There may be some modification of this condition where the foundation of the school requires them to make provision for a particular group—for instance, the sons of clergymen, but in general the principle that no boy may be debarred from admission by reason of financial circumstance is an overriding one, and with this goes control of fees, and the exacting of a standard of ability for admission.

---

[3] These schools may vary considerably in the extent of public aid and control, from ' aided ' and ' special agreement ' status, where the school provides the buildings and the authority the running costs, to ' controlled ' status, where nearly all finance and control is local authority, the school retaining small independent powers—e.g. to give denominational religious instruction.

The fees of the school are, naturally, some thirty pounds a year below the cost.

The second method of using independent schools rests with the local authorities. Where the local authority has insufficient grammar school accommodation of its own, it may meet the grammar school needs of an area by a contract with the nearest independent school. This situation occurs in country areas, where there may be no school, or where the demand is insufficient to justify the provision of a complete state grammar school. It also occurs in heavily populated town areas, where the demand is great, and such arrangements are a supplement to local authority schools. Such schemes exist on a large scale with Dulwich College in South-east London, in Bedford county and town and until recently in Coventry, where there is an unusually generous supply of independent day schools. No conditions, or no standard conditions are attached, as far as the school is concerned. The school reserves a part of its entry for the local authority, and the latter pays the fees, and any supplementary charges, such as for books, which it may approve.

The state works by a system of alliance with independent bodies in its provision of adult education. University Extra-Mural departments and each district of the Worker's Educational Association are regarded as separate 'Responsible Bodies' by the Ministry. They organize courses themselves, and appoint their own lecturers, and are aided, when the courses are of a standard approved by the Ministry, by grants equal to 75 per cent of the fees and travelling expenses of the lecturers.

The Universities

Public finance of universities is in general on a different basis, and takes two forms: first, the provision of scholarships or grants to students; and second, direct grants to universities. The provision of aid to students may take various forms—supplementing with a maintenance grant a scholarship financed by private funds, state scholarships, Ministry of Education grants to intending teachers, local authority scholarships and grants, either supplementary or full. All such grants are subject to a means test, and the national grants come through the Ministry of Education. The local awards are grant-aided by the Ministry, but the principles on which they are awarded are the concern of the local authority, and there may be considerable differences in the methods and the scale of such awards between different authorities. But both national and local grants work through a system of private enterprise, and have the effect of increasing effective demand for education. They give money to those who haven't sufficient, and who want to go to a university, and are thought worthy to study there.

The direct grant to universities is under the guidance, if not control, of a unique institution—the University Grants Committee, which consists mainly of university teachers, though not appointed as or acting as representatives. The committee is strictly advisory to the Treasury, but its advice carries considerable weight, and is based on inspection and visitation of all universities and colleges at the period when they are preparing their quinquennial estimates. After discussion with each university, a recommended grant for a five-year period is decided on, and if the Treasury accepts the recommendation, it is paid. There is no detailed accountancy of the money so spent, as is the case with Government departments: Parliament approves a global sum, and universities have considerable though not absolute discretion in the spending of it. Hence it is a departure from the usual practices involved in the principle of democratic control of public money. It would be impossible to generalize about the principles on which the grant is based beyond saying that the committee tries to assess both the needs and the qualities of each institution, and may, in addition to its general grant, allot earmarked grants to particular universities for particular purposes. By and large, the grants to universities are a system of aid without control: they do not displace private financial independence, nor do they impose conditions on it, like the direct grant regulations for schools—to a very large extent, universities remain financially and academically independent.

The Incidence of State Provision

From this brief summary of the facts of the situation, we may distinguish two main forms of state provision of education. First, the state may provide education in its own schools and institutions, fully under its own control. Second, it may work, in one way or another, through a system of private enterprise in education. The incidence of either form of state provision may be seen by contrasting it with the situation which would exist if education were left entirely to private enterprise. And the starting-point of such a comparison is to analyse the nature of the demand for education.

The Nature of the Demand

To the economist, and to the supplier of any article under a system of private enterprise, ' demand ' means ' effective demand '—that is, it consists of people who want something and who have the money to pay for it. In private-enterprise education, therefore, ' effective demand ' consists of those parents who want education for their children and who are able and willing to pay for it. But there is one important difference between the demand for education and the demand for other commodities and services. When a man wants a motor-car, and can buy one, thus constituting an ' effective demand ' for motor-cars, he uses it himself, and is *directly* satisfied or dissatisfied with his purchase. He himself wanted it, and he himself can judge how far his purchase satisfies his want. It is otherwise with education: it is the parent who wants and pays for the education, it is the child who receives it, but it is the parent who has to judge whether he is satisfied with his purchase. The relationship between demand and its satisfaction in education is therefore an indirect one, and private enterprise in education rests essentially on the assumption that the parent is capable of assessing the real value of the education which his child receives, and of adjusting his ' effective demand ' accordingly.

This assumption is rarely, if ever, entirely valid, and very little reflection is needed to see that it may often be very wide of the mark. Since the parent does not himself receive the education, he must be guided by what he takes to be the signs, symptoms, or hall-marks of good education either in his child or, commonly, in the institution providing the education. He may thus value good manners more than rapid progress in science, physical development more than a knowledge of the classics, the boys whom his son meets more than either factor. He may like the appearance of a school with an ancient and attractive main building, he may find the head master, housemaster, or form-master congenial and pleasant people, he may enjoy a good dramatic performance put on by the school, or he may find the Sunday-evening chapel service impressive and worthy of respect. He may, more rarely, value the examination successes of the school, but he is unlikely to compare them with those of other schools. Similarly, he may know something of the careers record of the school, but, again, he is unlikely to compare it with those of other schools. He may be a schoolmaster in a state school who automatically assumes that an independent school will be better in every way than his own. He may be an educational psychologist who periodically tests the ' Intelligence ' of his child, and assesses his progress accordingly.

In all these cases, the parent is doing his best according to his lights. Not being the recipient of the education he has purchased, he pays attention to its hall-marks. Where these hall-marks are approximately a true indication of the value of the education given, then the parental demand is a genuine demand for education. Where they are not, then the demand is not for education, but for what appears to the parent to be education, and supply will be adjusted accordingly to produce not education but what parents think are the signs of education. To this extent, there is a diversion of resources which purport to provide education, from providing education proper to providing something else.

The parental demand for education is not the only demand for education in any community. The community itself may demand education, in that it wants skilled scientists and technicians, or able administrators. It may feel that, to maximize its economic welfare, no talents or abilities in any individual member of the community, which may be put to its service, should be allowed to waste untrained and uncultivated. It may want all citizens in a democracy to be literate. Under pure private enterprise such a demand may exist, but be ineffective, not because the community does not value it and would not be prepared to pay for it, but because its value to an individual cannot be computed, and therefore there is no *individual* effective demand—an essential condition of supply under private enterprise.

Lying behind these two conceptions of demand, there may be fundamentally different conceptions of what constitutes ' economic welfare ': that it means, on the one hand, ' what individuals want '; or, on the other, ' what individuals ought to have if their material welfare is to be maximized '. Although the problem may be looked at in this light, it is unnecessary to do so, for it has always been recognized, even by the most classical of economists and the most rigid individualists, that there is, for certain things like law and order, a communal demand which cannot be satisfied by the mechanism of private enterprise. It is fairly clear that education comes in part, though not entirely, into this category. It cannot be denied that there is a communal demand for education, but this by itself can also lead to difficulties. The state may, in satisfaction of the communal demand, select and try to educate the ablest children. But if these children are unwilling to learn, and uninterested in a lengthy period of education, if they leave before their courses are completed and prefer to earn a living, then the resources devoted to them have been very largely wasted. Education, in fact, is a service for which there is both an individual and a communal demand, and it is in relation to both that we must consider various methods of supplying it.

The price of supplying education under private enterprise, as of supplying everything else, must cover the costs, and, other things being equal, there will be an incentive to keep those costs as low as possible. It may be noticed at the outset that these costs will probably vary significantly in different localities. A rural area where children have to travel to school adds the cost of transport to the parents' bill and to the true cost of education. A densely populated area avoids this, but may have other effects. Large schools with resulting economies are possible, and perhaps better education in the form of a larger variety of Sixth Form courses can be supplied at a lower cost, owing to the more economic staff-pupil ratio obtained. But land may be costly, because in demand from industry and housing, and so also may be the incidence of rates in such areas. Academic staff may be expensive, because a district is unattractive to live in, or because, being overcrowded, the cost of housing is high. Finally, if the area is poor, the demand for education may be low. By contrast, a less populous but more wealthy area, constituting a higher effective demand, will tend to get more educational resources devoted to it. The high demand balances the higher costs of running a medium-size school. And some of these costs may not be higher, if the district attracts academic staff by reason of, for instance, the proximity of a university. All these factors, taken together with the local variations in effective demand, will influence the geographical distribution of resources for education under private enterprise.

Private Enterprise

A school under private enterprise conducts its affairs like any other undertaking in private enterprise—it tries to get the maximum return for its expenditure by making the most efficient use possible of its buildings, staff, and other resources. It is running at optimum efficiency if by no conceivable change in its allocation of resources could it increase its output of education, if we may so describe it. Such a distribution of resources is individual to each school : each school allocates resources to suit the particular parental market it is dealing with at any given time. A consequence of this is that academic and financial decisions are to a large extent in the hands of a single authority—the head master and his governors. Since most academic decisions have a financial side to them, this may be regarded as an advantage : not only the desirability of academic changes is considered, but how far they are worth the cost, when balanced against competing claims on scarce resources. Thus private enterprise in education means that each school acts as an individual unit with considerable flexibility in the way in which it allocates resources, and with financial responsibility for its decisions. But it must always be remembered that its allocation of resources is in satisfaction of *parental* demand, which, as we saw, may diverge considerably from being a genuine demand for education. An optimum arrangement of resources in satisfaction of parental demands must not therefore be equated with an optimum arrangement of resources in satisfaction of the true demand for education.

Where private enterprise provides a boarding and not a day school, it is automatically in competition with all other boarding schools in the country, and, to the extent that the competition is perfect, all schools are impelled to keep their costs and therefore their fees as low as possible.   The allegiance of Old Boys, and of particular groups associated with the foundation of particular schools, may render this competition imperfect, but it is none the less there, with boarding schools, for the whole country is their potential market.   A day school, on the other hand, serves a limited local market, and monopoly conditions may easily arise.   If the effective demand for grammar school education in an area is only sufficient to make one school pay, then that school can charge monopoly fees, and gain a monopoly profit over its costs.   This situation can occur widely, owing to the fact that one grammar school can be as small as three hundred pupils, or as large as one thousand pupils, and still remain one unit.   Large towns might produce competition, but they might also produce agreed fees between several schools.   Rural areas might be at the mercy of one school, but, if between two towns, they might get the advantages of competition between them.   Generally speaking, day-school education tends to produce monopoly conditions.

Direct Grant Schools

With these considerations in mind, we can turn to the first kind of state provision of education, *through* the private-enterprise system, but not displacing it.   Part of this aid may increase not effective demand, but the possibility of effective demand; this would be true of income-tax rebates to parents, irrespective of whether they spent the money on education.   Part of the aid directly increases effective demand; this is true of scholarships and grants to universities or to independent schools, for they reduce the price of education.   In both cases the system of private enterprise remains unchanged except by the factor of increased effective demand.

The Direct Grant regulations in England go further than this.   They start with a thirty pounds *per capita* grant for each pupil.   Although this is made to the school, it has the same effect as a scholarship to the parent, and it increases effective demand by making possible a reduction in fees.   In part, the forty pounds per pupil in the Sixth Form has the same result: it does not produce lower fees for Sixth Form pupils, but the pupil gets more expensive education in return for the same fee.   But it also affects the school's distribution of resources and encourages it to build up large Sixth Forms.   Owing to the staff-pupil ratios involved, a large Sixth Form is, in any case, more economic to run than a small one, and if in addition the school's grant increases with the size of the Sixth Form, the financial advantages are multiplied.

Thus, on the supply side, this grant diverts resources from pure satisfaction of parental demand to a more relevant element in good grammar school education.

Still more important are two other conditions imposed upon Direct Grant grammar schools. The first is that the fees charged are approved and controlled by the Ministry of Education : this prevents the exaction of a monopoly price and limits public liabilities in respect of free places and aid to ' residuary ' place-holders. The second is that the boys admitted must be at least the same standard in ability as would secure them a grammar school place in the area : this has the effect of diverting the private demand for education until it is identified with the communal demand—that is, limited to the able boys whom, in any case, the community would want to educate. Taken in conjunction with the other results of the direct grant, this is very important. The *per capita* grant means lower fees for everyone. The subsidy to needy parents still further increases effective demand. The minimum standard exacted reduces demand by an educational not a financial criterion, and it becomes the able children of keen parents who are the pupils of direct grant grammar schools. This is perhaps, in the end, the truest of all the demands for education.

State provision of education by means of state-owned schools is not subject to the price-mechanism, and is consequently not influenced by the effective demand of parents. It has to rely upon some other test than the test of the market—those wanting education and able and willing to pay for it. And, since public education is usually conceived as a service to the community, it is with the communal rather than the private demand for education that it is preoccupied. In pursuance of this aim, it offers education to those able to profit from it, irrespective of parental desire and ability to pay. Hence state education necessarily depends upon some system of diagnosis by which the able children are selected. To be fully effective, it would also need a system for selecting the keen children as well as the able, so that education was not provided for those who were indifferent to it, or more interested in earning their living at the earliest opportunity. To some extent, the test of the market provides this test of keenness, in private enterprise : a parent who pays for education may be presumed to value it, and it is probably correct to infer a similar attitude in his children. The state may, by selecting the able, still get keen pupils, but it has no test by which to judge keenness, and it may therefore select ability combined with indolence or indifference.[4]

---

[4] This is also possible with the ' free ' places in Direct Grant Schools.

Local Authority Control

Owing to the system of grants in aid, the state is free to distribute its educational facilities as it wishes among different localities : in this respect it has a distinct advantage over private enterprise. It may, if it wishes, give the advantage to the wealthy areas, on the grounds that they pay most of the taxes. It may allocate more than proportionate provision to expanding industrial areas, to attract people to live there, and to provide skilled labour for the future. Or it may follow a policy of providing equal opportunity for education in all areas.

With state education in England, the responsible authority is the county or county borough, with few exceptions. The financial unit is not the school, but the local education authority : this body is responsible for both raising and spending the money. Since each body deals with a large number of schools,[5] it can obtain the advantages of bulk purchase of things like stationery, and may be a monopoly demand, or quasi-monopoly demand for certain kinds of building. But with the unit being the local authority and not the school, there is also, partly as a consequence of bulk purchase, a tendency to standardization in provision of education. All schools in an area may be built to the same design, by the same firm. More than this, improvements required for a school tend to be regarded in the same standardized form, as improvements required for all grammar schools or all primary schools. For instance, all grammar schools in an area may require improved laboratory facilities, and also new kitchen canteens, owing to the expansion of school meals. This will normally be regarded as a general demand, not as a demand from each individual school. A general decision may be taken, in itself perfectly correct, to build laboratories. But with an individual school, with a small Science Sixth Form, but an increased rural catchment area expanding the need for school meals, this is not the best allocation of resources; it is, in fact, uneconomic as regards the needs of that particular school. Again, the decision of the authority may equally be to build neither laboratories nor canteens because the cost is too great. But the cost which tends to be considered is not the cost of one but of several laboratories, or canteens. Or, it may decide to build both for all : with individual schools this may be extravagant provision of something for which there is only a small demand.

A second characteristic of local authority control of the supply of education is that the final responsible decisions must always be made

---

[5] Local authorities vary considerably in the number of their schools from large counties like Lancashire (forty-five grammar schools) to small county boroughs like West Hartlepool (two grammar schools).

by a lay, and not a professional, body. Public money is being spent, and public money must be under democratic control—under the control of the elected county councillors. The limited time which such people have to give to public affairs increases the tendency to give standardized decisions rather than individual decisions for individual schools. It also means that there is some inflexibility in time: estimates are considered once a year, and tend to remain fixed for that period. Finally, being lay controlled, the decisions may not always be wise ones. The principal danger is that the lay body is dependent upon professional advice in deciding what is desirable in the way of educational improvements. It has too often to accept the opinion of the expert, and, in doing so, finds it difficult to judge, not whether something is desirable, but *how* desirable it is, compared with other things. There may be an element of irresponsible decision in this way : things are provided if thought desirable, with less counting of the cost, and with less accurate balancing of competing claims, than would take place under professional control. In all these ways the allocation of resources will usually be less than the optimum one within each individual school.

General Reflections

The crux of the matter in state-owned and controlled education lies therefore in two factors; first, that the responsible financial authority deals with an area and not with a school; and, second, that it is an elected non-professional body. These two factors are interdependent. It would be possible to avoid the first by strengthening the powers of head teachers and of their particular governing bodies. But this would collide with the second principle, for, to the extent to which head teachers and governing bodies gained power, so would the democratic body lose it. Yet, in the light of this discussion, the efficiency of state education in meeting either the parental or the communal demand for education is questionable. The principle of democratic control of public money and the methods of strict accountancy have a long history behind them, and have lain at the root of many constitutional conflicts. But, in modern times, the extent and objects of public expenditure differ so radically from those of earlier days, when this principle was formulated, that we may well have to adopt a less rigid attitude. In England the Universities Grants Committee with the universities, and the Direct Grant system with the schools, are examples of the kind of compromise which can be affected.

Some compromise may equally be necessary on the side of taxation. Education is but a small part of the modern budget, but the total tax burden is so heavy that the modern community looks askance at suggestions for increased taxation, and is ever clamorous for a reduc-tion. The result is, as many will testify, that services such as educa-tion get less than they require for their efficient operation. The real difficulty lies in the nature of the demand for education : since it is neither individual nor communal, the satisfaction of communal de-mand by state education brings benefits which can be imputed to individuals unlike the benefits of purely communal goods like national defence. In these circumstances, unsatisfied private demand—the parents who send their children to independent schools—is less and less willing to finance by taxation an extension of the range and quality of public education. To such parents its incidence on the private demand for education too often appears to be capricious, and the only safe way lies in private enterprise arrangements. A possible compromise is to finance public education by a composite charge—in part a tax, falling on all according to their means, in part a price, falling on the user, just as the water rate is compounded of a basic tax, and an excess price. This is really what is involved in the Direct Grant system. Taxation pays for the *per capita* grants, and for the subsidies according to means. The parent in addition pays a price, according to the sub-sidized fees. An extension of such compromise methods might well increase and improve state provision of education by making greater funds more readily available.

In the light of this discussion, neither private enterprise nor public education is wholly satisfactory. Private enterprise is efficient in allocating resources to meet a given demand, but it does not question this demand, and so it ignores the demand of the poor and may divert resources from education to meet the prejudices and whims of wealthy parents. Public education is not efficient in allocating resources, and it ignores parental demand, and so leaves it unsatisfied, in so far as its efforts to satisfy the communal demand do not coincide with the wishes of parents. If, as we have argued, both demands for education are valid, then it is difficult to see how either method of providing education will be, by itself, satisfactory. It is in the mixed control of state and private enterprise on the one hand, and in the composite finance of tax and price on the other, that the best hope lies for the public provision of education to meet the full demand for it, in the most effective and economic manner.

W. H. BURSTON.

CHAPTER TEN

National Activity and the Tax System in Education: United States

NATIONAL activity in the United States shows a distinct tendency towards integration and concentration. Almost every business has extended its interests beyond local boundaries; many are organized on a nation-wide basis. The educational system, including its tax machine, has remained decentralized, because education is a state activity in the federal system and because states have responded to a strong desire to keep the control of education close to the people by establishing a local governmental and tax system for schools.

In order to view the tax system for education in relation to national activity, three broad areas should be described: the mechanism of control by state and local government, the social and economic forces which impinge on taxation, and the resultant tax system. Although each of the parts is integrated with the others, this article will discuss them in sequence. The first section will describe briefly the system of local control of education and will indicate very generally its meaning for taxation. The second section will summarize some of the social and economic forces which exert pressures upon the tax structure for education. The final section will describe and analyse briefly the actual tax system which has resulted from the interplay of the various pressures mentioned in sections one and two.

The Control of Educational Policy and Taxation

Education is one of the governmental functions which is reserved to the several states by the federal constitution. State constitutions, in turn, generally provide that the state shall establish a system of education. Even though there has been a national policy of encouraging education in territories and in certain special areas of national interest, it remains for the state to determine basic policy for education and to decide upon the method which is to be used to support education. Thus, there are at least forty-eight systems of education in the United States.

Local Control of Education

States, in discharging their responsibility, have chosen to organize local school districts and have delegated to them substantial powers to formulate educational policy and to tax. In so doing, states have responded to an intense feeling on the part of the people in favour of local control. Apparently developed over a long period of time, it is a very potent factor in any considerations dealing with changing the pattern of educational organization. This delegation of responsibility to school districts has created a unique pattern of government. In the next few paragraphs the development of local control will be presented, followed by a brief description of the inter-governmental relations brought about by the creation of school districts.

Development of local control. Local control grew out of colonial efforts to establish schools for children in isolated towns and hamlets along a wilderness frontier. As early as 1647, the Massachusetts Colony required that towns provide for education, and gave them power to tax in order to support it. Later colonial and early state laws provided for the formation of school districts and gave their governing boards power to tax to support education, and power to supervise and control policy. Because the population was relatively isolated, due to poor transportation, districts were frequently organized to provide education for children in a neighbourhood within walking distance of a one-room school. These school districts were often smaller than the units through which the few other governmental services that were needed at the time functioned.

Control of policy and taxation for education were intimately connected in the early school districts; the same board exercised both powers. Generally speaking, schools enjoyed considerable freedom to spend money on the things local citizens thought worth while, without much reference to other governing authorities. Citizens, through their representatives, could tax themselves according to their willingness to pay and their desire for the service. The conviction has grown that this is the genius of the educational system in the United States. A strong tradition has developed to keep the control of policy close to the home; people feel that they want a strong voice in how their children are educated and that they want educational authorities to be highly responsive to their wishes. There is a definite conviction that local school boards are more responsible and responsive in their planning for schools if all or part of the funds required to support their plans are raised locally. Many people also feel that citizens take greater interest in efficient and effective school operation when they pay directly for schools by local taxation. Because local control is highly valued, some small school districts have persisted even though it has been clearly demonstrated that they are too small to provide adequate facilities. Even when they are reorganized, the desire to give citizens a voice in educational policy has tended to keep school districts independent of other local governments.

The school district and its relation to other levels of government. School districts derive their powers from the state, not from the federal government. Districts operate the schools, therefore, within the limits of a definite framework, which is delineated by a number of regulations and mandates. For example, states make substantial grants to local school districts and give them power to tax. However, districts have usually been restricted to a few specific taxes, primarily the general property tax; and a ceiling has sometimes been placed on the tax rate. In most states, local districts are expected to raise the major proportion of school funds through local taxation. In fact, state grants are looked upon as aids to districts rather than as the state's fair share of educational expense.

It is also necessary to see the school district in relation to other local governments to understand the financial situation. As a general rule, school districts are separate governing units which are not related to other local government. They may be conterminous with other units, but this is more the exception than the rule. The school district's power to tax is also independent of powers to tax which have been delegated to other units. Instead of a single local level of government, there are in the United States several, each operating under its own grant of power from the state. It is not unusual, for example, to find a school district embracing several other governmental units or a city divided into several school districts. Thus, a taxpayer may well be paying as many as five or six different local taxes upon his property.

In summary, there is a separate local government for schools which establishes educational policies, decides how much money is needed for the school, and levies taxes upon the district according to the amounts needed. There are varying degrees of autonomy, depending upon the location of the district. The important fact is that there is neither a national tax system for schools nor in all respects is there a state tax system for schools. The system is based, in fact, upon some hundred thousand small units, most of them with some sort of independent tax powers.

Changes in the Social and Economic Structure which affect Taxation for Education

Population changes have created many pressures upon the tax system for education. Small local tax jurisdictions are affected more severely than regional or national jurisdictions by population shifts. If the tax jurisdiction for education corresponded with the nation or

with regions like a metropolitan area which show marked integration, the problem created by population change would be minimized.

There has been a tremendous increase in population in the United
States since 1800. Recent spurts indicate that this increase will continue. The more people there are, the more education will cost.
Hence, more money must be raised by taxation. If the wealth or
income against which taxes are levied does not change proportionately,
taxes will bear more or less heavily upon the taxpayer. The likelihood
of disproportionate changes in taxable wealth and population growth
is greater when tax jurisdictions are small. Many school districts
where taxable wealth is stable have found that an increase in population has brought with it a growing tax burden. Even in units as large
as a state, growth in population may have a similar effect.

The age-composition of the population also changes. Lately there
has been an increasing number of older people in the population and
an increasing number of very young. Proportionately, the working-
age population has decreased, and the burden of supporting the non-
working population has begun to fall upon a relatively smaller group.
To-day the working group must, therefore, spend more of its efforts
than previously doing this. Since the old and young use more of the
tax-supported facilities like schools and hospitals, there is an increasing
need for tax money from this comparatively small taxpaying group.

The most persistent general population shift has been from rural
regions to urban centres. For rural districts this meant a decline in
school population which, provided wealth did not decline faster than
population, lessened, up to a point, the tax burden. But when school
populations are small, schools tend to be economically inefficient.
Loss in efficiency can cause school costs to rise and force an increase
in taxation upon the remaining rural residents. Urban centres, on the
other hand, get more people and face the consequent problem of providing more of everything. The greater complexity of urban life
requires an extension of school services—such as attendance enforce-
ment—and of other governmental services, all of which increase the
tax burden. In the last two or three decades there has been a movement of population towards the periphery of urban centres, which has
increased the need for new services there, consequently increasing the
tax burden. The urban centre which has lost population may find its
tax problems compounded. It must still pay for capital improvements
which were installed to accommodate the larger population, but some
of that population has escaped its responsibility for paying by moving
away; those who remain must pay higher taxes. If the urban population has maintained its size by in-migration to offset the out-migration,
the former is usually a poorer group than the one it replaced. The

new population has less ability to pay taxes and may also have greater needs for public welfare. The result of this shift in population is often a heavier tax burden in the urban centre.

With suburbanization there has been a tendency to form homogeneous communities, each with a specialized function relating to the region; thus, people live in one section and work in another. School districts and other governmental units cut the integrated area into illogical pieces. Some communities are able to raise large amounts by taxation, but have little need to do so; others need money, and except by taxes at confiscatory levels cannot raise enough locally.

A further compounding of the population problem arises when racial and ethnic minorities are introduced into any area. In order to induct them into the prevailing culture, a greater expenditure is often required. But the tendency to discriminate against strangers and people unlike oneself operates to prevent an increase in taxes to help such groups integrate and acquire greater work efficiency through education. Lack of opportunity tends to reduce the minorities' economic capacity and their ability to help themselves by taxation. A pattern of poverty which is difficult to overcome is set up in one part of the district or region which sooner or later affects other parts and lowers the economic capacity of the whole.

Changes in the Economy

There has been a remarkable growth in the economy. For about fifty years there has been an average increase of 2 to 3 per cent in the national product each year. Whatever its cause, this growth in productivity has made possible an increasing standard of living which has brought with it marked changes in patterns of daily living and personal expenditure. Viewed locally, economic growth has generally favoured the tax system, but growth has been unequal and some communities declined in taxable wealth, especially where natural resources have been exhausted or new methods of production have caused industries to migrate.

Growth has been accompanied by a change in the nature of the economy. As a rural agrarian nation the value of property was clearly related to its ability to produce, and property ownership was a good indication of wealth. Now the United States has become one of the great manufacturing nations. This change helped to shift the economy towards a money one, where wealth is more likely to be represented by the contents of a safe-deposit vault than by land, and where good will and a sound credit rating are avidly sought. Moreover, the value of goods produced in a factory is more likely to be related to the time and effort put into their production than to the value of the land or buildings and equipment used. An increasing proportion of the population derives its income from wages—spent in a variety of ways other than in the accumulation of property. The effect of the shift to a money economy upon property as an indicator of wealth and as the chief base of taxation is rather obvious. Tax limitations and district organization force schools to tax property, yet property holdings are becoming less tangible and more difficult to locate and assess, while other values are becoming important as indices of ability to pay. Districts where people are ' wealthy ' are faced with great difficulty in taxing the evidences of this ' wealth '.

A concentration of economic power is found in the modern corporation, which has become the device for organizing the huge quantities of labour, capital, and material necessary in the modern manufacturing processes. Control of these resources automatically gives power to the corporation. Decisions made by a board of directors far away from the manufacturing location greatly influence economic developments there, yet localities are unable to participate in these decisions. Corporate powers transcend political boundaries, and corporations can rather easily arrange their operations to avoid local taxation on any indications of wealth other than real property.

Increased productivity per worker has made it possible to release people to spend their time either in leisure or in service-type occupations. The problem of taxing the part of the nation's wealth represented by the services which one person performs for another is quite different from that of taxing property.

The national economy to-day is more than ever based upon consumer wants. To fulfil their part, consumers must be induced to spend, and to do so must have highly liquid assets. Since the average consumer has relatively few savings, the key need is for credit with which to buy durable goods. The result has been a marked increase in consumer credit. There is hardly any ordinary citizen who does not owe several merchants and dealers in his community some money and who is not paying against a loan from a bank or other financial institution. Pay-checks are allocated to weekly and monthly payments for this or that as soon as they are received. Pressured day and night to expand his spending and promised easy-payment terms, the average taxpayer has committed his income for many months in advance. The pressure, of course, stresses material gains. Taxes for education are unwelcome, because they reduce the amount that can be spent according to individual tastes and because education does not produce immediate material gains. The continual efforts to show the material value of education in order to 'sell' it to the people are one result of this economic situation. Local districts feel the effects of instalment-plan living a little more than other levels of government because they have not yet hit upon instalment-plan taxation—exemplified by income taxes which are deducted from the weekly pay-check.

Another illustration of economic change, or rather of a force directing and influencing it, is the rapid improvement in transportation and communication. This has brought about much greater interdependence among communities of a particular region. Production and distribution facilities have been relocated so that they are advantageously related to markets, supplies, and labour forces. Since industry now has a wider choice in selecting the location of a plant, and since the latter's presence is economically advantageous, communities compete with each other to encourage corporations to locate within their borders. The inducement is sometimes in the form of a tax exemption. Larger tax jurisdictions are less inclined than smaller ones to offer inducements. Almost every jurisdiction smaller than the nation, however, is conscious that its tax structure may encourage or discourage new economic developments within its borders.

Even if there were no variations from place to place in the impact of economic change and growth, there would still remain the problem of adjusting local tax systems to variations in rates of growth and erratic fluctuations like deflation and inflation. Because they must balance the budget for operating expenses, school districts find a sudden change in the economy sharply affects their ability to raise money. This is especially true since property (on which much of the money is raised) is notoriously slow to respond to inflation and deflation. During inflation the people have money to pay, but the tax base does not reflect the increase. High tax-rates are needed to produce sufficient revenue for schools, but legal limitations on the tax-rate and taxpayer reluctance may make it impossible to increase rates enough to produce the required income. During deflation there is less actual ability to pay, but values remain high and seem capable of providing enough money, yet when taxes are levied at a high rate during deflation, tax delinquency increases and districts fail to raise the money they need.

Increasing Impact of the Federal Government

The outstanding change in governmental activity in recent years has been the increasing power of the national or federal government. In 1914, only about 25 per cent of all tax moneys were levied and collected by the federal government, now 75 per cent of them are so collected. This increase reflects both the greater efficiency of the federal tax machine and the very much higher level of federal spending. More and more commerce has become inter-state in nature and has come within the power of national government to regulate and to tax. Extensive spending for national defence has made the federal government one of private industry's biggest customers. Its pay-roll is by far the largest in the nation. The federal government, indeed, now has a tremendous influence upon the economy. Local districts are, of course, indirectly affected by this in many ways. The effect upon willingness to pay taxes is, however, quite direct. When the taxpayer is faced with heavy federal taxation, he is likely to look askance at increases in his local tax bill. Since he can more directly control the level of local taxation, he is inclined to put the brakes on local spending to offset the increase he feels in national taxation. Almost all taxes are paid from income, and income that is used to pay federal taxes is not available to pay local taxes.

The Development of the School Tax System

The changes in the social and economic conditions previously described have placed several demands upon the school tax system. Most important is the need to raise more money. The proportion of the national income spent on education has remained about the same, between $2\frac{1}{2}$ and 3 per cent, during the past twenty or thirty years, but the actual sums spent have more than doubled. Over-all increases in expenditure and changes in the relative value of different forms of wealth create a need for higher taxes and different taxation structures. Changing patterns of living and economic integration require either new tax jurisdictions, which correspond to regions, or taxation by central government. Not all of these demands can be met simply by changing the tax system. Sometimes the desire for local control conflicts with the most straightforward method of revising the tax system. Sometimes political considerations are more important than improving the tax system. The tax system for schools is, therefore, the resultant of an interplay of factors. It revolves about the word property tax.

Tests of a Sound Tax System

There are four general tests which provide a rough idea of whether a particular tax or tax system is sound. Each of them will be illustrated as it applies to the general property tax. Briefly stated the tests are : Is the tax adequate; does it raise enough revenue? Is the tax efficient to administer? Is the tax equitable? What are the economic effects of the tax? It should not be inferred that a tax which fails to meet these tests should be discarded or is useless. Whether or not a particular tax is put into practice depends upon the specific purpose for which it is designed. Thus, a federal tax upon gamblers has been imposed even though gambling is illegal in most states. The principal aim of this tax is to provide a convenient legal weapon against gambling.

The Property Tax

The most effective tax which a small tax jurisdiction can levy is the property tax. Historically, local government has made extensive use of it. In 1932, about 80 per cent of local school revenue came from the property tax: to-day between 45 and 50 per cent. It will probably remain the key tax in local systems because it is one of the easiest to administer and can produce substantial revenue.

Briefly, the property tax is usually an *ad valorem* tax upon all property, real and personal, tangible and intangible; it is a direct and impersonal tax. Exemptions have in a few cases reduced the base of taxation, so that in some places property tax has come to mean a tax on real estate only.

Adequacy of the property tax. Tax adequacy may be phrased as the question: " Will the tax raise enough money?" In terms of modern tax theory as applied to the national economy this is an over-simplification, but for a local system, where control of the economy is not a practical consideration, the concept is useful.

The property tax is generally adequate; however, it no longer brings in enough revenue to carry the whole burden of education. Many of the social and economic forces already discussed act to limit its adequacy. On the other hand, changes in the tax system have been made to counter-balance these forces and restore its vigour. One of the most difficult problems is the unequal distribution of property values among school districts. As a result of this distribution, some districts find the property tax inadequate while others are able to raise money with great ease. Generally speaking, this tax can be made more adequate when the taxing jurisdiction is increased in size; this is, of course, an averaging process but it effectively taps the resources of extremely wealthy, small districts which would ordinarily apply very low rates of taxation to raise the money they need. Increasing the size of a tax jurisdiction works contrary to the principle of local control; as size increases local control will at some point become ineffective. As mentioned, property taxes also tend to be inadequate during periods of rapid economic change, especially during inflation or deflation. This inadequacy is due to the stability of the tax; ordinarily one of its strong points as a locally administered tax.

School districts face several limitations; many of the consequent problems could be overcome only by extensive governmental reorganization. States, as has been pointed out, place limits on the rates which may be applied by school districts and exempt from taxation certain types of property and certain classes of taxpayer. Both reduce the adequacy of the property tax. Other local governing units, also, use the same property-tax base as the school district. The property tax must, therefore, be considered in terms of adequacy to support all local government rather than schools alone, even when school districts are independent taxing units.

Administering the property tax. A sound tax is one which can be administered efficiently. This is achieved when the cost of collection is small in proportion to the amount of tax collected, when the tax-payer can comply with the tax easily and at low cost in terms of money and time, and when the tax is difficult to avoid or evade.

The property tax is at once easy and difficult to administer. Although there are exceptions, small local units can in general administer it better than any other. Because of this, many experts consider the property tax the key to local control.

The administration of the property tax involves three basic steps: locating the property to be taxed, assessing the value of the property, and levying the tax. Real property is easy to locate; personal property, especially if it is small or easily transported, is more difficult; and intangible property, such as stock certificates, may be nearly impossible to find on assessment day. Unless the assessor can find the property he cannot assess it. Once the property has been located, its accurate valuation is a highly technical job. A large staff of experts and consultants is necessary. It should be pointed out that small local tax jurisdictions seldom have a competent assessor, let alone the staff required to assess properly all forms of property. The result is that most property assessments do not accurately reflect true value. Competitive and political factors also enter into assessment practices. Extremely unhealthy political situations arise where assessors are elected and the assessment of property at a low value becomes a political favour.

Generally speaking, however, a real property tax can be administered fairly well. Taxes on other forms of property, on the other hand, are not as easy to administer.

Equitability of the property tax. Although the equitability of a tax is related to the ethical standard of the time, there is general agreement now that a tax ought to accord equal tax treatment to those taxpayers who are in similar economic positions, and that it ought to relate either to the ability to pay the tax or to the amount of benefit received from the service supported by the tax. On the whole, a well-administered property tax may be reasonably equitable in a local tax system. A school does provide a benefit to the people of a community, but the relation of this benefit to the value of property is not so clear-cut, for example, as the provision of a water system. The benefit from education is diffuse and accrues to the people of neighbouring school districts and to the nation generally as well as to the home district. The property tax for schools is, therefore, not necessarily equitable in relation to benefit. Ability to pay taxes has generally been considered closely related to property ownership, but as ability to perform services for others has become important in the economy, property ownership has become a less important measure. There is some evidence that the property tax bears more heavily upon low-income groups and is, therefore, regressive or inversely related to ability. It is not clear whether this regressiveness is the result of poor administration or the result of inherent qualities of the tax.

Furthermore, in evaluating ability to pay, what must be determined is who pays the property tax or, in the technical sense, the incidence of the tax. Does the taxpayer, against whose property the tax is levied, shift all or part of the tax to someone else? Experts tend to agree that the extent of this is small except in the case of rental and corporately owned properties. When property is sold, however, the buyer may insist upon a lower price than otherwise would be expected in anticipation of the effect of taxation upon his return from the property. Tax capitalization such as this is a kind of shifting. Judged on the basis of ability to pay, the property tax is inequitable to the degree that assessment is poorly done, and to the degrees to which shifting is possible and to which some taxpayers enjoy exemptions not available to others. However, if exemptions are clearly related to ability to pay, as in the case of disabled workers, the exemption may be considered equitable.

Effects of property tax upon the economy. One of the tests of the desirability of a tax is its expected effect on the economy. The fact that school districts are small units without co-ordinated tax policies and limited to a few taxes makes this test of minor importance, excepting the possibility that some individuals and corporations will move to avoid high property taxation. But property taxation for schools does tend to affect the use of other tax devices by the nation to regulate the national economy. Since districts must, because of legal restriction, live within their means much as a family does, they tend to tax less than is desirable from a national regulatory point of view during inflation and more during deflation. Given this generalization, appropriate compensatory measures can be taken provided the cost of local government does not fluctuate much more widely than do other costs and values. Locally, the level of taxation on property may encourage or discourage a particular type of activity. Undoubtedly, high taxation upon property within a central city area may influence some concerns to move towards the lower-tax suburban regions. A kind of rough justice applies, however, for employees soon move to the same area, bringing greater demands for services and consequently higher taxation, often even higher than taxes paid in the city. Only by moving to districts of high industrial concentration and low residential density do commercial activities find refuge from property taxes at high rates.

Improving the property tax. Actually, many of the faults of property taxation for schools rise from the fact that school districts are small local units. But since local control is considered essential, and since, therefore, relatively small size is inevitable, the faults cannot be corrected solely by district reorganization. Administration of the property tax has been improved substantially by making state units responsible for assessment and by giving the assessor a civil service status, free of political control. Local control does not suffer, because the local district still decides how much money is to be raised and levies the tax accordingly. It is so difficult even for trained assessors to locate and assess personal property that some states have entirely exempted such property from taxation. The tax base is thus reduced and some method of compensating for the loss is required. The real property tax, however, comes much closer to meeting the specification of a good tax than the general property tax. Some consideration has also been given to exempting certain classes of real property from local taxation, making them taxable only by the state. This device can be used to reduce the advantage of industrial concentration in a few low-tax-rate districts.

State Assistance to Improve Local Tax Structure

State grants. State grants or state aid to local school districts have become one of the most common and most effective ways of improving the local tax situation. They have proved useful in solving the problem of providing sufficient funds for school districts while still maintaining local control. In this way, the state's greater taxing powers are made available to the school district and the state's ability to collect more efficiently certain types of taxes is also tapped.

Broadly speaking, there are three general types of state grant: equalization grants, lump-sum grants, and matching grants. Equalization grants reduce inequality by taking into account local ability to raise taxes and local need. Need is usually measured by the number of children to be educated. Low-ability districts are granted more funds than high-ability districts of equal need. Equalization aid treats districts in such a way that education is supported as though they all had equal tax resources. Lump-sum grants allocate a fixed sum of money for each unit of need regardless of wealth. All districts get some tax help under this sort of grant, but wealthier districts tend to benefit more, in proportion to their actual need for money, than do poor ones. Matching grants provide that the state will contribute in proportion to the local contribution. If a locality raises one-half of the money for a service, the state may agree to grant the other half. This relieves the burden only in those districts which can, in the first place, tax themselves enough to raise their share of the cost. Matching grants also encourage expenditure on unnecessary local services. In this way, tax money may be drained from worthy projects and spent on non-essentials.

Each of the foregoing methods of granting state moneys to local districts has its particular advantages. Most states use some combination of them, depending upon their fiscal policy. The important thing is that grants do not supplant local taxation. Local taxation remains as the key to control. Districts remain free to spend their moneys as they choose and to raise taxes locally to provide services which they think are important. On the other hand, the state's greater ability to tax is effectively used to support education in a decentralized system. Grants can also be used in the same way to bring the greater taxing powers of the federal government to the assistance of the states.

Sharing state taxes. Another way in which the state may help overcome some of the local tax system's administration difficulties is to levy and collect the tax and return all or part of the money to the district in which it was collected. This method reduces competitive taxation among local units and provides much more effective administration of taxes on sales and income. There is, however, considerable difficulty involved in returning the tax to the place of its collection. Actually, the lump-sum technique of granting state money is generally used as a device to share taxes collected by the state. This technique, as was pointed out before, gives some districts more money than they need, while others get too little.

Shifting governmental functions from the local towards the state level. Some services and functions of the government can be performed much more effectively at a more central level than the local district. If the state assigns some of these activities—maintenance of highways, for example—to another level of government, pressure is removed from the local tax system. In education there has been some shifting. Actually, shifts of activities outside the scope of education have done more to relieve the burden upon local taxation than have shifts in the sphere of education. As functions or services are shifted to other levels, a certain amount of local control is given up, but as long as districts continue to control the major aspects of elementary and secondary education, it is unlikely that people will feel local control has been seriously weakened.

Tax co-ordination. Tax co-ordination is a general term for a number of devices—separation of tax bases, tax deductibility, tax credits, supplemental taxes, and state administration—that a state can adopt to improve the local tax situation. These devices have the general effect of lightening the burden on the local tax-base by reducing the weight of taxation at another level, by making some of the states' ability to levy certain taxes available to the locality, or by increasing the efficiency of tax administration.

There is a trend towards giving local units exclusive use of property taxes by ceasing to levy them at the state level. Separate use of a tax-base by one level of government reduces the burden on the class of taxpayers affected and makes it easier for local government to plan a tax programme commensurate with local taxpaying ability. States and the federal government have also provided that certain taxes paid to one level of government may be deducted from income which is to be taxed at another level. Tax deductibility reduces the net cost of local taxes to the taxpayer. Closely related to deductibility are credit devices which provide that a proportion of a tax paid locally may be credited towards a similar tax levied by the state. Taxpayers must pay the tax no matter which jurisdiction actually gets the proceeds. Tax crediting discourages avoidance by migration from one local jurisdiction to another. The state machinery can be used to collect a tax which is difficult to administer locally if the state permits the locality to add a levy of its own to a state levy on a particular tax-base. The state collects the money and gives the proceeds to the local district. This method is similar to sharing, except that the locality decides how much tax to levy and the state merely acts as a collecting agent for what amounts to a surtax. States may also use their tax machine to help local districts administer taxes. Wisconsin has used a system of state assessment of property very effectively for some time. The local unit benefits from more efficient and accurate property valuation, and saves the cost of maintaining a local assessment system too.

Local Non-property Taxes

States, in their efforts to keep control of taxation in the hands of local authorities, have granted some powers to levy non-property taxes to local governments. Usually the taxes permitted are on sales or on income, but there are other taxes, most of them designed to meet specific local conditions, such as the stock-transfer tax, which makes it possible for New York to tax the transactions of the exchanges in that city. Experts, generally speaking, do not favour the use of local non-property taxes when they devise ideal tax plans. There is, however, a distinct trend towards their use locally. This probably reflects the great need for funds to support local government and to supplement the local property tax.

Non-property taxes produce substantial revenue, especially in large cities and counties. Non-property taxes provide a way to tap economic resources no longer closely related to property values; therefore, they help reach more of the local resources. But difficulties in their use make the non-property tax of questionable value to small local units. Taxes upon retail sales and upon pay-rolls (income taxes collected at their source) are quite easy to administer, but in small jurisdictions avoidance and evasion are likely to be very high. Income earned outside the jurisdiction and from sources other than wages rather easily evades local taxation. Sales taxes can be avoided by making purchases elsewhere. This can be reduced somewhat by imposing a ' use ' tax upon items which are subject to the sales tax but which have been purchased outside the local jurisdiction.

Non-property taxes bear more heavily upon the poor than upon the rich. Regressiveness is one of the chief reasons why local non-property taxes are not favoured in ideal plans. From the economic point of view, relatively few concrete data are available to show the effects of local non-property taxation. One may surmise that high local non-property taxation tends to encourage migration from a high-tax area. This should occur more readily from small tax jurisdictions and in situations where transportation enables the migrant to enjoy most of the advantages he received in the high-tax community. Business will not be affected by personal income taxes, but almost all the other taxes tend to hurt business if one assumes that purchasers can easily buy elsewhere and business cannot shift the tax. Local businesses, which must compete with business in non-tax or low-tax areas, will be somewhat adversely affected, either by a reduction in profit because they have absorbed the cost of the tax, or by a loss in sales because their prices are higher than those in the neighbouring area.

Co-operation among Local Tax Jurisdictions

School districts are usually only one of several local tax jurisdictions sharing all or parts of the same tax-base. There may be no legal requirement that they co-ordinate their activities, but among themselves local jurisdictions must consider the over-all effects of their taxes upon taxpayers and must endeavour to provide their respective services with a minimum of duplication. Most of the co-operation is done by informal agreement, but districts can arrange the transfer of money from one unit to another by entering into a contract which permits one unit to pay for a service performed by another unit. In this way two units can make more efficient use of the same tax-base or can arrange to share the tax-base when they are not conterminous. An interesting example of such contractual arrangements has developed in connexion with the provision of specialized educational services. In order to provide those which can be used only part-time and are too expensive in small districts, several districts may agree to employ the specialist and share in the expense. Co-operation of this sort has grown in some places to the point where state legislatures have passed laws permitting the establishment of units which employ specialists and contract with local districts for their services. These co-operative units are some-times aided by the state to encourage their establishment. Thus again, local control is achieved within a framework which provides substan-tial state moneys.

National activity has a pronounced influence upon the tax machine for education. In the highly decentralized system of taxation described in this article, the influence is most sharply seen in the pressure which it places upon small local jurisdictions having little control over the tax machine they use. The resulting tax structure must be bolstered in many ways in order to provide sufficient funds for education. Local control of education has been preserved even though substantial funds have been granted by other levels of government. In a centralized tax system, many of the same pressures may be felt, but the solution to the tax problem is likely to be quite different. National governments can anticipate change and can provide for changes in the tax structure to yield a certain economic effect more directly than can local govern-ments.

J. ERVITI.

GENERAL REFERENCES

O. H. Brownlee and Edward D. Allen, *Economics of Public Finance*, 2nd edn. (New York, 1954).

Clarence Heer, *Federal Aid and the Tax Problem* (Staff Study Number 4. Pre-pared for the Advisory Committee on Education, Washington, D.C. U.S. Government Printing Office, 1939).

Mabel Newcomer, *Taxation and Fiscal Policy* (New York, Columbia University Press, 1940).

Philip E. Taylor, *The Economics of Public Finance*, rev. edn. (New York, The Macmillan Company, 1953).

Education as a Demand on Resources Competing with Other Activities

How much a country can afford for education depends on many factors. The most important is the output of goods and services, that is, the national income, in turn related to the size of the population, the proportion of the population in the labour market, the amount of unemployment, the productivity of labour and capital, and the intelligence of management. A second relevant factor is the distribution of the income : the more skewed the distribution of income the easier it may be to raise revenue, though frequently maldistribution of income is accompanied by archaic tax systems striking the many poor instead of the few rich. Again, with large inequalities the demand for education may be small. A third factor is the nature of the tax system. Under the modern tax system, with its great emphasis on direct taxation, a given income can yield much more than an equal amount of taxation would have yielded fifty years ago. For example, in the early part of the century, state and local governments of the United States raised about 1 billion dollars in revenue, and most of its tax revenue (in 1902, $706 million of $860 million of taxes) from the General Property Tax (GPT). Federal revenues were but one-half billion dollars, with customs and excise duties providing roughly equal amounts and accounting for the most part of the revenue. Total taxes were about 10 per cent of the national income of the period. By the early 1950's, the major taxes were direct and the major tax power was the federal government, which concentrated largely on taxes that responded to income. By 1954, government was raising $90 billion, with the federal government accounting for $63·5 billion, or more than two-thirds. Of the latter sum, $45 billion were in direct corporate and income taxes. Even in state and local taxes, the importance of more flexible taxes than the GPT had increased : with the GPT accounting for only $10 billion, or 11 per cent of all taxes of all governments, as compared with about 50 per cent fifty years ago. That governments can raise so much more money than fifty years ago is explained first by the rise of income and second by the revolutionary changes in the tax structure. Whereas fifty years ago the tax bill was less than $2 billion in the United States and 10 per cent of income, it is now about $90 billion and 30 per cent of the national income.

Alternative Demands

A final factor of great importance in determining the amount of money available for education is the alternative demands upon government. Obviously as the military, the combustion engine, health, and development of natural resources put increased burdens on government, the amounts available for education are likely to be influenced. But we should note that whereas education is a demand for labour and other resources, a large part of the social services introduced in recent years (e.g., unemployment insurance) are transfer payments and hence do not consume labour or materials as education does.

The Distribution of Responsibilities for Education among Governments

In the United States, the major responsibility for education rests with local governments, which pay about 60 per cent of the bill, and state governments pay most of the remainder. This is perhaps the most unfortunate aspect of American educational finance. Local governments, largely responsible for public school education, are hampered by the fact that their revenues come primarily from the GPT (60 per cent of all local taxes), which is an inflexible tax responding inadequately to the rise of prices and income. As goes the GPT, so goes American education. In an inflationary economy, with costs rising and revenue responding slowly, periodic crises follow. I do not mean to imply that local governments, given their tax system, are without blame. Many local governments fail to raise the revenue that they should in support of education: they are often victimized by real-estate lobbies and taxpayers generally.

The Development of Spending Patterns

It is interesting to compare the major relative change in outlays on the part of state and local governments of the United States. The outlay on education, over fifty years, is up from 23 to 28 per cent of the total (from $874 to $7,756 million). Highways account for roughly the same percentage (16 and 15); but public welfare is up from 3 to 9 per cent, and housing and natural resources from less than 1 per cent to 4 per cent. Relatively, general control and interest on debt have been cut greatly.[1] But note that the interest on debt is also a transfer

_____

[1] Figures from *Historical Statistics of the United States, 1789–1945* (U.S. Department of Commerce, U.S. Census, 1949), and *Historical Statistics on State and Local Government Finances, 1902–1953* (1955); and *Survey of Current Business* (July, 1955).

item, though not in the same sense for local as for national government.

The great expansion of central government activity is of much significance. In the United States, the large rise in outlays has been for national security, social security, and the development of natural resources. For the federal government, the major outlays for 1955–6 are as follows.[2]

	Billion Dollars
Major national security	38·7
International affairs and finance	2·1
Veterans' service and benefits	4·8
Welfare, health, and education	2·4
Agriculture and natural resources	4·4
Commerce and manpower	2·8
General government	1·7
Interest	6·8
TOTAL	63·7

In 1900, security and general government were the major items. The other items in this list are relatively new or have grown at a tremendous rate; and the burden of security was minor in 1900 compared with the present. As a result of the Great Depression and three major wars, the federal government's responsibilities have become much more important; and with that development, the federal government has arrogated to itself the most productive revenues, with the result that the financial problems of state and local government become more and more serious. Their responsibilities have not been cut in the same degree as the federal government has usurped financial resources. This disproportion between financial resources and responsibility is felt especially in education. To some extent the federal government has atoned by providing grants-in-aid—amounting to $2·6 billion in 1953, but $305 million for education.[3]

SOCIAL WELFARE EXPENDITURES, TOTAL ALL LEVELS OF GOVERNMENT
AND PER CENT BY U.S. FEDERAL GOVERNMENT, 1950–51

	$ Million	Percentage Federal Contribution
All	23,367	41
Veterans' programme	5,506	94
Social insurance	4,642	58
Public aid	2,583	46
Health and medical	2,512	13
Education	7,627	2

Source: Social Security Bulletin (February, 1953), p. 8.

[2] Review of the 1956 Budget (Bureau of the Budget), p. 29.
[3] Historical Statistics on State and Local Government Finances, p. 19.

In this connexion, it should be noted that, according as the responsibility for a function is divided between the federal (central) and other governments, the function is well or badly financed. For example, in the United States, veterans are well provided for, the reason being, in large part, that the responsibility lies primarily with the federal government; but education is another matter.

Expenditures and Motivation

Expenditures on education are related, then, to the allocation of responsibilities for education among various types of governments, on the national income, its distribution, the conflicting demands on the government—these are probably the major factors. But there are others of some importance.

One important item is the attitude towards education. When motivation is strong, more money is likely to be spent on education. In the United States, for example, elementary school education is almost universal, and 85 per cent of those of secondary school age go to school (60 per cent graduate), and about 25 per cent go to IHL.[4]

In the United States, the motivation is to a considerable extent economic. The view is widely held that education contributes to a. higher income, and hence education is held to pay. That vocational aspects of education are stressed more is evident in the changing curriculum, and in higher education in the trend towards vocational education. Thus, from 1901–05 to 1951–3 the percentage of bachelors and first professional degrees changed as follows[5]:

	1901–05	1951–53
Humanities and arts	13·3	9·8
Engineering	3·3	9·6
Applied biology	0·3	5·3
Business and commerce	0·2	14·3
Education	0·4	19·2

Against these substantial movements towards vocationalism, the professional field, even of health and law, lost ground relatively. In the former, at least, the explanation in large part is the restriction of entry.

It is scarcely necessary to add that the British and other European countries discourage the march to higher education that prevails in the United States. The likely candidates are selected at a relatively

---

[4] Figures based on Oxtoby, Mugge, and Wolff, "Enrollment and Graduate Trends: From Grade School to Ph.D.," *School and Society*, October 11th, 1952, pp. 225–8; and *Fact Book on Manpower*, U.S. Department of Labor, B.L.S. (1954), p. 13.

[5] " America's Resources of Specialized Talent " (*The Report of the Commission on Human Resources and Advanced Training*, 1954), pp. 294–5.

early age. The fact that eighty-five thousand is the target figure for Great Britain as compared with 3-4 million in the United States (with population only three times as high) perhaps also explains the much higher proportion of graduates in the arts in England. Whereas American IHL graduated only 9·8 per cent of its students in the humanities and arts, in England the proportion in the arts was 44 per cent, and in *pure* science 21 per cent.[6]

There is, indeed, much evidence that with greater educational achievement incomes rise. For example, in a recent year 36 per cent of those with sixteen years' or more schooling had incomes of $5,000 or over; but only 0·2 per cent of those with no schooling, 12 per cent of those with seven to eight years of schooling; and 24 per cent with twelve years of schooling had incomes of $5,000 or over.[7]

WAGE AND SALARY INCOME FOR MALES 25–64, BY YEARS OF SCHOOLING COMPLETED—NATIVE WHITE MALES

Income	Percentage Distribution			
	Schooling			
	No School	7–8 Years	12 Years	16 Years or more
All . . .	1·2	37	16	5·8
No income . . .	3·2	39	11	4·3
$1,500–1,999 . .	0·3	34	21	6·7
$3,000–4,999 . .	0·1	20	23	24·5
$5,000 and over . .	0·2	12	24	35·7

These material gains of education are likely to decline as the numbers with education increase; and there are already signs in the much larger rise in pay of farmers, factory workers, and others *vis-à-vis* the white-collar workers that the trend is in this direction. In view of the fact that the number of living college graduates in the United States will have increased by ten times from 1910 to 1960, and of high school graduates by fourteen times, it is surprising that the relative economic gains of education have stood up as well as they have.

[6] Dodds, Hacker, and Rogers, *Government Assistance to Universities in Great Britain* (1952), pp. 106–7; also cf. *The Problems Facing the British Universities* (Nuffield College Report, 1948).

[7] Calculated from the Report of the President's Commission on Higher Education : *Higher Education for American Democracy*, VI, p. 7.

	Living High School Graduates (000's)	Living College Graduates (000's)	Percentage Population aged 21 and over
1910 .	2,660	696	1·4
1930 .	9,780	1,737	2·4
1940 .	19,030	3,213	3·9
1950 .	29,550	5,230	5·4
1960 .	39,800	7,680	7·4

Source: Calculated by the author for the American Textbook Publishers Institute from material in Reports of the Office of Education (*Statistics of State School Systems,* 1949–50); FSA., *Statistics of Higher Education, etc.,* 1949–50; *Statistical Abstract of the U.S.,* U.S. Census, *Illustrative Projections of the Population, 1950 to 1960;* and President's Commission on the Health Needs of the Nation, *Building America's Health,* 1952, p. 35.

Paying the Bill

It does not follow that just because the average American wants more education he (she) is prepared to pay for it. The fact is, there is much evidence that he (she) is not prepared to pay the educational bill. In part, the explanation of inadequate resources for education, given the demand for it, arises from the faulty methods of financing. It is not easy to raise additional revenue from the general property taxes; and state governments, especially alerted to inter-state competition for employment and sales, are loath to increase their contributions to education. They are fearful that higher taxes will mean a loss of business to competitive states.

But outlays are insufficient. This is evident in the pay of teachers. In a period during which the average American has increased his real income by 50 per cent, the real income of teachers has remained roughly unchanged. In view of the fact that school enrolment is to rise by 40 per cent in ten years, and enrolment in institutions of higher learning to rise by 100 per cent in fifteen years, and in view of the fact that the backlog in school construction required by 1965 is estimated at $32 billion (the current backlog is about $11 billion), it is clear that the public is not pumping enough cash into the schools and colleges. It prefers to increase outlays on eating out, on bizarre automobiles, and on gambling to providing adequate resources for education. It is an interesting fact that teachers, with an average schooling of 15½ years, earned a salary of $3,725, whereas the average worker, with a schooling of 9 years, received $3,590 per year, and the average factory worker, $4,051. From 1939–40 to 1951–2, the average salary of a teacher rose by 5 per cent (corrected for prices) and over a period of fifty years, real income of professors in large universities declined by 2 per cent and of teachers in big city high schools by 1 per cent, while pay of workers in seven different industries rose from 107 to 163 per cent.[8]

The Education Bill

No country has an educational bill equal to that of the United States. The amount involved is of the order of $12·5 billion, inclusive of $2·5 billion for higher education and $1 billion for private grade and secondary schools.[9]

In Great Britain, in 1951–2, public outlay on education was £328 million, or 2·2 per cent of the national income. The corresponding figure for the United States is about $9 billion, or somewhat less than 3 per cent of the national income. (Private outlays are, however, more important in the United States than in the United Kingdom.) For all public services the British outlay in 1951–2 was £2,011 million (13·7 per cent of the national income), and education (£328·3 million) accounted for 16 per cent of the total. In the United States the public outlay for education (1950–51) were $7·6 billion, or 32 per cent of the total. Hence it is clear that public education is relatively more important in relation to both national income and total outlays on social services in the United States than in Great Britain. The great importance of education in the United States is italicized even more when it is noted that social services accounted for 9 per cent of national income in the United States and close to 14 per cent in the United Kingdom. In other words, despite the much greater drain on the economy of social services in the United Kingdom than in the United States, education absorbed a larger part of national income in the United States.

In part, the differences in the structure of expeditures for social service arise from variations in the needs and ideologies of the two peoples as well as variations in the structures of the governments. There are, for example, large differences in the percentage of social-service outlay.

---

[8] *The Forty-Eight State School Systems* (Council for State Governments, 1949), p. 70; *Financing Public Education in the Decade Ahead* (National Citizens Committee on the Public School, 1954), pp. 37 and 57; *Emergency Federal Aid for School Construction* (Senate Hearings, Senate Committee on Labor and Public Welfare, 1955), pp. 46, 67; *Statistics of City School Systems*, Chapter 3, p. 14 (U.S. Department of Health, Education and Welfare); *Teaching Salaries Then and Now* (The Seventh Company, 1955 Prelim.), p. 16.

[9] *Financing Public Education in Decade Ahead*, p. 51; and *Finances of Higher Education: Statistical Summary for 1951–52* (U.S. Department of Health, Education, and Welfare).

PERCENTAGE SOCIAL-SERVICE OUTLAYS (EARLY 1950'S)

	United Kingdom	United States
Food and nutritive subsidies .	20	Negligible
Education	17	33
Health, hospital, etc. . .	24	11
Social–security services .	28	31
Veterans	4 [1]	24

[1] *War pensions only.*

In general, the British spend heavily on food subsidies (since the early 'fifties greatly reduced), health, and hospitals; the United States, on education and veterans. Undoubtedly the large outlay on veterans in the United States and on health in Great Britain increases the difficulties of spending on education in both countries. In the United States, veterans profited from federal outlays of $2,121 million on pensions and compensation (British outlays on war pensions were but £75 million), $691 million on health and medical services, $2,012 million on education, and $328 million for welfare and other purposes. In addition, state and local governments spent $334 million on veterans.[10]

Responsibility of Central versus other Government

In comparisons of educational finance one other aspect should be noted. The financing of social services is much more a non-central government responsibility in the United States than in Great Britain—with resultant troublesome problems of the optimum allocation of resources in the United States. There, the federal government financed but 41 per cent of all social services in 1950–1 (and almost half of these were insurance programmes) and only 23 per cent of the educational bill (primarily higher and vocation, educational, defence, etc.). In the United Kingdom the central government financed 63 per cent of the cost of social services, though (1949–50) grants for school education from the central government were but £144 million (local authorities spent £237 million).[11]

---

[10] " Statistics for Social Welfare Programs in the United States," *Social Security Bulletin* (February, 1953), p. 8; and " Cost of the British Social Services," *Ibid.*, p. 13. The items compared are not exactly similar, but the broad general conclusions still hold.

[11] References above and *Education, 1900–1950* (The Report of the Ministry of Education for the Year 1950), p. 32.

Enrolments at Different Levels

Varying costs for education depend in part upon the demand for education in turn related to the economic capacity to pay. The relative costs are also related to the number of children of school age as a percentage of the total population.

Enrolment in schools as a percentage of the population aged 5–14 varies from 115 in France to 13 in French Morocco. The percentages for some important countries are as follow : Mexico, 40; Brazil, 41; India, 27; Burma, 15; Japan, 101; Germany, 100; Italy, 73; Sweden, 86; England and Wales, 105; Australia, 109.[12] In general, attendance *vis-à-vis* enrolment tends to be smaller for the under-developed countries than for the others. Hence, the differences here noted are greater than they seem to be.

Much depends upon the ratio of children of school age to the total population. There are great variations among states in the United States, with the agricultural states having to educate a much larger part of the population than the non-agricultural states. Among countries, also, the differences are striking. Whereas some countries have five times as many in the productive age-group 20–69 as in the group 5–14, others have less than twice as many. It is the richer countries that tend to have the smallest number to educate relative to the numbers in the productive age-group.

PERCENTAGE OF POPULATION

	In Age-group 5–14	In Age-group 20–69
Belgium (1949)	12·9	65·0
France (1950)	13·1	63·1
Sweden (1947)	13·1	65·0
England and Wales (1948) . .	13·0	65·3
United States (1949) . . .	16·5	61·1
Venezuela (1945) . . .	25·6	46·6
India (1931)	24·6	49·6
Malaya (1947)	27·0	49·4
Egypt (1937)	25·9	49·4

Source: Preliminary Report on the World Social Situation (UN, 1952), p. 65.

In general, when there is relatively little primary education, there is little post-primary education. In independent countries, post-

---

[12] *Basic Facts and Figures* (UNESCO, 1954), pp. 30–1.

primary education tends to be relatively more important than in dependent countries.

"In the majority of independent countries of a less-developed economy, primary school enrolment is five to fifteen times as great as post-primary enrolment . . . and it is generally only between two and five times as great as in the more-developed independent countries. Differences in school systems and age-structure between less-developed and more-developed areas must, of course, be borne in mind. . . ." [13]

Secondary school enrolment for some countries in relation to population is given below (around 1950):

	Enrolled 000's	Population (million)	Percentage Enrolled
Turkey . . .	139	21·5	0·7
France . . .	1,227	42·2	2·9
Germany (West) . .	1,250	48·1	2·7
Greece . . .	239	7·8	0·3
Italy . . .	1,111	46·6	2·4
Spain	347	28·1	1·2
England and Wales .	1,872	43·8	4·3
Australia . . .	238	8·4	2·8
Union of South Africa .	84	12·7	0·7
Mexico . . .	150	26·3	0·6
United States . .	6,452	154·3	4·2
Argentina . .	158	17·6	0·9
Paraguay . . .	8	1·42	0·6
Iran	51	19·1	0·3
India	5,394	367·0	1·5

Source: Computed from Statistical Yearbook (UN, 1953), Table 1, and Basic Facts and Figures (UNESCO), Table 4.

An examination of the above table reveals that the percentage enrolled in secondary schools varies from 0·3 per cent in Iran to more than 4 per cent for the United States and England and Wales. The differences between the United States and the more advanced countries of Europe are much less than is generally supposed. But the under-developed countries seem to have from one-tenth to one-fifth as many in secondary schools relative to the population generally as the most-developed countries. When allowance is made for the much larger proportion of young in the under-developed countries, then the differences are even greater than suggested by the crude figures.

Variations in the percentage of the population of those of college age in institutions of higher learning (IHL) are, of course, much greater than in the secondary school population. Here the differences in the standard of living play an important part. When there are large numbers of college graduates, the effects on the standard of living are marked; and when the incomes are high, it is possible to send many more to IHL.

Enrolment in Institutions of Higher Learning and National Income

It is not easy to compare the incomes of different nations; in part because the foreign exchange-rates do not give an accurate picture of relative purchasing power and in part because a dollar or a pound sterling in a highly developed country means something entirely different from what it means in an under-developed country. The dollar in the United States buys luxuries, and an entirely different basket of goods from that in Indonesia. The cost of which basket of goods do we try to measure? If the British national income is £10 billion, the population 50 million, and the exchange-rate is $3 = £1$, and the United States income $350 billion, population 150 million, it does not follow that the *per capita* income of the United States is 3·9 times the British; and a comparison of the United States and Indonesia is subject to much greater reservations.

$$\frac{10 \text{ billion}}{50 \text{ million}} = £200 \text{ per capita} = \$600 \text{ for U.K.}$$

$$\frac{350 \text{ billion}}{150 \text{ million}} = \$2,333 \text{ for the U.S.A.}$$

Hence, United States *per capita* income seems to be 390 per cent of the United Kingdom *per capita* income. On the basis of this kind of comparison it was found that with the United States *per capita* income at 100, the United Kingdom income in 1950 would be 37, French 35, German 26, and Italian 12. But on the basis of new techniques which more accurately measure relative purchasing power, it was found that the British *per capita* national income was from 53 to 63 per cent (the range determined by comparing on the basis of one country's basket first and the others next) of the America level, the French 42–53, the German 33–43, and the Italian 22–30. In another comparison, it was revealed that *per capita* consumption in the United States was more than three-and-a-half times the consumption of fifteen European countries, with the range for 1953 (1951–2 prices) being $171 for Portugal and $877 for Denmark. In an early post-war year, it was estimated that *per capita* income of Asiatic countries was around $50, though this is an estimate subject to all kinds of reservations.[14]

In the light of these differences of income, it might well be expected that there would be large variations in the relative numbers at institutions of higher learning. The percentage of enrolment in IHL in relation to population (around 1950) for several countries was as follows:

U.S.A.	1·50
Argentina	0·45
France	0·34
England and Wales	0·23
Mexico	0·14
India	0·12

Source: Computed from above.

The United States, it will be noted, has a higher education population relatively 12 + times as large as India's and 6½ times that of England and Wales. The large proportion of students in IHL in the United States results in much larger outlays on education than would otherwise be experienced. Roughly 20 per cent of educational outlays are for higher education in the United States. With about 7 per cent of the total enrolment in school and IHL, the students in IHL account for 20 per cent of the educational outlays. The costs of higher education are much greater than is assumed here, for there are large losses of income involved in not working. Since the average member of the labour market earns about $3,500, the loss of income times the numbers enrolled may be put at roughly 9 billion additional dollars.

According to a study of the United Nations, 1 person in 75 in North America in 1949–50 was enrolled in an institution of higher learning (this proportion is inflated to some extent by the large numbers of veterans enrolled in this year in the United States and the classification as IHL in North America for some institutions which might not be so classified elsewhere). In 1937–8, the proportion was 1 to 115 in North America. In the same year the proportion was about 1 in 350 in Europe, 1 in 725 in Latin America, 1 in 1,250 in the Middle East, and 1 in 1,100–1,200 in Asia. In Africa, among its indigenous population, the proportion probably does not exceed 1 in 20,000.[15]

On the basis of current estimates, a doubling of enrolment at

---

[14] Basic data supplied by the Executive Branch, *The Mutual Security Program for Fiscal Year 1954* (1953), p. 61; *Foreign Assets and Liabilities of the United States, and Its International Transactions* (Report to the Senate Committee on Finance, 1948), Table D.3; and M. Gilbert and I. B. Kravis, *An International Comparison of National Products and Their Purchasing Power* (Organization of European Economic Co-operation, 1954), p. 27.

[15] *Preliminary Report on the World Social Situation* (UN), p. 69.

roughly 5 million at IHL is expected in the United States within the next fifteen years. At present costs (assuming no rise of prices and no improvements of standards), the cost of higher education would rise to $5 billion, or from one-third to one-quarter of total educational costs. It is likely that should enrolment increase as projected (and the rise projected is based largely on the increase in numbers of college age), then a much larger relative burden would be put upon the taxpayer. At present, public institutions account for roughly one-half of the enrolment. The inability of private institutions to provide the plant required for this enrolment may result in public institutions absorbing most of the additional enrolment and hence accounting for close to 75 per cent of the total.[16]

Other Educational Outlays

Education extends beyond the schools and colleges, with adult education accounting for an increasing stake—and especially as the numbers in the age-groups rise. It is well, therefore, to consider briefly some relevant outlays outside of the schools and colleges. Adult education is on the move in many countries. Thus, an official estimate puts the enrolment in England and Wales in classes for adults held by " responsible bodies " at 163,000 in 1948-9. But I shall concentrate here on reading materials.[17]

In the United States, books and maps account for outlays of $531 million, and magazines, newspapers, and sheet music, $1,708 million, the total equalling about 20 per cent of all outlays for schools and IHL. It might even be held that the $2·7 billion spent on radio and television is partly educational. British outlays for books were £35 million, for newspapers £64 million, or in all (books, newspapers, and magazines) roughly 1·45 per cent of all consumption expenditures, as compared with 0·97 per cent for the United States. The British clearly spend more, relatively speaking, for literature of various kinds. The British outlays for books are relatively about twice those for the U.S.A.[18]

In part the explanation of the larger outlays on books and suchlike in Great Britain must be associated with the low prices of this kind

---

[16] Cf. *The Impending Tidal Wave of Students* (American Association of Collegiate Registrars and Admission Officers, 1954); and *Higher Education for American Democracy* (A Report of the President's Commission for Higher Education, 1947), I, pp. 42-3.
[17] *Education, 1900–1950* (The Report of the Ministry of Education), Ch. 5.
[18] *National Income* (U.S. Department of Commerce, 1954), pp. 206-7; and *National Income and Expenditures, 1946–1953* (UN, Central Statistical Office, 1954), pp. 32-3.

of material in the United Kingdom—associated in turn with low wage-rates and much smaller overhead and distributive costs.

Health is also an important and increasing responsibility of the schools. The school authorities assume responsibilities not only for health examinations and medical care but also for proper feeding. In an excellent survey of British developments since the early part of the century, Mr. Lowndes concludes:

"The history of the school medical service belongs rather to a study of the awakening of the national conscience in regard to the public health than to a study of growth of the public service of education. Moreover, no feature of our educational system is more fully documented. . . ."

And the author comments on a fall of 30 per cent in the death-rate of children aged 5 to 15 in a period of twenty-seven years.[19]

Outlays on Capital

Especially troublesome for both schools and institutions of higher learning are capital needs. As enrolment expands, capital outlays become a serious problem. Depressions followed by war aggravate the problem. According to modern theories of finance, the depressed countries should have encouraged public improvements, including the building of schools in the Great Depression. But everywhere, orthodox canons of finance prevailed, and it was not generally accepted that in periods of unemployment outlays would not only provide the needed schools, roads, and so on, but would actually raise income and reduce unemployment. Instead, in all Western countries the authorities allowed losses of labour and capital that could not be re-couped later.

In the war and post-war periods incomes rose greatly, and the resources were available for school and college construction. But there were numerous obstacles. First, construction costs tended to rise much more than all other prices. The construction dollar is an especially depreciated one. Second, and related, most countries have embarked on ambitious investment programmes, some stimulated by government outlays and others by private enterprise. The emphasis has been upon investments directly associated with the improvement of the national economy; and in most of the programmes capital outlay for the social services did not receive a high priority. The emphasis was on higher productivity in industry: for example, more power, improved transportation, mechanization of agriculture, and automation. With this kind of competition, the school boards found it increasingly difficult to meet current needs and make up for the losses incurred

---

[19] G. A. N. Lowndes, *The Silent Social Revolution*, 1947 edn., p. 225.

during the Depression and World War II. In this connexion, it might be noted that for public schools in the United States, capital outlays account for 25 per cent of the total outlays; and if the large backlog were to be treated, the percentage would be higher.

The Problem of the Under-developed Countries

Under-developed countries are confronted with especially vexing problems. They are short of capital and are fortunate indeed if they can attract one to two billion dollars of foreign capital per year. But their annual needs are estimated by official agencies as high as $10 billion per year. Domestic savings are small, and especially so because of the low incomes and poor organization of the capital market. An effective manner of raising capital is through inflation, a process of squeezing the consumer out of the market for goods and services. But in the end inflation reduces voluntary savings.

With low incomes, the under-developed countries spend relatively less on social services. Like the more advanced countries fifty to a hundred years ago, they spend much less on social services relative to national income and concentrate their social services largely upon education and relief. They will ultimately experience the revolution that has occurred in the Western powers and notably in Great Britain and Scandinavia, where social insurance, subsidies, and the like become an increasing part of the social-service budget and of income.[20]

The Educational Dollar

At different times and in different places the educational dollar is spent in varying ways. As has been noted, the poor countries tend to concentrate on primary education, the explanation being that their resources are limited and the advantages of education are not widely appreciated. In the Western countries, there is an approach towards universal secondary education, though for economic and other reasons the goal is still far off, even in the United States. The democratic principle of equal opportunity for all has stimulated the trek to institutions of higher learning in the United States, with the result that they perform a somewhat different task from that in European countries and also that the enrolment of 7–8 per cent of the population tends to bring in many of limited capacity—though it should be noted that only about 40 per cent of those within the top 25 per cent in intelli-

---

[20] For a good discussion of these issues, see N. T. Wang, "Some Problems of International Comparison of Public School Expenditures", to be published in *Indian Economic Review; Report on International Definition and Standards and Levels of Living* (UN); and U. K. Hicks, *British Public Finance, 1880–1952* (1954).

gence tests survive the sixteenth year of school. (Many of the potentially best students do not even enter college.)

School and college authorities with limited resources seek to make the most effective use of their resources. With great demands for health, recreational, and other services, there is a tendency to save on such costs as teachers' salaries and good classrooms. When teachers are not well organized, the teachers' relative position suffers; but in a full-employment economy, the authorities have to make concessions or they have to get on with inexperienced and incompetent teachers. It is an interesting fact that but one-half of the United States school budget goes to salaries of teachers, superintendents, and other personnel, and even a smaller part of the budget of IHL.

The economics of education is, then, largely a problem of the resources that can be mobilized for our schools and colleges in relation to other claims upon the economy, and how the funds made available are allocated among the claimants: elementary schools, secondary, IHL, adults, nutrition, recreation, and medical; and also among teaching staff, administration, maintenance, new construction, amongst other things.

SEYMOUR E. HARRIS.

CHAPTER TWELVE

The Reform of English Education under the 1944 Education Act

THIS was an act of faith rather than of sober judgment. No doubt the intentions of those who framed the 1944 Education Act were admirable. Public opinion, sharpened by the unifying experiences of total warfare, was strongly in favour of so extending education as to give all children equal opportunities. Pressure from all sides to reorganize public education without delay was great. Thus, during a fight for existence, the final policy discussions took place; before ultimate victory the Act which has been named the greatest piece of legislation in educational history was passed. But the conditions which gave the Act its impetus also made the working out of its detailed implications difficult. Moreover, they might have been unpalatable to a war-weary public. In any case, the magnitude of the proposed programme either was not appreciated, or—and this is more likely—was withheld from the general public during the war. What would be involved was either never made clear by successive post-war governments or went unheeded.

Some eleven years later it is apparent that the large gaps in terms of what was proposed still exist; for this reason the English educational system is often criticized. Little attention has been paid, however, to the nature and extent of post-war educational investment in terms of recurring economic crises, or of the resources put into education compared with those made available for the Health Service, for example. Not much has been written on the effect of these policies on the national economy. Has education made, or been able to make, its proper contribution to increased national prosperity? It is in these terms that some of the significant provisions of the 1944 Education Act will be analysed.

The Post-war Situation

The Act proposed to extend educational services on a very broad front. No aspect of pre-war public education was to remain untouched. Nursery schools were to be part of the primary system, secondary schooling was to be reorganized, and further education beyond the compulsory attendance age was to be provided on a large scale. Each stage—primary, secondary, and further—of the educational process was to make heavy demands on the nation's resources of manpower, buildings, and equipment. Conditions at the end of the war were not auspicious and brought into being a number of committees to investigate the problems of reconstruction.

Crucial to all this was the country's changed economic position, due to the loss of foreign investments during the war. The United Kingdom has always had to import basic materials of one sort or another, but after the Second World War, to " a greater extent than ever before, we shall have to pay for them [imports] by the export of goods and services. For as a result of two world wars we have had to sacrifice by far the greater part of the foreign investments which we built up over many years when we were the leading creditor country of the world ".[1] The country's prosperity now depended on exports—in particular on the " export of manufactured goods of high quality ". Some previously profitable exports had become negligible. Statistics [2] show how the coal exported dropped from nearly fifty million tons in 1938 to less than ten million tons in 1946. Rather similar figures could be quoted for other important basic industries. The effect was twofold: there was an acute shortage both of exportable materials and of those basic commodities—timber, steel, concrete, coal, etc.—on which to build a successful export trade of high-quality goods.

Everywhere the labour problem was acute, the demand was obviously going to be far greater than the supply. Whilst industrial mobility was restricted, the direction of workers into essential industries was never introduced—workers could be selective in their jobs. During the war years the labour force in the mines had dropped by nearly 100,000. Despite a fourfold increase in the average weekly wage of miners, many recruiting drives, additional incentives, and benefits, the pre-war figure of men on colliery books has not yet been reached. Numbers, indeed, continued to fall. There were " 5,700 men less on the average in 1954 than in 1953. . . . The country's high industrial activity, with the great demand for manpower in less arduous employment, is the main cause of this difficulty. . . . No old extractive industry, suffering, as the coal industry is, from inadequate development work in the last thirty years, could compete successfully with such simultaneous factors as a rapidly falling manpower and a rapidly increasing demand for its products . . . coal is being imported ".[3] Against this must be recorded the fact that the percentage of coal cut mechanic-

[1] *Employment Policy* (H.M.S.O., May, 1944), Cmd. 6527.
[2] *50 Questions and Answers on British Coal* (National Coal Board, April, 1955).
[3] N.C.B. Chairman's speech to the National Union of Miners Conference, July 5th, 1955 (Public Relations, National Coal Board).

ally had risen from about 60 in 1939 to over 83 in 1953. Nevertheless, the total output never in any one year reached the 1939 figure.[4]

No doubt other industries suffered from acute shortage of labour, scarcity of materials, and inadequate investment in mass-production machinery during the inter-war years. In a Command paper of May, 1944, policies to meet this situation were outlined. They were designed to prevent the production of unessentials interfering with that of essentials; and to cut down home consumption. Rationing and price controls were to remain; costs were to be stabilized; saving was to be encouraged; and the use of capital controlled.[5] Nevertheless, successive Chancellors, whether Labour or Conservative, urged the imperative need to step up industrial production for export if the economy was to be stabilized.

Unfortunately, some industrial practices which had grown up under entirely different circumstances continued to be used. There has been opposition by trade unionists to the recruitment of trainees, especially foreigners. In the Command paper it was appreciated that " If any retraining schemes are to be a success there must be the fullest co-operation between employers and Trade Unions. Difficulties have arisen in the past because some sections of industry have been reluctant to admit trainees . . . [to] safeguard employment of existing workers and their wage standards, and to maintain a proper standard of skill. In some cases the difficulty has been increased by competition between Unions ".[6]

Although the leaders of the trade union movement have, on the whole, set their faces against strikes, many unofficial ones have taken place.[7] One of their most serious aspects has been the apparent inability of one side to communicate with the other. Both sides often have seemed to be arguing about different things. Too often, at the human level, action and counteraction seem to be based on prejudice, underlying hostility, impatience, and a general lack of trust on both sides.

There is perhaps a growing realization that under inflationary pressure, a nation's industry cannot be maintained at the highest level of efficiency and productivity if relations between management and labour remain similar to what they were in the days of unemployment. The Chairman of the Coal Board, Sir Hubert Houldsworth, suggested more than once that the problems of manpower and production could

---

[4] *50 Questions and Answers on British Coal, op. cit. supra.*
[5] *Employment Policy* (H.M.S.O., May, 1944), Cmd. 6527.
[6] Cmd. 6527, *op. cit. supra.*
[7] *The Annual Abstract of Statistics* (H.M.S.O., 1954) shows no year since the war has been as free from working days lost through stoppages as 1938.

be ameliorated by an " increase in co-operation between management and men at many pits. . . . This is more a matter of human approach than of organization, although organization must be perfected and play its part ".[8] Even so, the Joint Committee on Human Relations in Industry maintained that, " despite increasing recognition of the importance of the human factor in industrial affairs, research into the human relations problems of industry has developed relatively little. . . ." [9] Generally speaking, the problem is one of determining under what social, traditional, economic, and cultural conditions incentive-payment schemes in industry lead to maximum productivity. One project being carried out by Manchester University " is not concerned with incentive-payment schemes in any narrow sense, but with production norms determined not so much by technical or economic considerations as by the attitudes of workers and management. Studies in America show that these conventional norms of production, based on social attitudes, exist in many industries, and that they are important in affecting the level of output and the operation of incentive schemes ".[10] Projects on the " effective communication of information and ideas within the management hierarchy, and the relations between line management and function specialists," [11] were seen as important related aspects of the problem. Two further factors were being investigated : the human problems which slow down or prevent the effective and rapid introduction of new scientific techniques, and the complexities of recruiting available talent and developing to the full its skills in management and supervision. In short, some solutions to the fundamental problem of production have to be sought in education.

Technical and Scientific Manpower—the Social Demand

If the resources that could be placed at the disposal of education were limited by the general economic situation, there remained the problem of the most efficient allocation within education of those available. Discussions before and immediately after the end of hostilities emphasized that one of the most serious problems would be the recruitment and training of scientific and technical personnel. The post-war economy depended for its stability as much as on anything on the quality and quantity of these people. " Never before ", stated the Barlow Committee *Report*, " has the importance of science been more widely recognized or so many hopes of future progress and wel-

---

[8] N.C.B. Chairman's speech, *op. cit. supra*.

[9] *First Report of the Joint Committee on Human Relations in Industry, March, 1953, to March, 1954* (London, H.M.S.O., 1954), p. 2.

[10] *Ibid.*, p. 3.

[11] *Ibid.*, p. 4.

fare founded upon the scientist ".[12] This committee, appointed in December, 1945, concerned itself with the recruitment of qualified scientists—either those with a degree or members of recognized institutions. The task was twofold : to bring back qualified scientists from the forces and guide them into occupations " according to the needs of reconstruction ", and to see how sufficient scientists could be trained to meet the "nation's requirements during the reconstruction period and thereafter ". In the light of its analysis the Barlow Committee recommended that the output of scientists should be doubled, estimated that between 1950 and 1955 fifteen thousand more teachers would be needed, and that by 1955 there would be a total demand for some ninety thousand scientists. This figure compared with the forty-five thousand registered scientists in 1945. But the demand exceeded by far the expectations of the committee; by 1950 the output of scientists had been more than doubled. But in 1956 there was still a grave shortage.[13] Estimates indicate that of the three thousand extra graduate science teachers needed before 1960, less than half will be available at the present rate of supply.

The Barlow Committee made clear that the quality of science graduates should not be sacrificed to increased numbers, and pointed out that only one in five of those who could benefit from a university education in fact received it. This made it possible for the committee to urge that the increased demand for science students should not be met at the expense of the humanities. The claim is perhaps substantiated by glancing at the number of university students per thousand of population in other industrialized European countries.[14] The United Kingdom, with 1·5 per thousand of population, comes very low in the list. There is evidence to suggest that this is not due only to lack of accommodation, equipment, and staff. In an attempt to maintain academic standards some institutions are not making full use of their available facilities.

The same serious shortage exists in engineering. In 1955 it was reported that the total number of graduates recruited was " some 25 .

---

[12] *Scientific Man-Power* (London, H.M.S.O., May, 1946), Cmd. 6824.
[13] *Technical Education* (H.M.S.O., London, February, 1956), Cmd. 9703; and *Ministry of Labour Gazette*, in which (December, 1954) over four thousand vacancies for qualified scientists were recorded by the Scientific and Technical Register.
[14] *Current School Enrolment Statistics* (UNESCO, June, 1955), and *Whitaker's Almanack, 1955*. Belgium, 2·5 students per thousand population; Denmark, 4·7; German Federal Republic, 2·4; Italy, 4·3; France, 3·3; Spain, 2·5; Sweden, 3·5; Switzerland, 3·2. (N.B.—This gives only rough comparisons as classification varies.)

per cent below the number required, the reason generally being that insufficient applicants were available." [15]

But industry needs other grades of trained men as well as graduates. Figures in *The Economist* showed that in mid-1955, in the engineering, shipbuilding, and vehicle-making industries, there were three to four vacancies for every person unemployed.[16]   Many of the skilled technicians in these industries are recruited through apprenticeships. Two types might be distinguished : ' student apprenticeships ' whose products might be named ' professional technologists,' and the craft or trade apprenticeships. Industrialists were just as concerned about the number and quality of recruits for these schemes as they were about graduates. Indeed, not enough people were being trained at any of the three levels. Again the question is : Is there enough talent available in the population of boys and girls to meet the demands of industry? If not, what are the orders of priority? The Advisory Council on Scientific Policy's *Report* (1955) indicated that industrialists were by no means unanimous in their opinions. Some thought, for example, that the effect of university expansion was to ' cream off ' from apprenticeship schemes too many of the brighter boys. University expansion was necessary, but not at the expense of apprentice schemes and only if the universities became, at the post-graduate level, more conscious of the needs of industry.

There were claims that the needs of industry could best be met by a large expansion of technical college work; one industrialist compared the number of Higher National Certificates awarded in the United Kingdom (some eight thousand in 1953–4) with the annual number of people in America who received a first degree (about four hundred thousand in 1950, of whom 150,000 were available to industry).[17] The two awards mentioned were regarded as equivalent qualifications. Figures for the output of similarly trained technologists from the U.S.S.R. are even more striking.[18]

The question of who shall train the various grades of technician is complicated by problems of how they shall be trained. Some industrialists felt that university training was not meeting industrial requirements, and that certainly post-graduate university research was less desirable for a man on graduation than entry into the rough and tumble of industry. The desirable qualities looked for in an engineering

---

[15] *Report on the Recruitment of Scientists and Engineers by the Engineering Industry* (Advisory Council on Scientific Policy), (London, H.M.S.O., 1955).

[16] *The Economist* (November 12th, 1955).

[17] *Advisory Council on Scientific Policy, op. cit. supra.*

[18] Nicholas De Witt, *Soviet Professional Manpower* (National Science Foundation, Washington, D.C., 1955), see also Cmd. 9703, *op. cit.*, Appendix A.

graduate were not in dispute, but in the face of competing demands for qualified men, several industrialists made plain their view that the expansion of science and engineering departments in universities must be achieved by diverting some of the very able men from other faculties. " It is unlikely that men of this calibre [university men with academic prowess, personality, and powers of leadership] are being missed by the university selection machinery and it is probable that the numbers can only be increased by diverting the very able men from other faculties such as Arts and Classics...." [19]

The committee evaluating the divergent views accepted that (a) there was a need to expand university departments, and that there would be an ever-increasing demand by industry for scientists and technologists trained to the graduate level, and (b) the talent available in the population was sufficient to meet the needs both of universities (in all faculties) and of technical apprenticeships. More children could be persuaded to stay at school for sixth form study, and there a " balanced attitude towards the different ways of training to become an engineer " [20] should be maintained.

In summary, after the war " the position of Great Britain as a leading industrial nation [was] . . . being endangered by failure to secure the fullest possible application of science to industry, and this failure is partly due to deficiencies in education ".[21] This may be primarily due to the fact that not enough of the nation's resources are, or were, invested in education. But within the limits of its resources the deficiencies of education might be of three kinds. First, the structure of the system might be such that young people leaving school are inefficiently distributed in accordance with industrial and economic needs. Secondly, the structure and its subsequent distributive effect might do nothing to improve human relations within industry and may, in fact, increase tensions, decrease co-operation, and thus affect output. Finally, what is taught and how it is taught affect the rate at which young people can be assimilated into industrial and adult life. It also raises the question of who shall undertake the kinds of training that are essential if this country is to survive as a leading industrial and democratic nation. How far has the 1944 Act met these post-war social demands?

The Extension of Education Services

Whilst the 1944 Act proposed to reorganize education under three heads—primary, secondary, and further—changes affecting secondary

---

[19] Advisory Council on Scientific Policy, op. cit. supra.
[20] Ibid., p. 13.
[21] Percy Report, Technical Education (London, H.M.S.O., 1945).

schooling are, generally, the most pertinent to this analysis. Two aspects of the proposed extensions, although important, will not therefore be considered in detail. Local authorities were to submit in their development plans details of nursery schools designed to meet the needs of pupils who had not yet reached the age of 5.[22] War-time needs had resulted in a very considerable increase in the number of nursery schools and the opening of day nurseries. At the end of March, 1945, there were some fifteen hundred day nurseries, in addition to over a hundred twenty-four-hour nurseries.[23] L.E.A.s were also running nearly eight hundred nursery classes. These institutions were evidently playing an important part in the nation's economy. During the first three years after the war's end the number of women in the armed services and civil employment dropped by a million—many of these were married women.[24] Despite the continuing demand for industrial workers, the majority of day nurseries were closed down or converted into nursery schools, and by 1953–4 only 486 of the latter were operating, with twenty-three thousand children in attendance.[25] It is difficult to assess how many young mothers, anxious to have either full- or part-time jobs, do not work because there is neither a day nursery nor a nursery school for their young children. There is every reason to believe that the demand for these schools is great, although obviously it is not restricted to mothers who wish to work. But more nursery schools would enable the number of workers to be increased. When in the interests of economy L.E.A.s proposed to close some of these schools, the Minister of Education asked them to review their decision in the light of local conditions, "including the extent to which mothers of children attending the schools were in full-time employment".[26] The same report stated that some nursery schools had been closed. This action had been taken, however, on the ground that the accommodation was urgently needed for children of statutory school age. The wisdom of the choice is debatable. Yet in nursery education, as elsewhere, the Act is explicitly concerned with the "needs of pupils", and makes no reference to the economic prosperity of the nation.

Economic stringency also curtailed the programme of further educa-

---

[22] *The 1944 Education Act* (Part II, sections 9(4) and 11(2)(e)).

[23] *Summary Report of the Ministry of Health: Year ending 31 March, 1945* (London, H.M.S.O., December, 1945), Cmd. 6710.

[24] *Annual Abstract of Statistics* (H.M.S.O., London), Nos. 88 and 91.

[25] *Education in 1954: Report of the Ministry of Education* (London, H.M.S.O., 1955), Cmd. 9521.

[26] *Education in 1952: Report of the Ministry of Education* (London, H.M.S.O., June, 1953), Cmd. 8835.

tion envisaged in the Act. The numbers [27] of part-time and evening students (above the statutory school-leaving age) attending various institutions of further education give some indication of the demand. A large proportion of this is, of course, for vocational training; fees in many cases being small, they do not represent a large personal investment, but many industrial firms make heavy investments in the training of personnel through day-release schemes and through their own apprenticeship schemes. The Act provided that this demand should be met by local authorities, who were required to secure the adequate " full-time education for persons over compulsory school age " [28] and for the leisure-time occupation of such persons as are willing and able to benefit from them.

Colleges of further education were to provide vocational instruction for young people. It was also recognized, if not sufficiently emphasized, that some kind of education beyond the compulsory attendance age was necessary in a complex industrial society to prepare members for citizenship.

County colleges were to do this in compulsory part-time (one day a week) courses for adolescents up to the age of 18 who were not in full-time attendance elsewhere. The education was to be such as would, at one and the same time, " increase the happiness and welfare of the individuals " and " be for the good of the country and the communities that comprise it ".[29] Young people were to be helped to adjust to their jobs, their complex industrial communities, and to ' life ' through a mixture of physical education, practical work, general subjects, and electives. The latter would be " especially useful for laying the foundations of social activities ". This policy could be criticized as placing too much emphasis on ' individual needs ', even though they were given a social context. Nevertheless, in county colleges young people from different types of school, and from a variety of jobs, could have been brought together and given the opportunity of acquiring some of the social knowledge and skills necessary in a complex industrial democratic society. Here future managers and skilled workers might have met. Problems of human relations in industry, the economic structure of the country, and its political institutions could be studied, the responsibilities of democratic living examined. Since county colleges have failed to materialize, young people pick up their ' social ' knowledge in a variety of places, but chiefly within a highly

---

[27] In 1953-4 : Part-time day students, 372,000; evening students 1,860,000.
[28] *Further Education*, Ministry of Education Pamphlet No. 8 (London, H.M.S.O., 1947).
[29] *Youth's Opportunity*, Ministry of Education Pamphlet No. 3 (London, H.M.S.O., 1946).

structured industrial set-up. The norms of output, behaviour, and so on, are set by conflicting groups—with serious economic consequences.

Parental Demand for ' Secondary ' Schooling

Among other things, it is in relation to the failure to establish county colleges that the present structure of ' secondary ' education is so deficient. Its extension under the Act has, of course, been most controversial. Of the three proposed stages, it has perhaps the most direct bearing on national well-being. In fact, it operates as an instrument of occupational selection. What is taught in ' secondary ' schools and how it is taught greatly influence the attitudes of young people entering industry, commerce, and the professions. Whether this education should be vocational or not is therefore a matter of debate. Furthermore, unlike primary education, ' secondary ' education is selective, or discriminatory, and therefore as a part of compulsory schooling is the one in which inequalities of opportunity are most keenly felt.

In the following brief account of the growth of the ' secondary ' stage some attempt has been made to analyse the parental demand for education and the economic reasons for it. In the light of this, what has been done in education since 1944 can be judged.

The cry "secondary education for all" finds expression through organizations like the trade unions and the Labour Party; this demand has been either for secondary technical schools providing first-rate vocational instruction, or for common schools into which all children from a particular geographical area would go irrespective of ability or parental income. When, from the turn of the nineteenth century, non-vocational, somewhat classically biased selective ' secondary ' schools developed, labour leaders rightly demanded an extension of these. They were not to be fobbed off with technical, vocational, or trade schools. Thus the development between 1902 and 1939 showed three main trends. First, there was a substantial increase in the number of ' secondary ' schools and in the number of pupils in them. There was, furthermore, a considerable rise in the proportion of pupils entering them from public elementary schools: by 1938 this was as high as 81 per cent, of whom more than half, i.e., 57.4 per cent, paid no fees.[30] The third trend was that the proportion of free places or special places had risen steadily, so that of the total admissions to grant-aided ' secondary ' schools nearly 70 per cent had Free or Special places. Of these, nearly 80 per cent paid no fees, about 10 received no exemption, and the rest paid partial fees. In this year, altogether some 470,000 pupils were in ' secondary ' schools, about 19 per cent of the 11–17-

---

[30] *Education in 1938: Report of the Board of Education* (London, H.M.S.O., May, 1939), Cmd. 6013.

and-above age-group of children in publicly maintained schools. Thus the opportunities for 'secondary' education had been increased considerably for clever children from the elementary schools. Transfer took place on the basis of scholarship results at 11 or slightly older.

Just less than half the pupils (about 47 per cent) paid fees. They were quite modest, ranging from five guineas a year in a few local authority schools to over thirty guineas in some foundation schools. For the most part, fees were between six and twelve guineas a year.[31] These schools catered for—and in turn sustained and enlarged—the growing middle class. Because of the advantages 'secondary' education conferred upon its recipients (cf. pupils who went to elementary schools until the age of 14), parents were prepared to pay, if necessary at some sacrifice, for it. The return on their investment in terms of occupational advantage, social advancement, and ultimately greater economic security for their children can be appreciated by a brief catalogue of occupations open only to pupils from 'secondary' and 'Public' (private, independent, fee-charging) schools. All the professions requiring university training—medicine, law, university, and 'secondary' school teaching, scientific research, and so on—were closed to pupils from elementary schools. Increasingly, teacher training colleges were becoming restricted to those with a 'secondary' education. Banking, accountancy, and other occupations associated with professional bodies demanded similar educational qualifications on entry. These schools also gave considerable advantage to those pupils who aspired to commercial work, either as representatives or as clerical workers in industry. In short, practically all 'white-collar' jobs were filled by 'secondary' school pupils.

It need only be mentioned that these occupations were specially attractive in England during the 1930's. In periods of unemployment, economic depression, and deflation, those who have fixed, pensionable, salaried positions are very favoured. Understandably, 'secondary' education was in great demand. It did not matter that the curriculum was rather formal, that teaching was stereotyped, that the amount of science taught was woefully small. A greater dose of education, as such, gave a person a greater chance of security, a pension, better conditions of work, and a higher standard of living.

Evidently, the 'secondary' schools were middle-class schools; socially desirable as well as economically advantageous, they were able to compete in many ways with the more famous older established 'Public' schools. They were also in demand by the workers. An alternative for labour leaders was the common, or comprehensive secondary, school. The principle of this kind of school, into which

---

[31] *Ibid.*, p. 132.

all children go irrespective of ability, has been held with a steadfastness that does credit to those who have constantly urged the provision of greater equality of educational opportunity. The difficulties of maintaining it will, perhaps, be better appreciated when the position of the influential ' Public' schools is discussed later.

Meeting the Demand

In fact, the historical development of education in England had created a popular demand for schools which could compete with the ' Public' schools—exclusive institutions for a socially or economically privileged few. The provision of post-primary education in the 1944 Act was based on a series of reports dating from 1926. Very little *new* thinking emerged from them, and hardly any sociological analysis. The programme was one of expansion in terms of the " needs of the pupils". But these were so narrowly conceived as to disregard almost completely the vocational aspirations of other than the ' white-collar' workers.

" Child-centred " Schools

The Hadow Committee (1926) virtually proposed to set up " child-centred schools ". These should, however, not be confused with the similarly named American schools, for there the structure of the common school gave the concept an entirely different meaning. In fact, post-primary education in England " should be envisaged so far as possible as a single whole, within which there will be a variety of types of education supplied, but which will be marked by the common characteristic that its aim is to provide for the needs of children who are entering and passing through the stage of adolescence ".[32] Structurally a multi-partite scheme was proposed; the existing junior technical and trade schools were to continue as before. In the *Spens Report*,[33] a more strictly tripartite scheme of grammar, technical, and modern schools was advocated, and the *Norwood Report* [34] justified it in the abilities of " particular groups of pupils ". Those children who were interested in learning for its own sake should go to the grammar schools, those " whose interests and abilities lie markedly in the field of applied science and applied art " should attend technical schools; finally, a pupil who " deals more easily with concrete things than with ideas . . .", whose horizon " is near " and whose movement " within a limited area . . . is generally slow, though it may be surpris-

---

[32] *Hadow Report: Education of the Adolescent* (London, H.M.S.O., 1926), Chapter III, section 87.

[33] *Spens Report: Secondary Education* (London, H.M.S.O., 1938).

[34] *Norwood Report: Curriculum and Examinations in Secondary Schools* (London, H.M.S.O., 1943).

ingly rapid in seizing a particular point or in taking up a special line ",
should attend, with his fellows, a modern school. This, for better or
worse, was ' the mixture as before '.

Child-centred education makes claims to be based on what is best for
the child. Historically, in England, education has been more concerned with a child's character (and, strangely, this has involved an
ability to pass examinations) than with him as a potential adult
worker. Consequently the *Hadow Report* went no further than to
suggest a liberal, humane education provided for modern school children by "means of a curriculum containing large opportunities for
practical work and related to living interests ".[35] Only the last two
years, however, should be given over to a practical bias, and even
this should not aim at giving a technical or vocational education.
" ' Realistic ' studies " should be used " as an instrument of general
education." [36] A very different outlook exists in America.[37]

Under its principles of curriculum development, the *Spens Report*
placed the training of the individual first, but then included his training as a democratic citizen and as a future worker. The *Norwood
Report*, however, countered criticism of the traditional liberal education by pointing out how adaptable ' secondary ' school pupils had
shown themselves to be during the war. It is a large step—but one
that is implied—to assume that these pupils were what they were
because of their school education and that it had met the requirement
that "the curriculum must fit the child, and not the child the curriculum." [38]

All these views are based on an archaic, if highly reputable, philosophy, ameliorated by a somewhat warmer regard for and appreciation
of children as growing organisms. The reports ignored almost completely the economic and social implications of their proposals. In
the 'thirties, it is perhaps understandable that many people felt that
the economic stability of Britain and the Empire had been built up
largely on the commercial and industrial enterprise of leaders trained
in a liberal, largely unspecialized tradition. England remained relatively prosperous, with large foreign investments, and was able,
through the dole, to keep from starvation her three million unemployed. The possibilities of reducing adult unemployment by further
investment in education was rejected by industrialists. A new pattern
of education for England, in face of contemporary or future economic
circumstances, was not seriously considered in official reports.

It is not surprising, therefore, that the 1944 Act made it the duty of

---

[35] Hadow, *op. cit. supra*, Chapter III, section 93.
[36] *Ibid.*, p. 85.   [37] See note 56, p. 250.
[38] Norwood, *op. cit. supra*, p. 9.

every local education authority to provide sufficient schools in their area to " afford for all pupils opportunities for education offering such varieties of instruction and training as may be desirable in view of their different ages, abilities, and aptitudes. . . ." [39] No fees were to be charged, and in principle parents had the right to select the kind of education they desired for their children.   Clause 76 of the Act stated: "So far as is compatible with the provision of efficient instruction and training and the avoidance of unreasonable public expenditure, pupils are to be educated in accordance with the wishes of their parents." But the direct participation of parents in the formal process of education is negligible in English state schools.   Joint effort in the organization of curriculum, in methods of teaching, and in the content of lessons (except in religion, where there is a conscience clause) has not been part of the tradition.   It is usually made clear to parents in the growing number of parent-teacher associations that on these questions the word of the 'expert' is law.   The desires of parents within the state system can be expressed only through the structure of the schools and in their ability to contract out if they can afford to, either by sending their children to non-state schools or by educating them privately. The problem is to extend the area of activity in which the parent might participate without infringing the professional rights of teachers. In the event, all three reports gave support to the tripartite system. Parents were thus, in theory, able to select one of three types of school but were unable to choose between various educational offerings.

The Adequacy of the Building Programme

The choice of parents has been seriously limited.   Since the war, as before, the demand has been for grammar schooling.   Apart from the traditional advantages, this was not difficult to understand.   Between the wars the majority of educational investment had been in ' secondary ' schools.   Relatively little had been spent on selective post-primary schools (central and technical), and even less on the old elementary schools, many of which had been built during the elementary school expansion of the late nineteenth century.   Many of these old buildings lacked specialist rooms, were often inadequately heated, and in general made it possible to pursue instruction only in the three R's, plus a watered-down ' secondary ' curriculum containing very little science. A halt was called in 1938 on ' secondary ' school building, so that more of the other post-primary building could take place.[40]

In the event, the economics of the reorganization were simple.   There

---

[39] *1944 Education Act* (Part II, section 1(b)), p. 5,
[40] *Education in 1938, op. cit. supra.*

already existed comparatively new ' secondary ' schools carrying out programmes now proposed for grammar schools; there were a number of old, and a few new, technical and trade schools, and a large number of comparatively old buildings which before the Act had housed pupils enjoying post-primary but elementary education : the selective central schools, the non-selective central schools, and the higher tops or senior departments of existing elementary schools. Least immediate disturbance would be created by renaming the ' secondary ' schools ' grammar '; retaining the technical schools as such, and calling the rest ' secondary modern ' schools. This is what happened in a large number of cases. Understandably, and inevitably, it increased the demand for grammar schools. The prospects of rehousing secondary modern schools were indeed not rosy.

During the war, over five thousand schools were destroyed or badly damaged. In addition, by the end of March, 1945, "more than a million houses in Greater London and South-East England had been destroyed or damaged".[41] This situation called for special measures: "The Government decided to treat the first two years after the end of hostilities in Europe as a period of national emergency . . . and proposed to take measures with the object of increasing the numbers of men in the building trade from the current level of 337,000 (compared with about 1,000,000 before the war) to 800,000 by the end of the first year after the defeat of Germany."[42] Evidently schools had to take their place in an order of building priorities. Shortages of cement, steel, and timber added to the acute shortage of employees in slowing down the process of replacing out-of-date school buildings and putting up new ones. By the end of 1948 the temporary housing programme had been virtually completed, and the number of vacancies notified by building and civil engineering contractors had been reduced to forty thousand, yet in this year slightly less than 1 per cent of the total value of building and civil work authorized was for hospitals and schools.[43] The low priority accorded to educational buildings was brought out more vividly in an article in *The Economist* discussing Mr. Philip Redfern's paper to the Royal Statistical Society. With due allowances for depreciation, obsolescence, and so on, Britain's capital investments in agriculture, public utilities, transport and communications, manufacturing and distribution, housing, and public social services were compared. The latter were in the worst position except for

---

[41] *Summary Report of the Ministry of Health: Year Ending March, 1945* (London, H.M.S.O., December, 1945), Cmd. 6710.

[42] Cmd. 6609 (London, H.M.S.O., March, 1945).

[43] *Summary Report of the Ministry of Works* (London, H.M.S.O., June, 1949), Cmd. 7698.

agriculture. The article concluded: "This total result marks wide divergences between the different classes. Net investment in housing has been impressive—too impressive." [44] Housing, of course, became central in the election campaign of 1951. And since the war, health schemes had received greater attention than education.

This serious decline in investment took place in a period when the school-leaving age was raised from 14 to 15, and when the rapid increase in births after the war was beginning to show itself in the primary schools. A great many of the resources available for education were put into meeting these 'emergencies'. But even in 1954 *The Economist* reported that in more than 40 per cent of all primary classes there was overcrowding—and " by official definition a primary class is not overcrowded until it consists of over 40 pupils, which by any common-sense standard is far too large ".[45] In addition, two-thirds of the secondary school classes were overcrowded—with more than thirty pupils.

Raising the school-leaving age not only threw an additional burden on educational resources but also withheld from an already starved labour market nearly a quarter of a million youngsters. Many of them resented the delay in entering gainful employment, and the situation was made worse by the fact that some teachers were ill-prepared to provide, in the extra year, courses which had relevance either to pupil interests or to social needs.

The Recruitment of Teachers

The renamed secondary modern schools suffered from a further disadvantage. Prior to 1944, teachers had been paid more or less according to the school in which they taught—there were elementary school teachers and ' secondary ' school masters. The elementary school teachers' salary scale was much lower than that of the ' secondary ' teachers. Qualifications were also different. On the whole, ' secondary ' schools employed university graduates with three or four years' training; the other post-primary schools employed teachers with two years of training in training colleges. The market value of the former was much higher than that of the latter. But Burnham Committee proposals in 1944 tied teaching salaries after the war to a basic and common scale, with increments for additional training, i.e., graduates. These increments were, in the early post-war era, too small to win to the profession in large numbers the highly qualified graduate who had found his way into the pre-war ' secondary ' schools. This was particularly true of science graduates, whose economic position in the teaching profession bore no relation to the salary they could command in other

---

[44] " Britain's Capital Formation ", *The Economist* (January 22nd, 1955).
[45] " Towards Longer Schooldays ", *The Economist* (May 8th, 1954), Vol. CLXXI.

occupations. The general shortage of teachers was met by the emergency training scheme, during which over thirty thousand teachers were trained in one-year courses. Generally speaking, this dilution weakened the bargaining position of teachers as a whole without filling the vital gaps in the science-teaching corps. No other profession lost its scarcity value, and therefore its economic power, by halving in this way the minimum period of qualifying training. This reduction occurred at a time when the amount of knowledge a teacher should have has increased enormously, particularly in science and the social studies.

The failure to maintain salary differentials within the teaching profession in line with market values seriously decreased the ability of the educational system to compete at all for certain types of teacher. The supply of mathematics and science teachers was, and is, completely inadequate. More generous technical college scales have drawn many of the better-qualified graduates away from the grammar schools. The plight of the secondary modern schools was even worse. Understandably, graduates continued to move into grammar schools. Until they were adequately staffed there was little hope that the modern schools would attract many graduates, and certainly not the best of them. As the supply of arts graduates improves, no doubt the situation will change. P.E.P.'s report showed what a large proportion of them went into teaching—but few science graduates were attracted to it.[46]

' Parity of Esteem ' and the Devaluation of Skill

In terms, then, of tradition, buildings, equipment, and staffing the secondary modern school had, and has, little prestige. Since 1944, attempts have been made to create a demand for this type of school. Policy statements have wished to accord ' parity of esteem ' to all types of secondary education. This objective can be achieved at the verbal level. In practice, esteem is a measure of public demand; parity of esteem will be enjoyed by the secondary modern school only when there are as many parents who want their children to attend it as there are parents who want their children to go to a grammar school. This is patently not the case. Few parents to-day who won places to pre-war ' secondary ' schools want their children to have an inferior education and so reduce their occupational opportunities. Many of these parents are no doubt aware of the economic advantages that their liberal, traditional, humane education gave them. They still hope, rightly or wrongly, that a grammar school education will safeguard or enhance the social and, to some extent, the economic position of their children. In the changed economic circumstances of post-war England they might be mistaken, but they are right in thinking that secondary

<hr>

[46] " Graduates' Jobs ", *Planning* (P.E.P.), Vol. XXI, October 24th, 1955.

modern schools have nothing better to offer. It cannot have whilst its aims, methods, and curricular offerings are pale copies of the grammar and 'Public' school. With less favourable facilities, how can the secondary modern school compete with these schools in preparing its pupils for universities or 'white-collar' jobs?

The specialized nature of the demand for secondary education is reflected in the public criticism of intelligence tests as methods of selection at 11+. It suggests that they are unacceptable, invalid, and unreliable. The movement of workers to areas with good grammar school provision is another indication of this demand.

Since all fees to publicly maintained schools were abolished, new criteria of selection have had to be used. They are " age, aptitude, and ability ". Albeit sufficiently general and vague as to defy definition, they imply the presence in human beings of rather specific, innate, and measurable qualities. To assume that certain tests measure what is there is one thing; then to use the results as a predictive instrument is another. But this, it seems to me, is often what is done. Selection tests are used to predict the future success of children in school and subsequently, without any regard for the socio-economic and familial circumstances in which they will be working. (Successful predictions in the natural sciences involve an accurate statement and control of the specific conditions under which the predicted event will take place.) If, after selection at 11, subsequent success is measured in series of academic examinations, then some consideration of the incentives to succeed in grammar schools is important. If they are high at 11, are they necessarily so as the school-leaving age approaches? The curricula of grammar schools have an important bearing on this question.

For to-day the 'white-collar' jobs are not, of course, as economically desirable as they were, although they may retain considerable social prestige. Since the war, inflationary pressures, high income-tax, and over-employment have lowered the relative position of salaried workers. The greatest scarcity of labour was in engineering and associated industries. In the middle of 1955 there were almost 500,000 unfilled industrial vacancies. The number of unemployed was of the order of 150,000.[47] In this situation, reading, writing, and arithmetic conferred no particular advantage on the potential industrial worker. He was in demand, and not, as in the 'thirties, competing for too few jobs. School leavers have had no difficulty in finding employment. What is a matter of grave social concern is the distribution of young workers. Immediate economic returns encourage many of them to go into unskilled work, dissuade them from taking further courses of instruction, and discourage them from taking trade or student

---

[47] *The Economist* (November 12th, 1955).

apprenticeships. Wage differentials between skilled and unskilled workers have steadily declined over the past fifty years, partly as a result of trade union policy.

A serious problem has been created. It was discussed in *The Economist* under the title " The Devaluation of Skill ". Under inflation, differentials have been narrowed so that the wage of the skilled worker in engineering to that of the unskilled worker as a percentage has been reduced from 172 in 1900 to 119 in 1946 and 116 in 1954.[48] The writer suggested that the case for saying that less " formal training for industrial trades and crafts " was now necessary had not been proven. "Technological change has largely retired some hand skills, but it has immensely widened the range of skills that its attendants require; . . . evidence is certainly insufficient to establish the hypothesis of any absolute decline in modern industry's demand for skill; on the whole, the indications tend the other way. But will enough people acquire skill if the price for doing so continues to fall?"[49] What contribution are the schools making to the solution of this problem? It could be argued that schools should give far more pupils the technical and—of equal importance—the social skills needed by industry.

Of course, many occupations are still closed to secondary modern school pupils. They are denied the social prestige of most 'white-collar' jobs. But many of them can earn higher wages as unskilled workers in industry than the 'white-collared' worker—particularly the trainee. There is little economic incentive to succeed academically in secondary modern schools. Apathy may turn into hostility if the futility of what is being taught strikes home. Any resentment at being rejected at 11 may turn into a bitterness tinged with scorn. These attitudes may be carried over into adult life.

This indifference to what is offered in the name of education might be changed if the skills needed to gain promotion in industry were taught. These are a combination of technical skill in the operation and maintenance of machinery, applied intelligence in the handling of men, and a social knowledge of how to get on with fellow workers and superiors so that a group can function harmoniously.

This economic situation also affects the grammar schools. Opportunities of employment being what they are, pupils who find the work in school either difficult or apparently unrelated to any of the problems they are facing drop out, to take up employment before finishing the grammar school course. The seriousness of this for industry has been pointed out. The wastage involved is revealed by figures of pupils

---

[48] " The Devaluation of Skill," *The Economist* (June 4th, 1955).

[49] *Ibid.*, p. 870.

throughout England who leave grammar schools before completing the course.[50] Figures for 1947 showed only a slight improvement in the percentage of early leavers from grammar schools on the figures for 1930 (a year of acute economic depression). There was virtually no improvement in the percentages staying at school until they were 17 or 18, despite the raised leaving age, and the fact that the 1944 Act was designed to make entry to these schools on ability and not on ability to pay. The returns do not seem very high. Examination successes[51] lead to much the same view. Several conclusions are possible. Perhaps the methods of selection to-day are no more reliable than when payment of fees was an important criterion. We might be wrong in assuming that a larger proportion of pupils than were in grammar schools pre-war can cope adequately with the work there. Or it is possible that the incentives to succeed are fast disappearing? There are differences of opinion on all these points of view.

If greater numbers than at present are capable of benefiting from grammar school and the university education as it now is, we are driven back to the question of incentives—social and economic—and to the adequacy of what is taught in English schools in terms of parental (and pupil) demand and of social and industrial need. " In a sense," the writer in *The Economist* remarked, " one ought to be down in the dumps about education; for there is no doubt that its present inadequacy, both in quality and duration, is a great source of national weakness." [52] The situation was compared unfavourably with that in America, where educational opportunity of a less scholarly type has been widely extended. Whatever disadvantages this has had, " the result has been to create a large educational middle class of men and women who, without ever coming within sight of being scholars or scientists, have nevertheless been trained far beyond the elementary level. Nobody who has had the opportunity of observing the strength and vitality that are thereby given to the American community can fail to want to build a similar educational middle class in Britain, where it is still woefully small ". Too often the achievements of the average American high school product are compared with those of an average English grammar school pupil—the comparison should be with the secondary modern school pupil.

---

[50] *Early Leaving: A Report of the Central Advisory Council for Education* (England), (London, H.M.S.O., 1954).

[51] *Education in 1938* and *Education in 1954*. Exact comparisons are difficult because the form of the statistical tables has been changed.

[52] " Towards Longer Schooldays," *The Economist, op. cit. supra.*

The Distribution of Resources

Quite obviously the economic resources of post-war England could not match those of America. But it is important to consider whether the meagre resources available for education were used in a way likely to improve the economic situation by creating a larger educational middle class and preparing young workers for industry.

Perhaps the rapid increase in the number of children of primary school age could not have been foreseen. It meant, however, that between 1945 and 1952, 928 new primary departments had been completed compared with 194 completed secondary departments.[53] Raising the school-leaving age involved building six and a half thousand rooms to accommodate pupils retained in secondary schools from 14 to 15. Apart from these demands on resources, statistics show that at least from 1950 the educational building programme provided for substantially more secondary modern school places than for either grammar or technical school places. Some seventeen times as many modern school places were provided in 1952 as technical school places, and four times as many as grammar school places. The ratio improved in 1954 (8 to 1 for technical places), but evidently the large majority of resources was still being put into schools for which there was no demand, and whose curriculum was not designed to give vocational instruction, or to guide school leavers towards occupations vital to the nation's economy. A total of 1,185,360 pupils in secondary modern schools should be compared with a mere 90,132 in technical schools (*Education in 1954*). It can be appreciated that the cost of secondary school building is greater than that of primary schools, but it is debatable whether the cost, and therefore the resources invested, of technical school building are more than those of modern school building.

No doubt the most serious problem, if far greater emphasis than at present were placed on providing technical schools, would be the shortage of qualified staff. The report on *Technical Education* (H.M.S.O., 1956) disappoints by not making this problem central. Nevertheless, industry has to find teachers for its extensive apprenticeship schemes. Much on-the-job training could with advantage be provided, as in the U.S.A. and the U.S.S.R., in secondary technical schools.

It perhaps needs reiterating that this failure to invest in technical education took place in spite of the frequent official and unofficial statements urging the need for more technically trained people at all levels. The greatest single obstacle to building up substantial technical training in schools has been the kind of psycho-philosophy implicit in

---

[53] *Education in 1952* (London, H.M.S.O., 1953).

the three important reports on secondary education and in the English educational tradition. Many influential people have felt that technical and vocational instruction cannot be the core and base of a broad general education. Moreover, a large proportion of highly paid and responsible positions has consistently been held by persons with little or no scientific training.[54] These views have influenced the kind of technical education given in many institutions. It has been criticized by industry as being unrelated to industrial problems. In spite of the Advisory Council on Scientific Policy's statement that "Industry in all its branches should be encouraged still further to recognize the value of University graduates",[55] many industrialists were not disposed to accept post-graduate scientists because of the ' pure ' character of their university research experience.

The ' pure ' criterion of sound technical education spreads down to secondary schools. There is an emphasis on ' principles ' rather than on applied vocational training. Some indication of the difference in the American attitude towards vocational education can be gauged from the statement of John Dewey in a letter to the New Republic (1915): " I would go farther than he is apparently willing to go," wrote Dewey, " in holding that education should be vocational . . . that a separation of trade education and general education of youth has the inevitable tendency to make both kinds of training narrower, less significant and less effective than the schooling in which the material and traditional education is re-organized to utilize the industrial subject-matter—active, scientific and social—of the present-day environment." [56]

The limited view of technology and vocational studies and their role in education have meant that very little attention is paid to science in secondary modern schools; certainly it could not be said to be the central core of the curriculum. Some people would agree with Dewey in objecting " to the identification of vocation with such trades as can be learned before the age of, say, eighteen or twenty; and to the identification of education with the acquisition of specialized skills in the management of machines at the expense of an industrial intelligence based on science and a knowledge of social problems and conditions ".[57] They might feel that important as training technicians

---

[54] Letter from Stanley Mayne, General Secretary, Institution of Professional Civil Servants (Manchester Guardian, Saturday, December 10th, 1955), stated that the remuneration of scientific officers in the Civil Service is, on the whole, less than for officers in the administrative class with similar qualifications.

[55] Annual Report of the Advisory Council on Scientific Policy, 1948–9 (London, H.M.S.O., July, 1949), Cmd. 7755.

[56] Letter in New Republic (Vol. III, May–July, 1915).

[57] Ibid.

is, of equal importance is the development and release of 'industrial intelligence' through scientific and social studies. Innumerable judgments, political, ethical, social, and economic, have to be made to-day, if they are to be rational, on some knowledge of science and its implications. This knowledge cannot be taught in a few isolated lessons by teachers who have a rudimentary acquaintance of the content of science, its methods and techniques of investigation. A great deal of money would be needed to build up a corps of teachers.

Under the 1944 Act the county colleges were, perhaps, to fulfil this need. " In this scientific and industrial age," according to the Ministry pamphlet, " the pattern of our lives is complex. . . . There is a danger that the over-intricate pattern will become ill-proportioned and out of joint. . . . We must be efficient in our work, for upon this depends our standard of life and that of our neighbours at home and abroad." [58] Through further education and with the co-operation of industry and commerce an adequate system of vocational preparation was to be developed. The failure to open county colleges has thrown an added responsibility on to the secondary modern school.

Meanwhile, with these serious deficiencies on the educational side of the system, very considerable resources have been put into the provision of lunches, milk, medical, and dental services through the schools. The latter two services seem in some ways to duplicate the expensive and extensive Health Service. Of the former, it involved an investment, when building materials were scarce, of twenty-two million pounds—only twelve million were spent in accommodating the pupils kept on when the school-leaving age was raised. The emphasis on the 'welfare' side of educational distribution reflected the strength of the post-war demand for health services and the priority given them among the competing claims on real resources.

Comprehensive Schools and the ' Public ' Schools

The tripartite system is open to grave objections. It has failed to develop a large educational middle class, and has helped to sharpen class differences. Yet the solution cannot be to send more and more children to grammar schools unless the curricular offerings of these schools are radically altered—the wastage in these schools has already been mentioned. Until the curriculum of the grammar schools is revised there is little hope that secondary modern schools can develop along different lines. Only a very considerable increase in the number of technical schools—for which there is a growing parental demand— could salvage the system. As it is, the latter is fulfilling none of the

---

[58] *Further Education*, Ministry of Education Pamphlet No. 8 (London, H.M.S.O., 1947), p. 5.

three roles education might be expected to play in increased national prosperity. Very little initial training of specialists and technical workers is done, so that most of it has to be done after school before they can be fully absorbed into industry. The system is not guiding sufficient pupils towards skilled industrial occupations. Finally, it is not providing the social education necessary to make industry, and the economy, ' tick ', whilst at the same time safeguarding democratic institutions. To achieve the first and second objectives there should be more technical and commercial education, and to achieve the third —if for economic reasons county colleges cannot be established—there should be common schools for children in the formative years of adolescence. The emphasis in these schools should be on the acquisi- tion of social skills. Attention should be paid to the training of pupils in the ability to take democratic decisions, to appreciate the wider implications of science and technology, and to understand as far as possible the basic principles of the nation's economy.

This does not mean that comprehensive schools should be as large, e.g. as those of the London County Council. The view that the com- mon school should be large is often based on the belief that the widest possible range of subjects should be offered, that some of the pupils should reach the same academic standards at 15 as the brightest grammar school pupils, and that only in this way can adequate Sixth Forms develop. My belief is that schools, at least up to the age of 15, should not be selective; that a common core of learning should be pre- sent, and that the emphasis should be on social and economic living. The curriculum might be based on Herbert Spencer's views; one which helps to prepare children to face the problems of personal, occupa- tional, aesthetic, and leisure-time activities. Clearly to have a large unselective school in which the emphasis is on those aspects of learn- ing which have traditionally been carried out in smaller selective grammar schools is grossly inefficient. American experience [59] is that the schools doing the job of preparing university students best are the smaller suburban schools, not the large comprehensive city schools. In the former the homogeneity of the pupil population, parental back- ground, and support and the economic environment will all play im- portant parts in the success of the teaching. I visualize the common school as a reasonably small regional school serving all the children of the immediate locality. The courses would be largely unspecialized.

Specialist studies after the school-leaving age could take place in separate institutions. Junior colleges of the type proposed for Croy- don, where this specialized study could take place, have a great deal

---

[59] *General Education in a Free Society* (Harvard University Press, 1946).

to recommend them. The process of selection could, if the feeding schools were non-selective, be delayed until the compulsory leaving age. The utilization of highly qualified staff, specialist accommodation, and so on would be much more efficient than at present. The segregation at 15 of children into secondary grammar colleges (leading to university studies), technical colleges (for student apprenticeships and some university studies), and colleges for commercial and other vocational training would not be open to the same moral objections of doing so at 11. The technical difficulties of reliable, valid, and acceptable selection would be considerably reduced.

These institutions would not run counter to the 'Public' school tradition of having highly qualified teachers devoting the whole of their attention to Sixth Form work. In many grammar schools this is too widely spread at the moment. It would be possible in an urban area and with such a scheme to attract a sufficient number of well-qualified arts and science graduates to do adequately the job of preparing pupils for the universities (many of which are complaining of the poor quality of student they are now receiving). At the moment, Sixth Forms are spread throughout an urban area, in many cases the classes are too small to provide intellectual stimulus, the work is duplicated several times throughout the area, and the quality of teaching varies enormously. The failure in some schools to provide certain science courses through lack of qualified teachers makes the whole process inefficient. Furthermore, few people would argue that *every* graduate is capable of teaching the most able Sixth Form students. Yet in few grammar schools is it possible for qualified persons to devote all their time to Sixth Form teaching; their energy is often dissipated, leaving them little time to maintain and enhance their own scholarship. The tasks of preparing specialists could undoubtedly be undertaken with much less waste in institutions similar to the proposed junior colleges. This kind of organization would distribute available resources much more economically.

Of course, critics maintain that this would destroy the *ethos* of the grammar schools, that it would deprive them of leadership, and so on. Are the secondary modern schools to be deprived of this kind of leadership at the expense of the grammar schools? Are there not opportunities in a common secondary school enrolling children from 11 to 15 for the exercise of leadership? Is there no leadership to be found in the American junior high schools? Do the American senior high schools fail to develop in three years any *esprit de corps*, any scholarship, or any social learning? Only a rash person would give unfavourable answers to all these questions.

The Position of the ' Public ' Schools

An important factor in the reorganization of the English system is the presence of the private and ' Public ' independent schools. The 1944 Act made it possible, under certain conditions, for privately owned-and-run schools to remain open and continue to charge fees. This accords with clause 76, which stated that pupils should be educated in terms of the wishes of their parents. It gave to that section of the community who can afford the very high fees charged by the best of these schools an opportunity denied to the rest of English society. No doubt, many parents regard the payment of high fees as an investment. Dr. Hans has shown [60] what positions of power, importance, and wealth are occupied by products of the famous ' Public ' schools. Parents who pay these fees may complain that in addition they help to support an educational system from which they derive no benefit through general and local taxation. Yet since the war an increasing number of parents in England seem to have thought that this heavy investment in education, even though involving considerable sacrifices on their part, was worth while. There probably remain many who would be prepared to make a direct investment in education by paying the kind of moderate fee (adjusted to present-day money values) which were common in the pre-war fee-paying grammar or ' secondary ' school. Denied this opportunity, some have their children coached for the 11 + selection tests with possibly harmful effects.

The difficulty remains that if the tripartite system were discarded, common or comprehensive schools would be in direct competition with the ' Public ' schools and would be at some disadvantage. Many of the latter are, of course, large, but their pupil populations are fairly homogeneous socially, in outlook, in ambition, and so on. This would not be the case in the state common school. The quality of the staff in ' Public ' schools depends on the willingness of the consumers to pay the price of high teacher salaries, adequate specialist accommodation, and a low teacher-pupil ratio. It is generally better than is to be expected in a state school. Conditions make it possible to select able boys for special attention from a very early age. The *ethos* of the schools makes it possible for less able boys to progress academically at their own rate without undue feelings of failure. Attendance at one of them, indeed, often confers a status considerably higher than great academic success in a state institution. Opportunities are provided for the kind of education, general, vocational, and specialist, that their parents demand and for which they are willing to pay. Perhaps only

---

[60] N. Hans, " Independent Schools and the Liberal Professions," *Year Book of Education,* 1950 (Evans Bros.).

a few of these schools have smaller science than classical sides. A letter from Mr. W. Hamilton, Chairman of the Headmasters' Conference (*Times Educational Supplement*, November 18th, 1955), showed how balanced were the science and arts Sixth Forms in independent and direct-grant schools. No doubt many very able boys are encouraged to take up classical or modern studies, but equal numbers now pursue scientific courses: a reflection of parental and social demand. There is little doubt that the ' Public ' schools offer their pupils experience in making democratic decisions through a variety of activities and institutions. The high quality of the education provided has to be paid for. It is difficult to estimate their *per capita* expenditure on education because many of them are well endowed, receive many bequests, and so on; tuition fees might reflect only part of it. But in 1951–2 *fees* for day pupils in independent schools ranged from about £67 per annum to £175. Typical in London schools were fees of £75. Preparatory school fees also showed wide variations, but were of the same order as in the ' Public ' schools. State secondary schools *cost* £43.2 per pupil to run, and state primary schools *cost* £24.3 per pupil in the same year.[61] It is impossible to imagine new comprehensive schools providing as good an ' education ' as the established ' Public ' schools unless *per capita* expenditures were at least as high. State investment would indeed have to be much greater than at present.

There is a danger that the large comprehensive schools with children from 11 to 18 would feel obliged to compete academically with the ' Public ' schools. This they can do less successfully than the present grammar schools unless they are organized to select for special attention the pupils who would obviously have gained admission to a grammar school. Furthermore, an unconscionable amount of time would have to be spent on academic learning. The sense of failure which is implicit in much of what the secondary modern school does would be carried over to the common school. There is a danger that in attempting to compete, comprehensive schools would defeat their purpose of providing social education and equality of opportunity. Any proposed reorganization of state schools should take this factor into account.

The Problem of Investment

No system of public education will effectively meet the demands of the country until far more money than at present is invested in it. It must be made possible for the educational services to compete successfully with other services for well-qualified personnel, especially

---

[61] *Whitaker's Almanack, 1952.*

scientists and mathematicians. Far more money should be spent on buildings and equipment. More time would have to be devoted to the training of teachers, and the qualifications of all of them raised to rank with a university degree. More teachers are needed for the state system if it is to provide as good education as the best private institutions.

This kind of investment can be made only if a higher priority is given to education in the list of competing services. At the moment the defence and health services are chief among these. The latter, which employs as general practitioners only a tenth of the number of teachers, costs annually more than education.

At the same time, money spent on tobacco and beer cannot be spent on schools. The public demand for education which would give it a higher priority will come about only when (a) the role of education in the national economy is appreciated, and (b) when the education offered gives some recognizable advantage to the recipient. That is to say, greater support will be given to education when the returns on the investment are real and apparent.

To achieve this may involve a considerable re-allocation of resources within the school system. Educational policy must, it seems to me, reflect parental demand. I have tried to point out that the 1944 Act has not done this. One way of gauging public demand would be to reintroduce fees. A generous scholarship system would make it possible for any very able boy or girl, however poor, to go to the school of his choice. Fees would be a selective device for the many academically marginal cases.

This assumes that the tripartite system continues to operate and that grammar schools and, to an increasing extent, technical schools continue to be those in demand. A system of common schools up to the compulsory leaving age would be better. The common school would be followed by a variety of secondary schools or junior colleges rather on American lines. Such a system would offer some prospect of meeting the various challenges within a democracy of social cohesion, academic achievement, industrial requirements, and economy efficiency. It should be flexible enough to respond, without capitulating, to public expectations. For greater investment in education will depend on this. Eventually, the public will pay only for what it wants.

BRIAN HOLMES.

CHAPTER THIRTEEN

Greek Economy and the Educational Budget

THE aim of this study is not to make a detailed analysis of the budget of the Greek state regarding expenditure on education—an aspect that should not be overlooked—but rather to examine the interdependence of the education of Greece and her economy. Education and economy constitute two great social forces and contribute enormously to the enhancement of 'culture' and 'civilization', as long as they work harmoniously together.

Use is purposely made of both terms 'culture' and 'civilization' to indicate their complementary role in human progress. 'Culture' refers more to spiritual, intellectual, and artistic values. By 'civilization' is meant more the practical, technical, and material aspects of our daily needs and preoccupation. Both make for a complete life. Education cannot, without damage to its main object, neglect either of these two kinds of values. This is 'total education.'

By way of explanation in these introductory words, it is with 'total education' in Greece as affected by economic factors to-day, and *vice versa*, that we shall try to follow up our problem here. For education, as a basic force in society, viewed only from the angle of its totality can reveal its true bearings on our life and its permanent influence on man, from birth to death.

Greek Education in its Relation to the State Budget

As has already been mentioned, no effort will be made here to enter into the complicated and multitudinous details concerning the way the annual Greek budget is allocated into different items covering this or that expenditure on education. We shall give just a few statistics (especially as percentages) absolutely indispensable for the further treatment of our subject.

The available statistics as to state expenditure refer to the budgetary year of 1953-4, in the form which was approved by Parliament on September 5th, 1953. According to that estimate, out of 10,751,000,000 new *drachmae* [1] or 358,366,666 dollars that represent the entire expenditure of the Greek state for that year, 628,364,400 *drachmae* or $20,945,480 were allocated to the Ministry of Education. But not even the whole of this sum is for purely educational purposes. Some 60

---

[1] 84 *drachmae* = £1; 30 *drachmae* = $1.

million *drachmae* ($2 million) are given for ecclesiastical, archaeo-
logical, and similar purposes. On the other hand, according to information received, the amount allocated to the Ministry of Education
was increased by the end of that budgetary year by about 3 million
dollars. Also, it should be mentioned that the pensions paid to retired
teachers or to their families, amounting to about 2 million dollars,
appear under the expenditures of the Ministry of Finance, while some
other items, like expenses in case of illness of teachers, are paid by the
Ministry of Social Welfare. On the whole, however, the allocation of
the budget to the Ministry of Education does not exceed the 6 per cent
or at maximum 7 per cent of the entire state expenditures.

If we now divide the total sum spent on education by the number
of the student population—approximately one million—covering all
kinds of schools from nursery to university, we find that the Greek
State spends about 630 *drachmae* or 21 dollars for each pupil or
student annually. Or again, if we divide the annual allocation to the
Ministry of Education among the 7 million of the adult population (19
years of age and above), then each Greek grown-up citizen pays in the
way of taxation exactly 90 *drachmae* or 3 dollars a year for public
education, that is, hardly one-quarter of a *drachma* or one cent (of a
dollar) per day.

If we attempt finally to find out how many of these 21 million
dollars go to the three main branches of the educational system, as outlined above, then we find:

(1) For *primary education* 350 *million drachmae* ($11,666,666) are
spent, or 57 per cent of the entire annual allocation to the Ministry of
Education.

(2) For *secondary* and *vocational education*: 105 million drachmae
($3,500,000)=16 per cent.

(3) For *higher education*: 65 million drachmae ($2,166,666)=about
10 per cent.

Altogether, 83 per cent of the annual budget of the Ministry of
Education is spent on these three and covers a large proportion of
teachers' salaries and, in part, the cost of buildings, equipment, etc.
Almost *nine-tenths* of this 83 per cent goes for salaries and, of course,
very little remains for other purposes.

Needs of Greek Education as Affected by the Economy of the Country

It is impossible to give real education to over a million children,
even at the primary level (up to the age of 12), with so little money.
But there is a widespread need for reform.

Yet, there is always a stumbling-block: the chronic lack of the necessary funds, resulting from the unstable situation of the country ever

since the end of World War I.   This situation is the result of a series of events : the defeat of Greece in Asia Minor (1922); the influx of millions of impoverished refugees as a result of it; the dictatorship of 1925; the war against the invader in 1940; the capitulation before a second most powerful assailant, and the dreary period of the four-year triple occupation (German, Italian, and Bulgarian).

Greece was exhausted, the whole country lay waste.   Scarcely freed (October 1944) when another danger—communism—appeared from within and without.   While all other countries of Western Europe began—thanks to the American gesture (unique in human history) known as the Marshall Plan—their reconstruction, Greece had again to fight on (as she had done before, between 1919 and 1922) until the end of 1949 against the new enemy, and she had to feed, clothe, and give shelter to seven hundred thousand new refugees who fled to urban centres from the northern frontiers of the country.

Real reconstruction in Greece began, therefore (to some extent building all over again, what had been already rebuilt), only at the end of 1949, that is, hardly seven years ago.   Thousands of schools and churches, hundreds of entire villages, bridges, and so forth, had been destroyed.   The work accomplished since then, with the help of the Marshall Plan, has been significant in spite of the many and different unavoidable shortcomings resulting from the prolonged hard and un-stable conditions that had prevailed.

But fate intervened !   A series of earthquakes during the last two years struck different parts of Greece and thus retarded the reconstruction and progress of the country.

This unfortunately is the sad picture that can be drawn of Greece at the present moment, when other countries, some greater, richer, and better organized than Greece, have made wonderful progress, especially through the help they have also received from the U.S.A.

Under these circumstances education in Greece, like all other aspects of national life, has suffered a great deal.   Yet, in spite of all these drawbacks, Greece can make rapid progress if, first, a more systematic and up-to-date organization is introduced; if, second, the pace is quickened in the process of decentralization and self-government which has already begun; if, finally, the many and different natural resources of the country are intensively exploited for the benefit of all.

Let me give now a few concrete examples illustrating, as I see it, some of the most urgent needs Greek education faces to-day.[2]

(1) *First, and above all*, there should begin an immediate *reorganiza-*

---

[2] For more details see my book, *Our Most Urgent Educational Problems* (Athens, Greece, 1954) (in Greek); also, *Memorandum*, sent to the Ministry of Education (Greece), August, 1954.

tion of our administrative system in education and an *ad hoc* preparation for their job of those holding responsible administrative positions
both at the centre and in the provinces. Some such measures as the
following could be taken : the offering of a series of courses in school
administration; the sending of officials abroad to see how things
are being done elsewhere; and the inviting of foreign consultants,
specialists in school administration, to study our situation and advise
on the course to follow.

(2) The Greek *Ministry of Education* should give up all matters
pertaining to church, archaeology, theatre, fine arts, music, and similar activities, and it should occupy itself strictly and thoroughly with
purely educational problems. For these, in any case, are both
numerous and difficult to tackle.

(3) The *Supreme Board of Education* should be completely reorganized. Its tasks should consist mainly in advising on fundamental
questions of the country, in following up the progress made abroad,
in suggesting, without forgetting any sound traditions of the Greek
people, the introduction of the appropriate new methods in teaching,
in examinations, and the enrichment of the Ministry of Education with
new departments made necessary to-day. The reconstruction of Greece
cannot be achieved unless education steps in and prepares adequately
the human potential required for this purpose.

(4) The systematic *introduction of practical vocational education* for
(almost 90 per cent of the child population) all boys and girls who do
not continue their schooling beyond the 12th year of their age. Further, all services dealing with vocational education should be concentrated in the Ministry of Education.

(5) The *reorganization of the teachers' training colleges* so that they
meet the modern requirements, both in teaching and in administration.

(6) The realization of the importance of *special education*, of *adult
education*, of *nurseries* and *kindergarten* and their systematic further
organization or their introduction into our educational system.

(7) The *erecting of school buildings* well equipped and meeting
modern educational demands as indicated by school architects.

(8) The systematic organization of *the libraries of the country*, both
public and in schools, under the supervision of specialized librarians, of
whom we are in great need.

(9) The increase of money spent on *scholarships*.

(10) Education should go back to the Greek people to whom it belongs by way of *decentralization and self-government*. This should
take place in such a way that the central authority does not cease to
give guidance, on such a vital national question, after consulting local
authorities.

Ways Out of the Difficulty

In order to put into effect all these reforms now, the 21 or 25 million dollars allocated to the Ministry of Education are hardly enough to take care of even one of its problems, namely, the proper payment of the teachers' salaries. Is there, then, any way out?

First, there are *the contributions of the parents*, the free and voluntary contributions, over and above the taxes paid, in the case of primary education which is compulsory and is supposed to be financed by the state; the *payment of tuition fees*, rather low in the case of public secondary schools (at which attendance is free) and high in higher education. Very often the financial assistance on the part of the citizens to put up a school building, to care for its upkeep, takes the organized form of a P.T.A. (a Parent-Teacher Association). It should be mentioned here that two-thirds of the expenses of the great number of school buildings constructed between 1928 and 1932, when a special loan was contracted with Sweden, were covered by contributions of the Greek communities and municipalities.

Second, *private initiative* steps in. Some people, moved by ideological motives, others, and perhaps there are more of these, by expectations of a profitable enterprise, set up *private schools*, and private education is, of course, more expensive. Its drawback lies in the fact that not all children of a given society profit by it, as is the case with public education.

Third, *foreign schools* are also established. They, too, help especially through the introduction of new methods in education, when their work is not hampered by too much official intervention.

Fourth, *donations* made by social-minded wealthy people contribute a lot. Greece is really proud of her national benefactors, particularly in the field of education. Very often donations of that nature come from foreign countries (books and so on from the U.S.A., help through the British-Canadian *Save the Children Fund*, through the Swedish *Rädda Barnen*, etc.). Also, international organizations like the Red Cross, the Y.M.C.A., and the Y.W.C.A. do immensely good work along these lines.

Fifth, the efforts made through *adult education* (mentioned above).

With the contribution of all these non-governmental or semi-public agencies the sum spent on education, that is on 'total education', exceeds by far the very inadequate sum spent by the state.

Since this is the case, would it not be better if formal education, adult education, and the educational efforts mentioned in this last section, came under the systematic influence and far-sighted survey of the new Board of Education we proposed so that nothing is wasted or unnecessarily duplicated, but beautifully co-ordinated?

And, as a corollary to the above, since it is the people who pay for education in one way or other, since it is the whole of society that is going to profit or lose from the kind of education citizens receive, then why not allow local authorities to assume gradually, through wise decentralization and self-government, the responsibility for education, thus allowing the central Government plenty of time and leisure to think out, experiment, and suggest the best ways and means of developing education, of ' total education ', as has already been suggested?

Finally, I should like to point out the following: that *education, whatever part of the world we are thinking of, should become the earnest concern of everybody—of all nations.* If for our physical well-being we have set up a *World Health Organization,* if for the effective defence of our countries we have felt the need to pool our forces, if against the misuse of atomic energy we are (as at Geneva) meeting together, why not then push a little further the noble aim of UNESCO and tackle internationally, but in a more positive and more effective way, the problem of education, namely, that of *giving to each human being, regardless of race, colour, creed, or social rank, the education his or her abilities and inclinations are capable of?*

Let me conclude this little study by quoting a few lines from a speech I delivered at Teachers College, Columbia (July, 1952), on the subject, *Democracy and a Stable World Order*: " Fighting illiteracy is of course a noble aim, but, if we care to promote the cause of democracy and that of social mindedness, then steps—especially of financial nature—should be taken *towards raising obligatory education in all countries, members of UNESCO, to the 15th year of age, and also towards providing a partly obligatory vocational education until the 18th year of every child in the world.* In that way the main and indispensable requirements for general and vocational education will have been guaranteed."

Greece and many other countries cannot meet by themselves the adequate education the citizen of a civilized country needs to-day.

Education is the greatest and most hopeful force humanity possesses. Let us use it properly and unselfishly. It is only then that the peaceful use of atomic energy will also be better guaranteed.

THEODORE HARALAMBIDES.

CHAPTER FOURTEEN

Secondary Education for All: New Zealand—Maoris

NEW ZEALAND has accepted politically the full consequences of secondary education for all. Attendance at school has been compulsory up to the age of 15 years since 1943, but free education is available to all to the age of 19 years, and in addition pupils who qualify, by accrediting or by examination, for entrance to the university have their tuition fees for full degree or diploma courses of four or five years reimbursed provided they do reasonably well in their work. The privilege of extended secondary education is taken advantage of by an ever-increasing proportion of the population, and any further increase in the age for compulsory attendance would probably have only minor consequences.

The state provides for about 83 per cent of secondary pupils in its own institutions, the remaining 17 per cent being provided for in private schools, of which Catholic schools account for 10 per cent.

The rapidly increasing population since World War II has proved a heavy burden in all three sectors: (1) finance, (2) buildings and equipment, and (3) trained teachers. Finance has been provided for a heavy building programme and industry has up to the present been able to cope with its task, although in the financial year 1954–5, of the building grant of £6½ million [1] authorized by the Government, only a little more than £5 million could be spent. The problem of teacher supply and training has proved more difficult. It is obvious that this should be so when one considers that students entering the teachers' training colleges in 1955 at the minimum age of 17 years were born in 1938 or earlier. For the three years 1936–8 the total births were 28,476; 29,985; and 30,942, compared with totals of 51,928; 51,943; and 54,135 for 1952–4. To cater for the surge in school entrants the usual device of short training courses of one year for older students has been employed, but this source seems near exhaustion.

The problem of competition with other employing agencies is probably more acute in New Zealand than in most other countries. The increase in population is now annually over 2¼ per cent, and the main weight of the increase is on the younger range of the population. The provision of teachers for secondary schools is much more difficult than for primary schools. The source is an earlier birth-rate group still less

---

[1] £1 New Zealand=approximately $2.80.

productive than that of 1936–8, and the incentives to enter the secondary service have up to the present been much less generous than for entrants to primary teaching. For the primary service adequate subsistence allowances have always been provided during the full training period, while secondary entrants have been drawn from students who have either paid their own way at the university or have received government bursaries of £70 a year for three or four years. This allowance has proved so inadequate that this year the Government has altered the bursary system to one of studentships and the students will be paid an allowance of £185 a year for two years and £285 a year for the following two years while at the university, and £530 per annum for men and £455 for women in the fifth year, which is spent at a teachers' training college. A boarding allowance of £40 per annum is also paid for the first four years to students obliged to live away from home. The consequences of this action will not be felt for several years. It is a helpful measure as far as the secondary teaching service is concerned, but it is naturally to be expected that other government departments such as the Ministry of Works, the Agriculture Department, and the Department of Scientific and Industrial Research will ask for similar concessions to provide the trained personnel they require.

Economic Problems

As indicated above, the provision of education for all is in New Zealand a major item of national expenditure. The estimates for 1955–6 provide £27 million for general education purposes in addition to £6½ million for buildings. The total expenditure by the Government is estimated to be £327 million, which includes the expenditure under social security, and certain trading departments such as railways, post office, government life insurance, and so on, whose receipts materially reduce the burden. Education is thus responsible for some 10 per cent of the crude national expenditure.

Special economic problems centre largely round the salaries payable to graduates to the various professions, but here a confusion arises due to social and prestige elements which make a purely economic solution difficult to assess.

Medicine has in New Zealand always had a social as well as an economic attraction and there is no dearth of candidates who in the main pay their own way except as to university tuition fees, which are refunded by the Government in most cases. Here it may be repeated that university education in New Zealand is virtually free to all who qualify for university entrance. In fact, a small bursary of £30 per annum is also paid in the case of satisfactory pupils who have spent an extra year in the Sixth Form after qualifying for entrance. The number of medical students admitted annually is determined by the facilities available at the sole Medical School—at the University of Otago in Dunedin. This enables a degree of selection of candidates which ensures that, intellectually at least, the quality of medical students is well above the average. The Dental School, also located in Dunedin, provides graduates for dental services but its popularity has never been as high as that of its sister profession.

Engineering ranks high as a profession to students of good ability, and here again the profession has its popularity increased by a rising social prestige. One unfortunate effect is becoming serious, however, the loss to other countries of trained engineers who are attracted by financial offers much higher than those available in New Zealand. The exodus of locally trained engineers is assuming serious dimensions. In New Zealand as elsewhere the problem of the technician is a serious one, and here the solution is being found by the Education Department in consultation with the Institution of Engineers in the establishment of a new qualification to be called the New Zealand Certificate in Engineering. The course for this will be provided in senior technical schools.

The sole university School of Architecture, located in Auckland, provides reasonably for the needs of New Zealand and its prestige compares with that of engineering.

The scientific field is in much the same position as that of engineering. The popularity of a career in scientific research is undoubted and although the financial rewards are not commensurate with the arduous training called for, a large percentage of the best students enter upon university studies in science with a purely scientific career in view. Here, likewise, there is an exodus overseas of the best types, who seek further experience there and usually do not return.

Although New Zealand is mainly an agricultural country, and there are two schools of agriculture of university rank, the professional side of agricultural studies does not seem to attract a sufficient number of students of first-class ability. Avenues of employment are to be found mainly in the Agriculture Department which, with the Department of Scientific and Industrial Research, conducts institutes devoted to research in problems of primary industry. In spite of a number of distinguished research scientists employed in these institutions, the status of the profession does not appear to equal that in most other branches of science, pure and applied. A few graduates find places in secondary teaching, but even in the secondary schools the study of elementary agriculture appears to languish. This may be a passing phase. The real success of the two schools lies in their short courses on certain technical aspects of farming, from which important economic advantages result.

New fields of growing significance are those of the social sciences, though it is too early yet to assess their status in the economic sphere. Several government departments, such as Education, Justice, Labour and Employment, require young people trained in welfare work and psychology, and there is a growing awareness of the importance of this work.

The professions of law and accountancy continue to attract an adequate number of students, though the economic rewards available militate against their choice by the best students. Such students usually attend university classes as a part-time activity and gain practical experience of their profession at the same time. The rewards of lawyers and accountants vary enormously among themselves, but the inference remains that the popularity of the professions is not particularly high from a purely economic point of view. There is a growing field for employment, however, in government departments, particularly that of Finance.

The problem of the usual arts student is economically obscure. Language and classics, and that group of the social sciences including history and geography, have decreased in popularity among students of the highest calibre except with that minority which find a natural devotion to these studies. The field of employment is narrow, teaching being easily the most important. There are accordingly fewer problems here in the supply of teachers of such subjects, though the quality of the average supply is a disquieting phenomenon. Such graduates are encouraged by higher initial salaries to join government departments.

This leads us, then, to the general crisis in teaching in secondary schools. Potential teachers in mathematics and the sciences find more attractive avenues of employment and the supply of adequate teachers of such subjects shows a dangerous tendency to dry up. In girls' schools the matter is very serious indeed, and the effect on future entrants to the university is causing much concern. A fall in standards which may take decades to correct may be the consequence of this neglect by science graduates of teaching as a career.

The Education of Marginal and Submarginal Groups

The New Zealand Government makes no difference in the emphasis it places on the intellectual quality of its secondary pupils. There is, in fact, some criticism that undue attention is being paid to the low-intelligence layer of the population, to the detriment in some degree of the more gifted pupils. The courses of study provided for pupils of average and below-average intelligence are well adapted to their powers. Excellent provision both in equipment and in teaching staff is available in such subjects as woodwork and metalwork, needlework and general homecraft studies, and crafts of a wide range, while the definition of social studies and elementary science is well adapted to their needs. The popularity of such courses is undoubted, and pupils even in this group show the same desire to pursue their schooling for a much greater length of time than is demanded by the compulsory attendance regulation. I think it is fair to say that the population as a whole has accepted the view that a school career of the longest duration reasonable has values for all. In fact the extraordinary development of Parent-Teacher Associations is largely due to widespread demands for the full realization of what might be done by a comprehensive system of education, and the consequences in increased taxation are fully accepted.

It may be mentioned here that there is no broad distinction in New Zealand between secondary academic and secondary technical schools. The usual school is comprehensive and caters for pupils of all aptitudes and abilities. In the larger centres of population provision is made for both co-educational and single sex schools.

The Education of Maoris

The Maori population of New Zealand, over 131,000 out of a total of 2,120,000, is increasing at a faster rate than that of the Europeans, averaging 3·3 per cent per annum for the past five years against 2·2 per cent per annum for Europeans.

The full privileges of the European population are available to Maoris and special privileges are provided in Maori village schools in the matter of additional equipment for practical education in the primary schools and special facilities in hygiene, together with free textbooks and other school materials, while bursaries for secondary education and higher studies at the university are available for Maoris who at the same time can compete for other privileges with the rest of the population. These special privileges are beginning to show results. The number of Maoris completing secondary courses is increasing, and the number embarking on university studies shows an upward tendency.

It may be remarked here that there are definite signs of a kind of renaissance among Maoris. In early days of the white domination, the tribal leaders threw out able personalities who shared with the Europeans the government of the country. Significant names such as those of Sir Apirana Ngata, Sir James Carrol, Sir Maui Pomare, all of whom were scholars and Ministers of the Crown, and Sir Peter Buck, a world-renowned anthropologist, come to mind. Then followed a period of torpor, when the natural tribal leaders seemed to lose heart and lost authority. This period seems now to be ending and a greater interest is being shown by the Maoris themselves in their own destiny, and they are showing greater awareness of the values to be obtained from higher educational studies. The breakdown of the tribal organizations, largely due to the movement of large Maori populations to cities and country towns, and the consequent closer contact with the new civilization, are making the Maori more conscious of his privileges and duties. In the economic sphere the Maori is entering certain occupations in important numbers. Gangs employed on road building and building labourers are heavily reinforced by Maori workers, who show special capacity in the management of heavy tractor machinery, bulldozers, and the like. At the same time an encouraging number of young Maoris are finding employment in clerical duties in government and private offices. The standard of farming is rising too, and although the Maori farmer is in general less efficient than his European neighbour, there are adequate signs that he is learning more of modern techniques. There is very much to be done in housing and general social conditions and the standard of Maori hygiene is still backward, but the work of the Health Department and the Maori Affairs Department, as well as the progressive approach of the Education Department, should bear fruit in the near future.

Conclusion

A democratic country cannot organize any social structure to make full use of the potential capacity of its citizens. The laws of the market and the desires of the individual have full sway. The sole recourse of Government is to provide such rewards as will ensure that all social activities are catered for. It appears that the main criticism that can be made against the New Zealand system of education is that too little attention has been paid to the pupils of the highest intelligence, both in their early education and in the rewards made available to them on the completion of their school and university studies.

H. HENDERSON.

CHAPTER FIFTEEN

Economic Aspects of the Reform of Indian Education

THE Departments of Education at the state level were established in India in 1854-5—almost exactly a hundred years ago—with the object of organizing a proper educational system for the country. Their primary object was defined as the spread of Western science and literature, preferably through the medium of the English language. For this purpose, it was proposed that universities be established at Calcutta, Bombay, and Madras, and at other places when necessary, and a graded system of education be organized beginning with the primary school and ending with the degree college affiliated to the university. It was further laid down that, while there was no objection to establishing government schools and colleges for this purpose, it would be more desirable, on financial grounds, to encourage private enterprise—missionary and Indian—by adopting a suitable system of grants-in-aid. It was envisaged that the government would sanction a considerable increase in expenditure—in 1854, the total educational expenditure from government funds was only about £100,000—in order to carry out this programme.

It is not possible to envy the administrators in their task. Here was a vast continent, with a multiplicity of religions, races, and languages, and a population of about 200 million, which was increasing at the terrific rate of about 1 per cent per annum and in which, owing to the short span of average life, the number of children of school-going age was proportionately larger than in European societies. Moreover, the general social pattern was highly stratified and the educational attainments of the different strata showed great inequalities.

The general poverty of the people and their rather deep-rooted conservatism formed serious obstacles to progress, and the scatter of the population over tens of thousands of small villages, with poor means of communication, created great administrative difficulties. But while the problem and difficulties were enormous, the resources—human and financial—at the disposal of the authorities were meagre in the extreme. Thus the programme of educational expansion could be adequately financed neither by the government nor by any private resources.

A problem of such magnitude and difficulty needed far-sighted and competent handling. But the history of Indian education, during the last hundred years, shows that the administrators concerned failed to rise to the occasion. They were responsible for making two major errors—failure to take effective steps to raise the standard of living of the people, and failure to accord a sufficiently high priority to education. This was due, largely, to reasons which were inherent in the situation and the nature of the British rule itself. Both these factors deserve closer analysis.

The Allocation to Education

Let us take the problem of the standard of living first. It is obvious that the measure of educational facilities provided in a country is intimately related to the national dividend, and mass education can progress only in proportion to the rise in the standard of living. A low national dividend cuts educational progress at both ends. It reduces the taxable capacity of the people and restricts the total revenues of the state, thus making a reduction of educational expenditure inevitable. On the other hand, it also restricts the capacity of the average parent to spend on education and this leads to the premature withdrawal of children from schools, as their earnings are looked upon as indispensable to the family budget.

The present survey is, however, primarily concerned with the second failure, viz., the low priority accorded to education in the distribution of government revenue. The Departments of Education in India were never really given a fair chance to work out their ideas, as they were all born under the gloomy star of financial stringency. Most of the annual reports of the Directors of Public Instruction make painful reading on account of their perpetual lament about the lack of adequate funds, and remind one of poor Oliver Twist, who was always asking for more and was almost always refused! Starting in 1854–5, with a grant of about £100,000,[1] by 1870–71 the total government grant for education had increased only to £657,100. In this year, education ceased to be the responsibility of the central government of India and was made the concern of the states. Thirty years later, by the end of the century, it had risen to £1,039,100. The drive for educational reform organized by Lord Curzon at the opening of the present century, and maintained to varying degrees by his successors, led to a comparatively more rapid increase during the next two decades, so that the total educational grant in 1921–2 was £6,017,335. Education was then transferred to the control of Indian ministers at the state level and this improved the situation to some extent, especially after provincial autonomy was introduced in 1937 and Congress

---

[1] According to the usual convention, a *rupee* was taken as 2 shillings up to 1902; thereafter it is taken as equivalent to 1s. 6d.

Ministries came into power in most states. The government grant for education increased to £8,242,347 in 1936–7 and to £17,305,936 in 1946–7—the year in which British power was withdrawn from the country.

However, the correct measure of the *educational effort* which an administration is making and the priority which it accords to education is not the *absolute* amount of government grant for education but its ratio to the total expenditure incurred. Considered from this point of view, we find that this percentage has varied from 0·3 (in 1854–5) to 6·1 in 1936–7. It is obvious that with such small allotments, education could not—in no country and under no circumstances—progress satisfactorily.

Sources of Revenue

Two other criteria may be applied to determine the importance given to education in the total economy of the country—the share of the total educational expenditure which the government is prepared to bear from its own funds and the expenditure per head of the population. Accurate figures are not available, but it is reasonably correct to say that, between 1780 and 1813, the government was prepared to bear practically the total expenditure on education. But, as education began to expand, the assistance of other sources was invoked. Fees began to be charged and came to be looked upon as an important source of revenue. Missionary enterprise and the voluntary efforts of the people were encouraged, and thus the resources of the missions and private philanthropy were fully utilized. When the demand for education increased still further, local rates for education were levied in rural areas and municipalities were required to contribute their share. Private enterprise, which now conducted the bulk of the educational institutions in the country, was, therefore, compelled to raise a considerable portion of its expenses through public charity. All these measures tended to reduce the government's share of the total expenditure to a marked degree. It had fallen to about 80 per cent in 1854, touched the lowest mark of 26 per cent in 1901, and was about 45 per cent in 1947. Such a policy, under the economic circumstances obtaining in the country, shows that the government accorded a low priority to education in its scheme of values. According to the second criterion, i.e., educational expenditure incurred per head of the population, the situation is shown to be no more favourable. In 1870–71, this was about a penny, but after seventy-five weary years it had only risen in 1947 to 1s. 2d. *per capita*. Judged by any standards, and in view of starting almost from scratch, this small increase cannot be regarded as evidence of due priority being accorded to educational development.

The reasons for the low priority are not far to seek. Prior to 1833, the East India Company was a commercial body. Hence its natural desire to maintain a high level of profits, coupled with the claims of expenditure on wars and the consolidation of the Empire, left but a small margin for developmental expenditure like that on education. Thereafter, till 1870–71, the finances of the government of India were in sorry shape, partly because the tax structure of the period, inherited from the earlier rulers, was defective and partly because the system of financial centralization, which had been introduced in 1833, proved to be extremely wasteful in practice. Consequently, the government of India had a series of deficit budgets during this period.

These general difficulties, and the continuance of the old policy of according higher priority to defence and the maintenance of law and order, left little scope for securing money for even essential developments. Even among these developmental activities, imperial needs like railways, roads, bridges, and the organization of the postal system were given higher priority than education. Later, between 1901 and 1913, when the financial position improved, the largest part of the available surplus was used first for imperial needs like the army, a smaller portion was allocated to developmental needs connected with imperial purposes, and a much smaller part to education. Thus it seems obvious that the small grants allocated to education were not due mainly to the paucity of total government resources or the difficulty of making a choice between one type of developmental work and another, but were the direct and inevitable consequence of the imperialistic policies.

The Responsibility of Educationists

It is clear from this sketchy survey that the progress of education under British rule suffered greatly from two extraneous factors over which educationists had little control—the failure to raise the standard of living of the people and failure to accord due priority to education. But these were not the only reasons that prevented proper educational development. The experience of other countries and the history of Indian education in recent years show that, even within the limitations set by the poverty of the people and the small government grants for education, better results could have been obtained if educationists had not committed certain serious mistakes of their own and thus made a bad situation worse.

When an educational administrator is called upon to perform his task, his first approach to the problem should be primarily that of an educationist. He should prepare his scheme according to his lights, calculate its financial implications, and then ask for adequate financial grants. If the amount required is not available—which is often the case—he has to decide an order of priorities. He has necessarily to cut and prune his proposals and to make a hard choice between several conflicting demands within the educational system. His choice is hard, because it is always a choice between two good things and he has to decide which is the more urgent. This is the essence of wise educational administration, and it is the wisdom of decisions on such issues which determines the proper direction of educational progress in an under-developed economy.

A very important choice of this type had to be made by the Education Departments at the very outset. There was at the time a system of indigenous education which, in spite of all its shortcomings, had a certain innate vitality of its own which had enabled it to survive decades of misrule and anarchy. This system might have been improved, developed, and expanded into a national system of education. Advice to this effect had been given by competent educators like William Adam and in his Dispatch of 1854. But the Education Departments ignored this advice and decided to start new schools of their own. The result was that the old indigenous system disappeared from the scene by the end of the nineteenth century. This affected education in two ways. It compelled the Departments to start educational work *ab initio*, as if the country had no educational system in pre-British days, and thus greatly increased the magnitude of the problem. Secondly, it added to the total cost of the programme, because the maintenance of the new Departmental schools was much costlier than the payment of grants-in-aid to indigenous schools. It is true that the Departmental schools were, in many ways, superior to the indigenous schools. But even that could not justify letting the latter die of inanition.

If the literature of the period is studied carefully, it would be seen that many of the voluntary schools of England at the beginning of the nineteenth century were really no better than these indigenous schools. But England started on the basis of the existing voluntary schools, increased the provision of educational facilities in them and then turned to the improvement of the quality of schooling. To-day India might perhaps have been better off educationally if the Education Departments had decided to build on the basis of the indigenous schools and then to expand and improve them as more funds became available. But as this was not done, the ' better ' became an enemy of ' good ' and the development of Indian education suffered irreparably.

The second important choice which the Education Departments

were called upon to make, on purely financial grounds, related to the problem of mass education. Between 1813 and 1854 the available funds were extremely small, and hence the question of any programme of mass education could not even be entertained. Macaulay, therefore, put the view that the government should educate only a limited *class* of Indians and leave it to them to educate the masses. " We must at present do our best to form a class ", he wrote, in his famous Minute, " who may be interpreters between us and the millions whom we govern—a class of persons Indian in blood and colour, but English in tastes, in opinions, in morals, and in intellect." This view dominated the scene till 1854, when Wood's Education Dispatch deprecated the previous direction of the efforts of the government almost exclusively towards providing high education for a very small number of ' natives ' drawn, for the most part, from the higher classes. This Dispatch laid down that, in the future, the attention of the government should be devoted to the manner in which useful and practical knowledge, suited to every station of life, could best be conveyed to the great mass of the people, who were incapable of obtaining any education worthy of the name by their own unaided efforts. This declaration envisaged the abandonment of the ' Downward Filtration ' theory. But, unfortunately, this directive was never obeyed in practice and, until the end of the nineteenth century, when Curzon revised the decision, the Departments of Education concentrated on the education of a *class* and generally neglected the education of the *masses*.

This policy produced several undesirable results. Secondary and college education was unduly emphasized and received a proportionately larger share of funds, and the expansion of primary education was held up. Even in 1901–2, only 29.5 per cent of the total educational expenditure was devoted to primary education, while normally it should account for about two-thirds of the total educational expenditure in any well-planned educational system. As a result, Indian education became top-heavy and a gulf was created between the highly educated *intelligentsia* and the almost illiterate masses. This socio-cultural schism also led to certain other social evils and maladjustments which need not, however, be discussed here.

The third important question which the Education Departments were called upon to decide, related to the choice of principal agency for the spread of education. The Departments would have preferred to conduct the bulk of the educational institutions through their own agency, but, as the direct maintenance of such institutions was much costlier than the payments of grants-in-aid to private associations, it was decided, on financial grounds, to encourage private enterprise to take on this responsibility and to restrict the direct educational activities of the

Department to the minimum. This, however, gave a wrong orientation to the educational system as a whole. Private enterprise had limited financial resources and, therefore, the educational institutions started by it were usually of the academic type, and not professional and vocational schools and colleges. These are, of course, very costly to establish and maintain, so that there was an over-emphasis on general education, to the neglect of vocational education. Even within this field, training in the ' black-coated ' professions of law, medicine, and teaching received greater attention than technical and industrial education, and the industrial development of the country was seriously handicapped.

Another important result of this policy was that, comparatively speaking, the rural areas came to be neglected. Private enterprise was restricted largely to cities and towns, which were more vocal and politically conscious and had the necessary personnel and funds. Government schools, too few in number, were mostly concentrated in urban areas. This created a gulf between urban and rural conditions which had many repercussions on the developing pattern of national life. The education of the backward classes also suffered as a result of this over-emphasis on private enterprise. It was only the advanced classes who had the necessary resources to organize schools, and their efforts were mostly restricted to the higher and the middle classes and hardly touched the backward classes.

The fourth important conflict of this period is that of quality *versus* quantity. As the available funds were limited, the point at issue always was whether they should be spent on the improvement of educational institutions by ensuring better pay-scales for teachers, better training facilities and equipment, and so on, or utilized for securing expansion. A careful study of the policy followed during the last hundred years shows that there was a shift of emphasis from time to time. It may well be argued that this was not a very suitable policy for a country where the education of the masses had been very largely neglected, and an all-out attempt should have been launched to make up the leeway, as was done in many Western countries in the nineteenth century. In actual fact, however, what happened was that the policy of mass education was never adopted and, even qualitatively, education remained very poor.

As a result of the various mistakes of commission and omission discussed above, the development of education during this period was far from satisfactory. After an educational effort spread over about 150 years, the percentage of literacy, according to the census of 1941, was about 12, and, in 1946-7, only one village out of three was provided with some sort of a school, while the percentage of pupils enrolled to the total population was only 6·3.

The Economic Problem of Education since 1947

With the attainment of independence in 1947, the problem of educational finance assumed a different complexion. In the earlier days, the major conflict of demands was between imperial and developmental needs, but now the conflict arose between various types of developmental needs. Between 1947 and 1952, the problems arising out of the Partition had to be given top priority—the rehabilitation of refugees, the settlement of certain outstanding problems with Pakistan, the organization of international relationships, the integration of hundreds of small feudatory states into convenient units of modern administration, and the crisis of the food situation. It was not, therefore, possible to devote as much attention and as many resources to educational reconstruction as would have been ordinarily expected from a national government. In spite of these difficulties, however, the total educational expenditure in India increased to more than £83 million in 1951–2. In other words, the *increase* in the total educational expenditure within five years of the attainment of freedom was even larger than the *total* educational expenditure incurred in British India in the last year of British administration. This in itself is an indication of the comparatively higher priority given to education by the national government.

In 1951–2, the *First Five-Year Plan* was adopted. In this plan, first priority had to be given to the development of agriculture. Similarly, high priority was given to industrial and technical projects calculated to raise the standard of living of the people. While education was regarded as the most important of the social services, the social services as such had to take a back seat. The total cost of the plan was estimated at about £1,000 million, of which the social services as a whole received about £170 million and education was allotted about half of this, i.e., £82 million only, that is, about 8 per cent of the plan funds. It may be pointed out, however, that the amount actually spent on education during this period, according to the revised plan, is likely to be considerably higher.

In the *Second Five-Year Plan*, which is still under discussion, the total allocation is expected to be about £3,000 million. The food situation in the country is now comparatively easier, the controls have been lifted, and the prices of food-grains have come down. The problem of unemployment has, however, become very acute, and the question of raising the standard of living continues to occupy top priority. So the greatest emphasis must be given to industrial and technological development, although the idea of a balanced and co-ordinated planning has to be kept in view. Under these circumstances, it has been anticipated that education is likely to get a somewhat higher percentage of the total funds under the second plan.

In spite of this comparatively low priority accorded to education since 1947, the total educational expenditure in India increased by more than 100 per cent between 1946–7 and 1951–2. It was not unusual for unimaginative administrators and others to say that the cost of a good educational programme for India would run into ' astronomical figures ', and that the time required to achieve it would have to be counted in centuries. The *Sargent Report* had, for the first time, grappled with the problem realistically and pointed out that this reform was not only possible but *must* be carried through. The experience of the last seven years has confirmed the feasibility of spending the large amounts needed for the purpose, and there is reason to hope that, if the progress continues at the present pace and the anticipated increase in the total national wealth is achieved, a good system of education will be established in the country in about two decades.

Central Government Activity

Several factors have contributed to the large increase in the total educational expenditure during the last seven years. Although education is primarily a responsibility of the state governments under the Indian Constitution, the central government has been taking a keen and active interest in its expansion and improvement. It has assumed a certain measure of direct responsibility in several spheres. It has set up a number of scientific research institutions and National Laboratories and is giving considerable financial support to the development of technical education as well as vocational courses at the secondary level. It has established a University Grants Commission, given considerable financial assistance to the universities, and instituted a large number of scholarships at various levels. Under the *Five-Year Plan*, it has decided to give large grants-in-aid to state governments for various approved programmes of educational reconstruction, such as the expansion of primary education, the conversion of primary schools into basic schools, the improvement in the training and status of teachers, the expansion of social education and the development of the backward classes. This is being done on a much larger scale than ever before in the history of Indian education.

The state governments, too, are making serious attempts to expand and improve education. The target recommended is that each state government should spend about 20 per cent of its total revenue on education. In some states the standard has already been reached, in others it is still considerably lower, but all are striving to reach it as quickly as possible. The same keenness is also evident to some extent among the local bodies, whose total expenditure on education is rapidly expanding. Private enterprise, too, is in evidence to a much greater extent than in the past, not so much in the form of educational investment by the philanthropic rich as in the form of *popular* contributions being made in money, labour, land and buildings for establishing educational institutions. The response made in recent years by the people in this respect has no parallel in history. In 1948, the Indian Income Tax Act was amended and donations to charitable purposes (including education) up to a certain percentage of the total income were exempted from taxation. This measure has also given some impetus to private charities. Lastly, foreign assistance has become available in increasing measure and organizations like the Ford Foundation have come forward to help the development of certain significant educational projects. It is true that the finances now available for education are still very inadequate as compared to the total requirements. They are, however, considerably larger than was the case in the recent past, and the hope has been created now that the solution of the difficult problem of educational finance is no longer such a utopian dream as it seemed to be a decade ago.

Future Problems

Although the total educational expenditure in India has thus increased materially during the last few years, the educational needs of the country are so large that several conflicting demands arise within the educational field, and one of the most difficult problems which educational administrators have to face at the moment is the distribution of funds between them. Priorities have, therefore, to be decided at every level. The government of India has accorded priority to development of technical education and scientific research, the improvement of universities, the encouragement of Basic Education, the establishment of multi-purpose secondary schools with a vocational bias, the development of higher education in rural areas, educational experiments at various levels, and educational planning and co-ordination. In state programmes of education, priorities are being accorded to the expansion of primary education, the development of Basic Education, and the general improvement of secondary education. So far as the backward classes are concerned, priority is being given, at the state level, to primary and secondary education and the government of India is giving special assistance at the university level in the form of scholarships.

One general trend has now become apparent. As stated already, the emphasis, during the British period, shifted from quality to quantity and *vice versa* from time to time, but now the old *conflict* between the claims of quality and quantity is not so sharp. There is general dissatisfaction with several aspects of the existing system of education, and a popular as well as professional demand that the *quality* of instruction should be radically improved. Similarly, the pressure of democratic forces calls for an early and large-scale *expansion* of educational facilities in as short a time as possible. The situation, therefore, demands a simultaneous and well-balanced advance in quality as well as in quantity. Perhaps it may on the whole be true to say that the politicians are more inclined to favour expansion, while the educationists are exercised about the urgent need for consolidation and qualitative improvement. They feel that a mere multiplication of the kind of schools that obtain to-day—and invite criticism all round—would be a dubious blessing. It is, therefore, obvious that measures will have to be taken to bring into being, as expeditiously as possible, an educational system that has both greater amplitude and a deeper social purpose, and whose standards are distinctly higher than at present.

K. G. SAIYIDAIN.

J. P. NAIK.

CHAPTER SIXTEEN

The Five-Year Plans in Argentina

THE Perón regime has been overthrown by a revolution and we Argentinians may begin to appraise what has been done in the various aspects of the nation's life. Sometimes the task will show the face of drama, often a disgusting one, but if we are to gain anything at all from the general suffering, we must be sure of what we have; and we already know that something positive has been left. A fair appraisal will demand many months of accurate research to obtain the real facts and to check the several falsified figures we have been given, but any final judgment should rest with history.

Those of us who never submitted our minds and will to the harangues of governmental propaganda because we knew how tainted was the basis of the system, must now, more than ever, try to be just and objective in our analysis.

We are firmer than ever in our faith in education, and knowing the many ways in which the other social factors act upon it, we should say from the very beginning that some new features have appeared in our social body which may and must be capitalized to the benefit of our educational efforts.

The regime put down by the recent upheaval had, as a vital necessity, constantly to appeal to the opinion and support of the masses. This made great numbers of people politically conscious. They are consequently now much more conscious of political, economic, and social events, and, therefore, may understand more easily the importance and the impact of education both in its relationship to other aspects of social life, and in the promotion of progress and welfare generally.

The second great fact we may try to use is that the former government, in its efforts to seize the people's will for its own profit, had repeatedly insisted upon the need to make the spirit of education conform to the Peronist doctrine in order to produce so-called general happiness. False as this statement was, nevertheless it attracted the interest of many people who had not considered the problem before. Now education can be made a star performer in the circus ring.

If the new educational authorities make steady and sound use of these two facts, they may convert into long-range advantages the many disadvantages that education itself has suffered.

Characteristics of the Argentinian System of Education

The Argentinian system of education has the following general characteristics:

(1) Higher education depends on and is supported only by the federal government.

(2) Elementary and secondary education are provided and supported by the federal, provincial, and municipal governments, and by private institutions.

(3) The attendance at the primary common school is compulsory from 6 to 14 years of age.

(4) Education is free of any fees in all official schools, including universities.

Before 1943 the Department of Education directed the progress of education according to several special laws: (a) Avellaneda's Law for Universities; (b) a number of decrees for secondary education, and (c) Law 1420 or the Common Education Law, for elementary education. During the provisional government of June 1943 to June 1946, all the schools and universities were managed by the government through supervisors.

From June 1946 to September 1955, education was directed according to the rules of the First and Second Five-Year Plans, which tended to a centralized management by the Federal Ministry of Education, though apparently each educational body had its own independence.

It is the purpose of this article to show and briefly analyse the facts and principles underlying practice in the field of Argentinian education over the last ten years.

New Buildings and Teachers' Salaries

If it is true that the figures representing the amount of money spent on education have grown enormously in the last decade, it should be pointed out that the value of the money in 1955 is several times less than it was in 1943. The official index numbers show, making the figure in 1943 equal 100, that in 1955 the cost of living was 700. So the acquisitive value of money is now a seventh of what it was.

The former Minister of Education said last August that in 1943 the federal government spent in education 286 million *pesos*[1] and that in 1955 the budget would be 2,197 million. If we multiply the first figure by seven we get 2,002 million, an amount not very far from 2,197. (We should add that it is generally accepted that the index number 1955=700 is below reality, and that it would be in 1955=1,000.)

It is also necessary to point out that in the last twelve years the population of the country has increased from 15 to 19 million people,

---

[1] 1955, 39 *pesos*=2.8 U.S. dollars=1 pound sterling.

and, consequently, the education needs have also risen in proportion. So, from an objective viewpoint, our educational budget has not been increased in order to meet the necessities and in no way represents a real improvement of the services in the field. To meet this over-all and fair assessment would put the federal budget for education at not less than 3,000 million *pesos*. If anything was done during this decade, it was only at the expense of the salaries of all those engaged in the task. In fact, the increase in teachers' salaries is far below that in the cost of living. As one of the many proofs we can give, let us take that of the teachers of elementary schools. The top salary of one of those teachers in 1943 was $312. Now a teacher in the same category receives $1,390. But if we multiply 312 by 7 (official index number for the cost of living in 1955) we get $2,184, and we see that $1,390 is more or less only two-thirds of what the salary should be in order to match the cost of living. And in 1943 all people agreed that $312 was far from being a just remuneration for teachers.

This reduction in the real salaries of all categories of teachers, from primary school to university professors, has permitted the building of many schools throughout the country. This is a positive asset, but it was paid for mainly by a deterioration in the standard of living of teachers, who, in order to keep pace with expenses, had to work extra hours as private teachers or in other fields.

As we have said, many figures made public by the former authorities do not represent the real facts, and are in need of more accurate readjustment. Let us take a single example—in a booklet issued by the Ministry of Education in 1952 appears the following statement : " In 1946 the total number of students in the different schools depending on the federal government was 1,267,459. Now the number is 1,512,184." But the last Perón Minister of Education said in August 1955 : ". . . in 1955 . . . we have 3,994,225 students, almost a million more than in 1946. . . ." So the Minister gives as a fact that in 1946 we had something more than 2,900,000 students. Comparing this figure with that given in the pamphlet mentioned before, we cannot help but be confused.

The same exaggerated figures appear in other fields. We know and understand that an authoritarian government, as was the Perón regime, needed to exaggerate what was being done in order to show the people how great it was. But nevertheless, we must begin again and check the figures. It will be a hard task, but not an impossible one.

The fundamental principle underlying the educational programme during the Five-Year Plans was that of winning over the mind and will of youth to the national doctrine. Of course, the purpose was camouflaged under attractive words or slogans : " happiness of the people ",

" greatness of the Nation ", " in Argentina the only privileged ones are the children ", " better than speaking is acting, and better than promises are facts ", and so on. But the spirit of the ' doctrine ' was a disguised totalitarian one. All that has been done has, in the final analysis, this imprint, and demagogic and cynical procedures were characteristic features of the regime. It would be good to remember that while the name of Dr. Bernardo A. Houssay—a Nobel prize winner in physiology—was almost forbidden in our Press, President Perón himself went to the airport to welcome Pascual Pérez, a winner of a prize fight.

Summary

At this early stage the balance sheet of the Perón regime appears to be as follows :

(1) The number of schools built for educational purposes was substantially increased, though the places where they were built were not always suited to their specific functions.

(2) The federal educational budget is far below the real needs.

(3) The intensive propaganda favouring the regime and pointing to two of its representatives—Perón and his late wife—did not succeed in distorting to any dangerous extent the spirit of the youngsters.

(4) The repetitious insistence on making education a corner-stone of the regime, by waving the flags of progress and welfare of the people, has set a basis for future, real improvements.

(5) The spirit of the teachers was not conquered by totalitarianism, and we hope that a few months of good critical work will establish a normal pattern of action.

(6) The lesson was hard and teachers must think deeply about their responsibilities as barriers and defenders against any attacks on liberty.

(7) In this sense the university has an important role to play.

ALFREDO M. GHIOLDI.

THE GROWTH OF EDUCATIONAL PROVISION IN ARGENTINA

Type	Number of Establishments		Teachers		Students	
	1943	1955	1943	1955	1943	1955
KINDERGARTEN						
Official	42	850	266	2,001	4,734	43,037
Private	57	338	—	721	2,895	20,196
TOTAL . . .	99	1,188	266	2,722	7,629	63,233

PRIMARY SCHOOLS

	1943	1955	1943	1955	1943	1955
Common and other schools . .	13,294	16,476	73,299	111,258	1,958,707	2,603,116
Adult Schools . . .	352	561	1,270	4,943	32,870	51,512
TOTAL .	13,646	17,037	74,569	116,201	1,991,577	2,654,628

TEACHERS' COLLEGES

	1943	1955	1943	1955	1943	1955
The Federal Ministry of Education . . .	23	22	247	636	3,591	3,430
The Provinces . . .	—	11	—	91	—	469
TOTAL . .	23	33	247	727	3,591	3,899

UNIVERSITIES

	1943	1955	1943	1955	1943	1955
The Federal Ministry of Education						
University of Buenos Aires .	6	10	843	1,336	17,287	77,785
La Plata . .	10	11	415	666	10,275	20,146
Córdoba . .	6	7	316	538	6,461	12,473
Litoral . .	6	13	332	618	6,854	18,794
Tucumán .	4	13	112	396	1,255	3,954
Cuyo . .	7	15	177	468	1,020	3,743
Southern Institute of Technology	—	4	—	111	—	804
The National Commission of Apprenticeship National University for Workers' Regional Schools	—	8	—	176	—	1,510
TOTAL . . .	39	81	2,195	4,309	431,52	139,209

SECONDARY SCHOOLS

Type of Support	Number of Establishments		Teachers		Students	
	1943	1955	1943	1955	1943	1955
OFFICIAL						
The Ministry of Education						
High schools ⎫						
Normal schools ⎬	201	388	11,019	24,179	74,458	156,238
Commercial schools ⎭						
Technical schools . .	120	263	2,237	7,275	24,466	53,165
Art schools . . .	8	10	386	373	2,590	3,154
Apprenticeship schools .	—	196	—	3,104	—	45,708
Miscellaneous schools						
(adult, in clinics, etc.) .	209	241	962	1,674	40,404	56,428
The Provinces						
High schools ⎫						
Normal schools ⎬	—	132	—	1,590	—	14,805
Commercial schools ⎭						
Technical schools . .	—	342	—	3,144	—	41,699
For adults . . .	—	341	—	—	—	43,378
The Municipal Control						
High schools . .	—	58	—	301	—	8,712
Technical schools . .	—	32	—	192	—	3,312
The University						
High schools . .	28	60	1,565	3,411	18,771	22,982
Technical schools . .	—	31	—	511	—	7,652
PRIVATE						
High schools . . .	234	274	2,097	4,624	17,621	30,117
Normal schools . .	107	194	2,061	3,697	18,564	32,745
Commercial schools . .	102	146	1,362	2,720	5,105	16,086
Technical schools . .	96	68	659	627	5,259	7,030
TOTAL . .	1,105	2,277	22,348	57,422	207,011	543,207

PROBLEMS OF MANAGEMENT

No fundamental distinction is made in this section between publicly managed and privately managed education. The problems are similar in both cases. The severity differs and the solutions naturally reflect the fact that the resources of voluntary and private educational institutions are usually very much less than those of the public institutions. Indeed, wherever the state is taking over the responsibilities for education previously discharged by private institutions the problem of state support for the latter arises. Under some circumstances, when there is a strong plea for equality of educational opportunity, this is a major problem.

The first part of this section examines the task of providing *Equality of Opportunity in Education*. It recognizes that there are special problems associated with racial, linguistic, social (caste and class) diversity. Further, that geographical conditions, systems of taxation and social attitudes might make it difficult to provide adequate educational facilities for all citizens of a country. For all these affect both the possibility of raising resources and effectiveness of the distribution. Case studies are taken from South Africa, Iraq, and the United Kingdom. The strength of the desire to provide equality of opportunity in the United States and the diversity of problems associated with meeting this demand is analysed in four articles under the general heading *Educational Opportunity in the United States*. Each expert considers a particular aspect of a vast and complicated problem.

Case studies in the second part of this section deal with fiscal management. These are theoretical articles in which the policies and practices of administrating acquired resources are discussed. A distinction is drawn in institutional organization between policy forming groups and administrators responsible for the implementation of policy. Further questions relate to the ways in which public opinion is ventilated, how public support is secured, how administrative action is checked and controlled, and finally how the departments are organized and staffed.

Another field of interest is that of budgetary formation and control. Who is responsible for budget formation and what procedures are used? What is the period of planning? What procedures are used to control the budget? What are the limits to local expenditure? These and questions concerned with accounting systems, audits, and so on are mentioned in articles from England, France, the United States and from a representative American University. Aspects of administrative procedures are reviewed under such headings as: the management of revenue, the management of expenditure, the management of buildings, and the management of personnel.

The third part is concerned with *Educational Provision through Private Agencies and Supplementary Services.* Four main topics are discussed in case studies. The first, by Mr. Evans, illustrates how in England the Church took the initiative in opening training colleges and providing schools. The second, by Dr. Idenburg, deals with the principles of reconciling the right of religious denominations to run their own schools with their need for financial support from the state. A great deal of education is provided in institutions other than the schools, universities and colleges. Dr. King describes how supplementary services are provided in England and the armed forces. Finally, in two articles, aspects of the training of executives in the United States are presented by Dean Lockley and Mr. Corless. All these articles reflect the extent to which educational provision is made under the auspices and control of institutions other than those regarded as strictly and formally educational.

Finally, the very big question of how teachers are paid is considered. Everywhere, the salaries paid to teachers represent a major proportion of the cost of education in money economies. No longer is it possible to attract to the profession well-qualified people in large numbers by offering rewards such as security of tenure, long holidays, pensions and high social prestige. The status and social value of the *guru* was reflected in the support he received from his students and the community. More and more these values are reflected in the amount of money that the community are prepared to make available for the payment of teachers' salaries. Here, a world survey is given by Mr. Fernig of UNESCO. This is followed by accounts of how teacher salary scales and schedules are negotiated in England, the United States, and Norway. In a second part to the article dealing with the United States Mr. Hubbard gives a comprehensive summary of salary schedules there.

THE EDITORS.

CHAPTER ONE

Equalizing the Burden

THE problem of educational finance has become in recent years not merely one of economics and public finance, but increasingly one of education itself. In brief, the problem is how to make available as much as possible of the nation's resources to equalize educational opportunity on a national scale, without weakening the sense of responsibility of the local community for taking an interest in its schools, and without destroying the initiative of the teachers.

The *cash nexus* inevitably involves control; and the nature of the control can vitally affect the nature and spirit of the educative process. The worship of Mammon in the temple of education, however necessary in many cases, involves also the worship of other gods, often to the detriment of the worship of education in its highest form. We shall return to this aspect at the conclusion of this chapter.

The Problem of Sparsely Populated Countries

Though basically the problem is much the same in all countries, we shall, in what follows, deal more particularly with the problem as it confronts the younger countries where education has come to serve large, sparsely populated areas as well as large cities as, for example, in Australia, New Zealand, and South Africa. These countries had no strong forms of organized local government and education, and education developed practically without any local machinery for financing it. The choice was between no educational facilities at all, except through private schools or missionary endeavour, or provision by the state alone.

For interesting historical reasons these countries chose state provision as the mainstay of their education, in contrast with the United States of America and Canada (which also have large, sparsely populated areas to cater for), where local support and local control are characteristics of their educational systems.

In the discussion which follows, the Union of South Africa will be used as an example, because it illustrates how a system of centralized

finance has grown up out of the keen desire to bring good education
to its citizens in sparsely populated areas and to minister to the needs
of racially different and backward peoples within its borders. Before
doing so, certain general principles, which are virtually truisms, must
be stated.

The Main Factors

The *quality* as well as the *quantity* of education in any particular
country depends very largely upon :

(*a*) the economic resources of that country,

(*b*) the extent to which those resources are made available for
education, and

(*c*) the *method* by which the available resources are administered.

Considerations (*b*) and (*c*) are each in turn conditioned by the political structure of the country and by *the attitude of the people towards
the school as an institution and by the value they place on education
in general.*

By *quantity* is meant not merely the number of scholars enrolled,
but also how high they climb up the educational ladder. For example,
amongst the Natives in Africa, the vast bulk of those who go to
school are in the sub-standards, and comparison of their numbers with
pupils attending school in European countries would have little significance. The *extent* of education when measured in any country
should therefore be measured vertically as well as horizontally.

By *quality* is meant the relative excellence of the instruction offered,
not just to the few but to the many. It connotes also the degree to
which such education is diversified and articulated in order to provide
for the needs of individuals of widely differing capacities and levels of
intelligence.

The Economic Factor

All this, however, requires an economic basis. For example, with
the discovery of gold in the Transvaal during the last quarter of the
previous century, education developed in a phenomenal way in that
province (at that time still a Boer Republic). Gold meant more money
in the treasury and higher salaries to teachers. Higher salaries
attracted better teachers, and thus the quality of the instruction was
gradually improved.

Before this windfall the provision of education had been of a rudimentary nature, barely sufficient to meet the needs of a dominantly
farming community of Dutch Reformed persuasion.

The Boers were ardent Protestants and placed great store by education as a means of gaining Church membership and individual salva-

tion. Hence they did not hesitate to devote as much as possible of the newly found revenue of the state to the improvement of education, not only at the primary and secondary levels, but also at the higher and technical levels to provide for the needs of a rapidly growing industrial community on the Witwatersrand.

When later (1910) the Transvaal became incorporated as one of the four provinces in the Union of South Africa, it continued to set the pace in spending money on education. It was ahead of the other provinces in stepping up the training and the qualifications of teachers. It could do so because it offered better salaries than the other provinces. This in turn proved probably the most vital single factor determining the quality of education in South Africa.

The Public's Attitude to Education

Economic resources, therefore, do play an important role in determining the amount spent on education. This is by no means, however, the sole factor. There is, for example, hardly a country which, for its size and its population, possesses greater agricultural and mineral resources than Colombia. These are far greater than the economic resources of South Africa. Yet this country has remained relatively backward in comparison with, say, the Dominions of Australia, New Zealand, and South Africa. It spends, in relation to its national income, very little on education. In consequence its education is at a lower level, quantitatively as well as qualitatively, than the above-mentioned Dominions.

This applies in general also to some other states in South America.

The question arises, why do they devote so little of their national income to education, whereas South Africa, which is also a relatively undeveloped country and has only in recent times emerged from colonialism, ranks second highest in the world as regards the percentage of its national income which it devotes to public education? [1]

Is it not that non-economic factors, such as tradition and the people's attitude towards education, also play a role?

In this comparison, religion seems to be an important factor determining a people's attitude towards public education. For example, public education in younger countries settled dominantly by Protestants has developed much faster than in countries settled dominantly by Roman Catholics, as was the case in Latin America.

Following the injunction of Martin Luther, Protestant countries have always strongly supported public education of the masses. Protestants believed profoundly that literacy and the ability to read the Scriptures were essential for every individual in order to become a member of the

---

[1] *Public Expenditure on Education* (UNESCO/ST/R/11, Paris, 1953).

Church and to gain salvation of his soul in the hereafter. Presbyterian Scotland is famous for the many teachers it has sent all over the English-speaking world. Probably no single group of men has contributed more to the advance of education in the English-speaking Dominions and colonies than Scottish teachers.

In short, if a people believe in public education, they are generally prepared to make big economic sacrifices for it.

The Pooling of Resources

Another general principle is that an educational system must be large enough to be adequately financed. To ensure the equable distribution of educational opportunities, the resources of the country as a whole must be pooled. This is necessary to ensure the adequate training and remuneration of teachers, effective supervision, and adequate buildings and equipment.

The country may, of course, be sub-divided into smaller units for administrative purposes. But unless these are in some way or other anchored financially to the bigger whole, so as to ensure at least a certain minimum of financial support for the schools within that unit, the educational facilities within these separate units may suffer considerably. According to this principle, the education of the children of a particular area who are, after all, the future citizens of the nation, should not be jeopardized by the precarious economics of the area in which they happen to be born.

These great inequalities were prevalent in the past and are still present in some parts of the United States, where the schools were often dependent almost completely on the tax resources of the local county unit. And as these local districts varied tremendously *inter alia* in taxable wealth, one finds a similarly extreme variation between the educational offerings in these local districts. The best schools *I* have ever seen were in the United States, but so were also the worst *I* have ever seen.

It is to remedy these extreme local inequalities and to guarantee to every child in the state at least a certain minimum programme of education, that most of the forty-eight states have stepped in with a certain amount of financial support of the local community's schools. In some states, state aid is given in proportion to the educational need without regard to the ability of the locality to pay. In other states both the factors of the locality's *need* and of its *ability to pay* are taken into account.

One of the questions which arises from this is whether the use of state funds to equalize the burden of a minimum programme involved in equalizing opportunity, with no reward for the locality's effort to pay, promises as great educational progress as the use of state funds for rewarding local effort, with the resulting incomplete equalization of burden.

This question, to which various answers have been given in the different states, has been fairly intensively studied over the last thirty years in the United States of America. Lack of space does not allow an account of these here. The most original and stimulating of these studies have been led by Paul Mort of Teachers College, Columbia University, who was also Associate Director of the National Survey of School Finance in the United States of America.[2]

The same problem has, of course, arisen at the federal level as a result of the great inequality amongst the states themselves of resources with which to pay for what may be regarded as a satisfactory minimum programme from a *national* point of view—some states spending only one-fifth per pupil of what other states spend.

So great, however, is the fear that federal aid might bring with it federal interference with the autonomy of the states, that there has been a consistent resistance to equalization between the states on the lines of the equalization that the states themselves have achieved with regard to local districts within the states. So that, apart from federal aid in respect of certain specific objects like agricultural education and Americanization programmes, the United States of America is still far away from any national basis of equalizing the burden of financing the public schools.

The Union of South Africa

The administrative system of the Union of South Africa differs from that of the United States of America and of the Dominions of Canada and Australia. The four provinces, viz. the Cape, Natal, the Orange Free State, and Transvaal, are constituted into a *Union and not a Federation* like the above-mentioned countries. That is, when Union was formed in 1910, the provinces retained only certain limited functions, chief of which are primary and secondary education—i.e. ' education other than higher '. They retain these powers at the pleasure of the Union Government, and even the exercise of these powers is subject to the over-riding power of the Union Parliament.

Since the formation of Union, the Union Government has, from time to time, taken over certain educational functions which it con-

---

[2] Paul R. Mort, *The Measurement of Educational Need—A Basis for Distributing State Aid* (1924); *State Support for Public Education* (1935); *Federal Support for Public Education* (1936); Paul R. Mort and F. Cornell, *Adaptability of Public School Systems* (1938). (All these are published by the Bureau of Publications, Teachers College, Columbia University.)

sidered should, in the interests of the nation, be taken care of on a national basis. These functions included (besides university education) technical and vocational education, agricultural education, special education, and even nursery schools and child welfare. Teacher training is, however, given in training colleges under the provincial administrations, as well as in the education faculties of the universities.

Equalizing Educational Opportunity between Provinces

The important point to note is that the Union Government subsidizes the provinces to the extent of about 50 per cent of their budgets. To this extent the nation's resources as a whole are pooled in order to ensure that the primary and secondary education of the nation's children is kept up to a good standard. There are no strings tied to the Union's contribution. In no way has the Union Government ever prescribed to the provincial administrations how they should run their schools. In order, however, that the Union Government should not be automatically committed to unrestricted expenditure to match everything a province may wish to put up, a brake is put on the Union's commitment. A general limitation is that " if the net expenditure of a province in respect of any financial year exceeds the net expenditure of the financial year immediately preceding by more than 5 per cent [whether a general subsidy at the rate of 50 per cent was paid on the whole amount or not] the general subsidy of the excess above 5 per cent shall be calculated at 33 ⅓ per cent."

Despite this restriction on subsidy from the Union, the money spent (excluding capital expenditure) on primary and secondary education in the provinces grew from £25 million in 1948 to £39 million in 1952. (These are the latest published figures.) To-day this figure probably stands near to £45 million.

During the same period the Union's commitments on its own educational ventures, e.g. higher, technical, vocational, and special education, grew from £6¼ million to £7⅓ million.

It is doubtful whether the development of education in general in the Union would have gone on at such a high rate if the financial resources of the whole country were not made available for education at all levels.

But what is more important is that, while no province is debarred from using its own tax resources to develop its own schools, the Union subsidy made it possible for all to achieve a far higher general standard of education than would have been possible had each province been dependent solely on its own resources. The taxable resources of the four provinces differ considerably. For example, the taxable income *per caput* of the school population (all races) for the

Transvaal Province is more than twice as high as that of the Cape Province and the Orange Free State, and is about 1·6 times as high as that of Natal.

It should be noted that by sharing a province's expenditure on a 50 per cent basis, the Union does not in fact wipe out the inequalities between the provinces. The richer province will still get more in subsidy from the Union because it has, out of its own resources, more to spend. And the poorer province will automatically get less because it has, itself, from its own taxable resources, less to spend.

A refinement of the basis of Union subsidy to the provinces could be made if one were to take into account (on the lines of what has been done on the so-called "Mort plan" within some of the American States):

(a) a province's *ability to pay*, and

(b) its *educational need*, measured in terms of sparsity and the presence of large backward groups of population.

It has been found in South Africa that as soon as one gets outside centres of 2,500 population, the cost of providing educational facilities more or less of the same standard as in towns of 2,500 and over rises very sharply. In proportion, therefore, as a province has a large amount of ' ruralness ', its education will cost more.

Both these factors (a) and (b) can be objectively assessed, and it should be quite feasible to devise a subsidy formula which will take into account a province's own ability to pay as well as compensate it for ' ruralness '. This would certainly provide a more equitable basis of subsidy than the present rather rough and ready one. At any rate it would be anchored to hard facts which are relevant to the situation, and could not be so easily manipulated politically.

This is an aspect which will repay research in other countries as well as in South Africa.

Nevertheless there can be no question that, rough and ready as the present basis is, it has helped South Africa to guarantee minima and to achieve a far greater degree of equalization of educational opportunity, as between one province and another, than if each had been left to its own resources, as they were before Union was formed.

If one were to take as an index of educational opportunity the proportion of the European population who go on to university (to any university), one finds that in the two poorest provinces (the Cape Province and the Orange Free State), one in 160 of the population go as full-time students to university (to any university) as compared with one in 200 for Transvaal and one in 220 for Natal. It would seem, therefore, that as a result of equalizing the financial resources available between the provinces, the amount of taxable wealth in any province has not been allowed to become the crucial factor determining educational opportunity in that province. The decisive factors here would rather seem to be tradition, belief in education, and the economic demand for the products of the schools.

Ministering to a Heterogeneous Population

This spreading of the burden of financing education over the whole body politic in order to equalize educational opportunities has a further and special significance in a *multi-racial society* like South Africa.

The Union of South Africa has a population of roughly 13 million, constituted as follows :

European	2,700,000
Native (or African) . . .	8,800,000
Asiatic	380,000
Coloured	1,120,000

From this it will be seen that about four-fifths of the population of South Africa are non-European and about one-fifth European. Of the European population, 20·5 per cent are receiving education; of the Asiatic and Coloured 19·3 per cent, and of the African Natives 11 per cent.[3]

From the time of the earliest missionary efforts, about three hundred years ago, in South Africa, up to the present day, it has been the responsibility of the relatively small European population to bear the main burden of financing the education of the non-European population, most of whom are still very backward. It is obvious, of course, that through his labour the non-European has contributed to the wealth of the European out of which the latter had to find the money to provide for educational services. The indirect contribution by the non-European in this way has over the last century become increasingly greater as he became integrated into the white man's economic system. Though the non-European contribution through direct taxation to the revenue of the country is very small when compared with that paid by the European, he probably makes quite a considerable contribution through indirect taxation. Exactly how much would be very difficult to assess.

The bulk of the non-European population consists of African Natives, the large majority of whom still live in a relatively primitive state and on a rather low level of subsistence economically.

---

[3] It is generally accepted that 20 per cent of a country's population constitutes the proportion of children of school-going age.

Despite what has been done by missionary sacrifice supported by public funds to bring the Gospel and the fruits of European education to the African Native in his *kraals,* much has still to be done.   Only a little more than half the number of Native children of school-going age are to-day able to attend schools because of lack of facilities, i.e. school buildings and trained teachers.   Nevertheless, about nine hundred and fifty thousand Native children now attend state and state-aided schools.   About twenty-two thousand teachers are employed in these schools.   In the Cape Province all the teachers are fully trained.   All except a small percentage in the other provinces are fully trained. During 1955, £8,650,000 was being spent on Native education.

There is no territory or colony or protectorate in the whole of Africa where the education of the African Native has advanced to the same extent as it has done in the Union of South Africa.

Probably one of the best designed medical schools in the British Commonwealth has just been completed at the University of Natal at a cost of £450,000, paid for by the Union Government.   It is primarily intended for Africans, who receive very generous bursaries and loans to take the seven-year medical degree course.

As for the Indian (Asiatic) population in South Africa, fifty times as much per head of population is spent by South Africa on their education as in India.   In South Africa nearly all Indian children of school-going age are at school.   In India about a third are at school.   Four times as high a percentage of the Indian population in South Africa go to university as in India.

The Incidence of Taxation

The main source of revenue of the South African Government is derived from income-tax on individuals and companies.   This is paid by only about two hundred thousand individuals and two thousand companies.   This is out of a population of thirteen million.   This small proportion of the population paid £116 million (1952 figures) in income-tax towards the country's inland revenue.   Native taxes contributed £1½ million pounds.   Of those who pay income-tax, at least 95 per cent are European.   The main incidence, therefore, of direct taxation, which is the chief source of the nation's revenue, falls on the white population and on a very small section of that white population.

Education and National Income

Because such a large proportion of South Africa's population of thirteen million still lives on a relatively low level of economic productivity, it is to be expected that its national income per head of population, viz about £100 or $280, is low when compared with the United States of America and with the Dominions with homogeneously white populations and a high standard of living.

A comparison, therefore, of the absolute amounts spent on education in these countries or even in countries with lower standards of living than South Africa is not very meaningful. It would seem, therefore, that the best way in which to assess the effort which a country like South Africa has put into bringing education to the backward as well as to the advanced sections of its heterogeneous population is to see what proportion of its national income is devoted to education.

Though South Africa's national income per head of population is about £100 and that of the United States is over £700 and Canada's over £450, South Africa spends 4 per cent of its national income on education, as against the United States' 3.7 per cent and Canada's 3 per cent. South Africa's *per caput* national income is less than a third of that of Australia and New Zealand, yet it spends more than twice as big a proportion of its national income on education as those two Dominions.

South Africa has much the same handicaps in bringing education to its non-European masses as have countries like Egypt and India, where the incidence of illiteracy is high. Not only are those countries poor as regards *per caput* national income (Egypt about £42 and India about £20), but they also spend a very low percentage on education, i.e. 1.3 per cent in the case of Egypt, and 0.5 per cent in the case of India.

From the above it would seem that we have further evidence that the general level of education in any country is conditioned as much by the value which the people place on education and upon the sacrifices they are prepared to make to bring it to the whole population, as it is dependent upon a country's economic resources. The degree to which these resources are tapped, and the store a people place on education, are in their turn dependent upon the efficiency of the country's school system. These factors interact in a circle of causality.

Adaptability

To be effective in any country, the school system must be sensitive and responsive to the country's needs. And where, in young countries like South Africa, there is rapid economic development and a continual process of acculturation between different racial groups, it is essential that finance and control are so balanced that adaptability is guaranteed.

As has been pointed out before, where central financial support is necessary to equalize the burden of cost as well as of the service rendered amongst communities of widely different economic status, the danger is that all policy-making also becomes centralized. This breeds bureaucracy at the centre and apathy on the periphery.

This is what is gradually happening in South Africa. It is to a large extent the penalty that South Africa is paying for being so effective in ' equalizing the burden ' within each province. Because all the funds (e.g. teachers' salaries) are dispensed from the central office of the provincial capital—which in one province is as far as eight hundred miles away from the farthest school in the province—all control of the schools is centralized. The local school committees and school boards, which in years gone by had considerable financial responsibility for the schools, have no taxing powers and are no longer responsible for financing education. They sometimes raise money by voluntary effort by means of fêtes, bazaars, and concerts to pay for minor extra amenities at the school. In the Cape, Transvaal, and the Orange Free State, local school committees and district school boards still exist as historical relics of a regime when they had more powers. To-day their chief function is the selection of teachers, subject to the approval of the Department, where the appointments are finally made. Natal has no local authorities for education. Everything is controlled by the Department of Education at the provincial capital.

Centralized finance means control by the state. On the ground that " he who pays the piper calls the tune ", the state can become authoritarian and impress a whole ideology on the schools. This is what is happening to the Native schools since the Union Department of Native Affairs has taken over all Native education from the provincial education departments. But even where liberal democratic principles are still recognized, as in the field of European education in South Africa, centralized control tends to put a premium on standardization and conformity. It often sprouts from mere administrative tidy-mindedness, to which officials in control of funds tend to become addicted. This invariably results in the stifling of initiative amongst the teaching staff and affects in a subtle way the whole spirit of education.

It becomes " a matter of rules, regulations, and inspection, in which the machine assumes greater importance than human beings. But education, soundly conceived, cannot be reduced to a machine; it is something that results from the impact of personalities—both teachers' and pupils'—and to this end variety within a common framework is more important than uniformity and standardization." [4]

Just how to bring about this variety or adaptability is the problem. Centralized control frowns on new ideas. Innovations—whether in

---

[4] I. L. Kandel, *Types of Administration* (Melbourne University Press, 1938), p. 15.

method, content, or organization of teaching—are always bothersome to those in authority. It becomes a struggle between the priest on the one hand and the prophet on the other. The priest is there to conserve and *to maintain what is*, by adherence to ritual. The prophet often flouts ritual. He sees into the future and perceives what is lacking in the present system. He makes his voice heard and does something about it. Thus progress is achieved, though not without sacrifice. Prophets are often stoned, crucified, or burnt at the stake. Priests never. Yet both are necessary in education.

To be effective in any community, education has a twofold function: (a) to reproduce the type, and (b) to provide for growth beyond the type. It is the latter function which is most endangered by centralized finance. Those tender shoots—the growing-points in the educational system—are so often stunted and even killed off by the cold blasts of officialdom. They must at all costs be preserved. This can be done only by reconciling centralization of support with a considerable degree of decentralization of policy-making. To achieve this, one must cultivate an enlightened interest in education amongst the people themselves.

E. G. MALHERBE.

CHAPTER TWO

The Education of Nomadic Tribes in Iraq

FROM its early history, Iraq has provided harbours on the edge of the desert for nomadic tribes coming from the Arabian Peninsula. The plains of Iraq, with the Rivers Tigris and Euphrates and their tributaries irrigating them, always attracted nomadic tribes known as Bedouins from Arabia. The mountains of Iraq in the north always provided homes and grazing-ground for the Kurdish nomadic tribes who move into Persia or Turkey during the summer season. This continuous flow of tribes in the past has been the source which always provided fresh blood for the body of Iraq. The settled peoples of the towns and villages, whether Arab or Kurd, proudly trace their ancestry to well-known tribes. Not only that, but tribal life, tradition, and character have had a strong impact on the non-tribal population.

Tribesmen, whether Arab or Kurd, provide the country with men of strength, courage, endurance, and chivalry. At the same time they become a source of friction with the settled people, whose farms they may invade and whose security they may disturb. At best, nomadic life is very wasteful to human life and productivity, for the nomads hardly achieve much more than raising sheep and cattle. Tribal feuds and tribal codes of honour take a goodly toll of human life—especially of the womenfolk.

But nomadism has been progressively and rapidly shrinking in Iraq with the development of modern roads and modern means of transportation, with the use of aviation in preventing tribal feuds, and with the steady penetration of government control and order in tribal areas.

The majority of the population of Iraq is of tribal descent. Most of the Bedouin tribes have, in the course of recent history, settled to agriculture and very few tribes, like the Shammer, Anizeh, and Dhafir, have remained nomadic. The tribes of Jaf in the Sulaymanyeh district, Girdi, Herki—tribes in the Erbil district—and Bouli and Atrushi in the Mosul district, are examples of important Kurdish tribes who still practice nomadism. Practically all Kurdish tribes lend themselves to agriculture and settle in villages except for the summer season. In other words, Kurdish nomadism is mainly *seasonal* and not perpetual, a fact which is of significance in any educational planning.

There is no accurate census of the nomadic population in Iraq as yet, for the tribes do not lend themselves to census and never reveal their real numbers. A very rough estimate would be that Iraq possesses some quarter of a million nomads, of both Arab (Bedouin) and Kurdish origin, who are not settled as yet and whose education presents a problem. There are a number of reasons why tribal education should be pushed through in Iraq as quickly as possible. The first is that the impact on tribes of modern inventions, including automobiles, radios, aeroplanes, and water-pumps, has been very deep. Tribal chiefs who participate in the affairs of the state through membership in Parliament feel that their nomadic life is an anachronism in the modern age. Conversations which the writer recently had with some tribal chiefs, both Bedouins and Kurdish, definitely reveal that the tribes want modern education and they want to be settled on land with full participation in the modern life of the country.

The second reason is that Iraq as a modern state, evolving towards Westernization, cannot afford to leave a section of its population to continue to live in relatively primitive conditions and remain a continual source of disturbance of peace and order in the country. For nomadic tribesmen who shun settled life think of the government and its control as an evil which interferes with their freedom and happiness. The tribes loathe paying taxes on their sheep and cattle to a government whose services are not seen and probably not appreciated by them. Their loyalty to the state has to be built up by modern education and by the modern social and economic services which a modern state provides. The tribal men have to be made productive, loyal citizens of a modern state. Iraq cannot afford to let this process be delayed.

The third reason is Iraq's urgent need for workmen. Within the last few years Iraq's revenue from petroleum has been steadily rising. It has reached over seventy million pounds, some two hundred million dollars, in the year 1955. Iraq is the first country in the Middle East to devote 70 per cent of this amount to major development projects. For this purpose a Development Board has been established which plans these capital works. Irrigation and flood control have been the first concern of this Board. Dams are being constructed which will bring vast areas of arid land under cultivation. Agricultural and industrial development is also a major concern of this Board. The Board plans for the expansion of roads and communications, schools, hospitals and preventive health measures, including the drainage of swamps and the provision of disinfected water for all rural areas. Now, according to the plans of the Development Board, Iraq, which in the past contained at least four times its present population, needs every tribal member to be settled and become active as a citizen in a modern society. This makes tribal education and tribal settlement a matter of importance and urgency.

In the summer of 1953 the writer had the privilege of travelling for six days on mule-back accompanying His Majesty the King of Iraq in the mountains of Kurdistan in the sub-district of Rawanduz. In the areas through which we travelled, no automobile roads are constructed as yet. It was a pleasure to see that beautiful country, the home of many a nomadic Kurdish tribe. We enjoyed the hospitality of these Kurdish tribes and admired their fine character. We felt that here lies a great wealth of material, as well as human, resources in Iraq which have not as yet been tapped. To do that the construction of roads would be the first requisite. This year we learnt that automobile roads are already under construction to the nearest tribal harbour—Sidakan. Thus the Development Board is already paving the way for the liquidation of nomadism in Kurdistan. Land settlement and land distribution will do much to terminate the existence of nomadic life in Iraq.

The Present Position

The present-day position of tribal education generally consists of its traditional method of bringing up a child to know the geography of the district in which the tribe moves; the history of the tribe and its relationships with the other tribes; methods of warfare and horsemanship; the grazing of sheep and cattle; tribal folk-lore, and the rudiments of Islamic religion. Usually one *Mullah*, a religious teacher, or *Sayed*, a descendant of the Prophet, join or frequent each tribe and look after their spiritual welfare. The chief of the tribe (if he himself does not happen to do so) must have someone with him who can read and write.

Besides, modern education has already touched some tribes. Most tribal chiefs send their sons to town and cities for modern schooling. Some Kurdish tribes avail themselves of the schools opened in the villages in which they settle the greater part of the year. But this is not a common practice. In other words, the overwhelming majority of tribal children remain without any form of schooling. Although the Iraq Government has enacted an educational law which makes six years' elementary education compulsory for all children of school age, it has not so far provided the facilities for the universal implementation of this law, and this holds especially true with regard to nomadic tribes. In 1933 some attempt was made at opening peripatetic or roving schools with some nomadic tribes. The one with the Shammer Bedouin tribe, opened at the request of Sheikh Ajil Al Yawar, a wise and distinguished chief of his tribe, and the one with the Harkyeh, a well-known Kurdish tribe, in the district of Sulaymanyeh, are good examples. These schools had to be in tents which moved with the tribe. School equipment, as well as the teacher, was mounted on camel-back in the case of the Bedouins, and on mule-back in the case of the Kurdish tribes. But these peripatetic schools did not survive long, depending on the continued interest of the chief; the availability of teachers who could endure the hardships of nomadic life, as well as the durability of the enthusiasm of the Ministry of Education in the promotion of such schools. None of these things contributed to the permanency of these schools.

How could the Problems be Tackled To-day?

The Development Board has to proceed vigorously, providing land and pastural grounds for all tribes. This should go hand in hand with projects of irrigation, afforestation, and land distribution. Artesian wells are being bored in districts where river irrigation is not available to make permanent pasture possible for tribal settlement. All this could be achieved under the new six-year development programme for the country, to which over three hundred million *dinars* (a *dinar* equals a pound sterling), nearly a billion dollars, have been allotted. Once these tribes are settled, then a suitable educational programme should be worked out for them. The basic problem, however, is to decide what sort of education is suitable for the tribal population if they are to settle. It would be a grave mistake to extend to them the system now prevailing in Iraq without basic modifications. The present system, as it stands to-day, is too bookish, formal, and not directly related to life. It is already doing much harm in creating a big bulk of white-collared young men who abhor labour and who form a discontented and unhappy group. The present system does not emphasize character education, nor the spiritual life of the nation.

The programmes which are proposed for the tribes of Iraq consist of the following :

(1) Tribal elementary schools should be co-educational. For it is possible for boys and girls to attend school together in Iraq. It should emphasize, besides the three R's, hand work, agricultural work, animal care, practical hygiene, sports and native art, as well as a strong emphasis on character and religious education.

(2) At least two teachers' colleges for men and another two for women should be established to prepare teachers for tribal areas. These institutions should emphasize the techniques for broadening tribal loyalty, so as to make it emerge into state loyalty, and they should promote tribal democratic tradition. They should promote tribal inclination to agriculture and other productive pursuits, as well as encourage tribal arts, sports, and folk-lore. These teachers should

be especially prepared in community leadership and social service. Women teachers should be especially prepared in child-care and home economics. Scout-life should be one of the outstanding features of these teachers' colleges.

(3) Peoples' colleges that would take adults and give them courses in civics, religion, agriculture, animal husbandry, hygiene, child-care, and fine arts should be encouraged.

(4) Gifted boys should be selected from the elementary schools and sent, at government expense, to boarding secondary schools, where they should have an academic education which prepares them for the professions and leadership in agriculture, medicine, engineering, administration, and technical education, as well as the Army.

(5) There must be established, in the new tribal settlements, community houses in the form of Houses of the People which should be frequented instead of the coffee-shops. In these they should enjoy seeing cultural films, listen to the radio, hear a periodic lecture, or see an art exhibition.

(6) Suitable games, village fairs, and national festivities should be encouraged.

To achieve all this, co-ordinated planning is required by the Development Board, which must enlist the participation of the Department of Miri Sirf (land distribution) as well as the Ministries of Agriculture, Health, Education, and Interior. The administration in Iraq needs a new orientation towards tribal settlement and new community development. This requires high-level political planning. In this way the nomadic tribes of Iraq will not only stop being a source of trouble to peace and stability, but they will prove to be a positive force in building up the country, which badly needs to increase its population and is hard hit by a shortage of labour.

MOHAMMED FADHIL JAMALI.

CHAPTER THREE

The Finance of State Education in the United Kingdom

EDUCATION facilities in the United Kingdom are provided for the most part by the state, so that decisions about the size and scope of these facilities depend on political as well as market factors. The government in power lays down the requirements of the educational programme, such as minimum standards and the relative priorities to be assigned to each type of education, the attention to be paid to safeguarding religious and cultural minorities, and so on. The necessary economic consequence of this complex of decisions regarding education is that it implies the use of the community's resources in a particular way, to the exclusion of other possible alternative uses. At the same time the fact that the decisions are taken by public authorities means that the necessary control over the use of resources must be determined by the employment of some system of taxation, which reduces the purchasing power of individuals and increases that of the state at either the central or the local authority level.

It is this latter aspect of education provision that is considered in this article; that is, we are concerned with the fiscal problems of education, with the ways in which funds for the provision of education are in fact raised and spent, and with their consequences for such matters as the distribution of incomes between persons and regions. This is not to say that there are no economic issues of interest concerned with the ' resources ' aspect of education provision. Indeed, it may be useful to begin with some discussion of the fundamental question, since it bears on later discussion.

In Table I below we measure the claim of education on our annual output by the total of current expenditure and of capital expenditure for education purposes expressed as a percentage of the gross national product.[1]

---

[1] Some of the items included under 1 in this table (such as scholarships and university grants) represent transfer payments, *i.e.*, money grants from the government to individuals or institutions rather than direct payments by the government for services rendered. However, in the case of education both types of payment can reasonably be considered to represent a direct claim on the community's resources; universities can be treated for our purpose as ' spending agents ' of the government, and scholars (perhaps with less validity) as factors of production attracted by the scholarships from other employment. While it is common practice to exclude transfer payments from comparisons of this kind, we have thought it less misleading to include them. The size of these transfer payments in comparison with direct purchases by the government can be seen from Table II on p. 312.

TABLE I

GOVERNMENT EXPENDITURE ON EDUCATION, U.K. (1937–8 TO 1954).

	1937–8 (£mn.)	1950 (£mn.)	1954 (£mn.)
1. Current expenditure	116	348	503
2. Capital expenditure	10	48	74
3. Total	126	396	577
4. 3 as percentage of gross national product at factor cost	2·4	3·4	3·7

Sources: (i) 1937–8: based on A. T. Peacock and P. Browning, " The Social Services in Great Britain and the Redistribution of Income " in Income Redistribution and Social Policy, ed. A. T. Peacock, 1953.
(ii) 1950 and 1954: based on Blue Book on National Income and Expenditure, 1955.

The figures in row 4 of Table I inevitably give rise to speculation as to whether the percentage of the community's resources being devoted to education is ' too high ' or ' too low '. But no *technical* answer to this question can be provided either by economists or by education experts; it is impossible to lay down universally acceptable criteria for ' optimal ' education services based, for example, on the teacher-pupil ratio, or the number of square feet per pupil in schools, or the ' correct ' school-leaving age. So-called ' optimum ' standards based on such criteria leave out of account the alternative ways in which resources devoted to education might be used. This is well illustrated by a comparison of the situation of different countries; the standard of education services provided in the United Kingdom would be an intolerable burden on the present resources of, say, Colombia. Equally, there is room for wide differences of opinion as to what resources should be sacrificed to provide which types and amounts of education in any community at any time. Thus, in the conditions of full employment that have obtained in the United Kingdom since the war, improved standards in the provision of any type of education have been made possible only by the loss of resources to, say, the building of factories and plant, or by the loss of scientists to industry; and so on.

This does not mean that nothing useful can be said about the volume of the community's resources to be devoted to education; the realization of the economic problem involved does help us to formulate both question and answers more carefully. Thus Professor Judges, who is fully aware of the economic problem, makes a persuasive case for greater expenditure on education, precisely on the grounds that it would increase our productive efficiency in the long run, quite apart from cultural and spiritual gains.[2]

Similar considerations apply when we examine the problems created by the existing methods of finance of education, which is the main subject of this contribution. No absolute agreed criteria can be stated which would tell us either who should be taxed and by how much in order to provide for education, or how the benefits should be distributed. Any particular method of finance can be judged by the economist only by the establishment of the policy objectives actually being aimed at, and comparison of these with the actual effects of the methods adopted. For these reasons, subsequent discussion will take existing education standards as a datum and will devote attention to the implications of the fiscal procedures by which the requisite education resources are provided.

Financial Relations of Central and Local Government

Before examining the finance of education something should be said about the financial relations of central and local government.

British public administration (and with it the administration and finance of education) is the responsibility of the central government and of local authorities (county councils, county boroughs, and so on) whose relationship with the central government has many of the characteristics of a federation. Local authorities have a fair amount of autonomy except in matters concerning which Parliament places specific obligations upon them; in respect of many services, including education, they make it possible for the central government to avoid the centralization of detailed administration, while general supervision and control increasingly are exercised from the centre.

The supervisory powers of the central government have been reinforced during the present century by the increasing dependence of local authorities upon central government finance. The main source of local government income is the local rate—a tax levied on the occupiers of land and buildings [3]—and the considerable increase in the financial burden of their statutory obligations has found local authorities unable to raise adequate revenues from this tax, so that they have become increasingly dependent for financial assistance on grants pro-

---

[2] A. V. Judges, "The Social Cost of an Education Programme" in *Looking Forward in Education*, ed. A. V. Judges (Faber & Faber, Ltd., London), 1955.

[3] Occupied property in local areas is given a 'rateable value', which is an assessment of the income derived from such property. The sum of these values is the total 'rateable value' of the area. The local rate is a tax on these assessed values, usually expressed as a 'rate per £'. Thus, if the local rate was 10s. in the £, the occupier of a property with a rateable value of £50 would pay £25 in rates.

vided by the central government out of general taxation. The grant system has come to be regarded by the central government both as a means of controlling the nature and the standard of the services provided by local authorities, and as a means of ' equalizing ' the financial burden imposed upon individual authorities by the provision of such services. Accordingly, central government financial assistance has taken a variety of forms and has been subjected to a variety of conditions; these reflect the multiple, and possibly conflicting, objectives of the assistance, and the changes over time in these objectives. As we shall see, the finance of education has been one of the important factors in the developing pattern of grant aid.

Following Chester,[4] the various forms of assistance may be classified in the following way. Grants may be *conditional*, that is, their payment depends on the performance of specified duties, or (less usually) grants may be *unconditional*. They may be completely *specific*, as with those made to meet defined expenses such as the salary of a particular employee (*e.g.*, the detailed grants given before 1921 in respect of particular types of education, such as the teaching of cookery); or, again, they may be *general*, that is paid without reference to the nature of expenditure. They may be *fixed* or *variable*, and the variability may take several forms, *e.g.*, a grant may be proportionate to local authority expenditure of a particular type, as in the case of one part of the present education main grant, or proportionate to the physical amount of the service provided. Lastly, the grant may be related to the means (*i.e.*, rate revenue) of the authority concerned (as with the present education main grant) or may take no account of means at all.

It is impossible to outline in a paragraph the evolution of the grant system in the United Kingdom, but the understanding of education finance depends on some knowledge of its history. Briefly, the pattern of development has been for grants to be provided first of all as a stimulus to the development of particular services, and therefore to be conditional, more or less specific, and bearing some relation to total expenditure by the local authority on the service concerned. Once a grant of this kind becomes established, however, it must bring with it supervision of local authority expenditure in order to ensure that the conditions of the grant are being complied with; both a system of audit and a system of inspection and the authorization are the concomitants of grants of this kind. With the success of this ' encouragement ' type of grant in establishing minimum standards of service, the administrative apparatus can be used to ensure that legally prescribed stan-

---

[4] D. N. Chester, *Central and Local Government: Financial and Administrative Relations*, Chapter V (Macmillan, 1951).

dards are universally maintained, and the financial assistance required by local authorities to meet their legal obligations can become more general in nature. The process extends to the replacement of 'encouragement' grants by 'block' grants, which are less specifically (if at all) related to the performance of particular tasks, but are conditional only upon the general willingness of the local authority to meet its statutory obligations, and are also related to some extent to the differing financial resources of different authorities. The final outcome of this process in the United Kingdom has been the introduction of general exchequer grants. The first of these was the General Exchequer Grant of 1929. This was both a resources and an equalization grant. It was replaced in 1949 by the present Exchequer Equalization Grant, in which the equalization is more pronounced. It is paid to authorities whose rateable value falls below a weighted national average. Other local authorities get nothing, and the grant formula, which is discussed in more detail below, is aimed at removing differences between the rate-burdens of those who benefit.

Education Grants to Local Authorities

The relevance of this rather lengthy description is that education is now by far the most important single item of local government expenditure, representing to-day about 40 per cent of the total. This fact alone implies that it must exercise a major influence on the present structure of the grant system as a whole.

The finance of education has followed the general evolutionary pattern. To-day, the bulk of central government aid to local authorities for education is given in the form of a general grant, although some subsidiary conditional grants (e.g., for school meals) still exist. However, education remains unique among the important local authority services in never having been assimilated into the general exchequer grant system just described. Consequently, the general grant made solely for education comprises a considerable part of total local government revenues, being now much larger than any other single grant (including the Exchequer Equalization Grant), and accounting for some 50 per cent of the total grant payments from central to local authorities.

Section 100 of the 1944 Education Act authorized regulations by which the grant aid to any local authority is to be calculated. The formula now used has three elements :

(a) the authorities receive £6 per unit of the average number of pupils in maintained and assisted schools;

(b) to this is added 60 per cent of 'net recognizable expenditure' (*i.e.*, expenditure on education recognized as qualifying for the grant under the Act); and

(*c*) from this total is deducted the product of a 30*d*.[5] rate.

An example will show how this formula operates. Let us assume that the net recognizable expenditure of an authority is £250,000. Then its ' education accounts ' could be drawn up as follows :

+	*Thousands of Pounds*	−	*Thousands of Pounds*
£6 per unit of average number of pupils on registers (6,000)	36	Net recognizable expenditure	250
60 per cent of net recognizable expenditure	150		
Less product of 30*d*. rate[1] (say) . .	−40		
	——110		
Balance to be met by local authority .	104		
	250		250

[1] *I.e., authority has a rateable value of £320,000.*

For most authorities the main determinant of the size of the grant is clearly the net recognizable expenditure undertaken, and some writers have tended to stress the fact that education is financed primarily on a percentage grant basis. Nevertheless, the grant does to some extent take the different circumstances of individual authorities into account. The ' pupil ' element varies to some extent with the differing needs of authorities, and the product of a 30*d*. rate takes account of the wealth of authorities, at least in a rough-and-ready way. There are also subsidiary education grants, which are related to needs. For example, subject to certain conditions, school meals and milk services attract a 100 per cent grant, as do local authority provisions for the training of teachers. It is also relevant, of course, that (as has already been explained) the Exchequer Equalization Grant cannot be allocated to specific services. It is paid according to a formula whose purpose is to help those local authorities who would otherwise be able to maintain services of a satisfactory standard only by recourse to relatively heavy rates. Consequently, this grant contributes towards the finance of education by those authorities who are entitled to receive it.[6]

Having explained the sources from which the revenues for the finance of local education are derived, let us examine in more detail the redistributive effects of these methods, to discover who bears the burden of taxes to finance education and who receives its benefits.

---

[5] 30*d*. = 35 U.S. cents.
[6] This is discussed in greater detail below.

Two kinds of redistribution can usefully be considered : First, how the methods of finance adopted affect the *distribution of incomes between persons,* and then how these methods affect the *relative burden imposed on individual local authorities by the provision of education.*

Allocation of Burdens and Benefits by Incomes

Table II gives details of the current expenditure of central and local government on education for selected years. The table is not given in the detail we would like, due to the limitations of the available statistics. It includes one estimate, which is necessary because it is not possible to allocate the Exchequer Equalization Grant to particular local authority services. For those authorities who receive it, the Grant operates as a general supplement for *all* expenditures, irrespective of purpose. Thus the grant in effect serves to meet a *proportion* of all local authority expenditures. Accordingly, we have considered it most reasonable to assume that the proportion of total education expenditure met out of the Exchequer Grant is the same as the proportion of all expenditures met in that way. Despite this difficulty, the table provides some useful information about the redistributive effects of education finance both as between income groups and as between geographical (*i.e.,* local authority) areas.

The table demonstrates that there has been a marked shift in the proportion of expenditure on education financed from central government revenues. In so far as the central government raises revenue from direct taxes, particularly progressive income taxes and death duties, it may be presumed that a shift towards central government finance of education will mean that an increasing proportion of education expenditure is financed by the higher-income groups. Unfortunately, the matter is not as simple as that, although we hope to show that this presumption is a much more reasonable one than others that have been made. For example, it has been argued that the poor largely pay for their own education. This statement is not tenable.

Three difficult problems arise in trying to allocate the burdens and benefits of the present system of finance of education more precisely between individuals. These concern the indentification of the taxes which finance education, the determination of the incidence of these taxes, and the allocation of the benefits from education expenditure. We shall see that there is no ' right ' solution to these problems; we can proceed further only by making what seem to be the most reasonable assumptions that are possible.

TABLE II

CURRENT EXPENDITURE ON EDUCATION, U.K. (1937–54) (£mn.)

Receipts				*Payments*			
	1937–8	*1950*	*1954*		*1937–8*	*1950*	*1954*
1. From Central Government:				3. By Central Government:			
(a) Central government expenditure met from general taxation	2	59	65	(a) Goods and services	2	22	27
(b) Grants to local authorities met from general taxation:				(b) Transfers:			
(i) General education grant		147	223	(i) Scholarships, etc.		14	4
(ii) Specific grants	56	28	40	(ii) University grants, etc.	—		
(iii) Proportion of non-allocable grants		11	15			23	34
2. From Local Government:				4. By Local Government:			
(a) Proportion of local rates and income from property	58	103	160	(a) Goods and services	112	250	381
				(b) Transfers:			
				(i) Scholarships, etc.	2	13	20
				(ii) School meals and milk	—	26	37
TOTAL	£116	£348	£503	TOTAL	£116	£348	£503

Sources: (i) 1937–8: Peacock and Browning, *loc. cit.*
(ii) 1950 and 1954: based on *Blue Book of National Income and Expenditure*, 1955.

The first problem is that of finding the appropriate taxes to finance education. In contrast to the finance, say, of national insurance, there are no central government taxes ear-marked for the financing of education; there is no modern equivalent of ' whisky money '—the grant received by local authorities for technical education under the Local Taxation Act of 1890 (from the proceeds of a tax on spirits). Since we cannot allocate particular tax sources to education, the most satisfactory procedure, in our view, is one similar to the one already adopted in allocating the Exchequer Equalization Grant. That is, we assume that the raising of revenues for the finance of education does not alter the *proportions* of the different taxes raised to meet *all* forms of expenditure, including education. Thus we assume that education is financed, so to speak, by a segment of each individual tax raised by the central government. This seems much more reasonable than to assume, say, that a particular tax, such as the purchase tax, is devoted to the finance of education alone. The problem is less difficult when we turn to the expenditure on education that comes from local authorities' own revenues. We know that the part of education expenditure that is borne by local authorities must come from one tax, the local rate, or from local authority income from property.

The second problem arises after we have decided upon the appropriate division of taxes. It is concerned with the technical problem of tax incidence. Can we say with any certainty who bears these taxes, in the senses that particular persons have their money incomes reduced or the prices of the goods they buy increased by them? We cannot consider this question in any detail here, but we feel it necessary to warn the reader that the common assumptions that income taxes are borne by income receivers and that taxes on commodities are passed forward to consumers are not universally accepted by economists, although we shall follow the usual practice of adopting them for this study. This is not the only difficulty about incidence. Statistical problems are bound to arise in trying to classify consumers and different types of income receivers, wage earners, and so on, according to the particular income groups to which they belong. In any case, data for the United Kingdom are inadequate for firm conclusions to be drawn. Further assumptions have therefore to be made, and the estimates given later need to be read with this in mind.

The third problem relates to the allocation of benefits. It would seem a relatively simple matter to perform this allocation, compared with the difficulties connected with taxes. It is true that we have sufficient information about the distribution of children according to income groups to allow us to perform a rough allocation of expenditure according to the proportion of children in each group. But is this the appropriate procedure? There is, of course, the obvious difficulty that benefits in terms of the outlay on each child are not homogeneous. Different types and grades of education require different *per capita* outlays. But there is a more fundamental point. Does it really make sense to allocate the benefits of education to individuals at all? Are not the benefits of education received, at least in part, by society as a whole irrespective of income group?

This last question must surely be answered in the affirmative, but the allocation of benefits to particular individuals can still be defended, since the benefits to society accrue as an indirect consequence of the utilization of education by the individuals concerned.[7]

The reader may feel that it would be better at this stage to close with the statement that the allocation of burdens and benefits is impossible. However, for those who are prepared to accept the assumptions outlined in the previous paragraphs despite their arbitrariness, the figures in Table III, based on the study by Peacock and Browning, may be of interest. We have taken only three broad income bands: up to £499 per annum, £500 to £1,999 per annum, and £2,000 and above per annum. Unfortunately it is not possible to use calendar-year figures in Table III; instead the fiscal year 1950–1 is taken and figures relate to Great Britain and not to the United Kingdom (*i.e.*, Northern Ireland is excluded). Grants to universities and certain minor education expenditures are omitted from the table.

TABLE III

ALLOCATIONS OF RECEIPTS AND PAYMENTS IN THE EDUCATION BUDGET, 1950–1.
(£mn.)

	Taxes Paid				Benefits Received		
	£0–£499	£500–£1,999	£2,000 and over		£0–£499	£500–£1,999	£2,000 and over
Central Government: Direct Taxes	11·2	31·0	66·5	Goods and services	188·4	54·1	—[1]
Taxes on expenditure	65·4	21·2	6·4	Transfers	35·4	10·2	—
Local Government: Local rates and income from property	60·3	18·0	8·1				
TOTALS	136·9	70·2	81·0	TOTALS	223·8	64·3	—

[1] '—' *means negligible.*

Granted our assumptions, therefore, the ' poor '—that is, those with incomes of £500 and below in 1950–1—paid about 61 per cent of the cost of their education, the difference being made up very slightly by

[7] For a more extensive discussion of this point, see A. T. Peacock and P. Browning, *op. cit.*, pp. 154–5. It is also relevant that the extent to which the benefits of education are ' individual ' rather than ' social ' differs according to the type of education being considered—contrast, for example, technical and classical education. On this point, see M. Friedman, " The Role of Government in Education " in *Economics and the Public Interest*, ed. Solo, 1955.

the middle-income group, but largely by the ' rich '—that is, those with £2,000 a year or more. It is interesting to contrast this percentage with the percentage paid by the ' poor ' towards all social services. According to the study upon which we have based our results, the ' poor ' paid £897 million towards all such services, and received £1,607 million in benefits. That is to say, they paid about 55 per cent of the total cost of social services from which they directly benefited. The explanation of this difference in percentage is very simple; education is now the main social service provided by local authorities and still relies upon receipts from a regressive tax, the local rate, while other major social services, and particularly the National Health Service, are primarily financed out of central government taxation.

Equalizing the Burden between Local Authorities

We now turn from examination of the distribution of the burdens and benefits of education between income groups to the problem of the effect of central government assistance on equalizing the burden of education finance as between different local authorities; that is, between the inhabitants of different geographical areas. There are two questions of interest. First, how the *absolute level* of the rate-income required by all local authorities from their ratepayers for the provision of education is affected by central government subventions. Second, how the *relative burden* of education expenditures on different individual local authorities is affected by the " equalizing " formulae by which the size of government grants to them is determined.

Table II (page 312) brings out the great size of the general education grant relative to other sources of local authority education finance, and particularly relative to the Exchequer Equalization Grant (item 1(b) (iii) for 1950 and 1954) which, on our assumption, is estimated to provide only about 3½ per cent of the revenue for local authorities' expenditure on education. The point is reinforced by the fact that in 1950 the entire Exchequer Equalization Grant for the United Kingdom was £58 million, or only about one-fifth of all local authorities' expenditure on education, so that the grant would not have been the most important source of education finance, even on the extreme assumption that it was devoted exclusively to that purpose. Since, further, the terms of the education main grant ensure that approximately 60 per cent of education expenditure must be met by the central government for all local authorities, the overwhelming importance of the education main grant in ameliorating the absolute burden of education expenditure upon local governments, and hence in reducing the general level of rates, is quite evident.

It remains to discover how the form of central government grants affects the relative burden of financing education as between one local authority and another. Two questions arise : how does the grant system affect the rates required to be levied by different local authorities in order to finance any given level of expenditure, and how does the system account for variations in the actual cost of financing education in different local areas? Of course, our study will tell us the extent to which grants operate to raise ' poor ' areas to parity with ' rich ' areas in the provision of education *only if rate income provides a satisfactory index of relative wealth, and only if we can make fairly specific statements about the relative costs of providing education in different areas.* Nevertheless, some interesting conclusions can be drawn, even when all the qualifications have been taken into account.

The central government grants attempt to take into account the ' wealth ' or ' resources ' of different local authority areas by the inclusion of a weighting for ' rate-resources ' in the grant formulæ. As we have already pointed out, this method of weighting is found both in the education main grant and in the Exchequer Equalization Grant. In order to assess the combined effect of the two weighting factors, it is convenient to begin with the unconditional Equalization Grant.

The formula for this grant is weighted to take account of differences in rate-resources in such a fashion that local authorities with rate-resources above the weighted national average get nothing.[8] The aim of the formula is to make such grant payments as will achieve parity in the rate-burdens of the remaining (' poorer ') authorities, parity being defined as a situation where the same increase in rate poundage is needed in order to finance a given increase in expenditure. We have already noted the small size of the Exchequer Equalization Grant in comparison with total education expenditure by local authorities. We must not be led by this to assume that its equalizing function can be measured by its relative importance as a source of finance. Its importance as an ' equalizer ' will be better understood if it is appreciated that local authority expenditure on education financed by local rates in 1954 was about £112 million,[9] or only 26 per cent of all such expenditure. Of this total of £112 million only about 60 per cent is affected by the Equalization Grant, the remaining 40 per cent being

---

[8] The actual population of local authority areas is adjusted to take account of varying numbers of children and varying sparsity of population from one area to another before rateable value per head (*i.e.*, ' rate-resources ') is calculated. It is the rate poundage ' adjusted ' for these factors that the Grant operates to ' equalize '.

[9] It will be observed that this figure is less than that shown in Table II [2(a)], as being spent by local authorities from their own resources. That item includes expenditure out of income from property, etc., estimated at £48 million, which has to be excluded when considering rate-burdens.

rate-revenue raised for education purposes by local authorities who do not qualify for the Grant because their rate-resources are above the weighted national average. Consequently, the Grant does nothing to equalize the rate-burden of education between those who do not qualify, or between those qualified to receive it, considered as a group, and those not so qualified. But it is quite large enough to equalize the rate-burden of education expenditure as between ' poorer ' authorities who qualify for the Grant. Woodham [10] has calculated that, in the year 1949–50, £16 million of the Grant would have been enough to achieve complete equalization of the rate-burdens imposed by education of all authorities receiving the Grant in England and Wales.

We have seen how the main education grant discriminates against authorities with high rateable values by a deduction equal to the proceeds of a rate of 30d. Unlike the Equalization Grant, however, the education main grant is paid to all local authorities. Consequently, rateable value can have a double effect upon the total grant received by a local authority, once through the Exchequer Grant in the manner described, and again through the education main grant. This dual system means that those authorities who benefit from both grants are over-compensated, in the sense that the burden of expenditure on education falling on their rates becomes not only equal to, but actually *falls below*, that of other authorities who receive only the education main grant. Woodham [11] demonstrates that, if local authorities had similar education costs per scholar, and similar proportions of scholars to population, then the Exchequer Equalization Grant alone would bring about a formal equalization of the rate poundages for financing education, in respect of authorities in receipt of this Grant. The effect of the additional weighting for rateable value in the education main grant is to favour the ' poorer ' authorities even further. Consequently, all authorities receiving both grants are over-compensated as against those who receive only the education grant, and the ' poorer ' of the authorities receiving both grants are over-compensated in relation to the ' less poor ' in that group. In the case of authorities receiving only the education grant, the ' resources ' element in that grant is too small to bring about an equalization of their relative rate-burdens. On the other hand, as we shall see, the ' cost ' elements in the education grant may discriminate in favour of such ' richer ' areas, and so act as an offset to the effect of the ' resources ' elements.

The different *costs* of providing similar education facilities are taken into account in some of the specific grants for education, such as the

---

[10] J. B. Woodham, *Educational Rates and the Education and Equalization Grants* (Institute of Municipal Treasurers and Accountants), p. 58.

[11] *Op. cit.*, pp. 38–45.

grant for school meals. The weighting factor for children in the education main grant also tends to offset high costs, to the extent that these costs vary with the number of schoolchildren per head of population in the area. But while it is clear that the payment of £6 per scholar increases the relative size of the grant of areas with many children, it is also clear that their education costs will remain higher than those areas with fewer children to the extent that the £6 per scholar is inadequate to offset the extra costs of educating more children, since less than 60 per cent of the excess over £6 is accounted for by the other elements in the main grant. Furthermore, education costs do not vary solely because of variations in the numbers of schoolchildren; different authorities have both varying problems in providing a given standard of education and varying conceptions of the standard they wish to provide. In this latter regard, it is clear that the 60 per cent element in the grant will be greater, the higher the standard of education provided. ' Rich ' authorities can thus obtain higher grants to the extent that they elect to provide standards of education above the average—as many of them do.

One final factor that might possibly be considered to act as an offset to the high education costs of local authorities with many schoolchildren is the population weighting in the Exchequer Equalization Grant, since the population of each local authority is weighted for the number of children under 15 years in such a way that those areas are favoured which have more than the national average number of children per head. It is questionable, however, whether this weighting should be considered in connexion with our problem. If we try to discover the intentions of the Equalization Grant, we find no clear evidence that the children weighting was introduced with education specifically in mind. Indeed, there is some evidence to support a contrary conclusion. Children involve local authorities in expenditure on services other than education, such as maternity and child welfare services. Furthermore, the children weighting is not affected by the proportion of children actually being educated, or by variations between authorities in actual education expenditure per head on children. This reasoning is supported by the fact that the earlier General Exchequer Grant introduced in 1929 included a similar children weighting which was generally assumed to operate simply as an index of relative wealth or poverty. We take the view, therefore, that it is misleading to attempt a detailed estimation of the effects of the children factor in the Equalization Grant upon the burden of education in particular local areas. Any such attempt must require not only the separation of that part of the Equalization Grant attributable to the children weighting in individual areas, but also arbitrary assumptions

regarding the proportion of the figure so obtained that should be allocated to education rather than to other services from which children
benefit. It seems more plausible to treat the children weighting simply
as a factor affecting the total value of the grant given, without attempting to impute the benefit to particular local authority services.[12]

General Conclusions

Our analysis suggests certain tentative conclusions of a general
nature, and raises some questions about the relationship between objectives and methods in education finance.

The fact that there is reason to suppose that persons in lower-income
groups finance a greater proportion of the education services they
receive than they do of other social services, while interesting, does not
in itself support any particular policy recommendation. There is no
' right ' proportion, and it is unreasonable to consider any individual
service *in vacuo* when examining tax burdens : what matters is the
effect of the tax and benefit system considered as a whole.

There is something more specific to be said about local authority
finance. Since the rate element in the Equalization Grant was intended
to take care of the equalization of rate burdens for ' poorer ' authorities, there seems little reason for a similar ' resources ' factor in the
education main grant. The only possible justification would seem to
lie in a belief that rateable value is too conservative an index of the
wealth or poverty of local authorities. No such suggestion was made
when the grants were introduced, and even if it were held it appears
to indicate the need for an adjustment of the Equalization Grant
formula rather than for a separate weighting in the education main
grant.

The grant formulæ, while producing over-compensation (in rate-
burdens) as between ' poorer ' authorities receiving the Equalization
Grant and as between all such authorities and ' richer ' authorities,
simultaneously discriminate (through the 60 per cent element) in
favour of ' rich ' authorities who are able and willing to incur high
education expenditures. Thus, while elimination of the rate element
from the education grant formula would be useful, the grants would

---

[12] It is worth noting that in the detailed study by Woodham to which we have
referred, a different view is taken. Woodham recognizes some of the difficulties, but argues that the rateable-value factor in the Grant now takes adequate
care of ' wealth ' or ' poverty ', and that the payments due to children weighting
can therefore be separated and distributed over the services concerned with
children. He allocates 61 per cent of the total ' weighting ' payments to education, and thus attempts to show how the children factor affects education
finance in the case of individual authorities. The calculations are interesting,
but, in our view, misleading for reasons given above.

still be ill-conceived in the context of any specific 'equalizing' function. The reason for this is perhaps to be found in their history. The emphasis on the equalizing function of the main unconditional grant, the Equalization Grant, led to the creation of a grant formula which, while adequate for this limited purpose, could not deal with the other equally important function of central government aid, namely, the subsidization of local authorities as a whole. The education main grant can be considered not unreasonably as operating to meet this deficiency. If this is so, it is permissible to ask whether any separate grant for education is necessary at all, and whether the education main grant could not be replaced by a simple *per capita* or similar payment incorporated in the unconditional Exchequer Equalization Grant. Adequate supervisory and regulatory powers now exist for the central government to be able to ensure the maintenance of minimum educational standards, and the unconditional grant would give scope for imagination and enterprise to individual education authorities. Such a change would also enable the unconditional grant to be devised in such a way as to reflect more precisely the views of Parliament about the combined objectives of equalization and subvention.

The whole question of the need for subsidizing education according to area and income group raises the fundamental issue of the *raison d'être* of a nationalized education service. In the United Kingdom it appears to be taken for granted that the future development of educational facilities lies within the orbit of the state. While the present authors would not question the need for subsidizing the education of individuals, they would point out that this is not in itself an argument for a nationalized service. With adequate safeguards, a community which accepts the need for such education might meet it by providing a direct subsidy to individuals, leaving them free to 'spend' their education resources as they thought fit. Apart from providing more individual freedom in the choice of facilities, this would bring the redistributive aspects of the problem within the direct provenance of the central government.

This suggestion, which is considered in detail by Professor Friedman,[13] raises issues which cannot be considered in a short study. But we mention it here in order to bring home to the reader the fact that the question of equalizing the burden of education provision between individuals is quite a separate one from that of the method of education provision itself.

ALAN T. PEACOCK.
JACK WISEMAN.

---

[13] See M. Friedman, *loc. cit.*

CHAPTER FOUR

Educational Opportunity : United States of America

PART ONE: EFFICIENT ADMINISTRATION AND EXPENDITURE

IN this chapter, the problem of efficient administration and expenditure in education is divided into three parts: (1) *Functions of Creative Leadership*, (2) *Basic Issues of Organization*, and (3) *Special Problems of Financial Administration and Control*.

Creative Leadership in Education

Basic Considerations

The function of creative leadership is by far the most important aspect of efficient administration and expenditure. It is too often neglected. School administrators, who are to be creative leaders, must look not only to current analyses of society but also to the social philosophies and economic thought of both the past and the present, which influence public thinking as to the role of education in society. From these sources come the best guides for school administrators who would be leaders in developing educational programmes, appropriate in scope and content to meet ever-changing social and individual needs. These sources will help to answer such questions as: why public appropriations for education came about slowly and even now are pitifully small in some communities; why have governmental costs greatly increased in recent years?; why the new attitude towards public expenditures?; what is the role of education in a changing society?

Theory of Government—Its Effects on Public Expenditure

Efficient administration and expenditure in education involve social and fiscal concepts of a most profound character. No narrow or limited approach will suffice.

The temptation, rooted in past considerations and supported by conditions in many societies even to-day, is to put the emphasis upon confining public expenditure to the lowest practical minimum and to a meticulous accounting for the meagre allocations made. This attitude has its roots in the history of past governmental performance and economic theory.

When a government is characterized by tyranny and the exploitation of the rank and file by a small ruling class, public expenditure results in little benefit to the general welfare. Taxation becomes merely another means for the oppression of the masses and the maintenance of privilege for the classes.

Tyranny in government, as encountered in the past, as well as the hypotheses of leading economists of the time, explain the extreme conservatism which prevailed at the close of the eighteenth century. For example, Adam Smith's doctrine of *laissez-faire* or non-interference of government with the laws of supply and demand, and Ricardo's ' iron law of wages ' which would give the worker the least possible amount for him to live, placed no responsibility on government or employer for the well-being of the common man. This explains why not only society in general but liberal thinkers were fearful of government.

Adam Smith's *Wealth of Nations* and The Constitution of the United States both bear the date 1776. One readily perceives why the latter was built upon a series of checks and balances between the major functions of government, and why, even then, the states refused to ratify this Constitution until a series of fundamental rights were added in the first ten Amendments. People were fearful of government.

Similarly, one can account for the slow adoption of the Reform Acts of Britain during the nineteenth century.

Not only was there fear of government in which a small exploiting class was in control, but also, on the part of even some socially motivated citizens, there was the fear of the tyranny of the masses which might develop even under democratic regimes. For example, Alexander Hamilton, one of the early statesmen in the United States, held that " when the minds of the unthinking populace are loosened from their attachment to ancient establishments and courses, they . . . are apt more or less to run into anarchy ". Hence Hamilton held that while " the people should have their voice in an Assembly ", they should be governed by a few.

During the past century, fear of government in general and taxation in particular as instruments of tyranny have gradually been reduced as in more and more nations the chief function of government is coming to be the promotion of the general welfare of the governed.

At the same time, conservatism towards governmental activity is also fostered by certain contemporary developments. The modern despotisms which have arisen in recent years, buttressed by the technology of free regimes but lacking their moral principles, once again emphasize the potentiality of government as a vehicle of despotism.

To-day, people for the most part, and particularly those in democratic countries, recognize the power of government to improve their individual and social status. This recognition, along with many other factors, has enormously increased governmental expenditures throughout the world.

In the United States, for example, total public expenditure, at all levels of government, rose from $13 billion in 1932 to $107 billion in 1953:

GOVERNMENTAL EXPENDITURES—FEDERAL, STATE, AND LOCAL—IN THE
UNITED STATES, 1932-53
(In millions of dollars)

Year	Federal	State and Local	Total
1932	4,659	8,406	13,065
1942	34,046	10,034	44,080
1946	60,448	14,067	74,515
1948	33,069	21,260	54,329
1950	39,606	27,905	67,511
1953	73,982	32,937	106,919

The above expenditures represent a large increase, even after correction for population growth and rises in prices are taken into account. In other words, the proportion of the national product ticketed for expenditure under public auspices has substantially increased.

From the foregoing, it is clear that in the United States, although factors rooted in history as well as those which occur in the contemporary scene tend to counsel conservatism in public expenditure, the latter has greatly increased, both in amount and in proportion of income. This is true even after deducting the enormous expenditures for national defence.

New Attitude towards Government and Public Expenditure

Behind the phenomenon of greatly increased governmental activities and expenditures is a series of influences. As democracy has advanced and the people have become the masters rather than the victims of government, they are less fearful of tyranny and exploitation. The removal of a property qualification for voting tends to support public expenditure. For example, failure to-day to provide substantial fire and police protection in great cities is unthinkable.

Factors affecting life resulting from industrialization and urbanization have also been highly influential. The social consequences of depression periods in an industrial, as compared with an agrarian, economy are so severe in their effects on the individual that they cannot be ignored.

The accumulation of scientific knowledge inevitably has results in other spheres of public action; witness, for example, the building of tens of thousands of miles of expensive modern roads following the development of the automobile. Today, no civilized community would tolerate the scourges which ravaged populations in the past when scientific knowledge in fields of sanitation, health protection, and medicine makes them almost wholly preventable. Hence governments at all levels are expending increasingly large amounts for public-health measures. The desire for better standards of performance in many governmental activities also leads to increased expenditures. The humanitarian motive has caused government to develop and finance activities ranging from maternity care to old-age pensions.

The nature of some enterprises, as it concerns both the capital required and the risks involved, makes them feasible only under public auspices. The development of the atomic bomb is the most dramatic, but not the only, example. Fear of war leads to national preparedness on a gigantic scale, regardless of the cost involved.

To summarize, there are some forces rooted in the past and in situations existing to-day which find expression in slogans such as : " The less government, the better ", and " Public expenditure is inherently unproductive and wasteful ". These often have a vigorous and, at times, salutary effect in preventing ill-considered public expenditure. There are even more powerful forces which tend to increase public expenditure. In nations such as those of north-western Europe and the United States, public enterprise and taxation are less feared as sources of tyranny and arbitrary power. The prevailing view is that an abundant life for the common man cannot be achieved without relying somewhat upon government in a number of spheres formerly reserved for private and individual action.

Furthermore, it is widely felt that the number and complexity of the problems of present-day, advanced, interdependent societies call for action of a type which can be performed better through governmental and quasi-governmental action. In short, people are coming to look upon government as a means of promoting the general welfare through positive action.

Education for All or for the Few

How have the above countervailing forces affected theory and practice concerning appropriations for education?

In dealing with this question, one must take a position as to the significance and importance of education in the modern world. There are, to be sure, a wide range of viewpoints, both as between nations and within nations on this issue.

Historically, education frequently has been a privilege of the few, especially when offered to the children and youth of the ruling and wealthy classes, to equip them for leadership, while for the masses it was limited both in scope and in amount. The object was to achieve certain social controls whereby the rank and file, through limited training, would be equipped for lowly roles in society. This conception of education, designed to maintain the *status quo*, has been very slow to disappear in some countries.

The battle to make education less of a class institution as to organization, content, and financial support was a vigorous one. It was fought fiercely both in Britain and in the United States during the nineteenth and has continued into the twentieth century. In both countries, the battle to support education through public taxation, rather than through individual resources, has clearly been won. The principle that some schooling should be provided for all, regardless of social status, is also generally accepted.

The structural organization of education varies widely between different nations. In the United States, for example, it is substantially less class-oriented than in some countries; and secondary education, although far short of achieving perfection, is rapidly becoming universal. More than half of those who enter high school, graduate. In 1955, 2,700,000 students enrolled in post-high school institutions in the United States.

Some argue that if technical and professional education is provided for all who have the capacity and willingness to achieve it, there will be an over-supply of trained workers. This theory assumes that there is a fixed and limited supply of work. The object should be to create an economic organization which is constantly clamouring for workers to perform a multiplicity of worth-while things. The regimes which have unemployed skilled workers are those which have the greatest undeveloped need for such services : take India, for example. On the other hand, in countries such as the United States, which are making abundant use of trained workers, few if any of these are unemployed.

Others fear that if all youths can choose the callings for which they will train, there will be imbalances in the various callings. This situation can be prevented by the collection and dissemination of facts concerning present over- and under-supply of workers in different fields and careful estimates of future needs, and through guidance programmes which will lead youths into expanding fields of service. The maintenance of proper standards of training for admission will also help. Finally, the law of supply and demand, as it affects wages, will tend to correct imbalances, especially if effective procedures for retraining and relocating workers are provided. In any case, the 'right to choose ' should be maintained for all those willing and able to meet the standards set up by society for admission to professional and skilled callings. An artificial maintenance of shortages should not prevail.

There is also the perennial question of whether the wider diffusion of educational opportunity results in lowering the quality of education, and especially the preparation of the gifted and potential leaders.

Some fear that proper education of the gifted is not possible in a pattern of universal education. Experience shows that it is possible. Adequate education of the gifted can be met by various means, such as counselling and guidance, differentiation of curricula, special groupings of the gifted, and maintenance of high standards and full performance, small classes, special assignments, and especially trained teachers who can capitalize on the breadth of interests and special abilities of the gifted, and see that they work up to full capacity.

These special provisions for the gifted in a programme of universal education call for additional expenditures. In the long run, however, these are more than self-liquidating because of the beneficial results to society. The need for trained leadership and skilled manpower is coming to be so clearly recognized in industrialized nations that the education of gifted children and youths is receiving special attention —but, as yet, far less than it deserves.

Issues such as the foregoing concerning the degree to which social and economic status, as opposed to ability and diligence, should determine the amount and content of instruction, and the degree of diffusion of education and its structural organization, constitute the fundamental considerations which determine its efficiency.

These questions will be given different answers in different societies, even in those which have as much in common as Britain and the United States—even more so in regimes as different as those in northwestern Europe, Asia, Latin America, and Africa.

Interrelationships of Education and Economics

Are there any relatively universal policies and principles concerning education which offer guidance as to its role in modern societies, particularly those in which the democratic and technological factors are characteristic?

First, it would seem that an increasing amount of education, both of the type designed to equip for the broader responsibilities of individual and social life and to prepare for technical and professional competence, is essential. The growing scope and complexity of governmental and private activities make increasing demands upon the individual whether performing as a citizen, a member of a family, or as a worker. Science and technology result in an unceasing and increasing demand for technically and professionally trained persons as well as those equipped for leadership in public and private enterprises. Whether one thinks of maintaining and improving the domestic economy or of national security in a dangerous world, this seems to be true.

In fact, the necessity of more and more education, although its content may differ widely, seems to be recognized as essential in both totalitarian regimes and those of the free world, regardless of their state of development.

Second, it would appear that the cost of increased amounts of education of the right kind cannot wisely be looked upon as a mere levy against a nation's economy. Rather, it represents a productive investment which more than pays for itself in a purely economic sense. This hypothesis is supported by data of various types.

It is not necessarily the nations with the most abundant natural resources which achieve the highest standards of living. Technology or the application of science to economic production and the general provision of educational opportunity appear to be the essential factors in a high level of economic productivity.

There is also a direct relationship between individual earned incomes and the amount of schooling completed. In the United States, for example, in 1949 the median income of all males 25 years of age and over who had completed five to seven years of elementary school was $2,035; for those who had completed one to three years of high school, $2,917; four years of high school, $3,285; one to three years of college, $3,522; and for those who had completed four or more years of college, $4,407.

It should be remembered that the factors involved in the preceding paragraphs and their relationships are exceedingly complex. Cause and effect are more difficult to assess in complex social phenomena than in the physical sciences.

For example, it is probable that neither technology nor education are solely causative in their effects on each other, or in their effects in increasing productivity. Rather, the process is one of continuing interaction. When some factor such as leadership results in even a slight increase in the quantity and quality of education, the effect is, other things being equal, increased productivity.

Improved technology makes it feasible to spend more for education. If this expenditure is for the right kind of education, and if it is efficiently administered, the effect is to increase the efficiency of the economy. This hypothesis is supported by a comparison of individual earned incomes, in societies with advanced economies and educational systems, with those in countries undeveloped in these respects. By and large, educated citizens generally act far more efficiently, whether performing as consumers or as producers, than those who are un-educated. For example, the educated citizen is a more intelligent consumer and demands high-quality products. He is more likely to adopt sanitary and healthy measures, both individual and social, which guard his life and energy. The industrial worker, trained for his job and having at his command modern mechanical equipment, is constantly increasing his productivity. The intelligent farmer, using modern equipment and bringing science to bear upon the protection and im-provement of his crops and livestock, is far more productive than the ignorant peasant motivated by superstition and using antiquated equipment.

The question might be raised as to whether there is a point of diminishing returns in infusing education into a dynamic industrial economy. This is an interesting theoretical speculation. The facts would seem to indicate that no society has yet reached this point. In the United States, for example, where a relatively high level of expen-diture for education was maintained in 1900, the past fifty years have been marked by parallel rapid increases in educational expenditure and in *per capita* expenditure. Also, recent researches in the United States give more than a speculative basis for the conclusion that there is a positive relation between quality of education and level of expenditure.

Third, it would appear that the full capitalization of education from an economic, and doubtless from other points of view, requires that it be widely diffused and not be denied anyone who has the capacity and the will to take it.

Acceptance of these concepts does not imply that all should receive the same kind and amount of schooling. Rather it means that a differentiated curriculum offering should be available to take account of varying capacity, interest, and need, and that no artificial barriers of class or financial circumstances should prevent anyone from going as far as his ability and diligence will permit.

Making Education Effectively Free to Able and Willing Students

The achievement of effectively free education requires more than provision of classroom instruction without cost to those in attendance. There are additional costs, such as suitable clothing, incidental fees, and board and room, unless a youth is able to live at home. The family also loses the wages which might be expected after a youth reaches the age of possible employment. As a result, lack of family financial ability and family need may prevent youths from obtaining the education which the interests of society demand.

Recent studies in the United States reveal that half of the top 25 per cent of those who graduate from high school do not go on to college, largely because of lack of family finances. As a result, tens of thousands of youths who should ultimately receive specialized training fail to do so. This is one of the chief reasons for the shortage of technical and professional manpower in the United States. A situation such as this can be corrected by providing scholarships or other financial aid to those who are able and willing to continue their education, but who are prevented by lack of means.

Equalization of School Costs in Communities of Varying Economic Ability

There must be a fiscal mechanism whereby the revenue in any given school jurisdiction is not dependent solely upon its tax capacity. Otherwise, under the wide disparities in taxable wealth per pupil, in local communities, children who happen to live in the poorer communities will obtain sub-standard educational opportunity, unless their communities tax themselves at a relatively high rate, a phenomenon which does not ordinarily happen in such localities. Accordingly, the source of tax revenue should involve a wide geographic area such as the national government or, as in the case of the United States, the governments of the states as well as the nation.

At this point, a policy decision must be made. As the larger jurisdiction is brought into the picture for purposes of financing, will it also take over the control and administration of education? And will the role of the local authority in these respects be either decreased or abolished? It would be most unfortunate if this happened. Experience shows that such centralization of control and administration is by no means necessary. Rather, the superior jurisdiction can : (1) define a minimum of financial support per pupil for all localities which is considered essential for general well-being; (2) require the localities to levy a reasonable and uniform rate of taxation towards financing this minimum; and (3) from the central treasury apportion the difference between the amount so raised and the amount required to finance the minimum. The control exercised by the central authority can be largely limited to requiring the maintenance of the minimum of financial support. The determination of the educational programme, both as to content and as to method, the appointment of teachers and school executives, and other aspects of basic school control and administration, can be left in, or delegated to, the locality. The locality, in addition, can be left free to go beyond the centrally prescribed minima, financial and otherwise, on its own resources. In fact, the central jurisdiction should encourage, but not coerce, it to do so.

Arguments For and Against Centralized Control

What are the inherit merits and demerits of centralized *versus* de-centralized control in the development and the administration of public education?   Most authorities would probably agree that in undeveloped, static societies, in which the people in sub-jurisdictions generally have little appreciation of the value of schooling and meagre resources for its financing, the central government must play the major role in the control and support of education, if it is to be pro-vided in any appreciable amount.

In more advanced nations, the role of the central government can be much less prominent.   In such societies, the issue is not between extreme centralization or decentralization of government.   Rather, it is one of achieving a proper distribution of the various functions in-volved in the maintenance of an efficient system of education among two or more levels of government.

Providing the local jurisdiction is of reasonable size and its people possess substantial appreciation of the importance of good schools, a very high degree of responsibility can be placed in the locality.   This permits experimentation and flexibility in the development of educa-tional programmes and augments local interest in education which is desirable.   Substantial local responsibility in education, assuming reasonable citizen intelligence, gives some protection against the cap-ture of the education of youth by the political party which happens to be in power in the central government.

There are certain functions, however, which a central government can perform most effectively.   It can even out the disparities in the level of support which will inevitably result from wide differences in financial ability of local communities.   It can initiate new areas of educational service.   It can conduct researches and deliberations by citizens of national perspective, which offer a basis for the develop-ment and implementation of educational policy.

Summary

The foregoing are some of the basic considerations to which the school executive who would exert creative leadership must give careful attention.   They add up to efficient administration and expenditure in education and offer guidance in providing sufficient support.   In modern industrial societies, unwise limitation of educational expendi-ture may result in economic waste as well as other social liabilities. Poor education may ultimately cost far more than good education. Efficient administration, therefore, will constantly seek guidance from all possible sources as to the amount and quality of education which will represent just treatment of the individual and fulfilment of the needs of society.

Basic Issues of Organization

The working philosophy of school administrators will be largely shaped by answers to the fundamental issues discussed above. The stand which the general public, statesmen, and leaders in many fields, as well as educators, take on these issues determines the educational programme and whether adequate appropriations for its financial support are provided.

In addition to the above major issues, there are others concerned with organization for the effective financing of education. These issues are important and must not be overlooked. Space permits the discussion of only a limited number. Some are questions of general organization; however, since they have special significance for finance, they will be included here.

Should the Schools be Fiscally Independent?

The degree of separation or independence of school government from other departments of government varies between and within nations. In most parts of the world, education is merely one department of government co-ordinated with other functions in the general hierarchy of organization.

In the United States a considerable degree of separation exists at the state and especially at the local level of government. The local board of education may be directly elected by the people and given full responsibility, limited only by very general state legislation, for the control and financing of education. The board adopts a budget and the tax to support it must be levied. The theory here is that since education is the foundation of all good government, it should receive its mandates directly from the people, and it should be guarded as fully as possible from partisan misuse.

When the schools are fiscally independent of other local government, the question arises as to the limitation of local expenditure for education. Some would maintain that so far as current expenditures are concerned, as opposed to incurring debt, directly elected local school board members should have full power. Others argue for a review of proposed school expenditure, either by a higher level of government or by some general local governmental body.

What should be the Relation of the Public to the School Budget?

To what degree should the public, as opposed to administrative officials, be involved in the development of the school budget?

Most would agree that the amount expended for education should represent the will of the people, usually expressed through some responsible representative committee, board, or legislature. In some instances, however, the tendency is to look upon the actual preparation of the budget, up to the point of review and acceptance or rejection, as an executive function. This is perhaps essential when the budget is that for a nation or for one of the states of the United States. Some participation, however, by the legislative arm of government and by a considerable percentage of local citizens can be of considerable value. This is especially true when major administrative responsibility for the schools and substantial financial support are delegated to the locality.

In the United States, in some relatively small communities, the board of education presents the school budget to the people in a general meeting for approval or rejection. This procedure usually works out well educationally and fiscally. In the United States the trend is towards continuous educational planning as a basis for budgetary requests. This may involve the appointment of citizen advisory committees, wide distribution of information as to present school costs and needed additional expenditures, and the employment of outside consultative experts on various phases of the educational programme. Corresponding procedures have also been employed at the state level. The 1955 White House Conference on Education, preceded by forty-eight state and hundreds of local conferences, represented a similar tendency at the federal level. Such procedures, when well conducted, result in budgets which are based upon careful planning and well-conceived educational objectives. They also result in more intelligent support of education by the public.

As the educational programme expands, the necessity of developing effective means for involving citizens in the determination of programme and policy, or of at least acquainting them with it, increases.

There is, of course, an opposing viewpoint, namely that the general public should be concerned with only the most general issues of educational policy. Everything else should be a matter of professional determination by school executives and teachers. The issue here is doubtless one of degree. On the one hand, the public makes a mistake in attempting to deal directly with matters which only the professionally prepared person can effectively perform. On the other hand, history warns against giving too much control of education to any one group—economic, political, or religious. This should be especially guarded against as the importance of education and its power in the shaping of thought and action in modern cultures increase.

What should be the Relation between Educational and Business Executives in a School System?

The issue of the relation of officers responsible for the educational programme, as opposed to those in charge of the business and financial affairs of a school system, is often crucial. In the United States the prevailing theory is that all administration should be centred in one professionally trained executive, the superintendent of schools, to whom all assistants charged with educational or financial phases of the school programme should report directly.

The danger of dual administrative control is that financial administration will become an end in itself, and the emphasis will be upon keeping down costs and exercising meticulous controls which lack educational justification.

Some hold that a business and financial officer, co-ordinate with the official in charge of the school programme, is necessary to achieve appropriate economy in budgetary requests and the avoidance of waste. It would seem that these objectives do not demand dual control. They can best be achieved through continuous study of the educational programme, and through financial analyses which raise questions concerning economy and efficiency. This study and these analyses are among the major responsibilities of the business executive. He should avoid carping criticism and exaggeration of the importance of minor items which tend to lower morale and result in friction. Maintenance of good morale among employees avoids the worst kind of waste, namely, poor workmanship—in this case poor teaching and school administration. The attitude of the professional personnel as a whole should be to balance the value of objects of proposed expenditure against their cost.

How Organize the Curriculum to Achieve Good Education and Efficient Expenditure?

The tendency constantly to add to the educational programme without eliminating services no longer needed should be kept under control. Retention of obsolete areas of instruction and services, which have little justification except that they have been offered for a long period of time, is as unfortunate as the failure to make additions to, and adaptations in, the school programme demanded by changing conditions. This is one of the first warnings to heed in modernizing curricula. The addition of laboratory science and vocational courses, as well as those in such fields as music and art, usually cost more than many traditional courses because, in addition to a classroom, a teacher, and a book, they call for equipment and materials.

Social analyses and surveys of community and individual needs will reveal whether such courses are demanded in a particular school. If they are, the additional cost should not be a deterrent. Outmoded courses are wasteful, not only of school funds but also of pupils' and teachers' time and energy. Efficient expenditure calls for curricula which meet educational objectives agreed upon after careful study, research, and discussion. Long-term or future, as well as immediate, objectives must be considered if efficient school administration and expenditure are to be achieved.

The danger of over-specialization carried into the lower schools from the university is always substantial. Specialization in the university, particularly at the graduate level, is essential. When this emphasis is carried into the elementary and secondary school programmes, the tendency may be towards an undesirable multiplication of courses, and the maintenance of small enrolments in classes where the chief concern is specialization of subject-matter instead of the well-rounded education of the pupil or student. When the foregoing occur, the result is both unnecessary expenditure and ineffective education.

Special Problems of Financial Administration and Control

In addition to the above fundamental issues, such as the role of education in society and questions of organization, or the relation of education to other departments of government, there are a large number of detailed problems of financial administration and control, namely, problems of the business management of education which must be handled wisely if efficient administration and expenditure are to be achieved. These problems have largely to do with the safeguarding, accounting for, and wise expenditure of school appropriations. In governmental activities the profit motive is eliminated, and efficiency must be sought as a matter of deliberate policy, if optimum use of resources is to be attained. The unfortunate tendency on the part of some administrators, however, is to become so involved in economies and competence of management that they lose sight of their larger educational responsibilities. In all problems of business administration, attention should be centred at all times upon the purposes which the schools are expected to attain.

Principles of financial management and experience in school business administration offer certain definite guides to action. Space permits only brief mention of some of them. The following are relatively routine procedures which are recognized as essential for economy and efficiency.

(1) Arrangements should be made for obtaining and accounting for all income from taxation and other sources which is due for the financing of schools. Means of checking actual receipts against those which

should be expected are required at this point. Such careful accounting for income will prevent losses due to carelessness or dishonesty.

(2) All funds received should be promptly placed in a depository or school account in which the procedures are such as to guarantee against loss. When conditions justify, interest on deposits should be realized.

(3) A carefully organized, functional system of accounting for all expenditures is essential. This should guarantee that services and goods for which expenditures are made are actually received. Analyses of expenditures by functions should be made to offer leads as to possible imbalances, and at the same time wastes in expenditures may be identified and corrected. The danger of accounting for the sake of accounting should be guarded against. The organization of accounting and reports based upon it should be justifiable as performing essential functions. These should also serve as means of necessary budgetary control, that is, means of guaranteeing that expenditures will not exceed appropriations *in toto*, and in major categories, except as official authorization of supplementary appropriations or transfers are made.

(4) Brief, meaningful reports which have a functional relation to the school programme and finance should be regularly prepared for the public, for governing boards, and for the professional staff. These should contain illustrations, diagrams, and other effective means of presenting factual and other material.

(5) An insurance programme should be adopted to guard against loss of property by fire and other causes, and to protect the community and personnel against suits for damages. Officials who handle considerable sums should be bonded.

(6) Provision should be made for a careful audit of all accounts to guard against losses due to mistakes or misuse of funds and to certify that accounting is complete and accurate.

(7) In administering all of the foregoing, the purposes for which schools are maintained should be kept clearly in mind and the first objectives should be to serve those purposes; the importance of maintaining morale should not be overlooked; there should be a desire to anticipate and prevent, through constructive measures, waste and misuse of funds or property. This is preferable by far to the discovery of such after they have occurred.

A fine balance should be sought between the maintenance of good practices, understood by the rank and file of those engaged in the educational enterprise as contributing to economy and efficiency, as opposed to those which are of little financial significance and sometimes merely represent the exercise of petty power through the financial mechanism.

Economy should not be confused with reduced expenditures. True economy in education is the wise and prudent spending of money for the kind of education which will enhance the productive capacity of a nation, ensure wise consumption of goods and services, increase individual, physical, and spiritual well-being, and promote not only national welfare but also international understanding and good will. The cost is heavy, but handsome dividends result from wise and efficient administration of and expenditure for an adequate amount of the right kind of education.

JOHN K. NORTON.

PART TWO: EQUALITY OF OPPORTUNITY, MINORITY GROUPS, STATE SUPPORT, FEDERAL AID

THE first section of this paper deals with seven fiscally related issues that are central to the concept of equality of opportunity as it has evolved over the years in the United States. The second section deals with two additional issues.

Connotations of the Term ' Equality of Opportunity '

The term 'equality of opportunity' as applied to fiscal considerations in the schools of the United States has a variety of connotations.

Availability of Schools

' Equality of opportunity' historically connotes the physical availability of schools to all children. This accounts for the organization of one-teacher schools first throughout the New England states, and later in the newer states. The objective was to have a school within walking distance of every child. Since the American states early substituted residence on farms for village-centred living, meeting this demand represented a large capital investment. In the states where farms were large, as in the South, there was less divergence from the European village pattern of living and therefore less apparent need for this early manifestation of equality of opportunity.

Freedom to Attend School

Equality of opportunity connotes the freeing of children and young people from the demands of home and occupation. When most people were concerned with agriculture this was in part achieved by holding school during the period of low activity on the farm and for short school terms. These adjustments doubtless did a great deal to establish the assumption on the part of parents that their children should be freed for schooling for a part of the year. Relatively late in the evolution of the school system, as technological advances reduced the need for children on farms and in other occupations, these expectations were supplemented by compulsory school attendance laws. The slack in time for children was taken up by increasing the months in the school year and by extending the period of compulsory school attendance. ' Equality of opportunity ' in this sense was enhanced quite as truly by the limiting of work opportunities for children and young people as by the direct desire to extend the scope of education.

Assurance of Normative Opportunities within a State

Equality of opportunity during the past half-century has come more and more to connote that no child shall be denied the kind of educational opportunity which is generally accepted as good by the communities in his state that are neither especially handicapped nor especially favoured economically. This conception seems to have had its origin in the political decision to operate and finance schools by community units, a decision that resulted in marked community differences in ability to support schools. Some communities were extremely wealthy; some extremely poor. The great mass of communities, of course, including most of the large cities, clustered about the state average. Equality of opportunity thus came to mean assuring to the ' poor ' communities (through state financial aid) a programme comparable to that which could be thought of as representing the great central group in the state.

Adequate versus Normative Guarantees

In recent years this connotation has been experiencing a significant change. As dealt with above, attention was on the privilege of children, not on the adequacy of the programme. Now more and more the idea comes to the fore of establishing as a minimum for all a programme of education adequate for our times. This takes the form of considering the possibility of building, towards expenditure for all, not less than some minimum which may be higher than any community in the state now attains. As an example, the Rhode Island 1955 Finance Act sets a minimum level of support higher than that yet achieved by any community of the state, save one. Clearly, such consideration diligently pursued would achieve the justice the old equalization laws sought to achieve, as an incident to achieving vastly more.

This idea is not entirely new. Similar steps were taken more than a quarter of a century ago in Delaware and North Carolina, but they were one-shot affairs designed more to correct a great state lag behind the nation than to achieve an educational level that could be defended in terms of present-day needs.

Complementary Values

The American states are no exception to the rule that no society is controlled by a single value. Accordingly, carrying even so deep-rooted a value as equality of opportunity to its logical conclusion—

sameness of opportunity—brings it into conflict with other values. A value cherished in the American way of doing things is the right of the community to make educational decisions. The legal system encourages this. Accordingly, differences in school offerings among communities are the result of differences in interest and vigour quite as much as differences in ability. In the central mass of communities, vigour differences have a much greater influence than ability differences. A community of average wealth by exercising greater tax vigour will find itself supporting schools as well as an able community that exercises less than average vigour. Accordingly, the tests of equality customarily applied can be misleading. They usually take the form of comparisons on such items as expenditure per pupil. Quite clearly, except for the communities where there is a definite economic shortage, the variations noted will be due more to differences in community concern than to economic differences. Viewing such distributions, the high expenditures on the scale must be thought of as favourable, representing, as they do, communities that have exercised initiative with adequate economic ability. They do not represent inequality in the sense used here. Low expenditures as compared with the central mass of the state are the test of inequality. But it cannot be assumed that they are due solely to economic lack and are therefore correctable by state aid (or by building up the economies of the communities) solely. Where the difficulty is lack of vigour the correction is central leadership, or more often, the cheaper and not always effective device of state mandates for minimum effort.

National Equality of Opportunity

The conception of assuring an adequate, rather than a normative, programme to all has appeared in incipient form in considerations of federal aid to education. The great lacks revealed by World War I jolted many people from the comfortable ' state ' frame of reference. As yet nothing has occurred in federal legislation that can be classed as an over-all response. Steps have been taken to correct lacks in limited areas; viz. teaching of agriculture and mechanical arts. The Federal Government has contented itself with these nudgings. Constantly proposals have been before the Congress that attacked the problem of equalizing the burden of support up to what might be considered national normative practice. But the voices calling for the national assurance of an adequate minimum have been few. Perhaps the recent dissatisfactions in states with the idea of equalizing the normative will eventually bear fruit. A goodly number of people, the writer included, believe that such fruit is essential to our national well-being. It may

even be that the adequacy approach may have in it the national appeal
that the more limited normative approach has lacked.

Identifying Equalization Aid

Most 'equalization laws' carry more aid for non-equalization purposes than for equalization purposes. A word on these other purposes
may help to clarify the equality concept. Whatever their avowed
purpose, the root causes underlying state-aid proposals are in two fiscal
maladjustments.

At the roots of equalization aid is the difference in economic ability
among school districts within a state. The negative effects are found
in the communities of low economic ability. They can be corrected
by aid to the poorer districts. In practice in American states this is
achieved by assuring all communities a normative foundation programme, either by complete state support for such a programme (as in
Delaware and North Carolina) or by some plan of state and local
sharing of the cost. The task can be satisfactorily done by requiring
all districts to contribute towards the 'foundation programme' at the
rate which the ablest large district would require completely to support it. State aid beyond this is not necessary to equalization. Of the
state funds required, the people in the ablest districts get nothing; the
poorest perhaps as much as 80 per cent of the cost of the foundation
programme. Districts above average wealth get back less than they
pay into the state; districts of less than average wealth get back more
than they pay in—the poor ones much more.

Accordingly, any aid the ablest district gets is for purposes other than
equalization. Most 'equalization laws' pay money to the rich as well
as to the poor. Such additional aid is paid in proportion to wealth. No
matter how much additional aid is paid, the poorest district will get
very little additional. Even if the state pays the whole cost of the
foundation programme, the poorest district will receive only the
difference between, say, the 80 per cent required for equalization and
100 per cent. The additional aid in all districts, rich and poor, is
money collected from the districts and sent back to them in approximately the same amounts as collected.

The fiscal justification of this is in the need for broadening the local
tax base, a need arising from the fact that a practical tax base for
school districts is too limited in scope. An analysis of so-called equalization laws shows that typically the aid they carry for broadening the
tax base of all communities is in excess of the actual equalization aid.

Associated Issues

This section treats two issues in which fiscal considerations are not
central.

Applications within Districts

As attention has come to be centred more and more on individual differences in mental ability, talent, and home background, the concept of equality of opportunity has taken on specialized meanings for school districts where the same tax base is available for all. Here it has taken the form of making special provisions for the handicapped, often requiring expenditures far in excess of those made on normal children. In the large cities, which partake more of the nature of centralized-state systems than of the as-yet-typical American community school district, the attention of central offices tends to be centred more on the under-privileged areas. The equalization of opportunity in this sense comes fully into its own in our large cities. It has been said that our large cities give not only equal opportunity (to the handicapped, the socially under-privileged), but 'equaller' opportunity. The lack is in giving too little regard to other values— by no means in giving too high regard to the equality value.

Another facet of this connotation is in giving direct financial aid to economically under-privileged children. This is a practice of long standing in all types of school districts. It takes the form of aid for clothing, lunches, eye-glasses, and medical care provided for children whose families are handicapped financially.

Minority Groups

It is only in the sameness test that the treatment of minority groups in the American school system can be thought of as differentially bad. In terms of adequacy for our times, the education of all groups falls behind. Within the framework of states the problem has become less and less one of a differentiation in financial support. In certain whole states operating separate schools for Negroes the expenditure level for Negroes is higher than that for whites. So it is now more centrally a social problem than an educational problem. In most of the states there is no legal separation of schools. What segregation there is results from population clustering. The legal separation in the states that practise separation as policy is in turn deeply rooted in social outlook. It remains to be seen whether the action of the United States Supreme Court in outlawing such separation will hasten the solution of the deeply ramifying social issues. Here we have a manifestation exactly the opposite of that of large populations which on their own choose to operate private schools and thus segregate their children from those of their neighbours. Here the principle of equality would not seem to be assuring the same to all, but rather assuring to all *the choice* of segregation or non-segregation. The issue seems to transcend the educational considerations. PAUL R. MORT.

PART THREE: THE SITUATION IN THE RURAL UNITED STATES

THE problems of rural education in the United States are many and some of them are serious. The varied nature of the problems is caused by historical, economic, sociological, and administrative factors. There is no national system of education in the United States. Education is a function reserved to the states and territories. Despite many similarities among the states there are in actuality 48 state and three territorial systems of education, with variations in the degree and methods by which state aid to schools is channelled to local districts, in the qualifications demanded of teachers, in the degree of freedom given local districts in curriculum determination, and in other ways. Each local district has its own governing board.

Some of the differences among the states stem from sharp differences in their economic resources. In 1929 the average *per capita* income of the highest state was 3·9 times that of the lowest. In the 1930's this spread increased to 5·1 times, but in the last decade has fluctuated between 2·6 and 2·9 times. The low states are largely rural and southern.

The pattern of rural education in the United States was set by the historical factors existing in a new, sparsely settled continent. The modal school for many decades was a one-room structure in which one teacher taught all subjects offered to all elementary grades. At the turn of the century there were over two hundred thousand such schools. With the coming of the automobile and the hard-surfaced road, making school consolidation possible, the number of such schools has rapidly declined, to 75,000 in 1950 and probably slightly less than 50,000 as of 1955. The decline, however, has been at uneven rates among the states. The reason for this in areas of low population density is obvious. However, in a few other rural states the cultural attitudes of the people have strongly opposed removing the primary school from the immediate neighbourhood of the few children eligible to attend it. Occasionally absurd situations arose. In one wheat-belt state one year, due to migration and consolidation of farms, almost a hundred one-teacher schools opened with no pupils on the roll. Now, however, procedures for effective school consolidation are available in practically all states. Consolidation involves transportation of pupils, and in the United States as a whole nine million children are transported daily to and from school in 130,000 buses at an annual cost of $300 million.[1]

The situation described resulted, of course, in disparities in educational opportunity, not only among states but between rural and urban schools within states. The best single measure of the latter is the census report on the median number of years of schooling completed by persons of several age-groups. These data for 1940 and 1950 are given in the table below. This table shows that the spread between farm and urban has increased. For those born in 1875 or before it was

MEDIAN YEARS OF SCHOOL COMPLETED BY PERSONS IN SELECTED AGE-GROUPS FOR THE UNITED STATES FOR URBAN, RURAL NON-FARM, AND RURAL FARM, 1940 AND 1950

Age-group (years)	Urban		Rural Non-farm		Rural Farm	
	1940	1950	1940	1950	1940	1950
20 to 24 . . .	12·0	12·1	10·7	11·2	8·8	9·9
35 to 39 . . .	9·0	11·2	8·8	9·2	8·2	8·7
75 and over . .	8·2	8·4	8·0	7·8	6·5	7·0
Total 25 and over .	8·8	10·2	8·6	8·8	8·1	8·6

1·4 years, as measured in 1950, but 2·5 years for the 35- to 39-year-olds. This had dropped to 2·2 years for the youngest group of adults, a rough measure of the fact that rural education in the United States has begun to improve and to increase its holding power. The rural non-farm population, i.e. those in villages of less than 2,500 population, is closer to the urban and has also improved its relative position.

This measure is inevitably crude. It takes no account of differences in length of term between rural and urban, once about a month, now very slight; nor of differences in the training of teachers, where the city still has a considerable lead.

Real Estate and State Support

These differences relate to the variations in wealth and in state-aid policy already alluded to. The traditional, and in most states still the chief, source of school revenue is the tax upon real estate and other forms of real property located within the district the school serves. This clearly introduces the possibilities of inequality. Even within some of the more prosperous rural states it has been found that there was twice as much taxable wealth behind each child in that fourth of

---

[1] £1 = approximately $2.80.

the school districts which led the state as in the bottom fourth. This resulted either in a lighter burden on the taxpayer in the wealthier districts as compared to the poorer, or in inequality in educational opportunity.

Facts like these stimulated all over the Union a demand that state aid to local school districts should equalize the burden of educating the children and youth of the state. A great deal of attention has been given to this problem and several different formulae have been developed, as would be expected in an area as diversified as the United States, in which there is no federal control of education. In the main the different schemes fall into three categories:

(1) An allotment from the state to the local school districts involving a specified sum per teacher, per operating classroom, or per pupil, or one based on average daily attendance.

(2) A formula that, beyond some minimum payment on some such basis as has just been described, gives additional funds in proportion to the economic needs of the several districts. This is the usual formula where the objective is to equalize educational opportunity throughout the state.

(3) A few states have taken over the major share of the burden of education within their boundaries. In these cases the state pays for a reasonable minimum programme in all school districts, but in one or two cases wealthy districts, either rural or urban, are granted permission to levy a small additional local tax to enrich their programme if the voters approve.

The trend over the last thirty years has been for increasing state support of education. In 1925 only 15 per cent of public school revenues came from state sources. In 1936 the proportion was 29.4 per cent; in 1947–8 it was 39 per cent. In 1950–51 it was estimated that between 43 and 44 per cent of school costs would be met by the states. To-day the figure is probably very close to 50 per cent. While this is helpful to harassed local school boards, the fact remains that in 1937–8 state and local revenues for schools represented 3.24 per cent of total income of the states, while in 1949–50 it was only 2.39 per cent. This decline of less than one percentage point represents a drop of 26 per cent in the proportion of income allocated to schools.[2]

The effect of this trend can be illustrated from two sample states, one in the south, largely rural, the other New York, which with California leads in per-pupil expenditure. In the southern state, schools with

---

[2] Professor Francis Cornell, address before the annual meeting of the Association of School Business Officials, September 26th, 1950. For details see United States Office of Education Circular 274, *Public School Finance Program of the Forty-Five States* (Washington, D.C., 1950).

per-pupil costs of $35 or less in 1939–40 spent slightly more than twice
this sum in 1946–7. Those which had exceeded $55 per pupil in 1939–
40 had increased their per-pupil expenditures only 37 per cent by the
later year. In New York, on the other hand, where the median cost in
1939–40 was $150 per pupil, the gain by 1946–7 for school districts
above the median was barely 50 per cent. However, those districts
that had spent less than $100 gained up to 84 per cent by the later
period. Both these cases illustrate in part the effect of equalization.

Federal Aid

Federal aid to general education in the United States is practically
non-existent save for certain special situations where military or war
industrial developments have greatly inflated school enrolments. This
is largely confined to help in providing necessary new buildings and
facilities. There is, however, federal aid for vocational education in
agriculture, home economics, trades and industry, and the distributive
occupations, on a matching basis. This legislation has been in force
since 1914.

There has been continued agitation in the United States for federal
aid to general education for over thirty-five years. The arguments
advanced fall into three categories. There is first of all the patent
disparity in wealth among the states. The southern and more rural
states spend a far higher proportion of their total tax income on education than do the more urbanized, industrial states, but even so are
unable to offer equality of opportunity. In the southern states this
inability is partly because these states operate two school systems, one
for white children, the other for Negroes. This is in process of changing because of the desegregation decision of the Supreme Court in May
1954. It should be added that most southern states for some years
there has been only one salary scale, and that since Negroes tend to
teach longer than whites, and hence more take graduate work, there
are some states in which Negro teachers are better paid on average
than their white colleagues.

In the second place the more rural states have more children in proportion to population than have the others. In the 1930's the number
of children of school age per one thousand of the population in the
most biologically fertile states was approximately twice what it was
in New York and California. Thus each adult had a numerically
heavier burden to carry in furnishing education in the states with high
birth-rates than in those with low. Finally it is pointed out that, since
about half the rural children migrated to the cities when they joined
the labour force, the rural area was bearing the cost of rearing and
educating a considerable fraction of the cities' labour supply. It was

estimated that in an average year the costs so incurred equalled from 12 to 16 per cent of the net farm income.

The opposition to federal aid to education has stressed the constitutional argument that education is a state function and hence federal grants might not be legal. Religious issues have also been injected into the discussion. Roman Catholics, who comprise over 16 per cent of the population of the United States, have argued that if federal aid to education is ever granted it should benefit all the children, including those in parochial schools. Since the separation of church and state is not only embedded in the American Constitution but is also one of the most strongly held of American cultural values, there are many who would forgo federal aid to the schools, necessary as they believe it to be, rather than see any such aid go to church schools. Finally, there are some who fear that federal aid to education would result in federal control.

These issues have been considered by a number of national commissions in the last thirty-five years, some official under appointment by the President of the United States, and more, citizen bodies. Without exception they have urged that the Federal Government extend aid to schools through the various state departments of education. Such legislation has twice passed one House of Congress but never both.

The fear of federal control grows partly out of the unfortunate fact that the federal Office of Education does exert a considerable degree of control over the vocational education curriculum. This is not an inevitable pattern. Through the United States Department of Agriculture, federal aid is given to rural adult education organized as the extension service. Control is lodged wholly in the several state colleges of agriculture even though federal funds make up 40 per cent of the nearly $90 million cost.

Problems of Administration

The issue of the control of education raises questions as to the relationships among the various authorities. As one would expect from the varied administrative patterns already noted, this matter cannot be discussed in all its ramifications within the limits of this article.

Except in vocational education and some special situations the federal Office of Education has few important administrative duties. Its function is largely to serve as a clearing-house of information, as a compiler of educational data on a national basis from reports required from the states, and as a research agency. Its national leadership is and must be exerted by indirection and suggestion except in certain action programmes where special conditions prevail.

In the states, relations with the local districts vary from a high degree of control where there are state systems, to very little. In some cases a state curriculum has been adopted and only approved textbooks may be used. In some states the administrative unit is the county, but the county superintendent of schools may be either an appointed ' civil servant ' responsible to, and sometimes an employee of, the state Board of Education, or elected by the people. Among the functions of the state Board of Education where there is no state system the following are frequently found : disbursement of state aid to local districts, approval of building plans so as to safeguard health and prevent fires, formulation of qualifications for various grades of teachers' certificates, auditing of state appropriations, research, and assisting local systems when requested with respect to specific problems through specialists.

It is quite apparent, therefore, that a great deal of autonomy characterizes American education. The effective local unit may be the school district, the county, or an intermediate unit which, like some counties, assists the component local districts with special services. The state educational agency enforces such state laws as there are which apply to all schools, but in the average situation it is more of a service and record-keeping agency than anything else. This situation grew out of cultural conditions existing when the United States was largely an agricultural nation. It would still undoubtedly be approved by a majority of the citizens if put to a vote. Except in times of emergency the American believes in holding the power of the state and federal governments in check, especially in those matters which touch his life intimately, as does the education of his children. The practical operation of this attitude does, however, result in handicaps for the rural school. Some children whom it trains become farmers and farmers' wives, others enter the service occupations in the village or town centre of the rural communities, still others need curricula that will prepare them to enter the agricultural college or university. Finally a considerable group will enter the labour force of the city. The relatively small rural high school must therefore attempt to meet the demands of four groups. Half their pupils will sooner or later leave their home communities.

Migration from the Rural Areas

The inevitability of this migration is quite clear from many data. One illustration only can be given. As a result of extensive studies of manpower made during World War II it was found that in the more rural states there were from 150 to 200 young farm males potentially available to take over every hundred farms vacated by the retirement or death of their operators. In the industrial states, especially in New England, this ratio ranged from 110 to 100 per hundred vacated farms. This calculation took no account of enlarging farm size in the United States due to rapid mechanization. Average farm size in the United States has gone from 148 acres in 1920 to 210·5 in 1950. The census of agriculture under way as this is written will probably show it has reached about 225 acres. Thus in thirty-five years average farm size has gained 52 per cent, but total land in farms only about 10 per cent. Herein is the explanation for the decline in American farm population from over 30 million in 1940 to about 21 million in 1955. About 15 million persons left the farms for towns and cities during the 1940's, but because about 9 million moved in the opposite direction the net loss was 6 million. There was also an excess of births over deaths among the farm population. These trends have continued in the 1950's but at a less rapid tempo. Village population has thus far continued to increase, but none the less one in five moved during the year 1949, 40 per cent of them across county or state lines. These migrants had certain definite characteristics. Young women migrated a year or two younger than young men and were more likely to go to the city. The 20- to 24-year-olds are the most migratory age-group, with the 25- to 29-year-olds a close second. Each successive age-group contributes fewer migrants than the one just below it.

The detailed migration data from the 1950 United States Census have not yet been published, but since over-all trends are of a similar order to those in the five years before the 1940 census, attention will be given to these in terms of the group who were 20 to 29 years of age in 1935. In twenty of the twenty-four most rural states this age-group made up a highly disproportionate number of the out-migrants in relation to their share of the total population. They also accounted for a disproportionate share of the loss of these states through migration. When the states were ranked according to their gain and loss in population through out-migration of native-born inhabitants of this age-group, and also according to their support of education per classroom unit, a positive correlation of 0·51 resulted. This indicates a tendency for people to move from areas in which the level of educational support is below the national average to those in which it is above average.

It would appear that the more progressive states, educationally speaking, and especially the cities within them, can ill afford to be unconcerned about the level of education elsewhere. Migration could easily nullify some of the effects of a superior educational programme. There is also the problem of the adjustment of these rural people to urban living conditions, which is not always easily made and which sometimes results in regrettable social consequences.

It is often assumed that it is the better educated who migrate from the rural areas. This is likely to be true only in terms of the most disadvantaged counties, especially in the south. The departments of rural sociology in American agricultural colleges have made scores of detailed studies of the migration of rural youth. While, as indicated, there are a few exceptions, in nation-wide terms the tendency is for a slightly higher proportion than normal of the most able and the least able to go city-ward, and a somewhat smaller proportion of the middle group. Agriculture has become such a scientific occupation that able youth have real opportunity in becoming farmers in the good-soil areas of the nation.

With the diverse destinations of rural youth noted earlier, the problem both of the small school in terms of its curriculum and of the training of teachers for open country and village schools is pressing. Fortunately teacher education in the south and the less prosperous areas has been improved considerably, bringing the standard there more in line with the rest of the country. This, with the consolidation of rural schools, makes the provision in them of competent, trained teachers and adequate specialist equipment and physical plant more and more possible.

In summary, it may be said that rural education in the United States can look forward to gradual improvement. The traditions which have made tax upon real estate located within the school district the chief source of revenue have operated against the firmly held aim of providing equality of opportunity for all American children, to the disadvantage of those in rural areas. The trend towards broadening the economic basis of educational support through state funds has helped to remove some of the anomalies. The constant agitation for federal aid has reflected the desire of many people to raise the level of educational provision in less prosperous rural areas to that enjoyed in urban and wealthy rural communities.

Gradual improvement can, however, also be foreseen through the economic development of those parts of the country whose *per capita* income at the moment falls much below that of the areas with high and developed economic resources. A narrowing of this gap, a process now taking place, will make it increasingly possible to achieve 'equality of opportunity' whilst at the same time retaining a large measure of local economic support and control so traditionally American.

EDMUND DES. BRUNNER.

PART FOUR: THE NEGRO AND DESEGREGATION

WHEN the Negro was introduced into the American culture as a slave, a chattel to be bought and sold at the will of his owner, the foundations of a truncated society were laid. The Civil War brought an end to slavery as an institution, but the impact of the master-slave pattern of relationships—by then a firm part of the culture of the region—has persisted in varying degrees to this day. The abrupt shift of the Negro during the Reconstruction era from a slave to a temporary position of political power created animosities which have made more difficult the achievement of the status legally defined for the Negro by the 13th, 14th, and 15th Amendments to the Constitution of the United States.

It was inevitable in a society which generally believed the Negro race to be inherently inferior to the white race that separate schools would be created for each race. Indeed, during the era of slavery it was generally considered unnecessary to educate the Negro, except for the performance of his occupational duties. This was a responsibility of his owner. After the Negro was freed, controversies arose over whether or not he should be given the benefits of public schooling. Early educational opportunities for Negroes were due largely to efforts of church and philanthropic groups. As public education systems were developed following the Civil War, public schools gradually were established for Negroes. In each of the Southern states two distinct school systems grew up with the races sharply segregated by legal mandate. Separate school districts, however, were the exception. As a result, both school systems usually were under the same board of education and same administrative staff.

As was to be expected, quality differentials developed in the dual school systems which corresponded to the status of the two races in the Southern culture. It was not until 1896 that the question of segregation of the races in the public schools reached the United States Supreme Court. In the famous Plessy *versus* Ferguson case, which was concerned not with education but with the separation of the races in public conveyances, segregation in the public schools was simply referred to in the decision as a common practice. Thus, in a side comment, the doctrine of separate schools was given judicial sanction by the highest court in the land. It should be pointed out, however, that precedents established by various court decisions made it clear that separate schools were not to be different in quality.

While the separate half of the doctrine was rigorously observed throughout the South, the equal half was of less concern, with the result that within the same districts Negro schools were generally inferior to white schools. This meant that Negro schools in rural areas and in urban areas were usually not as good as white schools in the same areas. On the other hand, Negro schools in urban areas were often better than white schools in many rural areas. This is possible because of the fact that schools in urban areas are frequently better than rural schools.

A long series of court decisions beginning in the 1930's gradually broke down the legal walls of segregation in education. The culminating decree came in the famous May 1954 decision of the United States Supreme Court, which declared that separation of the races in the public schools on the basis of race alone is unconstitutional.

Social and Economic Change

The decision comes at a time when important changes in the Southern region are taking place at a rapid pace. The educational level of the population is rising at a fast *tempo*, the average age is moving upward, and the percentage of people above 65 is increasing rapidly. Many rural areas are sharply declining in density of population, while metropolitan areas are increasing in both number and population. Negroes are leaving rural areas and either concentrating in cities in the region or leaving the South for other regions. The percentage of Negro population in the region has declined steadily since 1900. Approximately one and a half million Negroes moved out of the Southern region during the decade of the 1940's.

The economy of the Southern region is also changing rapidly. Income levels are steadily approaching the national average. The region is becoming more industrialized, and the pattern of industry is becoming diversified. The character of agricultural pursuits is changing rapidly. Mechanization of farming and increases in the production of livestock are producing a new agricultural economy. Both industry and farming are requiring more skilled workers.

The value patterns of the region are undergoing change. The influences of two world wars, the mobility of population, and modern media of mass communication are giving the region a new cultural orientation. There is a trend towards more liberal political and economic thought. Religious views and practices are being adapted to modern conditions. New political alignments are developing, with the Negro rapidly becoming an important political influence. Labour unions are growing in power in the region. The status of the Negro has improved measurably during this era of unprecedented change.

Employment opportunities are better in scope and quality. Civil rights are exercised more frequently, and educational opportunities have been markedly improved.

It was into this scene of rapid social and economic change that the Supreme Court projected the decision which declared segregation in the public schools as public policy unconstitutional. Obviously the Court decree is but one of a number of forces which are bringing about a realignment in the position of the Negro. The uniqueness of the decision lies in the fact that it strikes at the heart of a long-established and legally sanctioned expression of the pattern of race relationships in the Southern region which involves the great social institution of public education, where the rigid walls of segregation had not been breached previously except on levels of higher education. A new legal principle was promulgated as a basis for this decision. This principle is that legal segregation on the basis of race alone is, within itself, discriminatory.

' Separate but Equal '

Before attempting to assess the economic impact of this decision, it is necessary to consider briefly the status of the bi-racial school systems at the time the Court decision was issued. This status is revealed by an examination of data related to public school enrolment and attendance, school expenditures, school buildings and facilities, instructional personnel, and some measures of the instructional programme for the two races.

Judged solely in terms of enrolment and attendance statistics, the problem of providing equal educational opportunities for the two races was virtually solved by 1952 and posed no economic burden. In 1950 the number of Negro children enrolled in the public schools of the Southern states was 92·4 per cent of the number of Negro children 6 to 17 years of age, as compared to 92·8 per cent of white children. Moreover, by 1952 the percentage of attendance of Negro children enrolled in school almost equalled the percentage of attendance for white children.

In the area of current expenditures, the picture was quite different. The average expenditure for instruction for white children in thirteen Southern states was $132.38 per child in average daily attendance. The expenditure for instruction for each Negro child in average daily attendance during the same year was $90.20. In 1940 these figures for the two races were $41.99 and $16.29 respectively. While the percentage gap between the expenditures for the two races had diminished, the dollar gap had actually increased.

Costs of instruction were nearer the same per pupil for both races than were expenditures for any other item in the budget. This is due for the most part to the adoption of single-salary schedules for teachers.

Differences in buildings and equipment for the two races were more distinctive than were differences in instructional costs. By 1952 the Southern region was moving towards equalization of facilities for the races, although a very substantial dollar gap remained. In 1952 the value per pupil in average daily attendance of school buildings and equipment was $454 for white pupils and $190 for Negro pupils. Twelve years before, the figures were $200 and $50 respectively (127 per cent for white pupils and 280 per cent for Negro pupils).

In 1940 the Negro teacher in thirteen Southern states had on the average 5·2 more pupils in average daily attendance than did the white teacher. By 1952 this number had decreased to 2·7 pupils. By 1952 Negro teachers in five Southern states had achieved a higher level of professional training, as measured by the number of years of college work completed, than had white teachers in those states. On a regional level the average number of years' training for Negroes was slightly less than the average for white teachers, being 3·8 years for white teachers and 3·5 years for Negroes. In 1940 the averages were 3·4 for white teachers and 2·4 for Negro teachers.

Some selected services which may be considered as indicative of the quality of educational programmes show that as a rule in 1952 these services were being provided in greater quantities and at greater cost for white pupils than for Negro pupils. For example, library books were more prevalent in white schools, although the percentage of increase in the number of volumes per pupil enrolled was greater for Negro pupils than for white pupils between 1940 and 1952. In 1940 there were 2·9 books per white pupil enrolled and 0·7 books per Negro pupil enrolled. Twelve years later there were 4·3 books per white pupil and 2 books per Negro pupil.

Although some indication of the financial aspects of integration in the public schools may be deduced from the statistics just given, literal interpretations would be highly misleading. If it is assumed that costs of educating Negroes are to be brought up to the level of white expenditures, costs of equalization in dollars and cents can be easily computed. The difference in cost of instruction per pupil in 1952 on a regional level was $32.18. Multiplying this sum by the number of Negro pupils in average daily attendance (1,902,001) yields the figure $61,206,392. Equalization of expenditures for instruction would of course require the expenditure of this additional sum annually.

The same kind of computation may be made for school buildings and equipment. The differential in favour of white students in 1952 was $264 per pupil in average daily attendance. Multiplying by the number of Negro pupils yields the sum of $502,128,264. Obviously this is not an expenditure which would have to be repeated annually.

Costs of instruction and capital equipment would account for the major outlay required to equalize white and Negro schools on a financial basis. Bringing expenditures in other items of the school budget up to present levels for white children would not require extensive increases in the total budget.

Desegregation

Obviously the ruling of the Supreme Court on segregation renders this computation of limited value. Since the ' separate but equal ' doctrine has been voided, the problem of equalization has been made much more complex. Even if the assumption is made that the dual school systems of the South are to be totally integrated, which the Court decision does not require, the resultant educational programme might or might not be as good as the previous programme for white pupils. In other words, equalization may raise the quality of the poorer schools or lower the quality of the better schools.

Making the assumptions that the cost of education for Negro pupils will be brought up to levels of cost for white students raises the problem of how to take into proper account such factors as housing patterns of the Negro population, density, and size of attendance centres. Obviously in areas (such as are found in many urban centres where, due to housing patterns, separate white and Negro communities exist) which make possible the establishment and maintenance of separate schools for each race without discrimination, integration would scarcely affect total school costs. On the other hand, in many areas, primarily rural, where Negroes are dispersed throughout a locality and where the dual system has resulted in numerous small schools with dual transportation systems, substantial financial savings might be effected by combining the schools. More effective use of existing facilities might also be possible in areas where population shifts have left some buildings overcrowded and others with unused space. The cost of administration and supervision would scarcely vary since both white and Negro schools are under the same administration.

Implementation of the Court's Decree

But the integration of the races in the public schools will scarcely be determined on the basis of economic factors. The implementation decrees of the Supreme Court, which place responsibility for initial steps in complying with the segregation ruling on the local school district and which recognize that variations in local conditions should be taken into account in implementing the decision, have generally been interpreted as taking the pressure off school officials to take immediate steps to comply with the Court rulings. Consistent with American principles of political democracy and home rule, the decree of the Court is to be implemented in terms of local conditions as determined, initially at least, by local authorities. The Court places upon each district the compulsion ultimately to integrate schools if necessary in order to avoid racial discrimination. For the present, the timing of such action is clearly a matter of local choice.

Subsequent Court action may be invoked to test the good faith of districts which appear dilatory in carrying out the Court's decrees. It is clear by now that in border states the integration issue will be resolved rather speedily and with little social upheaval. In the area commonly known as the Deep South the problem is much more serious, and a greater period of time will undoubtedly be required for carrying out the Court decrees. Among the important factors which will influence the rate at which integration can take place is the percentage of Negro population in the school district, the social and economic distance between the races, and prevalent patterns of racial relationships.

With limitations on employment possibilities of Negroes being gradually reduced and with changes in industrial and agricultural patterns calling for more and more technical skill in workers, the Negro requires education if he is not to be an economic liability. Enlightened leaders of both races have long regarded education as being the greatest need of the Negro if he is to make his maximum contribution to the economy of the region and to its citizenship. Herein lies the greatest long-term economic consequence of desegregation.

The increasing productivity of the region and better educational opportunities have already produced a higher income for Negroes. This permits better standards of living and results in improved health conditions, fewer welfare problems, and fewer delinquents. The Supreme Court's decision on integration hastens the making of decisions on a problem which has concerned thoughtful Southerners for years. The Court has simply enunciated a new rule to be followed in correcting the discrepancy in educational opportunities between the two races. In the long run any additional financial cost which may result from this decision will be far outweighed by the greater economic and civic productivity that better educational opportunities will undoubtedly enable Negroes to achieve.

TRUMAN M. PIERCE.

Fiscal Management in an English Local Education Authority

THE traditional opposition between education and finance has often led educationists to underestimate the value of sound financial principles in administration. It is not always easy for finance and education to understand each other's point of view. Those whose main preoccupation is financial matters sometimes find it difficult to understand that anything can be of value unless it can be measured in material or financial terms. Some finance officers regard it as their duty to do all that they can to prevent money being spent, which is a far from proper interpretation of their role in public service. In recent times some local government finance departments have been accused of seeking to secure for themselves in local government the position which the Treasury holds in relation to the Civil Service. It is generally agreed, however, that the duty of the local government finance department is, first, to protect the authority's funds and property; second, to ensure that the money available is economically and not wastefully expended; third, to prevent fraud and corruption (in public services, probity is perhaps more important than efficiency); fourth, to secure that expenditure is properly forecast and controlled; and fifth, to give information and advice in order to increase the efficiency of administration. These five functions are emphasized in different degrees in the three main branches of financial work: budgetary control, audit, and management accounting.

There are also reasons why finance for its part should tend to look askance at education. Since the Butler Education Act, monetary inflation combined with the expansion of the service has steadily raised the cost of education. It is widely believed that since more money is now spent the standard of education ought to have risen correspondingly. Whether or not the standard of education has risen is a matter which cannot be discussed here. It can, however, be shown that when present costs are compared with pre-war costs, with prices adjusted to allow for the fall in the value of money, the increased expenditure covers little more than the increase in the school population, together with the growth of particular services, such as aid to university students, technical education, and school meals. At the same time, a high proportion of costs is intractable : more than 70 per cent is made up of salaries and wages based on nationally or regionally determined scales. In the remaining expenditure are many fixed charges and there is, of course, an irreducible minimum for such things as the maintenance of buildings or for books, stationery, and apparatus. Again, although a great deal of school building has been carried out, by far the greater part of this has been simply to keep pace with the rising number of school children. A very substantial part of the school population is still taught in buildings which are not only obsolete but positively dilapidated.[1] In short, the main part of the education service, primary and secondary schools, has enjoyed few if any material benefits from the 1944 Act. This is not easily understood by finance, and some degree of mutual exasperation has resulted.

Education now represents a very high proportion, up to 30 per cent, of local authorities' expenditure. It has become by far the most important of local government services. Unlike some other large local services such as transport, there is no possibility of organizing it to produce a profit to the rates. Unfortunately, in a time of inflation a high and increasing level of expenditure does not necessarily mean that the quality of the service is improved. Those whose primary concern is finance may ask, not without reason, what the public is getting for its money. It is not always easy to show that there are good reasons why a service which is much more costly may in important respects be giving less benefits than before. Finally, local government remains saddled with a fiscal system based on principles evolved some three hundred years ago to deal with the important but limited problem of vagrancy. This is so inadequate to the needs of local government in the twentieth century, that cynics have argued that the only reason for its continuance is that it enables local finance committees to demonstrate the more convincingly that local government cannot bear the mounting cost of developing social services.

The essence of the English educational system is that it is a series of partnerships, a system in which power and control are distributed and not concentrated. The first and most important aspect of this is in the partnership between the government and local authorities, and this is reflected in the grant system. The difficulties of local authority finance and its need for new sources of revenue have led to an increasingly high proportion of the cost of education being borne by the state from taxes. In 1938, local rates bore 49 per cent; in 1953 only 40 per

---

[1] See the evidence given by the Manchester Education Committee to the Select Committee of the House of Commons on Estimates, 1953.

cent of the cost of the L.E.A. expenditure. Inevitably this has meant an increasing degree of control and supervision exercised by the Ministry of Education over local education authorities. It is not surprising that the main element in the complicated formula under which the Ministry's grant is paid to local education authorities should be that of percentage on expenditure. This is the method normally preferred by central authorities wishing to retain the power to direct educational policy, since local authorities can be influenced to spend in one direction rather than another by the simple device of varying the percentage of expenditure on different parts of the service. Block grant, an alternative system which may be used to give the maximum discretion to the subordinate authority, and capitation grant are also used to calculate the grant formula, which nevertheless remains essentially one based upon the percentage principle. Capitation grants may give more discretion to subordinate authorities than percentage grants, but they suffer from the disadvantage that they do not reflect differences in need between authorities but only differences in numbers.

Briefly, the education grant is made up of, first, a capitation grant based on the average numbers on registers, and, second, a grant of 60 per cent on the net recognizable expenditure of the authority. From the aggregate of these two, however, there is a deduction equivalent to the product of a rate of 30 pence in the £. This last is intended to vary the grant to authorities according to their own wealth or poverty, since the authority with low rate yield will suffer the lowest deduction. There is in addition an exchequer equalization grant, a block grant based upon another complicated formula and also intended to give additional exchequer aid to the poorer and less to the richer authorities. Two exceptions to the main education grant formula should also be noted. Local authorities recover the whole of their expenditure upon the training of teachers and contribute in accordance with the number of children in their schools towards a national pool from which this expenditure is met. Again, for school meals a grant is paid at the rate of 100 per cent on approved expenditure, food and overhead cost being treated quite separately. Since the central authority bears the whole cost it not unnaturally seeks to exercise a detailed control over expenditure, and the local authorities' position in school meals is reduced to little more than that of a local agency for a national service. Difficulties arising from the reluctance of both parties to recognize this fact and from the attempt to operate the system by approving or disapproving expenditure retrospectively in a time of constant inflation, has made of this a system which works with great discomfort to both sides. Attempts to abolish it have so far broken down because the central and local authorities have been unable to agree upon the proportions of the cost which each would bear under a more satisfactory system.

Estimates

Annual budgets remain the rule for expenditure from revenue, both in public services and in private business in this country. In view of the fact that the central authority pays for more than half of the service from its grant, it might be expected that the local education authorities' estimates of expenditure would be submitted to searching and detailed scrutiny. In fact, the forecast of income and expenditure and revised estimates submitted in prescribed form are seldom commented upon by the Ministry of Education. The reason for this is that the Ministry relies upon other methods of control. It is true that the letter calling for the submission of these estimates is normally accompanied by a homily couched in solemn terms upon the need for economy and explaining the precise grounds why on this particular occasion rigorous economy is more to be desired than ever. It appears that both depression and prosperity alike produce their own peculiarly cogent reasons for refraining from expenditure upon education. No doubt there are economic and fiscal circumstances in which local authorities would be encouraged to spend more than usual, but these circumstances, having yet to be experienced, can only be imagined.

There has been one occasion in recent years when authorities, having submitted their estimates, were asked to reduce them by an aggregate of 5 per cent, concentrating their economies upon certain items which the Minister regarded as of peripheral importance. This experiment has not been repeated. The word ' frills ' has been much used in criticism of the education service, with the implication that the cost is as high as it is because much money is wastefully or unnecessarily spent. As explained above, the bulk of educational expenditure is composed of fixed charges, particularly salaries and wages, and it is perverse to believe that major economies can come from reductions in minor items of expenditure. It is perhaps worth adding that ' frills ' are not in themselves normally regarded as unbecoming, and it is to be hoped that educationists will always resist the attempts to force them to adopt standards which are more appropriate to a charity institution than to a public service. Austerity is not in itself a virtue, and a good deal of what may be described as ' frills ' may be just those things which create a humane and civilizing atmosphere in the classroom.

The basis of Ministerial control over expenditure lies in the extent to which the broad lines of educational policy are laid down by law, by statutory regulations, and by Ministerial circulars or memoranda on particular issues.   Section 1 of the Education Act, 1944, gives the Minister powers of control and direction over local education authorities.   Much of the work of those authorities is now regulated by formulae, for example, those relating to payments between education authorities for the running of teacher training colleges and for the cost of new schools.   Until recently yet another formula limited the size of authorities' annual expenditure on minor building projects.   Since almost all salaries and wages paid by local authorities are fixed in detail by national bodies, it may well seem that there is no need for a detailed scrutiny by the Ministry of local authorities' annual estimates. Expenditure, once it has been incurred, is subject to a very exacting audit by government auditor in addition to the internal audit provided by local authorities themselves. Given the existence of H.M. Inspectors in each locality and the normal administrative co-operation between officers of the Ministry and those of local authorities, there is clearly no particular need for excessive Ministerial concern at the estimating stage.

It is perhaps also known to the Ministry that within the local authority itself the annual estimates are the subject of most prolonged and anxious inquiry, often lasting several months.   In one large city, for example, preparation of estimates for the year beginning in April starts in the previous September.   The estimates go through the education and finance committees in December and January, and are frequently reconsidered in February before receiving the approval of the City Council in March.

Let us consider these three stages.   It is worth repeating that properly prepared estimates are indispensable to good administration. Quite apart from any exclusively financial advantages which they may have, the preparation of the budget is an opportunity to review the whole service in detail.   Each heading in the estimate should be broken down into minute detail, the members of staff concerned with particular items of expenditure preparing their figures after considering what they have learnt about the needs of the service and the actual cost of providing it during previous years.   This principle, that of minute subdivision and the attribution of responsibility for every item to a particular person, or persons, is important in the control of expenditure as well as in formation of estimates.   Approval of estimates by committee is a process which probably varies in rigour according to the size, rather than the wealth, of the authority.   Estimates are usually prepared by officers in a form which calls attention to variations in expenditure between one year and another and which seeks to explain the reasons for such variations.   Normally a distinction is made between those variations which are due to such causes as rising prices and increasing school population or a wage award, and on the other hand to changes of policy resulting in higher expenditure or any proposals for the expansion of the service. The normal form of estimate is one which compares the actual expenditure for the previous financial year, the original estimate, and present estimate of expenditure for the current year, and finally the estimated expenditure for the forthcoming year. It is doubtful whether this purely historical-basis comparison is always the most profitable way of considering estimates. Nevertheless, for this particular purpose it is difficult to devise another. Indeed, it is exceedingly difficult in large authorities for members to be able to give sufficient time or to have sufficient knowledge to scrutinize estimates in detail.

Under standing orders, estimates must be scrutinized and co-ordinated by a finance committee. If it is difficult for members of a committee which is in day-to-day touch with a particular service to master the ramifications of its annual estimates, it is even more difficult for members of a finance committee to do the same for the estimates of every department of the authority. In practice, therefore, this kind of scrutiny is entrusted to the treasurer and his staff, and it is now widespread practice for them to have long discussions with service departments on the details of estimates before and frequently after these have reached the finance committee. Where the finance committee regards the estimates as excessive, as they frequently do, they normally seek to negotiate with their colleagues on other committees for an agreed amount by which the estimates may be reduced. Very properly, finance committees are reluctant to make specific proposals for such a purpose since this would involve them in interference with the policy of service committees. Where agreement is not reached or sought, finance committees may sometimes use the device of fixing the rate at a particular amount or of rationing committees to specific amounts. The service committees are then left to make the best use they can of the funds made available to them. The disadvantage of this method is its crudity. For example, where an education committee has to meet rising expenditure through an increase in the number of children, through higher costs, and through the expansion of part of its service under a statutory duty, then if its resources are fixed or if its increased resources are subject to certain limits, it can maintain its service as a whole only by reducing the standard of some parts.

It may be asked whether local authorities' estimates are merely estimates or whether, once approved, they represent the maximum of the funds available for expenditure under any one particular heading. Inconvenient and uncongenial as it may be, the latter is undoubtedly the correct interpretation. It is, of course, quite true that all the circumstances for a year or even eighteen months ahead can seldom be accurately foreseen when the budget is prepared. Standing orders, however, normally permit supplementary estimates which will be approved where it can be shown that they are due to circumstances which could not reasonably be foreseen when the budget was prepared. Similarly, some margin is allowed for error by the practice towards the end of the year of ' overs and unders ' (technically known as virement), which means the transfer of budget surpluses from one item to another to compensate for budgetary deficiencies. The use of items labelled ' contingencies ' is so shameful a confession of budgetary ineptitude that it is not even contemplated in well-organized authorities.

Budgetary Control

Once the estimates have been approved and the new financial year has begun, the immediate financial problem is to see that a proper control is exercised over expenditure. This involves budgetary control, a system of internal checks and a system of audit. If there has been the proper minute subdivision and allocation of responsibility in the framing of the budget, it should not be difficult to establish an effective system of budgetary control. The other main requisite is the rapid securing of information on how much expenditure has been incurred. Practice in authorities varies: in some, the expenditure statements are the responsibility of the treasurer's department: in others, they remain with the education department's finance section. Wherever they are, they must be rendered promptly if they are to be of value. The routine method is to give those responsible for expenditure a monthly statement of their commitments compared with their estimate for the whole year. Once again, the more minutely this can be subdivided, the more effective it is. Normally such statements are issued only during the second six months of the financial year. This comes just at the time when work is beginning on preparing estimates for the forthcoming financial year. In many authorities statements are made, at the half- and three-quarter-year, of expenditure under each main heading, compared with the estimate. Such statements are of little value unless interpreted by experience, e.g., expenditure on fuel and light in the period April–September is unlikely to amount to more than one-quarter. On the other hand, for certain other headings, such as university scholarships, the great bulk of the expenditure may fall in the first half of the year.

A particular difficulty arises in educational finance from the fact that expenditure is incurred at so many and at such widely dispersed points. The difficulties in financial control which this raises are, however, counteracted by the fact that most local education authorities are strict centralizers and allow a very small degree of delegation and discretion to their schools in the incurring of expenditure. School governors may appoint staffs, but the number whom they may employ is as a rule laid down by the educational authority itself. There may in some counties be considerable delegation of authority from county to division, but even this must be subject to a defined limit of total expenditure during the year. Books, stationery, apparatus, and other educational matters are in most authorities ordered by schools on requisition through the authorities' purchasing system. The officers responsible for handling these requisitions are normally made responsible for seeing that the quantities ordered do not exceed those to which the particular school is entitled in accordance with its capitation allowance. Many authorities retain what it is to be hoped is an obsolescent practice, under which administrative officers or school inspectors are made responsible for this work. In some places not only do they scrutinize the quantities ordered: they are supposed to see that schools order the kind of article which is approved by the central office. These practices are the more surprising since all but the smallest authorities work with contract suppliers and many of the larger authorities have their own supplies organizations. If supervision of what schools order, as opposed to the financial value of what they order, is thought necessary, it is surprising that it cannot be provided through specifications given to the contract suppliers or supplies departments.

It follows that since salaries and wages may be regulated by fixed establishment or other means and educational materials by capitation allowances, there is not a great deal of discretion left within which schools may incur obligations which will mean over-spending on the education authorities' estimates. Some margin, however, remains, and authorities have been much exercised in trying to devise some system of recording, in order to assist in controlling consumption by schools on such matters as fuel, lighting, and cleaning, or on food for school dinners.

During the last few years one authority, Hertfordshire, has decentralized its financial control over school allowances. In some ways, the Hertfordshire system departs sharply from accepted English practice. The method adopted is to give each school, college, or other institution a bank credit. The head of the school is himself free to order goods and to pay for them himself from this account. Repair and maintenance of school buildings and grounds are excluded from the scheme, but the allowance covers everything which the school spends on clerical assistance, general administration, school visits, games, and cleaning materials, as well as books, stationery, and apparatus. This system imposes a considerable amount of additional administration upon the heads; in fact, it is estimated to have saved the authority £5,000 a year in administrative costs. It might be expected that it would lead to an increase in audit staff, but this has not, in fact, proved to be necessary. Theoretically, it is wrong to take the risk of disbursing so much cash, even in the form of bank credits. Even more open to criticism is the lack of internal check, since accounts are certified as well as paid by the same person, the head of the school. It is understood, however, that both the education and financial authorities of the county are satisfied that no bad results have occurred by taking these risks. It would appear that Hertfordshire has been abundantly justified in putting into practice what is so often talked about, the freedom of the school.

No doubt the sense of freedom and responsibility which is conferred upon schools counteracts the greater possibilities of financial irregularity. There is no necessity for the system to lose the advantages either of a central supplies department, or of a supplies contractor, since schools may be given authority to buy either from the authority's own department or contractor or, if they think they can do better, elsewhere. It should be obvious that the schools are more concerned than anyone else to see that the money with which they are credited goes as far as possible.

One other unorthodoxy particularly popular with teachers is the fact that unspent balances may be carried forward into the next financial year. It is this rather than anything else which gives the impression that the Hertfordshire system is the beginning of a radical break with orthodox methods of local educational authorities' budgetary control.

At the other extreme are those authorities which rigidly insist upon the rule first made in the County Council Act of 1888 that no expenditure over £50 may be incurred without the sanction of the finance department. In county boroughs this figure may be substantially higher. This can be a stumbling-block to financial delegation. Some authorities, however, take what seems the reasonable view that if an item exceeding the statutory limit has been specifically included and approved in the annual estimates, no further authority is required. The difficulties of providing a proper system of delegation to divisional executives and still more to individual schools in authorities where such a rule, which takes no account of monetary inflation, is rigidly insisted upon, are very great.

The larger the number of people who are handling cash, the greater the possibility of accident, error, or peculation, the more complicated and extensive the task of audit, and the greater the risk to public funds. One of the principles which must be observed where cash is handled, or indeed where any kind of stock is controlled, is that of internal check. This means simply that neither cash, stock, nor financial operations are ever left entirely in the hands of one person or group, but that everyone with such responsibilities is able to rely upon the check of another member of the organization. This is a principle which has to be spread throughout the financial side of the administration. Particular support is given to it in the device of continuous stock checking. For this, full-time and permanent staff are appointed who give the whole of their time to checking stock, to advising on the writing-off of surplus and obsolete stock, and to securing that neither excessive nor dangerously small stocks of any article are held.

Audit

The third main principle in financial control is that of audit. Audit is often resented by teachers and not by teachers alone. Yet the very existence of regular audit is one of the chief means of protection to those who have to handle public money or public property, and the auditor should be regarded as a colleague whose advice is sought rather than as an agent of some form of secret police. Before one grumbles about the findings of auditors, it is essential to be sure that one has established sensible financial practices which give the auditors no reasonable grounds for complaining about the system as a whole. This is not to say that auditors do not, like the rest of us, have their preposterous moments, or that all their advice must necessarily be accepted. An auditor is always liable to a tendency to recommend an expenditure of half a crown in order to safeguard two shillings.

Audit in itself clearly is more adept at discovering than preventing fraud. Yet fraud can be discouraged by regular audit and, no less important, by an attitude throughout the administration of respect for financial efficiency. The prevention of fraud is in itself not the only benefit which derives from such an atmosphere. It also helps to protect those who have no fraudulent intention but who stumble into difficulties through carelessness or ignorance of financial practice.

Capital Expenditure

Nothing has been said so far specifically about capital expenditure; indeed, the whole emphasis has been upon revenue expenditure. The distinction between current and capital expenditure is not always easy to define. Capital work may be financed from loan or from revenue, and what is treated as capital in one authority may be paid for from revenue in another. With these reservations, it can be said that the capital estimates are a matter of far less concern to local authorities than are the revenue estimates. Capital estimates do not immediately affect the level of rate which has to be levied. Local authorities' building is paid for by loans on an annual redemption charge covering a period of some thirty years. English administrators who have sought to advise on the development of education in colonial territories have sometimes been forcibly struck, not to say dismayed, to discover that such arrangements are seldom possible overseas. It is indeed difficult to imagine that anything like the educational building programme of the last ten years would have been tolerated by the public in this country had it to be financed from revenue. Education officers will be familiar with the difficulty of explaining to parents that the £500 which cannot be found to carry out urgent repairs or improvements at the school which their children attend would still not be available if the authority had refused to spend a quarter of a million pounds on a new school in the adjoining neighbourhood. The decision to reduce the standards of new schools on the grounds that more money was needed to maintain existing schools would have been a disastrous one, since it would have fixed firmly upon the back of posterity many of the deficiencies from which we suffer to-day. The error has lain not here, but simply in our failing to find enough money out of revenue to keep existing schools in a reasonable state while simultaneously finding capital to build new schools for the additional children.

Annual capital budgets are always produced and it is customary to accompany this by a long forecast, for, say, five years. Educational building, however, which is almost the whole of educational authorities' capital development, is still controlled by annual programmes. This is a system which imposes great inconvenience upon local authorities, who necessarily have to plan their building requirements over a much longer term. To carry out a large building programme over a number of years it is necessary to have a stable architectural staff, a tried list of selected contractors who are available for large contracts, and some degree of standardization in both the plan and the specification of new buildings. None of these aims is facilitated by the system of annual programmes.

In other ways, however, the Ministry of Education has gone a long way towards meeting the needs of authorities. The Ministry's own procedure for approval of plans and quantities has been greatly simplified and now compares very favourably with the practice of most educational authorities. In addition, to give *post-hoc* approval to local authorities' plans, the Ministry now conducts what is in effect an advisory service, circulating ideas on the planning, design, and specification of schools, and giving useful comparisons in cost between one authority and another on such things as heating, lighting, and sanitary service for new buildings. Again, the Ministry exercises a broad control over furnishing and equipment on a cost-per-place basis. New building costs are, of course, controlled by this method. In spite of all this, local authorities find it exceedingly difficult to keep down the ever-swelling cost of building. Elaborate systems laid down in standing orders for competitive tendering do not always seem to accomplish their aims. There is much progress still to be made in the control of contractors' expenditure once a project has begun, and in securing that contractors adhere reasonably to some agreed time schedule for buildings. What is not always understood is that delay in building is one of the most potent means of raising cost.

Space does not allow a full discussion of purchasing procedures or the pros and cons of competitive tendering, but it should be noted that there is a constant struggle to find the right standard. The tendency of purchasers is always to adopt very high standards of quality in the belief that this gives the best value for money, particularly since public property tends to suffer rougher treatment than private property. On the other side there is always pressure to buy as cheaply as possible and to adopt standards which may be too low to be really economical. If the latter is carried too far the result is a permanent mediocrity, with nothing ever quite good enough to do its job properly. In a society where a greater and greater area of daily life is passing into the control of publicly financed or publicly subsidized organizations, the possible effects of this on our civilization are alarming. There is, after all, no reason, from a financial point of view, why a local authority should spend £40 on an original painting, even if it be believed that a painting is a necessity, when a greater area of wall can be covered by a reproduction for five guineas. It is only fair to say that such an attitude is by no means universally found among finance officers.

Nor does space allow discussion of such fascinating, if mundane, matters as machine accounting, verification of accounts, methods of collection and safeguarding of cash, and methods of paying weekly wages.

Expenditure and Greater Efficiency

Something must be said, however, about one other aspect of the subject, that which in industry is sometimes known as management accounting or efficiency audit. Here again, one of the main principles is that of speed. It is the duty of the accountant to produce the right information and to see that it is made accessible with all speed to those who can make most profitable use of it. Since public services lack the rough and ready and by no means infallible criterion of profit and loss account as a guide to efficiency, it is the more important for them to devise methods of setting their costs against a reasonable standard. One method by which this has been attempted is the collation by the Institute of Municipal Treasurers and Accountants of the cost per child of the education service broken down under a number of headings. Thus it is possible to see how the cost of keeping one child warm in school, let us say in Birmingham, compares with the same service in Manchester. These comparative figures have led to profitable investigations. Under other headings, however, their use is less apparent. If, for example, it is found that expenditure per child on teachers' salaries is greater in city A than in city B, does this show that city B is getting better value for money out of its teachers, or that city A has a more generous attitude to the staffing of its schools? Such a question may not be easy to answer directly, but may involve not only all the staffing ratios in the two cities but the relative average age, the numbers of men to women teachers, the numbers of graduates to non-graduates, qualified to non-qualified teachers in either city, and the ratio of class teachers to heads. Whatever conclusion may be reached, what is important is that this kind of inquiry should constantly be made. Comparative information is very much needed, but so far exceedingly difficult to obtain on the comparative cost of repairs and maintenance and decorating of schools. The Ministry's experience in comparing local authorities on costs of new building suggests that there may be exceedingly wide divergencies here. Once divergencies have been discovered, the way is open to finding, first, their cause, and then a method of eliminating the highest costs.

In conclusion, there is everything to be said for good financial practice, but nothing to be said for using finance in a purely restrictive way. The role of finance is not to stop expenditure but to see that money is wisely and honestly expended.

NORMAN FISHER.

CHAPTER SIX

Fiscal Management in France

THE way in which the French education service is financed is complex. It is by no means the result of a plan worked out in all its details at one and the same time and without thought for the past. On the contrary, it is closely connected with the history of France and her institutions. Even a cursory examination shows clearly the successive influences, which were sometimes in opposition to one another. For each new attempted organization had to incorporate certain historical elements which reflected a vastly different outlook. It can be said that the financial system of France is characteristic of the French mind; a mind full of contradictions, since it is both liberal (and thus favourable to local responsibility and initiative), and also, and above all, rationalist, and consequently reflects a belief in centralization.

We shall study in turn, from the point of view of the financial arrangements, primary education, secondary education, technical education, and advanced education. It so happens, moreover, that these divisions, arbitrary as they may seem, correspond to a certain reality. For the different problems raised by the organization of these different sections of education, and by the needs which they are designed to meet, were solved at different times and almost without connexion one with another. It should be stated immediately, however, that it was not the general problems of a state system of primary education that were the first to be considered: life and history develop in a way very different from that which simple logic would expect. In fact, higher and secondary education first attracted the attention of Napoleon I, and his decisions occupy an important place in French administration.

Primary Education

The first law dealing with a state primary school service was the *Guizot Law* of June 28th, 1833. Before the Revolution, primary education, organized by the Catholic Church, had been fairly widespread. The Revolutionary Assemblies had considered various projects, which they had not time to complete. So Guizot had to create something quite new. This is how, in his memoirs, he summarizes the essential administrative measures which he had adopted.

> Far from limiting itself to directing that primary, elementary, and schools for higher education should be established in all areas of the kingdom, the law further decreed that suitable accommodation and a fixed salary should every-

where be provided for teachers. Should the ordinary revenue of local authorities be insufficient for this purpose, it should be provided for by means of two special compulsory taxes, one of which should be voted for by the Municipal council, and the other by the General Council of the 'Départment'. If these taxes were not raised in this way, they would be ordered by royal decree. If it should happen that the local taxes were in themselves insufficient, the Minister of Education was to make up the deficit by means of a grant drawn from the credit provided for annually in respect of primary education in the government budget. The permanent existence of schools and the means of meeting their material needs were thus ensured, independently of the intelligence or eagerness of the people destined to benefit from them, and the central power would never be without weapons against their lack of willpower or their apathy.[1]

So this law had as its aim that every school should be set up as the result of local initiative. In this can be seen the influence of deputies (Members of Parliament) who were at that period very closely linked with local life and who—Guizot says this clearly—" were above all afraid of the influence of the priests, and the central power in the schools ". But how clearly, it can be seen by the very form which Guizot gives to his ideas, by the precautions he takes to make sure that in all circumstances the wish of the government shall prevail, that for him, as for Napoleon, as for the Kings of France, education was a matter for state control. For Louis XIV it was an organ for the conversion of Protestants and for instruction in the state religion; for Guizot it was a method of " supporting the Empire and ensuring constitutional monarchy by developing peoples' intelligence and spreading knowledge ".

The system which he envisaged—at least one school in each district, a minimum salary and suitable accommodation for each teacher, and a training college (*école normale*) for each department—seems necessary and logical to a French mind and doubtless it would to a German mind.

Other laws have been passed since : the *Falloux Law* of March 15th, 1850; above all the great laws which Jules Ferry carried through between 1882 and 1886, and which organized a compulsory, free, and undenominational system of primary education. The administration of this system has developed in the way to be expected, that is to say, the expenses borne by the state have increased, for since from the outset the state assured for itself nearly all the power, it is logical that all the expenses should devolve upon it. At present, the primary education system comprises : nursery schools for children between the ages of 2 and 6, primary schools for children between 6 and 14, and the *cours complémentaires* for children of 11 or 12 to 16 or 17.

All salaries, with the exception of those of the domestic staff (care-

---

[1] From F. Lévy Guizot, *Memoirs pour servir a l'histoire de mon temps* (Paris).

takers, women on duty in nursery schools, cleaners, canteen cooks, and
so on), are paid entirely by the state. But, as a survival of the *Guizot
Law*, the teachers' rent, or the money paid to them in *lieu* of rent, is
provided by the local authority.

The actual public primary school buildings belong to the local
authority, which must supply the money for new buildings and pay
for the upkeep of existing ones. But the state provides subsidies, which
may be as high as 85 per cent of the sum involved.

The running expenses of the schools (lighting, cleaning, school supplies, and so on) must be met by the local authority; however, the
government contributes to the provision of teaching materials by
grants, and by the distribution or loan of books, of educational
material, gramophone records, films, and so forth.

Extra duties have been undertaken by the schools, whose role at first
seemed limited to the instruction of children. In nearly all French
towns, and in many semi-rural districts, there now exist school canteens in which theoretically children have their midday meal [2]; these
canteens are under local control. Their expenses are met by contributions from families and by municipal credits. The government plays
its part by paying up to 50 per cent of the expenses incurred in building and equipping such canteens.

School medical services have been set up. In many cases the state
has had to bring pressure to bear upon local authorities to do this. For
this reason the government agrees to pay nearly all the running expenses, subsidizes, by up to 40 per cent, building expenses, and provides free supplies. Part of these expenses is repaid by local authorities
or departments by grants made for the purpose (*fonds de concours*).

Sometimes it happens that municipalities wish to organize instruction in special subjects in primary schools or *cours complémentaires*
(drawing, music, handicrafts, commercial subjects). They must be
prepared to meet all the expenses involved; the amount spent on these
lessons is particularly high in Paris and the Department of the Seine
(about 3,550 million *francs* [3] in 1955). But the development of technical education restricts any increase in these amounts. And the
government sometimes helps poor municipalities to finance projects
which they have undertaken.

Training colleges for men and women intending to be primary
school teachers are under the control of the departmental authority.

---

[2] It should be noticed that in France the school dinner ' hour ' usually lasts for
two hours; it is sometimes even two and a half hours. This corresponds to the
rhythm of French life, ill-suited to the demands of modern life. School canteens
are thus not essential, and are less widely used than in Anglo-Saxon countries.

[3] 980 francs = 2.8 U.S. dollars = £1 sterling.

(This is a survival of the *Guizot Law*.)   The state pays the salary of the staff and provides the scholarship for the pupils.   Grants may be made by the government to cover the cost of building and for the upkeep of existing structures.

Secondary Education

In general the *lycées* are controlled by the state and the *collèges* by the local authorities.   The law of March 15th, 1850 (known as the *Fallaux Law*), organized secondary education in France and was most anxious to ensure the freedom for private secondary education which the Revolution and Napoleon I had suppressed; Article 72 stipulates that *lycées* should be founded and maintained by the state, with the help of departments and towns.

The *collèges* were founded and are now maintained by the local authorities.   They can be subsidized by the state.   This meant that originally the salaries of teachers in *lycées* were paid by the state and those of teachers in *collèges* by the local authorities.

In actual fact, at the present time the state pays all salaries.   The only difference which exists, as far as finance is concerned, between *lycées* and *collèges* is that the upkeep of buildings and the purchase of supplies are in general met by the state in *lycées* and by local authorities where *collèges* are concerned.   But the state tends more and more, at the request of municipalities, to take upon itself expenses which should fall upon the towns.   The recent establishment of national *collèges* is symptomatic of a general development.

It is interesting, however, to note that each *lycée* works out its own financial estimates with the help of an administrative council, formed of employees of the government educational service and representatives of the local authority and of parents; the estimates are presented for the approval of the Minister of Education, who makes sure that it has been carefully checked before he supplies the necessary funds. Thus, sometimes, towns are encouraged, at the request of the administrative councils, to undertake expenses, usually not very large, which it would be difficult to obtain from the government.

The boarding-houses of *lycées* have special types of estimates in which account must be taken of the money received in the form of maintenance grants or scholarships paid by the state to certain boarders, and also of the sums paid in by the parents.   The boarding-houses of *collèges* are sometimes controlled by the local authority, sometimes by the heads of the schools concerned.

Thus the towns do not pay a large share of the expenses incurred by secondary schools.   The 1954 budget shows that of a total of 41,885 million *francs* spent, the state paid 40,430 million *francs* and the towns only 1,455 millions.

Technical and Vocational Education

Technical education has not long been in existence. The first official training colleges for apprentices date from 1880. They were controlled by the Ministry of Education. But a vocational educational system was developing, here and there, according to local needs and usually making use of the buildings of higher primary schools or those of the *cours complémentaires* of the primary schools. The financial law of 1892 stipulates that "higher vocational primary schools (*écoles primaires supérieures professionnelles*) in which the instruction given is specially concerned with industry or commerce will, in future, be controlled by the Ministry of Commerce and will be known as practical industrial and commercial schools". Technical education was thus outside the public system—a situation with all sorts of serious drawbacks. It also lacked resources needed for further development.

The law known as the *Astier Law* of 1919 introduced a tax on industry and wholesale businesses. This tax, known as the apprenticeship tax, was equal to four-thousandths of the salaries paid out. In 1920 technical education was brought into the general system and controlled by the Ministry of Education.

This apprenticeship tax is not allotted in the budget especially for technical education. It may be paid into the treasury, whose funds it will swell; it may be used by industrialists who need it in order to set up their own centres for apprentices; or paid out to any educational establishment it is desired to help. In the last two cases the government intervenes; it must supervise the establishment and equipment of private schools and inspect the way in which they are run and approve the special purposes for which it is proposed to use the taxes. In 1952, the apprenticeship tax produced 8,354 million *francs*, exemptions amounting to 6,366 million *francs* were granted. This latter amount was spent almost equally on private centres for technical education and on public establishments, chosen by private individuals for the receipt of their taxes.

At the present moment technical education is carried on in schools (*écoles supérieures*) amongst which are counted the former arts and trades schools (so well known among the lower classes of France), the national vocational schools, technical colleges, and the apprenticeship centres.

The cost of running and establishing the technical colleges (which alone have inherited, from the colleges of secondary education, the position of being controlled by the local authority) must be met partly by the municipalities. The expenses of all other establishments are met by the state. It is hardly surprising that local authorities try to change their colleges into national vocational schools in order to have nothing more to pay; they ask that apprenticeship centres should be set up. And these would frequently take the place of technical colleges if the government were not on its guard. The national technical colleges, entirely under state control, have been established during the last five or six years. Many towns claim that they have no money, so that their colleges may become national colleges.

If municipalities seem to have lost their desire to develop an educational system suited to their needs and by means of their own efforts, yet other bodies created by the economic evolution of the century—industrial and commercial committees, corporations, and so on—sometimes set in motion certain undertakings for which they accept some financial responsibility. In this way trade schools, in which the standard of work is high and strictly vocational, and with which private industry keeps in close touch, have been set up. The best example of this is the school for *hôteliers* in Paris.

Thus it can be seen that, in this particular field, groups of people living in the same area but representing different interests are gradually withdrawing from their responsibilities, and the influence of special groups linked by the same economic motive is growing.

Advanced Education

At the time of the French Revolution, the universities, which had shone gloriously in the Middle Ages, were utterly decadent. They were suppressed by the Revolutionary Assemblies who were not hostile to advanced education or to scientific research, but who were set resolutely against the corporations. They made many plans. Only two of them were realized: that of the training college for higher educational studies (*école normale supérieure*) and the *école polytechnique*.

By the decree of May 1st, 1808, Napoleon I gave new life to the old faculties: Law, Medicine, Science, and Arts, stipulating that they must be responsible for the teaching of " advanced knowledge and for the granting of degrees ".

The new faculties differed essentially from the old by their administrative position. They belonged to the state, were administered entirely and directly by the state; the fees paid by the students were paid to the state, which was responsible for all expenses. This system remained practically unaltered during the whole of the nineteenth century; it fell to a great administrator of the Third Republic, the philosopher Louis Liard, to establish the universities of France.

It was to do this that the law of July 11th, 1896, was formulated.

This brief law, containing only four articles, was very much to the point. The first article laid down that the ' groups of faculties ' should assume the name of ' university '. Official standing was thus given in the life of the country to universities which were referred to for the first time by this name in a state document. Article 2 established the University Council, a truly administrative council dealing with a new group which was to have its own life and be autonomous. Article 4—a most important one—stated that into the funds of each university should be paid all the fees for which the students were liable; fees paid for the course of study itself, for enrolment, for use of the library, and for practical work. All this money could be spent by the university on laboratory expenses, for libraries and various collections, to institute new branches of study, and on undertakings likely to be of use to the students.

So, to-day, universities have their own position in the state and are financially autonomous. A council, drawn from the university teachers, administers their finances. Their assets are first of all the fees paid by the students (with the exception of examination fees, which go to the government), a state subsidy, and finally grants, gifts, and bequests which the university may receive from the local powers that be. That is to say, groups like the chamber of commerce, or private individuals. On all this money the university depends to meet current expenses. It may also establish new branches of learning, and equip new laboratories, among other things. But the salaries of the greater part of the teaching staff are paid by the state, as are the student scholarships and the expenses incurred by university cities and restaurants run for students. Thus the larger part of all expenses is still met directly by the state. In 1954, to meet a total expenditure of 17,861 million *francs*, the universities themselves raised only 1,576 million *francs*. New buildings and the equipment of them are paid for by the state. Consequently the state has great authority over the running and development of the universities.

Quite a large number of the special kind of schools set up by the Revolutionary Assemblies are in existence to-day. The last of these schools to be opened is the National School for Administrators, whose aim is to ensure a flow of recruits for the administrative services of the state. Expenses of the schools are entirely met by the state.

Sources of Finance

In France, money allotted to education comes from :—
(1) The Treasury, supplied by various general amounts voted for by Parliament (direct or indirect taxation, loans);
(2) grants for special purposes (*fonds de concours*), groups of citizens

put at the disposal of the Minister for the Medical Care of Pupils, relatively large amounts of money (1,900 million *francs* in 1952);

(3) an increase of 0·30 per cent of the tax on production brought in
by the *Barange Law*, which (in a way quite in opposition to the normal
rules governing budgets and to settle the problem of private schools),
allows the sum of 1,300 *francs* per term to be set aside for each pupil
receiving primary education. The amounts of money thus collected
are paid out to the parents' associations in the case of private schools,
and to the Treasurer's office in the case of state schools. These
Treasurer's offices are controlled by the general committee. In 1954
the sum thus collected amounted to about 20 thousand million *francs*,
of which 13 thousand million *francs* were paid out to state schools;

(4) enrolment fees, examination fees and amounts paid by students
for diplomas;

(5) amounts paid by local authorities.

The financial share of the state is, as it has been seen, far the largest.
In effect, towns and departments try in every way to make the state
meet expenses which should really be their own responsibility. And
it is a sign of the times that Article 79 of the law of February 7th, 1953,
which completes the *Barange Law*, stipulates that the funds of the
departmental treasuries must be used first of all to pay that proportion
of the cost which local authorities must contribute to new buildings
and the repair of existing structures. It is an indirect way of relieving
local groups of a duty which originally seemed to devolve upon them.

The amount of government money destined for education is very
large: 324 thousand million *francs* in 1955, actually 8·64 per cent of
the amount spent by the nation, or 11·32 per cent of the civil expenses,
including subsidiary estimates (Post Office, broadcasting, and so on).
Of these 324 thousand million *francs*, 250 were ear-marked for current
expenses, 74 thousand were destined for new buildings.

Primary education swallows up the greater part of these sums: more
than 124 thousand million *francs*, or nearly 50 per cent of the total
amount. The amount spent on salaries (more than 197 thousand
millions or nearly 80 per cent) forms the largest single item. The next
largest is spent on grants for scholarship holders and students: this
forms a total of nearly 23 thousand millions, more than 8 per cent of
the total estimates.

These amounts are granted by the Assembly or by the Minister of
Education, who must, each year, present his estimates, giving details
of the needs he foresees. Since the estimates are voted on one section
at a time, the destination of each amount must be precisely stated.
Money cannot be diverted from one purpose to another, as far as
ordinary running expenses are concerned, without reference being

made to the Assembly, unless the sum involved be less than 10 per cent of the whole sum voted. This limits the freedom of the Minister.

He has greater freedom, however, as far as money destined for building is concerned. Transfers can be made from one section to another, any sums of money left over from one year can be carried over to the next. And the necessity of spreading out, over several years, expenses incurred for the building of large new premises has led to the practice of considering not only money to be paid out immediately but also the authorization of plans which may take years to complete.

All this expenditure can be undertaken only if it has first been approved directly by the Minister or by those in positions of authority subordinate to him but who have mandatory powers (for example the *Préfets* or *Recteurs*) granted to them by the Minister. Expenditure is examined on two different occasions. It is done both before money has been granted, and after it has been paid over.

The Minister of Education, like all Ministers, has working by his side a civil servant of high rank belonging to the Ministry of Finance called the Controller of Expenditure. He makes sure before he endorses the Minister's ordinances that the money being thus disposed of is really available, that the use for which it is to be put really conforms with the estimates, and that it is not an over-estimate.

Finally, an administrative account is drawn up with an explanation of every item of expenditure, and this is submitted to the general treasurer of each Department and to the Court of Accounts (*Cour des Comptes*). Any account which seems suspicious is carefully examined and explanations about it may be demanded.

Some Reflections

Such is the financial system regarding the state educational establishments of France. It was planned and put into practice by men who had a very high conception of the rights of the state. Local groups, still powerful in the nineteenth century, first forced them to put their plans into effect by the help of the local authorities, towns, and departments. But the projects of local groups were either prompted by the state or were examined and controlled by it and integrated into the general plan. The aim was to apply as uniformly as possible certain rules.

As the speed of transportation increased unbelievably, local groups gradually decreased in vitality; they lost their love of initiative and their habit of making efforts for the things they devised. So all power has slipped into the hands of the state, which pays all salaries and, on the whole, finances building projects. Only traces are left of an earlier state of affairs. The progressive assumption by the state of all the expenses of the education service seems to be the normal result of the present trend of development.

Even projects which eventually become realities are very often the result of careful work by civil servants employed by the Ministry of Education. Parents who have no official part to play in the solution of problems which concern the future of their children tend more and more to leave matters in the hands of the state and the specialists. Moreover, they have no powers except in the influence they may have over the Ministry.

Thus France is changing, and no longer consists of a whole made up of units, each of which has its own local base and its own life, elementary but complete, adapted to its needs. But she is becoming a whole, integrated state, and different elements in it meet to struggle or co-operate in Paris. Inevitably under such conditions new groups have been formed. The education committees are numerous and powerful and wield an enormous influence.

This centralized system, which had been created in the image of that drawn up formerly by the Catholic Church to spread a state religion, would be a danger to individual liberties if France in general, and members of French universities in particular, were not liberal in outlook, and if the new groups to which this system has given birth were not—whatever may have been said about them—remarkably public-spirited. It would be difficult, for example, to teach a state religion in France since all types of teachers have complete freedom of belief and their associations reflect most divergent tendencies.

The system is not without its advantages : the teaching profession is less badly paid in France than in many other countries where a variety of employers makes it difficult to organize powerful associations comprising large numbers.

It is efficient. At the present time France must make provision for a considerable increase in the number of pupils attending schools, both because of the increased birth-rate and because of the increased length of time spent studying. Needs have been examined. A plan has been made. Schools are being built at an increased rate.

It is economical. It is customary to say that things run by private enterprise are more economical than those carried on by the state. This is untrue as far as the running of schools is concerned. In the apprenticeship centres established by the state, each pupil costs about 80,000 *francs* a year. Certain centres for private industries or for nationalized undertakings have at their disposal a large staff, remarkable equipment; but each pupil costs about 300,000 *francs* a year.

Moreover, a certain uniformity of standard in buildings can be attained. Bulk buying at the same time on behalf of several districts has been agreed to. Costs have been lowered. A central service for the supply of school furniture also makes great economies possible.

It is regrettable that the rural districts and the towns of France have no longer the desire nor the means to lead a stronger and more independent life. It is regrettable that they have become used to relying on the government and asking for financial aid from it to meet problems they themselves should understand better than anyone else and the solutions of which will benefit them more than anyone else. This withdrawal of local groups from responsibility explains and follows the action of parents who abandon to the state the care of educating their children.

Moreover, since all educational problems have become, as it were, nationalized, the smallest difficulty finds its echo in Paris, gives rise to discussions, and arouses passions on a national level. It is well known that grants to private schools create difficult problems and cause regrettable divisions of opinion between Frenchmen.

The Ministry of Education (in French the word national is added to education in this context—a significant addition) is the faithful guardian of the rights of the state in the matter of education. Those who wish to break away from the guardianship of the state while at the same time gaining financial aid from it make application to other Ministries: for example, to the Ministry of Health or Agriculture. This fact gives rise to conflicts between Ministries, and passionate disputes take place before the National Assembly.

Perhaps it would be possible, while keeping the advantages of a centralized system, to mitigate its inconveniences. But this would be no easy task. Our educational system is, as Guizot saw and pointed out, the product of our history and our national character.

Roger Thabault.

CHAPTER SEVEN

Fiscal Management in the United States of America

FISCAL management in the public school systems of the United States is characterized by a wide variety of practices and procedures, a conglomeration of legal controls which have little uniformity, and the distribution of authority and responsibility among state and local administrative agencies which differs greatly among the states. This condition is the result of several factors, the most important of which are: (1) education is the responsibility of the individual states, therefore there are forty-eight separate and independent public school systems; (2) within the states the schools are organized in local administrative districts, which vary in number from twenty-four in one state to several thousand in other states, and in size from one-teacher rural districts with a few pupils to huge metropolitan systems with thousands of teachers and pupils; (3) rapidly changing social and economic conditions which have not occurred simultaneously or equally in different sections of the country; and (4) administrative reforms which have been developed out of extensive study of pressing financial problems but which have not been uniformly adopted. In attempting to describe and evaluate the administration of school finances in the United States, the best that can be done is to select those elements which are most common to the various states, to indicate the trends in practice, and to state the principles and criteria which are generally accepted.

Fiscal Controls

Basic to financial management is a great variety of controls which are imposed upon local school administration. Education is a function of state governments; local units of government have no authority or responsibility for the operation of schools. The school district is a quasi-corporation established by the state to perform a state function. School district officials are legal representatives of the state, and their powers, duties, and responsibilities are only those prescribed by statutes. It has been held in a long line of court decisions that the control of education is one of the sovereign powers of the state, and that the authority to determine educational policy resides in the state legislature.

Types of Fiscal Controls

Analyses of state systems of control over the administration of school funds show the following to be common : —

(1) Designation of the purposes for which school taxes may be levied and for which school funds may be spent.

(2) Limitations on local tax-rates and levies.

(3) Regulation and limitation on borrowing money.

(4) Prescription of procedures in budgeting, accounting, auditing, reporting, and protection of funds.

(5) Regulation of property assessment.

(6) Provision for review of budgets and tax-levies by some state agency or other local governmental agency.

(7) Requirements that local schools meet certain educational standards or provide certain services which may affect to a large degree the cost of education and the objects for which funds will be spent.

(8) Review and approval of capital expenditures, including approval of building plans and specifications.

(9) Establishment of local school districts and prescribing local administrative organizations which influence directly both economy in operation and efficiency in management.

(10) Regulation of the expenditure of grants-in-aid.

These controls may be expressed in the form of statutes and constitutional provisions or they may be exercised by state administrative agencies by reason of delegated authority. The types and combinations of controls are by no means uniform among the states. The lack of central control by the federal government and the fact that the state school systems were organized at different times and under different conditions and traditions have tended to maximize variations. There has long existed a basic issue as to what constitutes the proper sphere in which the state shall exercise authority and assume responsibility and what shall be left to local determination. Increasing activity of the federal government in education and the expansion of its grants-in-aid has raised the very controversial question of federal control.

Purposes of Fiscal Controls

The purposes of fiscal controls, while not always clear or effectively realized, may be summarized as follows : —

Protection of funds. The necessity of safe-guarding public funds is generally accepted. First, there must be protection against loss, embezzlement, fraud, and graft. Secondly, school funds should be used only for those purposes which are within the scope of the functions of the school. The protection of school funds involves the definition of authority and responsibility to collect and expend school revenues, bonding of school officials responsible for the custody and management of funds, provisions for auditing and reporting of financial transactions, and prescription of budgetary procedures. In the different states these controls have been adopted to varying degrees and are incorporated in statutory prescriptions or state administrative regulations or both.

Efficiency and economy in management. Efficiency and economy are to a large degree the product of sound administrative management. The fact that many local school systems have limited or no professional administrative service makes state control and supervision necessary if any degree of administrative efficiency is to be obtained. In many states there has been a tendency to extend state regulations and supervision rather than to modify local school administrative organization.

Protection of the taxpayer. All the states impose restrictions and limitations on local taxing authority; the power is limited to expressed purposes and must be exercised in accordance with prescribed regulations. The objectives of controls over taxation are to protect the taxpayer against discriminatory and confiscatory levies and to secure an equitable distribution of the tax burden. Controls designed to protect the taxpayer include : (1) definition of the purposes for which taxes may be levied; (2) limitations on tax-rates; (3) prescription of procedures for levying and collecting taxes; (4) review and approval of budgetary appropriations and tax-levies by state or other local agencies; (5) provisions for approving tax-rates by vote of the taxpayers; (6) designation of the sources of revenue and the types of taxes which may be used for school purposes; and (7) supervision of expenditures.

Equalization of educational opportunity. Local school systems vary greatly in their financial resources. The resulting differences in the quality of educational services provided for children and youth in the different localities and states have been the basic problem of school finance for the past half-century. Efforts to alleviate these inequalities through the reorganization of state systems of financial support and through extension of federal support have raised many issues of fiscal control. During the past twenty-five years practically all states substantially increased state financial grants to local school systems. In 1953–4 approximately 41 per cent of school revenues in the United States came from state sources. In the different states the proportion of revenue from state sources varied from less than 10 per cent to over 80 per cent. The method used for the distribution of state school funds may or may not involve special controls. It is generally agreed among authorities in school finance, however, that there is no justification for differentiating fiscal controls in terms of the sources of revenue.

Maintenance of educational standards. The formulation and enforce-ment of educational standards are obligations of the state. When local school systems are required to meet state standards for educational services there is usually some element of fiscal control involved. Both the purpose and the amount of school expenditure may be determined to a large degree by mandatory requirements and standards which have to be met. While these controls are indirect so far as finance is con-cerned, they operate to limit local administrative discretion in the allo-cation and expenditure of school funds. There are few restrictions, however, on the use of school funds for expanding the school curricu-lum or extending school services so long as the basic requirements are met and the resources are available. From the standpoint of fiscal control it is highly important that there be financial resources available to provide services and facilities which exceed the mandatory require-ments, and that there be freedom to utilize these resources.

Summary

The problems and issues of control involve all areas of fiscal management. It is generally recognized that fiscal authority must co-exist with operational responsibility if administration is to be effective and the greatest returns are to be received from the funds expended. Highly centralized control tends to produce a static uniformity which stultifies progress. On the other hand, local control without over-all regulation and supervision tends to lead to administrative chaos, with the consequent adverse effects on educational services. The problem is to preserve the values of local autonomy and local initiative and at the same time ensure the general welfare through state direction and control. The control of school finance is one of the most important aspects of this problem.

Administrative Organization

The administration of school finances operates through a number of state and local agencies, the organizational structure of which varies considerably from state to state. All these agencies derive their authority from the legislature and operate more or less independently of each other. There are, however, certain patterns of administration dealing with the more important phases of finance which are common to a number of states.

Local Administration

Authority and responsibility for the operation of schools are vested in local school boards.[1] These boards are agents of the state and derive

---

[1] These boards may be designated as boards of education, school commissions, school trustees, or school committees in the various states.

their authority from the state legislature. They are in no sense agents or divisions of municipal or county governments, although the members may be appointed by local governmental agencies and they may be subject to fiscal controls exercised by local governmental agencies.

The size of local boards of education varies from one to fifteen members, five being the most common number. The board members may be elected by popular vote or may be appointed by the mayor or city council or county commissioners in rural districts. In some states several methods of selecting board members are used; in other states all boards are elected by popular vote. It is generally accepted that election on a non-partisan ballot is the most desirable method of selecting board members.

The school district is the local administrative unit. These districts vary in size from small one-teacher elementary school districts to metropolitan districts which serve the largest cities. City and town school districts are usually coterminous with the municipality. In many instances, however, the small city and town districts may include contiguous rural territory. In twelve states the county serves as the basic school district. In four of these states, cities and towns are included in the county school unit; in the eight other states, cities and towns operate as independent districts. The latest estimate of the total number of local school districts in the United States is 59,270. In recent years there has been nation-wide emphasis on the reorganization of school districts, resulting in a decrease in numbers from approximately 127,000 in 1930 to less than half that number in 1954.

The relationship of size of district to cost and educational efficiency has been the subject of many studies. From these studies it is generally agreed that districts with fewer than twelve hundred pupils are deficient in educational services, and as the size decreases the *per capita* costs tend to increase. There is substantial evidence to indicate that both educational efficiency and economy in operation tend to increase as the enrolment increases up to ten thousand pupils. Approximately 64 per cent of the school districts in the United States have fewer than ten teachers; only 12 per cent have over forty teachers.

Another factor of considerable importance in financial and educational efficiency is the type and quality of administrative and supervisory services. In the smallest districts the board of education has to assume the entire responsibility for financial administration, often with little or no assistance from state supervisory agencies. In the districts large enough to employ a superintendent of schools, the details of fiscal management are delegated by the board to the superintendent and his assistants. The superintendent of schools has but limited legal status in most states; his duties and responsibilities are those delegated to him by the board of education. With a few exceptions,[2] the superintendent is elected by the board, serves at the pleasure of the board, and is responsible to the board for his administrative acts. In all cases the board is the legal fiscal authority; the superintendent has no discretionary authority independent of the board. In the large school systems, financial management may be in the charge of an assistant superintendent or a business manager who is responsible to the superintendent. In some of the systems the fiscal officer is co-ordinate with the superintendent and is directly responsible to the board. This type of organization is not considered desirable, in that it separates financial from educational administration. Division in administrative authority is not conducive to integrated policy and financial considerations are likely to dominate educational needs.

The position of the electorate is an important one in local financial administration. In fifteen states the voters exercise more or less direct control over the school budgets and tax-levies. In the New England states the town-meeting system operates in most of the communities except large cities. In New York and New Jersey similar systems of voter control operate. In other states, budgets, tax-levies, and other questions are acted on by the voters at the annual school meeting. In several states the school tax-levy must be submitted to the voters if it exceeds a maximum rate stipulated in the law. Another question that is almost universally referred to the voters is the issuance of bonds for the construction and equipment of school buildings.

The question of the extent to which the school budgets and tax-levies should be subject to direct voter control is a moot one. In the small rural districts it appears to operate satisfactorily. In the larger dis-tricts fiscal problems are more complex and it is more difficult for the voters to make an intelligent decision. Predominate opinion favours a well-organized representative school government with the public in-terest adequately protected through provisions for dissemination of information concerning school needs, etc., public meetings at which citizens can be heard, and the popular election of school board members.

Another factor of considerable importance in local administration is the control which municipal governments exercise over school budgets and tax-levies. There is provision for review of school budgets by local governmental bodies in twenty states. In some states the pro-vision for review applies to all districts, in others only to those districts of a certain class. The control involved in such reviews may vary from little or no authority to effect budget changes to complete authority over budgets and tax-levies. In about one-third of the larger

---

[2] In several states the superintendent is elected by popular vote for a fixed term but is responsible to the board of education.

cities the school budget is subject to review by municipal authorities. In about one-fifth of the cities the reviewing authority may disapprove the budget and require the board of education to change it. The mayor or the city council or both have responsibility for the review. In several states special tax boards or commissions approve school budgets. The relative merits of fiscal independence *versus* dependence of local boards of education has been the subject of a number of studies and numerous arguments, pro and con, have been advanced on this issue. From the standpoint of fiscal management and economy in operation the evidence is not conclusive in support of either system. Where real differences exist they favour fiscal independence. The separation of fiscal control from operational responsibility violates a basic principle of administration. The agency having fiscal control ultimately determines educational policy.

In summary, it may be stated that local boards of education exercise broad powers over financial matters. Within the restrictions prescribed by law and the limits of local financial resources, all boards have considerable discretion as to the amounts of money which may be spent and the kinds and quality of educational services which may be provided. The principal interest of the state is to ensure that basic standards of education are maintained and that acceptable administrative practices are followed. The principle of local autonomy in school government is well established and jealously guarded by the people. The basic problem in administrative organization is to establish local school units which permit efficient and economical operation and to provide adequate administrative services at the local level.

State Administration

State administration of public schools is vested in the state board of education, the state department of education, and, in some states, other boards or commissions to which certain functions may be assigned. The scope of authority and responsibility of state school administrative agencies varies considerably among the states.

State boards of education which are responsible for elementary and secondary schools have been established in forty-four states. State boards of education are quasi-legislative bodies with power to adopt rules and regulations which, in all but a few states, have the effect of law. The principal functions of state boards of education are : —

(1) Formulation of educational policies.
(2) Prescription of minimum standards of educational service.
(3) Regulation of the apportionment of state school funds.
(4) Regulation of teacher education and certification of teachers.

(5) Adoption of courses of study.

(6) Adoption of textbooks.

In the area of school finance the functions of state boards of education are limited to regulation of the distribution of state school funds, prescription of budgetary and accounting procedures, requirements of financial reports, and review of local school budgets. Beyond the review of local budgets, which is generally limited to correctness and conformance with legal requirements, state boards of education have no direct authority over, or responsibility for, school expenditures. In prescribing standards of educational facilities, adoption of courses of study, and in formulating general educational policies, the state board may exercise considerable indirect control over local school expenditures.

The state superintendent of public instruction [3] is the chief state school official, and the state department of education is the administrative agency in all states. The majority of state departments of education have some authority and responsibility in fiscal matters, but no single fiscal function is exercised by all state departments nor does any one state department exercise all the functions. The following fiscal functions are reported for the various states.[4]

Function	Number of States
(1) Approve local school bond issues	7
(2) Approve plans of local units for financing capital outlay	11
(3) Review and approve local school budgets	36
(4) Prepare formula for distributing general state grants	36
(5) Prepare formula for distributing special state grants	37
(6) Prepare formula for distributing federal funds	37
(7) Distribute general state funds in accordance with formula	44
(8) Distribute special state funds in accordance with formula	43
(9) Distribute federal funds in accordance with formula	44
(10) Manage and invest permanent school funds	8
(11) Audit local school accounts	11
(12) Check bonds of local school officials	9
(13) Check local school depositories	6
(14) Check local school tax-levies for compliance with law	15
(15) Advise local school officials on local finance problems and business administration	44
(16) Make studies of state and local finance problems and needs	44
(17) Prepare specifications for supplies and equipment used by local schools	18

[3] In several states the chief state school officer has the title of Commissioner of Education.

[4] Fred F. Beach, *The Functions of State Departments of Education* (Federal Security Agency, Office of Education, Misc. No. 12, Washington, D.C., 1950), p. 32.

Several of the fiscal functions listed above which are not performed by state departments of education are performed by other state agencies, such as state tax boards or commissioners, state finance boards, state auditors or treasurers, and state examiners or auditing boards. The services provided at the state level are by no means uniform in scope or quality. In only a few state departments is there a well-organized, adequately staffed division of finance. In about one-fourth of the states there is little state administration and supervision of school finance of any consequence.

Budgetary Procedures

Some type of budget is required in all local school systems. This may vary from a simple estimate of receipts and expenditures, prepared primarily for the purpose of determining the local school tax-levy, to elaborate documents. Properly conceived a budget is a plan for financing an educational programme for a stated period of time. When completely developed the budget consists of three parts: (1) an educational programme based on carefully formulated educational policies; (2) a spending plan which will effectively implement the educational policies; and (3) a financing plan which takes into account all the financial resources.

Preparation and Approval

Preparation of the budget is considered to be an executive function. While the board of education is the legal budgetary authority, the responsibility for preparing the budget is usually delegated to the superintendent of schools. In many school systems the preparation of the budget is a co-operative task in which the total administrative staff, and to some degree the instructional staff, participate.

The basic form and content of the budget document are prescribed by law or state regulation in the majority of states. While the form of the budget varies from school system to school system a complete budget document would include: (1) the budget message; (2) a general summary of the budget; (3) estimates of receipts; (4) estimates of expenditures; and (5) supporting schedules. The budget message may include such items as: (1) a statement of the scope of the educational programme to be provided in terms of services to be offered, pupil enrolment, and so on; (2) changes in policies which may affect the budget; (3) statement of the financial condition of the school system; (4) the capital expenditures to be undertaken; and (5) any other factors which may affect revenues or costs.

The budget summary usually gives a brief summary of anticipated receipts by source and estimated expenditures by character, with comparisons for previous years. Comparative tax-rates and levies for previous years may also be listed.

Anticipated receipts are listed by character and source. Expenditures are listed by character and object. Receipts and expenditures are listed in terms of the standard accounting classifications.

Supporting schedules would include salary and wage schedules, costs of the various types of personal services, unit costs (often compared with other school systems), proportionate parts of the school dollar spent for various types of services, bond schedules and interest payments, analyses of kinds and quantities of materials and supplies to be used, and any other information which may be pertinent in explaining the budget estimates.

When the budget has been prepared it is presented to the board of education for approval. Publication in some form is required in a number of states. Publication in newspapers of the budget summary, posting in public places, or placing the budget on file for public inspection may satisfy the requirements for publication. In many districts detailed budget summaries are prepared and distributed to interested citizens and civic organizations. Sixteen states require public hearings to be on the budget prior to adoption.

In fifteen states, the school budget must be submitted to the voters for approval in some classes of districts, usually the smaller districts. In ten states a state reviewing authority may reduce the budget total or any item in the budget. In twenty states the budgets of some or all school districts must be submitted to a city or county governmental agency or an independent tax board for approval. When the budget has been approved by the board of education and other reviewing authorities where such is required, it is a legal authorization to spend school funds for the purposes and in the amounts indicated in the budget.

Administration of Expenditures

The administration of expenditures is an executive responsibility which is usually delegated to the superintendent of schools and, in larger school systems, the business manager. Policies adopted by the board concerning salaries and wage scales, purchasing of supplies and equipment, operation and maintenance of plant, and standards of educational services are controlling factors. In some states it is required that the board formally approve each item of expenditure before bills or claims can be paid. In the small school districts which do not employ a superintendent, the board of education must assume responsibility for administering the budget.

An item of considerable importance is the extent to which the budget may be modified after adoption. Modifications may be made by transfer of funds or appropriations from one category to another or by making additional appropriations. Since the budget is usually made several months in advance of the period to which it applies, it is often necessary to make modifications even in the most carefully prepared budget. In some states the budget total may not be increased after its formal approval although transfers within the budget may be permitted. It is generally agreed that the board of education should not be rigidly held to the initial budget estimates, for to do so may prevent adjustment to unforeseen conditions and needs or restrict desirable modifications in educational services.

Allocation of funds among the various divisions and services of a large school system is an important and difficult problem. Divisions are usually made between elementary and secondary schools, but budget appropriations are seldom broken down school by school. In arriving at budget estimates careful analyses of the needs of individual schools may be made. In some items such as instructional supplies, estimates are made on a pupil-enrolment basis. Since few school systems have the financial resources to supply all needs and desires, the evaluation of the relative importance of the many elements which constitute a school programme is probably the most important part of planning and administering a school budget.

Control of Revenue

Budgetary estimates of expenditures become the basis for determining local tax-levies and tax-rates. The property-tax rate for schools may be set by the board of education or by a county or city official. In most states local school taxes are collected by county or city tax collectors and distributed to the school corporation. Collections and distributions are made half-yearly in most cases.

State grants may be distributed to local school systems annually or half-yearly. Some grants are made on a reimbursement basis and not distributed until after the end of the fiscal year.

The most common school fiscal year is from July 1st to June 30th. The tax year, however, does not always coincide with the fiscal year. Taxes may be levied and collected on a calendar-year basis. Since revenue is received periodically, it is necessary so to manage funds that money is available in periods between collections. If funds are not available to meet obligations, short-term borrowing must be used. The majority of states limit short-term loans to some stipulated percentage of anticipated revenue. The purposes for which such loans may be made, the interest-rates, the term of the loans, and the form of the obligation, i.e., notes or warrants, may be regulated.

Large capital expenditures for the construction and equipping of school buildings are generally financed by bond issues. Legal controls on bond issues include: (1) purposes for which bonds may be issued; (2) length of term; (3) type of bonds; (4) maximum rate of interest that may be paid; and (5) the requirement that the bond issue be approved by the voters of the district.

Accounting, Auditing, and Reporting

A fairly high degree of uniformity has been achieved in basic procedures and classifications used in school financial accounting. Although school accounting in the United States draws on the basic principles of commercial and general governmental accounting, a distinctive set of accounts adapted to the school enterprise has been developed. In several of the states the basic accounting forms are prescribed by the state administration and are required to be used in all school districts. All states require financial reports from local school systems and the United States Office of Education receives financial reports from all states.

Accounting for Receipts

Receipts are classified (1) as revenue or non-revenue, (2) by political subdivision from which received, and (3) by specific source of the money. Revenue receipts include all receipts which do not decrease assets or increase indebtedness. The principal sources are local taxes, state grants, tuition received from other districts, interest on deposits and investments, and contributions or gifts. Non-revenue receipts are those which decrease assets or increase indebtedness. Included are receipts from sale of property, insurance adjustments, sale of bonds, and short-term loans.

Another classification includes receipts from sale of textbooks, instructional supplies, school lunches, athletics, and other school activities or entertainments. Receipts from these sources are used to provide the respective services and are classified as revolving funds. Profits derived from such services and used for general operational purposes may be classified as revenue receipts.

In some states receipts must be segregated into separate funds and used only for designated purposes. Examples of such funds are salary funds, building funds, and bond funds. Best practices indicate that only three types of funds are necessary, namely, current operating funds to include all receipts used for operating expenses, bonds for the purpose of amortising bonded debt, and building-construction funds.

The basic forms for accounting for receipts are the receipts ledger with the appropriate headings and subdivisions, and the treasurer's record of receipts. The latter is a simple item record showing source and amount received. A record of deposits may also be kept showing the amount deposited in the banks which serve the school system.

Accounting for Expenditures

The basic classifications of expenditures are (1) current operation, (2) capital outlay, and (3) debt service. The commonly used subdivisions of these classifications are as follows:—

Current Operational Expense

Administration or general control. Instruction. Operation of buildings. Maintenance of buildings. Auxiliary services (e.g., health service, pupil transportation, and community services). Fixed charges.

Capital Outlay

Construction of new buildings and additions and alterations of old buildings. Purchase of land. Purchase of equipment other than replacements.

Debt Service

Principal and interest on bonded indebtedness.
Principal and interest on short-term operating loans.

Within the categories listed above expenditures are classified by object and location. The principal object classifications are (1) salaries and wages, (2) supplies and materials, (3) contractual services, and (4) non-personal services. Such items as insurance premiums, taxes, rents, payment to pension funds, and tuition payments to other districts are classified as fixed charges. Object classification may be further detailed by use of coded designations of individual items. Classification by location is largely dependent upon the size and complexity of the school system. The common allocations are by major divisions of the school system such as elementary schools, secondary schools, and special schools. In large school systems accounts may be kept by individual schools. Expenditures for administration may be divided on the basis of the various administrative offices and services. The detail of the break-down of school expenditures is dependent on the extent to which budgetary control and cost analyses are desired.

Analyses of Cost

Cost accounting has limited application in school fiscal management as compared with commercial enterprises. It is difficult to relate costs to quality of educational services and virtually impossible to determine the cost of the specific products of education. The cost per pupil in average daily attendance for current operation is the most widely used cost figure. Unit costs of supplies, materials, and equipment are valuable for preparing budget estimates and purchasing. Cost analyses are dependent upon the details of accounting classifications and the accounting services and facilities which are available. In the majority of school systems very little is done in cost accounting. The procedures and definitions used in cost accounting are not sufficiently uniform to afford valid comparisons of costs between school systems.

Internal Accounting

School systems are involved in a wide variety of activities and services not included in the operating accounts. School entertainments, inter-scholastic athletics, bookstores, lunch rooms, and extra-curricular activities involve large amounts of money in many schools. Accounting for these activities and services is usually separated from the basic accounting systems and handled in the individual schools. In some systems accounting control is maintained in the central business office. There is little uniformity in accounting for these services and activities. Generally such accounts are limited to simple records of receipts by source and expenditures by object. Separate budgets may be prepared for each activity or service. The audit of these accounts is usually separate from the audit of operating accounts, especially when the audit is done by state auditors. In only a few states is there any state supervision of the fiscal management of these activities and services.

Auditing

State requirements for auditing of school accounts vary from none to a requirement of an audit in every school system each year. In eleven states the state department of education is responsible for the audit. In thirteen states a state auditing agency makes the school audit. Several states require the audit to be made by public accountants at the expense of the local school systems. In some states, especially in the smaller districts, the audit may be made by committees of citizens selected for that purpose or by a committee of the board which audits the treasurer's books.

The purpose of the audit is to determine that all funds have been properly accounted for, that expenditures conform to legal requirements, and that there has been no misuse or loss of funds. Competent auditing requires a knowledge of the nature of the school business as well as of all the legal regulations which apply to the use of school money. There is general agreement among school finance authorities that the audit should in no way control educational policies or infringe on the discretionary authority of the board of education. The judgment of auditors as to the desirability of school expenditures should not rule over the judgment of the school authorities.

Financial Reports

All states require that an annual report of local school finances be filed with the state department of education. Such reports may vary from simple summaries of receipts and expenditures to detailed statistical reports. In most cases the financial report forms are based on the required accounting systems.

Local reports consist of those made by the administration to the board of education and to the public. Periodic statements of receipts, expenditures, and tax collections are the more important administrative reports. These reports serve to inform the board as to the current financial condition of the school system and provide a basis for budgetary control. Periodic balance statements of assets and liabilities in various fund accounts may also be made. The detail and frequency of administrative reports vary greatly among school systems.

Reports to the public are important in that they provide information to citizens concerning the financial condition and needs of the school system. In some states it is required that expenditures of the school system be published in local newspapers. In many school systems an annual financial report is distributed to taxpayers and school patrons. These reports usually give information concerning the school programme, enrolment statistics, costs compared with other school systems, as well as summaries of receipts, expenditures, and tax-levies. Special reports may be made on construction programmes, bond issues, and salary schedules.

Annual statistical and financial reports are filed by state departments of education with the United States Office of Education. These reports become the basis of many comparative and trend studies and provide a valuable collection of information concerning education in all states. The United States Office of Education publishes a *Biennial Survey of Education* giving the basic financial statistics of state school systems.

Summary

Important trends in the fiscal management of public school systems in the United States may be summarized as follows: —

(1) More adequate procedures in budgeting, accounting, and auditing are being developed. State departments of education, the United States Office of Education, and associations of school superintendents and business officials have been influential in these improvements.

(2) Reorganization of local school districts has resulted in improved local administrative services.

(3) Increased state financial support equalizes the tax burden for schools and increases the financial resources of local school systems. Greater leeway for local autonomy and initiative is a product of more

adequate resources at the disposal of school officials.

(4) Extension of state supervisory services and administrative assistance to local systems has resulted in improved fiscal management.

(5) There has been a marked increase in organized citizen participation in formulation of school policies and development of school programmes. Parent-teacher associations are active in many schools. Several thousand local citizens' committees and a number of state citizen committees have been organized under the leadership of the National Citizens Commission for Public Schools, which is a voluntary organization of citizens established to promote public participation in educational affairs. Greater attention is being given to public relations in most school systems, with particular emphasis on dissemination of information about the schools. Problems of finance receive major attention in these public relations programmes.

(6) Numerous research studies conducted by universities, state departments of education, and the United States Office of Education have contributed much to the understanding of fiscal problems and the development of effective administrative practices.

While fiscal management is deficient in many respects in the majority of local school systems, much improvement has been made in recent years. Satisfactory procedures have been developed in all areas of fiscal management and are being employed to an increasing degree, especially in the larger school systems.

RALEIGH W. HOLMSTEDT.

BIBLIOGRAPHY

1. National Conference of Professors of Educational Administration, *Problems and Issues in Public School Finance* (New York, N.Y., Bureau of Publications, Teachers College, 1952).

2. Paul R. Mort and Walter C. Reusser, *Public School Finance* (New York, N.Y., Bureau of Publications, Teachers College, 1951).

3. The Council of State Governments, *The Forty-eight State School Systems* (Chicago, Illinois, The Council, 1949).

4. Fred F. Beach and Robert F. Wills, *The State and Education* (U.S. Department of Health Education and Welfare, Office of Education, Washington, D.C., U.S. Government Printing Office, 1955).

5. Fred F. Beach, *The Functions of State Departments of Education* (Federal Security Agency, Office of Education, Misc. No. 12, Washington, D.C., U.S. Government Printing Office, 1950).

6. Edgar L. Morphet and Erick I. Lindman, *Public School Finance Programs of the Forty-eight States* (Federal Security Agency, Office of Education, Circular 274, Washington, D.C., U.S. Government Printing Office, 1950).

7. U.S. Office of Education, *Financial Accounting for Public Schools*, Circular 204 (Washington, D.C., U.S. Government Printing Office, 1948).

8. R. W. Holmstedt, "State Control of Public School Finance" (*Bulletin of the School of Education, Indiana University*, Volume XVI, No. 2, Bloomington, Indiana, 1940).

CHAPTER EIGHT

The Fiscal Management of New York University

NEW YORK UNIVERSITY is a large, complex, metropolitan, private institution governed by a self-perpetuating council of thirty-two members. Founded at Washington Square in 1831 as a school where " the artisan and the tradesman shall be as welcome as the children of the rich " and " on a liberal foundation, which shall correspond with the spirit and wants of our age ", the University now has thirteen schools, colleges, and divisions located in six geographical centres of instruction from Wall Street to the Bronx.

The University family is made up of four thousand faculty members and administrative officers, seventeen hundred clerical workers, and eight hundred plant employees. It enrols some fifty thousand students annually, of whom thirty-seven thousand are in attendance during any one term of the academic year. It is housed in buildings and grounds worth $45 million.

The chief administrative officers are the Chancellor, the Executive Vice Chancellor, and four Vice Chancellors: Vice Chancellor and Comptroller, Vice Chancellor and Secretary, Vice Chancellor for University Development, and Vice Chancellor for Medical Affairs. Other administrative officers of the central staff are the Director of the Budget, Business Manager, Bursar, Supervisor of Property, Director of Personnel, Supervisor of Purchases, Dean of Admissions and Registrar, and Director of Libraries.

Fiscal management in a privately supported university—in purpose, function, and organization—is not unlike that in public management. Indeed, there are striking similarities: in purpose, each is a non-profit institution; in function, each is engaged primarily in providing services. But there is a significant difference. The revenues of the privately supported university are not derived from taxes. It is similar to the large industrial corporation in that its revenues come from the sale of services—education—and from investments and the management of its properties. But the fundamental difference in this instance is that the university is a non-profit institution.

The organization for fiscal management at New York University is headed by the Chancellor, who is responsible, through the Council Committee on Finance, to the Council of the University. The Executive Vice Chancellor, as the chief academic officer of the University, is immediately responsible to the Chancellor for educational management in all its aspects, including fiscal administration. Budgetary administration is located in the Office of the Budget, which is a part of the Executive Vice Chancellor's office, rather than in the business or finance office.

The Director of the Budget, responsible immediately to the Chancellor and the Executive Vice Chancellor, is charged with the preparation and administration of the annual budget. Determination of budgetary policy is made by the Chancellor and the Executive Vice Chancellor, together with the Director of the Budget, and in conformity with the attitude of the Council.

The Office of the Vice Chancellor and Comptroller, responsible to the Chancellor and the Executive Vice Chancellor, has the function of business and fiscal administration. It contains the Offices of Business Manager, Bursar, Director of Accounts, Director of Personnel (non-faculty), Supervisor of Property, Supervisor of Purchases, and the University Auditor.

Fiscal management in a private university must be in the service of the educational programme. This is to say that fiscal administration exists only for the purpose of ensuring the fullest approximation of the primary goal of a university—the education of the youth who enters its doors. The philosophy of the financial officers of the university must be oriented to the primacy of educational values and to the constructive use of available funds for educational programmes.

Fiscal management, therefore, divides itself functionally into (1) providing adequate funds with which to realize, in so far as possible, the educational goals of the university, (2) allocating available funds among the several divisions in accordance with educational needs, and (3) supervising or controlling expenditures to the end that objectives are obtained.

Budgeting

A budget is a plan, a guide for discharging the various service obligations of the university and for providing funds to finance these services. It is through the budget that the Chancellor gives form and direction to the University's full educational programme. Budgeting in a university is essentially a form of applied economics, since it requires the allocation of scarce resources among competing needs. The budget process encompasses budget preparation, approval by the Council, and administration of the approved budget.

Income

Revenues are extremely important in a university. They are uniquely so in a privately supported institution. The kind of educational programme offered—its nature, quality, direction, purpose, and, finally, its value—depends largely upon the available revenues and upon their use. As resources are scarce in relation to need, programmes both old and new must be assessed from two points of view: (1) their value to the educational programme, and (2) how they can be financed.

Revenue sources in the privately supported, as distinct from the publicly supported, university are well established: tuition, endowment, gifts, and miscellaneous income from special services and activities such as government contracts, foundation grants, and fees from special programmes. The order of importance varies with the institution. New York University is especially concerned with tuition revenue, as this is the source of approximately one-half of its total annual income.

The Director of the Budget, in conference with the dean of each college or school and the Registrar, estimates the number of students for the ensuing year and the net tuition to be paid by each. When this process is completed for all units, the total of expected income from tuition has been determined.

Many factors will be considered at these conferences, among them actual enrolment for the last concluded year, estimated enrolment for the current year, and the difference in past and present enrolments, if any. In addition, factors for the next eighteen months will be considered: the number of high school graduates, the educational programme to be offered and its holding power, particularly beyond the freshman year; facilities for classroom instruction.

Revenues from endowment are relatively easy to determine. Since institutional investments are usually conservative, income from this source tends to be stable, fluctuating only in the total of endowments. Income from gifts during the year will be more difficult to estimate. There is usually a hard core of revenue from this source which does not decrease materially. However, an intensified drive may be planned among the alumni and friends of the university for a particular year. This may well increase income from gifts in that year. Gifts fall into two major categories—unrestricted and restricted. Every university prefers the former, for the obvious benefits which derive to it by being able to use this income to support programmes which, in the judgment of the administrative officers, need it most.

Miscellaneous and special income is predictable with a fair degree of accuracy. Its sources are fairly well-known: conferences, special institutes, the operation of clinics, testing services, book-store sales, and auxiliary services.

Government- and industry-sponsored research has become a significant item in many university budgets in the last fifteen years. Slightly
over 20 per cent of New York University's income comes from this
source. In estimating this income, the chief questions for speculation
are the level at which the government is expected to operate and
whether the University will be awarded contracts at the level of the
current year.

STATEMENT OF CONSOLIDATED INCOME

FOR THE YEAR ENDED JUNE 30TH, 1955

Endowments	$1,039,236.94
Students' fees, less refunds . . .	15,801,913.87
Dormitory rents	115,371.91
Gifts (including research grants) . .	2,634,909.68
Services to patients, etc. . . .	4,700,255.38
Research	6,884,849.44
Other income	3,169,625.84
TOTAL INCOME	$34,346,163.06

Expenditures

On the expenditure side, appropriations will ultimately conform to
the policy of the University administration and the Council. If the
policy decision is for a balanced budget, then expenditures may not
exceed revenues. On the other hand, it may be the policy to protect
programmes with a view to balancing the budget over a period of time,
though not annually. In the latter case, a determination must be made
as to a reasonable deficit, one which can be managed within a specified
period. All private universities in the United States have faced this
question in the last five years because of declining enrolments following the veteran ' bulge ', 1946–50, an inflationary economy, and high
fixed charges. In most instances, and New York University has been
no exception, there has been deficit financing. The alternatives are
reduction of programme, reduction of staff, increase in tuition, increasing revenues from gifts and other sources. The first two are not
acceptable as constructive policies. The third may or may not be
effective, and the fourth may or may not materialize.

Some privately supported universities operate on the policy that
each school, college, or division must carry itself at all times. New
York University, however, looks at the total University and the total
educational programme. It seeks to balance the University budget,
not that of each unit.

Preparation of the Expenditure Budget

The expense budget is prepared by the Director of the Budget after general policies have been determined in conference with the Chancellor and the Executive Vice Chancellor. Policies for the ensuing year are transmitted to the dean of each division. These instructions, or guide lines, will indicate, for example, whether a general salary increase is in pattern; changes in the total budget or in specific items such as printing and publications from the current year; salary policy on clerical and laboratory staffs; purchase of laboratory equipment or plant alterations.

Budget conferences begin annually early in December and continue through the first week in February. The first conferences are with the responsible administrative officers in the central administration : the Vice Chancellors, Business Manager, and Director of Libraries. As these are chiefly expense budgets, with little or no income potential, they can be prepared within established policy for the current year, to be reduced or increased as required by the situation.

The Director begins budget conferences for the schools with the academic deans shortly after January 1st. Since there are thirteen major schools, and the conference with each dean may last three hours, this process will continue for some four weeks. Each dean prepares requests for appropriations with substantiations generally in line with the instructions, but always pushing askings to the maximum to be allowed or slightly above. In the budget conference the diffences, if any, will be discussed and agreement as to the amount to be approved will be reached. Obviously, there will be times when it is not easy to reach agreement, especially if the total for the current year is being reduced.

After the final conference, each dean formally submits the budget for his unit to the Director of the Budget, who in turn forwards it to the Director of Accounts for consolidation into a total University budget. If the consolidated total for the University, both in estimated income and estimated expense, is within established policy, the University budget is submitted to the Chancellor for presentation to the Finance Committee of the Council. If approved, it is presented to the Council at its March meeting. The budget for the ensuing fiscal year —July 1st to June 30th—is thus put to bed.

The chief items of expense in the University budget are instructional costs : salaries, libraries, laboratories, and research; general charges of administration : amortization of bonds, interest, and staff benefits; plant maintenance; and office expenses : clerical salaries, student record recording, supplies, and so on.

STATEMENT OF CONSOLIDATED EXPENSE
FOR THE YEAR ENDED JUNE 30TH, 1955

Instruction	$23,486,148.41
General charges	5,046,655.36
Plant	3,465,440.39
Office	2,393,885.11
TOTAL EXPENSE	$34,392,129.27

Administration of the Budget

The chief administrative officer is the Director of the Budget. The general practice of budgetary administration requires, first, that each school, department, and office will confine its expenditures to the appropriations in its approved budget; and, second, that an appropriation is an authorization but not an order to spend the sum appropriated; third, that the total is fixed, but, upon approval by higher authority, transfers may be made as between objects or functions.

The first and primary responsibility for budgetary administration rests with the dean of each school and the head of each spending office. It is the dean, together with his department heads, who must determine needs for instruction, the number of courses and sections to be taught, and the available personnel to meet this need. In an institution with nearly four thousand members on the teaching staff, and with the number of faculty dependent upon enrolment, there must be many new appointments for part-time teaching each year, as well as for full-time. The budget of each school provides for the regular full-time staff, new positions, and makes appropriations for unfilled positions. In the day-to-day administration of the appropriation for instructional salaries, the deans recommend appointments to the Executive Vice Chancellor and the Director of the Budget. This will be a matter of routine for the part-time teaching staff, where rates of pay have been established. In the case of a full-time member to be added to the staff, the specific salary to be paid may become significant. In all such instances, there is prior discussion of the recommendation by the dean with the Executive Vice Chancellor and the Director of the Budget. In short, the Office of the Executive Vice Chancellor, and especially the Director of the Budget, are directly and immediately concerned with the administration of the instructional appropriation in all school budgets.

On the other hand, the expenditure of appropriations for laboratory equipment and supplies is the immediate responsibility of the department head and the dean, the only limitation being the total sum of the appropriation. However, in the instance of a piece of equipment costing some thousands of dollars, this will be brought to the attention of the Budget Director, inasmuch as the expenditure may have significant budgetary consequences before the end of the fiscal year, or it may require re-allocation of funds within the budget.

The budget for each school and administrative office includes an appropriation for clerical staff. Although the dean or the head of the office bears immediate responsibility for its expenditure, the Director of Personnel, a University officer responsible to the Vice Chancellor and Comptroller, has over-all supervision. In accordance with established policies, he approves salary increases, promotions, and fixes salaries for new appointees within salary classifications and within the limits of the specific appropriation.

Throughout the year and after the budget has been approved, decisions concerning it have to be made. For example, income may be less than estimated, requiring a tightening-up on expenditure. New or expanded programmes may be prepared, requiring budgetary changes. An increase in utility rates—telephone, electricity, fuel oil, coal—may call for reconsideration of the plant budget. The cost of construction and alterations may increase because of general wage increases or cost of materials; thus it is necessary to re-evaluate the need and determine whether to increase the budget or restrict the alteration programme. A dean may decide he would rather spend more on the clerical staff and less on teaching staff. This action requires the approval of the Budget Director for a transfer of funds from one purpose to another. The general policy is to require all deans and administrative officers to live within the totals for his unit, with considerable freedom to transfer from one specific appropriation within his budget to another during the course of the year. Obviously this policy is affected by the current status of the budget. It is administered more strictly when income is low, and especially if it is less than the sum estimated.

Budgetary accounting is an integral part of the accounting system. This function is performed by the Director of Accounts in the Office of the Vice Chancellor and Comptroller. A monthly financial control statement, prepared by the Director of Accounts, gives the financial picture of the University and is presented to the Finance Committee of the Council at its regular monthly meeting. This statement reflects the changed income condition, up or down, expenditures, the rate of expenditures compared with the previous year, and the relative financial position of the University at the end of each month throughout the fiscal year. The chief administrative officer of each spending unit receives monthly control statements for his unit by the tenth of every month.

Maximum effectiveness of financial management is achieved only when it is tied in closely with all other aspects of management. Fiscal officers must be alert to the value of the information they bring to the total management of the University. The decisions the Chancellor and Executive Vice Chancellor are required to make on educational programmes, purchase of new property, and so forth, should not be made without information on the financial condition of the University. Approximations, available in time to aid in this decision-making, are better than final and accurate reports that arrive only to have historical value.

Management of the University Staff

The over-all administration of policies concerning the instructional and research staff, such as appointments, salaries, staff benefits and tenure, rests with the Executive Vice Chancellor, who is primarily responsible for academic affairs.

The selection of teaching staff of the rank of Associate Professor and above is the combined responsibility of the head of the department, the dean of the college, and the Executive Vice Chancellor. Appointment to the lower ranks, instructor and assistant professor, is usually left to the heads of departments and the deans, as are all part-time appointments.

Administration of personnel policies for the non-teaching staff, clerical and supervisory employees, is the task of the Director of Personnel, who is responsible to the chief business officer, the Vice Chancellor and Comptroller. Also, all policies relating to the plant staff—elevator operators, porters, guards, and so on—are administered by the Supervisor of Property in the same office.

Faculty Salaries

University policy for faculty salaries is to provide a salary scale which will compare favourably with the best institutions in the country. That is to say, the minimum in each rank must be such as to attract the best to the faculty, and the maximum high enough to hold the best. Finally, it must be such as to provide adequate compensation for services rendered. The current salary scale is:

Instructors	.	.	.	.	$3,600–$5,000
Assistant professors	.	.	.	5,000– 7,000
Associate professors	.	.	.	6,500– 9,500
Professors	.	.	.	9,000–16,000

The salaries are for the academic year of nine months, though they are paid over twelve months. The summer months—June, July, and August—belong to the faculty member. Many are engaged in the summer sessions of the several schools of the University for extra compensation, others engage in activities outside the University, such as research, consulting, writing, and varied services to business, industry, the professions, and government.

New York University, located at the centre of a large metropolis and committed to a constructive and extensive programme of service to the community, has at its doors a vast resource of specialists upon which to draw for part-time instruction in selected fields such as business, corporate finance, indeed all the professions. The curriculum of the several schools is enriched and the educational service to the students, especially in the professional schools, is greatly improved by this practice. The University faculty thus includes many such persons who serve on a part-time basis for part-time compensation.

University salary policy does not provide for annual increments. Except in those years when increases across the board are announced, salary increments are on merit and limited by available revenues to be appropriated to this end. Always, even in deficit years, a number of the full-time staff will be given increases.

Staff Benefits

The ' fringe benefits ', as defined by unions in their bargaining with industry, have been rather fully extended to the faculty. In retirement pay, the University co-operates with the Teachers Insurance and Annuity Association of America in funding retirements plans at the rate of 15 per cent of the annual base salary, with the University contributing 7·5 per cent and the faculty member 7·5 per cent. When the government by law extended its Old Age and Survivors' Insurance to educational institutions, the New York University faculty approved the integration of TIAA and OASI at the combined rate of 15 per cent. These benefits are extended likewise to non-teaching faculty, such as persons on sponsored research projects. Participation is required of all full-time faculty in the rank of assistant professor or above; also of instructors with three years of continuous service to the University or those who have reached the age of 30. Hospital and medical insurance is available to all full-time faculty and staff through the Associated Hospital Service of New York at low monthly subscription rates.

Tenure may be acquired by all full-time faculty in the ranks of professor and associate professor. Appointment to the rank of assistant professor includes no right to permanent or continuous tenure; such appointments or re-appointments shall not, as a matter of general policy, exceed six years. All others—instructors, clinical and adjunct professors—are appointed for one year only and with no tenure rights.

Retirement is mandatory at age 65 for all administrative officers of the University. For the teaching staff, 65 is the retirement age except that under certain conditions, primarily programme requirements or need for his special services, a member of the teaching staff may be retained on a year-to-year appointment with a part-time teaching schedule. Usually, the professor will not be re-appointed for more than two years, but in no instance may he teach after age 70.

In order to permit a professor more readily to adjust to retirement, the University policy provides that an officer of instruction who has attained tenure may, one year prior to his 63rd birthday, elect to enter upon half-time service at half-salary effective September 1st following his 63rd birthday. He may continue on such basis through August 31st following his 67th birthday, at which time he shall be retired. The faculty member may also, one year prior to his 64th birthday, elect to enter upon half-time service at half-salary and continue on such basis through August 31st following his 66th birthday, at which time he shall be retired.

Clerical Staff

The University clerical staff of some seventeen hundred is distributed in numerous offices—some with a large number and others with only one secretary. Some are employed in the business offices and others in the offices of the academic departments of the several colleges. The Office of the Director of Accounts employs some seventy persons in this general category, the Office of the Bursar over a hundred; Dean of Admissions and Registrar some one hundred and eighty; there are over a hundred academic departments in the several schools each with one or more clerical workers; the offices of the deans and the research officers throughout the University require large numbers.

The University salary policy for clerical staff and junior administrators is based upon the current rates in the community. Each year the Director of Personnel studies these and brings to the budget conferences comparable data on which decisions of salary policy are made for the next fiscal year. In an effort to relate the clerical staff to the educational objective of the University, each full-time clerical employee is given remission of tuition for eight points of instruction per term, including the summer session.

There are two administrative groups in this general category who do not perform clerical functions: the Senior Administrative Group, including job-titles of building superintendent, supervisor, radio and television personnel, public information officers such as news and copy writers and editors in the University Press; the Junior Administrative Group, including those second in command to the above or in smaller offices.

The 'fringe benefits' of the faculty have been extended to the clerical staff with the exception of tenure. They are entitled to the plans for hospitalization and medical care, group insurance, and after one full year of employment to enter the retirement plan. Unlike the faculty, however, these benefits are voluntary.

Management of Buildings and Grounds

The task of managing buildings and grounds is extraordinarily complicated at New York University. The University's hundred and seven buildings are located in six different geographical locations in the city. The University Heights campus, of forty-six acres and thirty-nine buildings, is in the tradition of the campus college. The buildings are chiefly four-storey walk-up. The Washington Square centre consists of twenty-six buildings, of which sixteen are ten or more storeys in height and consequently have elevators. As these have been assembled over the years and many of them converted to educational use, the task of management is increased. The Dental Centre has seven buildings and the Medical Centre two. The Graduate School of Business Administration is located near Wall Street, and the Institute of Fine Arts is located in East 80th Street.

The management of this vast property is the responsibility of the Supervisor of Property, under the direction of the Vice Chancellor and Comptroller. He administers a budget of $3½ million annually. His staff is composed of building superintendents, plant employees, elevator operators, porters, guards, cleaning staff, engineers, painters, carpenters, electricians—indeed, all of the jobs to be found in a large business.

Painting, repairs to buildings, equipment, and its replacement are on a schedule. For example, painting of existing classrooms, offices, and laboratories is done on a schedule of two, three, and five years. This makes it possible to budget rather successfully at a certain level annually. The sum for painting on this schedule ranges from $75,000 per year up. Although some universities maintain their own crew of painters, the experience at New York University, where both systems have been used, is that contracting for annual paint jobs is more satisfactory and less expensive. In the first place, the painting of classrooms and offices should occur when university classes are not in session. This means moving in a large crew of workmen for relatively short periods of time. Classroom painting is an integral part of the instructional programme. From a purely business standpoint, it might be less expensive to standardize the painting of an institution into one or at least two colours. However, New York University provides multiple colours, with no two adjoining classrooms having the same colour of walls. Students and faculty respond favourably, even enthusiastically, to this.

Management of the plant involves the use of existing buildings, that is, the assignment of space. In order that this be related to the educational programme of the University, the assignment of all buildings used for educational purposes is in the hands of a university administrative committee consisting of the Director of the Budget as chairman, together with the Dean of Admissions and Registrar and the Supervisor of Property. The Committee reviews regularly assignments of space to classrooms, laboratories, offices, research, storage, and indeed for all purposes. It is necessary for the Committee to allocate classrooms to the several schools on the basis of their need. If there are not sufficient rooms to meet the need for a given hour, the Committee has to make a decision as to whether programmes will be reduced to available space or additional space will be rented in the neighbourhood.

Alterations of existing space must be approved by this Committee. The general principle, though exceptions are made, is that classroom space will not be reduced in order to make way for increased office use. Every effort is made to utilize available space to the maximum. This frequently requires an analysis of educational programmes to determine if they may function effectively at hours other than the peak ones from 9 a.m. to 1 p.m. and 6 to 10 p.m.

The management of the University's commercial property, which consists largely of apartment houses, is in the hands of the Business Manager under the Vice Chancellor and Comptroller. These properties may not become liabilities to the institution or to the annual operating budget. Rentals for such apartments are set in line with rentals of equivalent property in the neighbourhood. In the management of such rental properties, the University maintains a real-estate rental office, staffed by experienced rental agents whose sole job it is to keep the apartments rented and to supervise the maintenance of each property.

Purchasing

Purchasing throughout the University is centralized in the Office of the Supervisor of Purchases responsible to the Vice Chancellor and Comptroller. This is a large operation in volume and diversity of articles, and not inconsiderable in dollars. It ranges from the purchase of pencils and paper to automobiles and trucks; from dental chairs to executive office furniture; from dormitory beds to laboratory chemicals; from typewriters to an electronic computer such as New York University's 'Univac'. The expenditure in the average year approximates a million dollars, exclusive of purchases for plant alterations.

Purchase requisitions are initiated by the primary user, for example, the head of the chemistry department. With the approval of the dean or proper administrative authority, the requisition goes to the Purchasing Department. If the Director of Accounts certifies to the availability of adequate funds to cover the requisition, the purchase is made.

The Supervisor of Purchases buys in a competitive market and will secure competitive bids from at least three vendors in the instance of special purchases. He has freedom to select the vendor and determine the brand. In regular annual purchases, the office has established continuing relationships with the faculty user and with individual suppliers. Thus, for many items the purchasing transaction becomes routine. A central stores department is maintained by the Purchasing Department for regulation office supplies.

Faculty members are not permitted to negotiate on their own initiative for supplies, services, equipment, or alterations for their departments. The Purchasing Office maintains a constant study of prices and quality of all standard items used in the University. It seeks to hold down costs while improving the quality of items and services to faculty and students.

The purchase of office and laboratory equipment follows a fairly fixed procedure. In the case of office equipment—typewriters, desks, and adding machines—a schedule of replacement has been established. The number of new machines to be purchased in the next fiscal year, if the schedule is maintained, is known at budget-making time. The only question at this point is a budgetary decision as to whether the money is available to cover the estimated cost.

In so far as possible, appropriations for all additional equipment other than replacements will be included in the budget. But inevitably there are items to be purchased which were not anticipated. Sometimes this is the result of new programmes producing new revenue, but in other instances it is simply an additional item required by an existing programme. In the latter event, a decision has to be made whether to eliminate certain items already provided for in the budget or to increase the budget to take care of this additional unanticipated expenditure.

In conclusion, fiscal management of a privately supported university is a complex of responsibilities, frustrations, and rewards, resting upon a foundation of scarcity of funds, yet set in a framework of insistent and ever-expanding aspirations.

RAY F. HARVEY.

CHAPTER NINE

Church Schools and Training Colleges

ONE of the outstanding features in the history of education over the last hundred years has been the increasing control of education by the state. In most countries in Europe the state had become paramount by 1850, and highly centralized state systems assume control over the education of their future citizens. Where the religion and the people have been closely identified, there has been little difficulty or controversy in the transfer from voluntary bodies to the state, as for example in Norway, which is predominantly Evangelical Lutheran, and in Spain, predominantly Roman Catholic. But where there have been powerful religious and anti-religious or anti-clerical elements, controversy has been fiercely extended over many years, not only on doctrinal or denominational grounds but also on the principle underlying the old proverb "that he who pays the piper calls the tune". Under a system—or lack of it—in which non-compulsory education is supplied by voluntary bodies, the availability of education is governed by the willingness to pay for it by producers and consumers. Under a state system the tendency is towards universal, compulsory, and free education. The strain on the finances of the voluntary body, usually a religious denomination, becomes too great, and increased financial aid by the state inevitably brings with it increased control.

That this control of education by the state was slow to develop in England (and, indeed, did not reach its final stage until the Education Act of 1944) finds a partial explanation in the fierce controversies between the Anglicans and the Nonconformists, who between them controlled secondary and elementary education, and undertook what training of teachers was considered necessary. In 1870, for example, there were 6,724 Church of England elementary schools, and 2,074 other voluntary schools, denominational or undenominational. Long before England slowly evolved the concept and realization of the state, the churches were strongly entrenched in education. The secularization of their schools was resisted (a) because the two religious parties were bitterly opposed to an educational compromise offered by the state, and (b) they had sufficient financial resources to maintain their position. With the Education Act of 1870, however, the state took the first important step towards establishing control : this led to compulsory education (1876) and inevitably and eventually to free education. And although the expansionist period of voluntary (i.e., church-controlled) education continued for at least twelve years after the 1870 Act, the financial strain imposed on the churches in their provision of buildings, equipment and teachers became too great for them to preserve their independence in view of the state's development, and its development of compulsory, free education.

Even as early as 1833 a grant of £20,000 [1] had been voted by Parliament to assist the National Society and the British and Foreign School Society in " the erection of School Houses, for the Education of the Poorer Classes ", and with it the beginning of the government inspection of schools, although on a denominational basis, until 1870, for the voluntary bodies nominated the inspectors.

Education Acts and Voluntary Schools

The three great Education Acts of 1870, 1902, and 1918 aroused fierce denominational controversy, to a large extent avoided in 1944 because of the careful preparation for a compromise before the Act was debated in Parliament. The three main reasons for this controversy were :

(a) the interested parties insisted on religious education but differed violently on the form it should take;

(b) the voluntary system was so firmly established and owned so many schools that its co-operation was essential in the over-all planning of popular education. Never at any time has the ' climate ' of opinion allowed a Parliament to discuss the complete secularization of schools;

(c) essential as was the incorporating of the voluntary system into the state system, the state has had increasingly to subsidize the voluntary schools, for the continual raising of standards by the state imposed expenditure quite beyond the financial resources of the voluntary bodies. The controversy mentioned in (a) is closely linked with this, mainly because of the objections of the Nonconformists to the subsidizing of denominational schools (Anglican, but also, increasingly, Roman Catholic) out of public funds.

The relations between church and state have thus been a major issue in educational politics ever since the state began to be aware of its responsibilities.

The present administrative and financial agreement between the central authority and the voluntary bodies was embodied in the 1944 and 1946 Education Acts and subsequent Amending Acts, of which the chief is the Education (Miscellaneous Provisions) Act of 1953. The development of this agreement can be traced through previous Acts

---

[1] £1 = $2.80 approximately.

over the last century or so, but it is so complicated in administrative detail that at least two detailed guides [2] have been published, one for L.E.A.s and the other for the voluntary bodies. Only the broad outlines of the agreement can therefore be given here.

Excluding the small number of 'Special Agreement' voluntary schools, a product of the Education Act of 1936, voluntary schools of all denominations are placed in the two categories of (a) 'Aided' and (b) 'Controlled'.

(a) An 'Aided' school is a voluntary school the managers or governors of which have satisfied the Minister that they are able and willing, with the assistance of the maintenance contribution payable by him under the Act, to defray the expenses which would fall to be borne by them under the Act.

(b) A 'Controlled' school is a voluntary school the managers or governors of which are unable or unwilling to defray the expenses which would fall to be borne by them under the Act.

The main divisions of responsibility and control are as follows:

Aided School

(i) The governing body is composed of two-thirds foundation managers and one-third LEA appointments.

(ii) The LEA is responsible for all expenses of maintaining the school except for expenditure on altering school *buildings* to conform to the prescribed standard. This falls on the managers or governors, but the Minister will pay 50 per cent of such expenditure if approved by him.

(iii) Religious worship and instruction are under the control of the governing body, but parents can withdraw their children from both.

(iv) The governing body appoints the teachers, with certain sanctions by the LEA. It has the exclusive right to dismiss a teacher appointed by them to give religious instruction if in this respect he is unsuitable or inefficient.

Controlled School

(i) The governing body is composed of one-third foundation managers and two-thirds LEA appointments.

(ii) The LEA is responsible for all expenses of maintaining the school, including the cost of altering school buildings to conform to prescribed standards.

(iii) Religious *worship* must be carried out according to the provisions of the trust deed, religious *instruction* according to the 'agreed syllabus'. But religious instruction according to the trust deed may be given in not more than two periods a week, at the request of parents.

(iv) The appointment and dismissal of all teachers rests with the LEA, including teachers reserved to give religious instruction according to the trust deed. The appointment of a 'reserved' teacher is subject to the approval of the governing body, who may also require the LEA to dismiss him *qua* 'reserved' teacher.

---

[2] Alexander and Barraclough, *Country and Voluntary Schools* (Councils and Education Press, 2nd edn., 1953); Laidler, *Voluntary Schools* (The National Society and the S.P.C.K.).

In 1944 this compromise was rightly thought to be reasonable and generous : it was also hoped that the solution had settled the problem which had so bedevilled educational politics. Serious problems have, however, arisen over the last twelve years. The tremendous rise in costs, combined with the decline in parochial and congregational enthusiasm for denominational education, has made it increasingly difficult for the churches to maintain the ' aided ' schools and to bring them up to the prescribed standards. Many ' aided ' schools have, as a result, become controlled or fully maintained or, particularly in small villages, been closed, and it has been beyond the financial resources of the churches to build sufficient schools to meet the needs of a greatly increased child-population. The churches built the schools in the nineteenth century, the L.E.A.s in the twentieth. The comparative figures are significant :

	Voluntary Schools	LEA Schools
1938	10,533	10,563
1947	11,625	16,520
1951	11,107	16,846
1953	10,893	17,432

The Roman Catholic community has continued to expand in education, chiefly because it was late in the field of elementary education and because the agreements have given it substantial help. It is increasingly insistent on a revision of the compromise, because of the enormous burden placed upon its parishes in providing schools, and there exists, perhaps, a greater sense of urgency among them than in many Anglican parishes. They point out insistently that they are contributing twice over to a system of education which should be wholly a national responsibility.

Secondary Education

The other great problem which faces the voluntary bodies is the provision of secondary education. It must be remembered that the vast majority of voluntary schools were ' elementary ' schools, with an age-range of 5 to 14, and the adoption by the Board of Education of the recommendations of the *Hadow Report* meant the reorganization of elementary schools into primary and ' central ' or ' senior ' schools. The enormous expenditure required in building such schools or in adapting old ones was beyond the voluntary bodies, and although an attempt was made to solve the problem in the Education Act of 1936 with the new category of ' special agreement ' schools, and great strains were borne by the churches in the educational interests of their children, the reorganization was only piecemeal. The problem was aggra-

vated by the Education Act of 1944, which established secondary
education for all and raised the school-leaving age to 15. This has
made the biggest breach in the 'voluntary' position, for, putting
administrative difficulties aside, it is beyond the means of the churches
to provide secondary education for all the children who receive
primary education in their schools, although, in many dioceses, some
very fine secondary modern schools have been built.

The Training Colleges

The need for trained and educated teachers was realized in the early
nineteenth century only when it became obvious that the whole
system of elementary education would break down without them.
There were not enough teachers, even of the deplorably low personal
and professional qualities which had been accepted. As elementary
education was still in the hands of the voluntary bodies, it was they
who undertook the training of teachers, but from the beginning the
principle of financial help from the state was accepted, either by direct
grant or by the payment of students' fees. The relations, therefore,
between the central authority and the voluntary bodies over teacher
training were never so controversial as those over the schools, and, in
any case, the public have never been so interested in how teachers
were trained as in what they should teach.

The remarkable expansion of teacher training in the nineteenth
century was almost entirely the result of voluntary enthusiasm, and
when the central authority stepped in, in 1902, it was not because the
voluntary colleges had been found wanting but because more trained
teachers were needed than could be supplied on a voluntary basis.

The first training college was founded in 1840 by Dr. Kay, later Sir
James Kay-Shuttleworth, and was transferred in 1843 to the National
Society. The Committee of Council for Education gave a grant of
£10,000 to the National Society and the British and Foreign Bible
Society, and, in 1844, capitation building grants of £50 per place. The
' Queen's Scholarship ' system helped to finance the tuition as well as
the maintenance of the students.

By 1860 the number of voluntary training colleges had increased to
thirty-four, with places for 2,388 students. This was a very small proportion of those actually teaching, but it must be remembered that the
college-trained teachers were the *élite* of the elementary school staff.
The expansion was, however, abruptly checked with Sir Robert Lowe's
Revised Code of 1862, which stopped all building grants to training
colleges. No new colleges were founded between 1860 and 1870, and
total accommodation increased by only one hundred. With the easing
of the financial situation a few years later, however, the expansion

recommenced and, in 1880, the number had increased to forty-three (thirty Church of England, two undenominational, six undenominational and British and Foreign Bible Society, two Wesleyan, and three Roman Catholic), accommodating 3,272 students. In 1890, Day Training Colleges were established, attached to the universities, primarily to provide training without religious tests of entry. These, although not officially inspected as were the other colleges, received advice of Her Majesty's Inspectors, particularly on teaching practices.

By 1900 there were sixty-one voluntary training colleges, including the university Day Training Colleges. They were quite insufficient in number to meet the demands of universal compulsory elementary education and the new secondary education which was introduced by the 1902 Education Act, and although a few voluntary colleges were founded in the next ten years, the voluntary movement had now passed from its expansionist to its conservative phase. Since 1902, the expansion has been with the L.E.A., who were empowered to build and maintain training colleges, with a 75 per cent grant from the Board. By 1913, twenty such colleges were established; by 1937 there were a hundred and nine training colleges (voluntary, L.E.A., and university Departments of Education); by 1953 a hundred and fifty-one, of which only fifty-four are voluntary. As with their schools, the voluntary bodies paid the penalty of being pioneers. The L.E.A. colleges had better buildings and greater facilities for residential education and training than most of the voluntary colleges, whose buildings and facilities reflected only too unhappily the cabined, cribbed, and confined conception of teacher training of the nineteenth century, and the ' trail of cheapness ' which dogged them and the elementary schools they supplied. The exposure of inadequacies made in the *McNair Report* on teachers and youth leaders (1944) applied more to the voluntary than to the L.E.A. colleges.

Post-war Problems

The urgent need for teachers after the war emphasized, if there were any need of emphasis, the essential part played by the voluntary colleges in teacher training. That they had received financial aid from the central authorities since their inception obviated denominational controversies at a time when even greater help had to be given. In 1945, the Government implemented the recommendations of the *McNair Report* with unusual but understanding rapidity. A new arrangement was made by which the Ministry agreed to pay to existing voluntary training colleges capital grants up to 50 per cent of the cost of improvements and major extensions to buildings. In addition, the *per capita* grants were replaced by grants covering the entire cost of tuition and boarding, the Ministry devising a scheme of parents' contributions, according to means, towards the boarding fees.

If it had not been for this, the financial burden on voluntary resources would have been intolerable. Although much has still to be done, the voluntary colleges now compare well with the L.E.A. colleges, but the cost of this great post-war project has imposed a great strain, particularly on the Church of England, which is responsible through the Church Assembly and the National Society for twenty-six of the thirty-four voluntary colleges (the Roman Catholic authorities are responsible for thirteen colleges). The actual cost to the Church of England since 1945 of work completed and in actual progress is over £1 million, representing 50 per cent of the total cost, and a recent report estimates the cost of completing the task at nearly £1½ million at present prices. No doubt the church will undertake it.

The voluntary organizations, in particular the Anglican and Roman Catholic churches, are still a major force in the provision of education. Reform and development in education have never caused a pitched battle between religious and secular education, between the church and the state, and fierce as the controversies have been, they have been largely denominational. The great contribution towards education made by voluntary bodies helped to create the insistence on universal and compulsory education which they lacked the means to satisfy. The relationship between church and state has been a running agreement and not a running fight, but the more the voluntary bodies have accepted, of necessity, financial support from the central authority, the more, inevitably, have they had to yield control in all but strictly denominational matters. Looked at in another way, the voluntary bodies still own and maintain vast properties and contribute heavily of their limited financial resources to the state system of education, and as the state is, even to-day, still not paramount, it might well be argued that each party to the agreement is in obligation to the other.

A. A. EVANS.

CONCISE BIBLIOGRAPHY

W. P. Alexander and F. Barraclough, *County and Voluntary Schools* (Councils and Education Press, 2nd edn., 1953).

J. G. Laidler, *Voluntary Schools* (National Society and Society for Promoting Christian Knowledge, n.d.).

R. Armfelt, *The Structure of English Education* (1955).

C. Birchenough, *History of Elementary Education* (1930).

S. J. Curtis, *History of Education in Great Britain* (2nd edn., 1953).

W. O. Lester Smith, *To Whom Do Schools Belong?* (1945).

McNair Report on Teachers and Youth Leaders (H.M.S.O., 1944).

A. D. C. Peterson, *A Hundred Years of Education* (1952).

CHAPTER TEN

Financial Equalization in the Netherlands

IT might be useful at the outset to agree on terminology. In the Netherlands, schools established and maintained by public authorities (state or municipality) are called ' public ' schools. Schools established and maintained by the churches or by private organizations are called ' voluntary ' schools. It should be noted that by far the greater number of the Protestant voluntary schools in the Netherlands was founded by private organizations, whereas most Roman Catholic schools were founded by the churches. A great part of voluntary education, therefore, is not under the direct influence of the church. Parents, rather than the church, play the important part. Private schools run by private persons for their own benefit are very rare. They are not subsidized.

The State and School

After this preliminary statement, the philosophy governing the relationship between state and school in the Netherlands can be easily defined. Voluntary schools, provided they fulfil certain conditions, can claim financial assistance from public funds to meet the capital expenses as well as current expenses, under the same rules (or to an equivalent extent) as public schools. This system is called the system of financial equalization. We may add at once that what has been described above does not infringe the freedom of the voluntary schools in choice of teachers or of textbooks. Although the standard of the voluntary schools is guaranteed by the public authorities, the state has no authority in their religious affairs.

Such a system is, of course, the outcome of historical developments. Before the time was ripe for this solution, a hard battle in education had to be fought. Financial equalization was first granted to primary education by the Primary Education Act of 1920, which was preceded in 1917 by a change in the Constitution. Since then, the principle has been extended to other branches of education, and its application has been further refined and developed.

In the course of years, a great deal of experience was gained which has been used to improve the system. This is due to the character of the nation. The Dutch are not satisfied with partial solutions or vague arrangements. Our electoral system aims at proportional representation to the last degree of perfection; our taxation system tries to distribute burdens as fairly as possible. And when financial equalization between public and voluntary schools was accepted, the system was worked out in great detail in Acts of parliament and Royal decrees.

Religious and Social Background

Before drawing the main outlines—it is impossible here to give more than a rough sketch—I would like to make some remarks about the religious and social background of the system.

One of the characteristics of the Dutch nation is the great diversity of religious conceptions and political convictions. Speaking roughly, 40 per cent of the population are Protestants, 40 per cent are Roman Catholics, and 20 per cent belong to other denominations or have no religious affiliations. A dominating religious pattern is therefore lacking. In the Second Chamber (House of Commons) the Labour Party and the Roman Catholic Party occupy thirty seats each, two of the Protestant parties combined occupy twenty-one seats, and the rest of the seats are distributed among other, smaller, parties. Here, too, no dominating tendency prevails.

The Dutch are very conscious of this diversity. There is an urge for them to formulate a point of view and to define it in relation to other convictions. The consequences are seen in everyday life. The diversity is apparent in the great number of organizations of different shades of conviction.

After a long history it is now clear that, given this state of affairs, tolerance is the first condition for peaceful co-existence. This implies that any connexion of the state with a particular religious grouping must be avoided. The government does not choose between the various views and philosophies. This emerges clearly in the character of the public schools, whose purpose is described as follows: " School education, by teaching suitable and useful knowledge, is directed towards the development of the intellectual capacities of the children, their physical development, and their training in all Christian and social virtues." The common ground in this case is a practical Christian ethic which everybody can accept. The Primary Education Act further stipulates: " The teacher will refrain from teaching, doing, or allowing anything which conflicts with the respect due to the religious convictions of persons holding other views." We have taken this neutrality, too, to its logical conclusion: sacred history must not appear in the syllabus of the public schools. The churches must take care of that. School facilities are at their disposal for this purpose during school hours.

This cautious official attitude goes hand in hand with freedom of private initiative. Parents must decide in what spirit their child shall be educated at school. They are free to found the kind of schools they favour. This philosophy has also been followed to its logical conclusion. The Dutch have understood that formal freedom can be effective bondage if the means to realize freedom are lacking. In the last century the worker was theoretically free to make a contract where and how he liked; economically, however, he was obliged to accept shockingly bad conditions of employment. Freedom is freedom only if people are economically able to use it. This is not the case if people have to contribute, through taxation, to the cost of the public schools which they reject for their own children, and if they then have to find the resources to maintain a free school of their own choice. This freedom is even more meaningless for people who cannot spare any part of their income for this purpose. Should not the person who is less blessed with worldly goods be able to claim the same freedom as the wealthy?

These are some of the ideas which constitute the background of the system accepted in the Netherlands, a system which guarantees that the freedom of education, laid down in the Constitution in 1848, is *real* freedom.

By accepting this, our country has renounced the attractions of the common school. Our children go to one of several segregated schools. It is possible, in the Netherlands, to start one's life in a Roman Catholic family, to go to a Roman Catholic nursery school, and to spend one's entire school career, including the university, in Roman Catholic institutions. The same is possible for a Protestant child. It is not improbable that during this entire period he never meets a single person who has different convictions. This is the consequence of a principle of freedom consistently applied. Many people in the Netherlands are concerned about this. But few would for that reason abandon a system which they conceive as a consequence of democracy—of all political systems still the least obnoxious.

How does the System work?

Firstly, there are, as we have already mentioned, general conditions which apply equally to public and to voluntary schools. They concern school buildings, syllabi—although the voluntary schools are free in the choice of subjects related to the convictions of the school—number, competence, and legal status of the teaching staff; further, for schools other than primary schools, certain qualifications and school certificates are sometimes required before pupils are admitted. Public and voluntary education, therefore, are of the same standard. Generally there is no difference of social status either, although there are some voluntary schools where parents pay extra fees which are used to appoint more teachers than the number for which subsidies are given, or to improve the equipment of the school. Public and voluntary schools pay the same salaries to their teaching staff. There is no competition in this respect.

Reviewing the system in further detail, we find a difference between primary education and all other kinds of education. In primary education, the co-operation of the public authorities is acquired automatically, whereas in other fields of education it must be preceded by a decision about the viability of the school.

In what follows, we describe only the primary education system. For other schools there are different regulations, but the spirit in which they are made and applied is the same as that valid for primary education.

If an incorporated institution (e.g., a church) or association is to receive assistance in the foundation of a new primary school, it must, before everything else, provide proof that the school will be attended by :

125 pupils in a municipality of 100,000 or more inhabitants

100 pupils in a municipality of 50,000 to 99,999 inhabitants

75 pupils in a municipality of 25,000 to 49,999 inhabitants

50 pupils in a municipality of fewer than 25,000 inhabitants

A declaration by the parents or the guardians of the children is sufficient for this purpose. Under certain conditions only, the children may be those already attending another school.

The board must further guarantee 15 per cent of the costs of building the school. The school board gets interest on this sum. The guarantee is forfeited if the number of pupils in the school remains far below expectation. If any such case has ever occurred, it must be very exceptional. When the school board makes its request to the municipality with these papers in hand, the municipality is *obliged* to erect a building for the school board or to provide an existing building. There is no question of a judgment on desirability. The building becomes the property of the school association, which, of course, must use it for the purpose for which it was provided. When the system of financial equalization was first introduced, there were many school boards who already possessed buildings which had been erected at their own expense. They receive interest on the estimated value of the buildings.

When the school gets going, the central government indemnifies the school board for the salaries of the obligatory number of teachers, in exactly the same way as it indemnifies the municipal council for the salaries of teachers in public schools. Sometimes a municipality appoints extra teachers to its public schools at its own expense—either class teachers or teachers in certain subjects. In such cases, the school board receives a compensation from the municipal funds for an equivalent number of extra teachers.

The current expenses of the voluntary schools are paid by the municipality in the form of a given amount per pupil. The amount is generally equal to that spent on the public school or schools in that municipality. In special cases, where either the public school or the voluntary school has special liabilities making the amount due according to the regulations too high or too low for the needs of the voluntary school, exceptions can be made. The school board does not receive the compensation as a lump sum to dispose of freely. It has to present accounts of its expenditure to the municipality.

These are some of the main features of the system. Our paper, of course, leaves many questions open. We can say only that all these questions have found their answers in continually developing legislation, to which we may add that appeal is possible—sometimes even in two instances—from each decision of the central government or of the municipality concerning this system of compensation.

Costs of the System

Finally, let us see how the system has worked out. We will present the results mainly in the form of figures: figures about schools, pupils, and cost in terms of the kind of school.

	Primary Public Schools				Primary Denominational Schools			
Year	Number of Schools, %	Number of Pupils, %	Average Size	Costs, per Pupil, in Fls.[1]	Number of Schools, %	Number of Pupils, %	Average Size	Cost, per Pupil, in Fls.[1]
1880	71	75	147	13	29	25	120	0·6
1890	69	70	154	19	31	30	145	0·3
1900	68	69	163	24	32	31	156	5
1910	62	61	170	34	38	39	166	18
1920	56	54	165	115	44	46	170	82
1930	45	38	134	118	55	62	179	90
1940	36	30	138	92	64	70	178	80
1950	34	27	133	199	66	73	184	170
1952	33	28	146	227	67	72	191	201
1954	33	29	161	—	67	71	199	—

[1] £1 = approximately 10·69 florins.

The language of these figures—international and very accurate—should be easily understood. One question which is frequently posed we cannot answer precisely, however: Is not this system particularly expensive? The difficulty is that this question presupposes a yard-stick for justified normal expenditure which we do not possess. The system, of course, is considerably more expensive than a system of obligatory public schools which all pupils, without distinction, would attend. We may assume that one school of six hundred pupils is cheaper, per pupil, than three schools of two hundred pupils each, established in three separate buildings. In the Netherlands, however, even leaving aside the question of financial equalization, there is no great enthusiasm for very large schools. Even obligatory public schools could not, therefore, be very large. But they would certainly be larger than at present, where, besides the public schools, there are Protestant, Roman Catholic, and neutral schools, the Protestant schools, indeed, being subdivided among various denominations. It is true that the ultimate question, therefore, is, how much money people are willing to sacrifice for the freedom which this system offers them. Nobody who takes an interest in the development of Dutch education has not sometimes doubted the necessity of founding a certain school. Freedom, in the automatic system described, certainly includes the freedom to misuse. But—as we said before—nobody would be willing to sacrifice this freedom to a system in which diversity is suppressed, or in which there is a chance that the cherished convictions of conscience of the parents would be violated. That is why much discussion goes on in the Netherlands about the development of the system, but the principle is not seriously challenged.

PH. J. IDENBURG.

CHAPTER ELEVEN

Supplementary Services in the United Kingdom

ANY survey of supplementary services using British material as evidence must start by emphasizing that British developments are justified by history more often than by logic. A country planning its adult education, social advisory services, museums, and so on from a fresh start could be expected to use very different methods and institutions. Yet there has been a tendency in many countries to use British experiments either as blue-prints for their own developments or as touchstones for comparative purposes, and this appears to be specially true of adult education. Therefore a critical analysis of the British formula for reconciling peripheral services in education may have some general value.

Traditional Institutions

In the middle of the twentieth century some institutions of adult education can already boast a life of more than a hundred and twenty-five years, like the Mechanics' Institutes and the Adult Schools. Some colleges founded more than a century ago continue either in their original form, like the Working Men's College in Camden Town, London, or as parts of technical colleges or universities. The University Extension movement continues in great vigour, though with some changes in its activities, after a life of about eighty years. The Workers' Educational Association was founded in 1903, and began to undertake tutorial courses of university standard in 1908; yet its programme is currently heavier than it has ever been. During the past fifty years also the local education authorities have been undertaking increasing responsibilities in 'further' education of a professional kind and in 'adult' education of a personal kind. Many examining bodies set up by the technical and commercial professions exercise a profound influence on the type of education offered in most colleges for adults, although they do not conduct courses themselves. In addition, a very large number of voluntary societies—believed to number several thousands—participate in educational and social activity that during recent years has been encouraged by public money. This still does not take account of the general education usually coupled with the specialized training afforded in the armed services, in civil defence, and in such remedial institutions as hospitals and prisons. Nor does it cover the considerable amount of training activity within industrial firms, much of which provides education of general and personal value. Libraries, museums, and public information services are integral parts of the educational system and make demands on the funds available. Churches and trade unions also share in adult education.

It is obvious that such diverse contributors to education differ widely not only in the constituencies they serve and the methods used but in their aims and principles. Some frankly declare that they wish to correct the shortcomings of others, or make good the deficiencies of the statutory school system by a countervailing emphasis. Reconciliation of such differing participants in British education might seem at first sight impossible; but with the passing of time a *modus vivendi* has usually been reached, and partnerships have sometimes been established that have worked harmoniously for years. Therefore the rationalization sought by the Education Act of 1944 and other official planning has not been based upon any rigid system or formula; it has rather taken the form of encouraging desirable developments with money and advice, and of cutting out duplicate activity. Wherever existing institutions have been able to continue or develop a service effectively, they have been retained in a hardly changed form. Few innovations have been made, and most of these are really co-ordinations of existing services.

Organization under the 1944 Education Act

The basic element in the scheme of continuing education fostered by the 1944 Education Act is that the local education authorities are required to see that a complete provision for after-school education is made in their areas. This provision is to include facilities for further (i.e. professional), adult (i.e. liberal), and social or physical education. The validity of these distinctions may be disputed; but the intention to secure complete coverage is praiseworthy. Local education authorities are not called upon to provide all these services themselves; they are expected to encourage voluntary participants where appropriate, and to develop local activity in concert with their own in a programme which will secure approval by the Minister of Education. If approval is given, the Ministry of Education pays a large proportion of the expenditure incurred. In 1953–4, about £20,367,000 [1] was spent on further education by local education authorities in England, and about £781,000 in Wales. Approximately two-thirds of this amount was reimbursed by the Ministry of Education from central government taxation. The rest was met out of local taxation (rates). It is usually calculated that about half the teaching costs in ' further

---

[1] £1 = $2.80 approximately.

education ' (i.e. all types of continuing and adult education undertaken by local education authorities) are refunded by the Ministry of Education. This expenditure includes not only all the classes initiated by the local authorities themselves, but also many others which they have provided with teachers at the request of groups organized by voluntary societies. Local education authorities have discretion to adopt such classes or not; but they have no right of embargo beyond that of refusing financial support.

Many local education authorities pool their resources or facilities in adjacent areas, especially for advanced studies. Co-ordination of this kind is fostered by the ten Regional Advisory Councils for Further Education in England and Wales, whose responsibility is to secure co-operation between the L.E.A.s themselves, and between technical colleges and industry. In addition, eight national colleges have been founded (usually in close association with an existing L.E.A. technical college) to provide advanced courses in horology, foundry, rubber technology, heating and ventilating, leather work, food technology, aeronautics, and art. A central Advisory Council on Scientific Policy has since 1947 made many excellent recommendations for the pooling of educational facilities in research, teaching, libraries, and so on. Co-operation of this kind is greatly encouraged by developments since the 1944 Education Act, and is given impetus by the growing sense of need for improved opportunities in technical and industrial training. In Britain this burden falls squarely upon the local authorities. They are expected to provide in their technical colleges most of the technological instruction that in the United States would be found in universities, and in other countries would be found in nationally organized colleges of technology. This remark applies not only to technical matters in the strict sense, but also to collateral training such as education for management. Courses organized jointly by the British Institute of Management and the Ministry of Education are given at some seventy technical colleges.

Co-operation between the local education authorities and industry is fruitful. This not only takes the form of providing classes for workers under the age of 18 in ' day release ' classes on one day a week for ' general ' subjects; it may also consist of supplements such as English, arithmetic, drawing, or geography that are complementary to the firms' own apprenticeship or training schemes. In such cases the firms themselves provide the technical instruction; the local education authority provides the teachers for general education, and may do so on the firms' own premises. It should be noted that the Ministry of Education is represented by advisers on the boards of management of about twenty apprenticeship schemes. More use might be made of training within firms themselves but for the fact that most industrial enterprises in Britain are too small for this. The overwhelming majority of all firms employ fewer than five hundred workers. Even in technical matters this demands that training should be provided outside; for reasons of personal orientation training given outside, with its leaven of liberal considerations, seems to be increasingly the concern of the local technical college. The number of students in Ministry-aided institutions of further education continues to grow. During 1953-4 there were 59,000 full-time students, 1,860,000 evening students, and 326,000 part-time day students.

Out of approximately two-and-a-quarter millions thus counted, between one-twelfth and one-tenth are probably pursuing evening institute courses of general rather than professional interest—such as those in literature, music, world affairs, and manual or physical exercises. All of these pay quite uneconomic admission fees, and the burden is borne by local or central taxation. But we must add to this expenditure the amount contributed by the Ministry itself towards what is officially called ' Adult Education '. In 1953-4 some 7,190 courses of advanced ' liberal ' study with 142,779 students received grants totalling £343,000. Until August 1955 the Ministry of Education paid three-quarters of the approved expenditure on the teaching of ' liberal ' subjects by the following institutions : 27 residential colleges for adults maintained or aided by local education authorities, devoted to ' liberal ' studies, and catering for about 35,000 students annually in preponderantly short courses; the Extra-Mural Departments of 21 universities or university colleges responsible for University Extension work, or tutorial classes in conjunction with the Workers' Educational Association, and thus accommodating about 120,000 advanced students yearly; 5 direct-grant residential colleges with long-term courses for adults on a non-professional basis; 44 vacation courses each year for adults; and various other colleges and organizations. The Workers' Educational Association is the biggest of these. The sponsoring organizations thus supported are called ' Responsible Bodies ', and have a direct relationship with the Ministry of Education for grant purposes, although they are academically autonomous as long as the Ministry is satisfied that their work is ' liberal ' and of the high standard required. Neither towards Responsible Bodies nor towards Local Education Authorities has the Minister of Education any powers of direction in the matter of content or method of education; he is concerned only with securing appropriate standards and co-ordination. As from August 1st, 1955, the Minister of Education does not undertake to pay three-quarters of the teaching costs in ' Adult Education '; he will determine payment after taking account of standards, continuity and earnestness of work, co-ordination between the various providing bodies, and the amount of students' fees.

In short, the main financing bodies are the local education authorities (who also have local responsibility and initiative) and the Ministry of Education. The university extra-mural departments, as has just been mentioned, have most of their teaching costs borne by the Ministry and may also have considerable supplements from the local education authorities in whose areas they operate; but their overhead charges and administrative costs come out of university funds. University internal teaching and other costs are covered by awards apportioned to the various universities by the Universities Grants Committee—an autonomous body distributing money received from the Treasury, and taking account of each university's liabilities and resources. Most universities, in addition to their internal courses and their extra-mural departments' work, also provide extra-murally many single lectures or special courses on topics of particular public interest.

Voluntary Societies

Under one head or another it is possible for the local education authorities or the Ministry to support any existing form of adult education that seems to merit it. Most of the institutions mentioned in the second paragraph of this article are thus in receipt of public funds for at least part of their programmes; they are thus encouraged towards systematization and co-operation without direction. Many existing societies, only part of whose work can be classed as formal education, take advantage of these opportunities for having a tutor or occasional course, while continuing their less formally educative activities at their own expense. It is almost impossible to over-estimate the importance of the voluntary society in social or community education in Britain. In recognition of their contribution, the Ministry of Education has continued to make grants towards the erection or maintenance of village halls (128 were assisted during 1953-4) or community centres (14 during 1953-4). Grants totalling £164,324 were made by the Ministry of youth organizations during the same period. Some local authorities also make grants-in-aid. A few, like the Cambridgeshire Education Authority, have built 'village colleges' or similar institutions in towns to combine a school, an institute for adult education, and a community centre. National bodies like the Arts Council have done valuable work in fostering good programmes at such centres, which are also frequently the home of a citizens' advice bureau, a child-welfare clinic, or some other organ of a nationally sponsored educational organization. Not all educators are alert to the value of this kind of workshop for education, which nevertheless may become a mainly self-supporting forum of civic and personal interest much more congenial to the average adult than the classroom environment of the formal evening class—and of more immediate significance in education. After all, more people are likely to be reached through the activities of the National Federation of Women's Institutes, the Townswomen's Guilds, and so on than through the formal class—at any rate at first brush. If we make comparisons we can see that these organizations in Britain might be the best vehicle for such work as is undertaken in the United States by the Agricultural Extension, Home Economics, and 4-H services. In fact, some of their work already is systematized into formal classes, and is encouraged to academic ambition by the existence of an N.F.W.I. residential college (Denman College, near Abingdon). In any case, the complementary co-existence of many different kinds of personal and social education in one centre is an aim any local education authority could be proud to foster. It might extend the appeal of 'further education' to the 90 per cent of the population who still have no part in it, and commend formal 'adult education' to the still larger percentage remaining aloof.

Libraries and Museums

Libraries and museums are well-used tools of education. A few museums are administered centrally by the Ministry of Education, for historical reasons. Such are the Victoria and Albert Museum and the Science Museum. Each of these has about a million visitors a year. Other metropolitan museums such as the British Museum, the National Gallery, and others equally famous, are governed by boards of trustees and receive direct grants from the Treasury. The British Museum has a total annual budget of about £885,000; the British Museum of Natural History spends about £600,000 annually; a smaller gallery like the Tate has about £90,000 a year.

Most of our museums and libraries are locally administered. Many were founded by philanthropy during the past century; but they are now maintained or extended very generously by city and municipal corporations. For example, in 1955 the Liverpool City Council decided to spend £500,000 on rebuilding the public museums, and £270,000 on rebuilding the Picton Library. A new central library for Holborn in London will cost £200,000. Magnificent facilities are maintained by many cities, towns, and counties throughout the country, and are enriched by various devices for co-operation. For example, borrowers even in small towns and villages can usually secure special volumes from a county's central library or from the National Central Library in Bloomsbury, London. This library is able to draw on the libraries of increasing numbers of large business concerns for technical or commercial books and periodicals. On a smaller scale, about a hundred public libraries in West London have formed an organization called Co-operative Industrial, Commercial, and Information Services; they have agreed to exchange books, periodicals, and other information. As part of the scheme, each local library adds to its ordinary facilities a collection of books and information in some specialized field. The enterprise of librarians is rewarded by the increasing interest of borrowers in non-fiction volumes, many of them advanced. Some cities not only have excellent premises for reference books but supply information, even of a technical or professional kind, by telephone. Glasgow has over fifty thousand business inquiries a year.

During recent years the realization that the museum or library is an instrument of public education has become more vivid. Librarians link their usual services to other educational activities. Almost the whole of the expenditure is borne locally by the town or county council, though a small fraction of the formal education may qualify for other grants if it is organized in conjunction with university extra-mural departments or the Workers' Educational Association.

The British system of compromise between existing institutions and co-ordination for greater effectiveness produces its own problems. Some of these continue to arise because the devotees of any particular species of adult education naturally think that its way is the only way, and its constituency the most important one. The time is ripe for a careful study of ' further education ', ' adult education ', community education, and of training in relation to professions. In this way those who operate supplementary educational services, or who are their beneficiaries, may secure a system of adult education that is more effective technically, socially, and personally.

The Forces, Civil Service, and similar Services

It is obvious that in any military or para-military establishment a great deal of training is constantly undertaken, and that much of this may be of permanent personal value to its recipients. The almost universal mechanization of military operations, and the complete reliance of any armed command on complicated scientific instruments for the conduct of any warfare, necessitate a high level of specialized training in every branch of the services. For real effectiveness, little of this can be restricted merely to the job in hand; it entails a more general study of the basic principles—in mathematics, physics, electricity, telecommunications, and so on. For most trainees this type of instruction is a great advance on previous schooling. It is widely recognized, too, that part of the job of making an efficient combatant is the same as the job of making a good citizen, so that those responsible for training in the armed services can no longer completely distinguish between professional and personal education. It seems profitable to consider the aspect of personal and general training here rather than the professional military side, because the latter is much the same all over the world, and also because few worth-while details could be given.

Literacy and Examinations in the Services

At the lowest level, such problems as imperfect literacy are found. Despite universal compulsory schooling to the age of 15 in the United Kingdom, some 23 per cent of national service entrants in a recent year were found to be ' illiterate, sub-illiterate, or backward '. Most of these recruits, it should be remembered, were conscripts and therefore a cross-section of society. They received intensive training in Preliminary Education Centres, and 92 per cent of them were soon educated enough to be fit for military effectiveness and for participation in the regular compulsory education programme. Procedure in the Army may be quoted as an example. All men who have not already attained the level of the General Certificate of Education (the certificate indicating satisfactory completion of five years' work in a ' grammar school ' or academic high school, and reasonable attainment in an external examination) must undergo, as part of their normal training in working hours, a course of general education for at least one year. This should take them up to the level of the Army Certificate of Education, second class. The curriculum includes English, mathematics, current affairs, military geography, regimental history, and map reading. It is intended to promote all-round mental developments rather than the acquisition of facts or skills.

Men who so wish may proceed to the Army Certificate of Education, first class, which is considered to be about one year below the level of instruction required by the General Certificate of Education obtained in schools. All men with the appropriate aptitudes are encouraged to learn a trade wherever circumstances permit. Successful trainees can acquire civilian trade certificates of reputable professional organizations. Any serviceman who shows fitness and interest is permitted to attend evening institutes or polytechnics of the local education authority. Should the conditions of service make it impossible to follow a continuous course in person, facilities are given for following correspondence courses. But within the Army's own education service there are facilities for advanced technical study. There are twenty-nine Army Education Centres in the United Kingdom, eighteen in Germany, thirteen in the Middle East, and four in the Far East. These teach science subjects up to the level of the General Certificate of

Education. There are also Higher Education Centres offering similar subjects to a standard comparable with the first year's work in a British university. Those who wish to continue to study by correspondence can do so at a nominal fee which is a minute fraction of the real cost. Full opportunities are given for taking examinations. Books, both professional and general, are made available in almost all circumstances, and any specialist demand will also be met.

Each Army unit is given the fullest possible opportunity for formal and informal education, including discussions, informal talks, and films. Most of the educational work in the Army is done by the Royal Army Education Corps, most of whose members have either been civilian teachers or have comparable qualifications. Some of the specialized training and a fair proportion of the general education are given by approved civilian instructors. The satisfactoriness of the provision is assured by regular inspection of every unit.

The main responsibility for general education rests with the Central Committee for Adult Education in Her Majesty's forces. After wartime reorganization of the facilities and administration, the Central Committee became effective early in 1949; since then it has published a valuable annual report. It consists of representatives of the universities, the three services, the Workers' Educational Association, the local education authorities, the Ministry of Education, and the Scottish Educational Department.

Work of the Universities

In England, Scotland, Wales, and Northern Ireland the universities and university colleges have sponsored, each in their own extra-mural area, the work of assisting the ' adult ' or (general) education of forces personnel. In the London area, as an exception, the university is not so associated. The normal arrangements are as follows : (a) in areas with small traffic the work is done by the university extra-mural department as part of its normal provision; (b) in fourteen areas where the organization involved is considerable, a special committee for forces education is set up, and this is responsible to the governing body of the local extra-mural department. In the London area, a special committee organizing general education in the armed services is directly responsible to the Central Committee for Adult Education in H.M. Forces. The reason for this rather unusual arrangement is believed to be the unwillingness of the university to identify itself with the provision of courses in many subjects which are normally excluded from the extra-mural programme, and of other courses which (though in familiar subjects) may not consistently be of university standard. However, there has long been close liaison between the officers concerned on an informal basis, and assistance has been given in many ways.

Much of the instruction given under these auspices takes the form of single lectures (about four thousand of them being given in a single year); but the universities look with favour only on more sustained effort, so that the number of longer courses continues to grow. There has been a marked development of residential and centralized courses of special interest, lasting from one to twenty-four days. For students with special abilities a tutorial system has been developed. Some of the officer instructors in the Royal Army Education Corps themselves follow advanced courses of study for higher degrees in the nearest university. University professors and lecturers are from time to time invited to visit Army schools of education to give special residential courses either in subject-matter or in methods of adult education.

Specialist Training

Comparable arrangements are made in the other services; but special mention should be made of facilities for technical and specialist training in the Navy and Air Force. The Royal Naval College at Dartmouth is a 'Public' school or secondary school of great repute, where naval cadets are taught by civilian graduate teachers. Some of the subjects traditional in comparable English schools, such as Latin and Greek, are absent; instead there is an emphasis on seamanship, navigation, and engineering. The Royal Naval College at Greenwich (which again has civilian instructors) may be described as a university of technology— at least for some of its work. It teaches at an advanced level the sciences related to gunnery, navigation, engineering, electrical equipment and communication, and naval architecture. The Royal Naval Engineering College at Manadon is comparable. Both justifiably claim to give an education comparable in all respects with that offered in a university. At a considerably lower academic level there are other programmes for the training of boys as artificer apprentices in ships and training establishments ashore.

The Royal Air Force College at Cranwell was opened in 1919. Bebetween the two world wars the R.A.F. Education Service was developed like the comparable service in the Army; but since 1946 it has been reconstituted as the Education Branch of the Royal Air Force, a fully integrated part of the service. It obviously caters for the training and technical needs of all personnel; but it also takes great care of general education. As a rule, higher intellectual ability and attainment are required for general recruitment into the Royal Air Force. Appropriate technical training within the Service is of course compulsory. It may be given as part of the general training, or may be systematized, as in the varied apprenticeships available at schools of technical training. There are also facilities for administrative training, and for the training of education officers. Civilians already trained, and with high qualifications, are also recruited. General or personal education of R.A.F. men and women is considered to be primarily their own responsibility, although excellent facilities are available, and service time is provided for the purpose. However, young national service men are required to undergo at least two hours of instruction weekly— one hour in general education, and another in current affairs—in addition to the specialized training given. In their second year these young men have one hour of compulsory instruction.

Outside the armed services, the many civil defence organizations offer all recruits a thorough training in air-raid precautions, fire-fighting, or ambulance and hospital work. Courses in the last-named field may be of lasting value to many women who form part of the various nursing reserves.

For the Merchant Navy an excellent range of opportunities is provided by the Seafarers' Education Service, an organization established by Albert Mansbridge, the founder of the Workers' Educational Association. It maintains a library service, a system of correspondence courses, and a system of tutorial advice for merchant seamen. Though it receives public funds it is not publicly maintained.

Civil Service Facilities and Social Services

Within the Civil Service, many of whose branches are highly technical, a large amount of in-service training of a directly professional kind is given. But wherever possible the assumption is that personnel will be recruited who already possess the appropriate standard of general or scientific education, and that they will pursue any further instruction required in their own time. However, facilities are sometimes made available, immediately before the regular daily schedule of work or immediately after it, for teachers sent in by the local education authority to give classes in non-professional subjects. In addition, employees under the age of 18 are regularly sent out to the usual institutions of the L.E.A. for one-day 'release' programmes of instruction each week. Very few are afforded such facilities over the age of 18, except in very special cases, as when a civil servant is required to learn a foreign language at a university. There can be no doubt, however, that in the highest branches of the Civil Service recruited by the Department of Scientific and Industrial Research the opportunities for further training and research within the service are comparable with the facilities in research departments of universities. In recent years, personal mobility and academic exchange have been facilitated by making conditions of employment, pension rights, and so on within the technical branches similar to those of senior posts in universities.

Other public services dependent on one or other of the ministries may exercise a profound educational influence. The work of Youth Employment Officers and child-welfare workers should be specially mentioned. Ever since 1909 there have been juvenile employment exchanges, and in 1910 the Board of Education offered financial support for advisory bureaux serving young people under 17 years of age. The upper age-limit was later raised to 18. Both the Ministry of Labour and the local education authorities shared in the work of helping young people to find suitable employment; but the realization gradually grew that suitable placing should be regarded primarily as an educational function and a social service—a necessary corollary to fuller education opportunities. After an official inquiry, the 1948 Employment and Training Act imposed the responsibility for this function on the Ministry of Labour, except in areas where local education authorities had proved their determination to discharge it. A Central Youth Employment Executive was established, with national Youth Employment Councils for England, Scotland, and Wales. Executive and councils are paralleled at the local level. Every attempt is made to secure full local representation of industries, education, and persons actively interested in the welfare of young people. There are close links with the schools in most areas, and some authorities (e.g. Newcastle-upon-Tyne) have clearly established a very praiseworthy bridge between school and the further opportunities of adult life. The emphasis throughout is on education and social service, with follow-up observation and advice, rather than on manning the various industries. It is on the threshold of adult life that the effectiveness of our educational system is most questioned.

During the war the various ministries concerned with homes, food, health, and young children conducted vigorous educational campaigns for the more effective use of resources available. There is no doubt that such improvements as better nutritional habits and better methods of child-rearing have come to stay. Parents who in peace-time would never have made use of child-welfare clinics became accustomed to seeking advice and appreciating 'welfare foods', immunization, and other services. This tendency survived the war. An awakened public interest in neglected children was reinforced by the appointment of child-welfare officers in all counties, as well as by the activities of health visitors and others whose business it is to help parents to healthier home life. Even the material provision of free milk in schools and of school meals at about half the cost price has indirectly helped in food education. Unfortunately, as was shown by a report in *The Times* in September 1955, the use made of ' welfare foods ' and the accompanying advice distributed by clinics has greatly diminished since the responsibility for running them was transferred from the central government agencies to the local (county) authorities.

It would be wrong to omit reference to the excellent work of education undertaken in the prisons. The shock of arrest and trial might lead to bewilderment and resentment if not carefully followed by remedial training. Some criminals are clearly pathological cases, or victims of society. Others have taken to crime because it seemed an easier, if not the only, way of securing a living. Even those who seem most plainly culpable need to rediscover a worth-while position in life if they are not to become recidivists. For all these reasons a very efficient education service is maintained. The assistant governor of a prison may perhaps be fairly described as an education officer. Training is provided in occupations from the manual crafts upwards. Prisoners of higher intelligence are strongly encouraged to take part in programmes of lectures, discussions, and more continuous study. Instructors not in the prison service are brought in from outside. In those prisons and institutions where the inmates are of high intelligence, such as the well-known ' open prisons ', opportunities of almost university standard are available. Indeed, by correspondence courses, the provision of libraries, and special tutorial advice, prisoners have been successful in advanced professional examinations. A few have taken university degrees. The governors and assistant governors of prisons, and the comparable staff of Borstal institutions for young people, manifestly regard the task of rehabilitation by re-education as basic to their whole position. In hospitals (including mental hospitals) and centres of physical rehabilitation, similar remedial education is undertaken, but often under conditions of greater difficulty.

It is clear from the description given here of education in the armed forces that, even without an acknowledgment of public responsibility for a universal educational service, the purposes of the armed forces themselves could be only imperfectly achieved without wise expenditure on general education. Similarly, the need felt in the Civil Service and in all the industries of the nation for efficient and well-placed workers would clearly justify expenditure on educational services not at first sight directly bringing in an economic return. Equally, and quite apart from the humane intentions of a welfare state, the cost of health education or the remedial services in prisons will soon be covered if there is even a small reduction in the incidence of disease, social *malaise*, and crime. The expenditure is obvious, yet it may be *fictitious*, although the very real financial gain by improvements in society cannot be assessed statistically.　　　　　　　E. J. KING.

CHAPTER TWELVE

The Training of Executives in the United States

PART A: SUPPORT FROM INDUSTRY*

THE presently accepted pattern of planned executive development was proposed in 1927 by the late Dr. W. W. Charters in two papers for the American Management Association on the discovery and development of executive talent.[1]

Unfortunately, Dr. Charters' thesis was poorly timed for being put into practice. Mergers of corporations in the late 'twenties and the Great Depression of the early 'thirties created a surplus of executives, thereby discouraging recruiting and training for executive replacements. There were a few noteworthy exceptions, such as Consolidated Edison's programme of job rotation (" Merry-Go-Round ") to find places for surplus staff resulting from mergers of several utility companies, and Sears Roebuck & Company's forced training and development of a large number of managers for its shift-over from merchandising by mail order to local retail stores. Outside of the Alfred P. Sloan Fellowships at Massachusetts Institute of Technology, educators appeared to be unconcerned with the development of executives.

The Post-war Situation

". . . since World War II an important dimension has been added to corporate giving. It springs from the conviction that the education of people is important, that the colleges and universities from which business concerns get a large part of their executive leadership and technical management are legitimate objects for support." [2]

This attitude is almost a complete reversal of the indifference shown thirty years ago,[3] when it was half-heartedly proposed that " business co-operate with schools by such methods as :

---

* The author, George Corless, is Regional Director, Institute of International Education, Houston, Texas.

[1] Reprinted in *Handbook of Business Administration* (McGraw Hill Book Company, New York and London, 1931), pp. 1604-33.

[2] " Company Gifts to Colleges and Universities," Council for Financial Aid to Education, Inc. (New York), Leaflet No. 9, p. 3.

[3] " Collegiate Schools of Business," Committee Report, Series 8, American Management Association (New York, 1924).

" Sending to the schools instructional material of any nature that would be helpful to the school in their conduct of courses.

" Visiting the schools for the purpose of lecturing and consultation."[4]

The explosively expanding economy of the past decade started with a badly depleted reserve of both executives and potential replacements. Age was taking its toll of the experienced pre-depression group, and the returning military men needed an opportunity to secure business training in somewhat the same way they had learned the technologies of warfare. Corporations had grown larger, business had become more complex, processes were more technical, and competition for the consumer's dollar was keener than ever. Even more important, however, business executives needed a new social outlook and more effective skills in dealing with people, particularly employees, the public, and government.

Since 1943, Harvard's School of Business had offered a short (three-month) course in production management. The original purpose was to ease the transition from non-essential industries to war production. After considerable debate,[5] the school decided to make this course available in peace time to companies that were feeling the need of a broader background for their executives.

Over the past five years, courses similar to Harvard's Advanced Management Programme have been presented by more than twenty-five colleges and universities in the United States. Many of these were underwritten by business, but this proved to be unnecessary in almost every instance after the first session. These courses, varying in length from two weeks to three months, have become an integral part of the planned programmes of executive development for many companies.

Although they have been criticized as ' too little and too late ',[6] they must have a high plus value to induce hard-headed, cost-conscious managements to over-subscribe them session after session. The participants are regarded as employees on detached duty, with full salary and living expenses allowed. Incidentally, the fees are universally higher than those charged for regular college tuition, which latter is frequently below the cost of education offered.

These management courses may not reduce a school's deficit, but in many instances they are a substantial source of income to the faculty, who may teach in them during summer vacations.

---

[4] L. F. Urwick, "Management Education in American Business," American Management Association (New York, 1954), p. 15.

[5] Bursk, *Getting Things Done in Business* (Harvard University Press, Cambridge, 1953), pp. 109–19.

[6] L. F. Urwick, *op. cit.*, p. 35

The Support of Higher Education

Concurrently with the rise of interest in executive development was a growing appreciation of colleges as sources of executive leadership.

> In all its enterprises, our country is becoming more and more dependent upon college educated men and women. College graduates already constitute 10 per cent of our adult population. But they head three-fourths of our biggest industrial enterprises. Nearly seven-eighths of our oncoming business executives nowadays have college or university origins.[7]

During the past fifty years the proportion of college-age young people attending schools of higher education has risen from 4 per cent to 25 per cent. It is still increasing. This growing demand, during a period of rising costs for construction and maintenance and declining returns on endowments and investments, has created a critical problem for higher education in America. Seven years ago, Mr. Frank W. Abrams, then Chairman of the Board of Directors of Standard Oil Company (New Jersey), a company which was a pioneer in adopting a formalized programme for executive development, urged companies to accept their responsibility as corporate citizens. He was particularly concerned over the financial plight of American colleges and universities. A number of leading industrial groups or trade organizations have since endorsed this idea. For example, the Board of Directors of the National Association of Manufacturers in 1951 adopted this resolution:

> Business enterprises must find a way to support the whole educational programme effectively, regularly, and *now*.

The United States Chamber of Commerce officially and vigorously expressed itself in 1954:

> Business must assume a greater responsibility for the financing of institutions of higher education, liberal arts, technological and professional.[8]

Corporate contributions to education and planned executive development are both motivated by " the need and desire to ensure a continued flow of educated personnel into business and industry and the nation at large." [9]

According to the Council for Financial Aid to Education, an advisory and research group of business men, there is no ideal pattern of support for educational institutions. The Council lists a number of types of

---

[7] Wilson Martindale Compton, *What Happens to American Education Will Eventually Happen to America* (Council for Financial Aid to Education, New York, May 1955), p. 3.

[8] " Corporation Support of Higher Education," Council for Financial Aid to Education Inc. (New York), Leaflet No. 6, pp. 4–5.

[9] *Idem.*, Leaflet No. 9, p. 4.

grants on the basis of five principal criteria of interest. Two of them are specifically related to the problem of executive development :

(a) " Sources of company college-educated personnel.

(b) " Increasing educated manpower."

The other categories of motivating self-interest are less definite but may be fully as effective in raising the standards :

(c) " Location of principal employments.

(d) " Location of principal markets.

(e) " General interest in the future."

Among these grants, which are based on sources of college-educated personnel, are Columbia Broadcasting System's gifts of $72,000 to thirty-six of its executives' *alma maters*. General Electric Company has adopted the Corporate Alumnus plan of matching an employee's gift to the college or university where he was educated. General Electric expects to contribute $250,000 to $500,000 annually for scholarships and graduate fellowships.

Westinghouse Electric Corporation, United States Steel Corporation, and others have made large donations for buildings and facilities to institutions selected as principal sources of technically trained personnel. Proctor & Gamble Company grants scholarships to institutions of higher learning selected as principal sources of the company's college-educated personnel, while Lockheed Aircraft Corporation and E. I. du Pont de Nemours & Company give unrestricted funds to professional and technical schools recognized as principal sources of their technical personnel.

Scholarships

Despite the large enrolments in American colleges, many young people with the best minds in the nation cannot afford the cost of a college education. To meet this situation the largest independent college scholarship programme in the history of education goes into effect this year. The National Merit Scholarship Corporation has recently been granted $20,000,000 by the Ford Foundation, $500,000 by Carnegie Corporation, $600,000 by Sears Roebuck Foundation, and $30,000 by *Time* Inc. Ten million dollars are available immediately for scholarship purposes, while $8,000,000 are for matching an equal amount to be contributed by business institutions. Two million dollars are set aside for administrative expenses over the next decade.

The corporation will see to it that financial need will not bar a young man or young woman from college, if he or she is among the top several hundred high school seniors of the nation each year.

Students from some twenty-five thousand public and private high schools will be permitted to compete for scholarships. Merit will be the chief factor for selecting recipients of the awards. The amounts will be determined by need—from a token $100 annually to full coverage of a four-year college course. In addition, the colleges chosen by the scholarship winners will receive a cost-of-education supplementary grant, roughly equal to the cost of tuition.[10]

Standard Oil Company (New Jersey) and several wholly owned affiliated companies have organized the Esso Education Foundation to continue and to co-ordinate their programmes of financial assistance to privately supported colleges and universities. In 1954 the company broadened its support to education by making unrestricted grants for aid at the undergraduate level to one hundred and thirty-eight institutions. A total of all educational grants for the year was about $1,000,000. Esso companies have made initial pledges of $1,500,000 to the Foundation for 1955.[11]

Shell Oil Company has announced a unique programme to improve and expand the teaching of science and mathematics at the high school level. The Shell Companies Foundation, Inc., will underwrite summer seminars to be held annually at Stanford and Cornell Universities for sixty high school teachers.

Selection for " Shell Merit Fellowships for High School Science and Mathematics Teachers " will be based upon merit and demonstrated leadership qualities. Recipients will be reimbursed for travel and living expenses plus $500 in cash to make up for the loss of summer earnings. According to the announcement, " the programme seeks to inspire those science teachers who in turn can best inspire the scientists and science teachers of tomorrow." [12]

Church-related schools and colleges are also turning to business for support. In many states they have formed associations to pool their appeals. It is reported there are thirty-nine such groups. The attitude of many industrialists was expressed by Dr. Richard Gonzales, Director and Treasurer of the Humble Oil & Refining Company, before the fourth fund-raising meeting of the Texas Foundation for Voluntarily Supported Colleges and Universities. He said that:

> Education is the foundation of a society such as ours and diversity of educational institutions is a great asset to the nation. The graduates of church-affiliated schools make a contribution to my company, and I feel that it is justifiable that we should contribute to these institutions.[13]

The post-war executive-development movement through short

---

[10] " $20,000,000 Talent Search," editorial, New York Times, September 8th, 1955.
[11] Wall Street Journal, October 4th, 1955.
[12] Ibid., October 24th, 1955.
[13] Houston Post, September 13th, 1955.

courses in management has made business more aware of its dependence upon higher education and the necessity of financially supporting
the prime source of supply for future executives. The new attitude
was summarized by Mr. Harold McMillan, Past President of the
National Association of Manufacturers:

> American industry fully appreciates the stake it has in our colleges and uni-
> versities. Knowing how important education is in terms of potential
> managerial and executive personnel, industry wants to help.[14]
>
> GEORGE CORLESS.

PART B: EXECUTIVE DEVELOPMENT PROGRAMMES

PARTICULARLY since the end of the Second World War, executive training programmes have increased rapidly among collegiate institutions
in the United States. Although the schools of business there have the
fundamental purpose of inculcating an administrative point of view
in their students and of helping them acquire the basic business skills,
the former purpose is mediate rather than immediate. The new
graduate is trained as an accountant, as a personnel statistician, or as a
retail buyer. The administrative training is of indirect and remote
preparatory value only and, by the time the graduate has reached
managerial levels, may be diluted by time and made obsolete by
change.

There has, on the other hand, been an acute shortage of personnel
with administrative or managerial ability. Junior executives have not
been maturing rapidly enough into more responsible managers. This
famine of executive talent may be due to the consequential increase in
business activity since the war, with a resulting demand for more
executives. It may be due to the imposition of higher standards of
managerial skill brought about by the more complex business environment and by the greater regulative activity of the federal and state
governments in the United States. Even the flow of recipients with
advanced degrees from the graduate divisions of the schools of business has not been able to relieve the shortage.

As a result, the larger corporations have come to rely on the schools
of business for one kind or another of training programme which will
possibly hasten the maturation process of the junior executives. For

---

[14] " Progress and Problems in Corporate Giving," *Investors Reader* (70 Pine
Street, New York, June 29th, 1955), p. 2.

many years various of the schools, leaders among the group being the University of Minnesota and Marquette University, have offered a wide variety of short workshops or institutes. Such topics as *Human Relations for Supervisors*, the *Arbitration Process*, *Procedure Analysis*, *Motion Study*, and *Work Simplification* have been explained or explored in short sessions of one to three days. The extension or adult education division of a good many of the larger universities have included, as an objective, the carrying over of the results of study and research into the business community.

Executive Development Programmes

But the executive development programme *per se* is markedly different from the more familiar short sessions, and is largely a post-war phenomenon. There is no central registry for such programmes, and many of them have only local or regional publicity or patronage, so it is impossible to know how many such programmes there are. A reasonable estimate would put the number at somewhere around fifty. In general, they will run from four weeks to thirteen weeks. Generally, they bring the business men enrolling in them to the campus, and keep them not only busy but detached from their responsibilities for the entire period of time. In general, they are expensive programmes. Their tuition cost is likely to run from $500 to nearly $2,000. The cost is not necessarily related to the length of the programme or to the expenses of producing it.

The courses are not uniform in their level of intensity. Some of them are designed to be of service to men expected to reach top-management status within a reasonably short time. Some of them are designed to be useful to younger men just emerging into the junior executive or middle-management level. At the outset, the executive development programmes were intended to increase directly administrative skills by stressing the several basic fields of business. Attention was given to such subjects as the managerial use of accounting information, the capital budget, market structure, and investment policies. Although a number of the executive training programmes still deal with the specifics of managerial work, there appears to be a trend among those which have been in operation for several years to move to a more general approach. Increasingly, a greater proportion of the time of executive training programmes appears to be given over to the attempt to make business statesmen out of good administrative technicians.

The greatest problem in offering an executive training programme is the difficulty of finding professors who can communicate with fairly high-level executives. Typically the professor is a technical man. He comes to know a great deal about some specialization, and typically is engaged in explaining that specialization to students who are less mature and less experienced than he. When he is faced with an audience of probably greater maturity, broader experience, and unquestionably less intellectual docility, he may be disturbed and ineffective. Many men who are entirely effective in the classroom are unable to meet the demands of the executive development programme.

Teaching Techniques

Probably a majority of the better-known executive development programmes minimize the lecture as a teaching device, and rely on discussion. What has been learned through group dynamics is applied directly to this type of programme. Some effort is made to select participants of somewhat the same level in business, so that there will not be a feeling of inequality among them. Then every effort is made to make the sessions informal, so that there will be a minimum of tension among the participants. Staff and students alike are usually dressed in slacks and sports shirts. All are put on a first-name basis within the first few days. Rarely is the paraphernalia of the classroom present. Examinations and grading are typically not a part of the executive development programme; the writer knows of no such programme which gives university credit for successful completion. The content of the course is the sole reward. It might be added that participants are selected by their managements, and the tuition and other costs are usually paid by their employers. As a result, the participants feel a great obligation to do as well as they can. Attention is close and interest high throughout the programmes—a good showing may have a causal relationship to a business promotion!

Probably a good half of the executive development programmes use, to greater or lesser degree, the case-method of instruction, first applied to education for business by the Harvard Business School. And indeed, a number of the faculty members of the Harvard Business School are engaged as staff members of several of the programmes. In most cases, they take place during the summer months. The reasons for this scheduling are compelling. In the first place, faculty members are not free to devote their full time to such courses during the school terms. In the second place, most of the programmes use dormitory and classroom facilities not available during the normal school terms. And finally, the tradition of absence from business during summer-vacation periods seems to make the summer an easier time for business men to absent themselves from their offices. It may be remarked that few of them feel that they have had a vacation on completion of any of the executive development programmes. The work pace is often very much more intense and rapid than the most arduous graduate course.

The Cost of Executive Programmes

The pricing of executive development programmes appears to be on the basis of what the traffic will bear. It has been remarked that the high tuition charges of some make patronage of an executive training programme a disguised way of giving support to a collegiate institution by business. Two facts argue against this conclusion. In the first place, the tuition cost is a small part of the cost the corporation incurs in sending one of its executives along. His salary obviously continues throughout, and his work must be undertaken by others. There is likely to be some disorganization when a man deemed in line for promotion is withdrawn for a number of weeks. Corporations apparently think well enough of such programmes to incur a consequential cost above tuition fees. In the second place, it is typical that firms sending executives to them continue to do so after they have appraised the results on their executives. Many firms increase the number of men sent: some of them patronizing the same programme, and others sending men to different ones. Follow-up studies of graduates suggest that exceptionally capable people have, in general, been selected, and that their rates of progress are ahead of what would have been expected.

Some Typical Programmes

The oldest executive training programme is that at the Graduate School of Business Administration at Harvard University. It has two sessions of twelve and a half weeks a year, being one of the few which is carried on concurrently with the regular school terms. In each session, two groups of approximately eighty men each are registered. During the fall of 1955, the Harvard Business School was carrying on the twenty-eighth Advanced Management Programme. In it, the case-method of instruction is used almost exclusively. Members of the Harvard Business School faculty are assigned to the programme by rotation of some sort. The tuition charge is $1,000. Board and room are in addition to this.

The Institute of Business Economics at the University of Southern California will start its fifth summer in June 1956. It is carried on for six weeks during the earlier part of the summer, with two groups of thirty to thirty-five registrants each. The staff is drawn primarily from the faculty of the University. Tuition is $1,000, with an extra charge for room and board.

Northwestern University has an Institute for Management of four weeks' duration, with a tuition charge of $1,000. During the summer, three different sessions will be carried on, each with a limit of thirty participants.

Ohio State University offered an executive development programme for the first time in the summer of 1955. It was planned for a two-week session on each of two successive years, with a limit of forty participants and tuition fee of $500, including board and room. This programme is built around four subject-matter areas—General Administrative Management, Managerial Economics, Marketing Management, and Managerial Accounting.

Using the facilities of Arden House, Columbia University's Graduate School of Business puts on two sessions of its Executive Programme in Business Administration each summer. The sessions are six weeks in duration, with a limit of forty-eight participants, and a cost of $1,750, including tuition, room, and board.

Stanford University has carried on its Executive Development Programme since the summer of 1952. It is a nine-week session, beginning in the latter part of June.

Other universities offering similar courses are: the University of Western Ontario (Canada), the University of Buffalo, Carnegie Institute of Technology, Cornell University, the University of Georgia, the University of Hawaii, Ohio University, Oklahoma Agricultural and Mechanical College, University of Oklahoma, Pennsylvania State University, University of Pittsburgh, Washington University, and the University of Washington.

This is not at all an inclusive list, but will give some idea of the extent to which executive development programmes have been offered by the schools of business in the United States. The obvious final question concerning them is whether they will be a continuing part of the educational scene in the United States. Clearly, some of them are superficially thought through and inadequately staffed, and will not continue very many years. But the need they minister to is so great that it is likely that well-organized and competently conducted executive training programmes will be continued for a good many years.

Lawrence C. Lockley.

A World Survey

ALWAYS a lively topic, the teacher's salary has received still more attention in recent years, internationally as well as nationally. Despite the growing literature on the subject, it remains remarkably difficult to find facts and to master those already available in order to produce valid generalizations for an international YEAR BOOK. A short list of the main sources will be found at the end of this article. Two in particular, the studies published in 1953 and 1954 by UNESCO and the International Bureau of Education, contain a wide range of official information from which many of the examples cited here have been taken. The present article attempts to draw together the main aspects of the question in the form of a short international survey.

Who Pays the Teacher?

In the last analysis, of course, the tax-payer or the parent foots the bill. As public school systems have developed, the financial responsibility for education has been shifted from the smaller group (parents) to the larger (general public), paying rates and taxes.

The authority responsible for employing the public school teacher varies with the administrative pattern of the country. Classifying broadly, we find that in about half the states covered by the UNESCO-IBE surveys, a department of the central government is the employing authority. An intermediate level of government, such as a province or canton, is the employer in about one-quarter of the countries, chiefly those with a federal structure in respect of education. For the rest, countries favouring a decentralized school system, teachers are employed by local authorities. This summary view naturally obscures the wide range of practices found within single states, such as India and Switzerland, where almost all possible variations are found side by side. Similarly, there is a certain difference between primary and secondary teachers. Both in newly developing countries, where central government action bears more on secondary than on primary schools, and also in a few well-established systems where the secondary school teacher is readily accepted as a state official and his primary school colleague is not, we may note that administratively the employing authority for the former tends to be higher than for the latter.

For the most part, the authority employing the teacher is also responsible for paying him. However, in the financial arrangements between the different levels of government, funds for teachers' salaries are very often the subject of transfer from one level to another. In the decentralized school administration of Scandinavian countries, for example, the state subsidizes local or communal authorities in various ways, but with particular reference to teachers' salaries. The table below gives a schematic view of these systems : —

STATE GRANTS TO MUNICIPAL AND COMMUNAL AUTHORITIES IN RESPECT OF
EXPENDITURE ON TEACHERS' SALARIES
(*Percentages*)

Primary Schools

Denmark : 20 basic salary, plus other allowances—roughly 50, total outlay on teachers.

Finland : towns 25; rural communes 65–70; Iceland : towns 89; rural communes 92; Norway : towns 30–35; rural communes 55–85; Sweden : somewhat higher total grant than outlay on salaries.

Secondary Schools (where Municipal)

Denmark : roughly 50 total expenditure; Finland : roughly 80 total expenditure; Iceland : all are government schools; Norway : 50 outlay on salaries; Sweden : roughly 75 outlay on salaries.

A more general example may be taken from the Union of South Africa, where the provinces have charge of primary and secondary schooling. The Union Government subsidizes the provinces to the extent of 50 per cent of all public expenditure, including education, and thus assists the payment of teachers, even though this particular element of expenditure does not appear in the subsidy formula.

So far the public school teacher. The private school teacher, by definition, is paid by the person or body owning the school, with funds received from fees or endowments. The extent of state intervention varies. At one extreme are countries, like the U.S.A., where no public control is exercised over and no public funds are available to private education. However, most states have adopted laws for the registration and inspection of such schools. In countries such as New Zealand and the Philippines the matter ends there, and the teacher's salary remains a question of private contract. Somewhat greater pressure is found in Brazil, where special codes are laid down for the payment of private secondary school teachers, although not for primary teachers. But most countries permitting private education have adopted some form of state grant to recognized or efficient schools, at least for the compulsory school age-level and these grants are generally aimed in particular at teachers' salaries. The effect of subsidies in the Netherlands is to ensure the same salary level in private as in public schools.

For similar reasons the recent *Barangé Law* in France makes a per-pupil grant to private schools, mainly with a view to increasing salaries.

Salary Schedules

The principle seems fairly well established of having fixed salary schedules for public school teachers throughout a country or some major part of it. Something like three-quarters of the countries reported in the UNESCO-IBE inquiry fix secondary school teachers' salaries by statute for the country as a whole. There is less national uniformity in the case of primary teachers, but almost everywhere the idea of fixed schedules is applied.

Where national schedules obtain, the method of defining grade- or class-levels within the schedule and of fixing the basic salary for each grade varies widely with the administrative pattern and even the cultural outlook of the country. Among the factors which determine the grading, the following appear to be important. First, and most general, the teacher's qualifications. In under-developed countries where the school system is rapidly expanding, primary teachers are employed with a considerable variety of previous academic and professional training, and salary scales tend to be correspondingly complex: in Ceylon, for example, no less than fourteen different grades of primary school teacher are distinguished. The more developed school systems have standard methods of training teachers, and here the chief distinction is between the primary school (non-university trained) teacher and the secondary teacher who is graduate. The figures below

	Primary Teacher Scale		Secondary Teacher Scale	
	Min.	Max.	Min.	Max.
Belgium (Belgian *frs.* per year)	56,000	109,200	82,000	198,000
France (French *frs.* per year)	299,000	640,000	551,000	1,228,000
The Netherlands (*florins* per year)	2,784	4,830	3,840	7,800

Rates of Exchange

1	Belgian *franc*	=	2d. *sterling* =	0.02 U.S. *dollars*
970	French *francs*	=	£1 *sterling* =	2.80 U.S. *dollars*
1	Netherlands *florin*	=	2s. *sterling* =	0.26 U.S. *dollars*

for 1952–3, show the extreme positions in three highly developed European countries. Even in the U.S.A. state salary scales are based to some extent on the amount of university training of the teacher.

There is an obvious correlation between the teacher's qualifications and the level of the school or the nature of the subjects he is engaged to teach. These latter factors are often used as the basis for determining which grade the teacher shall have in the salary scale. Differences thus occur between lower and upper primary, lower and upper secondary classes, as well as between the general classroom teacher and the teacher of special and practical subjects.

Apart from qualifications, the main elements affecting the salary scale seem to be the geographical location of the school and sex. Such countries as Belgium and Sweden provide different basic scales for urban, semi-urban, and rural areas (Belgium) or for the several cost-of-living zones (Sweden). This is probably no more than an admission in the basic scale of what other countries achieve by elaborate allowances. In the main, cost-of-living allowances favour the urban teacher, although one or two cases exist of a differential scale favouring the rural teacher. Where no national salary schedules exist, as in the U.S.A. and Canada, the differing paying capacities of urban and rural communities produce a similar variation. Thus in Canada, for 1952–3, the median salary of all teachers in nine provinces was $2,510,[1] whereas the median for teachers in one-room rural schools was $1,923. This situation is probably true for most parts of the world.

The factor of sex appears to be less important, and most national salary schedules are basically the same for men and women, other things being equal. The present trend in this direction in Britain may be taken as representative. But once again, as with geographical location, allowances make for a difference, this time in favour of men.

While questions of training, level of school, locality, and sex all play a part in providing differential grades, it is probably true that in most countries there is greater variation within a given grade or class than between grades. Regular increments for length of service, granted either automatically or upon proof of efficiency, produce a possible salary range in each scale which overlaps the next higher scale. As between countries, there are remarkable differences in the ways. The schedules for different grades of teacher are constructed and applied. The range from minimum to maximum salary, expressed as the number of years it takes a teacher to reach the highest point on a given grade, may be ten or twelve years (parts of Canada, New Zealand, etc.) or as much as thirty-five to forty years (Austria, Italy). Moreover, the mere existence of a salary range does not mean that teachers are normally distributed over this range. For the few countries producing data on the point, the majority have most of their teachers on the

---

[1] 2.80 Canadian *dollars*=£1 sterling=2.80 U.S. *dollars*.

lowest steps—a reflection perhaps of the high rate of turnover in the profession. One of the effects of these variations is to make it difficult to arrive at a national ' average salary ' in regard to teachers.

Additional Costs

The teacher's salary, as reflected by a salary schedule, and the cost of employing a teacher are by no means the same thing. The salary schedule is a basic minimum, moving but slowly in times of rising living costs. We find in most parts of the world a fairly elaborate set of allowances to compensate for this stability or inertia. The cost-of-living allowance (amounting to as much as 270 per cent in Austria in 1952, where the basic scale was fixed in 1946) is the commonest of these arrangements. Although a permanent machinery for the adjustment of basic salaries, such as the Burnham Committee, is still the exception, there appears to be considerable flexibility in the fixing of allowances. Centralized countries assimilate teachers to other parts of the public service, and generally have an automatic means of adjusting cost-of-living allowances. In decentralized or federal countries, tribunals or courts play the part of deciding claims put forward by the teachers.

The other major element in paying the teacher is provision for social security. The interpretation given to this term varies from one state to another, but it is noteworthy that every country covered by the UNESCO-IBE surveys reported a pension scheme for teachers, with retirement and disability benefits. For public school teachers, at any rate, this means an additional charge on public funds, which is at times extended also to private school teachers. Other forms of welfare services, such as medical benefits, reduced travel and housing rates, and so on, occur widely. These items make it extremely difficult to arrive at an accurate estimate of the teacher's real wages.

Problems of Comparison

The survey so far has been based on the method of taking fairly broad aspects of the question and illustrating them by national examples. A more precise method of study runs into the difficulty of securing significant and comparable data.

In two countries where the teacher's salary is essentially a local responsibility, Canada and the U.S.A., considerable progress has been made in this type of study. The NEA Research Division in the U.S.A. has for years published biennial surveys on the salaries paid in urban school districts, and since the war pilot studies have been made on the rural situation. Their interest lies in the careful analysis, over many years, of the movement of teachers' salaries and the conversion of these salaries into real wages. (See this section, Chapter 15.)

In Canada the surveys made by the Canadian Education Association and the Dominion Bureau of Statistics also attempt to go beyond the mere compilation of salary data. A useful summary in the recently published *School Finance in Canada* [2] provides two sets of comparisons: between provinces and between teaching and other occupations in each province. The former comparison points up the remarkable variation in salaries through the country as a whole, not merely when median salaries per province are confronted, but also in respect of salary range. By using census data from 1950–1, the report then compares the incomes of seven occupation groups—professional agriculture, chemistry and metallurgy, law, medicine and surgery, accounting and auditing, nursing, teaching. This comparison establishes teachers' salaries as lower than any other except nursing; it also brings out the interesting point that in the group of eastern provinces, where teachers are paid much less than their colleagues to the west, the same differential does not exist for other occupation groups, again with the exception of nursing.

These two cases come from countries where the raw data on teachers' salaries are extremely difficult to gather, and perhaps illustrate sufficiently that it is, or should be, possible to establish relationships at three levels: between salaries and the cost of living; between salaries in different parts of a single country; and between teaching and other occupations. But in practice very few such surveys can be found. The result is that international comparison, which should be a fruitful method of analysing the problem, becomes almost impossible. The official data published in the UNESCO-IBE surveys are left in their raw form, with at most some generalization at the descriptive level. The manifest difficulty lies in comparing salaries when these are expressed in different national currencies, and when one knows that the purchasing power of money and accepted standards of living cannot be directly translated by converting these currencies into dollars or pounds.

Perhaps the only attempt to overcome such problems internationally is represented by Hammer's study *Teachers' Salaries*, published in 1953 by the World Organization of the Teaching Profession, a body that has now been replaced by the wider World Confederation. Hammer sent a *questionnaire* to a number of national teachers' associations, twenty-nine of which replied. The first difficulty was to fix the average salary in each country, since for the most part the detailed information allowing one to calculate averages and scatter is lacking. Having arrived at

---

[2] Canadian School Trustees' Association. Finance Research Committee. *School Finance in Canada 1955.* Secretary of the Committee, College of Education, Saskatoon, Saskatchewan.

some form of 'typical' salary, he then had to effect comparisons. This was done in several ways, the most striking being to relate the teacher's salary to the national income per head of population in each of the countries studied. By such a device the teacher's earning power is shown in terms of the existing and accepted standards of living within each country. Extreme caution must be used when interpreting data based on the successive application of averages, but Hammer's method appears to be the only likely one for arriving at any comparative analysis of the question. From his tabulation for twenty countries, the teacher's salary is below the figure required for supporting three dependants at the average standard of living for the country; in the wealthier countries teachers are relatively worse off than elsewhere.

General Factors in the Situation

With very few exceptions, national school systems are experiencing a critical shortage of teachers which shows little sign of improving. Two demographic elements contribute, the post-war population bulge and the smallness of the generation born in the 1930's (between the slump and the war) from which teachers have to be recruited. These set off a demand for teachers which has been carefully measured and predicted in many countries. At the same time, the general demand for man-power in the expanding economies of the 1950's makes it still more difficult to find an adequate supply of teachers. Theoretically, the situation should be reflected in some spectacular rise in the rewards offered to teachers. In fact, the records show that teachers' salaries have kept more or less at the average wage earned in each country, have risen progressively with the cost of living since 1945—but no more. Summing up this situation, the latest World Confederation of Organizations of the Teaching Profession report [3] says that the main effect of increased demand has been to raise beginning salaries rather than salary scales as a whole. This is certainly true. Moreover, the mere operation of the demand factor in respect of teachers cannot by itself lead to a general rise in salaries. All public education authorities have explored ways for increasing the supply of teachers—shortened courses, relaxed standards of certification, the employment of untrained teachers, the use of correspondence courses for supervision by an unqualified classroom 'sitter' (these measures are described in a single highly developed country). That such emergency measures have been applied successfully and conscientiously in some countries cannot be denied; but they do tend to focus attention on the recruiting problem, i.e., the starting salary, rather than on the total salary scale.

[3] World Confederation of Organizations of the Teaching Profession. *Status of the Teaching Profession* (Washington, D.C., 1955), p. 29.

To this should be added the rather special appeal of the teaching profession. The factors that decide a young person to become a teacher are many : the influence of his own teachers, the social status of teaching in many rural areas, ideals of service, and many more which are not connected in the short run with salary-levels.

One aspect of the supply problem is the position of teaching relative to other occupations. Analyses of how much more or less teachers earn than doctors, farmers, and artisans will indicate the economic and perhaps social status of these occupations in a given society; but the varying need for recruits as well as the differing opportunities for preparation make it impossible to compare outright the competing pull of these occupations on young people. The competition is more likely to make itself felt in particular branches of teaching, in relation to some allied or nearly alternative group of occupations, and that over a long period. An instance occurring at present is the shortage of secondary school teachers for mathematics and sciences. This has been signalled in a number of countries, including France, Scotland, and the U.S.A. Such teachers usually need to have a good university foundation, and may be attracted to better-paid industrial posts even after they have begun a teaching career. Similarly, India is facing a shortage of crafts teachers for her Basic schools—because these teachers when trained find it more profitable to set up as artisans in their own right. It is perhaps only natural that educational authorities, meeting separate portions of the overall problem of competition, should take steps to remedy the supply of teachers in that particular area—by training facilities or allowances—without engaging in the larger issue of the economic status of all teachers.

For in the last resort the question of paying teachers is a national one. What is involved is the educational budget of the state, or the sum-total of such budgets in a federal country. Education competes with other purposes of public expenditure, and its relative position changes very slowly. This is brought out by a recent UNESCO report, *Public Expenditure on Education*, where the education budget is examined as a percentage both of the national budget and of the national income. The factors governing the decision to accord any given percentage of public funds to education are numerous, and mostly extraneous to the educational situation as such. And within this somewhat rigid framework the position of the teacher's salary has to be considered as competing with other objects of education expenditure—the buildings, supplies, and services the teacher knows to be indispensable. Roughly salaries represent half the total outlay.

Against this inelastic situation, the bargaining power of teachers is itself somewhat limited. In many cases there are sharp distinctions between branches of the profession, such as primary and secondary teachers. And even with complete organization, the most vigorous form of trade-union action, the strike, is one which teachers tend to refrain from using. Teachers' organizations at the national and international levels have recognized that their salary scales cannot be separated from the question of social status, and that any improvement in salaries can be achieved only by increased public expenditure on education as a whole. Hence we find a growing emphasis on professional problems and standards on the part of the organizations. The Teachers' Charter recently adopted by the Joint Committee of International Teachers' Federations makes the case for better remuneration on the two grounds of social responsibilities and qualifications.

Compromising policies followed by administrations and by teachers in the majority of countries cannot, however, conceal the basic problem at issue : the shortage of teachers and the low economic status of the profession. It is this problem which has given rise to so much national and international debate in recent years. A listing of the most obvious examples may serve to indicate the level of interest. Two of the latest International Conferences on Public Education, convened by UNESCO and the IBE, dealt with primary and secondary teachers' salaries (in 1953 and 1954 respectively). These conferences are of an inter-governmental, consultative nature, and they produced recommendations to Ministries of Education which do not, of course, have any coercive force. Another international body, this time the International Labour Organization (which has the tripartite representation of governments, employers, and employees), went to work on the same question in 1954, when its Advisory Committee on Salaried Employees and Professional Workers made a report on the conditions of employment of teaching staff. On the side of the teachers themselves, particular importance may be attached to the efforts since the war to set up representative international bodies. The World Confederation of Organizations of the Teaching Profession made the subject of the teachers' status the main theme of its 1955 conference in Istambul. Another body, the Joint Committee of International Teachers' Federations, has for two years been preparing a Teachers' Charter and pressing for the official adoption of this document.

It would be superficial to dismiss these debates and reports as so much time wasted. There is a serious problem before our school systems, as serious as any in the past, and the fact that it becomes a matter of international concern is perhaps a healthy symptom.

LEO R. FERNIG.

CHAPTER FOURTEEN

Factors affecting Teachers' Salaries in England and Wales

This article is primarily concerned with teachers' salaries in England and Wales. While the situation for teachers follows much the same general pattern in Scotland and Northern Ireland, there are important differences in the education systems of the two countries which make it unwise to include the Scottish and Ulster teachers within the scope of all the observations which follow.

THE majority of teachers in England and Wales, like their colleagues in most other countries, are public servants. Their salaries are therefore affected by such factors as the nation's total wealth, the proportion of that wealth which the community is prepared to devote to social services, the order of priorities within that social expenditure at any given time, and the rate of economic expansion of the nation.

The position of British teachers differs from that of teachers in some countries, however, in so far as they are employed, not by the state, but by the local government authorities; this means that, even though the national government reimburses local authorities for approximately 60 per cent of their educational expenditure, the general state of local government finance is an additional factor affecting their salaries.

Since 1945 there have been major changes in British local government. In particular, a number of the services previously controlled by the local authorities have been taken over by the national government, or nationalized industries, and the impression has been given that the local authorities are much poorer in consequence. This is open to question; it is certainly arguable that the level of local rates has not increased as much as the general level of prices and personal services. On the other hand, it is undoubtedly true that because the education service now constitutes the biggest single item in local government expenditure, and because the increase in the child population makes annual increases in expenditure inevitable, the education estimates are always the subject of much debate and close scrutiny in the local council chambers. Those seeking to keep down local rates therefore may easily see education as the most likely source of possible economies.

Many teachers believe that this vulnerability to pressure from local

454

ratepayers is responsible for the comparatively low level of their salaries, and a factor militating against any major improvement in them. They therefore urge that teachers' salaries should be subject to a 100 per cent Treasury grant. There are, however, grave dangers in this proposal—for such a step would inevitably lead to a change in the status of the teacher; it would possibly limit the freedom teachers now enjoy by establishing a measure of central government control. It is also debatable whether teachers' salaries would, in fact, be improved if they were to be fully dependent on the Treasury. They might, however, be negotiated more speedily. Chancellors of the Exchequer in these days of ' buoyant revenue ' can usually count on a large budget surplus. This gives them room for manoeuvre and enables the Treasury to deal with applications for salary increases more quickly than the local authorities, whose rate levy is tied very closely to each year's estimated expenditure, and who have no ' slack ' to take up.

Salary Negotiations

So much for the financial framework within which the determination of teachers' salaries is set. But what of the factors which come into play in the negotiation of actual salary levels?

The teachers' work is ' non-productive ' and ' non-measurable ', in the narrow economic sense. One therefore has to rule out, in determining the general level of teachers' salaries, the sort of criteria which play their part in some other professions, in manufacturing industry and commerce. There are no means of assessing effort or efficiency, in terms of output, or cases handled, or personal services rendered. Salary levels do not respond to greater responsibilities in the same way that wages respond to greater output.

Conversely, teachers are not affected adversely, generally speaking, by the element of economic competition. In industry, commerce, and certain professions, effort and efficiency can mean the difference between prosperity and bankruptcy and, at times, between employment and unemployment. It has therefore been customary for some people in Britain to argue that, since this gives teachers a greater security of employment than others enjoy, this is taken into account in determining their salaries. After a decade of full employment, however, this argument has lost much of its force.

While assessment in terms of individual ability and effort is ruled out in the determination of general salary levels, it has played some part in the establishment of differentials in the salary scales. Certain differentials in the current salary scale rest on qualifications and experience, but some are based on the assumption of special responsibilities. Admittedly this is not a question of ' output ' in the normal sense, but it does amount to a reward for some responsibility over and above that carried by others. It is, incidentally, on this aspect of the existing salary scales that there is the greatest controversy among teachers. The controversy has been brought to a head by a recent increase in the allowances paid to teachers assuming responsibility for ' advanced ' work, a step taken by the authorities, prompted, no doubt, by a desire to overcome an acute shortage of science and mathematics masters.

Applying the strict ' market ' approach to the problem, suggestions were made to overcome the shortage by making the increased allowances payable only to science and mathematics teachers. This was resented by the teaching profession, with the result that the payment now goes to all teachers doing ' advanced ' work. But, as has been indicated, the increase has nevertheless caused considerable dissatisfaction in many schools.

Mention of the increased allowance for ' advanced ' work indicates one of the major factors involved in salary negotiations—the ' market ' test. The employers are guided by what they consider the salary level necessary to attract sufficient recruits of the right quality to the profession; the teachers do not dissent from this, but they place more emphasis on a salary level which would reflect the high regard in which the profession should be held, and which is comparable with that seen to be obtainable in other professions. There are, however, two complicating factors: the first is the difficulty in making direct comparisons between teachers and other professional groups; the second is that teachers, by virtue of their specialized training, are not generally either able or willing to transfer to other professions.

This does not mean, however, that the effect of salary levels on recruitment to and resignations from the profession is not felt in negotiations; indeed it is, but the repercussions would be greater if teachers were able to move more quickly into other fields of professional employment.

It would also be greater if British teachers, as a group, did not possess a strong sense of social responsibility. This is borne out, I think, by post-war developments. Since 1945, the United Kingdom has been suffering from an acute shortage of teachers, and this was especially serious immediately after the war. Here, then, was an excellent opportunity for the teachers to exploit their ' scarcity ' value, to attempt to secure very substantial salary advances. Instead, the profession gave its full co-operation to the Government in the introduction of an emergency training scheme designed to overcome the shortage as quickly as possible, thus demonstrating its willingness to place the welfare of the children above its own.

This sense of social responsibility has not always been matched by a willingness on the part of the public authorities—government and local education authorities—to treat teachers adequately in matters of salary and conditions of service. Indeed, the fact that they are public expenditure to avert economic crises. The salary cuts of the among the first to experience the effect of any attempts to restrict public expenditure to avert economic crises. The salary cuts of the nineteen-twenties and nineteen-thirties are cases in point. A more recent example occurred in 1949, when, owing to their rapidly deteriorating financial position, the teachers applied for a substantial salary increase; the local authorities recognized the merit in the teachers' case, but said they could not accede to it, owing to national financial and economic circumstances. It is quite clear from these experiences that the level of teachers' salaries at any given moment is not necessarily related to the operation of the law of ' supply and demand ', or to the merits of any case based upon personal merits or needs.

When all these factors have been taken into consideration, however, in the long run the status and remuneration of teachers depends on the nation's attitude to education and to the role of the teaching profession. To-day there are signs in the United Kingdom of a growing realization that education is vital to the nation's future prosperity. Arguments are advanced that the economic future of the country depends on the skill and training of the people and that this means ever-increasing expenditure on education and in particular better salaries to attract a sufficient number of suitable and qualified recruits to the teaching profession. Whether teachers themselves will benefit sufficiently from these laudable sentiments depends on the working of the salary-negotiating machinery and the principles underlying the teachers' salary structure.

The Negotiating Machinery

The task of determining the level of salaries for primary and secondary school teachers is the responsibility of the Burnham (Main) Committee. This committee was established under the 1944 Education Act and comprises representatives of the associations of local authorities and representatives of teachers organizations.

There was, of course, some form of national salary-negotiating machinery for many years prior to the 1944 Act. Its history goes back to 1919, when Mr. H. A. L. Fisher, the then President of the Board of Education, invited the N.U.T. and the L.E.A.s to co-operate in the formation of a Standing Joint Committee " to secure the orderly and progressive solution of the salary problem in Public Elementary Schools by agreement on a national basis ". This committee soon commenced work under the chairmanship of Lord Burnham, and its first Report recommended the adoption of a ' Provisional Minimum Scale '. This was a major step forward, for hitherto each local education authority had framed its own salary scale, with the result that 320 such scales were then in existence. Although there was no legal obligation for them to do so, in less than a year every L.E.A. in England and Wales which did not already have a better scale had adopted the provisional minimum scales. The first step to real national salary structure had been taken.

Later the committee framed four standard scales and each L.E.A. was asked by the committee to confer with its teachers with a view to a provisional agreement as to the scale ' appropriate to its area '. This introduction of a differentiation based on geographical location persisted as a feature of the salary scales until 1945, when it was all but completely abolished (the exception being a Special London Allowance).

While national negotiating machinery had replaced local bargaining, it was many years before a single, unified salary structure was created. The division between ' elementary ' and ' secondary ' systems of education which existed in England before 1944 was reproduced in the salary field and resulted in two sets of salary negotiations and two machines for negotiations.

The two salary scales were based on different criteria. The norm in the elementary schools was the two-year trained certificated teacher. The norm in the secondary school was the graduate teacher, who might or might not have been trained. These divisions inevitably led to many anomalies, some of which were due to the growth of senior work in elementary schools, in which category schools such as the ' selective central schools ' were included.

Fortunately the 1944 Education Act, which changed the structure of the education system, also helped to remove the anomalies and divisions in the salary field. The Act called for the integration of the school system; the division between ' elementary ' and ' secondary ' schools was abolished, and henceforth education in all its stages—primary, secondary, and further—was regarded as one continuous process. It was therefore logical that the Burnham machinery and the salary structure should follow the same pattern. The result was a consolidation of the machinery leading to one committee, the Main Committee, to deal with the salaries of teachers in all primary and secondary schools, and one salary scale common to all qualified teachers.[1]

The norm became the two-year trained qualified teacher and differentiation by types of school disappeared. Henceforth the structure was to be based on a common Basic Scale with additional payments according to qualifications, experience, and responsibilities.

Burnham Committee Procedure

Before describing in more detail the principles which from time to time have been enunciated for the determination of teachers' salaries, and those which actually feature in the current Burnham Agreement, it is necessary to mention the composition and procedure of the Burnham Committee and the relationship to it of the Minister of Education.

The Burnham Main Committee has a statutory basis as a result of the 1944 Act. Section 89 of the Act confers on it the duty of determining teachers' salaries on a national basis. The committee comprises an Authorities' Panel of representatives of local authorities, and a Teachers' Panel of representatives of teachers' organizations. Each panel acts as a self-contained unit. In the full committee there is no voting by individual representatives. Only when both panels agree is any decision recorded. Disagreement between the panels on any particular issue means that no decision on that issue is made and there is no provision for arbitration between the two sides.

When provisional agreement has been reached in the Burnham Committee, it is usual to submit the proposals to the constituent bodies represented on the committee in order to obtain endorsement of the action of their representatives.

If this endorsement is forthcoming, the settlement is then ratified by the committee and its recommendations are sent to the Minister of Education. If he approves them, he will issue a statutory order which compels L.E.A.s to pay teachers' salaries in accordance with the terms of the agreement. The Minister is not empowered to alter the recommendations. In effect he is asked to endorse and make operative a settlement reached by negotiation on a national basis between representatives of teachers and their employers.

There is not normally any provision for back-dating the operation of

---

[1] There are other committees responsible for negotiating salaries for other sections of the education service. Two of these have the same statutory basis as the Main Committee. They are the committees dealing with Establishments for Further Education and Teaching Staff in Farm Institutes. There are other committees which negotiate salaries for Inspectors, Organizers and Advisory Officers of Local Education Authorities and for Teaching Staff in Trained Colleges, which do not have a statutory basis, but whose agreements are accepted by the employers and employees in the same way as those of the Burnham Committee.

a new salary award. This is because each agreement has statutory force once it has been approved by the Minister and it is not possible, in law, for a new agreement to supersede, retrospectively, a previous agreement. Furthermore, the very rigid limits within which local government finance operates makes the idea of back payment anathema to the local authorities.

Principles Embodied in the Salary Agreements

As this procedure indicates, the title of the Burnham Committee somewhat belies its nature. It is not an independent body making impartial judgments on teachers' salaries, but a negotiating arena where employers and employees match their strength, the one side intent, generally speaking, on securing the maximum for the teaching profession; the other side, generally speaking, determined to concede no more than is absolutely inevitable. In so far as there are discernible principles embodied in the agreements reached by the committee, they have emerged, as befits the empirical nature of the British, after years of negotiation and the practical application of salary agreements, rather than as a result of conscious *a priori* deliberation on principles as such.

There have, of course, been attempts by other bodies to establish the principles on which teachers' salaries should be based, most notably those of two departmental committees for " Inquiry into the principles which should determine the fixing of salaries for teachers ", whose reports were published in 1918, and of the McNair Committee which was set up during the last war to consider the supply, recruitment, and training of teachers and youth leaders. The views on teachers' salaries expressed by the latter committee were of considerable importance, for they helped to secure the fundamental revisions in scales which followed the 1944 Act.

It was the view of the McNair Committee that teachers' salary scales should satisfy four main tests :

(a) a test of personal need : they should make possible the kind of life which teachers of the quality required ought to be enabled to live;

(b) a market test : they should bear a relationship to the earnings of other professions and occupations, so that the necessary supply of teachers of the right quality will be forthcoming;

(c) a professional test : they should not give rise to anomalies or injustices within the teaching profession; and

(d) an educational test : they should not have consequences which damage the efficiency of the education provided in any particular type of school or area.

As the committee's report showed, the scales existing prior to 1944 failed in several ways to meet these criteria. The teachers' organizations maintain that the same criticism is applicable to present-day salary levels, especially regarding the test of personal need and of the market.

In fairness, however, it must be said that certain changes advocated both by the McNair Committee and by the teachers' organizations have been carried out. The most important of these are the removal of differentiation according to area, and differentiation according to type of school, which were prominent, and educationally undesirable features of the pre-1944 salary scales. A third form of differentiation, that according to sex, is now in process of removal, for in 1955 the L.E.A.s began the gradual introduction of the principle of ' equal pay ' into the teaching profession. By 1961, there will be no discrimination against women teachers where salaries are concerned.

These post-war developments are a pointer to the principles which now govern teachers' salaries, and they indicate the trends towards what is now the fundamental principle of the salary structure—the Basic Scale. This is the scale for the ' qualified teacher ', the two-year trained qualified teacher, and it is this scale which determines the general level of teachers' salaries. For while additions and allowances are made for extended training, graduation, special qualifications, and similar reasons, the Basic Scale is the element common to all teachers and comprises, in almost all cases, the largest proportion of each teacher's salary.

Its virtues are that it put an end to the divisions created by the pre-1944 scales, that it was a logical development of the educational integration laid down in the 1944 Act and that it is a contribution to the creation of a unified teaching profession.

The Burnham Committee has always recognized the need for differentials in the salary structure. The introduction of the Basic Scale, far from undermining such differentials, helped to create a system with a more rational basis. The principles on which this is constructed are as follows :

(I) Additions in Respect of Responsibility

(a) Assistant Teachers

These allowances are given for special responsibility, special work of an advanced character, special academic, professional, or industrial qualifications, or for other reasons which in the opinion of the employing authority justify such allowances. Their payment is subject to the proviso that they shall not be granted in such a manner as would effect a general alteration in the operation of the salary scales. While the number of assistant teachers who may receive these allowances is a matter within the discretion of the L.E.A.s, there are two conditions to be satisfied :

(i) no allowance paid shall be at a rate of less than £40 per annum,[2]

(ii) the annual expenditure on the allowances shall be within a prescribed range for each school or department, together with a payment from a fund known as the ' area pool '.

(b) Head Teachers

The head teacher's salary comprises the amount receivable as a qualified teacher, together with a head teacher's allowance. The amount of this allowance is ascertained for each school by reference to the number of pupils on the roll classified in four age-groups, giving what is known as the ' unit total '. This system brings all primary and secondary schools, of whatever type, into a common scheme of assessment. In Scotland, the allowances are determined, in part, by the type of school, and the difference between, say, a primary school or a grammar school of the same size might be as much as £350.

(II) Additions for Graduation

Teachers possessing a university degree or its equivalent receive an addition to the Basic Scale. A further addition is received if the degree is a ' good ' honours degree.

(III) Additions in Respect of Experience

(a) Recognition of Service as an Unqualified Teacher and other Experience

Service as an unqualified teacher and other experience obtained prior to recognition as a qualified teacher is recognized on the basis of one increment for each period of three years. Experience of special value (other than teaching) to the teacher may be recognized on the basis of an increment for each year of such service.

(b) Addition for Extra Years of Study and/or Training

Under prescribed conditions, study and/or training in excess of two years is recognized by the addition of one increment for each extra year of study and/or training up to a maximum of three increments.

(IV) Additions in Respect of Area

There is an additional payment for teachers serving in schools in what is called the ' London area ', which is made up of the City of London and the Metropolitan Police District.

---

[2] This figure is taken from the 1954 Report, which is now being reviewed. All the figures and principles mentioned here may be modified.

Experience has shown that no set of rigid salary scales can fully cover every variety of circumstances because of the intensely local nature of education in England and Wales and the wide variety of organization within individual schools. Hence the discretionary clauses which the Burnham Agreement confers on L.E.A.s for the formulation of schemes of special allowances.

While some of the allowances or additional payments have caused controversy among teachers (particularly, at the present time, the special allowances for work of an advanced character and the demand in some areas for an allowance similar to the London Allowance), the general opinion of teachers is that, providing they are not extended to a point where they endanger the Basic Scale, and providing the payment is made for qualifications or responsibility that is not only real but apparent to all, they are generally accepted and approved. They offer a proper incentive to teachers to undertake duties of a specially responsible character and provide scope for the teacher with exceptional qualifications or exceptional responsibility.

Where dissatisfaction arises about salaries—and it is widespread at the present time—it is due not to the structure of the salary scale, but to the actual value of salaries. For these are such that to-day the majority of teachers find themselves worse off financially than they were pre-war, and at a decided disadvantage when compared with other professional groups.

RONALD GOULD.

CHAPTER FIFTEEN

Salary Scales in the United States

PART A: THE BASES OF BARGAINING

THE development of thoroughly satisfactory teacher salary scales in the United States has been hampered by the influence of two factors. The first is that teacher productivity is difficult to assess. Even when the desired outcomes of teaching are well established and clearly defined, it is difficult to appraise a given instructor's success in achieving these objectives. This difficulty is further complicated by the subjectivity and intangible character of the goals of education as presently conceived. That teachers should develop character is readily accepted. How successfully a particular teacher performs this duty is not so readily agreed to by those concerned.

A second factor causing considerable confusion and difficulty is the nature of educational organization in the states. Since its early days, the United States has stoutly maintained that the education of youth is a proper responsibility of each state and should be delegated to local communities or school districts. Accordingly, then, the various states have established state systems of education with primary authority vested in local bodies, called boards of education, made up of citizens residing within each school district. These boards must comply with certain general regulations issued by their respective state governments, but are granted a large measure of freedom in the administration of education locally. One of the major responsibilities of these boards of education is the staffing of local schools. The matter of salaries for these professional workers is an item of much concern. Because by nature education is closely related to government and, hence, to politics, the possibility of malpractice in personnel and financial matters is a danger. To reduce the difficulties arising as a result of these factors, teacher salary scales were developed and teacher tenure legislation was adopted. The latter guarantees to each teacher continued employment if his work is satisfactory. The former provides for teachers a guaranteed annual salary with stated increases. By ensuring continued employment with salary increases it was thought the position of the teacher could be divorced from the influence of political patronage or favouritism. The problem then became one of developing salary schedules which were realistic and practicable.

Salary Schedules

The typical schedule which developed involves two features. Placement on the schedule is based on level of preparation, while promotion within the schedule is dependent on experience gained. Schedules may include up to five different categories of preparation, as follows: (1) normal school (less than four years beyond the secondary school), (2) the bachelor's degree, (3) the master's degree, (4) a sixth year of preparation, and (5) the doctorate. Beginning teachers are placed on schedule according to their collegiate training and may subsequently move to a higher category upon completion of additional schooling. The assumption here is that additional training will result in improved classroom service.

Typically, promotion within each category is automatic, with annual increments of stated amounts until the salary ceiling is reached. In this provision it is presumed that a teacher's work will improve as he continues on the job. Local schedules frequently include additional requirements for promotion within categories. Typical among these is a requirement that teachers take additional college work to earn the annual increment. In some instances credit is given for travel during vacation periods. Other schedules have provisions for some kind of merit rating to govern promotions.

Many of the states have passed legislation defining a mandatory minimum for all districts within the state. While many districts understand this to be a desired salary schedule, the intention is that local districts shall go beyond this minimal scale whenever possible.

The year 1919 marked a turning-point in the development of teacher salary scales in the United States. The publication that year of a study by E. S. Evenden, *Teachers' Salaries and Salary Schedules in the United States*, stirred interest in this matter, and the years immediately following saw a marked increase in the number of local districts using schedules. There were significant changes, also, in the nature of them. Until that time it has been customary to pay higher salaries to males and to secondary school teachers. Soon no differentiation was made among teachers on the basis either of sex or of grade level taught. To-day most school systems in the United States have adopted the single-salary schedule principle with placement and promotion based solely on level of academic preparation and years of experience.

The Bargaining Position of Teachers

Various arguments are used by workers in their demands for increased salaries, but some of the traditional bargaining procedures open to employees have not been available to teachers seeking higher wages. It has been considered impossible, for example, to develop a practical profit-sharing method of rewarding the contribution made by teachers. There is little question of the direct and valuable benefits derived from excellence in teaching. Inability to measure these results immediately and with the necessary accuracy, however, has forced teachers largely to abandon this as a practical argument. Ability of the employer to pay is another wage-demand premise which has proved of little value to teachers bargaining for higher salaries. No doubt the work of teachers increases the economic well-being of society and hence enlarges its ability to pay for their services. Failure to demonstrate a mathematical relationship between the health of an economy and the work of teachers has rendered this approach as ineffective as that of profit-sharing.

Supply and demand has some effect in determining teacher salary levels but its influence is often remote. The current teacher shortage has caused some increases in teacher salaries as local districts try to maintain their supply of classroom workers. Too often, however, replacements of inferior quality are hired to replace teachers who resign to earn more elsewhere. The large number of teachers leaving the profession annually has caused much concern and has had its effect in increasing teachers' salaries. The evident result in this instance, however, has been the provision of higher salaries for beginning teachers rather than an increase in teaching salaries generally.

It is apparent that the socialistic character of education in the United States governs the type of argument which can be utilized successfully by teachers as they seek to improve their economic status. One common argument put forward is that society should place a higher value on education and increase the salaries of educational workers accordingly. Many will grant the validity of this argument, but in the absence of specific measures of the value of education they are content to allow the *status quo* to prevail. Their reply is that, to date, the schools have done quite an acceptable job without these higher salaries. This approach has therefore had negligible effect in upgrading salary scales.

A second argument frequently advanced is that higher salaries for teachers are required in order to attract to the profession the most promising young people. As long as able youth see greater financial possibilities in other fields of work, it is argued, they will not consider teaching a desirable career. This is frequently extended to include the necessity for recruiting a greater number of men for teaching positions by adding that if heads of family units cannot foresee the possibility of providing comfortably for their families, they will not seek employment in teaching. This reasoning has met with some success, particularly in increasing the salaries of beginning teachers.

Another line of attack to justify salary increases for teachers is that based on the cost of living. This argument has taken two approaches. It is frequently stated that teacher salary increases are required if teachers are to maintain their relative position in an economy characterized by steadily increasing living costs. Several studies have been made in which the comparative economic position of teachers among other workers is shown to have deteriorated over a period of years. This appears to be a useful argument in obtaining increases for teachers. Certain industrial concerns have introduced the cost-of-living principle as an integral part of their salary schedules. To date, the typical procedure in teacher salary scheduling has been to provide a cost-of-living bonus for all teachers in the district. For example, each teacher may be given a double increment to offset increased living costs. Another application of the cost-of-living argument is that teachers are entitled to a certain economic status within the community because of the nature of their work. When teachers' incomes are compared with those of doctors, dentists, lawyers, and other professionals, it is argued that teachers need salary increases in order to maintain a standard of living comparable to these groups. This argument for a professional-level wage is based on factual data, but there is considerable reluctance to consider it seriously when it is applied to an automatic salary schedule for all teachers. The common feeling is that some measure of merit is needed to determine which teachers are truly professional before any high-level salaries can be achieved.

Comparative Studies of Salary Scales

Probably the most widely used argument for increasing teachers' salaries in a given district is that of comparison with the salaries paid in other districts. Several reasons have been advanced to explain the extensive use of this procedure. One of these is operation of the supply-and-demand principle within the profession. Ability to compete for teacher personnel is seen as a reason for maintaining salary-schedule levels comparable to those of neighbouring districts. A second possible reason for the utilization of comparative studies is that there is much in common among districts of a given size. Thus it is argued that teachers in one district are entitled to receive salaries equivalent to those paid in another district of comparable size.

A trend towards increased use of comparisons in industrial bargaining is another reason for the success of this approach to teacher salary increases. An upward spiral in industrial wages, with one company following another in providing pay increases, is cited as a usable precedent for the presentation of comparisons among school districts in arguing for higher teacher salaries. The fact that comprehensive teacher salary data are obtainable has been a factor also in the success of this approach. Increasingly in recent years, through the National Education Association and the United States Office of Education, detailed information has been published showing the teacher salary schedules in effect in various districts. These reports have been used extensively in local salary-scale discussions.

Another explanation for the widespread use of comparative studies is the development of salary schedules, and in their upward revision is the apparent usefulness of this technique. In instances where some more noble reasons for raising teachers' salaries may have little practical effect in achieving such increases, the argument of comparison with some other district or group of districts has often accomplished the desired results. It is apparent that when some of the wealthier school districts grant salary increases to their teachers, these higher-income levels become the goal of poorer districts. Efforts are then made in communities of moderate ability to raise salaries in order to compete successfully for needed teachers and to retain those already employed. As the gap between leader districts and those behind narrows there is agitation once more to raise salaries in the more able districts. Continued operation of this principle, particularly in a period of teacher shortages, has resulted in steadily increasing salaries for all teachers.

There has been much discontent both within and without the profession over the basic scheduling principles now in effect. Proposals for improving these are many and varied. Those outside the profession cite the critical need for some measurement of productivity in teaching whereby better teachers may be singled out for higher pay. The profession has been reluctant to accept this proposal, but if a suitable measuring procedure could be developed there would no doubt be widespread support for it among teachers. To those in the profession the greatest need seems to be for some practical procedure to provide additional income for those who have greater financial need. Supplementary allowances for dependants is mentioned frequently as one possible solution. In many instances, however, the matter of dependants' allowances appears to be in violation of the accepted principle of equal pay for equal work. Unmistakably, however, there is agreement that teacher salary schedules are in need of improvement.

EUGENE L. HAMMER.

PART B: STATISTICAL SUMMARY

BIENNIALLY for thirty years the NEA Research Division has published summaries of the salaries paid in urban school systems. Analyses also have been made of salary schedules. This article is primarily concerned with salaries paid in public elementary and secondary schools, but some facts are available on salaries in colleges and universities.

Public Elementary and Secondary Schools

In the United States about nine in ten of the pupils enrolled in elementary and secondary schools are in public schools. The term 'public' means schools supported by revenues obtained largely from taxes; the term 'non-public' is applied both to private educational institutions and to those supported by churches. Elementary schools usually include kindergarten through Grade VI; secondary schools include Grades VII through XII (but in some areas of the country the elementary schools include all grades up through Grade VIII).

In 1954–5 the average salary of classroom teachers in public elementary schools was *estimated* to be $3,614; high school teachers, $4,194; and of all public school teachers, $3,816. These amounts were about 5 per cent higher than they were in 1953–4.

Salaries Paid in Urban Schools

Detailed information is most complete with regard to salaries paid in urban school systems. Table I shows the median salaries *paid* for several types of positions in the school year 1954–5. It should be kept in mind that in each case the 'median' is the midpoint of the distribution (half of the cases fall above that point and half below).

Table II shows the number and proportion of classroom teachers in urban schools who are paid less than $2,500, and the number and proportion who are paid $5,500 or more. For example, in the largest cities (over 500,000 population) less than one-tenth of 1 per cent of the salaries reported were less than $2,500; more than 12 per cent were paid $5,500 or more in 1954–5. Adding together the totals for urban places of all sizes shows the following:

Type of Position	Total Number Reported	Paid Less than $2,500 in 1954–5		Paid $5,500 or More in 1954–5	
		Number	Per cent	Number	Per cent
Elementary school classroom teachers	280,647	5,762	2·1	35,976	12·8
Junior high school classroom teachers	62,473	456	0·7	10,092	16·2
High school classroom teachers	137,602	1,143	0·8	36,136	26·3

TABLE I

MEDIAN SALARIES PAID IN URBAN SCHOOL SYSTEMS IN 1954–5
(Figures in parentheses show purchasing power)[1]

Type of Position	Population Groups					
	Over 500,000	100,000– 500,000	30,000– 100,000	10,000– 30,000	5,000– 10,000	2,500– 5,000
1	2	3	4	5	6	7
CLASSROOM TEACHERS						
Elementary school	\$ 5,110[2]	\$ 4,055[2]	\$ 4,028[2]	\$ 3,857	\$ 3,591	\$ 3,465
	(4,471)	(3,548)	(3,524)	(3,374)	(3,142)	(3,031)
Junior high school	4,931	4,311	4,382	4,103	3,751	3,579
	(4,314)	(3,772)	(3,834)	(3,590)	(3,282)	(3,131)
High school	5,864	4,650	4,686	4,385	4,021	3,848
	(5,130)	(4,068)	(4,100)	(3,836)	(3,518)	(3,367)
Total, all regular classroom teachers	5,287	4,213	4,242	4,034	3,745	3,613
	(4,626)	(3,686)	(3,711)	(3,529)	(3,276)	(3,161)
PRINCIPALS (SUPERVISING)[3]						
Elementary school	7,956	6,321	5,897	5,479	5,175	4,773
	(6,961)	(5,530)	(5,159)	(4,794)	(4,528)	(4,176)
Junior high school	8,600	6,870	6,500	5,888	5,262	4,650
	(7,524)	(6,010)	(5,687)	(5,151)	(4,604)	(4,068)
High school	9,692	7,373	7,255	6,366	5,607	5,171
	(8,479)	(6,451)	(6,347)	(5,570)	(4,906)	(4,524)
SUPERINTENDENTS OF SCHOOLS	20,750	14,000	11,400	9,033	7,557	6,623
	(18,154)	(12,248)	(9,974)	(7,903)	(6,612)	(5,794)
Percentage of urban areas reporting[4]	100·0	92·7	88·9	66·0	59·4	51·5

[1] *The Consumer Price Index is based on the years 1947 through 1949 as 100·0; in January 1955 the index was 114·3; this index, divided into the current dollars paid, gives the purchasing power in 1947–9 dollars.*

[2] *In the largest cities the salaries of kindergarten teachers are not included in the medians for elementary school teachers. Their addition would have had slight effect upon the medians in urban places above 30,000 population.*

[3] *'Supervising' is used to mean those giving half time or more to administration and supervision; those giving more than half time to classroom instructional duties are not reported here.*

[4] *The classification 'urban' covers most systems in cities of 2,500 or more population, county units systems in which there is a city of 30,000 or more population, and other systems where half or more of the population live in urban communities.*

Salaries Paid in Rural Schools

The term 'rural' is usually applied to schools located in communities of less than 2,500 population. Comprehensive data are not available on salaries paid to public school teachers in rural schools.

The NEA Research Division's study of 4,266 rural school teachers, made in the school year 1951–2, showed an average salary of $2,484. In the same year the *estimated* average salary of all public school teachers was $3,365.

By size and type of schools the averages for classroom teachers in public rural schools in 1951–2 were as follows:

Rural Elementary Schools					*Average Salary*
1-teacher schools	.	.	.	.	$2,208
2- and 3-teacher schools	.	.	.	.	2,423
4- to 10-teacher schools	.	.	.	.	2,538
Over 10-teacher schools	.	.	.	.	2,581
All schools	.	.	.	.	2,385
Rural Secondary Schools					
With 10 or fewer teachers		.	.	.	2,866
With over 10 teachers		.	.	.	2,917
All schools	.	.	.	.	2,894

The foregoing amounts are ' averages ' (arithmetical means) rather than medians. Generally speaking, on a regional basis the highest salaries in rural schools were reported from the states in the far west, and the lowest from states in the south-east. In all regions the average salaries of secondary school teachers were higher than for elementary school teachers.

Relative Value of Salaries Paid

Salaries have value in terms of what they will buy; that is, their purchasing power. Expenditures are made by an individual in an effort to maintain a level or standard of living which he believes he needs for his occupation and which the community expects him to maintain.

Purchasing Power. In the United States a federal agency issues periodically a series of figures known as the Consumer Price Index. It is calculated in terms of the cost of a basic list of goods and services purchased by the family of a city wage earner. In the currently used index, a value of 100 represents the weighted average prices of commodities for the three years 1947, 1948, and 1949. Figures in excess of 100 represent the increase in prices over the base period (1947–9). The index in January 1955 was 114·3. When this index is divided into the salary (expressed in current dollars), the quotient is the salary in dollars of 1947–9 value.

Table I includes the median salaries of various positions in urban school systems and (in parentheses) the purchasing power of each median. It may be noted in passing that the average salary of ele-

TABLE II

RELATIVELY LOW AND HIGH SALARIES, URBAN CLASSROOM TEACHERS IN 1954-5

Type of Position and Salary Level	Population Groups					
	Over 500,000	100,000– 500,000	30,000– 100,000	10,000 30,000	5,000– 10,000	2,500– 5,000
1	2	3	4	5	6	7
ELEMENTARY SCHOOL CLASSROOM TEACHERS						
(a) Number paid less than $2,500	6	1,502	1,091	1,349	1,291	523
(b) Percentage (a) is of total number reported	0·01	2·0	1·8	2·6	5·4	5·9
(c) Number paid $5,500 or more	23,628	5,850	3,879	2,146	394	79
(d) Percentage (c) is of total number reported	37·7	7·9	6·5	4·1	1·7	0·9
JUNIOR HIGH SCHOOL CLASSROOM TEACHERS[1]						
(a) Number paid less than $2,500	0	136	127	121	53	19
(b) Percentage (a) is of total number reported	0·0	0·8	0·7	1·3	2·0	2·2
(c) Number paid $5,500 or more	5,226	2,202	2,076	540	42	6
(d) Percentage (c) is of total number reported	36·4	12·4	11·9	5·7	1·6	0·7
HIGH SCHOOL CLASSROOM TEACHERS						
(a) Number paid less than $2,500	1	176	177	325	315	149
(b) Percentage (a) is of total number reported	0·003	0·5	0·6	1·2	2·1	2·5
(c) Number paid $5,500 or more	19,307	7,001	5,692	3,335	693	108
(d) Percentage (c) is of total number reported	64·7	21·5	20·5	12·4	4·7	1·8
ALL TEACHERS						
(a) Number paid less than $2,500	7	1,814	1,395	1,795	1,659	691
(b) Percentage (a) is of total number reported	0·007	1·5	1·3	2·0	4·0	4·4
(c) Number paid $5,500 or more	48,161	15,053	11,647	6,021	1,129	193
(d) Percentage (c) is of total number reported	45·1	12·1	11·1	6·8	2·7	1·2

[1] Junior high school teachers are reported under this category when separate schools are organized; otherwise, teachers of Grades VII and VIII are reported as elementary school teachers; and teachers of Grade IX as high school.

TABLE III

MEDIANS OF THE MINIMUM AND MAXIMUM SALARIES FOR CLASSROOM TEACHERS
SPECIFIED IN SALARY SCHEDULES OF URBAN SCHOOL SYSTEMS, 1954–5
(Public Elementary and Secondary Schools)

For Preparation Indicated	Population Group					
	Over 500,000	100,000– 500,000	30,000– 100,000	10,000– 30,000	5,000– 10,000	2,500– 5,000
1	2	3	4	5	6	7
BACHELOR'S DEGREE (or four years of college)						
Median of minima[1]	$3,400	$3,194	$3,264	$3,108	$3,110	$3,075
Median of maxima	5,540	5,035	4,911	4,706	4,550	4,275
MASTER'S DEGREE (or five years)						
Median of minima	3,533	3,375	3,474	3,313	3,300	3,286
Median of maxima	5,800	5,344	5,317	5,050	4,986	4,570
SIX YEARS of college preparation						
Median of minima	3,850	3,720	3,728	3,490	3,650	3,625
Median of maxima	6,100	6,050	5,786	5,500	5,950	5,400
HIGHEST, if above six years of preparation						
Median of minima	[2]	3,750	3,929	3,675	[2]	[2]
Median of maxima	[2]	5,967	5,850	5,650	[2]	[2]
Total number of urban communities in group	18	124	414	799	726	440
Number used as basis for tabulations	18	107	296	107[3]	77[3]	41[3]

[1] *The median is the midpoint; above and below fall 50 per cent of the items. It may be said to be 'the average' of practice.*

[2] *Where only a few urban places provided salaries for those with more than six years of preparation, the medians were not calculated.*

[3] *The medians for urban school systems below 30,000 in population are based upon a selection of urban places believed to be representative of the nation geographically and of places of varying economic ability to support public schools.*

mentary teachers in urban places of 500,000 population has more than doubled since the survey in 1940–1 (that is, from $2,434 to $5,110), but it has increased only 12 per cent in purchasing power. Such facts must be kept in mind in considering what may appear to be the relatively high salaries of public school teachers in the United States.

Level of Living. The salaries of teachers in the United States must also be considered in terms of the average income of other occupations and the changes in income of these lines of employment. For example, the estimated average earning of civilian employees in the federal government was $4,103 in 1953; a 222·6 per cent gain over 1939. The average income of all persons working for wages and salaries was $3,590 in 1953; a gain of 284·0 per cent over 1939. Meanwhile, the average salary of all teachers in public schools increased 254·6 per cent (that is, rose from $1,420 to $3,615). All these salaries are calculated on a calendar-year basis and, therefore, are not comparable to salaries given in the tables of this article. Comparisons with the incomes of other professional groups (such as physicians, lawyers, and dentists) show that despite the gains between 1939 and 1953, the average salary of teachers is still less than one-third of the average earnings of dentists, lawyers, and physicians, taken as a group. These comparisons, of course, are between teachers on salary in public employment and other professionals with individual practices. The fact remains, however, that in comparison with other occupational groups in the United States, teachers, on the basis of average salary, have not advanced beyond the relatively low economic status they held prior to 1940.

Salary Schedules in Urban School Systems

At least 96 per cent of the urban places reporting in the Research Division's biennial survey of 1954–5 had a definite salary schedule. Nearly all these were the ' single-salary or preparation type '. This means that classroom teachers in public schools are paid primarily on the basis of years of college preparation whether they teach in elementary or secondary schools. Men and women teachers, with comparable preparation and experience, are paid at the same rates.

Table III gives some idea of the characteristics of the urban salary schedules reported in 1954–5. The figures in this table are *medians* of the tabulated distributions. For example, the median of the *minima* for a teacher with a bachelor's degree in cities over 500,000 was $3,400; the *lowest* minimum reported by one city was $2,714; the *highest*, also from one district, was $3,940. Similarly for the other medians, it should be kept in mind that there is a range of practice among the urban communities in each population group.

Most salary schedules provide for an annual increase or increment leading from the minimum to the maximum for those who continue in employment and, in some places, who meet the special inservice requirements. Typical practice is for twelve to fourteen annual increments, ranging from about $200 in the largest communities to $100 in the smallest places.

Salaries of principals of schools are less frequently outlined in a salary schedule than those of classroom teachers. In some places, particularly in elementary schools, the base pay for principals is determined by training and experience as outlined in the classroom teachers' schedule, and then the individual is paid an additional sum, based on the enrolment of the school or the number of teachers supervised. Since most of the large urban places (100,000 population or more) have salary schedules for principals, a few comparisons can be made as of March 1955 from data from 134 places:

(1) The maximum salary scheduled for supervising elementary school principals ranges from 5 to 60 per cent above the maximum available to a classroom teacher with the M.A. degree (five years of college preparation); median, around 37 per cent.

(2) Maxima available to junior high school principals range from 22 to 76 per cent higher than the maximum available to classroom teachers with the M.A. degree; median, 46 per cent.

(3) Maxima scheduled for high-school principals range from 29 to 94 per cent higher than the maximum available to classroom teachers with the M.A. degree; median, 57 per cent.

The salaries of the superintendent, since he is the executive officer of the local board of education, is determined largely by negotiation. Studies by the NEA Research Division indicate that the relative difference has steadily decreased during the past twenty-five years between the average salary of all superintendents in each urban population group and the average teacher's salary in the same group. The salaries paid superintendents in the 134 cities in 1955 ranged from 175 to 488 per cent higher than the maximum available to a classroom teacher with the master's degree. The median was around 270 per cent. It must be kept in mind that superintendents are employed for twelve months, and that most classroom teachers are paid for the school year (about ten months).

Scheduled Salaries in Colleges and Universities

There are about 1,850 institutions of higher education in the United States. This figure includes both the public (supported largely by taxation) and the non-public (both private and church-sponsored). A study made in 1952–3 by the NEA Research Division obtained information from about 40 per cent of nearly eleven hundred degree-granting institutions; 69 per cent of those replying had salary schedules. Some of the general characteristics of these college and university salary schedules are shown in Tables IVA and IVB.

Again, it should be remembered that the figures shown are medians. For example, the median maximum shown for professors in state universities is $7,575, but two universities had scheduled maxima above $10,000; one had scheduled maxima below $6,000. Similar differences existed for other positions and other types of institutions.

About 54 per cent of the schedules were created by action of the

TABLE IVa

MEDIANS OF MINIMA AND MAXIMA IN SALARY SCHEDULES OF PUBLIC
COLLEGES AND UNIVERSITIES, 1952–3
(For nine months of the academic year)

Type of Position (and Median)	Type of Institution			
	State Universities	Land-grant Colleges	State Colleges	Teachers Colleges
1	2	3	4	5
INSTRUCTORS				
Median of minima	$3,317	$3,350	$3,050	$3,567
Median of maxima	4,517	4,517	4,150	4,363
ASSISTANT PROFESSORS				
Median of minima	3,890	4,050	3,725	4,063
Median of maxima	5,275	5,375	4,670	5,325
ASSOCIATE PROFESSORS				
Median of minima	4,850	4,950	4,250	4,600
Median of maxima	6,250	6,425	5,308	6,133
PROFESSORS				
Median of minima	6,025	6,017	4,950	5,417
Median of maxima	7,575	7,600	6,050	6,650
Number replying to questionnaire	40	35	56	77
Number with salary schedules	21	19	40	60

local board of the institution; 9 per cent by state law; 15 per cent by
action of the state board of education; the remainder by miscellaneous
officials and committees.

Unlike schedules for public school teachers, a number of the college
schedules have no increments specified, others depend upon the available funds, and still others have some kind of ' merit ' requirement.
Where sums were specified, they ranged from $50 to $720 among the
colleges reporting. Part of the lack of development of salary schedules
may arise from their recency—almost half of those reported had been
created since 1950.

Frame of Reference

A brief reminder of the organization and financing of public education is appropriate at this point because of the influence of these factors
upon salary rates. There are about 1,125,000 public school teachers
(classroom teachers, principals, and supervisors) employed by approximately sixty thousand local school districts or administrative units.
Except for the requirements of state minimum salary laws, decisions
on salary rates are made largely by local school directors, trustees or

TABLE IVʙ

MEDIANS OF MINIMA AND MAXIMA IN SALARY SCHEDULES OF NON-PUBLIC
COLLEGES AND UNIVERSITIES, 1952–3
(For nine months of the academic year)

Type of Position (and Median)	Type of Institution			
	Universities	Colleges (by Enrolment)		
		Under 500	500–999	1,000 or More
1	2	3	4	5
INSTRUCTORS				
Median of minima	$3,083	$2,717	$2,850	$3,033
Median of maxima	4,050	3,340	3,675	3,950
ASSISTANT PROFESSORS				
Median of minima	3,650	3,125	3,267	3,567
Median of maxima	4,950	3,790	4,088	4,560
ASSOCIATE PROFESSORS				
Median of minima	4,350	3,550	3,800	4,100
Median of maxima	5,900	4,325	4,533	5,100
PROFESSORS				
Median of minima	5,033	3,990	4,275	4,800
Median of maxima	7,033	5,015	5,090	6,080
Number replying to questionnaire	26	80	61	31
Number with salary schedules	20	57	42	22

boards of education. Funds for the support of public schools (including the cost of salaries) are provided by three governmental levels in the following average proportions for the nation as a whole: 57·9 per cent from local; 38·6 per cent from the state; and 3·5 per cent from the federal government. Taxes are usually levied by a municipality or county to supply local funds (the real-estate tax supplies about 53 per cent of all local funds). State funds are authorized by the state legislature; federal funds are authorized by the Congress.

Public colleges are supported by funds from one or more levels of government, by fees paid by students, by grants of money from individuals and groups, and by income from investments. In each college the salary rates are usually determined by its board of trustees or board of directors, except in certain state colleges, where a state-wide schedule has been authorized by a state board of higher education or similar agency.

FRANK W. HUBBARD.

CHAPTER SIXTEEN

Teachers in Norway

FOR much the same historical reasons as obtain in a number of countries, there is in Norway a marked distinction between grammar school teachers with a university degree on the one hand, and on the other, teachers in elementary and other ' lower ' schools.

Grammar School and Elementary School Teachers

The grammar school teachers usually have about seven years' study at the university, with examinations in one principal and two auxiliary subjects, after which they get the *Cand. Philol.* or the *Cand. Real.* degree, qualifying as *lektor*. A few take a shorter time and present themselves for examinations in three subjects only as ' auxiliary ' subjects and obtain the *Cand. Mag.* degree, which is the prescribed qualification of an *adjunkt*. Both categories have, after graduating, to go to the so-called ' Pedagogical Seminary ' for six months, where they study educational theory and get practical training. The course leads to an examination, after which the candidates receive their teacher's certificates.

Elementary school teachers receive their instruction in the subjects taught at school, and in the theory of education, as well as their practical training, either in a four-year training college on the basis of a completed elementary school education and some further study; or in a two-year college after a completed grammar school education.

As in large parts of the country the density of population is very low, many schools, both elementary and secondary, are small. Therefore elementary school teachers have, in principle, to cover the whole range of subjects taught, and it has also proved necessary for secondary school teachers to be capable of teaching at least three subjects.

All elementary and the greater number of secondary schools are municipal, though financially supported by the State. Private schools are of a negligible importance in Norway. Teachers in elementary schools and ' continuation schools ' are appointed by the municipal education committee, while grammar school teachers and heads, as well as the staff of state-owned special schools, are appointed by the Ministry (or the Government).

There was a lack of competent teachers for the secondary schools in the early 'twenties, and at present there is (for the same reasons as in many highly developed countries) a shortage of science masters, which will soon spread also to the teachers of humanities. Since the war there has been a totally inadequate supply of elementary school teachers. These circumstances have led to a certain dilution, which is recognized by teachers as a grave danger to their position. The situation is, however, different for the two classes of teachers; there has been, and is, a strong demand for admission to the teachers' colleges, so recruitment has been of high quality, and this tends to increase the self-confidence and prestige of elementary school teachers. On the other hand, the faculties of science and of humanities are ' open ', while a number of other studies, such as medicine, engineering, agricultural science, are ' closed '. Consequently the latter attract the best students, and the studies leading to the teaching profession are chosen mostly by young persons with less brilliant entrance examination results.

Obstacles to a Unified Profession

This is not the only influence at work tending to lower social, economic, and academic standards for teachers. Proposals have been made—and considered—to ' rationalize ' and shorten their studies for future secondary school teachers, as well as to facilitate the in-service (or other) training of elementary school teachers by which they may qualify for positions in the secondary schools. The view is also advanced that in the interest of a rapidly approaching unified system of post-elementary education, the barrier between the two categories of teachers should be broken down by introducing a new training scheme consisting of a common basis of general education with a variety of additional specialized training.

The grammar school teachers on the whole protest against any plan to introduce what they consider to be a lowering of standards. They have already fought their first skirmish : when, some years ago, the authorities began to give the titles of *lektor* and *adjunkt* to teachers of a non-academic or a lower academic standing, working mostly in vocational schools, the *Norsk Lektorlag* (Norwegian Grammar School Teachers' Association) opened a lawsuit against the Ministry, and in the end won its case before the Supreme Court of Justice. The victory was, however, not decisive, and the fight continues. The importance of titles as a means of keeping up social prestige and the principle of academic superiority is recognized by both parties.

The teachers in Norway did not take advantage of their strong position in the eyes of the public immediately after the war, during which they had been in the vanguard of the fight against nazification. So they found themselves in an unfavourable position when, in 1948, a new

comprehensive system of salary scales for the civil service was introduced. Only a minority of teachers at state-owned grammar schools
are actually civil servants, but the rest of the grammar school masters
have by law the same economic and other rights, and the regulations
governing civil service salaries are indirectly also applied to elementary
school teachers. As the latter, and the bulk of grammar school staff
are formally employees of the municipal authorities, they had in many
places succeeded in obtaining substantial 'municipal additions' to
their salaries. This fact was taken into account when the grammar
school teachers were given their place in the new salary scales system.
The municipalities, shortly after this, took concerted action to do away
with the extras, and made the *Storting* (Parliament) forbid them, leaving only an unsatisfactory transitional arrangement. The official
salaries were not sufficiently increased to counterbalance the loss of
'extras'. When new salary scales were later introduced for elementary school teachers, they represented a considerable improvement for
teachers in rural areas and small towns. But in the larger towns,
where the municipal extras had been important, the outcome of the
change was rather unsatisfactory. As a result of this the teachers in
the elementary schools of Oslo went on strike in the winter 1953-4.
Although supported by their own municipal authorities and public
opinion, the teachers came out of the strike with symbolic rather than
real gains. Like most conflicts on pay during the past few years, this
one also was made difficult and complicated by the fall in the purchasing power of the Norwegian crown.

Union Activity

The strike in Oslo led to a split in the teachers' ranks. Most elementary school teachers belong to the *Norges Lærerlag* (Norwegian Union
of Teachers—of both sexes: only a smaller group of women teachers
still keep the *Norges Lærerinneforbund* going), but as this organization
did not dare to risk the advantages already won for many of its members, especially in rural districts, it refused to support the strikers, and
practically all the elementary school teachers of Oslo broke away from
it. They represent about 10 per cent of the membership, and are still
strongly against their old organization.

The *Norsk Lektorlag* (comprising 90-95 per cent of the grammar
school teachers) has, during the last five years, often been on the verge
of strike action, but has succeeded by negotiation in obtaining considerable improvements for its members. This does not mean that they
are content, but as far as their position within the general salary
system is concerned they are not very far from what can at present be
demanded, considering the length of their studies and the nature of

their responsibilities compared with other professions. An exception should be made of head masters, whose salaries are obviously too low when compared with those of assistant teachers and of other professions.

Now that the salaries of the teachers are beginning to reach the right level within the salary system for the civil service, they can be improved and adapted to salaries in private enterprise only by joint action, with all falling within the frame of the system. This system is difficult because all the salaries in question are determined by the *Storting*, not by the executive power, and because civil servants have no right to strike.

The elementary school teachers' organizations are ' independent ', and negotiate on their own with the authorities, but always only to get into line with what has been decided for the civil service. The grammar school teachers, through their *Norsk Lektorlag*, belong to a top union, the *Embetsmennenes Landsforbund* (National Council of Higher Civil Servants). Formerly in competition, now mostly in friendly co-operation with the two unions of lower civil servants, this organization struggles for a level of salaries which is more in conformity with salaries in private enterprise. So far it has succeeded in having civil service salaries adapted to the continuous rise in living costs, but has not obtained further concessions, such as a fair share of the increased national income. And, as State authorities refuse to recognize comparisons further back than 1948, the tendency continues towards a slow evening-out (or down, rather) of salaries for academically educated people. Calculations, for example, of a grammar school teacher's whole-career income as compared with that of a skilled labourer have been tried as an arguing-point, but are not accepted as valid by the authorities.

In Norway, all civil servants (except a few in the very highest positions) are protected by the Constitution from dismissal by the administration. They can lose their job only by judgment passed in a court of justice. This security of tenure also applies to teachers. They usually get a permanent appointment after two to four years' service. Out of their salaries they pay 10 per cent to the civil service superannuation scheme, and are secured a pension of about two-thirds of their salary at the time of resignation. They have to retire at 70, and may do so any time after they are 65 (for women five years earlier). If they have to leave work before reaching the pension age, they receive an intermediary pension according to length of service. In case of illness, they receive full pay, usually up to six months, with a possibility of prolongation.

They also receive increments and rise by grades in the salary scale automatically by years. This is a much-used argument against the teachers' salary claims; they are guaranteed a steady rise in pay, irrespective of ability and efficiency, so they cannot expect to reach the top salaries given to persons in high positions for which there is an open competition. Proposals to introduce a system of promotion within the teaching profession have met with stubborn resistance, and it is true that one of the great advantages of the Norwegian system is the good *esprit de corps* resulting from complete equality amongst the professional staff. The teachers argue that in no other branch of public service are there so few chances of promotion to better-paid positions of leadership. Therefore, the grammar school teachers claim, and are near to obtaining, a top salary equal to that of persons in 'top positions' in the civil service. The fact that grammar school teachers' (*lektors*) salaries rise during eighteen years by about two-thirds (from 11,950 Norwegian crowns to 20,200 [1]) is resented by young teachers, but it is in line with the ordinary economic career of a university-trained civil servant.

The elementary school teachers are paid according to the number of teaching periods during the year, and thus their salaries vary a great deal, but do not rise very much with length of service.

For grammar school teachers there is complete equality between the sexes: men and women receive the same pay and have to give twenty-four lessons a week. Male elementary school teachers have to give thirty-six lessons, but women teachers only thirty, and receive thirty-thirty-sixths of the men's salaries.

Shortage does not carry with it any bargaining advantage to teachers in Norway. But an increased public interest in education, and the prospect of school reform, together with outspoken discontent among teachers, led to the appointment of a governmental commission in 1954 to consider the whole problem of economic and working conditions for all categories of teachers. This commission will make its recommendation in October 1955, but no radical proposals are expected.

A. St. Langeland.

---

[1] According to new scales proposed from October 1st, 1955: from 13,145 to 22,935—a Norwegian *crown* being equivalent to a *shilling* sterling.

SOCIO-ECONOMIC CONSEQUENCES AND DETERMINANTS

THERE is a widespread belief that economic progress and education are very closely related. Evidently, modern industry depends upon a constant supply of well-trained people—skilled technicians, technologists, clerks and executives. It is often felt that the development of a national system of education makes possible rapid economic, social and political advances. Throughout the world this conviction has stimulated an interest in Western education as an initiator of economic progress. It is a view that might be contrasted with the classical economic theories which point out that economic change precedes educational ones; the latter, in fact, invariably lag behind so that in an expanding economy, for example, there is likely to be a shortage of skilled workers and a delay in the inculcation of appropriate social attitudes in the face of changing methods of production. Both these hypotheses are useful in any analysis of the returns on educational investment. This section is, then, in two main parts. The first deals with the consequence of educational investment in Europe and the United States. In the second part problems typical of Africa, Asia and Latin America are discussed.

It is, indeed, difficult to measure the return on educational investment. It cannot be done simply in terms of economic efficiency through technical progress—there are various concepts of " a higher standard of living " and it is perhaps unwise to accept without reservation material standards. Education might lead, for example, to political and social stability, or it might increase instability and encourage social mobility; it might encourage conformism or make political control possible. Then the question arises, " How shall people choose and who shall speak for them?" On the one hand one objective might be realized in the continued production of a *literati*, artists and an intellectual *élite*—but it might mean that technical educational lags so far behind that the whole economy of the country and the way of life of its inhabitants are perforce modified. The interrelation between education and national economy indicates the possibilities and the limitations of social planning.

The effect of educational provision on production is indeed very complex. It is difficult to measure successive ' inputs ' of education and ' outputs ' in production. Generally the costs of non-utilization of trained personnel are high, as are the consequences of failure to train skilled workers. Further, the compulsory acquisition by the state of resources for education through taxation, might affect incentives to produce. Taxation levels often depend largely on high educational expenditures. In addition, taxation policy might also be affected by the redistribution of income consequent on the state provision of education. For education is provided for those who would otherwise be unable to afford it and their earning capacity is therefore enhanced. Taxation might in fact prove a disincentive. The important problem for society is that of reconciling its objectives in terms of educational provision with other objectives. There is no optimum level of expenditure on education independent of the use of resources in other directions—this level will differ from community to community depending on a system of priorities, the integrity of the government, the economic viability of the land and so on. Failure to appreciate this might lead to frustration on the part of those who think of education in isolation.

The effect of educational provision on social and vocational mobility is equally important. The structure of the educational system and the allocation of resources within it are significant determinants of the social structure, the number of people who move into skilled jobs and of the speed with which young people can be absorbed into industry. Schooling may create occupational incentives, social ambition or political awareness. It may make its pupils able and willing to adapt themselves to changing circumstances or predispose them to resist change. Undoubtedly, part of the return on educational investment is social and though it may be discerned, the processes of evaluating it are themselves social.

In the first study, Dr. Kiehn describes the close relationship between education and economic growth in nineteenth-century Germany. It is followed by a theoretical analysis of the possible returns on education, written by Dr. Harold Clark; most of the illustrations are drawn from the United States. Dr. Ginzberg discusses the effects of education in the United States on national efficiency. The last article in the first part, by Mrs. Jean Floud and Mr. Halsey, is an analysis of the English educational system in terms of its occupational consequences.

Dr. Raum describes the objectives of Bantu tribal education and some of the consequences—both social and personal—of introducing into these areas Western education. This is followed by Professor Madge's analysis of the social and economic determinants of education in a peasant society. Professor Lewis reviews the problems in these terms for the British colonial territories and M. Thabault for Morocco. Finally, the relationship between education and the economy in Latin America is reviewed by M. Julio Larrea.

THE EDITORS.

CHAPTER ONE

German Education and Economy in the Nineteenth Century *

ONLY recently has the close link between the economic development of Germany and education become the subject of scientific research. So far very little specialized work has been carried out. What follows —and particularly since it is so short—must be regarded only as a first attempt to survey the field.

One of the difficulties in attempting to give a brief account of the numerous and varied problems is that before 1871 there was no Germany in a national sense, with its own economy and education. Napoleon's policy of expansion in Europe had the effect after 1803 of considerably reducing the multi-coloured aspect of the German map. However, he could no more remove it than could the Congress of Vienna (1815), which put thirty-nine autonomous German states together in a federation under the leadership of Austria. Each of these states had a history of its own in its economic development and education. In Bismarck's German *Reich* many aspects of the Prussian development became characteristic. This is true not only of the oft-cited militarism but of the less frequently recalled policies of economic freedom and expansion. These and the generous educational plans under Frederick Wilhelm III are among the more positive outcomes of the Prussian period of reform which followed the collapse of 1806.

This planned 'revolution from the top'—initiated by Stein and taken over by Hardenberg—proposed to remedy the structural faults in public life due to the absolutism of Frederick the Great.

Developments between 1806 and 1834

Confined to the territory east of the Elbe, exposed to the economically disastrous effects of an anti-British economic policy, and occupied by French troops, Germany had few prospects of recovery. Stein's proposals were, therefore, optimistic, but not utopian. He wanted to give the population ethical reasons for resisting the unification of Europe by the Corsican usurper, and thus to initiate a renaissance of the people. At that time the concept of German national freedom

---

* This is a précis of a longer article.—THE EDITORS.

was deeply rooted in the eighteenth-century ideas of individual freedom. Moral freedom was placed before national independence. This
implied a release in Prussia of all those forces which, until then, had
been bound by absolutism.

The Stein-Hardenberg reform represented a political and economic
re-education of major importance : the liberation of the peasants, for
example, the reorganization of the towns on the French model, the
reform of the army, and a new policy of free trade. It put an end to
the traditional restrictions of the medieval guild-system. In this connexion the emancipation of the Jews in Prussia (1812) had very positive effects on the economic development of the country.

Naturally, within this framework new methods of education had to
be sought. Wilhelm v. Humboldt, a friend of the Weimar group, introduced, during his short term of office as head of the Prussian educational system (1809–10), reforms whose influence is still apparent. He
was a typical representative of the classical German neo-humanist
movement. He objected to any premature link between education
and vocational training and, therefore, rejected, for example, the industrial schools (Industrieschulen) which had been created late in the
eighteenth century. For him, the education of the nation implied
nothing more than a reorganization of the universities and institutions
of higher learning, together with a humane education of the type
advocated by the great Swiss, J. Heinrich Pestalozzi, whom the German elementary school teachers have come to regard as one of themselves.

The Prussian law of 1794—the product of enlightened absolutism—
had declared that all schools were to be the responsibility of the state.
Thus it was possible to alter the whole university system in terms of
philosophic idealism, to introduce into the grammar schools
(Gymnasia) the cult of Latin and Greek, and to reorganize the whole
of elementary education (which previously had been largely religious in emphasis) and teacher training into a national system of
' humanistic ' education.

Humboldt did not exclude the possibility of vocational training at
a later stage and accepted Pestalozzi's concept of " developing of all
talents " despite his opposition to the idea of ' usefulness ' and the fact
that he thought in terms of ' class '. He wanted to include vocational
training, but to keep it strictly separate. ' Training ' was to follow
' education ', and ' education ' certainly did not mean a fund of useful
knowledge. The all-important point was the spiritual formation of
the young generation. Later on, in professional life, " everybody can
be a good workman, soldier, or businessman only if, irrespective of his
particular vocation, he is a good, decent and—according to his station

in life—a well-educated man and citizen. If the school can help him to become that, he will easily learn later on what is necessary for his profession, but he will retain the freedom to switch from one job to another, as so often happens in life " (1809). Although Metternich's policy was to curb all these liberal tendencies, nevertheless the Prussian elementary schools and the training of their teachers developed comparatively well up to about 1840.

It should not be forgotten that, during this period, Prussian leaders were pursuing a policy of free trade. The impoverishment which followed the Napoleonic wars made them anxious to do everything possible to recover economically. Attempts were made to unify the country through progressive economic policies. First of all, the western areas of the Rhine and Westphalia, which had been territorially and culturally part of the French state, had to be absorbed. This was attempted, among other things, in the great Prussian customs reform of 1818. The Customs Union of 1834 represented a further considerable success for Prussia both economically and politically. It became important in the incipient process of European industrialization by adding, to the considerable potential of Upper Silesia, the whole of the Ruhr.

Just as important as the natural resources of these areas were their inhabitants. The more conservative population of the agricultural areas in the east were counterbalanced by a liberally minded, intellectually active, nationalistically inclined *bourgeoisie*. It accepted and absorbed into its school policy many new Prussian ideas.

But compared with the British economy, that of Germany was somewhat backward. In 1804, for example, three-quarters of the ten million Prussians lived in villages. And half of the urban population were, in fact, little more than rural people living in towns. Yet by the end of the century Germany had changed into a highly developed industrial state. This development was more than an ' economic process ', and can be understood only in terms of the German people, who were on the whole moral, economical, persevering, and easily encouraged to be industrious whenever there was a prospect of even modest success. Through better schooling children learned how to " use their own brains ", as Kant called it. Although long periods of war resulted in the neglect of both town and village, religiously inspired counter-influences developed. In the Protestant churches they were not, however, always strong enough to counteract the destructive influences of industrialization which began to show in the 'fifties.

The development began slowly, and little effect was felt up to 1834. The number of industrialists who were becoming rich was increasing, and they were becoming more important. But as most of them were

former craftsmen the old merchant class remained socially aloof. Only
where there were common interests did they co-operate. Nevertheless, in contrast to the desires of the various German princes, they
aimed at a comprehensive German customs union. It is not surprising
that at the time, and particularly in Prussia, it was the industrialists
who complained of the low standards of education. They recognized,
rightly, that their own craftsman-like empirical way of working was
one of the most serious obstacles to the successful development of
German industry. A new epoch in German education can consequently
be distinguished. Educational institutions developed which were supposed to provide what was missing in apprenticeships.

The apprentice tradition remained despite the increasing freedom of
trade, but the schools were no longer supposed only to pass on a certain fund of general knowledge; they now had to anticipate professional life and teach those things which could not easily be learned
by experience in later life. Thus the schools anticipated future
economic development and helped it on—they have done so time and
time again since then. Even during this first period, neo-humanist
traditions did not interfere with the development of a vocational
school system. The need was too obvious, and secondly, the enlightened German *bourgeoisie*, with deep roots, experienced a marked
revival under the influence of the liberal political movements in France
around 1840. Their tendency to think rationally and analytically—a
process necessary in science—found expression in the functional
design of the vocational school. To the neo-humanist idea of the
generally educated man was added that of the ' progressive specialist '.
Under this influence new vocational schools were being founded for
the masses. As in 1790, they were founded as Sunday schools by
working men's societies, Freemasons, and persons with a social conscience. Just as in England and the U.S.A., the idea was to promote
industrial, agricultural, and commercial development and at the same
time to help the young hard-working artisan.

It was not by accident that the densely populated areas like Saxony,
Würtemberg, and Baden were more advanced than Prussia. In Prussia,
and particularly in the more agricultural regions, the Sunday schools
retained for a long time their religious character. Side by side with
these schools, others developed for the young people going into the
higher occupational levels of trade, industry, building, forestry and
agriculture, commerce and shipping. These will be dealt with later.
What was becoming clear at this time has been described by Friedrich
List in his *Das Nationale System der politischen Oekonomie* (1841) and
aimed at " the education of Germans for Industry ". List points out
how an economic programme was at the same time also educational.

This way of thinking was the result of the synthesis between the neo-humanist Pestalozzian ideas and the most urgent economic requirements. From both an educational and an economic point of view, "every effort for the education of youth" represented an economic investment the return on which was greater productivity. Further, education was itself a productive activity in the economic sense. Undoubtedly this basic idea is the key to a great many problems in the economic history of nineteenth-century Germany.

The Second Epoch, from 1834 to 1871

During this period, the successful development of the newly created German trade within the continent of Europe coincided with the revolution in transportation brought about by the railways. The latter advanced industrialization. British industry had for a long time dominated the German market, but attempts were being made to become independent. In 1837, Borsig began to build locomotives in Berlin. Gradually it was possible to replace British engineers by Germans. To do this, however, training facilities were required on a large scale. This problem touched all types of non-vocational school, including secondary schools. For, as a preparation for the professions in trade and industry, a 'middle-class' school was claimed to be necessary. It should offer a thorough training in modern languages (and particularly in English), in mathematics, and in the physical sciences; in short, in everything which the somewhat detached humanistic *Gymnasia*, with their classical studies, could not supply.

It should not be overlooked, of course, that graduates from the *Gymnasia* could compete in medicine and in the new methods of research in the exact sciences. But the demands for a new type of school were usually based on a rejection of the German university approach. As early as 1834 the Prussian administrators had given in to these demands. A new type of school had been created, the so-called *Realschule*, in which (and they were modelled on the lines of the *Gymnasia*) a humanistic element was included. Even in these schools professional training was not included. Both types of *Realschule*, i.e., those in which Latin was taught and those in which it was not, proved themselves during the century so that, extended to the *Realgymnasia* and the *Ober-realschulen*, they were entitled late in the century to grant certificates that admitted their graduates to enter the unversities in the same way as *Gymnasia* graduates.

A similar change took place in higher education. Although on the whole the German universities during the nineteenth century were pretty conservative, nevertheless they accepted new tasks, particularly in the pure sciences. The results of the research done there were in fact applied in technical fields and contributed greatly to agriculture, forestry, building, machine construction, and in the initial use of electricity. How great this contribution was can be judged when the work of men like Gauss, Weber, and Justus Liebig is considered.

Chronologically " Beruf " schulen (then full-time vocational secondary schools) were the first to be created. They provided special vocational training in courses of one to three years, which were a sort of preparation for technically trained personnel of the foremen grade; men who in modern industry cannot be trained mechanically. A large number of vocational and technical schools was founded, often called polytechnics, for building, mining, agriculture, forestry, and commerce, which were often of the same standard as the Realschule. From the above, technological institutions like the Technische, Landwirtschaftliche, or Forstwirtschaftliche Hochschule (technical, agriculture, and forestry), the Bergakademie (mining), and the Handelshochschule (commercial) developed which, towards the end of the century, were to be ranked with the universities. In these developments together with the vocational Sunday schools the modern ' tripartite ' system of vocational and commercial schools can be discerned (a development influenced both by England and France). The novel feature about these schools, compared with their eighteenth-century predecessors, was that they were no longer the responsibility of professional organizations but of the state. In the 'sixties, persons with foresight within the Prussian Ministry of Commerce made plans on the basis of accurate calculations and analysis. Commercial circles offered encouragement, but remained critical observers.

About that time the reorganization of the Prussian Army and the introduction of modern weapons were undoubtedly important. The part, for example, that Krupp steel played in making guns for Bismarck's wars of unification is well known. Prussian Germany, at the time, went through all the internal crises experienced by England—the mother country of industrialism. The population rose amazingly. In spite of large-scale emigration to the United States, modern industrial towns began to shoot up—mirroring most convincingly industrial expansion. This expansion required only the decisive political foundation of the German Empire in 1871 for a jump to be made into world markets. To gain time and consolidate peacefully what he had acquired by force, Bismarck aimed at a ' European ' policy which would make the German Reich a member of the group of colonial powers without having international repercussions. All this introduced a thorough change into the German way of life. Particularly after 1888, under Wilhelm II, there was a danger that the increased material well-being would lead to an impoverishment of moral and spiritual values. After the end of the century, voices could be heard warning against this danger. With the sudden outbreak of the First World War in 1914, what can rightly be called the nineteenth century came to an end.

The Third Epoch, from 1871 to 1914

During this period the criticisms of the educators were particularly loud and harsh. The expansionist movement, so contrary to tradition, also entered the sphere of education. In 1872 a liberal school reform in Prussia attempted to do away with religious and traditional obstacles to the development of a modern school system which would train pupils at the secondary level for the middle range of occupations. For the next fifty years an overloaded curriculum helped to model the elementary school on secondary school lines (*kleine Realschule*).

In connexion with the social tensions between the *bourgeoisie* and the workers we may now explain what measures the state took for young people leaving school. Saxony was the first (1873) to introduce a state system of further education; in the following year Prussia, Baden, and Hessen did likewise. Others took a longer time—for example, Bavaria (1895). The fact that, particularly after 1878, so many *Berufsfachschulen* (full-time vocational secondary schools) were opened, may probably be traced back to the publication of the very critical *Briefe aus Philadelphia* which was published by Reuleaux, the director of the *Gewerbe Akademie* in Berlin, after the International Exhibition in Philadelphia (1876). In comparing the manufactured goods of other countries with those of Germany he called the latter, frankly, " cheap and bad ".

The following year the well-known economist, Karl Bücher of Leipzig, found unanimous support in German economic circles for his publication : *Die gewerbliche Bildungsfrage und der industrielle Rück-gang* (The Problem of Vocational Training and Economic Regression). He firmly demanded new vocational schools for industrial occupations, with opportunities, wherever possible, for workshop training. State authorities, clearly recognizing the importance of this, dipped deep into their pockets. That they were wise in doing so was proved by the rise in export figures at the turn of the century.

Further education of the type mentioned had not taken its final form, although it aimed at making young people more competent in economic matters and at raising their ability. But the methods that had been chosen were not the right ones and the results were consequently disappointing. What in fact happened was that the curriculum of the elementary schools was repeated. Intellectual drill in these schools took place in buildings that often closely resembled army barracks. It took the form of a rigid instruction-technique based on Herbartianism. From this strictly formal discipline, in the elementary schools and schools of further education, however, the German worker got the intellectual equipment which made it possible for him to absorb the ideas in Marxist Socialism and in other economic theories. The role of the army should be mentioned in this context. As the ' school of the nation ' for ' the education of Germans for industry ' it gave a drastic education in obedience aimed at co-operation and subordination through drill and hard field work in physical endurance and preparedness. Associated with the proverbial spirit of army comradeship, training in how to function as an integral part of a group undoubtedly helped to produce smoothness in the discipline of industrial teamwork. Furthermore, the elementary training in the artillery and navy helped a great many of the rural population, the uninstructed workers, to acquire a fund of simple technical knowledge which became important in their later professional life, and which often helped them to accept more readily technical improvements in agriculture.

Apart from the ' vocational ' schools in the narrow sense, the agricultural, domestic, and commercial schools, the so-called *Kunstgewerbeschulen* (arts, crafts, and applied arts) developed where designers in the furniture, textile, and similar trades were trained after having served their apprenticeship. In this respect, these schools could be compared with the middle vocational schools for shipbuilding, machine-construction, and building. The importance of schools of art of high school rank (the so-called *Akademien*) need not be discussed here. But the numerous commercial institutions should be discussed. From the beginning, chambers of commerce took care that there should be schools for young trainees. Voluntary institutions for the further training of commercial employees bear witness— in the second half of the century—to the great number of new and urgent tasks which arose as a result of the expansion of German trade, the import and export business, and the inevitable growth of commercial activity to deal with this industrial enterprise. These problems had to find their solutions in the schools.

In 1895, leading business men in Braunschweig formed a German Association for Commercial Education (*Deutschen Verband für das kaufmänlische Bildungswesen*), which, after the Second World War, again became important. Even to-day, state authorities are indebted to the association for many helpful suggestions in all aspects of professional practice. In certain common interests it co-operates successfully with an association for vocational education (*Deutsche Gesellschaft zur Förderung des gewerblichen Bildungswesens*). The role of the teachers' unions has also been significant. Many of their members in commercial and agricultural education are university graduates. It seems possible that other vocational teachers will soon have to reach the same academic standards.

Future Prospects

Towards the end of the century a great change set in which is of importance to-day. It will always be linked with the name of a Munich inspector of schools, Dr. Georg Kerschensteiner (1854–1932). Deeply attached to the idealist traditions of German education, but at vital points influenced by the practical outlook of the United States (particularly of John Dewey), Kerschensteiner began in 1895 to re-organize radically the whole system of further education in Bavaria so that it became a model for the rest of Germany. He divided all the schools and school classes according to special occupations. The new institutions got the name of *Berufsschulen* (part-time vocational secondary schools). The name was not new, but the purposes they served were. They had a double task of ' encouraging trade ' and pro-viding young people of both sexes with a ' humanistic ' education. Thus Kerschensteiner tried to link up, from the viewpoint of education, what Pestalozzi, Goethe, Schleiermacher, and Friedrich List had aimed at, with the manifold professional demands which had developed in Germany during the nineteenth century as a result of industrialization. Man and his ethical values could not be separated from his professional activity. Only the person who had received standards and values through his practical and theoretical training could become more than a specialist in the purely economic sense. Only such a person could remain human in the increasingly soulless processes of modern pro-duction. The task of such a *Berufsschule* was, according to Kerschen-steiner, more than giving the most efficient practical and theoretical professional training. It should prepare a young man through school life and the reflective absorption of ideas for democratic participation and partnership in work. Kerschensteiner's bold concept not only implied making professional life more ethical, but also envisaged a more ethical political climate through a moral approach to life. Up to 1914 these tentative beginnings remained largely empirical, and were realized on a large scale only in the educationally extremely active years of the Weimar Republic after the First World War. Not sur-prisingly, in the years 1933 to 1945 it was these schools particularly which were, though not destroyed, increasingly divorced from their original educational inspiration through being incorporated into Hitler's system.

To-day divided Germany is facing new and great tasks in vocational education. Unfortunately they are being dealt with from two mutually exclusive points of view. Western Germany attempts to guide its educational endeavours through the principle of the importance of the individual. In this it continues in the best European traditions of the nineteenth century, even in an era of mechanization and the approaching automation of the future atomic age.

LUDWIG KIEHN.

CHAPTER TWO

The Return on Educational Investment

For the past hundred and fifty years most economists have accepted as a matter of faith the position that the economic return on educational investment was high. Adam Smith made the statement some hundred and seventy-five years ago. Little effort has been made to develop proof of the argument. Anything approaching case-studies was non-existent. The statement has been made over and over again in the intervening years. The economists have repeated the statement and then passed on to other items of more immediate concern to them.

Some years ago I made a study of the opinions of economists regarding the effect of education on economic welfare. Practically every economist, regardless of his country of origin, stated that education was an important factor in increasing economic welfare. Once in a while there would be a sentence or two of discussion, and in very unusual cases there might be as much as a paragraph. The pattern does not vary much around the world. Among the economists of an earlier generation, T. N. Carver, Irvin Fisher, and John Bates Clark in the United States stated that education was economically important. Cannan in England, Cassells in Sweden, Walras in Switzerland, Gide in France, the Austrian, German, and Italian economists and others said much the same thing. In no case, however, was a careful analysis developed. The same position holds for the present generation of economists in Europe, North America, and in other parts of the world.

There are several reasons why the economists have not systematically studied the return on the educational investment. In the first place it is extraordinarily difficult to get the evidence. The factors that bring about economic advance are many and varied. One author who is particularly interested in studying the effect of capital on economic growth will assign a great role to capital. Another author, who is impressed with the *entrepreneur* will assign to him the major role in economic advance. Another author will be impressed with scientific development. Some of the older authors were impressed very greatly by the natural fertility of the land. Many economists have been greatly impressed by the total range of natural resources.

In addition, education was being provided for many reasons, and many kinds of education were being provided. Many varieties of it obviously could not and were not expected to make any economic return. Consequently, the economists could not discuss education as a whole except as a general average. This necessarily blurred the issue and made the analysis more difficult.

If the opinions of economists are any guide, however, it is safe to say that education has high economic value and will bring a high return on the investment; and probably any country in the modern world can assume this. To the next question, Will the return on the educational investment be higher than it will be on other items?, the economist will become very indefinite in his answer. His answer in general will mean that he does not know, and it could mean in part that the evidence is non-existent. Even admitting that completely satisfactory evidence is not available, the weight of opinion would still be that the return on education is extraordinarily high even as compared to the return on most other alternative items.

Many Kinds of Education

The problem is further complicated by the fact that much education is clearly provided for non-economic reasons. Some part of the educational programme is expected to raise the economic welfare either specifically or in general. On the other hand, in every country in the world a very large part of the educational programme is designed for other purposes. One or two illustrations may make the problem clearer.

A study of any of the great classical religions of the world is clearly important, and should be pursued somewhere within the educational structure. It is probably equally clear that, except by the most indirect and roundabout ways, such a study could not reasonably be expected to have any immediate effect, one way or the other, on the economic welfare of a country. The same would probably be true of opera, though, doubtlessly, a very strong case can be made for some people knowing and appreciating opera.

There are literally hundreds of reasons for providing various parts of the educational programme. Improving the level of economic welfare is only one reason. One part of the educational system designed for some entirely different purpose might or might not have an important economic effect. There would be no reason to assume that it does until some evidence is available. If the economic level in a country is to be raised by education, it would seem as though the part of the education expected to be particularly useful would have to be designed, at least to some extent, to accomplish this purpose.

Education in General has a Good Economic Effect

The above arguments do not mean that education generally does not

have desirable results. It undoubtedly does. The economic consequences are much less direct than could be obtained if one cared to
pay the price. It is undoubtedly safe to say that on the average the
total educational programme in any western country in the world
to-day has a beneficial effect upon the economy as a whole. Much
of this benefit, however, probably stems from a part of the programme.

A similar case can be made for education generally as it exists
around the world. Probably a much stronger case can be made for the
position that an educational programme can be designed to have an
even more powerful effect on the level of economic welfare of any
country. It is probably true that such a programme could rapidly
change the economic status of any undeveloped country in the world.
This assumes, of course, that the people would be interested in making
the change.

The evidence is also very strong that at least in the technical fields
a highly developed educational system pays enormous economic
returns in the developed industrial countries of the world. There are
good reasons to believe that education can have even a greater
economic effect in the high-income countries than it has ever had up
to the present time. The question seems to be almost entirely one of
how much of the educational effort will be devoted to types of programmes that might reasonably be expected to improve the economic
status of the country.

The Level of Economic Welfare

The *per capita* incomes in the richer countries of the world are some
eighteen or nineteen hundred dollars per year. The *per capita* incomes
in the poor countries of the world are thirty or forty dollars per year.
Quite obviously there are many reasons for these extreme differences
in income. There is every reason to assume, however, that a substantial fraction of the difference is caused by education. There are,
also, the best of reasons for believing that a properly designed educational system can very greatly increase the income of the country with
the nineteen hundred dollars *per capita* income as well as the one with
the thirty dollars *per capita* income. The rate of increase will depend
very largely upon how drastically the country is willing to change the
school system and what price it is willing to pay socially and culturally
to bring about the high income.

Probably no one would hold that the physical resources, the location
of the country, and many other items are not important. Such factors
are important. Perhaps the best way to state the matter is that all
other factors being as they are, there are the strongest reasons for be-

lieving that education properly designed can have a powerful effect in increasing the income of any country in the world.

The Development in the United States

The development in the United States is a very interesting case-study of the place of education in increasing economic welfare. The United States was relatively fortunate in having large physical resources. It also was fortunate from the economic standpoint in obtaining a large number of settlers who were industrious and believed in saving and hard work. The combination of these with other factors was such that income would probably have been reasonably high with a relatively poor school system.

On the other hand, there are many reasons to assume that the development of a widespread school system has been a major factor in pushing the income of the United States to a far higher level than it would have otherwise been. An analysis of three specific areas of education may help to illustrate this.

There are some kinds of economic activity that are extraordinarily difficult to carry on unless the population has a high degree of literacy. Most of the people must be able to read and write. One economic development that seems to depend upon this is a widespread mass consumption market. Unquestionably, a mass market has been an important factor in making possible mass production. Mass production made possible far lower factory cost and consequently higher consumption, higher wages, and a higher standard of living. The high incomes, in turn, have made possible even larger mass production and mass consumption.

Clearly literacy is not an adequate cause of these complicated phenomena. Many other countries in the world have a very high degree of literacy and have not developed a mass market as is in the United States. Literacy is not an adequate cause, but at least in the past it has probably been a necessary requirement of certain kinds of mass markets. Here we have a case where at least a minimum amount of education was probably a necessary factor in a major American economic advance.

The Use of Interchangeable Parts

A great deal has been made of the fact that the use of modern interchangeable parts—a fundamental part of mass production—depends not only upon substantial verbal literacy but on a fairly widespread competence in mechanical skill. Some students of the problem have gone so far as to say it is difficult to see how large-scale mass production of machinery with interchangeable parts is possible until the bulk of the population has both the verbal skill to read and the mechanical background to understand simple instructions about machinery.

Probably most economists would agree that the American economy as it now is could not exist without high standardization of a large number of parts entering into literally thousands of machines. If every mowing machine, combine, and tractor on our farms had to have specially made parts, American agriculture as we know it could not exist. A tractor or cotton-picker breaks down; the farmer gets into his truck and goes to town and buys a standardized part, comes back to the farm, inserts the part into the machine, and goes on working.

Schools and Agricultural Development

The United States is burdened with agricultural surpluses of almost all kinds. This seems to be a curious problem and one that quite obviously seems puzzling to most of the world. A recent United Nations report estimated that probably half the people of the world are hungry a large part of their lives. It might appear as though any country should have the necessary skill to deal with too much food. Nuisance though an agricultural surplus may be to the United States, basically it is a great tribute to part of the educational system.

It is an entirely reasonable assumption to make that if our elaborate programme of agricultural education had not been developed, we in the United States would not be bothered with agricultural surpluses. In fact, we might very well have been greatly bothered, as so much of the world is, by not having enough food.

For a hundred years the United States has been developing a remarkable system of agricultural schools. These schools have been devoted overwhelmingly to increasing production on the farm and they have succeeded almost beyond belief. They probably will shift some of their analysis to dealing with agricultural over-production, and over a period of time they will solve that problem also.

The development of the agricultural educational system is a remarkable illustration of what can be done to deal with a fairly complicated part of an economic order. About a hundred and fifty years ago, most American farmers worked as their ancestors before them; a son learned his farming from his father, who had learned it from his father. Some changes went on slowly but perhaps took generations to develop and spread. A century and a half ago the American farmer was still planting wheat in the way it was planted in Biblical times. The farmer carried on his shoulder a bag of grain, broadcast it, then he covered it up and hoped for the best. The wheat was cut by hand and thrashed by a flail; processes that had been used for thousands of years in the Middle East.

Changes of many kinds started in many places other than the school system. But about a century ago, the schools began to play a very active and important part in increasing agricultural output. Agricultural colleges were started in each state of the Union. These colleges began to accumulate all kinds of technical information. They developed better types of wheat and corn; they improved all kinds of agricultural implements; and they expanded the technical knowledge of better breeds of cattle.

Very soon after the establishment of the agricultural colleges, agricultural secondary schools were set up. In the past three-quarters of a century approximately ten thousand agricultural high schools have been built. This means that almost any boy or girl in a rural area of America has access to technically accurate and reasonably up-to-date agricultural information. The agricultural teacher has probably attended the agriculture college. He keeps up with the new technical material and passes it on down to the boys and girls in his classes.

Throughout this same century agricultural experimental stations were also established in every state in the Union. These experimental stations became highly specialized centres searching for better methods of carrying on practically every phase of farming. They tested out a hundred different methods of growing a crop. Testing plots by the thousands became a customary part of landscape around all these institutions. There is scarcely any important aspect of American farm life that has not felt the impact of the scientific research of the agriculture experiment station.

During this period, a whole educational system of extension workers has been set up by the agricultural colleges. In other words, the agricultural colleges made a determined and systematic effort to carry their knowledge back to every farming community in the state. Then a system of county agricultural agents was established. These agents were trained, agricultural experts. There is one in almost every agricultural county in the country; altogether there are about three thousand of them. Finally, many rural elementary schools began to deal with some important agriculture problems. Now we have a comprehensive programme of education reaching a very large proportion of the total agricultural population.

Here is a brief outline of the total system: A universal system of elementary education producing literacy for almost everyone and also some acquaintance with agriculture procedures. A system of agricultural high schools extending into practically every important agricultural community in the country, training hundreds of thousands of boys and girls to be experts in all phases of agricultural life. A system of agricultural colleges covering the entire country and providing for agricultural leadership and producing highly trained personnel. A system of agricultural experimental and research stations covering every section of the country, and dealing at a very high, advanced technical level with all kinds of problems facing the farmer. Finally, a system of adult and extension education reaching back into the local communities, taking the technical information back to the farmer and his wife. Here is a system of education designed to try to improve agriculture. The only comment that can be made on it is that it has been amazingly successful.

American agricultural production has increased greatly during the past fifteen years; at the same time the number of farms has gone down. This has meant a very great rise in output per farmer. This is achieved by using better machinery, better organization, better fertilizers, better seeds, better crops, better stock, by having better control of water supply, and a better understanding of a thousand other agricultural problems. A very large part of all this higher skill has been brought about by the educational system. There is no question that the return on this educational investment has been very great as far as the United States is concerned. This illustration in the United States provides a strong indication that almost any aspect of our economic life could probably be very greatly improved if a section of the school system was designed to accomplish this end.

The developments in American agriculture probably also provided one other important lesson. Farming in the United States has become so highly technical that the farmer needs not only to know how to grow his crops in the old way, but also to know innumerable new things. As an illustration, the modern farmer must know a great deal about the control of water, and the more knowledge he has in this field the better. Historically he has been dependent upon the rain for his water supply. We are probably getting close to a major change in this situation.

One might almost say that the dividing line between primitive and modern technical agriculture lies in the ability of the farmer to control his water supply. Seemingly, it is too important to be left to the accident of rainfall. But this is going to force him to know a great deal more about the problem than any farmer in the world has ever known.

The modern farmer must also be a very good business man. It is important that he should know how much capital he can afford to use. Should he buy a bigger and more expensive tractor? Should he go in with other farmers and buy an expensive combine? Should he buy a cotton-picker? When can he afford to borrow money to buy better equipment? How can he find out the best time to sell his crops and livestock? The modern farmer must have very good facilities for keeping in touch with the markets. He must also have the necessary skills to work with other people, because modern agricultural production and selling require the co-operation of many individuals.

The information in many of these fields changes with startling rapidity. Only a well-informed farmer has much chance of prospering or perhaps even of surviving. In agriculture we probably have moved from the situation in which a great deal of highly technical schooling was desirable to the place where it is necessary.

Along with everything else, he must also use a great deal more power equipment than previously. Practically all the farms in the United States to-day have electricity, and the amount of electrically driven power equipment is expanding very rapidly. The same is true of the quantity of gasoline-driven equipment. The farmer needs to be a fairly good engineer to-day in order to operate a farm; this, again, shifts and expands the type of technical training he must have.

The most technical of this machinery he can have repaired, and probably will have to have repaired, by an expert. On the other hand, he must be a competent judge of the workings of the machine and be able to make innumerable repairs. Above all, he must know how to maintain the machinery so that it will not break down. The analysis of the work of the farmer could continue almost indefinitely. Wherever we look at his work, we see increasingly that it is dependent upon a much higher level of education than formerly.

The Field of Engineering

Engineering is another field of American economic life where the return on educational investment has probably been very large. Somewhat over a hundred years ago the first of the modern schools of engineering was established in the United States. Since then, several hundred engineering schools and departments of engineering have been opened. In most colleges and universities strong departments of science have been developed. Without them it is almost inconceivable that American economic life could have advanced as it has. The return on the money spent on engineering and technical education in the United States has been very high.

A century ago most industries in the United States changed fairly slowly. An improvement in a water-power flour mill or cotton mill was largely the accidental result of some ingenious worker or owner. The rewards were high for successful changes and many improvements took place in this way. However, the rise of the engineering schools changed the total picture. Technically trained men became available in substantial numbers in industry. They began to see the need and importance of systematically developed research. During the course of the past half-century industry itself has set up thousands of research and developmental laboratories. Now nearly two hundred thousand technical people are employed in these centres and some hundreds of thousands as assistants.

The more advanced industries all over the country are rapidly expanding their own, and encouraging the expansion of other, training facilities of all kinds. There is no end in sight to the process. The more technically trained people we have, seemingly, the more rapid the advance and the greater the need for trained people. It seems as though the educational return on the engineering, technical, and scientific training has been extremely large. Everything indicates that the larger these expenditures become, the more profitable they are, and the more the reason to expand them even further.

Many of the more technical industries in America are making large expenditures for scientific research development and training. The chemical and oil industries are outstanding illustrations. The automobile industry, the steel industry, and many other basic industries are expanding their training facilities. In some of the newer fields, e.g., electronics and aviation, industries are dependent almost entirely upon their developmental and research programmes.

The general picture, then, seems to be fairly clear. The engineering and technical schools have expanded greatly. The scientific departments of colleges and universities have provided basic training that has been invaluable to economic life. Industry itself has entered the picture on a major scale and is making a very large investment in the expansion of research and training. It has further moved into the systematic training of its own labour force. All the available evidence indicates that there is no end in sight to this process. The returns seemingly have been high and from all indications will remain high far into the future.

Medical Schools

A fairly strong and similar case can be made for the schools which are trying to improve the health of the United States. There seems little doubt that the medical schools plus the other allied agencies have been major instruments in expanding the average life-span there. Of course, many other countries have similarly increased the length of life; some of them have highly developed health educational programmes and some have not.

But it seems reasonable to assume that the return on the money spent on health education has been fairly substantial. Undoubtedly, the general rise in economic conditions, which has brought about better working conditions, better diet, and better housing, has also been a major factor in contributing to the rise in life-expectancy. However, when all these factors are taken care of, it is still probable that the return on education for health has been great.

A Possible Programme

It must be repeated again that there are many reasons for providing an educational programme. As a country becomes richer, it can provide all kinds of education simply as consumer items. This means it provides certain types of education for the same reason that it provides experiences in art, music, and in many other fields. The society can afford them and wants them. Now this non-economic education will undoubtedly expand greatly as societies become richer and can afford it.

However, it is also important for any country, including the United States, to have some general idea of the type of educational expansion that will bring a relatively high economic return. Clearly, we do not know the answer to this question in any final terms. However, there are strong reasons for believing that certain kinds of education in certain amounts will return a very high dividend to society.

In general, an educational programme that gives promise of bringing a high economic return to the United States will look about like this. Widespread and almost universal elementary education seemingly will more than pay for itself. Presumably, this programme would provide the minimum skills for literacy, for use of the native language, and for basic arithmetical competency. If there is a small part of the population that cannot absorb all this, it can probably profit from a certain amount of training to increase manual skills in certain limited fields.

Elementary schooling also provides a very wide basis for very large numbers to move into secondary school. As far as the United States is concerned, the number graduated from high school probably should be increased very substantially above the present level. About 60 per cent graduate from high school; the percentage probably should rise to about 80. This is an effort to make the decision on economic grounds. Whether the last 10 or 20 per cent of the population should be graduated from the high school on other than economic grounds becomes a question of social policy.

It is undoubtedly important to keep a widespread general education available for most of these high school students. But, probably very substantial numbers are going to have to be given somewhat technical education for a variety of reasons. Certainly in the rural areas the agricultural high schools should remain. If the time ever comes when virtually everyone is graduated from high school and most people go to a technical institution, then the question can be raised whether most of the technical agricultural education should be moved above the secondary level.

Much the same attitude exists regarding the great cosmopolitan high school and also the technical high school within the cities. The programme should be kept as general as possible; but, on the other hand, for a large number of students it must provide the basis for an occupation. This applies to some extent to the commercial high school as well. Again, if the time ever comes when these communities are sending almost all their students through the secondary school and on through two years of technical training, they then might consider moving the technical work above the high school level. But economically, the far safer situation would seem to be a widespread provision at the high school level of technical education of many kinds, and at the same time encouraging as many people as possible to take more general courses.

Seemingly, some further substantial expansion of the college population is economically advantageous. Clearly, there can be an enormous expansion of college enrolment beyond the point that would pay an economic return. There are somewhat over 2½ million college students now and the estimates are that the number will almost double within the next generation. This will probably be a desirable move economically. The real answer will depend, of course, upon the distribution of these students within the various fields of higher education. There can be no question that a further great expansion in the engineering, technical, and scientific fields will bring a very great economic return. Probably a substantial expansion in the health field will pay economically. Some substantial increase both in numbers and in quality of the agricultural education will undoubtedly pay.

A fair case can probably be made that an increase in quality in college education generally will probably pay. At this point, however, we quickly run into the problem of adequate personnel. In the future it is not going to be possible to staff all the institutions that need high-grade ability with as many able people as they want. Some better method will have to be found to see that able people are reasonably well distributed in the light of what they would like to do and in the needs of the society. An educational system that could do this would bring a favourable economic return to any society. The educational system in some countries is so narrow that it leads the able students into a few fields, and these are usually ones that the society does not need very much.

There are other important aspects of the American educational system that could undoubtedly be expanded with great economic advantage. It must also be always kept in mind that many parts of the educational system should be expanded that would not normally be expected to provide an economic return.

Summary

An attempt to sum up the return on the educational investment in the United States would be briefly this. Seemingly, the widespread general education of the entire population through the elementary school is economically advantageous. Undoubtedly, many economic changes could be made that would improve the education, but something fairly close to universal secondary education would doubtlessly pay an economic return. There are some reasons to believe that the average level of education in the United States should be raised about two years above the level which now exists. Probably alternative ways of getting education should be developed—perhaps far more effective ways than the present kind the high school offers.

The evidence seems extremely strong that the technical, scientific, health, agriculture, and many similar fields will pay a very great return if they are expanded. Probably some expansion in the college population as a whole will be economically advantageous. The United States has received a very great return in the past from its educational expenditures. The prospects are that this will continue in the future. With reasonable attention to the matter, the United States should be able greatly to expand its general education at the same time as expanding its special and technical education. The return on the investment should remain high far into the future.

HAROLD F. CLARK.

CHAPTER THREE

Education and National Efficiency: The United States

ABOUT two years ago, when the National Manpower Council was engaged in its study of skilled manpower, its staff called a conference of leading American educators to explore the interrelations between secondary education and the way in which young people prepare for work and life. The staff hoped to learn from the educators what, in their opinion, had been the contribution of the schools to the economic progress of the country and how this contribution could be enhanced.

It was a disappointing conference, for the educators were not inclined to move from broad claims to detailed proofs of the ways in which an expanding educational system had contributed to the economy and welfare of society. One participant argued that the subject did not warrant exploration since it was self-evident that the prosperity of the nation was directly dependent upon the American educational system. In support, he pointed out that the expansion of the economy had coincided with the expansion of education.

The purpose of this paper is to probe more deeply into the connexions, past and present, between America's high level of economic productivity and her great and highly diversified educational system. The scale of this system is suggested by the fact that the teaching personnel in elementary and secondary schools numbers over one and a quarter million, and that there are more than eighteen hundred institutions of higher learning in the country, with a total faculty of approximately a quarter of a million. Two additional facts may help to reinforce this picture. In the fall of 1950 there were five and a half million pupils between the ages of 16 and 22 enrolled in all schools, representing 37 per cent of the total population in this age-group. In terms of expenditure, the educational effort of the country amounts to over 11 billion dollars.

It would be difficult to gainsay the conclusions dictated by this data —that Americans are currently investing very substantial resources in the maintenance and operation of a far-reaching educational system. However, impressive though these figures may be, alone they do not make very clear the particular contributions that education has been making to national efficiency. To explore the extent and limits of these contributions, it is necessary, first, to identify some of the outstanding characteristics of the American economy; next, to make explicit the salient features of the American educational effort; and then to study the relationship between the two. Since both the American economy and the American educational system are constantly in a state of flux, it will also be helpful to point to the major directions of likely change. And, finally, because of the international character of the YEAR BOOK, it would be well to sort out that part of the American experience which is unique and those lessons which may be transferable—in whole or in part—to other countries, whether industrial or non-industrial, that are struggling to raise the productivity of their economies.

The economist faces a difficult task when he seeks to select for special emphasis a few of the welter of factors responsible for the shape and functioning of the American economy. There is the danger —in fact, the certainty—that by restricting himself to a limited number of factors he will fail to provide himself with an adequate base for interpreting accurately such a highly specialized and productive economy. However, such a selective procedure is permissible when the reader is forewarned that the facets selected represent characteristic and essential elements, and that the author does not pretend to take in all that are of strategic importance. With this warning, three important aspects of the American economy may be briefly considered: the extent to which that economy is driven by the money-making propensities of large numbers of the society; secondly, the extent to which almost the entire society is willing to accept and adjust to change; and, finally, the strong motive power exercised by the prevailing belief in equality—that is, that men should be judged by what they do, not by who their parents were.

The Money-making Propensity

Without seeking to explain why so many Americans are deeply concerned with the making of money and more money (the simplest explanation might be that the American scene has been unique in terms of the opportunities it has offered people to make money), it would be difficult to deny the potency of this drive and the contribution that it makes to keeping the American economy highly dynamic. Of course, as the distinguished American economist, Frank H. Knight, pointed out many years ago, making money is not only work geared to improving the consumption levels of the individual and his family, but has become in the United States a sort of a game that pre-empts a man's leisure time as well as his working hours. It is not accidental that much American business is transacted round the luncheon-table, at cocktail bars, and on the golf links.

There is probably no other country in the world where the sons of middle-class and even wealthy parents are so encouraged early in childhood to engage in activities the end of which is the making of money. Here is seen the early and heavy indoctrination with respect to money-making activities. At the same time the extent to which these activities are turned into a game should be noticed. Every society must make a selection among the values it stresses. No society can be equally distinguished in all respects. Economic expansion and the increase of personal and national wealth are unquestionably at the forefront of American life, and have been from the earliest days of colonial settlement. There may come a point in American development when significant re-adjustments will take place, but as yet there is no evidence of this. Men give up the highest positions in government to enter or return to money-making activities. Talented young people turn their backs on academic careers or order to carve out successful niches for themselves in the world of business and so on.

The Value Placed on Change

The progress of a modern economy depends in very large measure on the rate at which improvements in technology take place and, equally important, on the speed with which these improvements are assimilated. An outstanding characteristic of American life is the high value placed upon change, in contrast to the value that other societies place upon custom and tradition. In the major industries of the country, labour has long been willing to accept technological changes, subject only to getting its share of the increases in profit due to increases in productivity. The American consumer is constantly on the look-out for new and improved products and places great faith in even the most modest changes in style or performance. To Americans, last year's car is an old car; a house constructed five years ago is an old house.

Another aspect of the American attitude towards change is reflected in the mobility of the population. Millions of people are constantly on the move. Year after year the South sees much of its surplus rural population leave for the major manufacturing cities of the North and, more recently, for the expanding far west. There have also been sizeable movements, although somewhat less spectacular, in the other regions of the country, from rural to urban communities and from one urban community to the next. A new plant located in one of the south-eastern states will find, on the day that it begins hiring, applicants who have come from a distance of a thousand miles. In short, we can see, then, that the employer with a new and improved process need not fear that his labour will refuse to accept it. The manufac-

turer with a new product need not fear that the public will turn it
down simply because it is new; its very newness will give him an edge
over competitors. It would be hard to exaggerate the contribution
that this cultural desire for the new, this pervasive social acceptance of
change, makes to the vitality of the economy.

The Concept of Equality

A third characteristic of the American economy that has contributed
greatly to its continuing vitality is summarized by the concept of
equality. Americans proceed on the assumption that what some men
have done others can do; that success is the result of a combination of
brains, initiative, hard work, and luck; and that there is no need to
respect a man only because of the accomplishments of his father or his
grandfather. The doctrine that a man can be whatever he wants to
be if is willing to strive has gone far to unleash the potential that is
locked up in many men born into modest circumstances. The ideal of
the self-made man, the son of immigrant parents who moves to the
top, has substantial validity in a country where literally thousands and
tens of thousands of children born into modest, or even poverty-
stricken, homes have made their way up the ladder.

Quite another aspect of this doctrine that every man can be as good
as any other is reflected in the consumption patterns of the population. With the exception of a few luxuries, there are no items purchased only by a particular class. America is the land of the mass
market. The aspiration of the American working man is to provide
for his family as many of the good things of life as his employer is able
to provide for his family. Automobiles, radios, television sets, college
education—all of these and other good things are good not only for
the minority, but for all. Much of American prosperity in recent
years is the result of the constant growth in demand by the population
as a whole for all kinds of consumer goods, consumer durables, and,
not least important, for private housing.

There is a further aspect of this equalitarian doctrine which warrants
consideration. The family corporation has been replaced in the United
States by the public corporation to the extent that nearly every large
enterprise in the country is managed by individuals who do not own it.
Management is becoming increasingly professionalized, and the
decisions of management more and more rationalized. Consequently,
no decisions play a larger part in the efficiency of American business
than the selection and development of key personnel. Although it
would be foolish to argue that all nepotism has been eliminated, or that
favouritism and personal factors play no role, it can be said that the
personnel practices of large corporations are becoming increasingly

objective. This means that a man can anticipate being rewarded and promoted according to his performance. He need not fear that his family or the schools which he attended will limit his progress.

Educational Opportunity and Vocationalism

The first, and undoubtedly the most outstanding, characteristic of the American educational system is the extent to which public funds have been used to support increasingly extended educational preparation for all young people. Within the last two decades there has been a gain of not less than three years in the amount of formal schooling that the average young person receives prior to entering work. At the present time this schooling averages slightly more than twelve years. The important points to note in this connexion are, first, that the support for this schooling comes from public funds and represents no untoward burden upon the poor, other than the very small contribution which they make through taxes, and, secondly, that the educational process has now been extended to provide on the average for more than the completion of high school. Still another point worth mentioning is the extent to which there has been no sex discrimination in the development of American education. Ever since 1870 the number of girls graduating from high school has been greater than the number of boys. At the collegiate and post-graduate level it is true that boys have consistently outnumbered girls, but the gap between the two has been substantially narrowed within recent decades.

The American educational structure has been characterized by a pronounced utilitarianism, in which the responsibility of the schools for preparing individuals for work and life was narrowly and specifically, rather than broadly, defined. The large-scale contributions of the federal government in making grants of land available to the states in the 1860's to facilitate the establishment and expansion of state universities was motivated by the understanding that the embryonic industrial economy of the United States would soon need more engineers and technicians. The importance of vocational education at the high school level was greatly stimulated by shortages of skilled manpower during World War I. Additional evidence of this vocational trend can be found in the great increases in enrolment at the collegiate level in recent decades in such 'practical' fields as engineering and business administration. The elaboration of professional schools at university centres is further testimony of the same trend. To-day the larger universities boast schools of journalism, business administration, hospital administration, social work, pharmacy, optometry, and dentistry, as well as the classical triad of law, medicine, and theology.

It is unlikely that up to 25 per cent of the appropriate age-group—

in some states it is now as high as 50 per cent—would have entered advanced courses at collegiate or university levels unless such courses had been rather closely geared to preparation for work. There is undoubtedly a close relationship between the vocational orientation of American education and the continued expansion in enrolment.

One of the most striking and perhaps unique features of the American educational system at every level, surely from the secondary level on, has been the difference in quality between institutions and even between departments within the same institution. This reflects the fact that the United States, although a single nation, spans an entire continent, and further reflects that financial support for public education has been exclusively local and by the states. The large variations in wealth and taxing power have been reflected inevitably in the educational systems of the several states and localities. At the collegiate and university level there have been at least three major types of institution : the famous, heavily endowed institutions, few in number but very important in terms of educational leadership; the many state-supported institutions, ranging from outstanding universities to poorly staffed teachers' colleges in states that have been hard-pressed to maintain their position in the expanding economy; and the ubiquitous private smaller colleges, many of which originally were denominational institutions, some well supported and well led, others poorly supported and with little intellectual leadership.

Academic Standards

In the face of the trend to draw ever larger numbers of the population into secondary schools, so that at the present time more than 55 per cent graduate from high school and 25 per cent of the males attend college, it has been next to impossible to maintain rigid standards. Many graduates of the poorer, smaller colleges would have been unable to gain admission to a good college. In turn, many high school graduates from weaker school systems would be unable to match first-year students at strong high schools. The same differences prevail at the upper end of the scale. A Ph.D. degree from one of the weaker universities simply does not represent the same achievements as a Ph.D. degree from a major institution.

Although there are obvious and deep-seated weaknesses in an educational system with this range in standards, there are also some important strengths in the very diversity of the system. Many students who would be unable to gain entrance to a good college are afforded, under this flexible structure, an opportunity not only to enter but to do well at a weaker institution. Many positions in society, even in a society that places as limited value on status and tradition as does the

United States, become open to individuals because they have some kind of college degree. Except in the sciences, an individual seeking work is seldom asked what he knows. Emphasis is placed merely upon his satisfactory completion of a required level of education, which often means that he has acquired a bachelor's degree. Moreover, individuals who have been handicapped by inadequate schooling are often able to compensate by an opportunity to continue their education. Although it is not easy even for a well-endowed student to develop his capacities in the absence of stimulating teachers and a strong curriculum, the fact remains that many are able to do so. Included among the most distinguished American scientists and scholars are a considerable number of men who are graduates of these weaker institutions.

Education and the Economy

We have now considered some major characteristics of the economy and of the American educational system; what connexion and inter-relations can be found between the two? More particularly, what can be said about the contribution of the American educational system to the vitality of the American economy? The drive for economic aggrandizement which is found among large numbers of the population is of strategic importance for the American economy; the equali-tarian bias of the American educational system strongly supports and encourages this underlying goal. Every youngster who comes to school is told not by a single teacher, but by many, that his future will be what he determines to make it. He learns about presidents who came from humble beginnings. The American school must be given major credit for inspiring the youth of each generation with the model of the self-made man. What this means is well illustrated by a table presented by Dael Wolfle in *America's Resources of Specialized Talent*, in which he estimates the distribution of college graduates according to the occupation of their fathers. Of 100 graduates, only about 40 come from the professional, semi-professional, and man-agerial classes, while the fathers of the remaining 60 are lower in the socio-economic scale: half are skilled, unskilled, or factory workers; the other half, farmers and clerical and related workers.

It is not necessary to believe that the constant prolongation of educa-tion is pure gain, to recognize that there are many advantages in a situation where young people are permitted to find themselves late in their adolescence rather than in a situation of having their life deter-mined for them by their educational accomplishments when they are 10 or 11. My associates and I have shown in our study of occupa-tional choice (*Occupational Choice, An Approach to a General Theory*) the serious handicaps under which the children of the poor grow up because they leave school before they have reached the emotional and intellectual maturity that enables them to choose their occupations wisely and to prepare themselves in accordance with their choices. At present, young people in certain states can secure their working papers at the age of 14, although 15 or 16 is typical. But it is important to note that the concept of public education is being stretched in the richest states, such as California and New York, to include fourteen years of free education for all. This means that a young person need not make any serious decisions about an occupation until he is 18. In California there is strong pressure to remove all vocational education from the high schools and re-locate it in the junior colleges. This would mean that a young person would not commit himself until his nineteenth year.

The most obvious and direct connexion between the sizeable and constantly expanding American investment in education and the economy is reflected in the levels of education and training that young people have completed at the time when they first look for work. In passing, note must be taken of the fact that this training process has been extended further in recent years by the introduction of compulsory military service, which means that young men serve between two and four years and much of this time is devoted to acquiring some sort of specialized skill. One of the most interesting findings of the National Manpower Council's recent study, *A Policy for Skilled Manpower*, was the extent to which large American corporations have shifted their interest over the last generation or two from young people who have completed a vocational course in high school to young people with substantial control over the fundamentals of mathematics, communication, and basic science. This attitude of employers has a simple explanation. They are interested in young people who have acquired a sound foundation; they are willing to undertake the specific skill instruction. It is possible to discount to a considerable extent the official statements of American industry about its serious predicament resulting from the fact that too few young men are graduating in engineering and in the sciences and that a still smaller number are becoming available immediately because of their military service obligations. Yet, there is no denying that American industry around the turn of the century employed one engineer for every 255 workers in manufacturing, mining, construction, transportation, and public utilities; twenty years later the ratio was much higher : it was one for every 78 workers; the most recent data, for 1950, show that industry employs one engineer for every 62 workers. The absorption by American industry of these large numbers of engineers is only one outstanding illustration of the general trend constantly to enlarge the number of staff personnel.

Deficiencies

Significant as the contributions of American education to the expansion of the American economy have been, it would be a serious misreading of the facts to omit to say that this contribution has fallen seriously short in several respects. One of the most striking shortcomings is the extent to which individuals with good intellectual potential are not educated and trained, despite the great public and private investment in education. In the most able sector of the population, not more than one out of every two young persons completes college. Although every young man or woman with the intellectual potential need not necessarily go to college to ensure his own personal development or his place in the economy and the society, the fact that so large a percentage fails to receive advanced training is of major concern to an increasingly large number of Americans. This concern is the deeper because, on the one hand, people have come to recognize the extent to which the progress of the economy and the security of the nation depend upon the development of its brainpower and, on the other, because it runs counter to American principles to admit that in many cases the barrier which prevents young people from going on with their education is financial. Because of the deep belief in the right of every individual to develop his potentialities to the full, the fact that so many are unable to do so because of straitened economic circumstances of their parents is a challenge that will not long remain unanswered.

Other weaknesses that cannot easily be rectified have developed in the secondary school system. Having turned the high school into a common school, the educators have had to develop all types of curricula in order to meet the varying intellectual, emotional, and vocational needs of the vastly expanded student body. In responding to these democratic pressures, many compromises and adjustments have been made which have not necessarily resulted in a sound educational foundation. It is not easy to generalize about any facet of American education because of its great variability. However, many well-informed observers have reached the conclusion that secondary schools need strengthening, and by this they usually mean two things: first, that more stress should be placed upon instruction in mathematics, language, and science; and secondly, that to ensure that students profit from such instruction it is definitely necessary to strengthen the teaching staffs. This, they believe, can be accomplished only if the salaries of teachers and the conditions under which they work are vastly improved. Because of the striking increases in enrolments that loom on the horizon as a result of the much increased birth-rate of the 1940's, this challenge is even more formidable.

World War II revealed one of the more serious consequences of primary and secondary education being originally the responsibility of localities and, now, to a great extent, the states. The well-to-do and highly industrialized regions of the nation suddenly realized that conditions in backward economic areas, such as the south-east and the south-west, had produced substantial numbers of young adults who were either totally illiterate or so poorly educated that the military forces, even during a major emergency, did not accept them for service. As Dr. Bray and I have shown in our book, *The Uneducated*, there is a close relationship between *per capita* income, expenditures for education, and illiteracy rates. Although the over-all problem is complicated in the south-east by the heavy concentration of Negroes, whose schooling has long lagged behind that of the white population, the roots of the problem go deeper. The population of the south-eastern states is prolific—the rural South has by far the highest birth-rates in the country, it has lagged far behind most other regions in industrialization, and it has far smaller revenues available for education.

One of the major issues facing the country that is certain to agitate the public and that may well lead to legislative action relates to the advantages of federal aid to education, the level of such aid, and the conditions under which it should be proffered. Were it not for two extraneous issues—whether federal funds should be available to parochial schools and, secondly, whether the granting of federal funds should be made contingent on the introduction of non-segregated practices in the South—there can be little question that substantial federal aid would have been forthcoming long before now. This much is certain; if the legislators can get around these two issues, federal aid of one sort or another will definitely be forthcoming to the states so that they can better cope with the marked rise in enrolments which coincides with a public awareness that education has been less well-nourished than it should have been during the past fifteen years of prosperity.

Within a few years the substantially increased enrolments will press against the facilities available for higher education. A public policy already exists regarding the expansion of state-supported colleges. Recognizing that the major costs of a college education are represented not by tuition but by the cost of living away from home, some of the wealthier and more far-sighted states have moved towards the establishment of junior colleges in communities large enough to provide a student body of reasonable size. At present the junior college can have three distinct objectives. It can represent two years of terminal education beyond high school in liberal arts studies; this type of institution provides half of the usual college course. In other instances it serves as a feeder to the larger colleges and universities in the state, thus reducing the living costs of some young people in acquiring baccalaureates. Thirdly, it is geared to providing a large number of vocationally oriented courses to prepare people more specifically to enter an occupation. Another objective which is likely to develop is that of providing refresher training and education for older women who will be entering or re-entering the labour market at the age of 35 to 40 after their children are no longer a major demand on their time. During the past few years this particular group of married women has represented one of the most important additions to the labour force, and there is every indication that more and more of them will seek employment in the future. It is no easy matter for a junior college to achieve all these objectives simultaneously; yet concentrating on one or two, leaves other community needs unprovided for.

The great strength of American education has been its expansion so that more and more citizens have acquired the appurtenances of learning. Although the United States has been able to develop at every level a small number of outstanding institutions and a considerable number of strong institutions, the system has also encouraged the survival of a very large number of weak institutions. One consequence of the increasing preoccupation of various leadership groups with education has been to create an increasing awareness that quantity and quality are antithetical concepts. Several of the nation's leading colleges have already announced their intention not to expand their facilities and their staffs to any substantial extent to meet the oncoming rush of students. They plan to maintain standards and do the best job they possibly can with a selected number of students. Another facet of this same awareness is the trend among the best engineering colleges to add a fifth year to the curriculum for the purpose of providing the student body with a broader education in the liberal arts and more fundamental grounding in advanced mathematics and physics. (See the National Manpower Council's *A Policy for Scientific and Professional Manpower*.) Still another piece of evidence is the repeated warnings of leading scientists that the present research and development programme is out of balance because it neglects basic research in favour of applied work.

Clearly most Americans do not exactly understand how an improved educational system can contribute to economic welfare and national security. Nevertheless, there is enough understanding of these interrelations to have built up substantial pressure for constructive action to ensure that a larger number of intellectually able people in the community have an opportunity to go on to college and graduate school; to strengthen the teaching staffs and improve the curriculum of secondary education; to provide financial assistance from the federal government to the poorer states so that they can more readily discharge their obligation to provide a reasonable level of public education for all of their citizens; to expand further the educational plant through the establishment of a larger number of junior or community colleges with the objective of providing more and more citizens with fourteen years of basic education; and, finally, to place more stress than heretofore on raising the quality of American education.

In seeking to understand the reasons that lie behind the phenomenal productivity of the American economy, it would be an error to neglect the unique factors in the American scene, factors that derive from the history of the country. The wealth of natural resources available cannot be over-emphasized. Freedom from rigid class structures and traditions, though on occasion a serious disability, has proved a great boon as far as the American economy is concerned, because of the encouragement thus given to individuals to develop their full potential.

The educational system must be given substantial credit for the ways in which it has contributed to the reality of the opportunity story. American schools have encouraged the individual to take his future in his own hands and set high aspirations for himself. Furthermore, the ever greater extension of the educational system has increasingly avoided the wastage which takes place when young people must make occupational decisions at too early an age. Young Americans have had the opportunity to mature emotionally and intellectually before they have had to commit themselves. Finally, the ability of large numbers of individuals to receive specialized training within the educational system at no cost at all, or at a very minimal cost, has prepared them to enter many preferred occupations. In short, the school system itself has been a major source of occupational mobility.

The ability of other countries to profit from the American lesson will depend upon the structure of their society, their economic well-being, and the extent to which their present educational system is developed. But every country in the world can profit by establishing the following as criteria for its educational system : that it should contribute as much as possible to the enlargement of personal opportunities, that it should avoid the necessity for premature commitments, and that it should provide at the lowest possible cost specialized training for all who are capable of profiting from it and who desire it.

ELI GINZBERG.

CHAPTER FOUR

Education and Occupation* : English Secondary Schools and the Supply of Labour

SINCE in a modern economy the quality and efficiency of the working population and the degree of vocational and social mobility very largely depend on the educational system, an analysis of its relation to the occupational structure must naturally dominate any discussion of the economic consequences of educational provision or any attempt to assess the effect of education on the national economy. It is our intention in this essay tentatively to explore the nature of this crucial relationship, and to illustrate it by reference to the present position in England.

Education and Occupational Structure

The efficient division of the working population among occupations requires both that there should be the right number of workers in each occupation and that the qualities of workers in each occupation should be as appropriate as possible—in short, that 'ability' and 'opportunity' should be matched as closely as possible. Education affects the efficiency of the distribution of labour by its influence on both 'ability' and 'opportunity'; the skill of labour at various levels reflects the scale and nature of educational provision, which also exercises a decisive influence on vocational choice and on movement between occupations i.e., on the adjustment of the supply to the demand for trained labour. Thus the relationship between the educational system and occupational structure is not a simple one. Moreover, it changes over time.

In the first place, the range of vocational opportunities and consequently the demands of the economy on the educational system are affected by the growth of industrialism. It is a general feature of most European economies that continuous, often accelerating, technical change constantly calls for the development of new occupations and the modification, decline, or obsolescence of old ones. The structure of opportunities is therefore not only heterogeneous but also varies according to the stage of development reached by the economy. Thus,

---

* A substantial part of this essay is based on a paper " Social Aspects of Vocational Guidance " in the forthcoming *Problèmes de Sociologie du Travail (II)*, ed. Pierre Naville (Paris).

for example, the part played by education in occupational and social selection will be much less pronounced in pre-industrial as against advanced-industrial societies, where the selective functions of education tend to predominate. Similarly, while it was reasonable for Marx to observe of the early stages of industrialism that " a general prohibition of child labour ", on which compulsory universal education depended, " is incompatible with the existence of large-scale industry ",[1] it can with equal truth be asserted of present-day technological society that such a prohibition is essential to the continuance of the economy.

In the second place, the relationship is extremely complex from the point of view of causation. Thus, while it may be true that during the past fifty years in England " development within secondary education has had to wait upon changes in the social structure ",[2] it would be naïve in the extreme to see the relationship as one of mechanical adaptation of education to the changing needs of the economy. The opposite position would be even more exposed to criticism, though by no means indefensible. For example, changes in educational provision can influence the distribution of income between occupations. Professor Phelps Brown has pointed out that international comparisons suggest that " save where there is immigrant peasant labour, the extension of education goes with a higher ratio of unskilled earnings to skilled ", and has argued that the possibilities of further equalization incomes by further advances in educational opportunity are by no means exhausted.[3]

Moreover, in so far as the technical needs of the economy do mould the educational system, the actual pattern of the influence is mediated through ideological interpretations and the clash of interest groups. Thus, the growth of the dissenting academies reflected the unequal sensitivity of different social groups to the changing technological basis of industry; the growth of elementary education ' for workmen and servants ' in the nineteenth century not only reflected the need for the development of a literate working class, but also, in the emphasis of its curriculum on docility and pious acceptance of station, the power of the ruling classes; and the contemporary movement towards ' parity of prestige ' for the different types of secondary school and towards the adoption of the comprehensive school, though it may be in part a response to changing economic needs, clearly also reflects political ideas.

---

[1] Marx Engels, *Selected Works* (Moscow, 1951), Vol. II, p. 33.
[2] O. Banks, *Parity and Prestige in English Secondary Education* (London, 1955), p. 239.
[3] " Prospects of Labour," *Economica*, 1949, p. 4.

Thirdly, the relationship between education and occupational structure must be seen in the context of the wider social structure. None of the relevant social institutions are alone and absolute in their effects. The influence through the school of the family, for example, will vary according to social class, according to its situation in town or country, according to its social, geographical, and occupational history, and acording to the existence or non-existence of state social services supporting its functions.

Finally, account must be taken of the fact that special conditions may distort the relationship in peculiar ways at particular times. There may be large-scale unemployment, as in most countries in the nineteen-thirties, or full employment, as in England to-day; and obviously the general level of employment affects not only the freedom of choice open to the individual, but also the structure of the labour market itself.

However, we cannot in this essay do justice to the relationship by treating it historically in terms of the changing structure of the economy and the social class system. We must confine ourselves to illustrating the discussion by brief reference to one aspect only of the position in England to-day—namely, the influence of education on vocational choice and the supply of labour. We shall leave aside the less tangible question of the influence of twentieth-century changes in education on the skill of the working population [4]; and we shall not discuss the relation of education to the occupational and social mobility of adult workers.[5]

A Fluid Labour Supply

It is an economic truism that the distribution of labour among occupations cannot, as Professor Hicks has put it, " be left to be settled according to the preferences of producers alone; the desires of consumers must also be taken into account." [6] But the proposition applies

---

[4] A less tangible question both because it has not been subject to investigation, so that present knowledge is limited, and because the effect of reform is necessarily very gradual. Professor Hicks has calculated that in 1924 not more than 40 per cent of the occupied male population are likely to have had any experience (in their school years) of the educational improvements which followed the Act of 1902, but by 1938 the proportion may have risen to 80 per cent; and that although the proportion of those who had experienced the effects of the 1918 Act will have been continually rising, it cannot have reached more than 40 per cent in 1938, and will take until about 1960 to work itself out fully. (*The Social Framework* (1952), p. 192.)

[5] See D. V. Glass (ed.), *Social Mobility in Britain* (Kegan Paul, 1954), Chapter X, for an analysis of the relation between education and mobility based on a national sample inquiry in 1949.

[6] *Op. cit.*, p. 60.

with particular force to the economy of the Welfare State. The principle of ' citizenship ' requires the greatest possible measure of freedom for every individual to develop his talents and to choose his vocation; but the needs of the economy for persons trained in appropriate numbers to fill posts at various levels of skill and responsibility must also be met. The provision of a basic equality of economic status among all citizens—of a minimum supply of essential goods and services—presupposes full employment and a high level of productivity and consequently an unavoidable degree of economic planning. Thus it is that although the 1944 Education Act embodies the maxim of extreme individualism, that each child shall receive an education suited to his aptitudes and abilities—with no mention of any obligation on the educational authorities to have regard to the needs of the economy for labour of particular kinds—there are, in fact, from time to time official attempts to estimate the need for teachers, doctors, nurses, scientists, or technicians and to stimulate the educational system to produce them in the required numbers.

In the long run, and theoretically, the apparent contradiction disappears : " Since every producer is also a consumer, it is to everyone's interest that (such) an adjustment should be made." [7] Even in the short run, the demands of the economy are less threatening to individual rights under the Education Act than appears at first sight. The intellectual requirements of occupations and the capacities of individuals cannot be directly equated, except possibly in the case of the relatively small number of occupations for which formal qualifications are required, and no economic system can be so organized as to allow everyone to use his full talents in his employment. Fortunately, however, the aptitudes and abilities of individuals are rarely specific, so that as long as there is freedom of vocational choice and of movement between occupations, they may be expected to find their way into positions which will stretch their capacities and enable them to make their maximum contribution to the needs of society.

Freedom of vocational choice and movement are both the citizen's right and the conditions of a fluid and economically distributed labour supply, which is, in turn, a prerequisite of the high level of economic prosperity on which the Welfare State depends. A high degree of vocational and social mobility (or, looked at in economic terms, the elimination of rigidities in the supply of labour) is, therefore, both a cardinal principle of policy and a condition of survival for the Welfare State.

The most useful general index of the extent to which mobility exists is some measure of the propensity of children to enter and remain in

---

[7] J. R. Hicks, *op. cit.*, p. 60.

occupations of the same or similar grade as those of their fathers. If this propensity did not exist at all, i.e., if all new entrants were candidates for all posts in industry, there would be no rigidity of supply (though there might be a scarcity of individuals with particular potentialities). However, the hereditary element in ability and the different intellectual requirements of different grades of occupation introduce a basic rigidity. The only feasible principle of policy is to seek to minimize the influence of factors other than differences in capacity on the distribution of individuals between occupations.

There are a number of such factors, other than differences in capacity, making for an association between the occupational grades of fathers and sons. The demographic and occupational structures themselves are primary determinants of the association. Thus, for example, the proportion of skilled to unskilled workers in the population and the differential fertility of the various occupational groups define the opportunities for the sons of unskilled workers to enter skilled occupations.[8] The localization of industry, consequent regional differences in occupational structure, and the tendency of labour, especially juvenile labour, to be immobile [9] are also relevant.

Other rigidities in supply derive, however, from the wider social structure—in particular, from the class structure as it finds expression in the relations between the family environments of individuals at different social levels and the educational system.

In any highly industrialized community the nature of the educational system has a special importance for the occupational structure. The influence of changes in the statutory length of school life on the supply of juvenile labour is obvious. More important is the fact that in an industrialized economy the educational system becomes the prime agency of occupational selection and mobility. The scale of enterprise limits the possibility of working up small concerns into

---

[8] It is possible to measure, for past periods, the extent to which occupational ' fluidity ' has existed between generations. It is necessary to know the occupational distribution of fathers and sons. Then the actual distribution of the sons may be compared with the distribution which would have occurred if occupational recruitment had been made by a random process. This latter defines the conditions of ' perfect mobility ', and has been used as a model in a recent British study. (See D. V. Glass (ed.), *op. cit.*)

[9] The extreme geographical immobility of juvenile labour was illustrated in an investigation (J. and S. Jewkes, *The Juvenile Labour Market* (London, 1938)) which showed that the unemployment rate in Warrington among juveniles was negligible in 1935, while, in St. Helens, *only ten miles away*, it was around 20 per cent. Since the Employment and Training Act of 1948, efforts have been made in the Youth Employment Service to foster mobility by maintenance grants, etc., to apprentices and learners who need to live away from home in order to train.

large through the ploughing back of profits, and multiplies the number
of ' black-coated ' jobs; the significance of apprenticeship and long
service as avenues of mobility declines, and formal educational qualifications, at least to the secondary level, are increasingly required of
entrants to all but the lowest class of occupations. This may be
differently expressed by saying that the greater the degree of industrialization the more are young people limited in their choice of
employment by their educational attainments, and the more difficult
it is for adults to move outside the range of occupations for which
their formal educational attainments equip them.

The Welfare State, on grounds both of political principle and of
economic expediency, has made a renewed attack through its educational policy on the problem of securing a close relationship between
ability and opportunity. The effort has met with a marked degree of
success; but, as will be argued below, the organizational framework of
English secondary education and the social assumptions which it
reflects are such as to set arbitrary limits to the degree of vocational
and social mobility which can be achieved.

Schooling and Vocational Choice in England

The English school system is heavily class-conditioned both historically and actually. In post-war years it has become the centre of fierce
controversy as the outstanding support of old, and an important source
of new, class differences. It exercises a remarkable influence on occupational recruitment, setting firm limits to the freedom of individual
choice and to the possibilities of fluidity in the supply of labour. It is
so organized as to demand that decisions which are critical for vocational choice are made at the age of 11 or 12, when they can reflect
only the largely class-conditioned family environment of the child. At
the secondary stage, children are not, except in the case of a small
minority attending ' comprehensive ' schools, allocated to various
secondary courses within a common school, but are selected for one
of the three types of secondary school (grammar, technical, or modern)
each of which has more or less specialized relations with institutions
of further education and the occupational structure.

The close association between type of secondary schooling, length
of school life, further education, and vocational choice is illustrated in
the table on p. 525.

The majority of modern, technical, and comprehensive school pupils
leave at 15, and in 1953 some three-fifths of boys under 16 entered
unspecified semi-skilled and unskilled employment; about one-third
entered apprenticeships or learnerships to skilled crafts, and about one
in twenty clerical employment. The ' superiority ' of the occupa-

BOYS LEAVING SCHOOL IN GREAT BRITAIN, 1953-4

Boys Leaving for	Age on Leaving School, or on First Entering Employment				
	14, 15	16	17	18	19
	Percentages				
(1) Further full-time education[1] at:					
(a) Universities	—	0·1	10·0	55·0	64·2
(b) Other institutions	1·6	3·3	8·2	12·6	10·6
(2) Paid employment[2]:					
(a) Apprenticeships or learnerships to skilled craft	32·4	37·4	25·8	32·4[3]	25·2[3]
(b) Employment leading to recognized professional qualifications	0·3	3·7	8·0		
(c) Clerical employment	5·3	25·4	20·4		
(d) Other employment	60·4	30·1	27·6		
TOTAL	100	100	100	100	100

[1] *Compiled from statistics of school-leavers in England and Wales for the educational year ending July 31st, 1953. Education in 1953 (Cmd. 9155).*

[2] *Compiled from statistics of class of employment entered by boys in Great Britain below the age of 18 in 1953. Ministry of Labour Gazette, Vol. LXII, December 12th, 1954.*

Note.—*In order to take account of the difference in the form of the statistics from these two sources, appropriate corrections have been made to those derived from Education in 1953 (Cmd. 9155).*

[3] *Percentage of boys leaving school "for paid employment and other reasons" (class of employment not specified). Education in 1953 (Cmd. 9155).*

tional distribution of those leaving school at 16 or above is marked. The majority of grammar school pupils, and rather less than half of technical school pupils, leave at 16, and the proportion of boys at this age who entered apprenticeships was somewhat higher than among the under 16's, whilst the proportion going into clerical employment was much higher; a much higher proportion also went into employment or full-time further education leading to recognized professional qualifications (e.g., law, accountancy, surveying, etc.). The proportion going into the professional occupations, either directly or following further education, was considerably higher among those who entered employment at 17 or later, of whom most had attended grammar schools.

From the point of view of the national economy, the most serious shortage is in the supply of persons capable of following the more skilled and responsible occupations, and the educational system is the

main source of rigidities here. It is true that, against the general background of full employment, shortages of juvenile labour have been
created by the raising of the school-leaving age and the expansion of
further education (both full-time in universities and other institutions,
and part-time in county colleges and technical institutes) and the introduction of compulsory national service. The resultant over-all
shortage has tended to up-grade the range of opportunities formerly
available to school-leavers, and a special feature of recent years has
been the multiplication of apprenticeship and learnership schemes in
many branches of industry with the aim of improving the conditions and prospects, and therefore the attractiveness, of a wide range
of industrial openings for the young wage-earner. However, the
selective system of secondary education continues to set artificial
limits to both the range of employment opportunities and the occupational aspirations of juveniles. Children are, in effect, graded
' superior ', ' mediocre ', or ' poor ' in intelligence and attainments at
the age of 11, educated accordingly for a few more years, and turned
over for guidance into employment as manual or non-manual workers
as their schooling dictates. Yet a knowledge of the real significance of
the processes of educational selection and their relationship to the
family environment of children and the occupational structure which
confronts them on leaving school opens up the possibility of a longer-
term educational and vocational guidance policy directed towards improving the supply of trained labour at all levels to meet the growing
demand for it.

Some 20–25 per cent of the age-group of 11-year-olds is selected for
education in grammar schools (though for particular districts the proportion may vary from as little as 10 per cent to as much as 50 per cent,
and the provision bears no necessary relation to the needs of the local
occupational structure). It is sometimes suggested that this minority
represents an intellectual *élite*—a broad-based aristocracy of brains. It is
true that it probably contains the best brains of the social classes who
do not send their children to independent schools, but it also represents virtually the entire reserve of potentially qualified manpower.
Less than 10 per cent of the age-group is admitted at 11 to technical
schools, and a still smaller fraction at 13. The remaining two-thirds
of the age-group continue their education in the secondary modern
schools, leaving for the most part at 15, to form the bulk of the supply
of manual workers, very few of whom are destined to climb subsequently into posts of more than minor responsibility in industry or
commerce.

Since 1945, when fees were abolished in all maintained secondary
schools, the process of selection for secondary education has been

based almost solely on objective tests of intelligence and attainments in English and Arithmetic. This has had the effect of relating the distribution of grammar school places very closely indeed to the distribution of intelligence (as measured by the tests). Social-class inequalities of opportunity of proceeding to grammar schools are therefore almost entirely a function of social-class differences in measured intelligence, and there have been marked changes in the social composition of the grammar schools. Ten years ago more than 50 per cent of pupils in these schools paid fees, and the children of non-manual workers outnumbered those of manual workers. Since all places were opened to competition by examination in 1945, however, there has been a considerable influx of working-class children into the schools. This represents an important increase in mobility—a probable potential weakening of the present association of paternal and filial occupational status. For the more successful of these pupils there is entrance to the universities, and thence to administrative or professional occupations. For the middle group of those leaving at 16 or 17 there are careers in banks and insurance offices, the executive and higher clerical grades of the Civil Service and similar occupations. Even for those who do not complete the minimum grammar school course, some form of minor white-collar occupation is the typical expectation.[10]

But the selection process, though within its limits ' objective ', is nevertheless, as is widely recognized, very imprecise. It is difficult to know how much weight to attach to differences of ability between the selected and the rejected children in the middle ranges of the examination hierarchy. Within only a narrow range of differences in average I.Q., working-class children, divided according to certain features of their family environment,[11] show marked differences in success at the selection examination. The influence on children's educational performance and prospects of crude economic disabilities has been much reduced by social amelioration and post-war full employment; more subtle attributes tend to distinguish the home backgrounds of successful from those of unsuccessful children. Thus, the working-class child

---

[10] Although an increasing minority is now beginning to take up industrial apprenticeships. Hitherto the occupational ambitions of grammar school pupils have not been directed towards industry. It is difficult to decide how much this has been due to the academic atmosphere and curriculum of the schools, the lack of co-operation of employers, the difficulties of apprenticeship regulations, or the prejudices of parents. But it is beyond doubt that the field of acceptable choice for the grammar school-leaver has been and remains restricted. (See O. Banks, *op. cit.*)

[11] E.g., family size, parents' attitudes towards education, etc. For fuller information on this and the following points concerning the relation of home background to educational performance, see J. Floud (ed.), A. H. Halsey, and F. M. Martin, *Social Class and Educational Opportunity* (Heinemann, 1956).

who secures a grammar school place tends to come from a small family, his father is more likely to have received some form of further education, his mother to have received something more than an elementary schooling, and, before marriage, to have followed an occupation ' superior ' to that of his father. These factors are reflected in a complex of attitudes favourable to educational success and social mobility, and differences of this kind in home background presumably underlie differences in motivation which, in the absence of gross economic handicaps, are the key to differences in performance in a substantial border-line range of ability.

In so far as the Welfare State succeeds in providing a basic equality of economic status for all citizens, we may expect that increasing numbers of homes will provide the moral or cultural support which makes for success at school. The pressure on the grammar schools is then likely to increase from this cause, as well as from the increase in the birth-rates of the post-war years. It is unlikely that the number of places will be expanded sufficiently to maintain the provision at its present level—in which case the unselected reserve of educable talent in the modern schools (i.e., in effect, the number of ' border-line ' children) will increase, and selection will become even less effective than at present.

The selective influence of differences in cultural background continues to operate among the selected minority of grammar school entrants. Social class plays a very important part in determining the use that children admitted to the grammar schools can make of the course or, from the point of view of the occupational structure, the extent to which they in fact manage to equip themselves for, and enter, the grade of occupation for which their ability makes them eligible.

A recent official inquiry [12] has estimated that one-third of the grammar school boys who are capable of reaching a standard of at least two passes at Advanced Level in the General Certificate of Education leave school before doing so, and that the influence of home background is the major cause. The 15 per cent of all school children originating from the professional and managerial classes account for 25 per cent of the grammar school population and contribute 43·7 per cent of those reaching the Sixth form of the grammar school, whereas the 12 per cent from the homes of unskilled manual workers account for 5·6 per cent of grammar school pupils and contribute only 1·5 per cent of the Sixth formers. The Council's report confirms earlier in-

---

[12] Central Advisory Council for Education (England), *Early Leaving* (H.M.S.O., December 1954).

quiries [13] which found that the child of the professional or business man admitted to a grammar school is likely to improve his academic status relative to others in his age-group, whilst the unskilled worker's child is likely to deteriorate. 'Wastage' from grammar schools, as the Central Advisory Council clearly recognized, is a social-class problem. The traditionally middle-class schools are evidently failing to assimilate large numbers of the able working-class children who win their way into them.

Selection is imprecise and is made at an arbitrary point in the scale of ability; yet it reinforces the differences both between and within social classes by fostering different levels of vocational aspiration among children attending different types of secondary school. Thus among a sample of lower-working-class boys in London grammar schools,[14] no fewer than two-thirds expected to rise considerably above their fathers in occupational status compared with 12 per cent of their comrades in secondary modern schools. Professor T. H. Marshall has commented on the results of this inquiry that " the boys from the humbler working-class homes may overrate their chances without fully realizing how ambitious their success has made them ".[15] Secondary modern school boys, on the other hand, are subjected to the inhibiting effects of rejection and their occupational aspirations are correspondingly lower. The limit of aspiration among these children seems to be the top of the manual working class from which, in the majority of cases, they originate. Powerful forces, grouped by Jahoda under the heading of " climate of opinion ", appear to limit their horizon.[16] Jahoda reports that among secondary modern school-leavers in Lancashire, office or clerical work was the kind of job most frequently rejected and half of those who rejected it did so because they considered themselves unqualified for it. In her study of vocational choice in Ealing, Miss M. D. Wilson found that fewer than 5 per cent of the pupils in her sample of secondary modern pupils chose

---

[13] A. H. Halsey and L. Gardner, "Selection for Secondary Education and Achievement in Four Grammar Schools", British Journal of Sociology, March 1953; G. Greenald, University of London, unpublished M.A. Thesis, 1954: " An Inquiry into the Influence of Sociological and Psychological Factors on Trend of Achievement in Grammar Schools."

[14] H. T. Himmelweit, A. H. Halsey, and A. N. Oppenheim, "The Views of Adolescents on Some Aspects of Social Class Structure", British Journal of Sociology, June 1952.

[15] T. H. Marshall, "Social Selection in the Welfare State", Eugenics Review, 1953.

[16] C. Jahoda, "Job Attitude and Job Choice among Secondary Modern School Leavers", Occupational Psychology, April and October, 1952.

occupations unsuited to their educational standing.[17]   She found the children " ambitious, but not excessively so ", by which she meant that they tended, as had been noted of children in earlier inquiries, to aim at the highest levels available to the group to which they belong, showing, as she expressed it, " a healthy desire to climb to the top of the tree, but little yearning to move to another part of the forest where there are taller trees ".   She also produced evidence to show that selection at 11+ produced a marked modification of vocational aspirations, the children directing their interests soon after their admission to secondary schools to the general field of occupations available to them —the modern school boys, for instance, turning ' realistically ' from occupational ' phantasies ' to skilled manual work.

Yet if selection for secondary education is as faulty as the evidence suggests, the profound effect of the segregation of children into different types of secondary school on their attitude to vocations must be deplored.

Reorganization of the System

Selection at 11+ and segregation into separate schools is evidently a form of vocational as well as educational selection undesirable, because premature.   It is sometimes defended in the post-war conditions of full competition for grammar school places as a promoter of social mobility [18] and as a desirable method of selecting the best brains of all classes to form a much-needed democratic *élite*.   In fact, the post-war expansion of opportunity for working-class children to enter grammar schools directs attention away from the dysfunctional aspects of the system which we have been describing.   What conclusions are we to draw from the discussion?

The most radical inference is that English secondary education should be reorganized along comprehensive lines.   There is indeed something to be said for the view that the common secondary school is best suited to the needs of a technological society—least likely to stand in the way of free vocational choice and movement, most likely to produce the maximum supply of skilled and responsible individuals particularly in the middle ranges of the occupational structure.   But these advantages could be reaped from such a reorganization only if the spirit as well as the form of English secondary education were changed.   The emphasis on selection—on the sifting, grading, and

---

[17] M. D. Wilson, "The Vocational Preferences of Secondary Modern School Children ", *The British Journal of Educational Psychology*, June and November, 1953.

[18] *Cf.* E. James, *Comprehensive Schools Today*, ed. R. Pedley (Councils and Education Press Ltd., London, 1954).

sorting of ability—during the school years would need to be severely modified, and the relation of the schools to the occupational structure would need to be made much more flexible. The task of occupational selection which is at present performed by the secondary schools, with the adverse economic effects which we have noted, would need to be shifted to post-school educational institutions, and the intensive preparation of the *élite* now undertaken by the grammar schools postponed.

These are large questions, with profound social and educational, as well as economic, implications, into which we cannot enter here. The debate on the comprehensive school is still in progress. Meantime, however, within the traditional organizational framework of secondary education much can be done in the same spirit to loosen the bonds that tie occupation to schooling. More than lip-service must be paid to the arbitrary and imprecise nature of selection—every effort must be made to mitigate its effects on vocational choice. Thus, the increasing tendency to encourage children to stay in modern schools to take advanced courses after the age of compulsory attendance is a step in the right direction—as are also any measures which may be adopted to open up a new route to positions of industrial and technical responsibility by creating new technical qualifications accessible to ex-modern school pupils through a reorganized system of technical colleges. Such measures will be the more successful in that the unselected reserve of educable talent in the modern schools is likely to grow for the reasons mentioned above.

It is also desirable that the policy of vocational guidance should be re-oriented in a deliberate attempt to increase the fluidity of the supply of labour. To be effective for this purpose guidance cannot afford to begin its work only at the end of the children's school days, concentrating on the end-products of the educational process. If boys and girls are to be candidates for the widest range of occupations for which their ability fits them, and if this involves overcoming obstacles to their educational progress arising out of their family environment, vocational guidance has to start much earlier in their careers and to be part and parcel of the school system rather than an offshoot of the Ministry of Labour. Vocational guidance in England has made impressive strides in the short period of its existence as a national service.[19] But it is perhaps an indication of progress yet to be made that Logan and Goldberg are able to report that among the majority (of a sample of 18-year-old boys in a London suburb) the Youth Employment

---

[19] Cf. *Ministry of Labour Gazette*, "The Youth Employment Service 1950–3", February 1954, p. 41. Also H. Higginbotham, *The Youth Employment Service* (London, 1951).

Service seemed to exert little influence on the choice of job, being mainly used as a convenient agency for the notification of vacancies in semi-skilled and unskilled work.[20]

The service has not merely to make contact with the heads of schools and with parents when the children leave school, but to extend the conception of its task to include counselling at all points in the school course and the building up for this purpose of a detailed knowledge of home circumstances. Traditionally, this work has been done by teachers in the schools, who frequently have very considerable knowledge, not merely of their pupils' abilities and aptitudes, but also of the sources and determinants in their home circumstances of their attitudes and interests, or apathy and ignorance. However, it is doubtful whether, with the greatly extended professional demands on teachers to-day, they can be expected to undertake in the course of their ordinary duties what may approximate, with a large number of pupils, to social case-work.

Vocational guidance, to be effective, must therefore extend back into the school, becoming in the first place educational guidance based on a full knowledge of home as well as school circumstances and also, if necessary, family guidance. This kind of social and educational case-work, directed towards popularizing unfamiliar educational objectives or occupational prospects amongst children and their families, can be extraordinarily effective, as may be seen by comparing the reactions to their grammar school course and the occupational destinies of working-class children in neighbouring schools distinguished only by the enthusiasm and competence in this direction of the head master. The question is whether a national guidance policy, aimed at stimulating the ambitions of the unselected school population and tackling the problem of social assimilation which underlies the wastage of able working-class children from the grammar schools, does not demand the appointment of counsellors or guidance officers to the staffs of all secondary schools who would undertake what teachers cannot ordinarily be expected to do as part of their daily work.

JEAN FLOUD.
A. H. HALSEY.

---

[20] R. and L. Logan and E. M. Goldberg, " Rising 18 in a London Suburb ", *British Journal of Sociology*, December 1953, p. 327. See also L. T. Wilkins, *The Employment of the Adolescent* (Central Office of Information, 1951).

CHAPTER FIVE

The Demand for and Support of Education in African Tribal Society

ONE of the untested beliefs we hold about Western civilization is that it alone is education-minded. A closer acquaintance with other cultures discloses that the zeal for education is not less alive in them. In the average African tribe of the Bantu-speaking area we can distinguish three types of education.

Informal Education

The informal education of the home aims at training the child in the norms of conduct appropriate to family and kinship groupings. The educators, represented by the parents, act under the demands of the tribal *ethos* in rearing their children. These demands are expressed in traditional folk-lore, its proverbs and tales, in the system of reverential restraints or taboos, in the current social comment on the actions of the children and the educational abilities of the parents. Every African father and mother tries to induce in his or her children a behaviour which corresponds to these demands. In doing so, they use a series of educational measures, such as rewards and punishments, and supplement these with linguistic tools, as for instance promises and threats and the story. The latter follows either a traditional fairy-tale pattern or is the elaboration of an historical topic or of a contemporary example. It stresses, *inter alia*, the advantages of diligence and heroism and the drawbacks of deceit and stubbornness. In the particular situation of the family these norms appear by no means as being imposed from the outside. They arise as essential demands within the social dialectic of the elementary family, so as to ensure its integration.

The assumption underlying this article is that education being a social value has a price placed on it. This price can be expressed only in the idiom of the culture to which it belongs. Since primitive culture does not express its values in monetary terms, it is necessary for us to describe in detail how concrete or ideological equivalents of money secure the benefits of education. One thing is certain even for such societies. Education is a value, for which the ' producers of education ', the parents and political leaders, are prepared to pay a price, and so are the teachers, who might be called the distributors of the commodity of education, as well as its consumers, the children, the novices of an initiation camp, the educands of tribal life. But education is a complex value, inasmuch as it consists of many parts and many aspects, which may be either offered with or subtracted from the commodity as a whole. Hence the determination of the cultural value of education is a difficult undertaking, because even were it possible to obtain figures for educational services from the national budget, very little would be revealed as to the status accorded to education within the cultural context concerned.

No information, for instance, exists on the amount of time spent on the education of their children by African parents. But it would not be surprising if a comparative time-study revealed that the primitive score is higher in this respect than that of the average Western parent. The parental efforts are prescribed in the traditional division of labour in educational matters. It gives the training of small children and girls up to their marriage to the mothers. Boys transfer to the tutelage of their fathers at about 6. This division imposes upon the parents definite duties in reaching the goal of education. Girls have to be taught to prepare the food and this in the widest sense of the term; they have to till the fields in order to produce the raw materials for the kitchen; they must be able to make the pots; they have to fetch water and firewood and cook and serve the dishes. The boys may learn a craft; they usually look after the livestock, beginning with sheep and goats while small and transferring to cattle in their teens. Apart from this, children must be made to learn the norms of kinship conduct, the reverential restraints customary towards various types of kin, the nature and extent of co-operative assistance in lineage and clan activities.

The time and effort which parents devote to training their children in these areas of life are a measure of the value education has in their society or in a particular family. In addition, African parents provide occasions for the celebration of ceremonies which accentuate certain traditionally accepted stages in the child's development. The food prepared for these events, the livestock slaughtered, the fees paid in kind to the ritual experts, present part of the educational bill each primitive family has to face. On these occasions parents have to submit to ritual abstentions from normally enjoyed ' pleasures ', like certain types of food, sexual intercourse, or selected occupations. These deprivations are willingly accepted by the parents to secure the well-being of their children. They should be listed as important items in assessing the value of primitive informal education. Other values which might compete with the demand for family education hardly exist under conditions unaffected by Western contact. For since this type of education is a basic requirement for the existence of the family, and is an essential of social life, it receives ' top priority '.

The African parent expects certain satisfactions from the successful transmission of the norms of family conduct. For instance, a woman has her efforts in training her daughter recognized in the widespread custom whereby her daughter's betrothed presents her with some small gift. Usually one of the cattle constituting the bride-price is ear-marked for the mother, and its name indicates that it is meant to compensate her for her parental care. Of course, the bride-price in itself is a recognition of the value of the young woman, and as the transaction affects the families rather than the bride and the groom, it is a measure of her value to the two contracting families.[1] Successful training in the economic activities, be it for the fundamental tribal enterprise or a private occupation, makes a child an asset to his parents. In an economy which does not know the accumulation of money savings, capital is represented by working hands, and economic power by the number of workmen an individual can command. Education in the moral sphere, if it results in the child's willing submission to family leadership and to co-operation with kinship groups, supplements occupational training and helps to maintain the child's individual skill as a factor contributing to the welfare of a defined social group. Sons who turn out well enhance their father's prestige at court and strengthen his influence in tribal councils. In short, in native society, children are to their parents important socio-economic assets because of their economic capacities and because of the links made possible with other clans through their marriages.

Parents are also given ideal rewards for their educational efforts. Families with a good reputation in educational matters have a higher standing in their community than families in which the education of the children is neglected. Such standing helps to promote the interests and influence of a family and its members in various ways. Fathers and mothers may receive honorary names referring to their children or to the establishment through their offspring of a new branch of the lineage. In ritual praises the successful education of their children may be mentioned. As spirit guardians, the fathers remain in an

---

[1] The function of the bride-price as an educational yard-stick is not its only function. In addition it compensates the woman's paternal family for the loss of the children which she will bear to her husband's lineage. It is also a kind of insurance against conduct which might break up the marriage. For if the husband misbehaves, his wife will leave him and the cattle are forfeited to his family. If the wife behaves badly, she will be sent back to her father and he has to return the cattle paid for her.

intimate personal relationship to some of their children, and mothers are not excluded from this privilege, although normally they are prevented by the prevalent patrilineal system from being made much of after their death. Guardian spirits are supposed to enter and guide persons in such occupations as divination or healing. Through the fictitious extension of parental control, parents after their death continue to hold sway over their children's fortunes, rewarding them from the beyond for the fulfilment of obligations and punishing them for the infraction of rules. Neglectful parents, on the other hand, are forgotten by their descendants and certainly they lose the satisfaction of controlling their children's fate posthumously.

Children have their value enhanced through the right kind of education. A well-mannered, diligent girl is spoken well of in her neighbourhood and is much sought after by suitors. While the bulk of the bride-price is fixed by tradition, variations are allowed for deductions and premiums. In most instances these are determined by differences in status, the daughter of a headman being assessed at a higher rate than that of a commoner. Yet men are willing to pay a higher price for a girl with a reputation of a good worker and a dutiful daughter. The good qualities of a well-bred son stand him in good stead. The chief will hear of him and invite him to his court. Educational value, we see, is not necessarily defined in money terms, such as high salary or marriage endowment, but also and perhaps more humanly and satisfactorily, in multiple social relations and intensity of appreciation. Of course, a 'cultured' child enjoys private satisfactions as well.

Ritual Accentuation

The second type of primitive education takes the form of the ritual accentuation of the life stages of a child, the celebration of his advance in knowledge and bodily strength as traditionally defined. Its aim is to secure the growing individual's association with the mystic forces of the physical environment and of his social universe. The essential feature of these ceremonies is the rhythmical repetition of rites which link the child with these forces. In many of these ceremonies indelible signs are marked on the educand's body, be it by means of circumcision, mutilations on lips, ears, or teeth, or scarifications. The function of such signs is to act as a badge, to make the owner enjoy the fellow-feeling of being a member of a powerful sodality, to remind him of his obligations to society, and legitimize his claims for help.

Parents are coerced by the tribal value system into the efforts and expenditure required for the organization of these ceremonies. Well-to-do parents may have 'private' celebrations for their child. But it is more convenient for a number of parents to club together and arrange communal ceremonies. Experts are engaged, and an isolated ritual site is prepared, food is accumulated and new clothes and ornaments obtained for the children against the time when they pass out as graduates. If competitive claims have to be met (e.g., for a hutbuilding, a wedding, or a funeral), the fees in kind, the food required, may not be available. It is then possible for the harried parent to borrow the wherewithal from kinsmen. Or the child's attendance at the ceremony is postponed even to the extent of his becoming over-age. Teasing and ridicule, the powerful motivating forces for conformity of conduct in primitive society, in the end make the demand for performing the ceremony overwhelming.

A great number of educators may be engaged in these ceremonies. Old men act as teachers of moral lessons. Priests perform sacred rites which appeal to and thank the ancestral deities. Operators with a knack of using the traditional tools carry out the incisions and scarifications. Mentors are hired to stay with the educands in the isolation huts and train them in the lore which is to be memorized. Supervisors are appointed to see that the novices submit to the taboo regime of the ceremony. All these experts are paid fees in kind and consider these fees a return on the expenses incurred when they trained for their job. In their professional training they stayed for an extended period with a recognized master of their craft. They collected goods to exchange them for the professional accoutrement and esoteric knowledge. They submit to the abstentions and abandon their normal economic pursuits for the period of the ceremony. It is understandable that the ' popular ' demand for the performing of the ceremonies frequently emanates from these functionaries, who wish to recoup themselves for the expenses of their training.

The educands, normally boys or girls of the same age, jointly undergo these rites of passage. If there is delay in the ceremony, it is caused by the poor state of the crop or some tribal circumstance, e.g., the death of the chief, or the threat of an intertribal conflict. Such occurrences necessitate the concentration of the economic resources on these more urgent matters. But adolescents may not agree with their seniors' judgment as to the pressing nature of the alternative enterprises. They may gather together, sing provocative songs, commit outrages, occasionally inflict self-mutilations and destroy property. In this way, they provoke their parents to hasten the ceremony. The educands are as ready to pay the price for this type of ritual education as their educators. Not only are they frequently called upon to build the ritual camp or hut. They must also submit to the hardships of the austere camp life, suffer the excruciating pain of the operation, attend to their wounds and observe the taboos of the isolation period. The intensity with which they demand these formative ceremonies compares favourably with the attitude of the average Western child towards school. Of course, the primitive child receives in return genuine satisfactions: the ceremonies introduce him to a higher status; a carefully adjusted increase in privileges and obligations admits him to wider social circles.

Preparation for Participation in Public Affairs

In the third type of education known in primitive society, the young men are trained for full participation in the public affairs of the tribe. The aim is to introduce the prospective tribesman to the legal procedures and principles of his people, and to acquaint him with the constitution and the power set-up of the tribe and with its relationship to political forces outside it. The promoters of this type of education are the chief and his councillors. As the jural and political organism under their control needs to adjust itself to emergent internal and external circumstances, the tribal guardians add new items to their public educational programme and thereby give the tribe vitality.

As in the case of the ceremonies, this type of public training has to be organized, and the efforts devoted to its successful achievement are a fair measure of the value ascribed to education. The sons of noblemen and commoners are called to attend the royal court for important law cases. They have to be entertained, are given lodging and food and drink at the chief's expense. No lectures are given to them, but the young men attend the court sittings, hear the comments of councillors and spectators, and gradually learn to form their own judgment.

Where military organizations existed, the training of the youths in the war-like practices was entrusted to the officers with experience. Having been enrolled, the young men were drafted to military camps. In their training they learned the movements of military formations in both attack and retreat, the handling of small and large contingents, the tactical and strategical considerations appropriate to the weapons, the terrain, the military organization and aims of their people. The commissariat was a complex affair and called on the highest organizational abilities of the leading tribesmen. The emoluments of the officers in charge and the cost of the commissariat may be considered educational expenditure. Further expenses were incurred at the commencement of a campaign, when the tribal magicians were called in to administer charms and distribute amulets.

The demands competing for recognition over and against education are difficult to define in primitive society, which lacks the convenient index of an annual budget with departmental votes, and scarcely knows the representation of sectional interests. Undoubtedly the meagre economic resources of a people are strained by the larger tribal ceremonies, such as initiation, which sometimes combines with the military course. An initiation may therefore be held only at intervals of several years, and in some tribes only once in a generation. At any rate the time for celebrating ceremonies is after the harvest, in times of plenty, or in the winter months, when no other occupations interfere with their performance. On the other hand, their value is considered so high that they cannot be altered or abbreviated. And since their curriculum deals with such vital topics as marriage, the control of human fortunes by the ancestral deities, and the relationship between kinship groups and tribal institutions, attendance is compulsory for everyone. A further indication of the high value placed on the formative ceremonies are the tests which are part of them. They are scarcely examinations of memorized knowledge, but methods of symbolically expressing the candidates' allegiance to the moral values of their society. The tests do not isolate the individual as do our examinations, but are, on the contrary, group or companionship tests binding those who undergo them together in insoluble and lifelong bonds of comradeship. A clash between the claims of ritual and public education is occasionally noticeable in tribal life. For instance, the Zulu king Shaka abolished circumcision because the long healing period interfered with the military preparedness of his troops. We have here, in incipient form, a conflict between different types of education, such as might occur in a modern society.

To sum up : it has been established that primitive education may be viewed as an ' economic ' process in which we distinguish the producers of the commodity ' education ', its distributors, and consumers. The producers of education, the parents and political leaders, the tribe itself, are interested in promoting education, they appraise its function, advertise its advantages, and create additional values to make it appeal to the consumers. The teachers and experts, as distributors and transmitters of education, really form part of the producing side, although they may be passive in the elaboration of the commodity. The children are the consumers. They acquire an education and have to pay a price for it which is defined in the value idiom of their culture. Education should not be viewed exclusively as consumer-goods, since those possessing education may use it for the creation of new values. It may therefore be classed with the cultural producer-goods.

The Competing Education of the White Man

With the advent of the white man an entirely new situation was created in the sphere of education. He offered an alternative education to supplant the indigenous education given in the family, the ceremonial camp, and the tribal institution. To use an analogy : the new masters did their best to offer their type of education at competitive prices and to depreciate the indigenous educational currency. Yet right from the earliest contacts with primitive peoples, there were far-seeing Westerners who realized the intrinsic value of the indigenous order. A great educational theoretician, Jean Jacques Rousseau, sensed that the simplicity of the social norms in primitive society made for easier recognition of the fundamental moral norms of human conduct. While, in his advocacy of the noble savage's way of life, he went too far and under-estimated the values of his own advanced culture, the white man on the spot fell into the opposite error. He rejected in vehement language certain striking features of native life and many of its educational practices. Doubts were, for instance, raised about the value of the tests of hardship during initiation and in the ethical significance of kinship conduct.

The creation of the demand for Western education was thus accompanied by attempts to show up the spuriousness of the claims of traditional education. It was comparatively easy to disprove the claim that ritual education established a mystical association with the forces of the universe, because the material and military superiority of the white man was achieved without it.

Nevertheless the tardiness of a positive response in the commencing stage of white-black contact is an historical fact. The reason for this may be seen in the type of education offered. The missionary trained their native adherents in reading and writing holy scripture, in learning the spiritual truths about sin and atonement. For these completely alien notions, the native convert had to pay with isolation from his own family and tribe and with the abandonment of traditional economic enterprises and age-long types of entertainment. The difficulties experienced by early missionaries in attracting buyers for their educational wares is shown in the desperate efforts made by them to induce children to attend. Bribes in the form of food, clothes, even money payments, were common; chiefs and parents had to be persuaded to accept education for their children. In those days a chief might send the most stupid children of an unimportant wife for a trial period by way of experiment, and not find it worth while to continue it for long. Had it not been that internecine warfare resulted in the displacement of many families, that the rule of tyrants alienated the affections of some of the subjects, and the belief in witchcraft brought on fierce persecutions, very few individuals would have found their way to the missionaries. Frequently their first clients were victims of the disturbed tribal conditions. The reward for aligning themselves with the ' messengers of peace ' and participating in their education was that these refugees secured themselves a place of hiding, which, however, was not always safe against tribal raids to recover them.

The other Western agency interested in the education of the native, but with quite a different aim, was the newly established colonial government. It desired the assistance of Africans in a subsidiary capacity as clerks, messengers, attendants. The natives who were persuaded to undertake training thereby cut themselves adrift from their tribe. They were rewarded for the loss of full-blooded participation in the activities of a society by the prestige of sharing ' the white man's burden ' and by being recognized as government employees.

Western education in Africa, as first presented by its early promoters, was by no means the ideal, full-sized commodity known in the metropolitan country, but an attenuated and abbreviated variety of it. Only gradually did these initial efforts grow out into attempts to train the African on European lines, to give him an all-round education, to transform him into a citizen subject to a new loyalty, and aware of the scope and depth of a modern culture.

Particular difficulties were experienced in training a suitable type of teacher at once conversant with the cultural background of his pupils and alive to the social needs of an emerging society. Considerable expense was incurred in rendering vernaculars into literary media. The equally important task of recognizing and utilizing the educational significance of the physical and social environment of the native pupils has never been systematically tackled for lack of funds. The buildings of schools in inaccessible areas, the establishment of hostels, the support of indigenous pupils swallowed considerable sums. The educational efforts of the missionaries were supported not by local resources but by contributions from overseas, and the colonial governments gave grants to missionary institutions because they were not in a position to support or build a state system of schools.

A frequent phenomenon of the early stages of Western education in Africa was the ' backsliding of pupils '. Having received training in European knowledge and skills, some African scholars would ' take to the bush ' after a promising start. While this fact shows up the difficulty of getting the advantages of Western education across the native mind, it also implies that educational expenditure was apt to be wasted in the early colonial situation. In the competition between the two value systems the indigenous one tenaciously boasted of certain advantages. While in childhood participation in Western ways is an exciting adventure, in adolescence it is realized that the price paid for such participation is excessive. The transfer involves the wholesale abandonment of native values; polygamy becomes an expensive luxury; the native's cattle fixation cannot be indulged in an urban area;

his love of many children—an economic advantage in his own set-up—becomes a burden difficult to bear for a small-salaried man. Loyalty to the tribe, necessitating regular gifts to the chief, is impossible.

Gradually, however, a situation developed in which a fair-sized proportion of the child population of a tribe would simultaneously participate in both systems of education, the indigenous and the Western. For this double standard the African is prepared to pay an enormous price. Hundreds and thousands of children meekly submit to being separated from their homes in order to attend school. They accept the strange diet and the curious routine of hostels with equanimity. Many Africans travel tremendous distances to enrol in the institution of their choice. In school, Africans are supported by contributions from parents, siblings, and other relatives, who deprive themselves of amenities and necessities of life to do so.

It is well-nigh impossible, without an exhaustive and intricate statistical investigation, to assess the financial status of, and the degree of priority given to, native education within early colonial economy. Competitive demands, putting such education in the background, were plentiful. Consequently the schooling offered at first was not up to Western standards. This is true with reference to equipment and facilities, to the skill of the teachers, and to the suitability of the curriculum offered. Indeed, education was sometimes blamed for the spirit of rebelliousness and the lack of co-operation on the part of the indigenous population. Western education as given to Africans also suffered under the handicap of having to start from scratch. The creation of a literary medium, the writing and publication of suitable textbooks, experiments in the types of school and the kinds of curricula which would meet the situation, could not refer to and utilize the tested principles and hard-won experience behind century-old European school systems. This fact alone accounts for the relatively high cost of establishing Western education.

We are therefore not surprised to find in the literature on education in colonies constant references to its shortcomings. The slow rate of increase in the proportion of children attending school, the difficulty of insisting on compulsory education as long as universal education is out of the question, the shortage of funds for the development of technical and special education, the drawback of an undifferentiated teaching establishment, the urgency of fundamental education through literacy campaigns and demonstration units, are instances in point.

Conflicts between Value Systems

In the meantime a revolutionary situation has arisen. It is characterized by the conflict between Western and African value systems and the intensification of this conflict by the emergence of an inter-mediate area of ' floating ' values unattached to any of the traditional systems. This conflict results from the juxtaposition of two fully integrated cultures and their transforming influence upon individuals caught up in the contact situation.

As to the educational programme devised for the African, there is conflict in the white camp as well as in the African camp. Among the whites the so-called ' integrationists ' demand the extension to the Africans of an education modelled entirely on the Western metro-politan pattern. Their reason may be either a belief in the uniformity of human needs and ideals or a conviction regarding the unchallenge-able superiority of Western civilization over primitive ways of life. The ' differentialists ' among the whites plump for an education trimmed to suit the African in his special circumstances. This may be considered desirable again for two contrasting reasons. They either wish to preserve and genuinely stimulate the creative genius of indi-genous culture, or hope to underpin and justify the order of privileged segregation of the white from the native. The conflict in the African camp may be said to centre in the struggle between the conservatives and the reformers. Among the conservatives are found the die-hard traditionalists, who are still opposed to modern education as a symbol of the Western way of life which countenances the demoralization of the native proletariat in the urban centres. Other conservatives are genuinely interested in retaining the spirit of the culture which their forefathers have created and which shows such an amazing vitality under the stress of culture contact. Among the reformers some realize that there is an urgent need for social and cultural adjustments within the African community, so that Africa can compete in the modern world on equal terms with other nations. Others are imbued with a radical spirit and would like to jettison traditional social machinery and the tenuous cultural bonds which help it to function.

To put it briefly, the conflict situation results in an intensification of the demand for education. It also increases the awareness of alterna-tive ideals of education. The uniformity of educational thought seems a matter of the past. Greatly differentiated values emerge. Such sectional strife is, one must hope, preparatory to a new synthesis on a higher level. This makes itself felt even in the only group which has not been affected by the century-old campaign for Western education. The die-hard traditionalists are driven to re-create the demand for tribal ceremonies and institutions of primitive education. They are often prepared to go to great lengths to pay for them. However, such revivals cannot now hope to be acceptable for large sections of native society unless they make concessions to Western education.

The establishment of a central revenue in a colonial territory places the financial support for native education on a sure footing. When the policy of co-operation between government and missions in the educational field becomes acceptable, the imbalance between willingness to help the native educationally and lack of resources on the part of the missionaries can be redressed. Where elected representatives enter colonial legislatures the budgeting for native education becomes a subject for political bargaining and as a result the vote agreed on is not always tailored to the needs of the indigenous populace. Certain pressure groups are interested in limiting the educational opportunities of the African to the academic courses, begrudging him the training in arts and crafts that might make him a competitor with organized trades. In some colonial territories expenditure on education is on a differential scale and works to the advantage of the white child, who is trained in a separate educational establishment. The justification for such a fiscal measure is sought in the differential contribution of the two racial groups to the national income. Its effect on the scholastic performance of the handicapped section has been asserted to be incalculable. In some countries the native education vote may be fixed by statute, and unless provisions exist for the granting of additional votes, the charge that the governments concerned are not genuinely interested in a rapid advance of native education may be raised. In the present conflict situation, the demands conceded by any government as legitimate are likely to be considered as utterly inadequate by the reformers, while the traditionalists might view a fraction of the planned expenditure sufficient to produce a social explosion.

Western education as a commodity for native populations in colonial territories is subject to great fluctuations in value. It is appreciated in those sections which have learned to make a living by it. It is decried by people to whom the graduates of Western institutions appear to be undermining the values of the old order. An element bringing high appreciation is its apparent scarcity, for it is still in limited supply. Because of this scarcity, an unequal distribution is almost a thing of necessity. This obviously enables some people to profit by it who are not really qualified to have a first call on educational resources and leads to the phenomenon of the ' educated ' snob in native society, i.e., of the person who vaunts an education which is of no use to him. The fact that, in conditions of scarcity, waste occurs is a danger sign, indicating that the available education does not yet answer the needs of the native peoples.

O. F. RAUM.

CHAPTER SIX

Education in a Peasant Society

" ALTHOUGH peasantry still constitutes almost three-fourths of the world's people and makes up the bulk of the population in the under-developed countries, it has been relatively neglected by social scientists as a special field of study : anthropologists have specialized in primitive or tribal societies; sociologists in urban societies; and rural sociologists in modern rural societies. Thus, the great majority of mankind has had no discipline to claim it as its own. A comparative science of peasantry is only now beginning to take form." [1]

Without splitting hairs on a definition of the peasant, one is bound to agree with Oscar Lewis both as to the great preponderance of the peasant or village style of living and as to the great gap in understanding and knowledge which separates this style from urban ideologists, be they politicians, administrators, educationists, or economists. From the point of view of all these, the peasant represents a sort of ' backwardness ' which is dangerous to the urban-centred economic system, both nationally and internationally.

The Transformation of Peasant Society

The science of economics, as we know it, developed as an attempt to understand and control the potent forces of industrialism and capitalism. Sometimes it has been over-involved in the economic institutions which are its subject-matter, and then has been fairly criticized as an ideology, or system of apologetics, rather than a critical science. But even when economists have been critical of economic assumptions and when they have advocated major changes in the organization of economic life, as did Marx or Keynes, their preoccupations have been with large-scale industry, because it was the biggest, most powerful, most socially significant phenomenon within their experience. In Britain, as Marx eloquently pointed out, the elimination of the peasant was the pre-condition of the industrial revolution and of intensive urbanization. In North America and some parts of Europe, agriculture itself has been developed on a quasi-industrial basis, on the grand scale and with ever-increasing aid from machines and fertilizers. In the U.S.S.R. not only has the pace of industrializa-

---

[1] O. Lewis, "Peasant Culture in India and Mexico ", in *Village India* (ed. McKim Marriott, University of Chicago Press, 1955), p. 145.

tion been forced but the concept of collective, large-scale agriculture has been imposed on a resistant peasantry by urban intellectuals.

In those countries which still have a majority of unurbanized, un-industrialized, un-collectivized peasants, economists may well feel that they are up against a problem which is dark and intractable. In India and China, for example, with their enormous and growing populations, industrialization, however necessary, can provide only a partial solution and, as has often been pointed out, may actually worsen the degree of under-employment in the countryside. Nor are large-scale, collective methods of agriculture appropriate for growing rice, the all-important crop in Asia. Therefore, under whatever political auspices, the peasant has to be accepted as a factor of long-term importance in the economic situation. Something has to be done for, with, and by the peasant.

It would be easy to say, by way of simplification, that what is needed is a sociological rather than an economic approach to this problem. There is indeed a sense in which this is true. One cannot make workable economic prescriptions for any society without taking into account its social organization and cultural values. But even for the sociologist, it is the economic problem that remains fundamental. The trouble is that the most original economic thinkers—and in consequence the general stream of economic thought—have been preoccupied with large-scale production, both because it has seemed to be increasingly ' inevitable ' and because, in one form or another, capitalist or socialist, it has appeared as the necessary pre-condition of social development and progress.

Marx, for instance, sees in the peasant and small craftsman a transitional stage: "This method of production presupposes a parcelling-out of the soil, a scattered ownership of the instruments of production. Just as it excludes concentration of these means into a few hands, so does it exclude co-operation, the division of labour within the process of production, the social mastery and regulation of the forces of nature, the free development of the social energies of production. It is only compatible with narrow limits for production and society, limits that are the outcome of spontaneous growth. The desire to perpetuate the existence of such limits would be, as Pecqueur has rightly said, ' a decree for the perpetuation of universal mediocrity.' " [2] He therefore looks forward to " the transformation of the pygmy property of the many into the tital property of the few " as the next stage, " terrible and grievous ", but inescapable, on the way to socialism.

Professor Mitrany has analysed the practical effects of this point of

---

[2] Karl Marx, *Capital* (Everyman Edition), p. 844.

view.[3] He has shown how integrally the dogma of the disappearing peasant has been received into Marxist theory as developed under Lenin and Stalin, and how it has been applied in Soviet policy. He has also described the strong peasant-oriented political movements which grew up in the countries of eastern Europe between the wars. Post-war developments in these countries suggest a conflict between Marxist dogmatism and peasant independence. The conflict is, of course, still unsolved. Concessions towards the smallholder alternate with collectivizing drives. Fortunately there is some evidence of a slow change both in the temper of Marxist politicians and in the status of the peasants. The former are less frightened and the latter are less isolated and parochial.

There may possibly come a day when agricultural technology all over the world is transformed so that existing forms of rural social organization are outmoded. Similarly there may come a day for colonizing the moon and the planets. But neither the one nor the other of these apocalypses is in sight. The best that can be hoped for, within planning distance, is the improved cultivation of our own world, and in this task we must largely depend on its countless millions of peasants. However, if we realistically accept peasant agriculture as a necessary ' method of production ' we can, in many ways, help to encourage a ' progressive ' peasantry. This, in fact, is the essential help which town and industry, intellectual and educationist, can bring to the countryside, or, as Oscar Lewis puts it, to " the great majority of mankind ".

Doreen Warriner, in her excellent and unique pre-war study [4] of the eastern European countries, showed very clearly the immense variation in the economic basis of peasant agriculture as between different regions, provinces, and localities. The nature of soil and climate, the development of land tenure and land reform, the density of population, the existence of urban and industrial markets for rural produce, all these and other variables combine to make a patchwork of uneven and contrasting zones. A prosperous peasant society may well adjoin another whose plight seems desperate. Similarly, quite different policies may be appropriate in different areas. Large-scale farming may be the answer in some cases, in others it may be necessary to break up large estates and distribute the land among small-holders. The most general need, however, on her showing, is for the existence of some measure of industry side by side with agriculture. Local conditions will, however, determine the degree of industrializa-

[3] David Mitrany, *Marx against the Peasant* (London, Weidenfeld & Nicolson, 1951).
[4] Doreen Warriner, *The Economics of Peasant Farming* (London, 1939).

tion that can be realistically aimed at. If raw materials, transport facilities, and sources of power are not readily obtainable, then industrial development will be correspondingly gradual. Yet it is to be noted that all over the world there is a sort of ground-swell of urbanization and mechanization going on, even under the least promising conditions. The peasant of the future will certainly be in closer touch with the towns and more familiar with machinery than his forebears.

Village Education

It is in this perspective that we have to look at the relevance of education to peasant societies. Since the war, the number of small peasant holdings must presumably have greatly increased, as a result of land reform in many countries, most notably in Asia. Whatever the eventual social basis of agriculture, the present trend is towards an intensified and partly modernized kind of small-scale farming. Where this is accompanied by organized co-operation between the farmers, the co-operative unit is small, and corresponds to local patterns of settlement, of which the village of about five hundred people is the most widespread. In such a village there may very well already exist a small primary school. In many cases, the simple building in which it is housed will have been provided at the expense and on the initiative of members of the village community. Ambivalent as is the attitude of peasants towards education, as towards other influences which emanate from the government and from the town, there are nearly always elements among them ready to receive and encourage it, if only in self-protection. The school, although it often remains partly alien to the community, is something which the community feels it cannot afford to be without.

Let us take the large, semi-urbanized village of Shamirpet, near Hyderabad, described by Dr. Dube [5] in one of the very few full-length studies of this numerically world-predominant type of community. " The school ", he writes, " is at present ill-housed; it has five classes meeting in two small rooms and only two masters, who teach both Urdu and Telugu as well as the other subjects of the primary school curriculum. Children of all communities now go to school and the old prejudice against admitting untouchable students is dying out. In recent years some Mala and Madiga (untouchable) boys joined the school, but most of them attended only in name, playing truant so consistently that they derived little benefit and eventually stopped going altogether. The school is ill-equipped, having some miserable-looking furniture, a few charts and maps and the inevitable blackboard. The master still wields his stick, and among other reasons this explains

---

[5] S. C. Dube, *Indian Village* (London, Routledge, 1955), p. 25.

perhaps the lack of enthusiasm on the part of the lower-class children and their parents for the school."

One of the divisions which Dr. Dube found in Shamirpet was that between educated and uneducated, each group having its defensive stereotyped opinions about the other. As examples of what uneducated villagers were heard to say, he quotes [6] :

" ' What use is education to us? After four years at the school all that our children learn is to hold a pen in their hands. What we really want them to learn is the holding of the plough firmly.'

" ' Everyone says, " Send your children to school; uneducated people are like animals; education makes them human beings ". But what do we get out of education? Boys learn to read and write, but they forget the traditional ways. They do not want to cultivate the family land, and are ashamed of their traditional profession. They all want jobs in the city. If things go on like this, what will be the future of the community?'

" ' We village people are simple. Education makes us crooked.' "

On the other hand, the educated minority in Shamirpet (only about eighty out of its two thousand five hundred inhabitants have attended village schools for four to six years) think on these lines :

" ' The illiterate villagers are simple, superstitious, and stupid. They believe anyone. Conditions in the village will never improve so long as they dominate the scene.'

" ' Why do petty government officers harass us so much? Only because we are illiterate.' "

There can, of course, be small doubt that the prestige of education will grow in this village, which, we note, " is to have a better school in the near future " [7]. It is part of India's national plan to increase the number of primary schools, and to convert existing primary schools into ' basic ' schools, in which the teaching has a vocational content, as advocated by Gandhi. So vast is the task of providing even a minimum of education for all the millions of Indian village children that progress in this direction will assuredly be slow, in spite of all the encouragement a serious-minded government can give it, and all the enthusiasm that at least a section of the village people feel for it in virtually every village. The important point to note at this stage is the existence in a very large number of villages of a school of a sort, with teachers of a sort, and an education-valuing minority.

Expenditure on Education

This phenomenon, which is characteristic of the peasant countries,

[6] *Ibid.*, p. 189.   [7] *Ibid.*, p. 226.

must now be looked at in relation to the general economic and ecological situation of the village and the peasant household. First of all, it must be looked at from above; from the vantage-point of Delhi or Karachi, Rangoon or Bangkok, or of an international body like ECAFE (Economic Commission for Asia and the Far East), established by the United Nations to collect and assess the facts of economic development in a great and populous but under-developed region of the world. In terms of national or international resources, how much can the economy afford to expend on education? Apart from the cost of buildings and equipment (which, especially in the tropics, need not be very great) there is the cost of training teachers and paying their salaries—a very large item. Also there is the concealed cost to the community of diverting to the routine task of teaching in primary schools a high proportion of the more literate, perhaps more able and intelligent, members of the population. A recent contribution to this YEAR BOOK [8] suggests that an expert educational administrator may feel that it is possible for a country to spend *too much*, in relation to its resources, on primary education: "Thailand, for instance, is a country which has got itself into difficulties as a result of its own good intentions. Over a generation ago, on a wave of enlightened uplift, primary schools were established all over the place and a large (one might almost say in the light of experience an indefensibly large) proportion of the national revenue was allocated to education. To-day all these village schools, if they are to be brought up to date, require not only better trained teachers but also modern equipment for creative activities. The provision of these will impose a financial burden which, even with outside help, the national exchequer will find almost impossible to bear."

I am not sure that I agree with the writer of the above that Thailand's investment in village schools has been indefensibly large, although much needs to be done—and indeed much is being done, at considerable cost—to improve their standard. In order to see whether the village school is 'an economic proposition', we must now look at it in a different way, that is to say from below, or in terms of the village economy rather than the national economy. This will involve a crude and tentative essay in the kind of ' village economics ' which I began by postulating as a necessary but undeveloped complement to the national, urban, industrial economics of which most politicians and administrators have a smattering. I shall draw for this on my own

---

[8] Sir John Sargent, "The Educational Aspects of Planning," *Year Book of Education* (Evans Bros., 1954), p. 240.

inadequate but at least first-hand observations of a number of village communities in north-east Thailand.[9]

Population and Productivity

In the first place, the village settlement has grown up where it is because local conditions of water and soil make it possible to raise the staple crop of rice in quantities just sufficient to feed the population. Owing to improved health conditions and child care, child mortality has been greatly reduced and the population is rapidly increasing. Also increasing, but as a rule less rapidly, is the amount of land under cultivation and the amount of paddy harvested. The important point to note in the ecological situation is the unequal increase in population and in agricultural productivity. Even within quite a small area there may be wide differences in the ratio between these two rates of increase, but peasant populations are relatively immobile and the surplus of population of one village does not readily move to another village with a surplus productive capacity. What is more likely to happen is that the relatively well-off villages continue to expand in numbers until they too have exploited the productive potential of their land to the limit that their agricultural technique (including the development of water resources) will permit; while from the relatively worse-off villages, there will be emigration to seek employment in the small towns, in Bangkok, or in far-away mines and plantations. Of course, when the pressure of population on land reaches a certain point, there is the possibility, even in happily unpolitical Thailand, of politically-oriented discontent.

The villagers, meanwhile, are not inactive nor are they, as is so often alleged, obstinately set in their ways. They try all sorts of means to increase food production. They do their best to cultivate marginal land. In this they are encouraged—though as yet not very effectively —by provincial officials of the Ministry of Agriculture and of the Irrigation Department. One great handicap is the absence of proved knowledge as to how even the most willing and enterprising of the villagers can augment their crops and improve their livestock. One great advantage, however, is the presence in the village of the threefold leadership provided by the elected headman, the chief priest of the village *wat* (or Buddhist monastic centre), and the head master of the village school. In Thailand the collaboration between these three appears to be in most cases excellent, and all three may fairly be said to work for the community. The village teachers of Thailand are

---

[9] For another account of village education in Thailand, this time in a village near Bangkok, see Lauriston Sharp *et al.*, *Siamese Rice Village* (Cornell Research Centre, Bangkok, 1953), pp. 68–77; see also John B. de Young, *Village Life in Modern Thailand* (University of California Press, 1956).

predominantly natives of the village in which they teach, or of a neighbouring village. This, and the fact that they combine their teaching
with a certain amount of small-scale farming, binds them to the community, which in turn trusts them and accords them something of the
respect traditionally paid to the priesthood. Yet these teachers also
have a foot in the urban camp. Their dress, deportment, language, and
ideas are more urban than those of the other villagers. They are the
first, or among the first, to acquire beds, bicycles, mosquito nets, and
radio sets. Apart from some adult literacy campaigns, little planned
use has as yet been made of the village teacher as a means for spreading knowledge which can increase village productivity. Yet an army
of these teachers is posted strategically throughout the population for
the diffusion of such knowledge.

The Village Teacher

My tentative analysis, then, is that, as matters stand, primary education is not making a very rapid or a very relevant contribution to the
urgent task of keeping village resources level with village population.
From this point of view, it is no more easy to justify expenditure on
village schools than on Buddhist monastic institutions and ceremonies.
Yet while the latter may well be important in holding the village
together in traditional style, the former (in alliance with village head-
men) may be equally important as centres of village economic progress.
One must probably face the fact that the small measure of literacy
they gain at school is of doubtful benefit to many village children. It
is a necessary first stage, however, for those who are able or lucky
enough to go on to a secondary or vocational education. Of even
greater significance to the economy, whether seen from above or
below, is the potential role of the school teacher as the informal
educator and innovator of the village community.

This is an aspect of the teacher that needs study not only in Thailand, but in the other peasant countries. In India it has been necessary
to train thousands of ' Village Level Workers ' to help spread the knowledge needed for increasing village productivity. Each VLW is
allotted a group of from five to ten villages. This approach is justified
where village teachers are relatively few, and their standards and
prestige relatively low. Even so, as numbers and standards improve,
the teachers will surely become the necessary allies of the VLWs. And
in countries like Thailand, with relatively advanced village schools,
there may not be the need for a special corps of VLWs. A smaller,
more highly trained body of Community Development Officers, each
responsible for from fifty to one hundred villages, might in such an
instance be a more logical administrative bridge between the provincial

departments (e.g., Health, Agriculture, Co-operatives) and the village leadership provided by the headman, head teacher, and head priest.

The immediate problem for education in a peasant society is, then, to give urgently needed help as soon as possible in the task of increasing productivity within the context of the (more or less) traditionally based but inevitably changing style of village life. This can partly be achieved by making the content of primary and post-primary education more relevant to village needs, more ' basic ', more vocational, more agricultural. Partly also, and certainly with more rapid results, it can be achieved by a more deliberate and planned mobilization of village teachers as the diffusers, not only by precept but by example, of methods and appliances which are of proven value to villagers. It is necessary to stress that the value of any innovations thus to be widely diffused must indeed first be thoroughly proved and tested under realistic trial conditions.

The improvement of village productivity and living conditions will not itself indefinitely close the gap between population and resources. That, at least, is the author's belief, and though contested by various anti-Malthusian groups, it is in principle accepted by the governments of India and Japan and it would seem also now by communist China. These countries are making it part of national policy to encourage birth control or family planning, to check the unprecedented rate of increase in their populations—a rate which is likely to become more rapid still with improved health practices, both public and private. A recently published report by P.E.P.[10] suggests that before being granted international aid or technical assistance, governments should be induced " to face their population problem realistically ". In other words, they should not be helped to reduce death-rates unless they attempt to control birth-rates. Such a condition for aid is not, it seems to me, itself very realistic. It is one thing for a government to face its population problems realistically; another thing for it to be capable of taking technically effective measures to promote birth control among peasants, especially under tropical conditions. However, it is certain that if and when techniques of contraception suitable for these conditions become available, it will fall not only to the embryonic health services of the peasant countries, but also to village leaders and perhaps especially the village teachers, to ensure that these techniques are placed within the reach and understanding of the villagers. Medical services will inevitably be spread even thinner on the ground than educational for a very long time to come. There may well have to be a division of labour by which it is the teacher, or other village leader,

---

[10] *World Population and Resources* (P.E.P. (Political and Economic Planning), London, 1955), p. 328.

who spreads and encourages the idea of family limitation and its advantages, while it is the nurse or doctor who provides the method or appliance. Only sustained educational work can possibly ensure that peasant men and women give contraception a trial, let alone practise it consistently. This, though a somewhat less immediately practicable justification for the existence and development of village education, may in the long run prove to be of supreme importance.

Finally, I would like to emphasize that the arguments here tentatively outlined are not thought of as necessarily valid for human society until the end of time. They represent a desire to look at the problems of the peasant ' majority of mankind' as at the moment they seem likely to persist for at least two or three generations. Beyond that it would be rash to make predictions. It is conceivable that Marx is right (and his view is shared, in a sense, by typical American opinion) and that the peasant style of life will be replaced by a more urban style, and that agriculture will become in the end universally large-scale and collective. All that can be asserted with confidence at this stage in human affairs is that the peasant element is likely to become more important before it begins to become less important. For this reason the role of education in the peasant context may prove crucial for world development as a whole.

CHARLES MADGE.

CHAPTER SEVEN

Problems in British Colonial Territories

COMMENTING, in 1924, upon the application of principles of educational development which he was advocating in *The Keystone*, Sir Gordon Guggisberg went so far as to remark, " It goes without saying that anything I write in this booklet applies to the Gold Coast and nowhere else ", and continued, " In the Gold Coast itself—the Colony, Ashanti and the Northern Territories—conditions vary so greatly as to necessitate caution in the application of the principles advocated in this booklet ". In the thirty years since those words were written much has happened to modify such strictures as Sir Gordon Guggisberg thought fit to put upon the application of his ideas. Even so, caution is still necessary when attempting to generalize about educational problems and practice in colonial territories.

The Demand for Education

In the various territories the influence of external factors on general policy has been very largely contributory to levelling out many differences. In this respect the most important influence has been that of the Advisory Committee on Education in the Colonies. Beginning in 1925 with the publication of the white paper *Cmd. 2374* on the *Policy of Native Education*, and continuing at intervals with the *Memorandum on Education of African Communities (1935)*, the *Memorandum on Mass Education in African Society (1944)*, the Committee established and developed principles of development which were supplemented by other reports and memoranda devoted to specific features of general and local problems.

Within the colonial territories themselves, the most potent influence on and stimulus to education arise from the overwhelming prospects that the changing political and economic circumstances offer to a person who can claim the necessary educational status for appointment. At the lowest level it has created a mushroom growth of private institutions purporting to provide commercial training; at the highest levels it has tended to make demands upon responsibility before the requisite experience has been gained. Qualification in the narrower sense of the term, rather than education in the broader sense, is tending to be the requisite and the measure of educational success.

The increasing need for employees skilled and capable of responding to training is beginning to exert an influence by demanding more effective selection techniques and by emphasizing the importance of certain skills and a competence in particular fields of knowledge as opposed to other skills and fields of knowledge. One area of industrial educational need, namely, effective communication, raises afresh the subject of language as a medium of instruction, and as a subject throughout the educational system. Schemes of adult literacy in African languages lead to demands for English. The diversity of tribal sources of manpower in industrial concerns such as mines and factories, and the activities of trades unions, nation-wide services such as the police, all pose serious questions and demand specific answers to the problem of communication from the educational system.

Social and Political Problems

Related to the educational problems caused by movements of the population associated with industrial changes is the social problem of delinquency arising from the loosening of traditional family and tribal controls. Education for leisure is becoming as necessary as education for employment. In the urbanized areas this particular problem is intensified by the intrusion of the cinema; setting new patterns of conduct and creating new tastes to be satisfied.

Political patronage, however, must be recognized as the most potent influence on educational development. With political control dependent upon majority representation based upon a nation-wide electoral role, every political party finds itself committed to a policy of educational development. This commitment is as much due to the normal adage of political competition and of promise to meet the explicit needs of the community, as it is due to the recognition by party leaders that in the long run an educated electorate is necessary if stable co-operation is to be won for the development of the country's resources. In this latter respect the manner in which changes in political responsibility affected the campaigns in the Gold Coast to win the co-operation of the farmers in the fight against the major cocoa diseases is a remarkable illustration of the significance of the relationship which exists between politics and educational progress.

At its best, political patronage has produced bold attacks on the problem of universal education and the development of technical and higher education. At its worst, it has resulted in giving sops, to pressure from constituents, by way of schools, particularly secondary schools, without regard for the best interests of the general community. Sometimes this has also involved giving scholarships for studies overseas, more to satisfy elements of personal patronage and the desire to be a ' have-been ' (a person who has been overseas) than always to satisfy a genuine need.

Political patronage exerts an influence of considerable importance in another direction, namely that of Africanization. The natural desire of any people moving towards political independence to be free of control (as implied in the continuance of expatriates in the administrative and the policy-making levels of government and social service) has resulted in demands for increased and accelerated facilities for training of Africans for such duties. One consequence has been a tendency to press forward with the more expensive features of an educational programme without full recognition of the long-term financial implications. An initial generosity in this respect is almost inevitably followed by a dangerous anxiety to reduce expenditure. The problem is further complicated by the economic consequences at the salary-paying stage of responsibility. Except in the Sudan, there has been a general unwillingness to realize that with the rate of expansion of services at present taking place, it is unlikely that most of the dependent territories in Africa can afford, for the generality of workers, terms and conditions of employment similar to expatriate rates. Yet the social and financial status of the individual is such a delicately balanced affair that there appears to be little prospect in the near future of satisfactory adjustments being made. The consequences of this situation are twofold. It tends to increase the cost of education and the competition for funds between education and other services.

The financial problem of education is complicated by the past pattern of financial provision, the changes taking place in local responsibility, and the lack of appreciation on the part of the community in general of the new needs. Until comparatively recently, financial support for education was derived from central government funds, local support was restricted to school fees, church contributions for capital and recurrent purposes, and a comparatively insignificant contribution through local authorities. The universalization of primary education has forced recognition of the need for a readjustment of financial responsibility. But few local authorities yet understand their responsibilities or have the machinery for the efficient development of a local rates system. Few people appreciate the necessity of paying rates for services they have in the past obtained without apparent payment, or have supported by direct payment of school fees or by contributions as church members due to shared ownership. This aspect of educational change has created its own facet of the educational problem, namely, the education of the community to understand its new responsibilities.

The Stimulus of Education and Advertising

The very success of developing a system of formal education has brought about further educational needs. The intellectual stimulus at any level, be it adult literacy or university education, creates an appetite which calls for further satisfaction. To meet this, provisions like easily available supplies of further reading matter, libraries, broadcasting, extra-mural classes, in their turn make demands on manpower and finance. An added complication, to which few professional educational workers give sufficient attention, is the powerful stimulus and competition provided by commercial advertising. In the absence of carefully assessed data, to generalize on the strength and importance of this factor would be foolish, but there can be little doubt that, on the one hand, the increasing pressure of the advertisement is rapidly giving specific shape to public tastes and interests, and, on the other hand, sets up an element of competition in respect of individual and communal financial resources.

Policy Making

The use, control, and satisfaction of these various stimuli in the field of education in the dependent territories are complicated by the fact that until recently policy making and executive responsibility lay almost entirely in the hands of professional administrators : for in this sense missionary workers and their local protégés were and are of that category of person equally with the civil cervant. With the establishment of elected legislatures the whole process of education has become subject to the comment and scrutiny of every man, be he knowledgeable or otherwise. The eighty-six-year-old dictum of Peacock's that the nonsense talked on education would outweigh all the nonsense talked on any other subject, still holds good. Nonsense talked can give rise to irritation and may be deplored, but in so far as it represents concern and interest about educational matters it is to be welcomed. In this respect the dependent territories are probably fortunate. Whilst such concern remains, legislatures are not likely to ignore or generally become apathetic about educational affairs.

The extent to which these various influences in respect of education are significant in different territories varies considerably. Much more attention has been paid by African territories to advice received from the Advisory Committee on Education in the Colonies than has been paid by some of the territories outside Africa. It is probably equally true to say that the influence on education of the Christian church has been stronger in Africa than in many other dependent territories. Within Africa itself, politics have and are exercising much greater immediate influence on education in the Gold Coast and Nigeria than elsewhere. Furthermore, at the present time, nationalism is a more potent influence on the language aspect of education in the Gold Coast than in the other territories, except possibly the Eastern Region of Nigeria. But the variations in importance are relative, and dangerous as it may be to generalize, it is probably safe to say that the educational situation as it exists in the Gold Coast is illustrative of the pattern to be found in the dependent territories elsewhere.

Educational Responsibility

One of the more significant post-war developments, the result in part of Colonial Office advice, in part of social and political influences, is the recognition of the range of educational responsibility. This is reflected in the Gold Coast by the Ministry of Education—being made responsible for the general supervision of the Education Department, the Department of Social Welfare, and the Prisons Department. It is also responsible in general for the relations between the government and such organizations as the Sports Council, the Library Board, the Boy Scouts, the Girl Guides, the British Council, and for the relations with the grant-aided institutions of independent status like the University College of the Gold Coast and the Kumasi College of Arts, Science, and Technology. What is most significant in this grouping of departments is the recognition that, whether proceeding in the home, school or colleges or through mass education and community development, education is as much a concern of the community as of the individual. This overall concept in part reflects a modern view of government responsibility which has come to the Gold Coast, as it has come to other dependent territories, from outside. In addition to the maintenance of law and order and defence, governments are now expected to maintain highly organized and expensive social services. But it is also a conception of communal responsibility comparable with an older tradition of tribal responsibility for the well-being of the individual and the community.

This conception of responsibility for education and its range has behind it a sense of purpose which arises from the intense and shared desire of the people for economic, social, political, and spiritual advance. Foremost amongst the recognized needs is that of the Africanization of leadership. The recognition of this resulted in a determination, shown by the community as a whole, to have for itself an institution of university status. The outcome is to be seen to-day in the existence of the University College of the Gold Coast, with its autonomous status, and with its promise of manpower fitted for the responsibilities of leadership in government, commerce and industry, church and education. The creation of the University College has introduced a new element into the educational scene. The production of trained men and women in numbers sufficient to meet needs is no longer dependent upon the availability of facilities in overseas universities. Furthermore, it has provided opportunities for study in the fields of economics, the physical, biological, and social sciences directly related to local community needs and interests. The significance of this is not yet fully realized, consequently there is at present a serious wastage and an inefficient use of available financial resources through students being encouraged to interrupt their studies at home and incur additional expense by going overseas. Over the whole field of education, this weakness may not appear great, but it illustrates the kind of complication which arises from the concatenation of political, social, and economic factors in a situation where the speed of change is greater than is the immediate accumulation of experience.

Technical Education

Whilst the importance of general university education has been fairly completely recognized, the value of technical education is still very much a matter of the intellectual assent by the few. Consequently, the rate of development of technical education has been much slower. This in part reflects the historical fact that the modern development of the Gold Coast began with the coming of traders and missionaries whose first need was for literate indigenous assistants speaking English—clerks, trading agents, catechists, ministers of religion, and teachers. In part it reflects the absence of industrial pressure for skilled technicians. Furthermore, most people still see the best opportunities of personal advance through the Civil Service, trade, law, and medicine, and are naturally attracted by the exalted status of black-coated employment. Therefore, the provision in the past for technical education (meagre though it was) proved more than adequate to meet the supply of candidates for technical training.

The establishment of a full range of technical institutions leading up to degree-level facilities in the Kumasi College of Arts, Science, and Technology, and the expansion of opportunities of skilled careers now taking place are to some extent beginning to redress the balance of those with a training in science. Probably, however, a more significant contribution to the extension and adequate use of facilities for technical training is likely to come in the immediate future from the application of personnel-selection techniques in trade and industry and the essential corollary of opportunities for training and promotion in trade and industry.

In this respect a lead has been given by the West African Command, recruiting, as it does very largely, from illiterate and the less-well-educated elements of the community. The Army has recognized that the dangers of wastage in training are high, furthermore selection for training for leadership in technical as well as administrative capacities demands a higher average potential for learning when the time available for training is short. The importance of this has also been recognized to some extent in the mining industry. The application of sound selection methods and follow-up training is likely to introduce into the community a new kind of worker whose personal success in industry and trade will set a premium on technical education in the future.

The most spectacular field of expansion, and the one in which is expressed the most direct political and social concern, however, is in the primary level of formal education. Here political action reflected rather than directed effort. By 1949 the determination of even comparatively isolated communities to have schooling for their children had resulted in a large number of primary schools coming into existence of which the Education Department had no specific cognizance. The approval given to a scheme of a six-year programme of free primary education resulted in an immediate increase of over 96,000 in the number of children attending school. The total number of children in the primary and middle schools, representing a total of ten years of schooling, rose during 1953 from 418,921 to 468,118. This spectacular rise represented a voluntary reaction to the availability of facilities.

This expansion of the primary system has had its obvious repercussions on teacher training and supervision. It is here, probably more than anywhere else, that the disparity between demands and a willingness to meet the obligations have been most marked. It is true that consideration has been given to the training and conditions of service of teachers, but failure to implement certain recommendations, and an unwillingness to give teacher training a high degree of priority when the first flush of enthusiasm had to be tempered by a degree of deceleration, have left the Education Department unable to provide for the expansion of trained personnel and have so reduced the possibilities of supervision that few schools, if any, are likely for some years to come to receive the benefit of inspection visits more frequently than once in two years. This weakness in development does not appear to be appreciated either by the politicians or by the community at large, though the former are having to answer fairly widespread complaints from their constituent members of lowered standards of education following the dilution of the teaching profession with untrained teachers.

Financial Implications

The financial implications of the extension of primary education were realized as early as 1950, when the committee set up to report on the grant-in-aid system for educational institutions pointed out that "the cost of secondary and technical education would be particularly heavy, but that, if the Gold Coast was to progress economically, it must produce technicians right up to the university level". Another costly item was the training of teachers for the primary schools. The government would do its best to finance these educational needs, but primary education would have to expand mainly by means of increased financial contribution from local sources. It was proposed gradually to transfer the management of the primary schools more and more to the local authorities. It was felt that this would "eliminate rivalry and ensure economy of resources". The municipal authorities of Accra and Kumasi have been able to go a considerable way in accepting the local responsibility thus visualized, but for the majority of the country, accepting responsibility locally for primary education is still a financial impossibility even when contributions from the central government are such as to ensure the payment of teachers' salaries. In many cases local resources cannot meet the demands made upon them for the provision of very modest local services, but more important, the educating of communities to understand the need for developing local government and paying for it lags behind the demands being made. In two areas, the ignorance of the people in this matter has resulted in local rioting.

The financial factor was vividly expressed in 1950 by the then Director of Education (the late Mr. T. Barton), in these words:

"Now since the year 1930 there has been a demand for primary education in the Gold Coast, and, indeed, throughout Africa which has grown steadily in intensity and which is, in fact, one of the great events of the world history of education in the present century. . . . The demand is so great that it is extremely difficult to produce teachers in sufficient numbers to satisfy it. We have greatly increased the output of trained teachers; but you must remember that as we increase the number there comes closer and closer walking behind us another worry—indeed a fiend such as you read of in *The Ancient Mariner*:

"'Like one, that on a lonesome road
Doth walk in fear and dread,
And having once turned round walks on,
And turns no more his head;
Because he knows, a frightful fiend
Doth close behind him tread.'

" The fiend which has walked so very closely behind education has been the fear that we should go on and on producing more and more teachers (each of them on incremental salary scales which mean a rise in the cost of education every year of many thousands of pounds) and that, at the end there should come a collapse because neither the Central Government nor the Local Authorities can find money to meet the salary bill."

Expenditures

In the period 1945–50, recurrent expenditure on grants in aid of education from the central government funds rose from £373,000 to £914,000. In 1950, total expenditure on education from central government funds was £2,249,000, to which should be added approximately another £50,000 for the prisons and social welfare services. For the year 1954–5, out of a budget of approximately £60 million, the sum of £4,579,740 was allocated to education. The financial fiend is ever present, and its presence is likely to be more closely felt as financial needs for such developments as the Volta hydro-electric scheme press more closely upon the central resources. The need for shedding the load upon local resources, important as it appeared to be in 1950, is all the greater to-day. This makes the task of educating the adult community to the needs of local responsibility a major priority.

In this latter respect the Gold Coast has shown a degree of initiative through the development of mass education and community development that promises to compensate for the fact that, as yet, the majority of the people have not had a school education. Apart from literacy and welfare campaigns of a self-help character, intensive programmes of community education dealing with local government, the paying of rates, the franchise, eradication of diseases in cocoa, have given a most encouraging measure of understanding of needs and prospects. The principles of voluntary self-help and local leadership which underlie the community-development programmes suggest possibilities of dealing with many of the educational problems and, in particular, with the basic problem of meeting the tensions which arise from the contradictory demands upon the country's resources which threaten elements of the general educational programme, either by competing for manpower and finance or more indirectly by offering alternate stimuli to individual ambition.

L. J. LEWIS.

CHAPTER EIGHT

The Effects of an External Stimulus upon Education in Morocco

IN 1912, when Morocco signed the Treaty of Fès with France, the former was a very poor country. Its inhabitants lived as the people of Europe lived in the Middle Ages. Travelling was a difficult and dangerous undertaking.

The population was largely rural. Its needs were provided for by the cultivation of barley and maize, while the rearing of sheep and goats supplied the other necessities of life. The standard of living was low; very few commodities were exchanged; money was little used and barter was a commonplace. This meant that commerce played only a small part in life, except in certain towns, such as Fès, in which nearly all the buying and selling took place. There were no industries, but in the towns there were artisans, of whom the number remained relatively small, for, although they produced fine work, there were few customers to buy it. State organization was reduced to a minimum, for the Sultans were fully occupied in maintaining their authority over tribes continually on the verge of rebellion.

It is hardly necessary to add that there existed no system of modern education as we know it, no public education system for the people, having as its aim the training of children both to appreciate culture and to play their part efficiently in the economic life of their country. But in all the towns and in the regions where life was not too precarious, *fquihs* were to be found teaching the Qu'ran to the children by the old traditional methods. They were usually ill paid by the parents and did not always fully understand what they taught. Sitting on the ground and swaying backwards and forwards, the children repeated at the top of their voices the words they were told to learn, and only too often they made a prodigious effort to do so, and the only result was that they were able to recite the sacred writings without making a mistake. Sometimes *fquihs* who were better educated and who were a little better paid taught the rudiments of classical Arabic as well as the Qu'ran. Their best pupils went to continue their studies at the Universities of Kairouan at Fès or of Ben Youssef at Marrakesh. There they became acquainted with the prophetic tradition (the *hadiths*), with law and legal practice, with grammar and rhetoric. It was a system of education well suited to the needs of a poor country whose inhabitants were pious, and of a country without commerce or industry, in which state organization was precarious and very limited.

To give the French their due, it must be admitted that when they undertook the modernization of Morocco, they immediately opened schools and tried to attract Moroccans to them. Lyautey was especially anxious that the sons of the most eminent men should be educated in order that they might take a share in the modernization of the administration of their country, and it was as a result of his influence that schools and colleges were first established for the wealthier section of the population. Special syllabuses were drawn up to accomplish this particular purpose in these schools, and special examinations were set. But the teachers in the private schools—the *fquihs*—fought against these schools, which were taking their very livelihood—their pupils—from them. It is true that in the towns the more enlightened middle classes understood more or less clearly the possible advantages of modern education and could fairly easily be persuaded to send their sons to the schools. This was far from the case in country districts. Local authorities were consequently forced, if they did not wish to leave their schools empty, to exact compulsory attendance from the sons of poor parents who needed their help in some shape or form. Thus it was necessary to make the people want a modern educational system; they had to be led to feel the need to know how to read, to write, and to do arithmetic.

In the achievement of this aim the external stimulus given by the actions and the presence of the French was all-important. It appears that the stimulus was given in three different ways :

(1) By means of changes in the economic system of Morocco.

(2) By the example set by the French section of the population.

(3) By technical and financial aid by France.

Changes in the Economic System of Morocco

With the help of loans guaranteed by the French State and originating for the most part from France, harbours, roads, and railways were constructed. The port of Casablanca is now well known all over the world. But all along the coast, at Port Lyautey, at Rabat-Salé, at Fedala, at Mazagan, at Safi, at Mogador, and at Agadir, building enterprises were started and brought to a successful conclusion, and as a result shipping of varying tonnage could come right into port. The construction of a network of roads covering several thousands of miles was immediately started at various points in the country. At last two companies, that of Tanger-Fès and also the Moroccan Railway Company, undertook the building of a railway system.

Less than fifteen years after the Treaty of Fès, and in spite of the desperate efforts which France had to make during the years 1914–18 to defend her very existence, a network of modern communications was in use in Morocco.

During the same period towns were supplied with sewage systems, drinking water, and electricity, and a working-class population, attracted by increasing industrialism, was forming there. But even country life was transformed. Large stretches of land were cleared and cultivated. Formerly the Moroccan inhabitants of the *bled* (village) were shepherds and despised farming ("Dishonour enters the tent along with the plough", said the Berbers). Now they were gradually becoming, with the help of the local authorities, and spurred on by the example of the French, farmers with a multiplicity of activities. Industry spread its tentacles as far as the *bled* in the shape of saw-mills, vegetable-fibre factories, and similar projects. Little by little an economic system based on the exchange of commodities took the place of the self-sufficiency of the past. The *souks* (markets) became more and more busy and more and more distant. The people's minds became ready to accept new ideas. The barriers which had enclosed the Moroccan world burst open. Travel became much more widespread. Fathers or young men who had left their district to earn their living in the town sent home money; their letters had to be written for them by public letter-writers and had to be read out to the recipients by other public letter-writers.

All these economic and social changes were maintained by the new administrative system which the French had drawn up in agreement with the central *Maghzen* (government) and prepared the ground excellently for modern schools, where pupils would not be taught only to recite the Qu'ran, but to read, write, and to do arithmetic.

The need for such an education system was not felt for some time—long after the economic changes had made the opening of schools logically necessary. In 1941 there were still only thirty-two thousand Moroccans attending these schools. Even to-day, when a school is opened where a tribe has but lately come into partial contact with a modern way of life which will eventually overturn the old-established habits, it is difficult to persuade parents to send their children to school. This reveals a surprising paradox. The school ought to precede economic changes, so that the children who attend it can play a full and effective part in economic life when they become adults. It ought to be adapted to the society of the future. Instead it can only follow economic changes. If care is not taken, it adapts itself spontaneously to the society of yesterday.

The Presence of the French

Even though, in 1944, there were only thirty-two thousand Mussulman Moroccans attending protectorate schools, their desire to have a large number of schools established very quickly became very strong. Ten years later there were more than two hundred and forty thousand, and even so, it cannot be said that all needs, especially in the towns, were satisfied. The presence of French people, giving, as they did, a constant example of how to adapt themselves to the demands of modern society, hastened the development of the minds of the Moroccans—a development which has been prepared for by the economic changes.

In the first place, *all* the French had their children educated : an example which the Moroccans wished to follow. Servants who worked in French households stood out among the working-class population because of their passionate interest in their children's studies. The cult of progress, which acted as a great spur on the people of France right up to the war of 1914, tended to spread among the people of Morocco.

On the other hand, Moroccan middle-class nationalist groups arising from the presence of the French were influenced by the ideology of the French. Urged on by fervent patriotism, and sometimes stirred up by foreign propaganda, they tried by every means in their power to educate the masses. They saw that education could be an instrument in the emancipation of their country.

The presence and example of the French provided particularly necessary stimuli where the education of girls was concerned. For a long time Moroccan parents refused to send their daughters to the school which the authorities put at their disposal. The role of women in a Mohammedan society is well known. And yet care had been taken to provide for them schools in which the traditional teaching of carpet making and embroidery had an important place. In 1944 fewer than ten thousand Moroccan girls were receiving a modern or semi-modern education. But the example of his Majesty Sultan Sidi Mohammed Ben Youssef soon dispersed prejudice. More than fifty thousand of the little girls or young women of Morocco are now in attendance at schools providing elementary or secondary education. Moreover, most families in large towns, especially in Casablanca, desire that their daughters, just as if they were French girls, should gain sufficient knowledge to allow them to practise some trade or profession. There are already midwives, teachers, social workers, and instructresses in housewifery to be found in Morocco. Quite a large number of Moroccan girls now pass a General Certificate of Education.

It is well known that the French State system of education is completely undenominational and secular. It holds resolutely to its aim

of providing an intellectual training which will prepare people for
the more important posts so far as secondary education is concerned,
and of developing practical efficiency. Thus it is essentially different
from the religious education system which was the only one known to
the Moroccans before 1912. It contains, however, traces of an earlier
state of society in which fostering the intellect was an end in itself,
for the pleasure and ease it gave to conversation in the *salons*.

Its efficacy attracted the Moroccans. But they did not remain un-
moved by those elements which were devoid of ulterior purpose.

As mentioned, Lyautey had tried to establish for the *élite* of
Moroccan society a system of secondary education that was essentially Moroccan and adapted as closely as possible to the country and
its immediate needs; at the same time the French in Morocco received
the same education as in Metropolitan France. His successors found
themselves obliged, owing to pressure from Neghzen and the young
Moroccans, to make it possible for those in the Mussulman schools to
take the French *baccalauréat* as well as the Mussulman diploma for
secondary education. Very soon pupils gave up taking the especially
created diploma : they preferred to sit for French examinations, and
later these were adapted to suit their needs. There is no doubt that
more careers are available and prospects are better for those who have
passed the *baccalauréat* than for those who take the Moroccan degree.
For the latter, openings are few, and this point was perhaps not given
sufficient consideration—for it is most important. Another factor,
however, stimulates the Moroccans' desire to take French examinations. Various signs point to the fact that among Moroccans exists an
uncritical belief in the magical power of knowledge. The ignorant are
quite ready to believe that a child's education consists in teaching him
secrets which will inevitably bring him success. Since, obviously, the
French do their best to give their children the most effective of these
secrets, French education should be copied as closely as possible. Even
better would be for the little Moroccans to have the same lessons as
the French and to sit side by side with them in the same schools. This
is one of the reasons why the Moroccans want their children to attend
classes in French schools.

Doubtless, the very enlightened leaders who pleaded vigorously for
popular education in Arabic, and yet sent their own children to French
schools, had (and certainly gave) other reasons to explain the paradox
shown in their conduct. They said that these schools were nearer to
their homes, and that they were attended by children who were better
looked after than in the Moroccan schools. They pointed out the
necessity for friendship between young French people and young
Moroccans. Moreover, they fully realized that the French language

was of wider use economically, and that it brought with it a widening of intellectual horizons and a greater scope for action. But, deep down, they were quite sure that if their children were in a French primary school or *lycée* they would have more chance of learning the secrets of a culture which has proved to be the strength of the Western world. It sometimes happens that students of medicine or science regret, as a result of contact with some of their French comrades, that they also did not learn Greek and Latin. It is in some ways extremely significant that one of the wisest and most thoughtful of the enlightened Moroccans should have made his daughter do advanced work in classics. She is now at the Sorbonne, working for the *agrégation*. For this she will have to take examinations in French language and literature and reach a very high standard in Greek and Latin. Thus the disinterested and philosophical elements in French university work have not left the Moroccans untouched. The best of them were likely to find in it a deep-seated harmony with their own religious or mystical tendencies.

The Help of France

In 1912 it was impossible to find on the spot Moroccans capable of teaching the newly introduced subjects, and of using modern methods designed to develop intelligence. Thus it was essential at first to appeal to the French to come to their aid. Consequently, at first, lessons were given in French. It is worth noting that in all the schools qualified Moroccan *fquihs*, teaching as colleagues of the French, were appointed to instruct the children in the Qu'ran and the Arabic language. But the teaching of science, of arithmetic, and even, at first, of history and geography could only be given in French. Very soon, however, young educated Moroccans became able to teach according to modern methods in Moroccan schools. But they are relatively few in number. In January 1955, out of a total of twelve thousand teachers (in primary, secondary, and advanced education), there were still only four thousand Moroccans. If, as it is desirable, the progress in education in Morocco is to continue, it will be very difficult for a long time ahead to manage to do without French teachers. This is made all the more difficult by the fact that when young Moroccans pass the *baccalauréat*, they nearly all choose to apply for posts that are better paid than those of teachers in primary or grammar schools. They try, by means of scholarships, to become doctors, pharmacists, lawyers, engineers. Such ambitions are praiseworthy, but to be achieved, they need the aid of a French teaching staff to give thorough and precise instruction. It may well be that in the Morocco of tomorrow it will be decided to give primary instruction at least in Arabic; this will be difficult and involve great risks.

Help given in the form of French teachers, indispensable at the beginning and, in our opinion, indispensable even now, tends to become less and less vital and urgent as far as the schools for Moroccans are concerned. But economic help from France remains essential.

The building up of a system of education is a very expensive affair, and it is obvious that in supplying the needs of a country where everything had to be done, the structure of an economic system, the building of harbours, the construction of roads, and help in the clearing and improvement of arable land, were all given precedence over the equipment of schools. As long as the Moroccan people were not too pressing in their demands, the proportion of the budget granted to education was not more than 7 or 8 per cent. In 1944 it had risen to nearly 10 per cent. It was possible to increase it gradually to nearly 17 per cent of the total allowed in the budget for running expenses. In 1954 the financial estimates for all running expenses rose to 59,844 million *francs*. Of this, education was allotted 10,580 million *francs*, or 17·67 per cent of the total. In addition, 32,377 million were granted for capital investment. The share of this destined for the public educational system was 3,500 million or 10·81 per cent. This represented an expected increase of more than a thousand million *francs* in the next financial estimates so far as running expenses were concerned.

This percentage increase in money available for education was obtained only after careful study and detailed discussion, for there were other aspects of national life which demanded great financial effort, such as hydraulic equipment, the development of a system of communications, both of which were sources of great wealth for the future. Of the money spent on equipment, 22·5 per cent was spent on the development of hydraulic power, 24 per cent on communications.

Such as it was, this budget could not have been balanced without the aid of France. Out of the 27,474 million *francs* destined for investment, a little more than 14,000 million, or more than 50 per cent, was obtained by advances from the section of the French Treasury concerned with economic expansion. This loan was granted on very favourable terms, since it had only to be repaid after twenty-five years, and the rate of interest was only 1·5 per cent. This meant that expenses which could not immediately be met could not have been undertaken without direct financial aid from France.

But this direct aid was perhaps not the most essential. It has several times been pointed out in this short study that there is a very close connexion between the economic life of a country and its educational system. Modern economy demands that the people should be educated; it forces everyone to realize how necessary education is, it obtains by the increased yield in taxation the resources which are indispensable; it provides employment for young people who have received a good education. If the economic life of a country is slowed down or stops, then the tax yield becomes less and there are fewer posts available. The whole problem of mass education is at stake.

Now, the Moroccan economic system could not develop without the aid of capital coming from abroad. In 1954, the French government spent in Morocco more than 40,000 million *francs*, largely for the army. Loans were granted from public or semi-public funds to firms which were taking part in the economic development of Morocco (dams, prospecting for petroleum, and so on) to a total of 16,000 million *francs*. French banks themselves have consented to make loans of more than 5,000 million *francs*. Private investments originating from France have risen to a total of more than 6,000 million *francs*. Thus a total of more than 70,000 million *francs* of French capital were spent or invested in Morocco in 1954. Aid from foreign countries, including the construction of American bases, has reached about 20 per cent of the French total.

France gives help in many other forms, since it allows some of Morocco's products to be imported free of customs duty. This help appears to be absolutely essential to the life of Morocco.

This cursory survey of the modern system of education set up in Morocco since 1912 has made it possible to show clearly how necessary an external stimulus was to ensure the rapid success of the undertaking. Had the French not been established in Morocco, had it not been for French capital, the Moroccan economic system would not have developed so quickly and in so satisfactory a manner, and the education of children on modern lines would for much longer have appeared useless. The example of the French helped the development of the Moroccan way of life considerably and persuaded the Moroccans to send their boys and girls to school. Financial aid from France was necessary to finance the establishment of a network of schools, which, incomplete though it still is, calls for a considerable expenditure. This help is still indispensable if the country is to live a full life and if it is to be able to offer well-educated young men the types of employment which they expect and which will make them feel that their efforts have been worth while.

ROGER THABAULT.

CHAPTER NINE

Economics and Education in Latin America

MODERN life characteristically emphasizes the economic aspect of human activity and the development of society. This has led to an appreciation of the importance of education in the improvement of material welfare. At present, large areas of Latin America could not be more desolate: a sickly and undernourished population—manual labourers who are underpaid—very poor salaries for craftsmen and for the great mass of civil servants—a poorly developed civic life—miserable support for education—a high percentage of infant mortality—children who are sent to work too early—exploitation of female labour, and hospitalization which often leads only to the grave. Yet most Latin-American countries are potentially rich. Wealth, however, is produced through a union of physical and intellectual activity, and neither is possible without healthy bodies. A fundamental question, therefore, is to consider the policy of the state towards the promotion of public health. Evidently in school buildings, timetables, and methods of teaching, attention should be paid to it. In addition, adequate health and medical services, school dining-rooms, cloakrooms, and playing-fields should be provided. All these exist in our countries, but only as examples to be shown to visitors. They are needed in vastly increased numbers.

Furthermore, there is an urgent need to revaluate manual work—the hand must be thought of as an extra brain which should be given the power of expressing the purpose and ideas of the will. We need more and better workshops. Our people must be taught to make use of oft-wasted materials, and to apply new techniques to the abundant raw materials. Yet at the same time, the danger of promoting a purely material and practical outlook on life must be avoided. Theory and practice, thought and action, ideal and reality, principles and techniques, are not mutually exclusive or opposed. On the contrary, they need to be united for true fulfilment. Life, indeed, has to be spiritualized and improved. Everywhere in the world to-day, many people are too preoccupied with making money as the sole criterion of success—or with converting into merchandise the most noble activities of the mind. These are signs that our culture has failed to attain maturity. Thus it is well known that politics may become simply a wealth-acquiring activity, corrupting itself by its ignorance of science and of deep and true knowledge.

School Farms

Too little has been done in rural areas everywhere to develop the school farm as indispensable to the rural school. Yet it could help to develop a deep love of the soil, it might promote a scientific interest in plants and animals, arouse admiration for living forms, and develop a lively understanding of the importance of the economic inter-dependence between the various regions of each country and the world as a whole. The habit of hard work and the confident expecta-tion that effort produces results are among the educational results of the school farm. Often, too, school co-operatives are born and grow in connexion with the farm. When Carleton Washburne, one of the great representatives of the new education, visited Ecuador, he saw in the rural training college of Uyumbicho, fifteen miles outside Quito, a fully-active school co-operative; later he saw in three different villages of the Republic the work of three old pupils of the college. He found in all these schools, co-operatives which were for him most signi-ficant seeds of a new Ecuador. John Dewey, the great defender of democratic ideas in education, found to his astonishment that the rural teachers of Mexico, in their formidable task of raising the economic, social, and rural-education levels of a post-revolution Mexico, were doing things which were closely related to his own ideas —and this without having read his theoretical works.

The theory of the rural school in Mexico was born of educational action. That is to say, these schools, perhaps the most interesting of all in Latin America, were not based on any *a priori* theory. The soldiers of the Revolution made themselves school teachers in order to sustain from within the military achievements of the Revolution. Strangely, the example of this Revolution fired the country folk to aim at raising the dignity, fruitfulness, maturity, and, indeed, the whole life of the countryside.

In all Latin-American countries the school co-operative has been the agency through which, from the lowest to the highest grades of society, the greatest benefits have been received. It has created in-centives to feelings of responsibility and solidarity. It is the very marrow of the educational organism, developing an outlook that is neither avaricious nor wasteful. Here the child and adolescent learn that money is a good servant, but a bad master. Nationally, the teach-ing of wise management of money is as important as teaching to read.

In general, our system of production is colonial in type both in its implied concepts about property and the administration of public finance. Taxation falls very heavily on the middle classes, for cultural reasons the largest consumers. They are never able to have what to them are prime necessities. They are usually classes which pretend or simulate an ease of life which is not, in fact, theirs. They maintain their social life on credits or loans which are not directly related to their income. Constitutionally, it is disastrous that in Latin America the least-privileged classes, namely the Indians and Negroes, consume very little. There is a close and constant relationship between race and social class, and equality before the law is not translated into equality in life.

Contrasts in Economy

Many contrasts are found in the ways of life of various Latin-American republics. Into some countries, the torrent of industrialization has penetrated. In others, methods of production are old-fashioned and obsolete. The Egyptian plough has not always been replaced by more modern agricultural machinery, and the soil awaits irrigation. Valleys which enjoy natural or artificial irrigation contrast with the intensely arid regions, or the high, bleak plateaux of the Andes. The greater part of the population lives on the land and lacks roads or highways to join the villages and small towns together. The differences in the level of civilization of individuals and regions within the same country are really astounding. Next to a man of the highest education is often seen an Indian whose life is little more than sub-human. Brazil faces the gigantic problem of its hinterland—the culture of her upper and middle classes has been established along part of the Atlantic coast. It has a European appearance. But the limitless interior, that ‘green ocean’, has not been incorporated into the national life. Even now, the great rivers are hardly settled—they remain wild. Nevertheless, in Brazil the problems of distance are overcome by the greatest technical invention of our time, the aeroplane; the newspapers of Rio de Janeiro reach the towns of the interior on the day of their publication.

In Brazil, too, production has been, as in colonial days, based on raw materials rather than on staple exports. Elsewhere, as in the Argentine or Mexico, there have been great developments in the utilization of raw materials. In some parts a tremendous and startlingly quick growth has taken place—as in São Paulo (Brazil), Monterrey (Mexico), and Cali in Colombia. And there are cities, like those of South Chile, where massive European immigration has made possible industrial development and has shown how important industries can be established. Heavy industries have been introduced into Brazil. At

Volta Redonda, for example, is one of the greatest centres of steel production in the world.

Confronted in Latin America with problems of such magnitude, the technical aid extended by the United Nations or its specialized agencies, like UNESCO, or by the U.S.A. through the Point Four plan, is like a drop of water in a large ocean. This is almost like saying that Latin-American countries are pessimistic, with little faith in their own destiny and without the will to save themselves. In the second place, it implies that the UN and the 'Good Neighbour' policy during its ten years of existence have not truly faced the problem of 'aid', except verbally and not through heroic action.

The disunited states of South America have not been able to overcome geographical barriers and transform them into links—the Pacific has always been an obstacle. The nations of the Atlantic coast have developed more quickly, and in the north have shown what resources can be drawn from both oceans. Further, there are tropical regions which certainly do not hamper, as used to be thought, development. Brazil, with her impressive modern hygiene, cleanliness, and good architecture, offers a dazzling contrast with the barbaric profusion of the tropics. And the railways have helped to dominate inhospitable nature, for previously, Latin America, like Africa, was little more than a coastal strip.

Connected with the 'Good Neighbour' policy, is the most obvious link between the U.S.A. and Latin America, the Organization of American States (which has replaced the Pan-American Union). But everyone knows that the Organization hardly goes beyond the views of officials with limited horizons, both in its ambitions and modest projects. For day-to-day purposes the U.S.A. prefers to treat with each government separately; for instance, in the matter of raising loans. As for the relations between the people themselves—nothing has been done. The government, unhappily, do not see beyond their own bureaucracy. Citizens are viewed only as pawns in the political set-up. No account is taken of the fact that they are only irritated by political activity or that politicians are flowers that fade in a day. Any balanced understanding of what is happening should pay due attention to cultural and political life as well as to the social psychology of the people concerned.

Inflation and Education

From the above data a few consequences can be deduced. Latin America imports commodities to the degree allowed by its cultural and industrial development, paying for them by the export of raw materials. The level of culture is expressed here by the capacity to consume. This means that these countries will become better markets for foreign goods as necessities, appetites, and ambitions are created. As it is, these regions are not very good markets. There are vast areas where misery and poverty incline people towards communism and religious fanaticism. Fifty million Indians, Negroes, and mestizos—more than a third of the total population—vegetate in a way that is almost grotesque. It is hardly necessary to stress that the prime need is the cultural development of the whole continent.

The process of inflation gives rise to a vicious circle. On the one hand, the cost of living increases, or, to put it in another way, the purchasing power of money falls. More money circulates (sometimes, as in Bolivia, rising to astronomical figures), but every day the misery of the mass of the people grows. Increases in salaries and wages alleviate the situation only very temporarily—once again the cost of living goes up, creating new difficulties and hardships. The black market grows—terrifying and sinister. Foreign currency is bought and hidden. Neither regulations concerning the circulation of money nor tariff laws to prevent importation succeed in holding the catastrophe in check. The government's revenue is never as great as estimated, for the rich hide their true profits; the result is that the state finds itself in ever greater financial difficulties. To cover the deficits, new taxes are devised; one of the more evident signs of inflation is the rapid growth of both public and private budgets, while at the same time the most elementary or fundamental needs remain unsatisfied.

Countries whose economy is more solidly based know how to control and limit the disaster. They enjoy high industrial productivity, a healthy monetary system, and have technicians able to direct economic life and public finance. The advice of the experts can be used to solve problems in collaboration with those who best understand what is going on. But in underdeveloped countries the impact of inflation is direct and terrible. The hopes of everyone are pinned on what are called 'strong executives', strong leaders who are dictators disguised as constitutional presidents. Such dictatorships are, above all, economic in nature. The national budgets formulated by parliaments are realized only in terms of the will of the president. Many provisions are declared to be ineffective. Taxes are not raised, but expenditures are incurred by giving privileges to friends, to political supporters, and to those unprincipled men who prosper under all political regimes.

We must stress that the real problem to be analysed first of all is the standard of living of the people. Chile, for example, is a country which is suffering from tremendous inflation and in which the value of the dollar has gone up fantastically; but the common people live better than in Ecuador, where the dollar has not changed for fifteen years.

The processes of inflation affect education in various ways. Without doubt, the most important is that a national budget provides wages and salaries for the administrative personnel and for the Army. The amount of money allocated for other things is small when viewed in the light of popular demand for or of the needs of education and of training. Consequently, the full scope of national education is not appreciated, or planned for in its depth or vastness. Often the solution is merely a panacea applied without proper consideration of the real requirements. For example, a few school buildings or new textbooks may be provided. Ministers of Education, who are nearly always politicians, and not educators, give support to a small and insignificant part of education rather than to its entire field of action.

In times of inflation, the tendency is to save on education and to consider it simply from a monetary point of view. Teachers, and especially those in secondary schools and universities, spend their time in all sorts of occupations having no connexion with one another. Or they give routine instruction in various outside establishments. Their teaching is converted into a mechanical routine.

The best and most able members of the teaching profession are not appointed to the higher posts. These are the perquisites of those who think of politics as their occupation. Membership of a political party, club, or *camarilla* or simply friendship or acquaintanceship with the President of the Republic or the Minister of Education leads most easily to the top posts.

In a climate of this kind the disinterested study of educational problems from a philosophic or scientific point of view does not prosper—nor can it. Nor is the climate favourable to the discussion of fundamental issues. And since the governments (whether they be military or not) notoriously tend towards totalitarianism, even the most judicious and balanced views are repressed if they run counter to those of the government. The administration of education during the ten years of the Perón regime in Argentina is a proof of this assertion. The higher and most responsible posts were barred to the best members of the profession for the crime of holding different ideas. Twelve hundred secondary and university teachers were dismissed without any legal justification.

In times of rapid inflation or deflation, governments seem to attempt to compensate for their administrative difficulties by official propaganda which is at once tendentious, self-laudatory, and demagogic. They systematically oppose the search for truth, and seem to desire complete silence from the whole country. They argue that peace and order are the supreme conditions for national happiness; but they ignore that peace and order are the desirable consequences of a respect for the rights of man, free discussion, and follow from the collaboration of those best able to help.   And the fact that the rulers accept the idea that order can come only from strong rather than just government brings with it the familiar consequence : the government is either a military dictatorship or one of civilians which maintains itself by granting to the Army all kinds of privileges within the national budget.   The salaries of officers are very high compared with those of other people.   In most of our countries not even the most famous educator gets more than a small fraction of a general's salary, while university professors barely receive what is given to the most junior second lieutenant.   As a result of this unsatisfactory remuneration, teaching is not considered as a career except in rare cases like Chile, Brazil, or Mexico.   Of these, Chile is the country which spends the largest percentage of its national income on education.   What is true of teachers' salaries is equally true of equipment and buildings. There is a lack of laboratories, audio-visual aids, libraries, workshops, playing-fields, and so forth.

Economic Policy, Education, and Democracy

With minor differences in wording, the constitutions of nearly all Latin-American countries state that education is ' obligatory, secular, and free '.   The degree to which these terms have meaning differs from country to country.   Education is obligatory, nevertheless from north to south no state has been able to eradicate illiteracy, in spite of the provision of both primary and adult education.   In Honduras 80 per cent of the population is illiterate, and even in the Argentine 10 per cent are illiterates.   Literacy campaigns directed toward the masses, as in Mexico or Brazil, have been in operation only a few years.   Yet popular demand is strong and urgent everywhere.   People ask for schools and for the improvement and extension of those which exist. Progressive governments pay attention to this demand of the population.   Nevertheless, in most countries at least half the children remain without schooling.   In countries in which methods of adult education have been improved and in which the concept of education is more comprehensive, it is urged that reading is not everything—that education must teach people to live, to spend their leisure time, to produce better, and to live more hopefully.   For it has been realized that skill in reading can have value only when people understand the processes to which reading can be applied and have learnt to understand what they read.   The semi-literate are a more serious problem than the completely illiterate.   This legion of semi-literates, who hardly know how to write their own names, are those who vote to elect the President of the Republic, deputies, senators, and municipal councillors. We see that a lack of political maturity is closely linked with a lack of culture and of economic freedom.

The principle of secular education is suffering blows of all kinds. Denominational Catholic education very often makes use of political and conservative forces to oppose the growth or even the maintenance of what has been achieved by the secular movement. The state's control of education is continually more lax, more permissive, and more innocuous, and in many countries Catholic education has begun to receive important financial aid from the state.

Public education is free to all within limits more restricted than one might think. From the elementary level upwards, the state does practically nothing more than pay the salaries of teachers and maintain inadequate buildings. Uruguay is the most advanced country in its provision of free education for all, and of all kinds of instruction. In addition, a promising child or young person without means receives all kinds of grants or aids.

In reality, the democratization of the state implies that opportunities for all individuals must be provided, so that they may enjoy the benefits of a variety of institutions. The children of workers and many of the children of the middle classes have been deprived, as were their fathers, of the benefits of culture. I am not thinking of the university, nor of secondary education, for often even the elementary school is denied them. Such are the existing privileges, that we can say that for every doctor, lawyer, or engineer who graduates in a university, there are left as cultural orphans great numbers of young people born in the humbler classes. Despotic regimes are characterized by the efforts they make to keep the children of workers in the deepest ignorance. Through this cruelty society has lost an immense human capital which potentially is both useful and fruitful to the general well-being. This situation is modified when progressive groups, democratic in sympathy, break down some of the privileges and assume the management of the state. Immediately they manifest interest in education : the numbers of schools and of teachers increase rapidly, modern buildings are erected, curricula and methods of teaching are changed, the health of children is looked after, and auxiliary services are created. The conditions of work of educators are improved. Opportunities to attain higher levels of instruction are made easier by a system of grants and scholarships and through the rise in the standard of living among the workers. The educational improvements which such progressive groups promote are not, however, only quantitative, there is also an improvement in quality. Through a democratic government the political, philosophical, and social orientation of education is modified to such a degree that the old school which promoted class divisions gives way to one which is available to all the children of all the people. In a word, what happens in such a case is the transformation of ' caste ' education into ' popular ' education.

That schoolmaster of genius, Domingos F. Sarmiento, had a passion for teaching and for civilizing his fellow-citizens. As President of the Argentine Republic, he was a teacher of his people and created the basis of their national feeling. He often said, " If the people are sovereign, the sovereign has to be educated."

He is in agreement here with Alexander von Humboldt, who commented on the peoples of this continent by saying they were " beggars seated on a golden stool ". He was thinking, of course, of their apparent inability to discover the natural and human wealth which was available.

But the idea of democracy has an inner meaning too. When society is based on the privileges of a minority and the benefits and gains attained through the exploitation of some men by others—while there are rich nations which exploit poor countries—while there are imperialist powers who rule and absorb the wealth of powerless colonial lands and decide their destiny—we cannot find real democracy. Seen from within, democracy is, above all, the realization of the idea that political power is not something that simply gives privileges, but also carries with it responsibility. In this it is the antithesis of totalitarian systems.

Economic Life

What place in an order of priorities does education occupy relative to other public services? In regimes based on force and devoted to ostentation and exhibitionism, education always comes far below what is called defence as well as below public works. In all countries which keep up or initiate frontier disputes, armaments absorb a large percentage of the national budget. Unpopular regimes which have given up the attempt to create confidence through discussion and reason maintain order by military means in the face of popular discontent and dissatisfaction. Educational needs are ignored, since teachers have neither the means nor the bayonets to make themselves heard.

The work of the schools is, above all, an attempt to spread light. It is a spiritual crusade, which yields its return only after many years. Public works, on the other hand, can be seen and are preferred as a means of strengthening governmental credit. In countries where the care of education is united to public health, as in Brazil, campaigns can be carried out simultaneously. In Uruguay, up to the present, social welfare is looked after by social workers, doctors, and teachers, who work in teams. Panama and Costa Rica are countries which have no army, but only a police force. These countries, for obvious reasons are able to devote the highest proportion (a third) of the national budget to education.

The fact that Mexico, through its revolution, united soldiers and teachers, generals and leaders of education, into a single political order showed how decisive the teachers' political judgment was in the political victory. In the congresses of the Union and of the various states there are always many teachers among the deputies, and quite often some teachers hold military rank.

This particular political situation has favoured an increase in the proportion of the budget allocated to education. It is worth noting that a general like Lázaro Cárdenas, who was one of Mexico's most brilliant presidents, had a civilian rather than a military frame of mind.

Returns from Education

Does education in any of its forms give a direct return for the expenditure on it? It may well be that the development in pupils of a greater humanity or of a more developed spirituality is not easily measured in concrete terms. Yet, nevertheless, it might lead to greater production. New manual activities, different ways of facing problems, may be, in fact, a fertile soil for more intelligent production. Healthy human bodies may be socially constructive. Elementary rural schools might give some return to the community, for they are used as classes for both children and adults. Secondary education of the classical and obsolete type, however, is far removed from vital and urgent national problems; it is said to produce leaders, but many of them may well live sheltered from the clamour of reality. Universities which have gone beyond the old framework of the so-called liberal professions and include scientific work and technology have a direct connexion with industrial and material production. The Rural University of Brazil, the Polytechnic Institute of Mexico, the Technical University of Valparaiso in Chile, and the Institute of Social Research of the National Free University of Mexico, as well as the University of Chile, provide significant examples of the new tendencies.

In all post-primary schools there is an urgent need to improve the rich traditional forms of craftsmanship, so that beautiful and useful things can be made on a large scale. It is necessary here to introduce new techniques which will accelerate the rate of work while promoting the creative capacity of the hands. Workshops are now being set up, for example, in ceramics and interior decoration. The organi-

zation of international exhibitions in the principal centres of Europe
and America may well develop and promote these hopeful tendencies.

Is official management and administration of the educational system
efficient and well directed?   It is not difficult to mention cases where
the administration costs more than the services which it organizes.
This is one of the weakest sides of bureaucracy.   Higher posts are
continually being created.   They do not lead to any real improvement,
since the object has usually been little more than to provide a salary
for a friend.   Private enterprises, however, are not like this—they are
subjected to efficient planning, which does away with useless or super-
fluous costs.   One particular point might well be mentioned here—the
desirability of employing foreign technicians or advisers and giving
them either direct or indirect responsibility in the direction of affairs
may well be questioned.   Far too often foreigners do not succeed in
really understanding the complexities of the Latin-American world,
and they are often unable to adapt themselves to its requirements.
Some of them seem to think that sightseeing is better than careful
study, or else, to make sure of keeping posts that pay them well, avoid
any disagreement with the authorities.   In any case, they may be inferior to the best native-born technicians, who are often overlooked by
their government.

As for those Latin Americans who control capital resources, they
seem to lack courage as well as initiative.   As a result, too much is
hoped for from foreign capital.   Fundamentally, economic development depends on the co-operative use of human resources.   Modern
capitalism should make a more human collaboration with the workers
possible and should lead to undertakings of social value.

Is there geographical and social mobility among the population?   Up
to a point, yes.   Everywhere many people attempt feverishly to earn
more.   Often they hardly take into account that the occupations they
seek are not within their capacity.   Improvements, jobs, professional
occupations are sought under the tremendous pressure of shortage of
cash, rather than as a result of any special ability.   Thus people are
often moving continually from one occupation to another, and there
are too few persons who are really qualified in their particular field.

There is reason to fear that the great religious tradition may find
itself corrupted by attempts to convert the Church into a political
force to conquer or retain power for a privileged class which has kept
the great masses of the people in backwardness, poverty, and ignorance.   Christianity cannot be ignored nor denied more effectively than
by this.   By its very definition, denominational education does not
seek to educate the poorest ranks of the people; in any case, it establishes itself only in the more important cities, where high fees can be

charged. It displays no interest in rural education or in that of sub-normal children. True tolerance would imply developing an equilibrium between various religious creeds, for monopoly leads to abuse.

In very few cases can one speak of a true educational policy relating to widely conceived plans except in those countries where a dictatorship laid long-range plans or where a progressive constitutional regime established by a revolution, laid weight on systematic planning. As an example of the first, one might mention the Perón five-year plans; of the second, the six-year plans in Mexico. For the rest, one can find nothing but sporadic and self-contradictory activity.

Towards Education for Economic Life

Three types of school administration are found: centralized, decentralized, mixed. In the centralized republics, the authorities, through the Ministers of Education, direct, control, and finance education. In countries organized on a federal basis, such as Mexico or Brazil, decentralization occurs. Thirdly, examples can be found in certain semi-autonomous provinces, of private colleges, universities, and cultural bodies which receive financial support from the state. One of the more serious problems in the whole continent is to consider ways in which the more prosperous states or provinces can provide aid for those which are weak or backward. There is no other way of promoting national cohesion. Collaboration has to be established between the regions. It may well be that the main achievement of fundamental education projects has been to give an example of this.

The beginnings of a really progressive educational administration can be perceived in the most advanced nations. In these countries, pseudo reforms are no longer regarded as satisfactory. Attempts to produce changes are controlled by investigation and experience. Change is not made just for the sake of change. A certain technical competence is now being found even in the offices of Ministers of Education. A significant example of this is the Ministry of Education of Brazil, where the Institute of Educational Studies is looked upon as the very hub around which all discussions and deliberations turn. The Institute is housed in the very heart of the ministry on one of the ten floors of its marvellous building. Officials are beginning to understand that there exists an interdependence between the factors that complicate the educational problems and the means that can be used to solve it. They are beginning to realize full well that the central pivot is the personality of the teacher and depends upon his training as well as upon the general social valuation of his mission. The government no longer plans merely as a result of discussions in the ministries, but after studying data brought forward by careful investigation and social reporting, so that a total picture is available. They look for relationships between the various aspects of social life—the cultural, the political, and the economic. On such firm ground, national life can grow and solid traditions can flourish.

Two books by Francisco Antonio Encina are worth noting. They are *Our Economic Inferiority* (1911) and *Economic Education* (1912). Encina is a teacher, a financier, historian, and businessman of wide and varied culture. Those who know his work realize that his descriptions and his analysis of the economic life of Chile are based upon balanced and acute observations. The qualities and defects of his people—above all, the mistaken orientation of their educational system—are made absolutely clear. To read the pages of these two books is to observe the life of Chile, so to speak, from the inside and to understand what made this rising nation decline towards the end of last century. They teach us to see that it lay in the hands of the Chileans themselves (and —why not say it?—of all Latin Americans) to improve their national life by reforming their education and by laying stress on the importance of productive labour. Encina's books demonstrate once more that economics is not a mysterious science. On the contrary, its teachings have to be understood by all.

Amanda Labarca, another eminent Latin-American educator, completes the Chilean scene with her two theoretical works, *The Bases of Educational Policy* and *The Improvement of Rural Life*. Both delve deeply into elements which go to make up the Chilean nation in order to find the cultural and educational cement that may bind its citizens together. From such works one learns that the true bases of economics rests on regional studies. Economics affect all the sectors of human life and we have to make clear the reciprocal interactions.

Socialist Education in Mexico

Two important concepts were enunciated by General Lázaro Cárdenas and by Dr. Ignacio García Téllez, President of the Republic and Minister of National Education, during one of the most interesting phases of present-day Mexican education. They state with precision and clarity the socialist position—itself the ripe fruit of the Revolution. General Lázaro Cárdenas said: "We believe that the Mexican Revolution has already reached such a social maturity that it is possible to consider the total aspect of national problems. Thus the Revolution laid the bases of a social education, but it did not do so in the belief that education is a phenomenon isolated from the social processes and that by itself it has to remedy all the troubles of the workers; it does so because the revolution was preoccupied at the same time in an active and lively way with the attempts to deal with the economic aspects of the lives of the workers in the fields and in the workshops. And because it tries, as a matter of course, to complete this economic and revolutionary structure, fortifying it in the minds of the children and young people through the medium of education. In the school the varied elements of economic life will be harmonized for the welfare of the proletariat; it is an education, moreover, in which the principles of self-interest will be gradually transformed into those of a more frankly socialist economy." And Minister García Telléz stated: " The constitutional reform dealt with in Article 3 implies, without doubt, an undertaking on the part of the political institutions of the Revolution and of all the organizations of the Federation of the States, and of the municipalities to continue ever faster to subject individualistic systems to the general control of a scientific programme directed by authorities, a programme which will arise from the true democracy of the workers."

These two statements of official policy are very different from most of those found in the political literature of Latin America. They both refer to Article 3 of the constitution, which described one of the more important postulates of the Revolution. In other words, they place the centre of political life in the masses of the people and emphasize the economic and social basis of the Revolution. From such concepts are derived a new system of ideas about education—socialized education. The influence of the economic environment, of the means of distribution, and of the production of wealth on the school is not overlooked. Nor is the influence which education has or might have on the environment and on those systems. (Incidentally, we should mention that the 1910 Revolution in Mexico consolidated by the Constitution of Querétaro in 1917 came before the Russian Revolution.)

On the other hand, the education of a people depends on the money provided for it by public authorities or private individuals. We all know, of course, that this is not the whole of education. Leaving this on one side, it still remains true that a country which allocates a good part of its public budget and of its private resources to education reveals its effective interest in that great enterprise. The identification, in the last century, of the state with the capitalist *bourgeoisie* led to the creation of a well-known type of school : one in which rural workers and the poor people of the cities had very few opportunities of learning. When other types of school, either in the countryside or in the neighbourhood of factories, were established, it was done to provide an education adequate to the various differing social groups, and not to meet the general needs arising from the physical or geographical environment. Social groups were not thought of as being specialized by the conditions of their environment—rather were they thought of as simply occupying different levels in the social hierarchy.

There is now no country in which the educational system is fully adapted either to classical capitalism or to individualism. Social democracy, trade unionism, the co-operative movement, as well as the effect of doctrines which, while stressing the need for reform are yet compatible with established capitalism, place a more or less visible imprint on the aims and methods of education.

The New Education, Economic Life and the Future

One of the more widely diffused forms of education—namely, the activity school—seeks in some of the schools found in several Latin-American countries to understand the natural and human environment through the study of the material aspects of life. It seeks to understand how that environment can be used for the benefit of the community and how it can be improved. Here might be formed habits of applying knowledge to the promotion of a sense of beauty or of social value. In rural schools the effects of over-grazing or of the burning of trees would be studied, for example. The activity school might, for example, encourage reafforestation. Once the facts have been noted and studied, the school would try to get the people of the neighbourhood to co-operate in the transplantation of seedlings.

To face the future demands men of vision and insight. To live for the future means to live the present fully, but to conceive life as one of constant change. No country in the world lacks its centres of true inspiration and dauntless effort. The history of Latin America has been above all biographical, a story of great men acting against the background of the masses. The struggle to-day represents the first efforts of the people themselves and thus implies the need for economic liberation. Wherever social movements have been deep and liberating, one finds the people on the march, directed by the best among them.

Education is now passing from the stage when it was that of ' caste ' to that of the great masses. The peoples everywhere are beginning to discover themselves, to become aware of what lies in them and to determine their own fate. And this marks an advance towards a deeper maturity; but such maturity must be a power for good. While the values of spirit must be given priority, this maturity affirms strongly the value of material goods and of economic justice. When these aims are realized, Latin America will be better able to bring its contribution to a world whose future is now so doubtful.

JULIO LARREA.

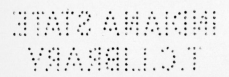

INDEX

A

ACCOUNTING, 25, 335, 381–95, 450
ACQUISITION of resources, see Resources
ACTIVITY schools, *Latin America*, 585
ACTS, 239; Astier 1919, 373; Avellanada (*Argentina*), 281; Barangé (*France*), 376, 447; Cole-Rice, 175; Colonial Welfare and Development, 85; Common Education (*Argentina*), 281; early *U.S.*, 198; Educational (*Iraq*), 302; Guizot 1833, 369; *Indian* Income, 278; Morrill, 155, 156; *the Netherlands* Primary Education 1920, 416, 417; New York State 1795, 171; salaries, 176; *Norwegian* Bank 1947, 177; *Rhode Island* 1955 Finance, 338; school attendance, *U.S.*, 337; *U.K.* 1870, 410, 1902 Education, 149, 410, 414; 1918, 410; 1936, 412; 1944, 149, 150, 152, 229–56, 309, 356, 366, 369, 409, 410, 413, 423–6, 457, 458, 459, 461; County Council 1888, 364; Employment and Training, 433; Local Taxation, 312; *U.S.*, 1805, 172, 1812, 172, 1877, 155, 1914, 156, Unification 1904, 173
ADMINISTRATION, 5, 65, 101, 228, 370, 410; central, 307, 329, 378, 446; control, 65, 69, 101, 334, 346; cost of, 354, *Latin America*, 582, *Greece*, 259, 260, *France*, 369, *India*, 274; local in *U.S.*, 197, 377; *Morocco*, 566; New York University, 396; organization, 23–7, 197, 281, 289, 383; in *Prussia*, 489; reform, 380; returns, 336; salaries, 449; *South Africa*, 292; State, *U.S.*, 386; *U.S.* superintendent of schools, 385
ADMINISTRATIVE, grants in *U.K.*, 308; skills in *U.S.*, 441
ADULT education, 93, 102, 225, 228, 422, 423, 425, 558; *Iraq*, 260, 261, 304
AFRICA, 77, 149, 157, 224, 289, 326, 483, 533–44, 556, 558
AGRICULTURE, 15, 68, 89, 110, 155, 158, 244, 265, 303, 337, 342, 345, 449, 450, 452, 545, 547, 553; education in *U.S.*, 499; *India*, 276; *Iraq*, 301; *Italy*, 118; *Morocco*, 566; size of *U.S.* farm, 348; *U.S.*, 221

ALLOCATION of benefits, *U.K.*, 313–14; see also Distribution
AMERICA, see *U.S.A.*
APATHY, 87–94
APPRENTICESHIPS, 100, 135, 234, 237, 373, 374, 424, 432, 488, 524, 525
ARGENTINA, 222, 224, 280–5, 574, 577
ARMED services, 14, 185, 214, 428, 514, 526, 561, 577
ASIA, 157, 224, 326, 483, 546, 548; South East, 81
AUDIT, 25, 335, 356, 381–95, 450; *U.K.*, 362; *U.S.*, 381
AUSTRALIA, 221, 222, 288, 290, 292
AUSTRIA, 138, 139, 142, 144, 145, 146, 448, 449, 485, 495
AUTOMATION, 87, 90

B

BASIC education, 278; *India*, 452; schools, 227
BELGIUM, 2, 138, 142, 221, 448
BOARDING schools, *Iraq*, 304
BOHEMIA, 138, 141
BOLIVIA, 576
BRAZIL, 22, 221, 446, 574, 578, 580, 583
BRITISH CARIBBEAN, 86
BRITISH WEST INDIES, 79, 81, 84, 86
BUDDHISM, 35, 37
BUDGETARY control, procedures, 388; *U.K.*, 362; *U.S.*, 332, 335
BUDGETS, 25, 195, 282, 381; *France*, 369–79; *Greece*, 257–62; *Latin America*, 577; school, 331; *U.K.*, 356, 360; *U.S.*, 380–95, 396–408
BUILDINGS, 12, 13, 89, 91, 110, 133, 140, 141, 153, 180, 189, 202, 203, 218, 226, 243, 245, 263, 282, 291, 306, 378, 490, 501, 572; construction of, in *France*, 371, 373; *Greece*, 259, 260; *Latin America*, 577, 579; *U.K.*, 242, 249, 414; *U.S.*, 354, 385; Foundations, 167; maintenance of, 357, 363, 389; programmes, 366; *U.S.* university courses, 441, 511
BULGARIA, 259
BURMA, 98, 221

C

CALVANISM, 34
CAMEROONS, 87–94